D1615794

Aviation Mechanic Series
Original Text by Dale Crane

Airframe
Systems

Fourth Edition

Keith Anderson
Technical Editor

AVIATION SUPPLIES & ACADEMICS, INC.
NEWCASTLE, WASHINGTON

Aviation Mechanic Series: Airframe Systems
Fourth Edition
Based on the original text by Dale Crane

Aviation Supplies & Academics, Inc.
7005 132nd Place SE
Newcastle, Washington 98059
asa@asa2fly.com I 425-235-1500 I asa2fly.com

ASA-AMT-SYS4
ISBN 978-1-64425-174-4

Additional formats available:
eBook EPUB   ISBN 978-1-64425-176-8
eBook PDF   ISBN 978-1-64425-177-8
eBundle ISBN 978-1-64425-175-1 (print + eBook PDF download code)

Printed in the United States of America
2026 2025 2024 2023 2022   9 8 7 6 5 4 3 2 1

Photo credits—Cover: Media_Works/stock.adobe.com. Figures 1-82 and 1-83: Keith Anderson. Figures 1-88 and 1-90: Simpson Electric Company. Figure 1-89: John Fluke Manufacturing Company, Inc. Figure 4-64: courtesy of RAPCO Inc. Figure 4-69: courtesy of Cessna Aircraft Co. Figure 4-71: iStock.com/hasansanci. Figure 5-29: courtesy of Lowrance Avionics, Inc. Figure 5-30: courtesy of Garmin International, Inc. Figure 5-35: courtesy of L-3 Communications Avionics Systems. Figure 5-44: courtesy of Rockwell Collins. Figure 5-45: iStock.com/atosan. Figure 5-51: courtesy of Dayton-Granger, Inc. (Kuflic Photography). Figure 5-52: https://commons.wikimedia.org/wiki/File:Wingletdetail.jpg, by Dennis N., public domain. Figures 5-54 and 5-56: courtesy of Dayton-Granger, Inc. (Ring Photography). Figure 9-4: icholakov—stock.adobe.com. Figure 9-5: Siraves Vorayos/Shutterstock.com.

Library of Congress Cataloging-in-Publication Data
Names: Crane, Dale, author. I Crane, Dale. Aviation mechanic series.
Title: Aviation mechanic series. Airframe systems / Dale Crane.
Other titles: Airframe systems
Description: Fourth edition. I Newcastle, Washington : Aviation Supplies & Academics, Inc., [2022] I Series:
    Aviation mechanic series I Includes index.
Identifiers: LCCN 2021044394 (print) I LCCN 2021044395 (ebook) I ISBN 9781644251744 (hardback) I
    ISBN 9781644251768 (epub) I ISBN 9781644251775 (pdf) I ISBN 9781644251751
Subjects: LCSH: Airframes--Maintenance and repair.
Classification: LCC TL671.9 .C66468 2022 (print) I LCC TL671.9 (ebook) I DDC 629.134/6--dc23
LC record available at https://lccn.loc.gov/2021044394
LC ebook record available at https://lccn.loc.gov/2021044395

Contents

About the Editorial Team
Fourth Edition

Based on the original text by:

Dale Crane

Dale Crane was involved in aviation for more than 50 years. His credentials include Airframe and Powerplant Mechanic, Designated Mechanic Examiner, Commercial Pilot, Flight Instructor (airplanes), and Advanced and Instrument Ground Instructor.

Dale began his career in the U.S. Navy as a mechanic and flight engineer in patrol bombers (PBYs). After World War II, he attended Parks Air College. After college, he worked as an instrument overhaul mechanic, instrument shop manager, and flight test instrumentation engineer. He spent the following 16 years as an instructor and then became director of an aviation maintenance school.

For 30 years, Dale was active as a writer of aviation technical materials and a consultant in developing aviation training programs. He participated with the FAA in the Aviation Mechanic Occupation Study and the Aviation Mechanic Textbook Study. ATEC presented to Dale Crane their special recognition award for "his contribution to the development of aviation technicians as a prolific author of specialized maintenance publications."

Dale Crane also received the FAA's Charles Taylor "Master Mechanic" Award for 50 years of service in and contributions to the aviation maintenance industry, and the recognition of his peers for his excellence in aircraft maintenance as a leader, educator, and aviation safety advocate.

Keith Anderson
LeTourneau University

Keith Anderson is an Associate Professor in the Applied Aviation Science Department in the College of Aviation and Aeronautical Science at LeTourneau University. He obtained his A&P certificate in 1983 and received his Inspection Authorization (IA) rating in 1997. He is a commercial pilot with Instrument Rating and is a certified flight instructor. He has an Associate Degree in Aviation Technology, a Bachelor of Science Degree in Electrical Engineering Technology, Aviation Option from LeTourneau University, and an MBA with Management Certificate from Corban University. He has been employed as a mechanic and director of maintenance at several maintenance facilities, including shops operating under Part 135 and Part 121. In addition to his maintenance experience, he flew for eight years for a non-profit mission organization in Venezuela and Guatemala and additionally served as chief inspector for one year for a non-governmental organization (NGO) in Uganda.

Following his overseas experiences, he was employed as a design engineer, director of engineering, and director of customer service for a company developing a new single-engine turboprop utility airplane, with additional duties as an Administrative Designated Engineering Representative (DER), and he was the primary point of contact with the FAA Aircraft Certification Office for the successful certification of the aircraft. Keith later became the vice president of engineering for a well-known company that developed supplemental type certificates (STCs) for corporate aircraft and also served as the director of engineering for an aircraft simulation company.

In addition to serving as technical editor for *Airframe Systems*, Keith is also the technical editor of the Aviation Mechanic Series *General* textbook and the *Aviation Mechanic Handbook*.

Linda S. Classen
Metro Tech, Instructor and Mechanic

Linda Classen is an Aviation Maintenance Instructor at Metro Technology Center in Oklahoma City. She has Private Pilot, Commercial, Instrument, and Certified Flight Instructor certificates. She holds a degree in journalism, and is a member of the Association for Women in Aviation Maintenance (AWAM), and the Professional Aviation Maintenance Association (PAMA).

Jerry Lee Foulk
LeTourneau University Instructor, FAA Designated Mechanic Examiner

Jerry Foulk has been an instructor of aviation maintenance since 1976, first at the Pittsburgh Institute of Aeronautics in Pennsylvania, at Moody Aviation in Elizabethton, Tennessee, and currently at LeTourneau University's School of Aeronautical Sciences in Longview, Texas (starting in 2003). He earned his B.S. degrees in Bible and in Aviation Technology from LeTourneau in 1976, and has also been an FAA Designated Mechanic Examiner since 1993. Jerry also was Technical Editor for the second and third editions of ASA's Aviation Mechanic Series *Powerplant* textbook by Dale Crane.

Stephen Roth
Embry-Riddle Aeronautical University

Stephen Roth earned a B.S. (Engineering Physics) at Cornell University and M.S. (Applied Physics) at Stanford University, then worked for several years as an engineer in ultrahigh vacuum and radiation detection. He returned to school to earn an M.D. Following a many-decade hiatus from flying, he became a private pilot and proceeded to earn the CFI certificate. After retiring from medical practice, he returned to school at Embry-Riddle Aeronautical University to earn an A&P. For the past several years he has taught courses in AMT, Human Factors and Computer Science at ERAU and has earned his commercial glider and seaplane ratings. Recently he joined the Aerospace Engineering and Research Center at ERAU, Eagle Works as Associate Director.

Donald Shaffer
Duncan Aviation

Don Shaffer attended Northwestern Michigan College, Western Michigan University and received a B.S. in Aviation Technology, and also Kalamazoo Valley Community College for an A.S. in Pre-Engineering. Don holds a commercial pilot license with ME/INST ratings. He has worked at Duncan Aviation for 17 years; eight of those years have been as a systems engineer designing avionics interface and modifications.

Peter A. Vosbury
Embry-Riddle Aeronautical University

Peter Vosbury attended Embry-Riddle Aeronautical University from 1968 to 1969 and completed the airframe and powerplant certification program there. From 1970 to 1973 he served on the carrier *U.S.S. Forrestal* as a turbine engine mechanic for the U.S. Navy. After the Navy, Peter went back to school and completed a Masters Degree in Education at the University of Central Florida. In 1976 he began teaching at Embry-Riddle in the AMT Department and in 2000 transferred to the Air Science Department, now teaching turbine engines and aircraft systems to professional pilot students. Peter Vosbury is the author of several books covering topics in math and physics, aviation regulations, weight and balance, and turbine engines, and has also participated in writing answers and explanations to the FAA A&P exams.

AIRCRAFT ELECTRICAL SYSTEMS

1

An Introduction to Aircraft Electrical Systems

An aviation mechanic (also referred to as an aviation maintenance technician or AMT) must have a solid foundation in basic electrical principles and a good working knowledge of the way these principles apply to complex systems. Electrical systems provide the muscle for retracting landing gears and starting engines and serve as the brains for *electronic* flight control and monitoring systems.

Basic electrical principles are covered in the *General* textbook of the Aviation Mechanic Series. In the *General* text, electricity is discussed from a theoretical point of view, with emphasis on its laws. Circuit analysis considers the variables in both AC and DC circuits.

The *Airframe Structures* and *Airframe Systems* textbooks of the Aviation Mechanic Series take up where the *General* text leaves off, including a brief review of electrical terms and facts, followed by the practical application of basic electrical principles to aircraft electrical systems.

The *Powerplant* textbook of the Aviation Mechanic Series covers practical aspects of the generation of electricity and some of the heavy-duty applications, such as engine starting systems.

Aircraft electrical systems covered here range from the simplest component schematics to logic flow charts used for systematic troubleshooting. The intent of this section is to present aircraft electrical systems in their most practical form.

No specific aircraft electrical schematics are used in this text, but the systems used have been adapted from actual aircraft. The procedures discussed are general in their nature, and this text must be considered as a reference document, not a service manual. Information issued by the aircraft manufacturer takes precedence over any procedure mentioned in this text.

One of the fundamental rules of aviation maintenance is that you must use the latest approved information, such as that furnished by the aircraft manufacturer when servicing any part of an aircraft. This is particularly true of electrical systems, as these systems and their components are far too expensive to risk damage as the result of improper servicing procedures. There are limits as to what an aircraft mechanic or technician can do in the repair of certain electrical or electronic components. Some of these can be repaired only by the manufacturer or by a repair station specifically authorized for this work.

To begin this study, we will examine the requirements for an aircraft electrical system and then review some terms and facts.

Electrical System Requirements

Title 14 of the Code of Federal Regulations, Part 23—*Airworthiness Standards: Normal Category Airplanes*—provides requirements and guidance for the certification of electrical systems in general aviation aircraft. The Normal

Category includes aircraft of up to 19 passengers and maximum certificated takeoff weights of 19,000 pounds or less. Basic requirements for aircraft electrical systems include:

- A power generation system that will supply the required power during all intended operating conditions.

- Design considerations so that no single failure of any power supply, distribution path, or system component will prevent the system from providing essential power for a continued safe flight and landing.

- Sufficient system capacity so that, should the primary power generation source fail, the essential loads will continue to operate long enough for a continued safe flight and landing.

- Lights that are installed so that they do not interfere with the flight crew.

- Position lights that are of the correct colors and intensities to provide sufficient visibility to allow other aircraft time to avoid collisions.

- Taxi and landing lights that allow for safe night operation.

- Riding lights on seaplanes and amphibian aircraft that include a white light that is visible in clear weather.

- Built-in lightning protection for critical systems.

- Electrical protection from high-intensity radiated fields (HIRF), which can occur near ground-based radio transmitters.

Review of Terms

Though by now you have a working knowledge of basic electricity, a brief review of some of the terms most commonly used in aircraft electrical systems should prove useful.

bus—A point in an aircraft electrical system supplied with power from the battery or the generator/alternator and from which the various circuits get their power.

conductor—A material that allows electrons to move freely from one atom to another within the material.

current—The assumed flow of electricity that is considered to move through an electrical circuit from the positive side of a battery to its negative side. This is opposite to the flow, or movement, of electrons. Current is measured in amperes (amps) and its symbol is the letter I. Current follows the arrowheads in the diode and transistor symbols.

When current flows through a conductor, three things happen: heat is produced in the conductor, a magnetic field surrounds the conductor, and voltage is dropped across the conductor.

diode—A solid-state device that acts as an electron check valve. Electrons can flow through a diode in one direction, but cannot flow through it in the opposite direction.

electron current. The actual flow of electrons in a circuit. Electrons flow from the negative terminal of a power source through the external circuit to its positive terminal. The arrowheads in semiconductor symbols point in the direction opposite to the flow of electron current.

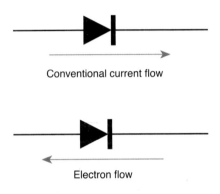

Conventional current flow

Electron flow

Figure 1-1. *Conventional current flows in the direction of the arrowheads of semiconductor diodes. Electron flow is in the opposite direction.*

conventional current. An assumed flow of electricity that is said to flow from the positive terminal of a power source, through the external circuit to its negative terminal. The arrowheads in semiconductor symbols point in the direction of conventional current flow.

schematic diagram. A diagram of an electrical system in which the system components are represented by symbols rather than drawings or pictures of the actual devices.

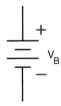

Figure 1-2. *Battery, or voltage source.*

electrons—Invisible negative electrical charges that actually move in an electrical circuit.

resistance—Opposition to the flow of current. The unit of resistance is the ohm, and its symbol is R.

voltage—Electrical pressure. The unit of voltage is the volt, and its symbol is either V (used in this text) or E (electromotive force).

voltage drop—The decrease in electrical pressure that occurs when current flows through a resistance.

Direction of Current Flow

One of the things that adds confusion to the study of electricity is the way electricity flows in a circuit.

Before much was known about electricity, its flow was compared to the flow of water in a river and was therefore called "current." As water currents flow from high to low, electrical current was considered to flow from positive (+) to negative (–). This was a reasonable conclusion, but was later determined to be wrong. Negatively charged electrons actually flow from negative to positive. This discovery was made only after countless textbooks about electricity had been written and symbols had been decided upon. Because of this, electrons in a circuit actually flow in the *opposite* direction to the way the arrowheads in the diode symbols point. This can be quite confusing.

In the *General* textbook, the term "electron flow" or "electrical current" was used to explain the basic principles of electricity. This *Airframe Systems* textbook (and many other modern texts on practical electricity) uses "conventional current," or simply "current." This is an assumed flow rather than an actual flow, and it travels from positive to negative, which allows us to visualize the flow in the direction of the arrowheads in the diode and transistor symbols. Considering the flow in this direction makes aircraft electrical systems much easier to understand. See Figure 1-1.

Electrical System Components

The most important tool for understanding an aircraft electrical system is the schematic diagram. This road map of the electrical system uses standardized symbols to represent the various components, arranged in a logical sequence with regard to the circuit operation. However, their placement in the schematic tells nothing about their physical location in the aircraft.

This text uses standard symbols to show the way aircraft electrical circuits are built. Chapter 1's Appendix A, beginning on page 95, show the most common symbols used in schematic diagrams of aircraft electrical systems.

DC Power Source

Figure 1-2 is the symbol for a battery. Conventional current leaves the positive (+) end and flows through the circuit to the negative (–) end. The long line is always the positive end of the battery.

Electrical Load

Figure 1-3 is the symbol for a resistor, or an electrical load. It may be an actual component, or it may be part of some other device. The filament in a light bulb and the heater element in a soldering iron are both resistances.

When current flows through a circuit, three things happen:

- A magnetic field surrounds the conductors that carry the current.
- Some of the energy used to push the current through the load is changed into heat, light, and/or mechanical energy.
- Some of the voltage is dropped across the load.

All conductors have some resistance, but in this study, the resistance of the system conductors is disregarded.

Figure 1-3. *Resistor, or an electrical load.*

Basic Electrical Circuit

Figure 1-4 shows a complete electrical circuit. The battery (V_B) supplies an electrical pressure (voltage) that forces current through the resistor (R). The arrows in the diagram show the direction of conventional current.

Note: In the symbols used in electricity, voltage is normally represented by the letter E, for electromotive force, but modern practice is to use the symbol V for voltage. As stated earlier, this text uses V, so don't be disturbed when you see E used for voltage in other books. The subscript B denotes battery voltage.

The current furnished by the battery follows the arrows. The resistor gets hot, and all of the voltage, or electrical pressure, from the battery is used up (dropped) across the resistor.

All electrical circuits must have three things:

- A source of electrical energy—the battery
- A load to change the electrical energy into mechanical energy, heat, and/or light—the resistor
- Conductors, or wires, that join the source and the load

In addition to these components, switches and fuses may be added for current control and circuit protection.

Circuit Control Devices

Circuit control devices are those components which start or stop the flow of current, direct it to various parts of the circuit, or increase or decrease the amount of its flow. These components may be mechanical, or—more frequently the case—semiconductor devices.

Switches

Figure 1-5 on the next page shows the symbols for some of the more common switches used in aircraft electrical systems. When a switch is open, current cannot flow in the circuit, but when it is closed, current can flow.

electromotive force (EMF). The force that causes electrons to move from one atom to another within an electrical circuit. Electromotive force is an electrical pressure, and it is measured in volts.

current. A general term used in this text for conventional current. See conventional current.

conductor. A material that allows electrons to move freely from one atom to another within the material.

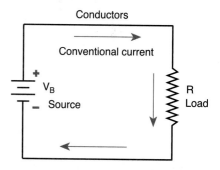

Figure 1-4. *A complete electrical circuit.*

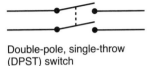

Single-pole, single-throw
(SPST) switch

Double-pole, single-throw
(DPST) switch

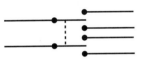

Single-pole, double-throw
(SPDT) switch

Double-pole, double-throw
(DPDT) switch

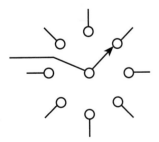

Single-pole, double-throw,
momentarily one position switch

Rotary wafer switch

Figure 1-5. *Switch symbols.*

In Figures 1-6 and 1-7, the symbol for a light bulb has replaced the resistor as the electrical load. Rays coming from the bulb show that current is flowing. When there are no rays, current is not flowing.

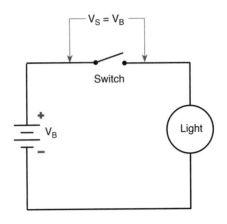

Figure 1-6. *This is an open circuit. No current is flowing and the light is off. All of the battery voltage is dropped across the open switch.*

Figure 1-7. *This is a closed circuit. The circuit is complete, current is flowing, and the light is lit. No voltage is dropped across the closed switch. All of the voltage is dropped across the light.*

Semiconductor Diodes

A semiconductor diode is an electron check valve that allows electrons to flow through it in one direction but blocks their flow in the opposite direction. Conventional current follows the direction of the arrowheads in the symbol. See Figure 1-8.

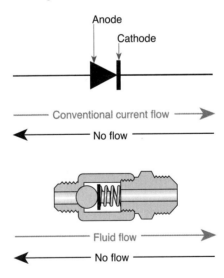

Figure 1-8. *A semiconductor diode controls current flow in an electrical circuit in the same way a check valve controls fluid flow in a hydraulic system. It allows flow in one direction but prevents its flow in the opposite direction. Conventional current flows through a diode in the direction shown by the arrowhead.*

When a diode is installed in a circuit in such a way that its anode is more positive than its cathode, it is forward-biased and current can flow through it. A diode causes a voltage drop across it as current flows through it, but, unlike with a resistor, this voltage drop does not change with the amount of current. A silicon diode has a relatively constant voltage drop of approximately 0.7 volt across it when current flows through it. The voltage drop across a germanium diode is about 0.3 volt.

When a diode is installed in a circuit in such a way that its anode is more negative than its cathode, it is reverse-biased and current flow is blocked. No current can flow through it until the voltage across it reaches a value, called the "peak inverse voltage." At this voltage, the diode breaks down and conducts current in its reverse direction. When this happens, an ordinary diode is normally destroyed.

semiconductor diode. A two-element electrical component that allows current to pass through it in one direction, but blocks its passage in the opposite direction. A diode acts in an electrical system in the same way a check valve acts in a hydraulic system.

reverse bias. A voltage placed across the PN junction in a semiconductor device with the positive voltage connected to the N-type material and the negative voltage to the P-type material.

forward bias. A condition of operation of a semiconductor device such as a diode or transistor in which a positive voltage is connected to the P-type material and a negative voltage to the N-type material.

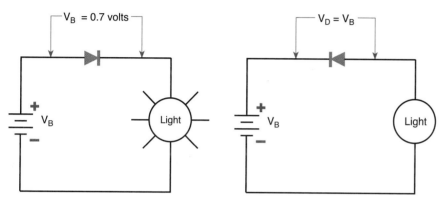

Figure 1-9. *A forward-biased diode acts as a closed switch, and current flows through it. There is a constant voltage drop of approximately 0.7 volt across a silicon diode.*

Figure 1-10. *A reverse-biased diode acts as an open switch. No current flows through it, and all of the battery voltage is dropped across the diode.*

Zener Diodes

Though an ordinary diode can be destroyed when current flows through it in its reverse direction, a zener diode is designed to have a specific breakdown voltage and to operate with current flowing through it in its reverse direction.

A reverse-biased zener diode is used as the voltage controlling component in an electronic voltage regulator used with a DC alternator. In Figure 1-12, the zener diode holds a load voltage constant as the input voltage changes. A 5-volt zener diode is installed in a 12-volt DC circuit in series with a resistor so that its cathode is more positive than its anode.

As soon as the voltage across the zener diode rises to 5 volts, it breaks down and conducts current to ground. Seven volts are dropped across the resistor,

zener diode. A special type of solid-state diode designed to have a specific breakdown voltage and to operate with current flowing through it in its reverse direction.

Figure 1-11. *A zener diode.*

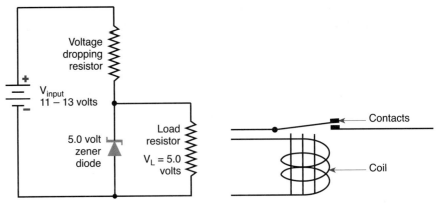

Figure 1-12. *A zener diode is used as a voltage-sensing unit.*

Figure 1-13. *An electromagnetic relay is a remotely operated switch that has a fixed core.*

and the voltage across the zener diode and the electrical load remains constant at 5 volts. If the source voltage drops to 11 volts, the voltage drop across the zener diode remains at 5 volts and the resistor now drops 6 volts. If the input voltage rises to 13 volts, the voltage across the zener still remains at 5 volts, but the voltage across the resistor rises to 8 volts.

A zener diode must always have a resistor in series with it to limit the current allowed to flow through it when it is conducting in its reverse direction, since its resistance drops to an extremely low value when it breaks down.

Relays and Solenoids

A relay is a magnetically operated switch that is able to carry a large amount of current through its contacts. It takes only a small amount of current flowing through the coil to produce the magnetic pull needed to close the contacts.

Any time current flows in a wire, a magnetic field surrounds the wire. If the wire is formed into a coil of many turns wound around a core of soft iron, the magnetic field is concentrated enough that just a small amount of current produces a pull strong enough to close the contacts of the relay. As soon as the current stops flowing through the coil, a spring snaps the contacts open. See Figure 1-13.

A solenoid is similar to a relay, except that its core is movable. Solenoid switches, also called contactors, are used in circuits that carry large amounts of current. The main battery contactor and the starter solenoid are both solenoid switches. A heavy cable carries the current from the battery through the starter solenoid contacts to the starter motor, but only a small wire is needed between the solenoid coil and the starter switch in the cockpit to cause the solenoid contacts to close.

Solenoid-operated valves are used in hydraulic and fuel systems. They can be opened or closed by a small switch located at some distance from the fluid lines themselves.

relay. An electrical component which uses a small amount of current flowing through a coil to produce a magnetic pull to close a set of contacts through which a large amount of current can flow. The core in a relay coil is fixed.

solenoid. An electrical component using a small amount of current flowing through a coil to produce a magnetic force that pulls an iron core into the center of the coil. The core may be attached to a set of heavy-duty electrical contacts, or it may be used to move a valve or other mechanical device.

contactor. A remotely actuated, heavy-duty electrical switch. Contactors are used in an aircraft electrical system to connect the battery to the main bus.

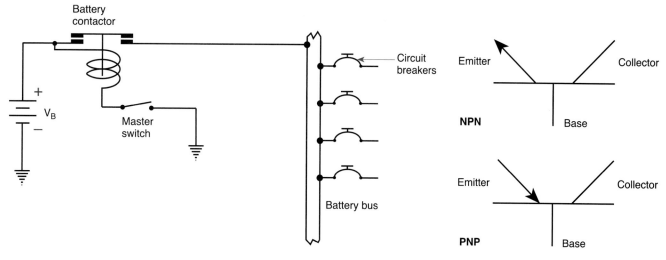

Figure 1-14. *A battery contactor is a remotely operated switch with a movable core. It connects the battery to the battery bus and is controlled by a very small flow of current through the master switch and the contactor coil.*

Figure 1-15. *Bipolar transistors.*

Bipolar Transistors

One of the most important developments in the field of electricity and electronics is the transistor. Transistors take the place of vacuum tubes and electromechanical relays. They do the same job, but do it better, use much less power, are more rugged, have a longer life, and are far less expensive.

There are two types of bipolar transistors, NPN and PNP, which differ in their construction and the way they are installed in electrical circuits. Figure 1-15 shows the symbols for these two types of transistors.

Transistors can be connected into a circuit so that they act much like a relay. Figure 1-16 shows a typical relay circuit, and the way an NPN transistor connected in a similar circuit performs the same functions as a relay.

The emitter of the NPN transistor in Figure 1-16 is connected to the negative terminal of the battery through the load, and the collector is connected to the positive terminal. When switch S_1 is closed, the base is connected to a voltage that is more positive than the emitter. A very small current flows into the base, and this causes a large current to flow through the collector and emitter and the load. When switch S_1 is open and no current is flowing through the base, there is no collector-emitter current to flow through the load.

It is easy to remember how a transistor acts as a switch: When the base and collector have the same polarity, the switch is ON; when there is no voltage on the base, or when its polarity is the same as that of the emitter, the switch is OFF.

A PNP transistor can be connected into the same kind of circuit as just seen, but the battery must be reversed so that the emitter is positive and the collector is negative. When the switch is closed, a small amount of current

bipolar transistor. A solid-state component in which the flow of current between its emitter and collector is controlled by a much smaller flow of current into or out of its base. Bipolar transistors may be of either the NPN or PNP type.

NPN transistor. A bipolar transistor made of a thin base of P-type silicon or germanium sandwiched between a collector and an emitter, both of which are made of N-type material.

PNP transistor. A bipolar transistor made of a thin base of N-type silicon or germanium sandwiched between a collector and an emitter, both of which are made of P-type material.

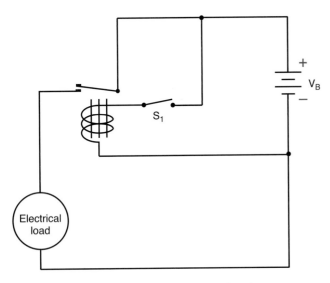

Small amount of current flowing through coil of a relay controls a much larger flow of current through the load.

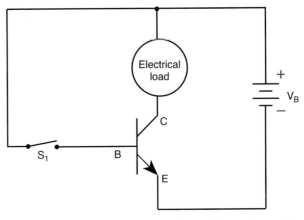

Very small amount of current flowing through base of a transistor controls a much larger flow of current through the load.

Figure 1-16. *A transistor acts much like an electrical relay.*

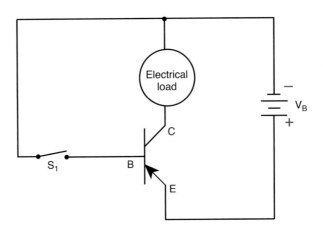

Figure 1-17. *A PNP transistor can work in the same way as the NPN transistor in Figure 1-16 if the battery polarity is reversed.*

base. The electrode of a bipolar transistor between the emitter and the collector. Controlling a small flow of electrons moving into or out of the base controls a much larger flow of electrons between the emitter and the collector.

potentiometer. A variable resistor having connections to both ends of the resistance element and to the wiper that moves across the resistance.

flows through the base, and a much larger current flows between the emitter and the collector. When the switch is opened, no base current flows, and no load current flows.

A transistor can be used not only as a switch, but also as a variable resistor. The switch circuit in Figure 1-16 can be replaced with a potentiometer across the voltage source, with the wiper connected to the base of the transistor, as shown in Figure 1-18.

This is an NPN transistor, and its base must be positive, the same as the collector, for it to conduct. When the wiper is at the bottom of the resistance element, the base of the transistor is negative, the same as the emitter. No current flows into the base, and no load current flows between the collector and the emitter.

When the wiper is moved to the top of the resistance, the base becomes positive, and the transistor conducts the maximum amount of load current. The amount of load current can be controlled by moving the wiper across the resistance. This kind of circuit is called an amplifier, because a very small change in base current can control a much larger change in load current.

Silicon Controlled Rectifier

A silicon controlled rectifier, or SCR, is a solid-state device that acts much like a diode that can be turned on with a short pulse of current.

The SCR has an anode, a cathode, and a gate. Current cannot flow through the SCR from the cathode to the anode or from the anode to the cathode until a pulse of positive current is sent into it through its gate. A positive pulse applied to the gate causes the SCR to conduct between its anode and its cathode. See Figure 1-19.

A holding coil, such as the one in Figure 1-20, requires only a pulse of current to close it. It remains closed until the main power circuit is momentarily opened.

When switch S_2 is closed, current flows through the relay coil to ground. This closes the contacts. As soon as the contacts are closed, current flows from the relay contact through the coil, and switch S_2 may be opened. The relay contacts remain closed with current flowing through the load until switch S_1 is momentarily opened. This breaks the ground to the relay coil and the relay contacts open, stopping all current through the load. See Figure 1-20.

An SCR does the same thing as a holding relay. Switch S_1 is normally closed, and voltage source V_B biases the SCR properly for it to conduct, but the SCR blocks all current until it is triggered by a momentary closing of switch S_2 in the gate circuit. When S_2 is closed, current flows through the gate resistor R_G into the gate of the SCR. Only a very short positive current pulse is needed to trigger the SCR into conducting. When the SCR conducts, current flows from the battery, through the SCR and the load, and back into the battery. Switch S_2 can be opened as soon as the SCR begins to conduct, and load current will continue to flow until switch S_1 is opened to stop it. Once the current is interrupted, no more can flow until S_2 is again closed.

An SCR can also act as a switch in an AC circuit. Figure 1-21 shows a simple circuit that allows a large amount of current to flow through the

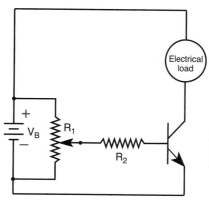

Figure 1-18. *A transistor varies the load current when its base current is varied. The greater the base-emitter current, the greater the collector-emitter, or load, current.*

amplifier. An electronic circuit in which a small change in voltage or current controls a much larger change in voltage or current.

silicon controlled rectifier (SCR). A semiconductor electron control device. An SCR blocks current flow in both directions until a pulse of positive voltage is applied to its gate. It then conducts in its forward direction, while continuing to block current in its reverse direction.

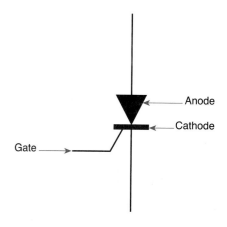

Figure 1-19. *A silicon controlled rectifier.*

holding relay. An electrical relay that is closed by sending a pulse of current through the coil. It remains closed until the current flowing through its contacts is interrupted. Also known as a latching relay.

electrical load. This large load current can be controlled by a very small control current, which can be carried through a small wire and controlled with a small switch.

The waveform of the input AC in the circuit shows that it rises from zero to a peak value in the positive direction, and then it changes direction and goes through zero to a peak value in the negative direction. Since an SCR blocks current flow in both directions before it is triggered, no current flows through the SCR as long as switch S_1 is open.

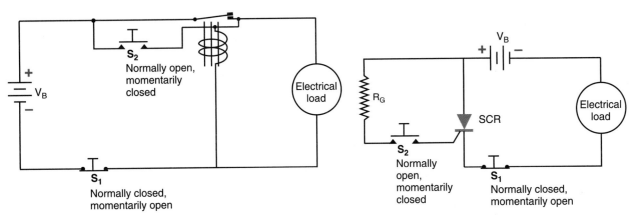

Contacts of a holding relay are closed by momentarily closing switch S_2. Current flows through load until switch S_1 is momentarily opened.

When switch S_2 is momentarily closed, the SCR is caused to conduct, and current flows through load until switch S_1 is momentarily opened.

Figure 1-20. *A silicon controlled rectifier acts as a holding relay.*

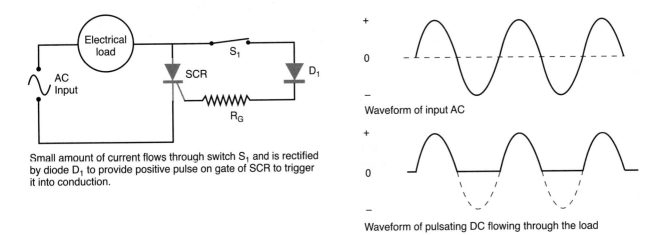

Small amount of current flows through switch S_1 and is rectified by diode D_1 to provide positive pulse on gate of SCR to trigger it into conduction.

Waveform of input AC

Waveform of pulsating DC flowing through the load

Figure 1-21. *An SCR installed in an AC circuit acts as a high-current half-wave rectifier for the load current.*

When switch S_1 is closed, diode D_1 allows current to flow to the gate during the half of the AC cycle when the current is positive. This small pulse of positive current triggers the SCR into conducting, and load current flows during the entire positive half of the cycle. The SCR stops conducting as soon as the AC drops to zero. No current flows during the negative half-cycle, but it starts to conduct again at the beginning of the positive half-cycle.

Circuit Arrangement

There are three types of electrical circuits used in an aircraft and each has its own unique characteristics. A series circuit is one in which there is only one path for the current to flow in from one side of the battery to the other. A parallel circuit has more than one complete path between the battery terminals. A complex circuit has some components in series and others in parallel.

Series Circuits

Figure 1-22 shows a series circuit. All of the components are connected in series, so all of the current must flow through each one of them. Voltage drops across each component until the sum of all of the voltage drops equals the voltage of the battery.

There is virtually no voltage drop across the closed switch S. The resistor changes some of the electrical energy from the battery into heat, and it drops some of the voltage. This voltage drop is called V_R.

The light changes energy from the battery into light and heat, and it drops voltage. This voltage drop is called V_L.

In a series circuit, the sum of all of the voltage drops is equal to the voltage of the battery.

$$V_R + V_L = V_B$$

Current is represented in an electrical formula with the letter I. In a series circuit, the current is the same everywhere in the circuit.

$$I_B = I_R = I_L$$

Parallel Circuits

In the parallel circuit in Figure 1-23, there are two complete paths for current to flow between terminals of the battery. When the current leaves the battery, it divides so that some flows through the resistor and some through the light. The voltage across the resistor (V_R) and the voltage across the light (V_L), are both the same as the voltage of the battery (V_B).

$$V_R = V_L = V_B$$

The current in a parallel circuit flowing through the battery (I_B) is equal to the sum of the currents flowing through the resistor (I_R) and the light (I_L).

$$I_B = I_R + I_L$$

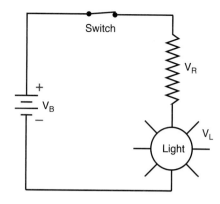

Figure 1-22. *In this closed series circuit, the sum of the voltage drops across the resistor and the light equals the voltage of the battery.*

series circuit. A method of connecting electrical components in such a way that all of the current flows through each of the components. There is only one path for current to flow.

series-parallel circuit. An electrical circuit in which some of the components are connected in parallel and others are connected in series.

parallel circuit. A method of connecting electrical components so that each component forms a complete path from one terminal of the source of electrical energy to the other terminal.

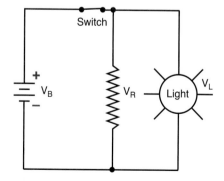

Figure 1-23. *In this closed parallel circuit, current from the battery divides, some flowing through the resistor and the rest flowing through the light.*

Complex Circuits

Many circuits in an aircraft electrical system are complex rather than simple series or parallel circuits. These circuits have some components in series and some in parallel. In Figure 1-24, the switch and resistor R_1 are in series with the parallel circuit consisting of the light and resistor R_2.

To better understand the voltage, current, and resistance relationships that exist in a complex circuit, review the section on series-parallel circuits in the *General* textbook of the Aviation Mechanic Series.

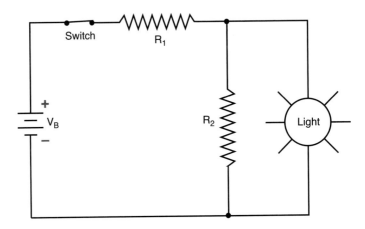

Figure 1-24. *In this complex circuit, the battery, switch, and resistor R_1 are in series with the parallel arrangement of resistor R_2 and the light.*

STUDY QUESTIONS: AN INTRODUCTION TO AIRCRAFT ELECTRICAL SYSTEMS

Answers are provided on page 99.

1. The letter symbol used to represent electrical current is _____ .

2. The letter symbol used to represent electrical pressure is _____ or _____ .

3. The letter symbol used to represent electrical resistance is _____ .

4. The point in an aircraft electrical system from which the various circuits get their power is called a/an _____ .

5. Three things that happen in an electrical circuit when current flows through it are:

    a._____

    b._____

    c._____

6. The longer line in the symbol for a battery indicates the _____ (positive or negative) terminal.

7. Electrons flowing in an electrical circuit flow in the _____ (same or opposite) direction as the arrowheads in a semiconductor diode symbol.

8. Conventional current in an electrical circuit is assumed to flow in the _____ (same or opposite) direction as the arrowheads in a semiconductor diode symbol.

9. Three things that must be included in all complete electrical circuits are:

   a._____

   b._____

   c._____

10. If the bar in the symbol for a semiconductor diode is connected to the negative terminal of a battery, the diode is _____ (forward or reverse) biased.

11. A forward-biased diode act as a/an _____ (open or closed) switch.

12. The voltage drop across a forward-biased silicon diode is approximately _____ volt.

13. The voltage drop across a forward-biased silicon diode _____ (does or does not) vary with the current flowing through it.

14. A semiconductor device that can be used as a voltage control is a/an _____ .

15. A zener diode used as a voltage regulator is _____ (forward or reverse) biased.

16. An electrical relay has a _____ (fixed or movable) core.

17. A solenoid has a _____ (fixed or movable) core.

18. When the base of an NPN transistor has the same polarity as the collector, the transistor acts as a/an _____ (open or closed) switch.

19. When a transistor is connected in an amplifier circuit, bringing its base polarity closer to that of the collector _____ (increases or decreases) the collector-emitter current.

20. A semiconductor device that acts in the same way as a holding relay is a _____ _____ .

21. In a complete series circuit, the sum of the voltage drops is the same as the applied voltage. This sentence is _____ (true or false).

(continued)

22. The voltage drop across an open switch in a series circuit is _____ (zero volts or battery voltage).

23. The voltage drop across a closed switch in a series circuit is _____ (zero volts or battery voltage).

24. The amount of current that flows through each path of a parallel circuit is determined by the _____ of the path.

25. The voltage across each path of a parallel circuit is equal to the _____ voltage.

Figure 1-25. *The ground symbol indicates that the electrical component is connected to the metal structure of the aircraft so it will form a return path for the current to the battery. Ground is considered to have zero electrical potential, and voltage measurements, both positive and negative, are referenced from it.*

ground. The voltage reference point in an aircraft electrical system. Ground has zero electrical potential. Voltage values, both positive and negative, are measured from ground. In the United Kingdom, ground is spoken of as "earth."

master switch. A switch in an aircraft electrical system that can disconnect the battery from the bus and open the generator or alternator field circuit.

Aircraft Electrical Power Circuits

Aircraft electrical systems are divided into two main classifications of circuits: power circuits and load circuits. Power circuits consist of the battery circuits, ground-power circuits, generator and alternator circuits, and distribution circuits up to the power buses.

Battery Circuits

All aircraft electrical circuits must have a complete path from one side of the battery through the load to the other side of the battery. Airplanes use a single-wire electrical system. In this type of system, one side of the battery, almost always the negative side, is connected to the structure of the aircraft with a heavy cable. All of the components are connected to the positive side of the battery through the proper circuit breakers and switches, and the circuit is completed by connecting the negative connection of the component to the metal of the aircraft structure.

In electrical schematics, the symbol that shows several parallel lines forming an inverted pyramid like that in Figure 1-25, is used to show that this point is connected to the aircraft structure. In American English, this is called ground; the British call it earth. It is the reference from which all voltage measurements in the aircraft are made.

In the circuit shown in Figure 1-26, the negative side of the battery is connected to ground and the positive side is connected to one of the contacts of the battery contactor and to one end of the contactor coil. The other end of the coil connects to ground through the master switch.

When the master switch is closed, current flows through the coil and produces a magnetic pull that closes the contacts. With the contacts closed, current flows to the battery bus, the point in the aircraft from which all other circuits get their power. The circuits are all connected to the bus through circuit breakers.

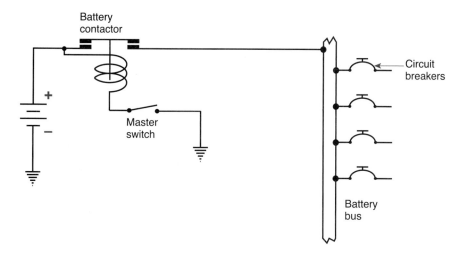

Push-to-reset, pull-to-open circuit breaker

Switch-type circuit breaker

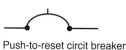

Push-to-reset circit breaker

Fuse

150-amp current limiter

Figure 1-26. *A typical battery circuit as found on a light airplane.*

Figure 1-27. *Electrical symbols used for circuit-protection devices.*

Circuit Protection Devices

Previous certification requirements, and generally accepted aircraft design conventions, utilize a device to open the circuit in the event of excessive current flow. This can be done with a current limiter, a fuse, or a circuit breaker. The primary function of a circuit protection device is to protect the wiring in the circuit. It should open the circuit before enough current flows to cause the insulation on the wire to melt or smoke. Some new aircraft designs are beginning to use electronic circuit breaker units (ECBUs) to protect circuits. The ECBU is a solid-state device that senses current flow and opens the circuit if it senses too much current. The advantage of an ECBU is that it has much faster response times and can greatly reduce weight due to fewer components and wiring.

Figure 1-27 shows the symbols used for circuit protection devices. Any time too much current flows, these devices open the circuit and stop the current.

Some circuit breakers have an operating handle or button that allows them to be used as a switch to open or close a circuit manually. Other circuit breakers have only a button, which pops out when the circuit is overloaded but can be pushed back in to restore the circuit. Depending on the design of the button, these push-to-reset circuit breakers may, or may not, be used to manually open a circuit. All circuit breakers have some means of showing when they have opened a circuit.

Some commercial and industrial motors are protected by automatic-reset circuit breakers that are opened by heat when excessive current flows. When the motor windings and the circuit breaker cool down, the circuit breaker automatically resets and allows current to flow again. Automatic-reset circuit breakers are not permitted in aircraft electrical circuits.

Circuit breakers approved for use in aircraft electrical circuits must be of the "trip-free" type and must require a manual operation to restore service

current limiter. An electrical component used to limit the amount of current a generator can produce. Some current limiters are a type of slow-blow fuse in the generator output. Other current limiters reduce the generator output voltage if the generator tries to put out more than its rated current.

circuit breaker. An electrical component that automatically opens a circuit any time excessive current flows through it.

A circuit breaker may be reset to restore the circuit after the fault causing the excessive current has been corrected.

trip-free circuit breaker. A circuit breaker that opens a circuit any time an excessive amount of current flows regardless of the position of the circuit breaker's operating handle.

after tripping. Trip-free circuit breakers cannot be manually held closed if a fault exists in the circuit they are protecting. All fuses and circuit breakers that protect circuits that are essential to flight must be located and identified so that they are replaceable or resettable in flight.

Some circuits are protected by fuses instead of circuit breakers. A fuse is simply a strip of low-melting-point wire enclosed in a small glass tube with a metal terminal on each end. When too much current flows through the fuse, the heat caused by the current melts the fuse wire and opens the circuit. A new fuse must be installed before current can flow again.

If fuses are used, there must be one spare fuse of each rating or 50% spare fuses of each rating, whichever is greater.

slow-blow fuse. An electrical fuse that allows a large amount of current to flow for a short length of time but melts to open the circuit if more than its rated current flows for a longer period.

Current limiters are high-current, slow-blow fuses that allow transient high currents, such as during motor starting, but will open when subjected to an excessive continuous current.

Induced Current Protection

Fuses and circuit breakers are installed in a circuit to protect the wiring; many electrical components have built-in fuses to protect them from an excessive amount of current.

There is another type of circuit hazard in aircraft that carry a large amount of electronic equipment. Solid-state electronic equipment is extremely vulnerable to spikes of high voltage that are induced into a circuit when a current flow is interrupted.

Before going too much further, let's review some very important facts about the magnetic field that surrounds a wire when current flows through it.

- Any time current flows through a conductor, it causes a magnetic field to surround the conductor. The more current there is, the stronger the magnetic field.

- Any time a conductor is crossed by a changing magnetic field, or is moved through a stationary magnetic field, a voltage is induced in it that causes current to flow through it. This is called induced current.

induced current. Electrical current produced in a conductor when the current through the conductor changes, or when it is moved through or crossed by a magnetic field.

- When the current flowing in a conductor changes, the magnetic field surrounding the conductor changes. As it builds up or collapses, it cuts across the conductor and generates a voltage that causes an induced current to flow.

- The amount of induced current is determined by the rate at which the magnetic field cuts across the conductor. The faster the current changes, the greater the induced current.

- Induced current always flows in the direction opposite to the flow of current that produced the magnetic field.

Consider the battery contactor shown in Figure 1-28. When current begins to flow through the contactor coil, a strong magnetic field builds up around the coil. This field surrounds the coil as long as current flows through it. But as soon as the switch between the coil and ground is opened, current stops flowing in the coil, and as it stops, the magnetic field collapses across all of the turns of wire in the coil. As the collapsing magnetic field cuts across the coil, it produces a short pulse, or spike, of very high voltage whose polarity is opposite to that of the battery. This voltage spike can damage any electronic equipment connected to the system when the master switch is opened. It can also damage the master switch by causing an arc to jump across the contacts as they are opening.

To prevent this kind of damage, a reverse-biased diode is connected across the contactor coil. During normal operation, no current can flow through it, but the high-voltage spike that is produced when the master switch is opened forward-biases the diode, and the induced current flows back through the contactor coil and is dissipated.

arcing. Sparking between a commutator and brush or between switch contacts that is caused by induced current when a circuit is broken.

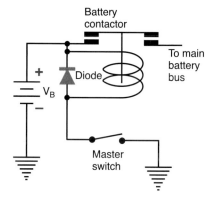

Figure 1-28. *A reverse-biased diode installed across the coil of the battery contactor allows the induced current that is produced when the master switch contacts open to be dissipated in the coil rather than arcing across the switch contacts.*

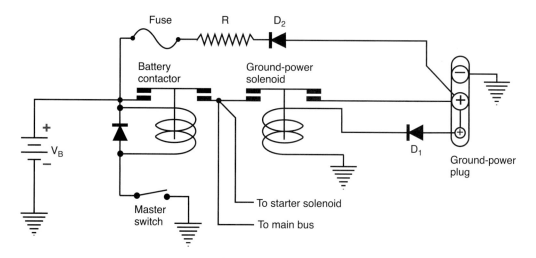

Figure 1-29. *A typical aircraft ground-power circuit.*

ground-power unit (GPU). A service component used to supply electrical power to an aircraft when it is being operated on the ground.

Ground-Power Circuit

The battery installed in an aircraft must be lightweight, and so it has a rather limited capacity. Because of this, it is often necessary to plug in a ground-power unit, or GPU, to provide electrical power for starting the engine and for operating some of the systems while the engine is not running.

It is extremely important that the polarity of the GPU be the same as that of the battery in the aircraft, as reversed polarity can damage much of the sensitive electronic equipment. The ground-power circuit shown in Figure 1-29 is made in such a way that no power can be connected to the aircraft if the polarities of the two sources are not correct.

The plug installed in the aircraft has three pins, with the two upper pins larger and longer than the bottom pin. The negative pin—the top pin in the diagram connects to the aircraft structure through a heavy cable. The middle pin is the positive pin, and it connects with a heavy cable to the contact of the ground-power solenoid. A small wire comes from this pin to diode D_2, resistor R, and a fuse connected in series. This wire then goes to the battery side of the battery contactor, to the same point where the coil of the battery contactor connects.

The GPU supplies power to the coil of the battery contactor so that it can be closed even if the battery in the aircraft is too low to close it. Closing this solenoid allows the GPU to charge the battery. It is important that the output voltage of the GPU be regulated so the battery will not be damaged by too high a voltage, which will cause an excessive charging rate.

Current flows from the positive pin of the ground-power plug to the battery coil through diode D_2, but this diode keeps the current from the battery from flowing back to the GPU plug. The resistor limits the current that can flow in this circuit to a value that is high enough to close the battery contactor, but not high enough to overcharge a fully charged battery. If there is a short circuit in the battery, the fuse will blow and open this circuit, preventing the battery relay from closing.

Sockets on the end of the ground-power cord make good contact with the two main pins in the ground-power plug. Then, as the sockets are pushed the rest of the way onto the plug, the short pin enters its socket and completes the circuit for the coil of the ground-power solenoid. Current from the GPU flows through diode D_1 to energize this coil. If the GPU has the wrong polarity, diode D_1 will block the current so that the GPU solenoid will not close.

When connecting or disconnecting external power to an aircraft, be sure to consult the aircraft flight manual or the manufacturer's maintenance instructions for the proper sequences. When external power is connected, some aircraft will automatically turn on the electrical system, even with the master switch turned off. To prevent unwanted actuation of systems, it is good practice to check the cockpit for the proper position of the flap handle and landing gear lever before applying power to the aircraft.

Power Generating Systems

The battery is installed in an aircraft only to provide electrical power for starting the engine and to furnish current to assist the alternator (or generator) when an extra heavy load is placed on the electrical system. It also furnishes field current for the alternator and helps start the alternator producing current.

For many years, DC generators were the prime source of electrical energy for aircraft as well as for automobiles. But with the advent of efficient solid-state diodes, the DC alternator has replaced the generator on almost all small and medium-size aircraft.

Alternators have two main advantages over generators: They normally have more pairs of field poles than generators do, allowing them to produce their rated current at a lower RPM; and their load current is produced in the fixed stator winding and then taken out through solid connections. Generators produce their load current in the rotating element, and it is taken out through carbon brushes riding on copper commutator segments.

When performing maintenance on power generation systems; you may need to measure the voltage being generated. The output of DC generators and alternators can be measured with a voltmeter between the output terminal and ground. On a DC generator, the output post is labeled as the B terminal, and on a DC alternator, the output post is labeled as the A terminal. When measuring these voltages with the engine running, safety is an important consideration. A long jumper wire with an insulated alligator clip is a handy tool for these situations.

In this section we will first consider DC alternator circuits, then DC generator circuits. In the section on large-aircraft electrical systems, AC alternator circuits are discussed. The theory of electrical generation is covered in the *General* textbook of the Aviation Mechanic Series, and the *Powerplant* textbook looks at the mechanisms and internal circuitry of generators and alternators, and their controls.

The DC Alternator Circuit

A DC alternator converts some of the aircraft engine's mechanical energy into electrical energy. A rotating electromagnetic field with four to eight pairs of poles is turned by the engine. The magnetic flux produced by this field cuts across some heavy windings, called stator coils, or stator windings, which are wound in slots in the housing of the alternator. As the magnetic field cuts across these windings, it produces three-phase alternating current in them. This alternating current is changed into direct current by six solid-state rectifier diodes mounted inside the alternator housing.

generator. A mechanical device that transforms mechanical energy into electrical energy by rotating a coil inside a magnetic field. As the conductors in the coil cut across the lines of magnetic flux, a voltage is generated that causes current to flow.

alternator. An electrical generator that produces alternating current. The popular DC alternator used on light aircraft produces three-phase AC in its stator windings. This AC is changed into DC by a six-diode, solid-state rectifier before it leaves the alternator.

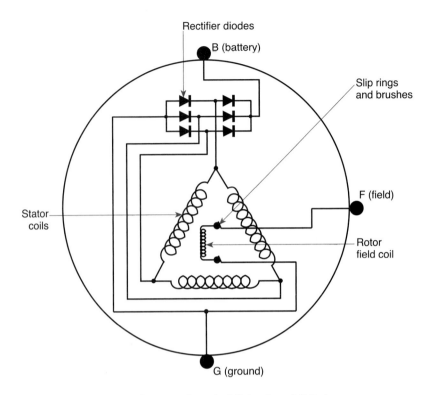

Figure 1-30. *The internal circuit of a typical light-aircraft DC alternator.*

The amount of voltage the alternator produces is controlled by a voltage regulator which acts much like a variable resistor between the battery bus and the coil in the alternator rotor. The strength of the magnetic field is controlled by the amount of current flowing through the field coil, and the voltage regulator varies this current to keep the alternator output voltage constant as the amount of current it produces changes with the electrical load. Figure 1-31 shows how the alternator ties into the electrical system at the main battery bus.

The B, or battery, terminal of the alternator connects to the main bus through a 100-amp circuit breaker. Since an alternator can be damaged if it produces electricity without a load connected to it, this circuit breaker must always be closed unless the alternator malfunctions. The field current is also supplied from this circuit breaker, so the alternator cannot be disconnected from the bus without also shutting off the field current.

The alternator field current flows through the alternator circuit breaker, then through a 5-amp alternator regulator circuit breaker, through the alternator side of the master switch, through the overvoltage protector, and into the voltage regulator at its B terminal.

The voltage regulator senses the voltage the alternator is producing. If this voltage is too high, it decreases the field current flowing to the coil in the rotor. If the output voltage is too low, it increases the current. The field

bus. A point within an electrical system from which the individual circuits get their power.

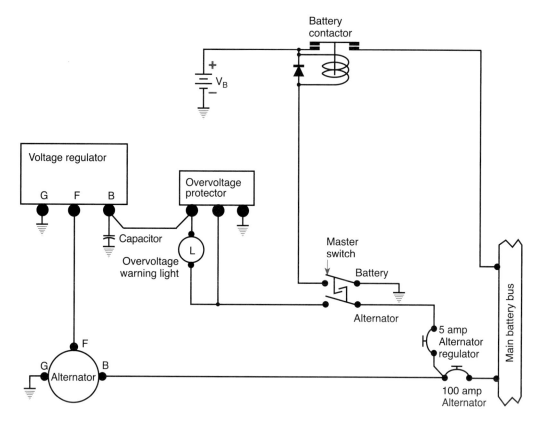

Figure 1-31. *A typical light-aircraft DC alternator system.*

current leaves the voltage regulator through its F terminal and flows to the F terminal of the alternator, to which the field is connected internally. The alternator and the voltage regulator are grounded through their G terminals.

The master switch is a double-pole, single-throw split-rocker switch that controls the battery circuit and the alternator field circuit at the same time. The rocker for this switch is split so that the battery side of the switch can be turned on without turning on the alternator side, but the alternator side cannot be turned on without also turning on the battery side. The alternator side can be turned off, as it would have to be if the alternator malfunctioned in flight, without turning off the battery side of the switch. You cannot turn off the battery side of the switch without also turning off the alternator field side.

The overvoltage protector is a device in the alternator field circuit that senses the voltage the alternator is producing; if this voltage gets too high, the overvoltage protector opens the field circuit, stopping any further output from the alternator.

The overvoltage warning light turns on when the master switch is first closed, and it turns off when the engine is started and the alternator produces the correct amount of voltage. If the voltage gets too high, the overvoltage protector opens the alternator field circuit, which turns on the overvoltage

split-rocker switch. An electrical switch whose operating rocker is split so one half of the switch can be opened without affecting the other half.

Split-rocker switches are used as aircraft master switches. The battery can be turned on without turning on the alternator, but the alternator cannot be turned on without also turning on the battery. The alternator can be turned off without turning off the battery, but the battery cannot be turned off without also turning off the alternator.

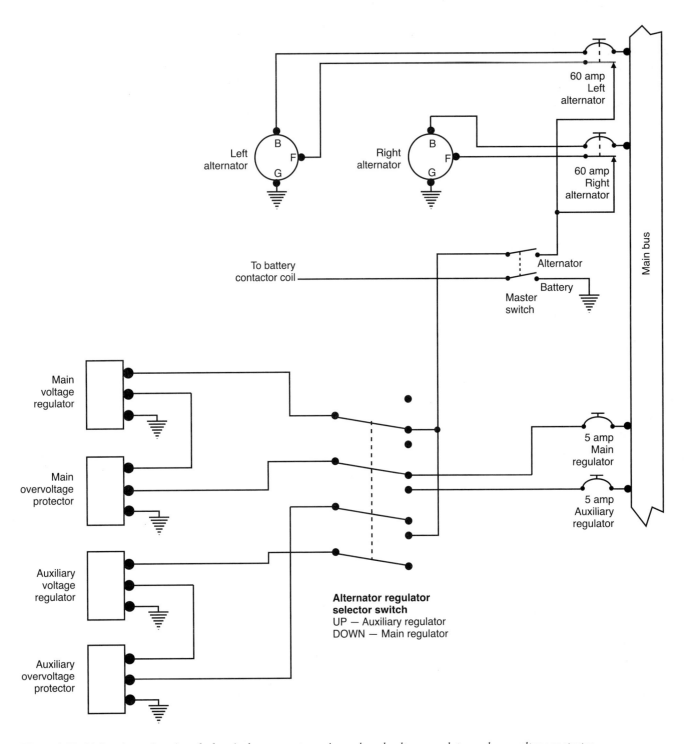

Figure 1-32. *Light twin-engine aircraft electrical power system using a shared voltage regulator and overvoltage protector.*

warning light, showing that the alternator has been shut off because of an overvoltage condition.

The capacitor installed between the battery input of the voltage regulator and ground acts as a shock absorber. During operation, the electric motors in the aircraft can produce a spike of voltage in the electrical system high enough for the overvoltage protector to sense, which prompts it to open the alternator field circuit, shutting off the alternator. To prevent this, the capacitor absorbs the spike so it will not trip the overvoltage protector.

Twin-Engine Alternator System Using a Shared Voltage Regulator

One of the simplest alternator systems for use in a twin-engine aircraft is one that uses a single voltage regulator to control the output of both alternators, so that they will increase their current output when the current load on the aircraft electrical system is heavy, or decrease their output current when the demand is low.

Figure 1-32 is a basic schematic diagram of such a system. The output from each of the alternators goes directly to the main bus through 60-amp circuit breakers. Notice in the diagram that each of these circuit breakers is connected to a normally open switch by a dashed line. This symbol indicates that the circuit breaker is mechanically linked to a precision switch, such as a Microswitch, whose contacts open when the circuit breaker is tripped, but are held closed when the circuit breaker is allowing current to flow. An alternator can be destroyed if it is operated into an open circuit, so when the circuit breaker opens, disconnecting the alternator output from the main bus, the Microswitch opens the alternator field circuit and stops the alternator from producing current.

The two Microswitches are connected in series with the field terminals of the two alternators. The two fields are connected to the alternator side of the aircraft master switch.

This alternator system has two voltage regulators, one main regulator and one auxiliary, or backup, regulator that can be switched into the system if the main regulator should fail. The alternator regulator selector switch is a four-pole, double-throw toggle switch. When the switch handle is in the down position, the main voltage regulator is in the circuit. When it is moved into the up position, the main voltage regulator is taken out of the circuit and the auxiliary voltage regulator takes its place.

When the main voltage regulator is selected, alternator field current flows from the main bus through a 5-amp main-regulator circuit breaker, through the regulator selector switch, then through the overvoltage protector. The current then flows through the voltage regulator back through the alternator selector switch, the alternator side of the master switch, and then through the Microswitches to the F terminals of both alternators.

If the main voltage regulator fails in flight, the pilot can switch the voltage regulator selector switch to the auxiliary-regulator position. The alternator field current will follow the same path to the selector switch, but from there

Microswitch. The registered trade name for a precision switch. Microswitches are used as limit switches in an aircraft electrical system.

overvoltage protector. A component in an aircraft electrical system that opens the alternator field circuit any time the alternator produces too high an output voltage.

it will flow through the auxiliary overvoltage protector and the auxiliary voltage regulator.

The overvoltage protectors are located in the alternator field circuits, so if the voltage regulator malfunctions and the alternators produce too high a voltage, the contacts inside the overvoltage protector will open the alternator field circuit. If that happens, both alternators will go off line until the auxiliary voltage regulator is selected.

Twin-Engine Alternator System Using Individual Voltage Regulators
A more modern control system for small twin-engine aircraft uses a solid-state voltage regulator and an overvoltage protector for each alternator. Figure 1-33 shows this type of system.

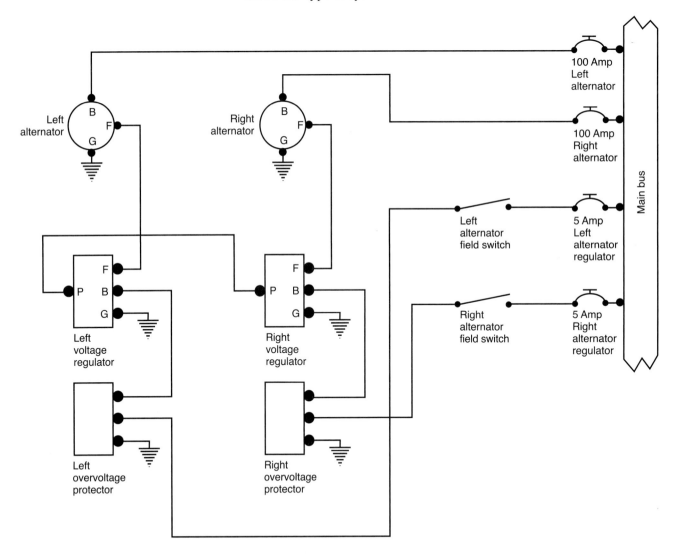

Figure 1-33. *Light twin-engine aircraft electrical power system using individual electronic voltage regulators and overvoltage protectors. The alternator paralleling circuit is built into the voltage regulators.*

The output of each alternator goes directly to the main bus through 100-amp circuit breakers. Field current is supplied to each alternator through its own 5-amp circuit breaker, alternator field switch, overvoltage protector, and voltage regulator.

This circuit has one feature that has not yet been discussed: the paralleling feature on the voltage regulators. The two regulators are connected through their P terminals so that circuits inside the regulators can compare the field voltages.

If one alternator is producing more current than the other, its field voltage will be higher. This difference is sensed by the circuitry inside the voltage regulators, which decreases the field current flowing to the high-output alternator and increases the field current sent to the low-output alternator. This adjusts the alternator output voltages so they share the load equally.

The overvoltage protectors sense each alternator's output voltage. If this voltage becomes too high, the overvoltage protector opens the alternator field circuit and shuts off the alternator.

The DC Generator Circuit

Because there are still a lot of older aircraft with DC generator systems installed, we need to understand these systems.

There are three basic differences between an alternator and a generator: the component in which the load current is generated, the type of rectifier used, and the method of field excitation.

Generator output current is produced in the rotating armature. The output current in an alternator is produced in the stationary stator.

Both generators and alternators produce AC, which must be changed into DC before it can be used. In a generator, this conversion is done by brushes and a commutator which act as a mechanical rectifier that switches between the various armature coils so that the current leaving the armature always flows in the same direction. An alternator produces three-phase AC in its stator windings, which is changed into DC by a six-diode solid-state rectifier mounted inside the alternator housing.

Generator fields are self-excited. This means that the field current comes from the armature. As the voltage produced in the armature rises, the field current rises and causes the armature voltage, and consequently the load current, to increase even more. If some provision were not made for limiting the current, a generator would burn itself out. For this reason, all generators must use some type of current limiter as well as a voltage regulator. Because alternator field current is supplied by the aircraft battery and the regulated output of the alternator, an alternator does not need a current limiter.

Most light aircraft use a basic electrical system that has been adapted from automobile systems. The generators and regulators are similar in appearance to those used in automobiles, but there are internal differences, differences in materials, and especially differences in the inspections used to certificate

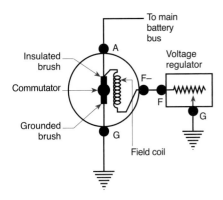

Voltage regulator used with A-circuit generator system is between shunt field and ground.

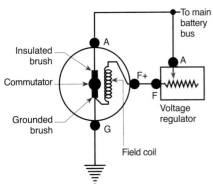

In B-circuit system, voltage regulator is between shunt field and armature.

Figure 1-34. *The placement of voltage regulators in the field circuits of generators for light aircraft.*

the components for use in aircraft. It is not permissible to use an automobile component in an FAA-certificated aircraft even though the parts do look alike.

There are two types of generator circuits used in aircraft electrical systems. Both are shown in Figure 1-34. The A-circuit's field coils are connected to the insulated brush inside the generator, and the voltage regulator acts as a variable resistor between the generator field and ground. In the B-circuit, the field coils are connected to the grounded brush, and the voltage regulator acts as a variable resistor between the generator field and the armature. The electrical systems that use these two types of generators work in the same way. The only difference is in the connection and servicing of the two systems. The fact that the components used in these different types of systems look much alike makes it very important that you use only the correct part number for the component when servicing these systems.

The generator control contains three units: the voltage regulator, the current limiter, and the reverse-current cutout. This unit is shown in Figure 1-35 and is described in more detail in the *Powerplant* textbook of the Aviation Mechanic Series.

The voltage regulator senses the generator output voltage, and its normally closed contacts vibrate open and closed many times a second, limiting the

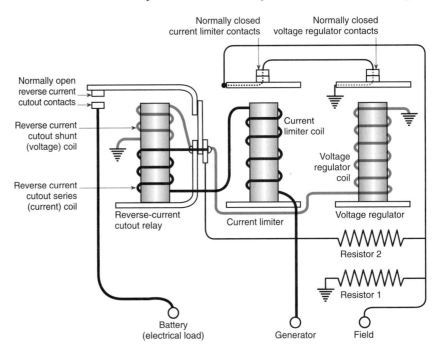

Figure 1-35. *An A-circuit, three-unit generator control such as is used on light aircraft.*

amount of current that can flow through the field. When the contacts are closed, the field current flows through the generator field coil, to ground through the contacts, and the output voltage increases. As the voltage increases, the magnetic field of the voltage regulator coil becomes strong enough to open the normally closed contacts, and the field current must then flow to ground through resistor 1. This increase in the field resistance decreases the field current and the generator output voltage drops enough to allow the contacts to close, repeating the cycle.

The current limiter is actuated by a coil in series with the armature output. When the generator puts out more than its rated current, the current limiter's normally closed contacts open and put a resistance in the field circuit to lower the generator output voltage to a level that will not produce excessive current.

The normally open contacts of the reverse-current cutout disconnect the generator from the aircraft bus when the generator voltage drops below that of the battery, and they automatically connect the generator to the bus when the generator voltage rises above that of the battery.

Simple Light-Aircraft Generator System

The A-circuit type generator system in Figure 1-36 is typical for most single-engine light airplanes.

The armature terminal of the generator connects to the G terminal of the generator control unit. The contacts of the reverse-current cutout are between the G and the B terminals. When the generator output reaches a specified voltage, the reverse-current cutout contacts close and connect the generator to the main bus.

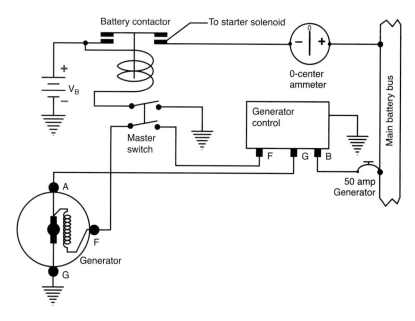

Figure 1-36. *Simple light-aircraft generator system.*

Field current produced in the generator flows from the field terminal of the generator, through the generator side of the master switch, into the F terminal of the control unit, and through the voltage regulator and current limiter contacts to ground. If either the voltage or the current are too high, one set of normally closed contacts opens and this field current must flow through the resistor to ground.

The zero-center ammeter shows the amount of current flowing either from the battery to the main bus (–) or from the generator through the main bus into the battery (+) to charge it.

Twin-Engine Generator System Using Vibrator-Type Voltage Regulators

The generator system shown in Figure 1-37 uses generators and regulators similar to those just discussed, except that the voltage regulator relay in the generator control has an extra coil wound on it through which paralleling current flows. This coil is connected between the regulator's P (paralleling) terminal and G (generator) terminal.

The paralleling relay unit contains two relays, whose coils are supplied with current from the G terminals of the two voltage regulators. This current

zero-center ammeter. An ammeter in a light aircraft electrical system located between the battery and the main bus. This ammeter shows the current flowing into or out of the battery.

vibrator-type voltage regulator. A type of voltage regulator used with a generator or alternator that intermittently places a resistance in the field circuit to control the voltage. A set of vibrating contacts puts the resistor in the circuit and takes it out several times a second.

paralleling circuit. A circuit in a multiengine aircraft electrical system that causes the generators or alternators to share the electrical load equally.

paralleling relay. A relay in a multiengine aircraft electrical system that controls a flow of control current which is used to keep the generators or alternators sharing the electrical load equally.

The relay opens automatically to shut off the flow of paralleling current any time the output of either alternator or generator drops to zero.

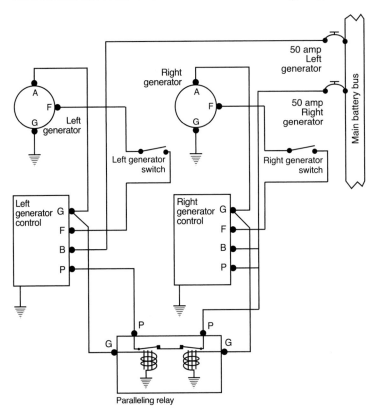

Figure 1-37. *Twin-engine aircraft generator system using vibrator-type voltage regulators and a paralleling relay.*

is supplied at the generator output voltage. The contacts of the relays are connected in series and to the P terminals of each of the voltage regulator units.

When both generators are operating and supplying current to the main bus, the two paralleling relays are closed and the paralleling coils in the two voltage regulators are connected. If the output voltage of one generator rises above that of the other, it will put out more current than the other. Current will flow through the paralleling coils from the generator producing the high voltage output to the one producing the lower voltage. The magnetic field caused by this current will aid the field from the voltage coil in the voltage regulator for the high generator and will oppose the field from the voltage coil in the voltage regulator for the low generator. This will decrease the voltage of the high generator and increase the voltage of the low generator so that they will share the load equally.

When the output voltage of either generator drops to near zero, the paralleling relay for that generator automatically opens the paralleling circuit so that the working generator will not be affected by the one not producing current.

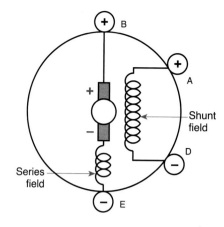

Figure 1-38. *Internal circuit of a compound-wound generator.*

Twin-Engine Generator System Using Carbon-Pile Voltage Regulators

Carbon-pile voltage regulators and heavy-duty, compound-wound generators with differential-voltage reverse-current cutout relays were used to produce current for all older large aircraft. While these systems are not used on aircraft now being produced, a lot of them are still in operation.

The generators used in these systems have both a shunt field used for voltage control and a series field wound in such a way that it helps minimize armature reaction that causes brush arcing as the generator load changes. The positive brushes are connected to terminal B, and the negative brushes are connected through the series field to terminal E (Figure 1-38). The positive end of the shunt field winding is connected to terminal A and its negative end is connected to terminal D. The carbon-pile voltage regulator used with this type of system acts as a variable resistor between the positive end of the field terminal, terminal A, and the armature output, terminal B.

The differential-voltage reverse-current cutout relay senses both the generator output voltage and the battery voltage, and its contacts close when the generator output is a specified amount higher than the battery voltage. The contacts remain closed until the generator output drops low enough that current flows from the battery back through the generator armature and the series field coils. This control unit has a switch terminal supplied with current from its generator terminal through a generator control switch mounted on the instrument panel. When this switch is closed, the generator can be connected to the main bus as soon as its voltage rises to the proper value. When this switch is open, the generator cannot be connected to the bus regardless of its voltage.

carbon-pile voltage regulator. A type of voltage regulator used with large aircraft generators.

Field current is controlled by varying the resistance of a stack of thin carbon disks. This resistance is varied by controlling the pressure on the stack with an electromagnet whose force is proportional to the generator output voltage.

differential-voltage reverse-current cutout. A type of reverse-current cutout switch used with heavy-duty electrical systems. This switch connects the generator to the electrical bus when the generator voltage is a specific amount higher than the battery voltage.

shunt winding. Field coils in an electric motor or generator that are connected in parallel with the armature.

generator series field. A set of heavy field windings in a generator connected in series with the armature. The magnetic field produced by the series windings is used to change the characteristics of the generator.

generator shunt field. A set of field windings in a generator connected in parallel with the armature. Varying the amount of current flowing in the shunt field windings controls the voltage output of the generator.

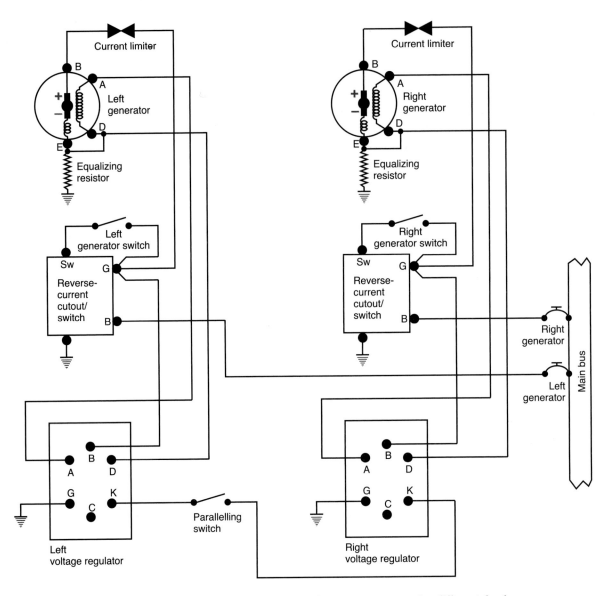

Figure 1-39. *Heavy-duty aircraft generator system using differential-voltage reverse-current cutout relays and carbon-pile voltage regulators.*

Figure 1-40. *Internal circuit of a carbon pile voltage regulator.*

A current limiter, a form of slow-blow fuse, is installed in the heavy cable between the B terminal of the generator and the G terminal of the reverse-current cutout. This type of current limiter allows current in excess of its rating to flow through it for a short time, but its fuse link will melt and open the circuit if its rated current flows through it for a longer than specified length of time. These current limiters are normally located in the engine nacelle, and cannot be changed in flight. The generator output current is carried into the main bus from the reverse-current cutout through a circuit breaker. See Figure 1-39.

The carbon-pile voltage regulator uses a stack of pure carbon disks inside a ceramic tube to act as a variable resistance in the shunt-field circuit to control the generator output. This stack of carbon disks, the carbon pile, is connected between terminals A and B of the regulator, which is between the armature output and the positive end of the shunt field (see Figure 1-40). The stack is held tightly compressed by a heavy spring to decrease its resistance.

Two coils, a voltage coil and a paralleling coil, are wound around an iron core so that the magnetic pull caused by current flowing through them attracts the armature, which pulls against the spring and loosens the pressure on the carbon stack. This increases the resistance of the carbon stack and decreases the current flowing in the field coils.

The voltage coil is connected between terminals B and G, so the current flowing through it is directly related to the output voltage the generator is producing. When this voltage rises above the value for which the regulator is set, its magnetic field pulls on the spring and loosens the carbon stack. Loosening the stack increases its resistance and decreases the field current. This lowers the generator output voltage.

Notice in Figure 1-39 that the E terminals of the two generators, the negative ends of the armatures, do not go directly to ground, but rather go to ground through equalizing resistors, also called equalizing shunts. These shunts are heavy-duty resistors that produce a voltage drop of 0.5 volt when the rated current of the generator flows through them. One end of each equalizing resistor connects to ground, and the other end connects to generator terminals E and D. This ground point of the generators is connected to terminal D of the voltage regulator, which connects to one end of the paralleling coil. The other end of the paralleling coil is connected to terminal K of the regulator. The K terminals of both regulators are connected through a cockpit-mounted paralleling switch.

The paralleling circuit ensures that the generators produce the same amount of current when both are connected to the main bus. All of the current the generators produce flows through the equalizing resistors and produces a voltage drop across them. When the generators are producing exactly the same amount of current, the voltage drops across the two equalizing resistors are the

equalizing resistor. A large resistor in the ground circuit of a heavy-duty aircraft generator through which all of the generator output current flows.

The voltage drop across this resistor is used to produce the current in the paralleling circuit that forces the generators to share the electrical load equally.

same and no current flows through the paralleling coils of the regulators. But if the left generator furnishes more current to the bus than the right generator does, for example, the top end of the left generator's equalizing resistor has a higher voltage than the top end of the right generator's equalizing resistor, and current flows through both of the paralleling coils.

The magnetic pull caused by the current in the paralleling coil of the left regulator aids the pull from the voltage coil and loosens the carbon stack in the left regulator. This decreases the left generator field current and lowers its output voltage. At the same time, the magnetic field from the paralleling coil in the right generator opposes the pull caused by the voltage coil, and the carbon pile tightens up so that its resistance decreases. The field current and the output voltage of the right generator increases until the generators share the load equally.

Turbine-Engine Starter-Generator System

Most of the smaller turbine engines installed in business jet airplanes have a combination starter-generator rather than a separate starter and generator. These units resemble heavy-duty, compound-wound DC generators, but they have an extra set of series windings. The series motor windings are switched into the circuit when the engine is started, but as soon as it is running, they are switched out.

Figure 1-42 shows a typical starter-generator circuit. When the start switch is placed in the START position, current flows through the start/ignition circuit breaker and the upper contacts of the start switch to the coil of the starter relay. This current produces a magnetic pull that closes the relay and allows

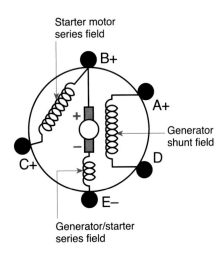

Figure 1-41. *Internal circuit of a turbine-engine starter-generator.*

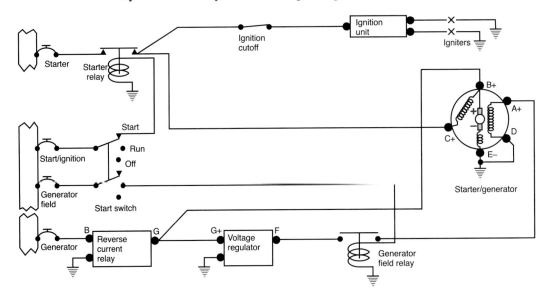

Figure 1-42. *Turbine-engine starter-generator system.*

current to flow to the starter-generator through its C+ terminal, the series motor windings, the armature, and the starter-generator series windings, to ground. At the same time, current flows through the ignition-cutoff switch into the igniter unit to provide the intense heat needed to ignite the fuel.

When ignition is achieved, the start switch is moved into the RUN position. Current flows from the bus through the generator field circuit breaker to the coil of the generator field relay, producing the magnetic pull needed to close the field relay contacts to connect the generator field to the voltage regulator. When generator field current flows, the generator produces current. As soon as the voltage builds up to the specified value, the contacts inside the reverse-current cutout relay close and the current produced in the generator flows from the B+ terminal through the reverse-current relay to the bus, through the generator circuit breaker.

When the start switch is placed in the OFF position, the current is shut off to the generator-field relay; it opens, disconnecting the generator field from the voltage regulator, and the generator stops producing load current.

starter-generator. A single-component starter and generator used on many of the smaller gas-turbine engines.

It is used as a starter, and when the engine is running, its circuitry is shifted so that it acts as a generator.

Voltage and Current Indicating Circuits

Almost all aircraft have some means of monitoring the current flow in some portion of the electrical system. The simplest system uses a zero-center ammeter connected between the system side of the battery contactor and the main bus, as shown in Figure 1-43. This type of system can be used only when the electrical loads on the aircraft are quite low, as the wire that carries all of the load current must go up to the ammeter on the instrument panel. Typically, this is an 8- or 10-gauge wire.

The ammeter has zero in the center of its scale, so it can deflect in either direction. When the battery is supplying all of the current, the ammeter deflects to the left, showing that the battery is being discharged. When the voltage of the alternator, which is connected to the main bus, is higher than that of the battery, the battery is being charged, and the ammeter deflects to the right. An ammeter in this location does not show the amount of current the alternator is producing.

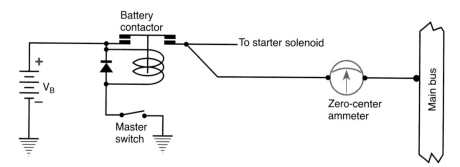

Figure 1-43. *A zero-center ammeter in this location gives an indication of the current flowing into or out of the battery.*

loadmeter. A current meter used in some aircraft electrical systems to show the amount of current the generator or alternator is producing. Loadmeters are calibrated in percent of the generator rated output.

millivoltmeter. An electrical instrument that measures voltage in units of millivolts (thousandths of a volt).

voltmeter multiplier. A precision resistor in series with a voltmeter mechanism used to extend the range of the basic meter or to allow a single meter to measure several ranges of voltage.

A loadmeter is a type of ammeter installed between the alternator output and the aircraft main bus. It does not give any indication of whether or not the battery is delivering current to the system, or whether it is receiving current from the alternator. The dial of the loadmeter is calibrated in terms of percentage of the alternator's rated output.

Figure 1-44 shows the way a loadmeter is connected into an alternator circuit. The loadmeter shunt is a precision resistor that has a large terminal on each end and two smaller terminals located between the larger ones. When the rated current for the alternator flows through the shunt, there is a fifty-millivolt (0.050-volt) drop between the two smaller terminals, which are connected to a millivoltmeter in the instrument panel with 20- or 22-gauge wire.

The millivoltmeter is calibrated in percentage from zero to 100 percent. If the aircraft is equipped with a 100-amp alternator and the loadmeter reads 50%, the alternator is supplying 50 amps of current to the main bus.

Some twin-engine aircraft have a volt-ammeter that can measure the current furnished by either the left or the right alternator and the current supplied by the battery, as well as the voltage on the aircraft electrical bus.

Figure 1-45 shows such a system, with an instrument shunt in the output of both alternators and a similar shunt in the cable between the battery contactor and the main bus. Small-gauge wires attach the three shunts to the instrument selector switch, and two small wires connect the switch to the volt-ammeter mounted in the instrument panel.

The pilot can read the amount of current being produced by the left or the right alternator or the amount of current the battery is furnishing to the system, as well as the voltage on the system bus.

The voltmeter multiplier is a precision resistor in series with the meter movement. It allows the millivoltmeter to read the voltage of the system.

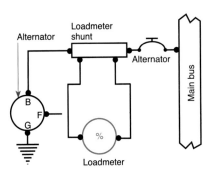

Figure 1-44. *A loadmeter in this location shows, in percentage of its rated output, the amount of current the alternator is producing.*

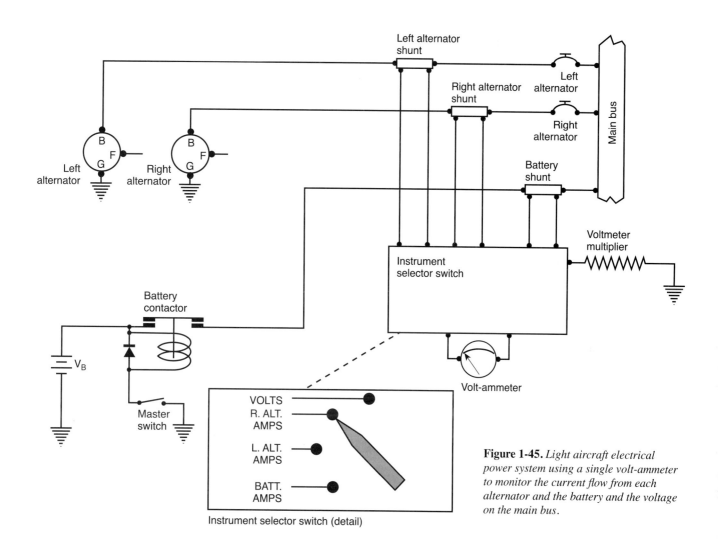

Figure 1-45. *Light aircraft electrical power system using a single volt-ammeter to monitor the current flow from each alternator and the battery and the voltage on the main bus.*

STUDY QUESTIONS: AIRCRAFT ELECTRICAL POWER CIRCUITS

Answers are provided on page 99.

26. The reference from which all voltage is measured in an aircraft electrical system is called the
_____.

27. Return current from devices installed in an aircraft electrical system flows back to the battery through the _____.

28. The battery terminal that is normally grounded is the _____ (negative or positive) terminal.

(continued)

29. Circuit breakers and fuses are installed in a circuit primarily to protect the _____ (wiring or circuit devices).

30. The one circuit in an aircraft electrical system that is not required to be protected by a circuit protection device is the main _____ circuit.

31. Circuit breakers used in aircraft electrical systems must be of the _____ type.

32. A trip-free circuit breaker _____ (can or cannot) be manually held closed in the presence of a fault.

33. Automatic reset circuit breakers _____ (are or are not) approved for use in aircraft electrical circuits.

34. An electrical circuit that has 12 fuses rated at 30 amps is required to carry at least _____ 30-amp fuses as spares.

35. Current that is induced into a conductor by a changing current in another nearby conductor is called _____ current.

36. The amount of current that is induced by a changing magnetic field is determined by the _____ of change of the magnetic field.

37. The direction of flow of induced current is _____ (the same as or opposite) that of the current that caused it.

38. The diode that is placed across the coil of a battery contactor is _____ (forward or reverse) biased by the battery.

39. Refer to Figure 1-29. The device that prevents the GPU from overcharging a fully charged battery is _____ .

40. Refer to Figure 1-29. The device that prevents the GPU from being connected to the aircraft electrical system if its polarity is incorrect is _____ .

41. Refer to Figure 1-29. The device that prevents the GPU from being connected to the aircraft electrical system if there is a short in the battery is _____ .

42. The prime source of electrical power in an aircraft is the _____ (battery or alternator).

43. The load current produced in a DC alternator is produced in the _____ (rotor or stator).

44. The voltage produced in the stator windings of a DC alternator is _____ (AC or DC).

45. DC electricity is produced in a DC alternator by the _____ .

46. If an alternator fails in flight and is disconnected from the main bus, the alternator field circuit should be _____ (opened or closed).

47. If an alternator produces too high a voltage, the overvoltage protector opens the _____ (load or field) circuit.

48. he load current produced in a DC generator is produced in the _____ (rotating or stationary) coils.

49. A DC alternator can produce its rated current at a lower RPM than a DC generator because of the greater number of _____ in the alternator.

50. DC electricity is taken from the armature by the _____ and _____ .

51. A DC alternator _____ (does or does not) require a current limiter.

52. A DC generator _____ (does or does not) require a current limiter.

53. In an A-circuit generator, the voltage regulator is between the field terminal of the generator and _____ (ground or the armature).

54. The three units in a generator control used with low-output DC generators are:

    a._____

    b._____

    c._____

55. The contacts of a reverse-current cutout relay are normally _____ (open or closed).

56. The contacts of a vibrator-type voltage regulator are normally _____ (open or closed).

57. The contacts of a vibrator-type current limiter are normally _____ (open or closed).

58. A carbon-pile voltage regulator acts as a variable _____ in the generator field circuit.

59. The output current produced by the two generators in a twin-engine installation are kept the same by the _____ circuit in the voltage regulators.

60. Current through the paralleling circuit in a twin-engine electrical system using carbon-pile voltage regulators is provided by the voltage drops across the _____ resistors.

61. Many general aviation turbine-powered aircraft combine the _____ and _____ into one single unit.

(continued)

62. The starter windings in a starter-generator are _____ (series or shunt) windings.

63. A zero-center ammeter _____ (does or does not) show the amount of current the alternator is producing.

64. A loadmeter is calibrated in _____ of the rated alternator or generator output.

Aircraft Electrical Load Circuits

The electrical systems just discussed are used to place electrical power on the main bus from the battery, the alternator, and the generator.

This section will examine some typical aircraft load circuits. A load circuit is simply any circuit that connects to the main electrical bus and provides a load for the electrical system. These circuits, all typical, are shown here to help illustrate the way these systems operate.

The Starter Circuit

continuous-duty solenoid. A solenoid-type switch designed to be kept energized by current flowing through its coil for an indefinite period of time. The battery contactor in an aircraft electrical system is a continuous-duty solenoid. Current flows through its coil all of the time the battery is connected to the electrical system.

intermittent-duty solenoid. A solenoid-type switch whose coil is designed for current to flow through it for only a short period of time. The coil will overheat if current flows through it too long.

The starter circuit differs from any other load circuit in the extremely large amount of current it carries. It is the only circuit in most aircraft electrical systems that is not required to have some kind of circuit protection device. The amount of current the starter motor needs to crank the engine is so high that it would be impractical to use any type of fuse or circuit breaker.

Though a starter solenoid is similar to a battery contactor, they are not normally interchangeable because the battery contactor must be energized the entire time the aircraft is operating, while the solenoid used for the starter is energized only when the engine is being cranked. The battery contactor is called a continuous-duty solenoid; the starter solenoid is called an intermittent-duty solenoid.

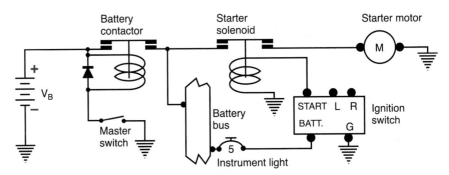

Figure 1-46. *A typical starter circuit for a light aircraft engine.*

One end of the starter solenoid coil goes to ground, usually inside the solenoid housing, and the other end connects to the terminal on the ignition switch marked START (Figure 1-46). Power comes from the battery bus through the circuit breaker and the BATT terminal of the ignition switch. Since so little current is used by the starter solenoid coil, and it is used for such a short time, it is often taken from a circuit breaker that is also used for some other circuit. For example, some aircraft tie the starter solenoid coil to the instrument light circuit breaker. When troubleshooting the starter circuit, you must have a wiring diagram of the aircraft so you know which circuit breaker this current comes from.

When the master switch is turned on, the battery contactor closes and power is supplied to the battery bus and the ignition switch. As soon as the ignition switch is placed in the START position, the starter solenoid closes and current flows to the starter motor to crank the engine.

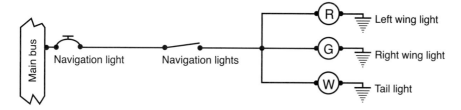

Figure 1-47. *Navigation light circuit typical for smaller aircraft.*

Navigation Light Circuit

Figure 1-47 shows a typical navigation light circuit. Note that navigation lights are also referred to as position lights. Current flows from the main bus through the 5-amp Navigation Light circuit breaker and the Navigation Light switch. The current then splits and flows through the red light on the aircraft's left wing tip, the green light on the right wing tip, and the white light on the tail.

This is an example of a series-parallel circuit. The three lights are connected in parallel with one another, and all three are in series with the switch and the circuit breaker.

Landing and Taxi Light Circuit

The circuit in Figure 1-48 is just slightly more complicated than that for the navigation lights. The landing light and the taxi light get their current from the main bus through their own circuit breakers. The landing light is connected to a 10-amp circuit breaker, and the taxi light circuit breaker is rated at 5 amps. The diode connected between the two sides of the switch is the reason for the difference between the ratings of the two circuit breakers.

The landing light shines ahead of the aircraft at the correct angle to light up the end of the runway when the aircraft is descending for a landing. The taxi light is aimed so that it shines ahead of the aircraft when it is taxiing. Both lights are on during landing, but only the taxi light is on during taxiing.

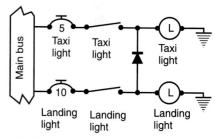

Circuit using two independent switches

Alternate switch arrangement

Circuit using a split rocker switch

Figure 1-48. *Landing light and taxi light circuits typical for smaller aircraft.*

When the landing-light switch is turned on, current flows from the main bus through the landing light circuit breaker, through the landing light switch to the landing light, and also through the diode to the taxi light. Both lights are on.

After the aircraft is on the ground, the pilot can turn the landing light off and the taxi light on. Current then flows through the taxi-light circuit breaker and the taxi-light switch and turns the taxi light on. The diode blocks current to the landing light.

Another way of doing the same thing is to use a special type of split-rocker switch. This is a double-pole, single-throw switch that turns on both lights when the landing-light side of the switch is depressed. The landing-light side of the switch can be turned off without affecting the taxi-light side, but when the taxi-light side of the switch is depressed, both lights turn off. The taxi light can also be turned on without affecting the landing light. When this type of switch is used, each light is connected to the bus through a 5-amp circuit breaker.

Landing Gear Actuation and Indicating Circuit

Figure 1-49 shows the circuit for the retractable landing gear system of a typical twin-engine airplane as it is with the aircraft on the ground. All three landing gear struts are down and locked and the gear-selector switch is in the GEAR-DOWN position.

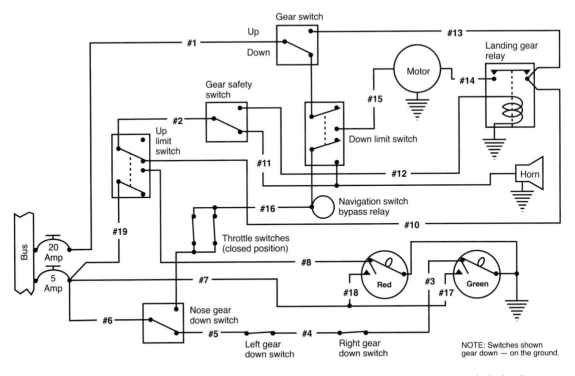

Figure 1-49. *Retractable landing gear control and indicating system. The airplane is on the ground, the landing gear handle is down, and all three landing gears are down and locked.*

Current for the green indicator light flows through the 5-amp circuit breaker, wire 6, the nose-gear down switch, wire 5, the left gear-down switch, wire 4, the right gear-down switch, and wire 3 to the green light, causing it to illuminate.

You will notice that the red and green lights both have two power terminals and one ground terminal. The lower power terminals of both lights receive power through the 5-amp circuit breaker and wires 7 and 17, or 7 and 18. When the lens of either light is pressed in, the circuit through wire 3 or 8 is opened and the circuit through wire 17 or 18 is closed. This sends current through the bulb to show that the filament is not burned out. This type of light fixture is called a press-to-test light.

When the aircraft takes off and the weight is off of the landing gear, the gear-safety switch (the squat switch) changes its position, as shown in Figure 1-50. When the pilot moves the landing-gear selector handle into the GEAR-UP position, its switch changes position, and the circuit is completed from the 20-amp circuit breaker through wires 1 and 13 to the right-hand terminal of the landing-gear relay.

press-to-test light fixture. An indicator light fixture whose lens can be pressed in to complete a circuit that tests the filament of the light bulb.

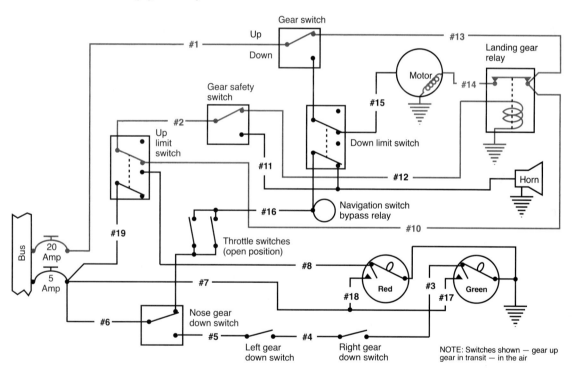

Figure 1-50. *The airplane is in the air, the landing gear handle is up, the landing gear is in transit, and the throttles are open.*

Current flows from this connection on the relay through wire 10, through the upper contacts of the up-limit switch, through the gear-safety switch, and through wire 12, to the coil of the landing-gear relay. This current produces a magnetic pull, which closes the relay so that current can flow through the relay contacts and the winding of the reversible DC motor to raise the landing gear.

As soon as the landing gear is released from its downlocks, the three landing-gear-down switches open and the green light goes out. The landing gear has not reached its up-and-locked position, so the red light is off.

Figure 1-51 shows the condition of the landing-gear circuit when the landing gear is up and locked in flight. The gear switch is in the GEAR-UP position and the up-limit switch is in the gear-up-and-locked position. There is no weight on the landing gear, so the gear safety switch is in the position shown here. The down-limit switch is not in the gear-down-and-locked position, and the three gear-down switches are open.

No current can flow to the relay coil because of the up-limit switch, and no current can flow to the gear-down side of the motor because of the

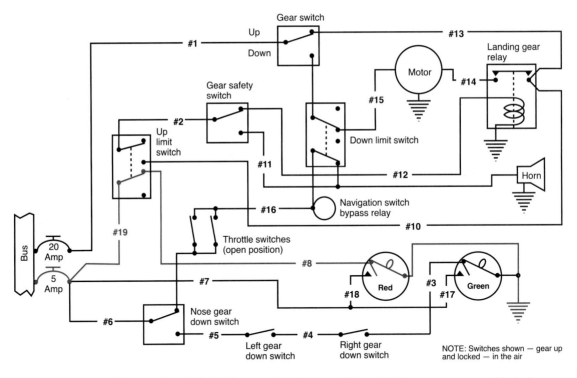

Figure 1-51. *The airplane is in the air, the landing gear handle is up, all three landing gears are up and locked, and the throttles are open.*

gear-selector switch. Current flows through the lower contacts of the up-limit switch, through wires 19 and 8, to the red light, showing that the landing gear is up and locked.

If either throttle is closed when the landing gear is not down and locked, current will flow through the nose-gear-down switch, the throttle switch, and the down-limit switch and will sound the gear-warning horn. This horn warns the pilot that the landing gear has not been lowered in preparation for landing.

When the landing-gear-selector switch is moved into the GEAR-DOWN position, current flows through it and the down-limit switch to the gear-down side of the reversible DC motor that lowers the landing gear. As soon as the gear is down and locked, the down-limit switch opens and shuts off the landing-gear motor. The three gear-down switches close and the green light comes on.

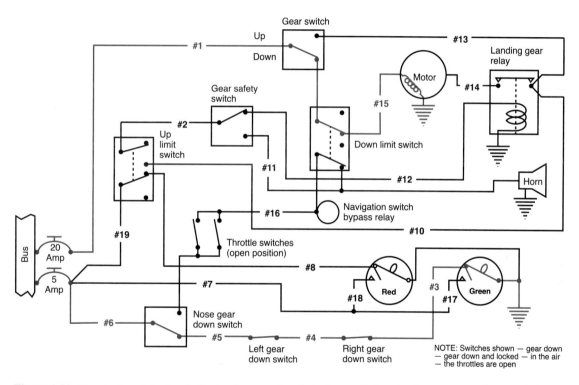

Figure 1-52. *The airplane is in the air, the landing gear handle is down, all three landing gears are down, and the throttles are open.*

Antiskid Brake System

The high landing speed of modern turbojet and turboprop airplanes, together with the small contact area between the tires and the runway, makes hydroplaning and brake skidding a real problem.

When the antiskid-control switch in Figure 1-53 is ON and the airplane is on the ground with the squat switches closed, current flows from the bus, through the antiskid-test circuit breaker and the antiskid-control circuit breaker, to the antiskid control box.

Each of the wheels has a wheel-speed sensor—a small AC generator—mounted inside the landing gear axle. The rotor for this generator is driven by a spring clip mounted in the inboard wheel bearing cover. Excitation for the sensor is supplied through the antiskid control box, and its AC output is returned to the control box. See Figure 1-53.

The frequency of the AC produced by the wheel-speed sensor is determined by the rotational speed of the wheel. The AC from each of the sensors is sent into the control box, where its frequency is compared with that from the other sensors, and with a built-in program tailored to the particular type of aircraft.

If any wheel starts to slow down faster than its mate or faster than the program allows, the control box sends a signal to the antiskid valve in the brake line for that wheel. The valve opens and allows fluid from the brake to flow back into the hydraulic system return manifold. As soon as the brake releases and the wheel stops slowing down, the valve closes and directs fluid back into the brake. The brake valve modulates, or turns off and on, to keep the tire on the threshold of a skid, but does not allow a skid to develop. See Figure 1-53.

When the aircraft is in the air and the antiskid-control switch is ON, current cannot flow to the antiskid control box because the squat switches mounted on the landing gear struts are open, removing the ground from the antiskid control circuit. The pilot can hold the brake pedals fully depressed, but no hydraulic pressure will reach the brakes because the antiskid valves are open, and the fluid flows into the hydraulic system return manifold.

As soon as the weight of the aircraft is on the landing gear and the squat switches close, current flows through the antiskid control box and energizes its computing circuits. The signals from the wheel-speed sensors are entered into the computing circuits, and when the wheels spin up to a specified speed or a specified number of seconds after the squat switches close, the antiskid valves close and direct hydraulic pressure into the brake. The computer senses the output of the wheel-speed sensors for a second or so to detect the braking action the runway provides, and then it applies pressure to the brakes. The control valves modulate the application of the brakes and bring the wheels to a stop at a rate that keeps them from skidding.

If, for any reason, one of the antiskid control valves dumps fluid back into the hydraulic system for a longer time than is allowed, the antiskid-failure light comes on, and the brake system returns to normal action without antiskid protection.

As soon as the aircraft slows to about 10 knots, the low-speed circuit in the antiskid control box deactivates the antiskid system, and braking is done as though no antiskid system were installed.

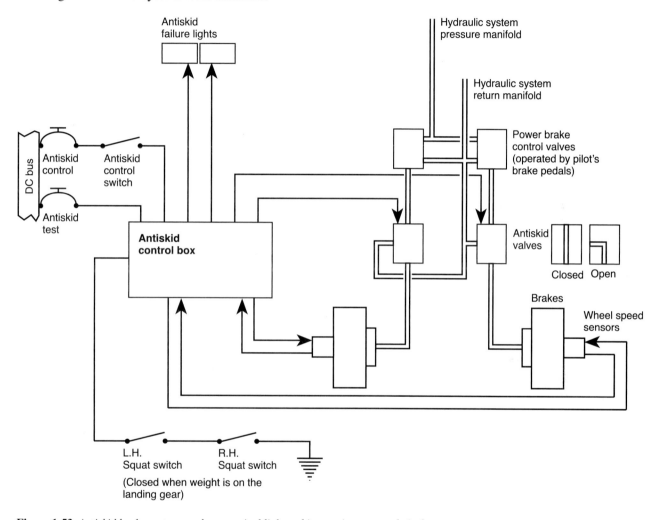

Figure 1-53. *Antiskid brake system used on a typical light turbine-engine-powered airplane.*

Electrical Propeller Deicing System

Many modern aircraft are certificated to fly into known icing conditions. They can do this because they are equipped with deicing systems to remove ice from the wings, the tail surfaces, and the propellers, and anti-icing systems to prevent the formation of ice on the windshield and pitot tube.

Deicing the propellers is done with an electrothermal system made of rubber boots bonded to the leading edge of the propeller blades. These boots have electrical heating elements embedded in them that are supplied with current from a propeller deicing timer.

Figure 1-54 shows a typical system used on a twin turboprop airplane. Current flows from the bus through a 20-amp prop deice circuit breaker switch into the deicer timer unit. When the manual-override relays are not energized, this current flows into the heating elements on the propeller blades through brushes riding on slip rings mounted on the propeller spinner bulkhead. The slip rings are connected to the heater elements through flexible conductors that allow the blades to change their pitch angle.

deicing system. A system in an aircraft that removes ice after it has formed. Propellers are deiced with heat produced when current flows through deicer boots bonded to the propeller blades.

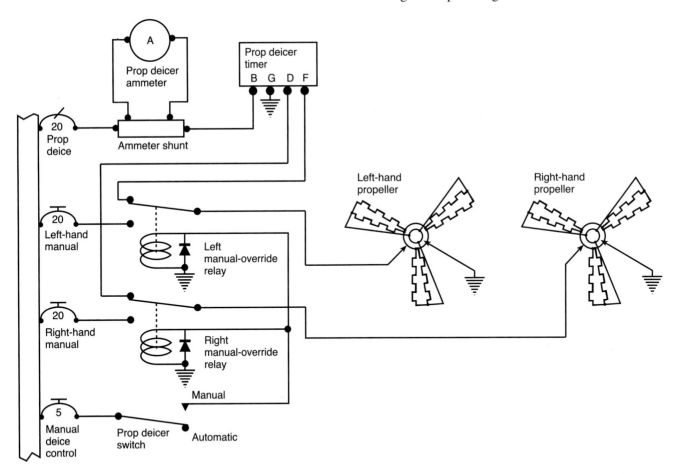

Figure 1-54. *Electrothermal propeller deicing system.*

The timer sends current through the right propeller for about 90 seconds, then shifts and sends current through the left propeller for 90 seconds.

Some propeller deicing systems have two separate heating elements on each blade. Current flows through the right-propeller outboard element for about 30 seconds, then through the right-propeller inboard element for the same length of time. After the right propeller is deiced, the timer shifts and sends current through the left-propeller outboard elements and then through the left-propeller inboard elements.

Current cycles of the two propellers are controlled by the timer if the propeller deicer switch is in the AUTOMATIC position. When the prop deicer switch is moved to its momentary MANUAL position, the two manual-override relays are energized and current flows directly from the bus to the blades without going through the timer.

The pilot can easily tell whether the deicing system is operating correctly in the AUTOMATIC mode by watching the propeller ammeter. It will show a flow of current each time one of the heater elements draws current.

Turbine-Engine Autoignition Circuit

The ignition system for a turbine engine is used only for starting the engine, but it is important that it be energized so that it can relight the engine if it should flameout. Autoignition systems such as the one shown in Figure 1-55 are installed on some turboprop engines to serve as a backup for takeoff and landing, during flight in conditions in which the engine is more likely to flameout.

The engine-start switch has three positions. In the ENGINE START AND IGNITION position, current flows to the generator control and to the coil of the starter relay, as well as to the coil of the ignition-power relay. Current flowing in the generator control opens the generator-field circuit for the starter-generator and connects the series starter winding to the electrical system. See Figure 1-42 on page 36. Current flowing in the coil of the ignition-power relay closes its contacts, allowing current to flow from the electrical bus to the ignition exciter unit and to a light on the annunciator panel, showing that the ignition is on.

When the engine-start switch is placed in the STARTER ONLY position to motor the engine without starting it, current flows to the coil of the starter-only relay and moves its contacts so that it no longer supplies a ground for the ignition-power relay. Since the ignition-power relay cannot be actuated, no current flows to the ignition exciters or to the ignition light on the annunciator panel. But current does flow to the generator control and to the coil of the starter relay.

In normal operation, when the autoignition-control switch is armed and the compressor-discharge pressure bellows have expanded and moved the switch contacts to the position that sends current to the autoignition-armed annunciator light, this light is on, informing the pilot that the circuit is armed, but the

autoignition system. A system on a turbine engine that automatically energizes the igniters to provide a relight if the engine should flame-out.

flameout. A condition in the operation of a gas turbine engine in which the fire in the engine unintentionally goes out.

annunciator panel. A panel of warning lights in plain sight of the pilot. These lights are identified by the name of the system they represent and are usually covered with colored lenses to show the meaning of the condition they announce.

igniters are not firing. In this position there is no current to the ignition-power relay. Should the compressor pressure drop, the compressor-discharge-pressure switch changes position, extinguishing the autoignition-armed light and sending current to the ignition-power relay, which closes the contacts in the ignition exciter circuit. The ignition-on light is illuminated and the igniters begin firing.

If the engine loses power and the compressor-discharge pressure drops below the specified value, the pressure-switch contacts shift and send current to the coil of the ignition-power relay. When this relay shifts position, current flows from the bus through the ignition-power circuit breaker to the ignition exciter and the ignition-on light on the annunciator panel.

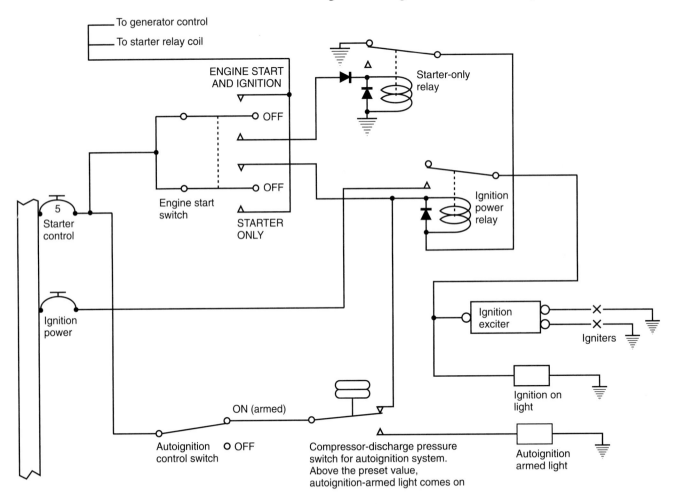

Figure 1-55. *Turbine-engine autoignition system.*

Reciprocating-Engine Starting and Ignition Circuit

The high voltage supplied to the spark plugs in an aircraft reciprocating engine is produced in a magneto. For a magneto to produce a spark hot enough to jump the gap in the spark plug, it must be turned at a high rate of speed. Magnetos on most small aircraft engines reach this high speed when the engine is being cranked by using an impulse coupling between the engine and the magneto. Most larger reciprocating engines use a vibrator to produce a pulsating direct current that is fed into the primary winding of one of the magneto coils. This pulsating DC induces a high-voltage AC in the secondary of the coil, and this high voltage is sent through the distributor to the correct spark plug.

Not only must the spark for starting the engine be hot, but it must also occur after the piston passes over its top-center position so the engine will not kick back. At one time, this late, or retarded, spark was produced by a trailing finger on the distributor rotor, but modern systems use a second set of breaker points in one of the magnetos to interrupt the pulsating DC after the piston has passed top center, producing a retarded spark in the cylinder.

Figure 1-56 shows a circuit used on many modern reciprocating-engine aircraft. When the ignition switch is in the OFF position, the primary coils of both the right and the left magnetos are grounded through the ignition switch. Current from the aircraft bus cannot reach the coil of the starter solenoid because the battery contacts inside the starter switch are open.

When the switch is placed in the spring-loaded START position, the primary circuit of the right magneto remains grounded, but the ground is opened on the left magneto. Current flows from the main bus through the battery contacts in the switch, to the coil of the starter solenoid, and then to the starting vibrator. The vibrator changes the DC flowing through its coil into pulsating DC. This pulsating DC flows through the BO contacts and the LR contacts of the switch to ground through the retard set of breaker points in the left magneto. Current also flows from the BO contacts through the L contacts of the switch to ground through the normal, or run, set of breaker points in the left magneto. These breaker points are in parallel with the primary coil of the left magneto. The closed retard breaker points short the coil to ground, which is the path followed by the pulsating DC. No current flows through the coil.

As the engine rotates to the correct advanced position for the magnetos to fire normally, the run breaker points open but current continues to flow to ground through the closed retard points. After the engine rotates far enough for the pistons to be in position for the spark to occur for starting, the retard points open and the pulsating DC flows to ground through the primary winding of the left magneto coil. When AC or pulsating DC flows through the primary winding of a transformer, such as the magneto coil, a high voltage is induced into the secondary winding. The secondary winding of the coil connects to the rotor of the distributor, a high-voltage selector switch, and high voltage goes to the correct spark plug.

retard breaker points. A set of breaker points in certain aircraft magnetos that are used to provide a late (retarded) spark for starting the engine.

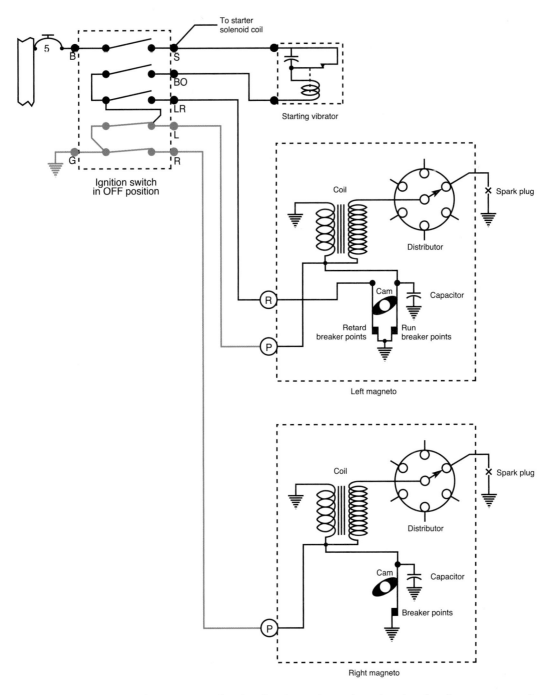

Figure 1-56A. *Starting and ignition system for aircraft reciprocating engine…(continued on the next two pages)*

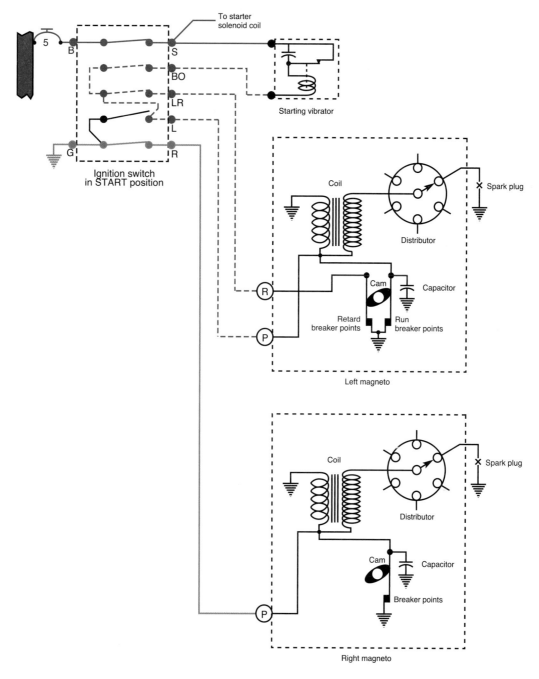

Figure 1-56B. *Starting and ignition system for aircraft reciprocating engine… (continued on the next page)*

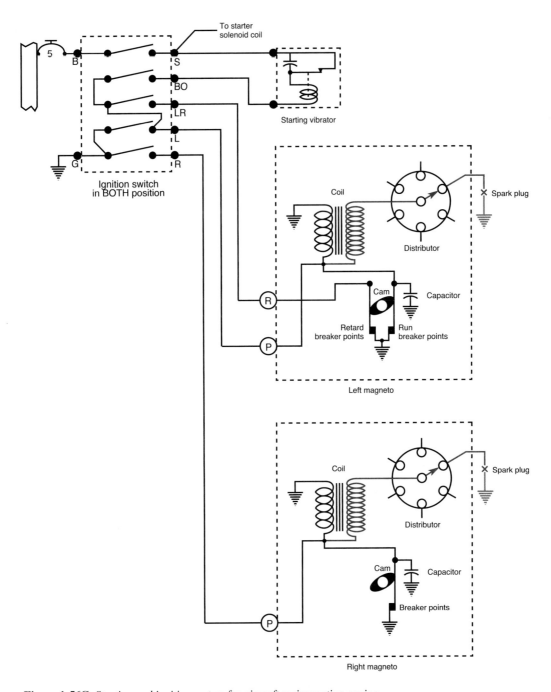

Figure 1-56C. *Starting and ignition system for aircraft reciprocating engine.*

As soon as the engine starts, the ignition switch is returned to the BOTH position and all of the contacts open, removing the ground from both of the magnetos and disconnecting the battery from the starter-relay coil and the vibrator. The L and R contacts in the switch can be closed individually in the course of a magneto check, to ground out the right and left magnetos.

Split-Bus Circuits for Avionics Protection

In the review of induced current beginning on page 20, we saw that any time current is shut off to a motor or a relay, the magnetic field that actuated these devices collapses, cuts across their windings, and induces a spike of high voltage in the electrical system. These high-voltage spikes can destroy any solid-state electronic equipment connected to the electrical system even when protected by a diode or capacitor.

To prevent damage to radio equipment, all radio equipment should be turned off before the engine is shut down, and a careful check made to be sure all of it is turned off before the engine is started. Most modern aircraft carry so much electronic equipment that it is possible to fail to turn off some system when the engine is started or shut down, or when the external power source is connected to the aircraft. To prevent this kind of damage, modern practice is to connect all of the voltage-sensitive electronic and avionic equipment to a separate bus and connect this bus to the main bus with either a switch-type circuit breaker or a relay.

Figure 1-57 shows a popular system that uses a switch-type circuit breaker to connect the avionics bus to the main bus. Before starting or shutting down the engine, the pilot opens the circuit breaker and all of the avionics equipment is isolated from the main bus. Any spikes of high voltage are absorbed by the battery, and there is no danger of damage to this equipment.

split bus. A type of electrical bus that allows all of the voltage-sensitive avionic equipment to be isolated from the rest of the aircraft electrical system when the engine is being started or when the ground-power unit is connected.

avionics. Electronic equipment installed in an aircraft.

Figure 1-57. *Avionics bus protected from inductive spikes by a switch-type circuit breaker.*

In another type of split-bus system, the two buses are joined with a normally closed relay that connects the two buses at all times except when the starter is being used or when the ground power source is plugged into the aircraft. Figure 1-58 shows how this system works. When the starter switch is placed in the START position, current flows through the diode and the coil and opens the relay. When the engine starts, the starter switch is released and the relay closes, connecting the avionics bus to the main bus.

When the external power source is plugged into the aircraft, current flows through its diode and energizes the relay, isolating the avionics bus from the main bus as long as the ground-power source is plugged in.

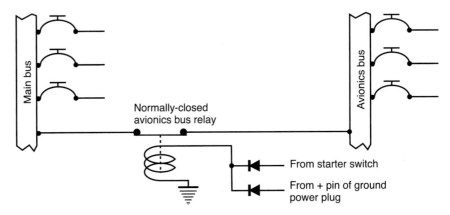

Figure 1-58. *Avionics bus protected from inductive spikes by a normally closed relay. This relay opens, isolating the avionics bus when the starter switch is closed or when the ground-power plug is connected.*

STUDY QUESTIONS: AIRCRAFT ELECTRICAL LOAD CIRCUITS

Answers are provided on page 99.

65. A battery contactor is a/an _____ (continuous or intermittent)-duty solenoid.

66. A starter solenoid is a/an _____ (continuous or intermittent)-duty solenoid.

67. Normally the only circuit in an aircraft electrical system that does not require a circuit breaker or fuse is the _____ circuit.

68. The navigation light circuit in Figure 1-47 is an example of a _____ (series, parallel, or complex) circuit.

69. In the landing light circuit shown in Figure 1-48 it _____ (is or is not) possible to turn on the landing light without the taxi light also coming on.

70. In the landing gear circuit shown in Figure 1-49, three switches that must be in the correct position for current to flow to the landing gear relay coil are:

   a._____

   b._____

   c._____

71. In the landing gear circuit shown in Figure 1-50, the landing gear warning horn _____ (will or will not) sound if only one throttle is pulled back to the idle position.

72. When the antiskid brake system shown in Figure 1-53 is operating properly, the aircraft cannot be landed with the brakes applied because the brakes cannot be applied until weight is on the landing gear and both _____ switches are closed.

73. According to the circuit of the propeller deicing system in Figure 1-54, the prop deicer ammeter shows the current flowing to the deicers when the system is operating _____ (manually or automatically).

74. In the turbine-engine autoignition circuit seen in Figure 1-55, the autoignition-armed light turns _____ (on or off) when the compressor-discharge pressure drops low enough for its pressure switch to supply power to the ignition power relay.

75. According to the reciprocating engine starting and ignition system seen in Figure 1-56B, the engine is started on the _____ (left or right) magneto.

76. Avionic equipment must be isolated from the aircraft electrical system when the engine is being started because of spikes of high _____ voltage.

Electrical Power Systems for Large Aircraft

The electrical systems for large turbojet transport aircraft are different than those used with smaller aircraft, primarily because these aircraft use alternating current for their primary power. The DC needed for charging the battery and for certain motor and instrument systems is produced by transformer-rectifier, or TR, units. They reduce the voltage of the AC produced by the engine-driven generators to 28 volts and then rectify it, or change it, from AC into DC. See Figure 1-59 on the next page.

Figure 1-59 shows a simplified block diagram of the electrical power system of a Boeing 727 jet transport airplane. Electrical power is produced by three 115-volt, three-phase, 400-hertz alternating-current generators driven by the engines through constant-speed drive (CSD) units. The CSDs hold the speed of the generators constant to keep the frequency of the AC they produce constant as the engine speed varies over their normal operating range.

transformer rectifier. A component in a large aircraft electrical system used to reduce the AC voltage and change it into DC for charging the battery and for operating DC equipment in the aircraft.

constant-speed drive. A special drive system used to connect an alternating current generator to an aircraft engine. The drive holds the generator speed (and thus its frequency) constant as the engine speed varies.

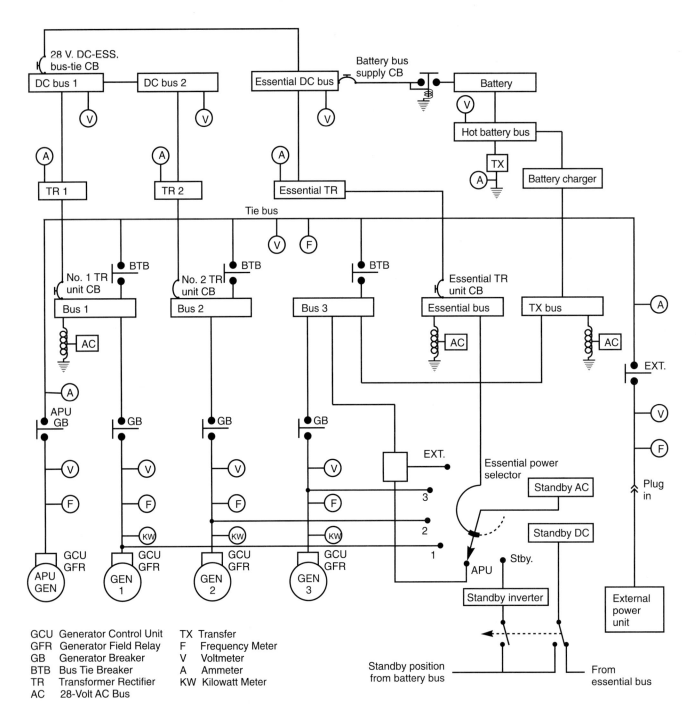

Figure 1-59. *Electrical system for a three-engine jet transport airplane.*

Each generator is connected to its own bus through a generator breaker (GB), and the three buses can be connected at the tie bus by the use of bus-tie breakers (BTB) that are controlled from the flight engineer's control panel.

Newer commercial aircraft combine the generator and constant speed unit (CSD) into a single assembly to reduce weight and size. This combined unit is called an integrated drive generator (IDG). See Figure 1-60.

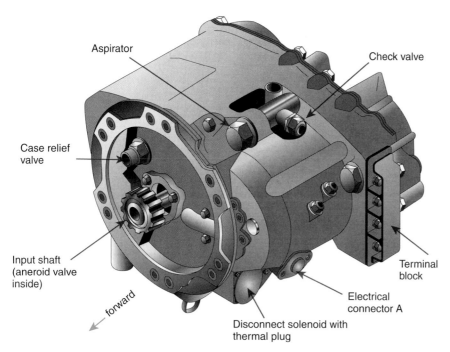

Figure 1-60. *Integrated drive generator.*

A turbine-powered auxiliary power unit (APU) drives a three-phase AC generator that can be connected to the tie bus through the APU generator breaker to supply electrical power to the aircraft when the engines are not running. The APU operates at a fixed RPM so it does not drive a CSD. An external power unit can also be connected to the aircraft, and its AC output can be connected to the tie bus through the EXT breaker.

All the circuits that are essential to the operation of the aircraft are connected to an essential bus, which can be supplied with AC from any of the three engine-driven generators: the APU; the external power unit; or a standby inverter that produces 115-volt, 400-hertz AC from 28-volt DC battery power. A selector switch on the panel allows the flight engineer to select the source of power for the essential bus.

auxiliary power unit (APU). A small turbine or reciprocating engine that drives a generator, hydraulic pump and air pump. The APU is installed in the aircraft and is used to supply electrical power, and air and hydraulic pressure when the main engines are not running.

essential bus. A bus that may be supplied with AC from any of the generators through a selector switch. It supplies current to the circuits that are essential to the operation of the aircraft.

TR unit. A transformer-rectifier unit. A TR unit reduces the voltage of alternating current and changes it into direct current.

Direct current is produced by two transformer-rectifier (TR) units that take AC from buses 1 and 2 and supply DC to DC buses 1 and 2. A third TR unit takes AC from the essential bus and produces DC for the essential DC bus.

The battery supplies power for starting the APU and for emergency operation of certain essential radio and instrument systems. The battery is kept charged by a battery-charger unit that receives its AC power from the AC transfer bus. Monitoring circuits inside the battery are connected into the battery-charger circuit so that if the battery temperature becomes too high, the charging current will automatically decrease.

The battery is connected to the hot battery bus at all times, but is automatically disconnected from most of the DC loads in normal operation. These loads are supplied from the two DC buses and the essential DC bus.

STUDY QUESTIONS: ELECTRICAL POWER SYSTEMS FOR LARGE AIRCRAFT

Answers are provided on page 99.

77. The generators installed on large turbojet aircraft produce _____ (AC or DC) electricity.

78. Direct current is produced in the electrical system seen in Figure 1-59 by the _____.

79. The frequency of the AC produced by generators driven by turbine engines is held constant by the _____ units.

80. Three measurements that are made of the output of the three main generators in Figure 1-59 are:

   a._____

   b._____

   c._____

81. Six sources of current that can be used to supply the essential bus in the electrical system shown in Figure 1-59 are:

   a._____

   b._____

   c._____

   d._____

   e._____

   f._____

82. The bus that is continuously supplied with battery power in the electrical system shown in Figure 1-59 is the _____ .

Inverters

Inverters are devices that convert DC power into AC power and are commonly used in smaller to medium-sized aircraft where AC power is needed for specific aircraft systems. Inverters are also used as back-up power systems on large transport category aircraft.

In most cases, 28-volt DC power is used as the input voltage, which is then converted to 115-volt, 400-Hz AC power. For smaller aircraft, this AC power is used for engine and flight instruments, windshield heating, and lighting systems. In larger aircraft, inverters are used in emergency situations to power essential AC loads.

There are two types of inverters found in aircraft: rotary and static. A rotary inverter uses DC input voltage to drive a DC motor. This motor drives an AC alternator that is on the same shaft as the DC motor. The output of the alternator provides the required AC voltage at 400 Hz. Rotary inverters will only be found on older aircraft as they are heavier and less efficient than new static inverters.

Static inverters, as the name implies, have no moving parts and use solid-state circuitry and transformers to convert the DC input voltage to an AC output voltage. An oscillator circuit is used to create the 400 Hz signal, which is then passed through a transformer to step the voltage up to the desired voltage and filtered to produce the desired sinusoidal wave form.

STUDY QUESTIONS: INVERTERS

Answers are provided on page 99.

83. An inverter converts _____ (AC or DC) power to _____ (AC or DC) power.

84. The standard AC power output of an inverter is _____ volts and _____ Hz.

85. The two types of inverters are _____ and _____.

86. The output frequency of 400 Hz from a static inverter is created by a(n) _____.

Aircraft Electrical System Installation

The installation of an electrical system in an aircraft differs greatly from non-aviation installations. Absolute dependability is of utmost importance, and this must be maintained in an environment of vibration and drastically changing temperatures. The weight of the electrical installation is critical, as every pound used in the electrical system costs a pound in payload.

This next section addresses the actual installation of the circuits.

Electrical Wire

The wire used in aircraft electrical systems must stand up under extremes of vibration and abrasion without breaking and without wearing away the insulation. Most of the wire installed in a civil aircraft meets Military Specifications and may be made of either copper or aluminum. Copper conductors are coated with tin, nickel, or silver to prevent oxidation and to facilitate soldering.

Both copper and aluminum wires are stranded for protection against breakage from vibration and, for low temperature installations, are encased in polyvinylchloride or nylon insulation. If the wire is to be used in a high-temperature environment, it must have glass braid insulation.

Wire size is measured according to the American Wire Gauge. The most common sizes range from AN-22 for wires that carry a small amount of current, to AN-0000 (pronounced "four aught") for battery cables that carry several hundred amps of current. In this numbering system, the smaller the number, the larger the wire. See Figure 1-61.

Figure 1-61 shows the current-carrying capability of both copper and aluminum wire. An aluminum wire must be about two wire-gauge numbers larger than a copper wire for it to carry the same amount of current. For example, an AL-4 aluminum wire should be used to replace an AN-6 copper wire if it is to carry the same amount of current. Six-gauge copper wire can carry 101 amps in free air; 4-gauge aluminum wire can carry 108 amps in the same installation.

A convenient rule of thumb regarding the current-carrying ability of copper aircraft wire is that each time you increase the wire size by four gauge numbers, you approximately double the current-carrying capability of the wire. A 20-gauge wire will carry 11 amps in free air, a 16-gauge wire will carry 22 amps, a 12-gauge wire will carry 41 amps, and an 8-gauge wire will carry 73 amps.

Aluminum wire is more susceptible than copper wire to breakage and corrosion. As a result, several limitations are placed on the use of aluminum wire in aircraft electrical systems, including:

- Aluminum wire is restricted to 6-gauge and larger.

- Aluminum wire should neither be attached to engine-mounted accessories nor installed in other areas of severe vibration.

- Aluminum wire should not be installed where frequent connections and disconnections are required. All installations of aluminum wire should be relatively permanent.

- Aluminum wire should not be used where the length of run is less than 3 feet.

- Aluminum wire should not be used in areas where corrosive fumes exist.

- Aluminum wire is not recommended for use in communications or navigation systems.

Copper Wire Current Carrying Capability

Wire Size	Maximum Amps Single Wire in Free Air	Maximum Amps Wire in Bundle or Conduit
AN-20	11	7.5
AN-18	16	10
AN-16	22	13
AN-14	32	17
AN-12	41	23
AN-10	55	33
AN-8	73	46
AN-6	101	60
AN-4	135	80
AN-2	181	100
AN-1	211	125
AN-0	245	150
AN-00	283	175
AN-000	328	200
AN-0000	380	225

Aluminum Wire Current Carrying Capability

Wire Size	Maximum Amps Single Wire in Free Air	Maximum Amps Wire in Bundle or Conduit
AL-6	83	50
AL-4	108	66
AL-2	152	90
AL-0	202	123
AL-00	235	145
AL-000	266	162
AL-0000	303	190

Figure 1-61. *Current-carrying capability of aircraft electrical wire.*

Selection of Wire Size

In any kind of electrical installation, it is important that the correct size of wire be used. When choosing wire size, two factors must be considered: the voltage drop caused by current flowing through the resistance of the wire, and the current-carrying capability of the wire. Current-carrying capability is determined by the amount of heat generated in the wire by the current flowing through it.

The Federal Aviation Administration has established a maximum allowable voltage drop for aircraft electrical systems, as shown in Figure 1-62.

It is possible to use Ohm's law to determine the wire size needed to meet the voltage-drop requirements, but the FAA has produced a handy chart that makes selection easier. This chart, shown in Figure 1-63, gives both the allowable voltage drop for any installation and a good indication of the wire's current-carrying capability.

The vertical lines in Figure 1-63 represent the various wire gauges. The horizontal lines are for the different lengths of wire that produce the maximum allowable voltage drop for continuous operation in each voltage system. The

Nominal System Voltage	Allowable Voltage Drop	
	Continuous Operation	Intermittent Operation
14	0.5	1.0
28	1.0	2.0
115	4.0	8.0
200	7.0	14.0

Figure 1-62. *Maximum allowable voltage drop for aircraft electrical systems.*

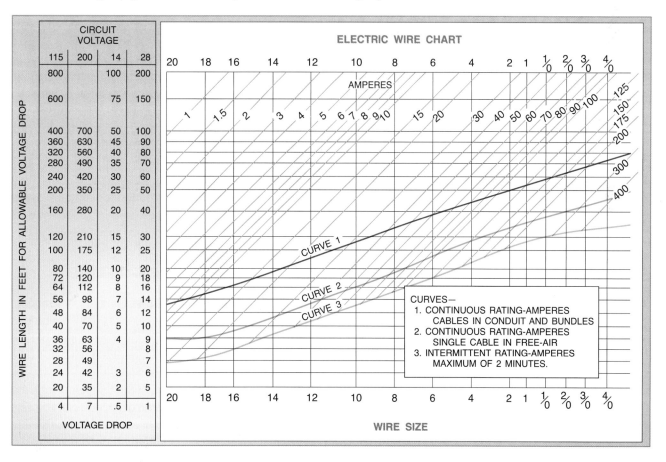

Figure 1-63. *Electrical wire size selection chart.*

diagonal lines represent the number of amps of current the wire carries. The three heavy curves across the center of the chart show the current-carrying limitations of the wires.

Use the chart in Figure 1-63 to find the size of copper wire needed for installation of a component that draws 20 amps continuously in a 28-volt system, if the wire needs to be 30 feet long and is to be installed in a bundle.

First, follow the 20-amp diagonal line down until it crosses the horizontal line for 30 feet in the 28-volt column. These two lines cross between the vertical lines for 12-gauge and 10-gauge wire. Always choose the larger wire when the lines cross between two wire sizes (in this case, the 10-gauge wire).

Follow the horizontal line from the intersection of the 20-amp current line and the 10-gauge wire line; it takes about 45 feet of this wire to give the maximum allowable 1-volt drop. Since the wire is only 30 feet long, we are perfectly safe as far as voltage drop is concerned.

The intersection of the 20-amp diagonal line and the 10-gauge vertical line is well above curve 1. This means that a 10-gauge copper wire can safely carry 20 amps when it is routed in a bundle or in conduit. (The chart in Figure 1-61 shows that a 10-gauge copper wire routed in a bundle can carry 33 amps.)

Now, assume that a battery in a 14-volt aircraft is installed in such a way that it requires a 15-foot cable to supply 200 amps to the starter.

First, see Figure 1-61; it shows that an AN-1 wire is needed to carry 200 amps in free air. Now, using Figure 1-63, follow the 200-amp diagonal line down until it crosses the 1-gauge vertical line. The intersection is between curves 2 and 3, which means that a 1-gauge wire can carry 200 amps if it is routed in free air and is used for intermittent operation (2 minutes or less). The starter is an intermittent load, and the starter cable will be run by itself in free air.

By projecting a horizontal line from this intersection to the column for a 14-volt system, we see that 16 feet of this wire will produce only a 0.5-volt drop when 200 amps flows through it, so the voltage drop in 15 feet of wire is well below the 1 volt allowed for an intermittent load in a 14-volt system. See Figure 1-62.

Special Types of Wire

PVC. Polyvinylchloride. A thermoplastic resin used to make transparent tubing for insulating electrical wires.

Most of the wire used in an aircraft electrical system is made of stranded, tinned copper and insulated with white polyvinylchloride (PVC) which is often covered with a clear nylon jacket. This type of wire is suitable for installations in which the temperature does not exceed 221°F (105°C). The insulation has a voltage rating of 1,000 volts.

If the wire is to be used in an application in which the temperature is too high for the PVC insulation some form of fluorocarbon insulation can be used. This insulation is normally good to a temperature of about 392°F (200°C).

When wires carry alternating current in an area where the electromagnetic field caused by the AC could interfere with other wires or with sensitive electronic equipment, the wires may be shielded. A shielded wire is one in which the stranded wire is insulated with PVC and then encased in a braid of tinned copper. Most shielded wire is covered with a clear PVC or nylon jacket to protect it from abrasion. Several individual wires grouped together and enclosed in a common shield is called a shielded cable; in certain applications, the wires inside the shield are twisted to further reduce the effect of the magnetic fields that surround the individual wires.

Coaxial cable, commonly called coax, is a type of shielded wire used between a radio antenna and the equipment and between other special types of electronic equipment. Coaxial cable is made of a solid or stranded center conductor surrounded by thick insulation. Around this inner insulation are one or two layers of tinned copper braid enclosed in an outer jacket of tough plastic to protect it from abrasion.

Coaxial cables are normally used to carry alternating current at radio frequencies. It is important when carrying this type of electrical signal that the two conductors (the inner conductor and the braid) be held so that they have the same center. Coaxial cable must not be crushed or bent with too small a bend radius or the relationship between the two conductors will be destroyed.

Normally, wire bundles are routed in straight lines throughout the aircraft following the structural members, but coaxial cable may be routed as directly as possible to minimize its length.

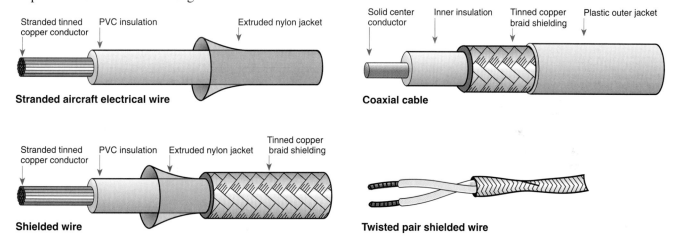

Figure 1-64. *Types of aircraft electrical wire.*

Soldering

Soldering of electrical wires in aircraft is not recommended, but there may be occasions when it is necessary. When multistranded, flexible aircraft wire is soldered, the solder is stiff and does not flex. Vibration of the wire in normal aircraft operations will cause stress at this location and may cause the wire to break.

Solder is an alloy of tin and lead, and its melting temperature is determined by the ratio of these two components. Solder for general aircraft applications is commonly an alloy of 50% tin and 50% lead, with a rosin flux core. The use of flux helps to clean the surface of the material and aids in the flow of solder when it reaches its melting point.

To get the best results in your soldering, always have a clean soldering tip and cover the tip with a thin layer of solder. This thin layer of solder on the tip is referred to as being tinned. The wire must then be heated to the melting point of the solder while the solder is applied to achieve a good bond.

Terminal and Connector Installation

The wiring for an aircraft electrical system is assembled into harnesses in the aircraft factory and is installed in the aircraft without the use of solder. Soldered connections are susceptible to corrosion and breakage caused by vibration. Permanently attached wires are fastened to terminal strips; wires that must be connected and disconnected frequently are terminated with AN or MS quick-disconnect connectors.

Quick-Disconnect Connectors

quick-disconnect connector. A type of wire connector used in aircraft electrical systems. The wires terminate inside an insulated plug with pins or sockets that mate with the opposite type of terminals in a similar plug. The two halves of the connector push together and are held tight with a special nut.

Wire bundles that connect an electrical or electronic component into an aircraft electrical system are usually terminated with quick-disconnect plugs that allow the component to be changed without disturbing the wiring. See Figure 1-65.

Wires carrying power to a component (hot wires) are fitted with connectors that have sockets. The mating connectors on the ground side of the circuit have pins. This minimizes the possibility of a short between a connector and ground when the connectors are separated.

The wires are installed in the pins or sockets of the connector by crimping or soldering, and the connector is reassembled. A cable clamp is screwed onto the end of the connector and all of the wires are securely clamped so that when the cable is handled, no strain is put on the wires where they are attached.

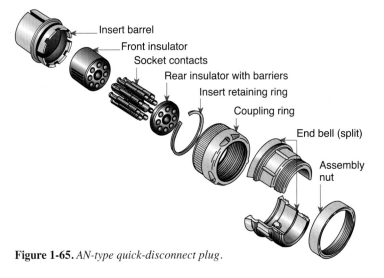

Insert barrel
Front insulator
Socket contacts
Rear insulator with barriers
Insert retaining ring
Coupling ring
End bell (split)
Assembly nut

Figure 1-65. *AN-type quick-disconnect plug.*

Wires are attached to most of the older quick-disconnect plugs by soldering, as shown in Figure 1-66. Be sure that only a resin-core solder is used. Acid-core solder causes corrosion. About ¹⁄₃₂-inch of bare wire is left between the top of the solder in the pots and the end of the insulation, to ensure that no solder wicks up into the strands of wire and destroys its flexibility where it is attached. After all of the wires are soldered into the connector, transparent PVC sleeving is slipped over the end of each wire and the pot into which the wire is soldered. These wires are then tied together with a spot tie of waxed linen or nylon cord.

Most modern quick-disconnect plugs use crimped-on tapered terminals that are pressed into tapered holes in the ends of the pins or sockets. A tapered pin is crimped onto the end of each wire to be inserted into the plug, and all necessary rings and clamps are slipped over the wires. A special insertion tool, shown in Figure 1-67, is used to force the tapered terminals into the holes and lock them in place. After the wires are in place, the connector is assembled and a wire clamp is tightened on the wire to take all of the strain.

Some components have two or more identical quick-disconnect plugs. In such cases, if the wrong socket is connected to the plug the equipment will not work, or worse, it may be damaged. To prevent this, the inserts in the connectors are designed so that they may be positioned in several different ways inside the shells. The last letter in the identification number marked on the shell is always one of the last letters in the alphabet, and it identifies the insert rotation. In Figure 1-68, the insert rotation letter is X, and the slot into which the key of the mating connector fits is near socket B. The inserts in both halves of the connector can be rotated so that the key and slot are near socket A. If this were done, the insert rotation identifier would be another letter, possibly Y. Only a plug with a Y identifier will fit into a socket with a Y identifier.

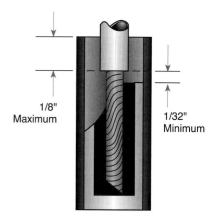

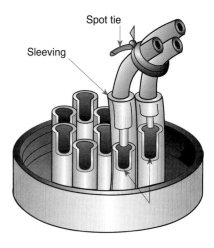

Figure 1-66. *Method of attaching wires in a quick-disconnect plug by soldering.*

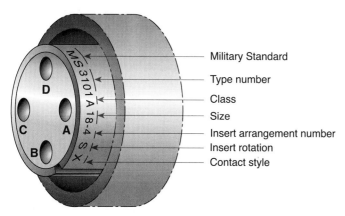

Figure 1-68. *Identification and insert orientation marking on a quick-disconnect connector.*

- Military Standard
- Type number
- Class
- Size
- Insert arrangement number
- Insert rotation
- Contact style

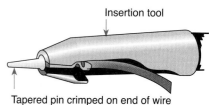

Insertion tool

Tapered pin crimped on end of wire

Figure 1-67. *Tapered pins are crimped onto the wires and are pushed into tapered holes in the connectors with a tool such as this.*

Terminal Strips

Wires which are installed when the aircraft is built and are disconnected only during a major repair or alteration are connected to terminal strips inside junction boxes. Most terminal strips in an aircraft electrical system are of the barrier type and are made of a phenolic plastic material. Barrier posts stick up between each terminal lug to keep the wires separated.

Most terminal lugs have 6-32, 8-32, or 10-32 machine screw threads and are held in the terminal strip with a flat washer and a cadmium-plated plain nut. Electrical power circuits normally use terminal lugs no smaller than 10-32, but most load circuits use smaller lugs.

Copper-wire terminals are placed directly on top of the nut, followed either by a plain washer and an elastic stop nut or by a plain washer, a split steel lockwasher, and a plain nut. The wire terminals are stacked on the studs, as shown in Figure 1-69, with no more than four terminals per stud. When it is necessary for more than four wires to be attached to a single point, a bus strip is used to join two studs, and the wires are divided between the studs. No single stud should have more than four terminal lugs or three terminal lugs and a bus strap.

Wire Terminals

Insulated crimp-on terminals are used on all wires connected to terminal strips. The insulation is stripped from the end of the wire, which is inserted into the terminal until the insulation butts up against the barrel of the terminal and the end of the wire sticks out slightly beyond the end of the barrel. When the terminal is crimped with a special crimping tool, the terminal sleeve grips the wire tightly enough to make a joint that is as strong as the wire itself.

Terminals approved for use in aircraft look much like automotive terminals but they are different. Aircraft terminals have a second metal sleeve inside the insulation that extends past the metal terminal barrel. When this portion of the sleeve is crimped with the proper tool, it grips the insulation firmly without compressing the wire itself, this relieves strain and prevents the wire from flexing at the point it is crimped into the barrel. See Figure 1-70.

The best aircraft wire strippers have a set of jaws with 360-degree cutting edges for each wire size. They cut through the insulation without nicking any of the wire strands, and as you continue to close the handles, the stripper pulls the cut insulation off the end of the wire without twisting the strands.

Aircraft terminal crimpers have a ratchet in the handles that prevent them from opening before they have completely closed, and spring-loaded jaws that compensate for different wire sizes to ensure that the proper compression is reached and prevents the terminal from being over-compressed. These tools also have two separate crimping patterns in one step, a cross crimp around the wire for a more uniform gripping of the wire, and a diamond pattern around the insulation of the wire for strain relief. These crimpers have replaceable dies that will crimp red, blue, and yellow terminals, for 22- through 10-gauge wire.

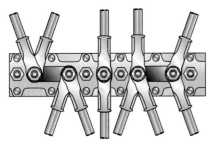

When it is necessary to connect more than 4 wires to a single point, 2 or more studs are connected with a bus strap.

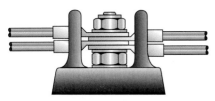

Correct method of stacking wire terminals on a stud

Figure 1-69. *A barrier-type terminal strip.*

The color of the insulation on the terminal indicates the wire size the terminal is designed to fit. A red terminal fits wire gauges from 22 through 18, blue terminals fit 16- and 14-gauge wires, and yellow terminals fit 12- and 10-gauge wires.

Terminals for wires larger than 10-gauge are non-insulated and are installed on the wires with an air-powered squeezer. After the terminal is squeezed onto the end of the wire, slip a piece of PVC tubing over the sleeve of the terminal and secure it by tying it in place with waxed string or by shrinking the insulation over the terminal with heat.

Large aluminum wires are installed in aluminum terminal lugs by the method shown in Figure 1-71. Strip the insulation from the end of the wire, being very careful to not nick any of the wire strands. (Any nicked strand will very likely break and reduce the current carrying capability of the wire.)

petrolatum-zinc dust compound. A special abrasive compound used inside an aluminum wire terminal that is being swaged onto a piece of aluminum electrical wire. When the terminal is compressed, the zinc dust abrades the oxides from the wire, and the petrolatum prevents oxygen reaching the wire so no more oxides can form.

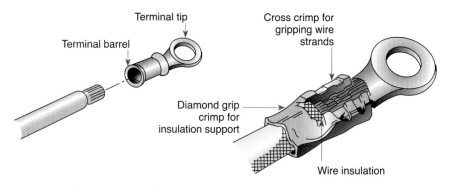

Figure 1-70. *Method of installing crimped-on terminals.*

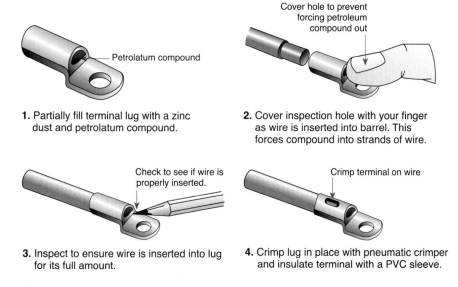

1. Partially fill terminal lug with a zinc dust and petrolatum compound.

2. Cover inspection hole with your finger as wire is inserted into barrel. This forces compound into strands of wire.

3. Inspect to ensure wire is inserted into lug for its full amount.

4. Crimp lug in place with pneumatic crimper and insulate terminal with a PVC sleeve.

Figure 1-71. *Installation of an aluminum terminal lug on a large aluminum electrical wire.*

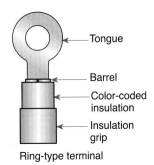

Tongue

Barrel

Color-coded insulation

Insulation grip

Ring-type terminal

Hook-type terminal

Slotted-type terminal

Figure 1-72. *Types of wire terminals.*

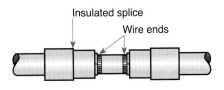

Insulated splice

Wire ends

Figure 1-73. *Insulated wire splice before it is crimped onto the wire.*

Partially fill the terminal with a petrolatum and zinc-dust compound and slip the wire into the terminal until the end of the wire shows in the inspection hole. As the wire is inserted into the terminal, the zinc-dust compound is forced back to cover the strands. When the terminal is crimped with a pneumatic crimper, the zinc dust abrades the oxide from the wire strands and the petrolatum keeps air away from the wire and prevents oxides from forming on the wire. After the terminal is crimped on, insulate the barrel with PVC tubing and either tie it in place or shrink it around the terminal with heat.

The three most popular types of wire terminals are ring, hook, and slotted terminals, shown in Figure 1-72. Most of the wires installed in an aircraft electrical system are terminated with ring-type terminals. If the nut on the terminal stud should become loose, the ring-type terminal will remain on the stud, whereas a hook or slotted terminal will slip off.

Wire Splices

At one time it was common practice to splice wires by wrapping the ends of the wires together and soldering them, but now almost all wire splicing is done with the proper size pre-insulated solderless splices. To install the terminals, strip the insulation off the ends of the wires, slip the ends of the two wires into the splice, and crimp the splice, using the proper crimping tool.

There should not be more than one splice in any wire segment between any two connections or other disconnect points. When several wires in a bundle are to be spliced, the wires should be cut so that the splices are staggered along the bundle, as in Figure 1-74.

Wire Identification

Wires installed in an aircraft are usually identified by a series of letters and numbers, including code letters for the circuit function, the number of the wire in the circuit, a letter to indicate the segment of the wire, a number for the wire gauge, and the letter N if the wire goes to ground. See Figures 1-75 and 1-76 for the interpretation of a wire identification number.

Most aircraft wires are identified near each end and at 12- to 15-inch intervals along their length. The numbers are stamped on the wire in the aircraft factory. If you must install a wire in the field, where you do not have access to a wire-stamping machine, write the wire number on a piece of pressure-sensitive tape and wrap the tape around the ends of the wire in the form of a small flag.

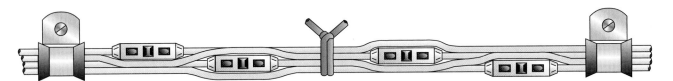

Figure 1-74. *Wire splices should be staggered when the wires are installed in a bundle.*

A **Armament**
B **Photographic**
C **Control Surface**
   CA - Automatic Pilot
   CC - Wing Flaps
   CD - Elevator Trim
D **Instrument (Other than Flight or Engine Instrument)**
   DA - Ammeter
   DB - Flap Position Indicator
   DC - Clock
   DD - Voltmeter
   DE - Outside Air Temperature
   DF - Flight Hour Meter
E **Engine Instrument**
   EA - Carburetor Air Temperature
   EB - Fuel Quantity Gage and Transmitter
   EC - Cylinder Head Temperature
   ED - Oil Pressure
   EE - Oil Temperature
   EF - Fuel Pressure
   EG - Tachometer
   EH - Torque Indicator
   EJ - Instrument Cluster
F **Flight Instrument**
   FA - Bank and Turn
   FB - Pitot Static Tube Heater and Stall Warning Heater
   FC - Stall Warning
   FD - Speed Control System
   FE - Indicator Lights
G **Landing Gear**
   GA - Actuator
   GB - Retraction
   GC - Warning Device (Horn)
   GD - Light Switches
   GE - Indicator Lights
H **Heating, Ventilating and Deicing**
   HA - Anti-icing
   HB - Cabin Heater
   HC - Cigar Lighter
   HD - Deice
   HE - Air Conditioners
   HF - Cabin Ventilation
J **Ignition**
   JA - Magneto
K **Engine Control**
   KA - Starter Control
   KB - Propeller Synchronizer
L **Lighting**
   LA Cabin

L **Lighting (cont'd)**
   LB - Instrument
   LC - Landing
   LD - Navigation
   LE - Taxi
   LF - Rotating Beacon
   LG - Radio
   LH - Deice
   LJ - Fuel Selector
   LK - Tail Floodlight
M **Miscellaneous**
   MA - Cowl Flaps
   MB - Electrically Operated Seats
   MC - Smoke Generator
   MD - Spray Equipment
   ME - Cabin Pressurization Equipment
   MF - Chem O_2 - Indicator
P **DC Power**
   PA - Battery Circuit
   PB - Generator Circuits
   PC - External Power Source
Q **Fuel and Oil**
   QA - Auxiliary Fuel Pump
   QB - Oil Dilution
   QC - Engine Primer
   QD - Main Fuel Pumps
   QE - Fuel Valves
R **Radio (Navigation and Communication)**
   RA - Instrument Landing
   RB - Command
   RC - Radio Direction Finding
   RD - VHF
   RE - Homing
   RF - Marker Beacon
   RG - Navigation
   RH - High Frequency
   RJ - Interphone
   RK - UHF
   RL - Low Frequency
   RM - Frequency Modulation
   RP - Audio System and Audio Amplifier
   RR - Distance Measuring Equipment (DME)
   RS - Airborne Public Address System
S **Radar**
U **Miscellaneous Electronic**
   UA - Identification - Friend or Foe
W **Warning and Emergency**
   WA - Flare Release
   WB - Chip Detector
   WC - Fire Detection System
X **AC Power**

Wire Number GE4B-22N

GE This wire is in the landing gear indicator light circuit. See Figure 1-76.

4 This is wire number 4 in this circuit.

B This is the second segment of wire number 4.

22 This is a 22-gauge wire.

N This wire is connected to aircraft ground.

Figure 1-75. *Interpretation of wire identification numbers.*

Figure 1-76. *Circuit function and circuit code identifiers for aircraft electrical wire.*

Wire Bundling

The complex wiring installed in a modern aircraft is not normally installed one wire at a time. Rather, the entire wiring assembly is made in the form of a harness on jig boards in the aircraft factory, and the harness is installed in the aircraft. If an aircraft is damaged to the extent that it must be rewired, it is usually more economical to buy a new harness and install it, rather than to install individual wires.

After an aircraft is in the field, new equipment is often added, requiring new wire bundles to be made up and installed. When making up a wire bundle, it is important that all of the wires be kept parallel and not allowed to cross over one another and make a messy-looking bundle. One way of keeping the wires straight is to use a guide made of the plastic insert from a discarded AN or MS connector. Slip the wires through the holes in the guide before they are secured into the connector. Then slip the guide along the wire bundle as you tie the wires together with nylon tie wraps or waxed nylon cord.

wire bundle. A compact group of electrical wires held together with special wrapping devices or with waxed string. These bundles are secured to the aircraft structure with special clamps.

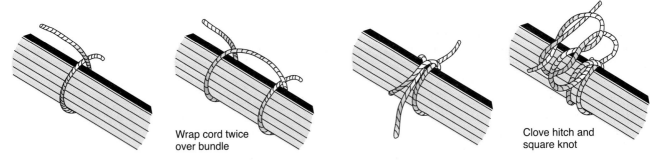

Wrap cord twice over bundle

Clove hitch and square knot

Figure 1-77. *Wire bundles can be tied together with waxed linen or nylon cord using two half hitches (a clove hitch) secured with a square knot.*

Junction Boxes

Terminal strips are mounted inside of junction boxes to protect the wires from physical damage and electrical short circuits. Junction boxes are usually made of aluminum alloy or stainless steel, and are installed at locations where they cannot be used as a step or the wire bundles used as a handhold. When possible, the boxes are mounted with their open side facing downward or at an angle so that any dropped nuts or washers will tend to fall out rather than wedge between the terminals.

The holes where the wires enter the junction box are fitted with protective grommets to prevent the wires from chafing, thereby damaging their insulation. Junction boxes are equipped with close-fitting lids to keep water and loose debris out and away from the wires.

Wiring Installation

When installing a wire bundle in an aircraft, use cushion clamps to attach the bundle to the aircraft structure. As mentioned above, be sure the bundles are not routed in a location where they are likely to be used as a handhold or where they can be damaged by persons entering or leaving the aircraft or by cargo or baggage being pulled across them or resting on them.

Wire bundles should not be routed below a battery or closer than 6 inches from the bilge of the fuselage (the lowest point where water can collect). Wire bundles should not be run closer than 3 inches from any control cable unless a suitable mechanical guard is installed over the wire so the cable cannot contact it.

If an electrical wire bundle is run through a compartment parallel to a line carrying a combustible fluid or oxygen, the bundle must be separated from the line as much as possible. The wires should be above the fluid line and must be no closer than 6 inches from the line.

Most wire installation in modern aircraft is open wiring. This means that the wires are bundled and fastened together, but are not installed in protective covering, such as a conduit. In some locations, however, such as wheel wells, where additional protection is needed for the wires, they are run through either a rigid or a flexible conduit.

When wires are run through rigid conduit, the ends of the conduit must have all burrs removed to prevent wire damage. The inside diameter of the conduit must be at least 25% greater than the outside diameter of the wire bundle in it, and the conduit must be bent carefully so that it does not collapse in the bend and decrease to less than 75% of its original diameter.

Wire bundles are often run inside a piece of clear PVC tubing for protection. A trick that makes this hard job easier is to use compressed air to blow some tire talcum through the tubing, then blow a length of rib lacing cord through it. Tie the end of the wire bundle to the rib lacing cord and pull it through.

Circuit Control and Protection Devices

The purpose of an electrical system in an aircraft is to create a flow of current that can perform work by the heat it produces or the magnetic field it causes. For this work to be done, the flow must be controlled and the system protected against an excess of either current or voltage.

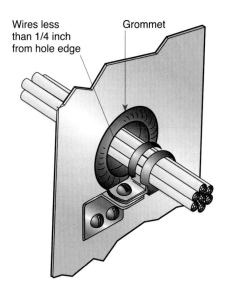

Figure 1-78. *When electrical wires pass through a bulkhead, the edges of the hole should be protected with a grommet, and the wire bundle secured with a cushioned clamp.*

open wiring. An electrical wiring installation in which the wires are tied together in bundles and clamped to the aircraft structure rather than being enclosed in conduit.

rigid conduit. Aluminum alloy or approved nonmetallic tubing used to house electrical wires in areas where they are subject to mechanical damage.

derated. Reduction in the rated voltage or current of an electrical device. Derating is done to extend the life or reliability of the device.

Type of Load	Derating Factors	
	24 VDC System	12 VDC System
Lamp	8	5
Inductive (relay–solenoid)	4	2
Resistive (heater)	2	1
Motor	3	2

Figure 1-79. *Switch derating factors.*

Wire AN Gauge Copper	Circuit Breaker (Amp.)	Fuse (Amp.)
22	5	5
20	7.5	5
18	10	10
16	15	10
14	20	15
12	25	20
10	35	30
8	50	50
6	80	70
4	100	70
2	125	100
1		150
0		150

Figures in parentheses may be substituted where protectors of the indicated rating are not available.

Figure 1-80. *Wire and circuit protection chart.*

Switches

All switches used in aircraft electrical systems must have sufficient contact capacity to break, make, and carry continuously the connected load current. Snap-action switches are preferred because their contacts open rapidly, regardless of the speed of the operating toggle or plunger. This rapid movement minimizes contact arcing.

The rating stamped on the switch housing is the amount of continuous current the switch can safely carry with the contacts closed. When switches are used in certain types of circuits, they must be derated by the factors shown in Figure 1-79.

A switch installed in a circuit that controls incandescent lamps is exposed to a very high inrush of current. When the lamp filament is cold, its resistance is very low. When the switch is first closed, the flow of current is 15 times more than the continuous current. As the filament heats up, its resistance increases and the current decreases. If the switch is not derated, the contacts may burn or weld shut when they are closed.

When a switch opens an inductive circuit, such as a relay or solenoid, the magnetic field surrounding the turns of the coil collapses and induces a high voltage that causes an arc across the contacts.

DC motors draw a large amount of current when the switch is first closed. As soon as the armature starts to turn, a back voltage, or counter EMF, is generated and the load current decreases. When the switch is opened to stop the motor, the magnetic field surrounding the coils collapses and induces a high voltage in the circuit.

A switch controlling a DC motor in a 24-volt system has a derating factor of 3. If the motor draws 4 amps for its normal operation, the switch must be rated at $4 \cdot 3 = 12$ amps to allow it to safely start and stop the motor.

Switches must be mounted in such a way that their operation is logical and consistent with other controls. For example, two-position ON-OFF switches should be mounted in such a way that the switch is turned on by an upward or forward movement of the control. If the switch controls movable aircraft elements, such as landing gear or flaps, the handle should move in the same direction as the desired motion. The operating control of switches whose inadvertent operation must be prevented should be covered with an appropriate guard.

Fuses and Circuit Breakers

Circuit protection devices such as fuses and circuit breakers are installed as close to the source of electrical energy as is practical. Their function is to protect the wiring. The circuit protection device should open the circuit before enough current flows to heat the wire and cause its insulation to smoke.

Figure 1-80 shows the size of fuse or circuit breaker that should be used to protect various sizes of wires.

Answers are provided on page 99.

87. A 20-gauge wire will carry _____ (more or less) current than an 18-gauge wire.

88. A continuous electrical load in a 28-volt electrical system is allowed to produce a voltage drop of _____ volt/s.

89. An intermittent electrical load in a 14-volt electrical system is allowed to produce a voltage drop of _____ volt/s.

90. If a 4-gauge copper wire routed in free air is to be replaced with an aluminum wire that is to carry the same amount of current, a _____-gauge aluminum wire will have to be used.

91. The smallest size aluminum wire recommended for use in aircraft electrical systems is _____-gauge.

92. When selecting the size wire to use in an aircraft electrical system, two things must be considered. These are:

    a._____

    b._____

93. Use the wire chart in Figure 1-63 on page 65 to find the wire size needed to carry a continuous load of 50 amps for 60 feet in a 28-volt electrical system. The wire is to be routed in a bundle. The smallest wire is a _____ gauge.

94. Use the wire chart in Figure 1-63 on page 65 to find the size electrical cable needed to carry an intermittent load of 150 amps for 20 feet in a 14-volt electrical system without exceeding a 1-volt drop. The smallest wire is a _____ gauge.

95. The electromagnetic field surrounding wires carrying alternating current can be prevented from interfering with sensitive electronic equipment by using _____ wires.

96. A radio transmitter is normally connected to its antenna with a _____ cable.

97. The half of an AN or MS quick-disconnect connector that carries the power is fitted with _____ (pins or sockets).

98. A barrier-type terminal strip should not have more than _____ terminals installed on any single lug.

99. If more than four wires need to be connected to a single point on a terminal strip, two or more lugs can be connected with a metal _____ .

(continued)

100. The correct size insulated terminal to use on a 18-gauge wire would have a _____ (what color) insulation.

101. The correct size insulated terminal to use on a 12-gauge wire would have a _____ (what color) insulation.

102. The type of wire terminal that should be installed on a barrier-type terminal strip is a _____ type.

103. Refer to Figure 1-76. Answer these questions about a wire identified as HD3A-20.

  a. This wire is in the _____ system.

  b. This is wire number _____ in this circuit.

  c. This is the _____ segment in this wire.

  d. This is a _____-gauge wire.

  e. This wire _____ (does or does not) go to ground.

104. The only type lubricant that should be used when pulling a wire bundle through a piece of polyvinyl tubing is _____ .

105. Wire bundles should be secured to the aircraft structure using _____ clamps.

106. If an electrical wire bundle is routed parallel to a fuel line, the wire bundle should be _____ (above or below) the fuel line.

107. A wire bundle should be no closer than _____ inches from any control cable unless a suitable mechanical guard is installed over the wire so the cable cannot contact it.

108. The maximum-diameter wire bundle that may be enclosed in a rigid conduit with an inside diameter of one inch is _____ inch.

109. The edges of a hole through which a wire bundle passes must be covered with a _____.

110. A switch used to control a 3-amp continuous flow of current in a 24-volt DC incandescent lamp circuit should be rated for at least _____ amps.

111. A switch used to control a 12-volt DC motor that draws a 3-amp continuous flow of current should be rated for at least _____ amps.

112. A circuit that is wired with an 18-gauge wire should be protected with a _____-amp circuit breaker.

General Inspection Procedures

The inspection of aircraft electrical systems will vary from aircraft to aircraft and becomes more complex as aircraft get larger. While the aircraft manufacturer's instructions should always be followed for specific systems, basic inspection processes will similar.

1. Inspect components for security of mounting hardware and inspect the mounting structure for cracks, corrosion, and cleanliness. Some locations of the aircraft, such as landing gear wheel wells, engine compartments, and areas below the floor, are prone to becoming dirty. A dirty surface can hide cracks and corrosion and should be cleaned as part of routine maintenance and inspection.

2. Check the attachment of wires to components for security and chafe protection. If a wire bundle or cable is attached to the component with a cannon plug, check the cannon plug for security and safety wire, as appropriate. Some cannon plugs will use safety wire (usually brass safety wire), while other cannon plugs are designed for use without safety wire.

3. Many electrical components use a short ground wire that goes from the component to the aircraft structure. Check the ground wire for security of attachment to the structure and clean any corrosion that may be present. Corrosion and loose connections will increase the resistance of the ground circuit and can cause intermittent or total failure of system operation.

4. Inspect terminal strips for security and verify that the nuts holding the wire terminals to the posts are tight and in good condition. There should never be more than four wire terminals on any one post.

5. Inspect wire bundles for security and chafe protection. Wire bundles should be contained with nylon cable ties, lacing cord, or protective sleeves and supported at regular intervals with Adel clamps to prevent sagging of the bundle. Check for burnt spots on the cable, which is an indication of wires shorting to ground or to each other. If wires are inside of a rigid conduit, check the conduit for security and chaffing and that drain holes are not plugged.

6. Check for adequate clearance of wires and bundles from moving controls and control cables (3 inches minimum clearance).

7. Wires should be routed above fuel lines, not below them. This prevents fuel leaks from dripping onto the wires.

DC Generators

You can find detailed inspection and maintenance instructions for DC generators in the manufacturer's instructions for continued airworthiness. The following instructions are general guidelines for inspection and maintenance. See Figures 1-81 and 1-82.

1. Inspect the generator for security of attachment.

2. If the generator is driven by a belt, check the belt for condition and proper tension.

3. Inspect the electrical terminals for condition and check security and condition of the attached wires and cables. Verify that the correct insulating boots are installed on the terminals.

4. Open the cover that provides access to the brushes. The condition of the brushes is very important as they provide the path for current flow between the rotor and the stator. Each brush will have a spring that provides the correct pressure on the brush as it contacts the rotor. The brushes will wear during normal operation, which leaves behind a dust of brush material. Clean out the dust with compressed air. Inspect the brushes for wear and replace the brushes when they reach their limits. Check the brush springs for proper tension by using a spring scale and verify that the tension is within the specified limits. See Figure 1-83.

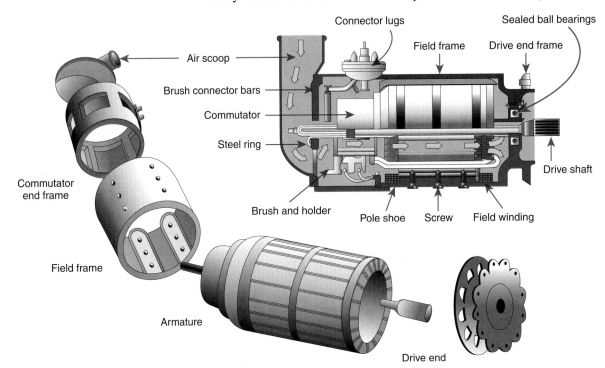

Figure 1-81. *DC generator.*

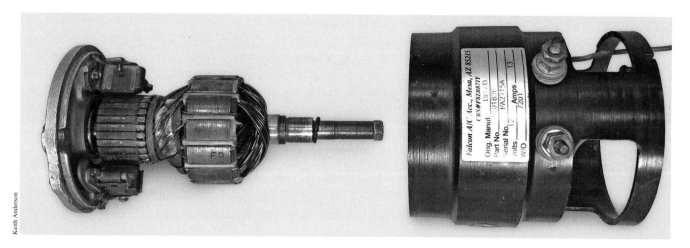

Figure 1-82. *DC generator.*

5. Inspect the rotor commutator for wear of the copper segments. The insulation between the segments is normally undercut by 0.020 inches to prevent interference with the brushes. If the commutator appears dark, this is caused by a film left behind by the brush wear. The commutator can be cleaned and polished with a plastic abrasive pad such as a Scotch-Brite™ pad.

6. On direct drive generators, check for oil inside the generator. If oil is present, check for an oil leak coming from the engine drive pad seal.

7. Check the output of the generator and voltage control system by running the engine and measuring the output of the generator with a voltmeter.

Figure 1-83. *DC generator brush and brush spring.*

Operational Check of Aircraft Exterior Lights

You can check the operation of aircraft exterior lights when the airplane is on the ground. First, turn on aircraft power by turning on the battery master switch. Next, turn on the switches for the desired light circuits. This includes navigation lights, anti-collision lights (including rotating beacons and strobe lights), and landing and taxi lights. Some aircraft may also have anti-ice lights which illuminate the leading edge of the wing, as well as logo lights, which shine on the vertical stabilizer to illuminate the company logo.

Further inspection of the lighting systems includes checking the condition and security of all switches, wiring, and lights.

Answers are provided on page 99.

113. Dirty surfaces can hide _____ and _____ and should be cleaned when conducting inspections.

114. Cannon plugs that are safety wired to prevent their loosening up usually use _____ safety wire.

115. Corrosion and loose connections of the ground circuit will cause a(n) _____ (increase or decrease) in the ground circuit.

116. Wire bundles are contained, or held together, with:

   a. _____

   b. _____

   c. _____

117. Wires should be routed _____ (above or below) fuel lines.

118. When inspecting generator drive belts, they should be inspected for _____ and _____.

119. When inspecting brushes in a generator, the dust from brush wear should be cleaned out with _____.

120. Insulation between segments of the commutator is normally undercut by _____ inches.

121. Oil inside of a direct drive generator is an indication of a failure of the _____.

Electrical System Troubleshooting

troubleshooting. A procedure used in aircraft maintenance in which the operation of a malfunctioning system is analyzed to find the reason for the malfunction and to find a method for returning the system to its condition of normal operation.

At one time, it was easy to see what was wrong with an ailing airplane, but much skill and knowledge were needed to get it back in the air. Today, the situation has drastically changed. With the complex systems used in modern aircraft, a high degree of knowledge and skill is needed to identify problems, but specialization has made it possible to get an aircraft back into the air quickly. Faulty components are sent to a shop where specialists with sophisticated test equipment can find and fix the trouble.

Remove and replace, or R and R, maintenance is the only way flight schedules can be maintained today. When an aircraft is down, it is the responsibility of the aviation mechanic to find out as quickly as possible which component is causing the trouble, remove it, and replace it with a component known to be good, in order to get the aircraft back into the air quickly. Maintenance of this type requires a good knowledge of systematic troubleshooting so that only the offending component is changed.

One major air carrier has recently stated that more than 60% of the "black boxes" removed from aircraft throughout their system have been sent to the shop only to find that there was nothing wrong with them. Needless to say, this is inefficient use of the mechanic's time, and it cannot be tolerated if the airline is to operate cost-effectively.

To help reduce unnecessary R and R of good components, this next section will describe how to develop a system of logical, or systematic, troubleshooting that will allow you to locate a problem and fix it in the shortest period of time.

When performing maintenance on live circuits or troubleshooting electrical systems, be careful to not short circuit power wires to ground or to other live circuits. General maintenance in areas that contain wires should be performed with caution so as to not damage wires or wire bundles. Whether performing maintenance or inspections, always inspect the aircraft wiring to verify secure installation and routing, as many problems can be prevented through good maintenance practices.

Rules for Systematic Troubleshooting

Efficient troubleshooting begins with a few very simple rules:

1. Know the way the system should operate. This sounds absurdly simple, but it is the secret of successful troubleshooting. You must know the way a component works. This includes knowledge of correct voltage and current at specified test points and the correct frequency and wave form of alternating current at these test points.

2. Observe the way the system is operating. Any difference between the way a system is operating and the way it should operate is an indication of trouble. Current or voltage that is too low or too high, or components that show signs of overheating, are indications that a system is not operating correctly.

3. Divide the system to find the trouble. Time is valuable in aviation maintenance; it is important that lost motion be kept to a minimum. When we know a system is not operating as it should, we must first find whether the trouble is in the beginning of the system or near its end. To do this, open the system near its middle and check the conditions there. If everything is OK at this point, the trouble is between there and the end. If things at that point are not as they should be, the trouble is between the power source and that point.

4. Look for the obvious problem first, and make all measurements at the points where they are easiest to make.

   Popped circuit breakers, blown fuses, and corroded ground connections are usually easy to check, and are the cause of many electrical system malfunctions.

black box. A term used for any portion of an electrical or electronic system that can be removed as a unit. A black box does not have to be a physical box.

Circuit breakers are sized to protect the wire and will open when excess current is detected. Excess current is often due to a malfunction in the component or a wire shorting to ground. Disconnect the wire at the component and reset the circuit breaker. If the circuit breaker doesn't pop, it is most likely that the component is at fault. If the circuit breaker still pops, there is a problem with the wire shorting to ground. Inspect the wire for obvious faults first. If nothing is obvious, you will need to disconnect both ends of the wire and check the wire with an ohmmeter to see if there is resistance or continuity between the wire and ground. If there is any resistance, it is an indication that the wire is shorted to ground.

A much more difficult problem to troubleshoot is when wires are in a bundle and are shorting to each other. If the wires go to the same system, this problem may show up as a popped circuit breaker or as intermittent or incorrect operation of the system. If the wires shorting together are from two different systems, a fault may show up in either, or both, systems. When troubleshooting a bundle with a suspected fault, disconnect both ends of the wire bundle. With an ohmmeter, first check between each wire in the cannon plug for a short to ground. If nothing is found, you will need to systematically check for resistance between each of the wires in the bundle. This can be done by putting one of the ohmmeter probes on one pin in the cannon plug and leaving it there while the other probe is moved to each of the other pins, checking for resistance. Next, move the first probe to the next pin and repeat the process. Continue doing this until all pins have been checked.

5. While most troubleshooting is done by measuring voltages, it is sometimes necessary to measure the resistance of a component. When making a measurement of resistance with an ohmmeter, the component being measured must be isolated from the circuit. This means you will need to disconnect one side of the component so that it is no longer part of the circuit. You can then measure across the component with the ohmmeter test leads to measure the resistance.

An Example of Systematic Troubleshooting

Let's examine a very simple troubleshooting problem. Most of the steps we will discuss will seem quite obvious, but bear with us. We are building a system that works on a simple inoperative dome light as well as on a malfunctioning ignition or alternator system.

In this example, the only information we have is a complaint left by a pilot that tells us "the dome light doesn't work." This is a simple problem, and in all probability, it is a burned-out bulb. But since we are analyzing systematic troubleshooting, let's not close our minds to all of the possibilities.

Below are some of the first points that might come to mind:

1. When troubleshooting a problem, you must know how the system SHOULD work: In this case, the dome light should light up.

2. You should know all of the possible problems that can keep the dome light from burning.

   a. Is there power on the airplane? There must be, or the pilot would have complained about more than just the dome light.

   b. Was the dome light switch turned on? Surely the pilot would have checked this.

   c. Is the bulb burned out? This is our most likely suspect, but let's not jump to conclusions.

   d. What else could be the problem? There are several other possibilities, including a bad switch, a bad connection, a broken wire, or a bad ground connection.

To make the most efficient use of your time, you must make only one trip to the airplane, and you must fix the problem on your first attempt. First, gather the tools and equipment you'll need. You'll need a copy of the wiring diagram for the dome light circuit; you can get a copy from the microfiche reader or from a service manual. And you'll need a spare bulb. You can get the correct part number from the circuit diagram. You will also need a multimeter (a volt-ohm-milliammeter, or VOM), and a screwdriver or two.

Before going any further, let's take a few minutes to consider the dome light circuit. Look at Figure 1-84 and answer the following questions:

1. Which circuit breaker supplies power to the dome light?
   Answer—Cabin lights

2. What other lights are on the same circuit breaker?
   Answer—L.H. Oxygen light, baggage compartment light, L. wing courtesy light

3. What is the part number of the dome light bulb?
   Answer—GE 313

Now you are ready to go to the airplane.

When you turn on the master switch, you hear the familiar "klunk" of the battery contactor, which tells you that there is electrical power on the main bus.

But, when you try the dome light switch, sure enough, the dome light doesn't light up. But the left-wing courtesy light does, so the baggage compartment light is probably burning too.

Next in line is the bulb and its ground circuit. Take the cover off of the dome light so you can see the bulb. Before taking the bulb out of the socket, make sure that the ground for the light is good. Using one of the test leads from your multimeter, touch one end to the outside of the lamp socket and the other end to some part of the aircraft that you know connects to the main structure and is not insulated with paint or a protective oxide coating. If the lamp burns with this temporary ground, you know the bulb is good and the trouble is in the ground circuit. The trouble could be:

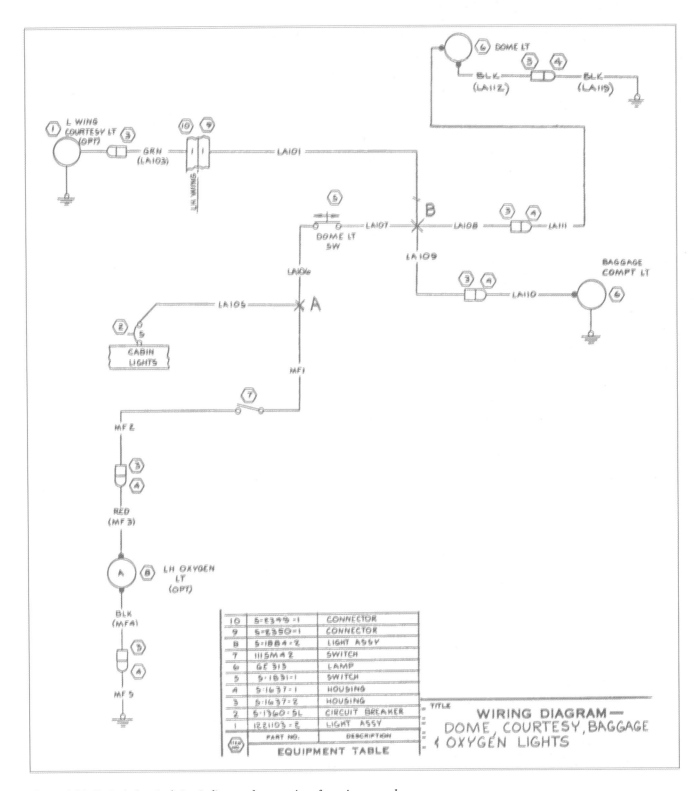

Figure 1-84. *Typical electrical circuit diagram from an aircraft service manual.*

1. At the point where the black wire, LA112, connects to the lamp socket

2. At the connection between the two sections of black wire

3. At the point where black wire, LA119, grounds to the aircraft structure

If this temporary ground did not cause the bulb to light up, it is time to take the bulb out of its socket and look at the filament. If it is broken, you have found the problem, and a new bulb will fix it. If the filament is not broken, check it for continuity. It is possible for a filament to look good and still be open. Switch the VOM to the low-resistance scale and measure the resistance of the filament. The amount of resistance is not important—you are just concerned that the filament has continuity. If the filament does have continuity, your problem is in the electrical system.

You now know that there is power through the dome light switch (since the left-wing courtesy light came on when you turned on the dome light switch), the lamp filament is good, and the ground for the light fixture is good. Now check to see whether there is power to the center contact of the dome light socket. Turn the selector switch on the VOM to the range of DC voltage that will allow the battery voltage to move the pointer up to around mid-scale. (The 24- or 50-volt scale is good for either a 12-volt or a 24-volt system.) Clip the black, or negative, lead to the outside of the lamp socket, and carefully touch the center contact with the red, or positive, lead. If there is power to the bulb, the meter will show the battery voltage. If there is no voltage at this point, check the wiring diagram. You will find that there are three possible places to look:

1. There could be a bad connection between wire LA111 and the lamp socket.

2. There could be a bad connection where wire LA111 joins wire LA108.

3. Wire LA108 could be loose where it joins wires LA101, LA107, and LA109. This is not likely, because the left-wing courtesy light burns, and it comes from the same point.

Begin by checking the easiest place to get to and work your way back to the point that has power. Now you can find the bad connection and fix it in the way the manufacturer recommends. Put the cover back over the dome light and turn the master switch off. The job has been finished in the shortest possible time.

Troubleshooting Voltage Rectifiers

Voltage rectifiers, often called bridge rectifiers, are used to change an AC voltage into a DC voltage. The most common uses of voltage rectifiers on aircraft are inside of DC alternators and in transformer-rectifier (TR) units, which are discussed in the section on Electrical Power Systems for Large Aircraft. Voltage rectifiers can be identified in electrical schematics by recognizing the diodes that are connected in a bridge circuit configuration. AC voltages in aircraft are usually 3-phase sine waves, which require a bridge rectifier with 6 diodes. Note the bridge rectifier diodes in Figure 1-85.

The diodes in a bridge rectifier act as check-valves of the alternating current, only allowing the current to go one direction, and thus ending up with direct current (DC) voltage. If one of the diodes fails, it can allow part of the alternating current to leak through to the DC side of the circuit. The easiest way to check for this type of failure is to set your voltmeter to the AC voltage scale and measure the DC voltage output. The voltmeter should read 0 AC volts. If there is a small AC voltage, one of the diodes has most likely failed.

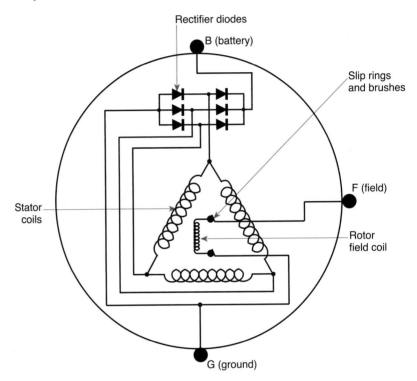

Figure 1-85. *Bridge rectifier diodes in a DC alternator.*

Troubleshooting Review

Now that you have completed a simple, but typical, troubleshooting problem, let's review a few basic points on how to make the most efficient use of your time when you have a problem like this:

1. Again, first of all, you must know what the system does when it is operating correctly.

2. Next, collect all of the information possible on the trouble. Ask the pilot or flight crew as many questions as possible. Did the problem happen suddenly? Did anything unusual happen before the trouble started? Have you noticed anything like this happening before? Was

there any unusual noise when the trouble started? Was there any smoke or unusual smell?

3. When you have all of the information from the flight crew, study the wiring diagram. Figure out all of the possible causes of the problem and plan your troubleshooting in a systematic way.

4. Work on the most likely causes first:
   • Blown fuses
   • Burned-out bulbs
   • Loose connections
   • Shorted or open diodes

5. When something is proven to be good, forget about it and keep looking until you find something that is not as it should be.

6. Remember that an aircraft electrical system is a high-performance system. To save weight, it uses the smallest wire possible and the lightest possible connectors and components, all of which are subjected to vibration that would shake an automobile system apart in a short time.

   Keep this in mind when you have a specially troublesome problem. Shake the connections and look for connections that appear to be good but which open up when they are vibrated.

7. If your troubleshooting requires a lot of power, such as you would need for landing lights, flap motors, or landing gear retraction motors, be sure to use a ground power supply, or GPU, so that you do not discharge the aircraft battery. When connecting the GPU, be sure to follow the aircraft manufacturer's instructions in detail. Airplanes differ in the way the GPUs are to be connected.

8. When a problem really has you stumped, draw a simple logic flow chart to help find where the trouble is.

Logic Flow Charts for Troubleshooting

Figure 1-86 shows a logic flow chart for the simple electrical system troubleshooting problem just discussed. This type of chart not only allows us to visualize the problem clearly, but it helps us see all of the alternatives.

An oval is used to show the beginning and the end of the problem. A diamond is used when there is a decision to be made. The instructions in a rectangle tell what to do next.

The first oval instructs us to turn the master switch on, and the last oval states that the job is done.

When the master switch is turned on, two possible conditions can occur. The battery relay will click, or it will not click. The first diamond depicts these two alternatives. If it clicks, there is power to the battery relay and you can follow the YES route to the next instruction. If it does not click, follow the NO route to the box that tells that the problem is between the battery and the

logic flow chart. A type of graphic chart that can be made up for a specific process or procedure to help follow the process through all of its logical steps.

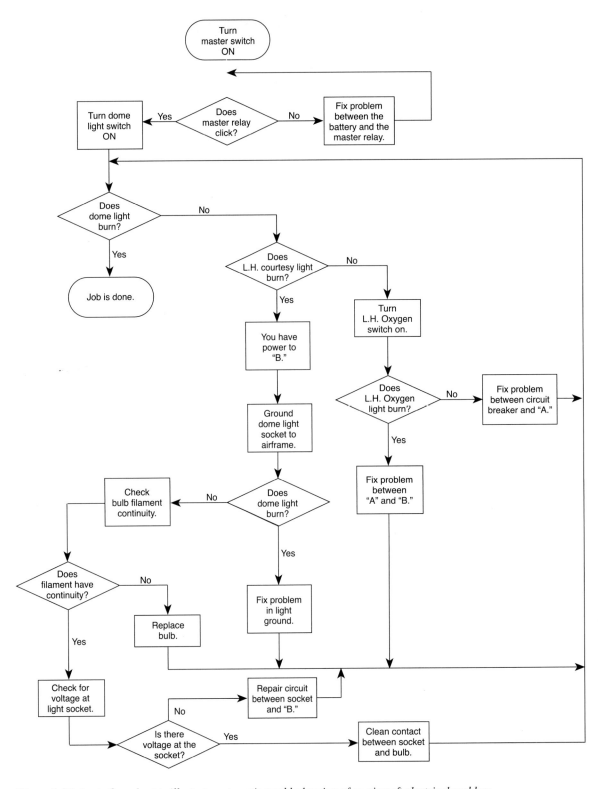

Figure 1-86. *Logic flow chart to illustrate systematic troubleshooting of an aircraft electrical problem.*

battery relay. The battery could be discharged, the battery ground connection could be loose or corroded, or there may be a loose or corroded connection between the battery and the master relay.

If there is power to the battery relay and it closes as it should, then turn on the dome light switch and go to the next diamond. If the dome light burns, follow the YES route to the oval that tells you that the job is done. If it does not burn, follow the NO route to the diamond that asks if the left-wing courtesy light is burning. If this light is burning there is power to point B on the circuit in Figure 1-84. Follow the next instruction, which tells you to ground the dome light socket to the airframe, and then go to the next diamond. If the dome light burns, go with the YES route and follow the next instruction to fix the problem in the light socket ground wire. When this is fixed, follow the line from the instruction box back to the diamond that asks if the dome light is burning. If it is burning, follow the YES route to the oval that tells you that the job is finished.

Now, go back to the third diamond that asks if the left-wing courtesy light is burning. If it is not burning, follow the NO route to the instruction box that tells you to turn the left-hand oxygen light on. Then go to the diamond that asks if the left-hand oxygen light is burning. If it is burning, the problem is between points A and B, and the most likely trouble spot is in the dome light switch itself. If the left-hand oxygen light is not burning, the problem is between the cabin lights circuit breaker and point A.

With a flow chart such as this, you can logically trace the steps that allow you to locate any trouble and fix it with the least amount of lost motion.

To make a flow chart, start with the first logical step in the operation of the system on which you are working (turn on the master switch) and end with the condition you want to occur (the dome light burns). Ask questions that can be answered YES or NO about every condition that exists between the beginning and the end of the problem. All YES answers should take you to the end, and all NO answers should require you to take some action that will put you back on the path to the solution.

Once you get into the habit of systematically analyzing your troubleshooting problems, you will be able to follow a logical sequence of action that will take you to a solution to the problem in the shortest time with the least amount of lost motion and expense.

Troubleshooting Tools

Because electrical system troubleshooting requires that you open up the system and measure values of voltage and current, you need specialized equipment. This can be as simple as a continuity light or as complex as an oscilloscope. Let's look at some of the most frequently used instruments.

Continuity Light

The simplest electrical system troubleshooting tool you can use is a "bug light," or continuity tester, consisting of two flashlight batteries, a 3-volt

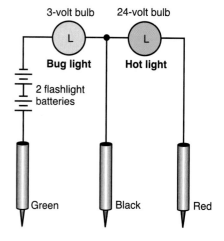

Figure 1-87. *A combination "bug light" and "hot light" is a handy tool for detecting continuity and power in an aircraft electrical system.*

continuity tester. A troubleshooting tool that consists of a battery, a light bulb, and test leads.

The test leads are connected to each end of the conductor under test, and if the bulb lights up, there is continuity. If it does not light up, the conductor is open.

Figure 1-88. *An analog multimeter of this type may be used for troubleshooting aircraft electrical systems.*

multimeter. An electrical test instrument that consists of a single current-measuring meter and all of the needed components to allow the meter to be used to measure voltage, resistance, and current.

Multimeters are available with either analog or digital-type displays.

digital multimeter. An electrical test instrument that can be used to measure voltage, current, and resistance. The indication is in the form of a liquid crystal display in discrete numbers.

analog-type indicator. An electrical meter that indicates values by the amount a pointer moves across a numerical scale.

flashlight bulb, and two test leads. With this simple homemade tool, you can trace wires through a system, locate shorts and open circuits, and quickly determine whether a fuse is good or bad.

Many technicians augment their bug light with a 24-volt bulb and another test lead. This part of the circuit is called a "hot light," and it is used to determine whether there is voltage in the part of the system you are testing. Since you want to know only if voltage is present, a 24-volt bulb will allow you to test both 12- and 24-volt systems.

When using the continuity tester, all electrical power must be off to the circuit. Connect the black test lead to one end of the circuit and the green lead to the other end. If there is continuity, the bulb will light up. If there is an open circuit, the bulb will not light.

Note: It is not a good policy when troubleshooting an aircraft electrical system to follow the automotive practice of piercing the insulation with a sharp needle point on the test lead to contact the wire for checking continuity or voltage. The insulation is different and there is a danger of damaging the small wire.

The hot light feature is handy for determining the presence of voltage at various points in the system. If you touch the red test leads of the hot light to the point you want to check for voltage, and the black lead to some ground point on the aircraft structure, the light will come on if there is voltage, or stay off if there is no voltage.

Multimeters

Continuity lights are simple, inexpensive to make, and can be easily carried in your toolbox, but they are limited in what they can do. The next logical choice in troubleshooting tools is a small, toolbox-size multimeter, about 2.5 inches deep by 3 inches wide, and less than 6 inches tall (See Figure 1-88). These multimeters measure AC and DC voltages, direct current in the milliamp range, and resistance. The meter sensitivity is 1,000 ohms per volt, which places too much load on the circuit for it to be used for making measurements in certain electronic circuits, but its ruggedness and small size make it ideal for troubleshooting aircraft electrical systems. The accuracy of this type of meter is about 3% of full scale for the DC measurements and 4% of full scale for AC measurements.

Digital Multimeter

The digital multimeter (DMM), such as the one in Figure 1-89, is a test instrument that has replaced the older analog multimeter. DMMs have circuits that convert analog values of voltage, current and resistance into a digital voltage, which is electronically manipulated to produce an indication in the form of discrete numbers in a liquid crystal display.

DMMs cover a wide range of AC and DC measurements with an extremely high input impedance—usually between 10 and 11 megohms. They can measure voltage, current, resistance, frequency, and capacitance. Their accuracy is much greater than the analog meters they have replaced. Good quality analog multimeters have an accuracy in the range of 3% of full scale indication while modern portable DMMs have an accuracy in the range of ±0.025%. The larger benchtop instruments are even far more accurate.

Microprocessor circuits in the DMM give it a wide range of features such as:

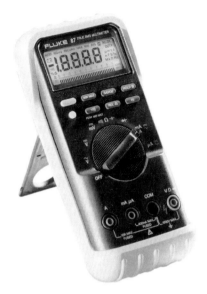

Figure 1-89. *Digital multimeters like this one have replaced analog instruments for many troubleshooting jobs. Their main advantages are their high input impedance and their inherent accuracy.*

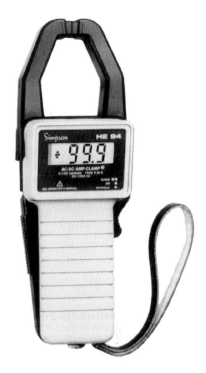

Figure 1-90. *This clamp-on ammeter measures current flowing through a conductor without having to open the circuit.*

- It may be used as a continuity tester that gives an audible sound when the circuit being tested has continuity.

- It has a current-limiting feature that allows it to measure the voltage drop across semiconductor junctions. This allows the DMM to be used to test semiconductor diodes and some transistors.

- It has a data acquisition feature that records maximum and minimum values taken over a period of time.

- It can sample and hold the most recent reading to be retained for examination after the instrument is removed from the circuit being tested.

- It covers a wide range of values and is autoranging so it automatically selects the correct range for the value being tested without the risk of damaging the instrument.

- It contains a bar graph that shows trends in changes in the values being measured.

Clamp-on Ammeter

One very handy tool for electrical-system troubleshooting is a clamp-on ammeter. This instrument has a set of jaws that can be opened, slipped over a current-carrying wire and then clamped shut. Current flowing in the wire produces a magnetic field that acts on a special type of semiconductor material to produce a voltage proportional to the strength of the magnetic field. The strength of this field is proportional to the amount of current flowing in the wire.

Clamp-on ammeters are also used for troubleshooting hydraulic and fuel systems that have electrically operated pumps. The load on a pump can be

clamp-on ammeter. An electrical instrument used to measure higher current without opening the circuit through which it is flowing.

The jaws of the ammeter are opened and slipped over the current-carrying wire and then clamped shut. Current flowing through the wire produces a magnetic field which induces a voltage in the ammeter that is proportional to the amount of current.

determined fairly well by the amount of current the pump motor is drawing. By clamping an ammeter over one of the wires supplying current to the pumps, you can determine which pumps are operating and get an idea of the amount of load they are carrying.

Oscilloscopes

oscilloscope. *An electrical instrument that displays the wave form of the electrical signal it is measuring.*

One of the most sophisticated pieces of test equipment used for aircraft electrical system troubleshooting is a digital oscilloscope. The display shows the wave form and frequency of the voltage being measured.

Modern electronic systems have made dual-trace oscilloscopes the most popular type of instrument. With a dual-trace oscilloscope, you can look at the signals on the input and output of a circuit at the same time. Oscilloscopes used for troubleshooting are hand-held devices that can easily be carried to the aircraft. Some digital multimeters include a built-in oscilloscope. These are commonly referred to as scope meters.

STUDY QUESTIONS: ELECTRICAL SYSTEM TROUBLESHOOTING

Answers are provided on page 99.

122. The four basic rules for systematic troubleshooting are:

    a. _____

    b. _____

    c. _____

    d. _____

123. One of the first things to check if an electrical component does not operate is the

    _____ .

124. A decision point in a logic flow chart is enclosed in a _____-shaped box.

125. Two characteristics of a digital multimeter that make it a valuable troubleshooting tool are its:

    a. _____

    b. _____

126. Trends in voltage and current changes are displayed on a digital multimeter by a _____ .

127. Current can be measured in a circuit without having to open the circuit if a/an _____-type ammeter is used.

128. Wave form and frequency of the voltage in an electric circuit can be observed with a/an

    _____ .

Appendix A—Electrical Symbols

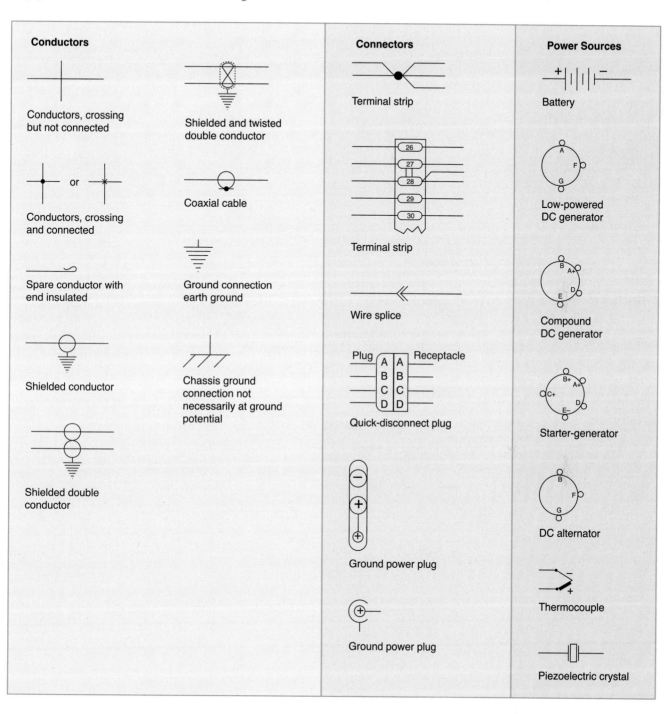

Conductors

Conductors, crossing but not connected

Conductors, crossing and connected

— or —

Spare conductor with end insulated

Shielded conductor

Shielded double conductor

Shielded and twisted double conductor

Coaxial cable

Ground connection earth ground

Chassis ground connection not necessarily at ground potential

Connectors

Terminal strip

26
27
28
29
30

Terminal strip

Wire splice

Plug   Receptacle
A   A
B   B
C   C
D   D

Quick-disconnect plug

Ground power plug

Ground power plug

Power Sources

+ | | | −

Battery

A
F
G

Low-powered DC generator

B
A+
E
D

Compound DC generator

B+
A+
C+
D
E−

Starter-generator

B
F
G

DC alternator

−
+

Thermocouple

Piezoelectric crystal

(continued)

Indicators

V
Voltmeter

A
Ammeter

W
Wattmeter

Ω
Ohmmeter

mA
Milliammeter

μa
Microammeter

Electrical Loads

Fixed resistor

Variable resistor — rheostat

Variable resistor — potentiometer

Tapped resistor

1 W
450 Ω
Resistor installed external to LRU
(Line replaceable unit)

T
Temperature-sensitive resistor

Heater element resistor

L
Lamp

Capacitors

Fixed, nonelectrolytic
capacitor

– +
Fixed, electrolytic
capacitor

Variable capacitor

Inductors

Air-core inductor

Iron-core inductor

Variable inductor

Autotransformer

Iron-core transformer

Air-core transformer

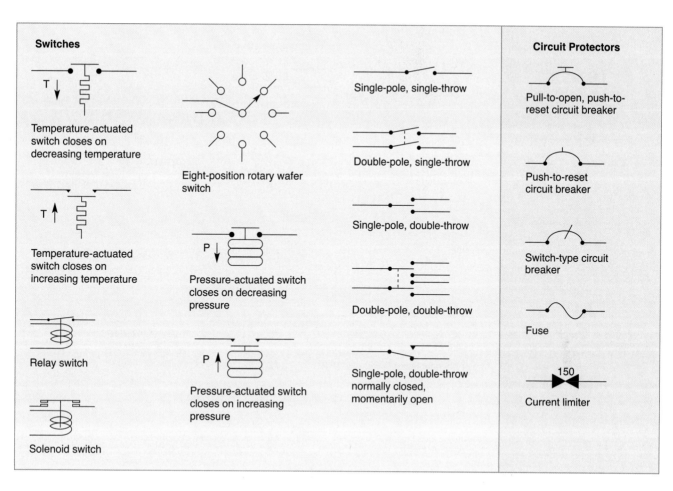

Switches

Temperature-actuated switch closes on decreasing temperature

Temperature-actuated switch closes on increasing temperature

Relay switch

Solenoid switch

Eight-position rotary wafer switch

Pressure-actuated switch closes on decreasing pressure

Pressure-actuated switch closes on increasing pressure

Single-pole, single-throw

Double-pole, single-throw

Single-pole, double-throw

Double-pole, double-throw

Single-pole, double-throw normally closed, momentarily open

Circuit Protectors

Pull-to-open, push-to-reset circuit breaker

Push-to-reset circuit breaker

Switch-type circuit breaker

Fuse

Current limiter

(continued)

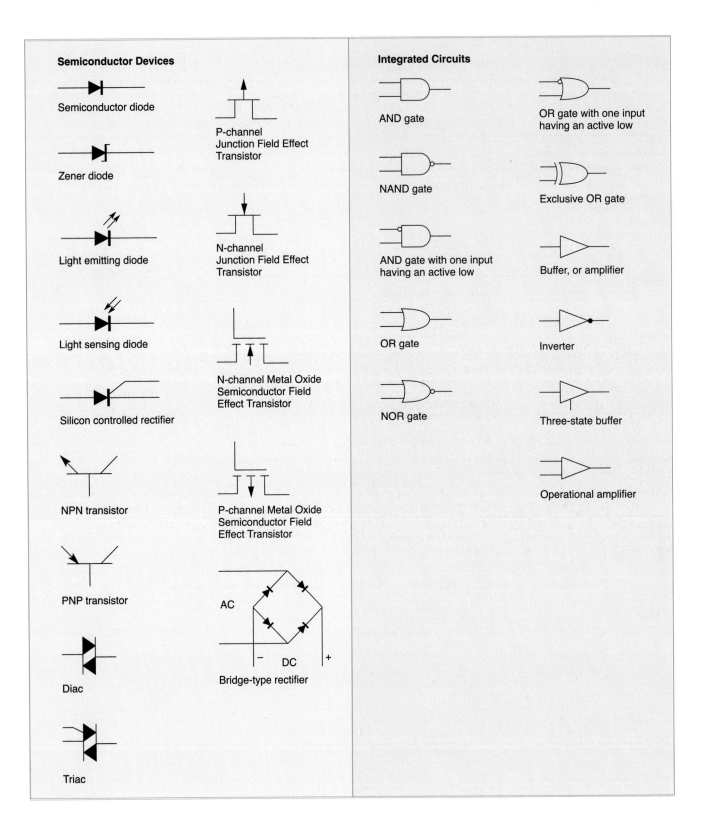

Semiconductor Devices

Semiconductor diode

Zener diode

Light emitting diode

Light sensing diode

Silicon controlled rectifier

NPN transistor

PNP transistor

Diac

Triac

P-channel
Junction Field Effect
Transistor

N-channel
Junction Field Effect
Transistor

N-channel Metal Oxide
Semiconductor Field
Effect Transistor

P-channel Metal Oxide
Semiconductor Field
Effect Transistor

AC

− DC +

Bridge-type rectifier

Integrated Circuits

AND gate

NAND gate

AND gate with one input
having an active low

OR gate

NOR gate

OR gate with one input
having an active low

Exclusive OR gate

Buffer, or amplifier

Inverter

Three-state buffer

Operational amplifier

Answers to Chapter 1 Study Questions

1. I
2. E, V
3. R
4. bus
5. a. heat is produced in the conductor
   b. magnetic field surrounds the conductor
   c. voltage is dropped across the load
6. positive
7. opposite
8. same
9. a. source of electrical energy
   b. an electrical load
   c. conductors to join the source with the load
10. forward
11. closed
12. 0.7
13. does not
14. zener diode
15. reverse
16. fixed
17. movable
18. closed
19. increases
20. silicon controlled rectifier
21. true
22. battery voltage
23. zero volts
24. resistance
25. battery
26. ground
27. aircraft structure
28. negative
29. wiring
30. starter
31. trip-free
32. cannot
33. are not
34. 6
35. induced
36. rate
37. opposite
38. reverse
39. resistor R
40. diode D_1
41. the fuse
42. alternator
43. stator
44. AC
45. diodes
46. opened
47. field
48. rotating
49. field poles
50. commutator, brushes
51. does not
52. does
53. ground
54. a. voltage regulator
   b. current limiter
   c. reverse-current cutout
55. open
56. closed
57. closed
58. resistor
59. paralleling
60. equalizing
61. starter, generator
62. series
63. does not
64. percent
65. continuous
66. intermittent
67. starter
68. complex
69. is not
70. a. gear switch
   b. up-limit switch
   c. gear safety switch
71. will
72. squat
73. automatically
74. off
75. left
76. induced
77. AC
78. TR units
79. constant-speed drive
80. a. voltage
   b. frequency
   c. power
81. a. external power unit
   b. generator 1
   c. generator 2
   d. generator 3
   e. auxiliary power unit
   f. standby inverter
82. hot battery bus
83. DC, AC
84. 115, 400
85. rotary, static
86. oscillator circuit

87. less
88. 1.0
89. 1.0
90. 2
91. 6
92. a. current-carrying
       capability
    b. allowable voltage drop
93. 4
94. 4
95. shielded
96. coaxial
97. sockets
98. 4
99. bus strap
100. red
101. yellow
102. ring
103. a. deicing
     b. 3
     c. first
     d. 20
     e. does not

104. tire talcum
105. cushion
106. above
107. 3
108. ¾
109. grommet
110. 24
111. 6
112. 10
113. cracks, corrosion
114. brass
115. increase
116. a. nylon cable ties
     b. lacing cord
     c. protective sleeves
117. above
118. condition, proper tension
119. compressed air
120. 0.020
121. engine drive pad seal

122. a. Know the way the system
        should operate.
     b. Observe the way the
        system is operating.
     c. Divide the system to find
        the trouble.
     d. Look for the obvious
        problems first.
123. circuit breaker
124. diamond
125. a. high input impedance
     b. high degree of accuracy
126. bar graph
127. clamp-on
128. oscilloscope

AIRCRAFT FUEL SYSTEMS

2

Fuel System Maintenance and Inspection   166

Aviation Fuels

Aircraft engines convert the chemical energy in fuel into heat energy. It is the function of the aircraft fuel system to store the fuel until it is needed, and then supply the engine with the volume of uncontaminated fuel that will allow it to develop the required power.

The development of aviation fuels has closely paralleled the development of aviation itself. In the early days of flying, the reciprocating engines used just about any type of gasoline that was available. But when more power was demanded of the lightweight aircraft engines, additives were mixed with the gasoline that allowed the engines to produce more power without detonating.

Turbine engines, with their voracious appetite for fuel, have led the petroleum industry to produce fuels that are especially adapted to the requirements of these engines.

This text discusses the basic requirements of fuels in aircraft fuel systems. The *Powerplant* textbook of the Aviation Mechanic Series discusses the actual chemical transformation that allows the engines to use these fuels.

Reciprocating Engine Fuel

Reciprocating engines were the primary power for aircraft up through World War II. The military services and the airlines used tremendous amounts of aviation gasoline in their high-powered engines, and private, or general, aviation used much less fuel in their low-powered engines. The two fuels used for the two types of engines differ in the additives they contain to suppress detonation.

After World War II the turbine engine became the standard propulsion system for the military and the airlines, and the demand for aviation gasoline has decreased drastically. The petroleum industry is finding it increasingly uneconomical to produce all the grades of aviation gasoline needed to supply small reciprocating-engine-powered aircraft. As a result, the older, lower-powered engines in the smaller aircraft use fuel that contains far more lead than they were designed to use. The unavailability of the correct fuel along with the high cost of aviation gasoline has propelled much research into the use of automotive gasoline in aircraft.

Aviation Gasoline Grades

When military and airline aircraft were powered by reciprocating engines, four grades of aviation gasoline were widely available. But now that most of the aircraft are turbine-powered, only three grades of aviation gasoline are produced, and two of these are being phased out. The petroleum industry would like to produce only one type of gasoline that would meet the needs of all gasoline engines.

hydrocarbon. An organic compound that contains only carbon and hydrogen. The vast majority of our fossil fuels such as gasoline and turbine-engine fuel are hydrocarbons.

fractional distillation. A method of separating the various components from a physical mixture of liquids.

The material to be separated is put into a container and its temperature is increased. The components having the lowest boiling points boil off first and are condensed. Then as the temperature is further raised, other components are removed. Kerosine, gasoline and other petroleum products are obtained by fractional distillation of crude oil.

octane rating. A rating of the antidetonation characteristics of a reciprocating engine fuel. It is based on the performance of the fuel in a special test engine. When a fuel is given a dual rating such as 80/87, the first number is its antidetonating rating with a lean fuel-air mixture, and the higher number is its rating with a rich mixture.

vapor lock. A condition in which vapors form in the fuel lines and block the flow of fuel to the carburetor.

vapor pressure. The pressure of the vapor above a liquid needed to prevent the liquid evaporating. Vapor pressure is always specified at a specific temperature.

Aviation Gasoline Characteristics

Aviation gasoline is a highly refined hydrocarbon fuel obtained by fractional distillation of crude petroleum. Its important characteristics are: purity, volatility, and antidetonation qualities.

Grade	Old Rating	Tetraethyl Lead Content ml/gallon	Color	Availability
80	80/87	0.5	Red	Being phased out
91			Blue	Phased out
100	100/130	4.0	Green	Being phased out
100LL		2.0	Blue	Available
115	115/145	4.6	Purple	Phased out

Figure 2-1. *Aviation gasoline grades.*

Purity

Every precaution is taken to ensure purity of aviation gasoline, but certain contaminants do get into it. The most prevalent contaminant is water. Fortunately, water is heavier than aviation gasoline and it settles to the bottom of the tank and to the lowest point in the fuel system. Aircraft fuel tanks are required to have a sump, or low area, where the water can collect, and these sumps are fitted with a quick drain valve so the pilot on a preflight inspection can drain water from these low points.

Water gets into the fuel tanks by condensation. If a fuel tank remains partially empty for several days, the changing temperature will cause air to be drawn into the tank, and this air will contain enough moisture to condense and settle to the bottom of the tank. All fuel tanks should be filled as soon after flight as possible to minimize condensation.

Jet engine fuels have a higher viscosity than aviation gasoline, and they hold contaminants in suspension better than gasoline, so water contamination causes additional problems with jet aircraft fuel systems. These problems are discussed in more detail in the section on jet engine fuel.

Volatility

Liquid gasoline will not burn. It must be vaporized so it will mix with oxygen in the air and form a combustible mixture. Aviation gasoline must be volatile enough to sufficiently vaporize in the engine induction system. If it does not vaporize readily enough, it can cause hard starting, poor acceleration, uneven fuel distribution, and excessive dilution of the oil in the crankcase. If it vaporizes too readily it can cause vapor lock, which prevents the flow of fuel to the engine.

The measure of the ease with which a fuel vaporizes is the Reid vapor pressure. This is the pressure of the vapor above the fuel required to prevent further vaporization at a specified temperature.

The vapor pressure allowed for aviation gasoline must be 5.5 to 7 psi at 100°F, which is lower than that of most automotive gasoline. If the vapor pressure of the fuel is too high, it is likely to vaporize in the lines in hot weather or high altitude and starve the engine of fuel.

Antidetonation Qualities

Detonation occurs in an aircraft engine when the fuel-air mixture inside the cylinders reaches its critical pressure and temperature and explodes rather than burning smoothly. The extreme pressures produced by detonation can cause severe structural damage to the engine.

Aviation gasoline is rated according to its antidetonation characteristics by its octane rating or performance number. The procedure for obtaining this rating is described in the section on Aviation Fuels in the *General* textbook of this Aviation Mechanic Series. This procedure compares the performance of the rated fuel to that of a fuel made up of a mixture of iso-octane and normal heptane. Grade 80 fuel has characteristics similar to that of a mixture of 80% iso-octane and 20% heptane, and grade 100 and 100LL have the same antidetonation characteristics as iso-octane.

Fuel Additives

Various grades of aviation gasolines differ in the types and amounts of additives they contain. The basic additive is tetraethyl lead (TEL) which increases the critical pressure and temperature of the fuel.

Not only does TEL improve the antidetonation characteristics of the fuel, but it provides the required lubrication for the valves. Engines that must use fuel with less lead than they are designed to use suffer from valve problems.

One problem associated with using a fuel with too much TEL is the buildup of lead deposits in the spark plugs. Other additives such as ethylene dibromide and tricresyl phosphate are used in leaded fuel to help scavenge the residue left from the lead.

Aromatic additives such as toluene, xylene, and benzene are used in some aviation gasoline to improve its antidetonation characteristics. Fuel that contains aromatic additives must be used only in fuel systems specifically approved for it, because these additives soften some of the rubber compounds used in fuel hoses and diaphragms.

Turbine Engine Fuels

There are two basic types of turbine engine fuel: Jet A and A-1, and Jet B. Jet A and A-1 are similar to commercial kerosine, having characteristics similar to those of military JP-5. They have a low vapor pressure and their flash points are between 110°F and 150°F. Their freezing points are −40°F for Jet A, −58°F for Jet A-1, and −55°F for JP-5.

Jet B is called a wide-cut fuel because it is a blend of gasoline and kerosine fractions, and it is similar to military JP-4. Jet B has a low freezing point,

detonation. An explosion, or uncontrolled burning inside the cylinder of a reciprocating engine. Detonation occurs when the pressure and temperature inside the cylinder become higher than the critical pressure and temperature of the fuel.

performance number. The antidetonation rating of a fuel that has a higher critical pressure and temperature than iso-octane (a rating of 100). Iso-octane that has been treated with varying amounts of tetraethyl lead is used as the reference.

normal heptane. A hydrocarbon, C_7H_{16}, with a very low critical pressure and temperature. Normal heptane is used as the low reference in measuring the antidetonation characteristics of a fuel.

iso-octane. A hydrocarbon, C_8H_{18}, which has a very high critical pressure and temperature. Iso-octane is used as the high reference for measuring the antidetonation characteristics of a fuel.

tetraethyl lead (TEL). A heavy, oily, poisonous liquid, $Pb(C_2H_5)_4$, that is mixed into aviation gasoline to increase its critical pressure and temperature.

ethylene dibromide. A chemical compound added to aviation gasoline to convert some of the deposits left by the tetraethyl lead into lead bromides. These bromides are volatile and will pass out of the engine with the exhaust gases.

tricresyl phosphate (TCP). A chemical compound, $(CH_3C_6H_4O)_3PO$, used in aviation gasoline to assist in scavenging the lead deposits left from the tetraethyl lead.

flash point. The temperature to which a material must be raised for it to ignite, but not continue to burn, when a flame is passed above it.

petroleum fractions. The various components of a hydrocarbon fuel that are separated by boiling them off at different temperatures in the process of fractional distillation.

around −60°F, and its vapor pressure is higher than that of kerosine, but lower than that of gasoline.

Turbine Fuel Volatility

Volatility of turbine fuel is important because it is a compromise between conflicting factors. Its volatility should be high enough for good cold weather starting and aerial restarting, but low enough to prevent vapor lock and to reduce fuel losses by evaporation.

Under normal temperature conditions, gasoline, with its 7-psi vapor pressure, can give off so much vapor in a closed container or tank that the fuel-air mixture is too rich to burn. Under these same conditions, the vapor given off by Jet B, with its 2- to 3-psi vapor pressure, will produce a fuel-air mixture that is explosive. Jet A, with its extremely low vapor pressure of around 0.125 psi, has such low volatility that under normal conditions it does not give off enough vapor to form an explosive fuel-air mixture.

Turbine Fuel Viscosity

Turbine fuel is more viscous than gasoline, so it holds contaminants and prevents their settling out in the tank sumps.

Water is held in an entrained state in turbine fuel, and at high altitude and low temperature, it can collect on the fuel strainers and freeze, blocking the flow of fuel.

Microbial Growth in Turbine Fuel Tanks

microbial contaminants. The scum that forms inside the fuel tanks of turbine-engine-powered aircraft that is caused by micro-organisms.

These micro-organisms live in water that condenses from the fuel, and they feed on the fuel. The scum they form clogs fuel filters, lines, and fuel controls and holds water in contact with the aluminum alloy structure. This causes corrosion.

Water in turbine fuel causes problems that do not exist in reciprocating engine fuel. During flight at high altitude and low temperature, water condenses out of the fuel and settles in the bottom of the fuel tank, where it collects around the sealant used in the seams of integral fuel tanks. Microscopic organisms live and multiply at the interface between the water and the fuel and form a scum that holds water in contact with the tank structure. Corrosion forms, with this water acting as the electrolyte.

To prevent the formation of the scum in the tanks, turbine fuel may be treated with a biocidal additive. This kills the microbes and bacteria and prevents their forming the scum. This additive may be put in at the refinery, or added into the fuel as it is pumped into the aircraft tanks.

Fuel Anti-Icing

anti-icing additive. A chemical added to the turbine-engine fuel used in some aircraft. This additive mixes with water that condenses from the fuel and lowers its freezing temperature so it will not freeze and block the fuel filters. It also acts as a biocidal agent and prevents the formation of microbial contamination in the tanks.

When water condenses out of the fuel and freezes on the fuel filters, it can shut off the flow to the engine. To prevent this, some aircraft use fuel heaters that are a form of heat exchanger. Compressor bleed air or hot engine oil flows through one part of the heater and fuel flows through another part. The air or oil gives up some of its heat to the fuel and raises its temperature enough to prevent ice from forming on the filter.

The fuel additive that prevents the formation of the microbial scum in the fuel tanks also acts as an anti-icing agent, or antifreeze. It mixes with the water that condenses out of the fuel and lowers its freezing point enough that it cannot freeze on the filters.

STUDY QUESTIONS: AVIATION FUELS

Answers are provided on page 169.

1. One of the basic differences between the various grades of aviation gasoline is in the amount of additive used to suppress _____ .

2. The most prevalent contaminant in aviation gasoline is _____ .

3. Jet engine fuels have a _____ (higher or lower) viscosity than aviation gasoline.

4. Hard starting, slow warm-up, poor acceleration, and uneven fuel distribution to the cylinders will result if the vapor pressure of the fuel is too _____ (high or low).

5. Gasoline does not vaporize easily if its vapor pressure is too _____ (high or low).

6. Aviation gasoline is not allowed to have a Reid vapor pressure higher than _____ psi at 100°F.

7. Most automotive gasoline has a _____ (higher or lower) vapor pressure than aviation gasoline.

8. The antidetonation characteristics of aviation gasoline are specified by its _____ rating or _____ number.

9. The basic fuel additive used to suppress detonation in a reciprocating engine is _____ .

10. Aromatic additives are used in aviation gasoline to increase the antidetonation characteristics of the fuel but they also cause deterioration of _____ parts.

11. The jet-engine fuel that is similar to kerosine is _____ (Jet A or Jet B).

12. Turbine engine fuels are more susceptible to water contamination than aviation gasoline because they are _____ (more or less) viscous than gasoline.

13. Micro-organisms live in the water which condenses and collects in the integral fuel tanks of a jet airplane. They form a scum that holds the water against the aluminum alloy structure and cause _____ .

14. The additive that is put into turbine engine fuel to kill the micro-organisms also acts as an _____ agent.

Fuel System Requirements

More aircraft accidents and incidents are attributable to fuel systems than to any other system in an aircraft. System mismanagement has caused engines to quit due to fuel starvation when fuel was still available in some of the other tanks. Bladder-type fuel tanks have partially collapsed, decreasing the amount of fuel that can be carried without warning the pilot of this shortage. Fuel systems serviced with the wrong grade of fuel have caused severe detonation and the loss of an engine on takeoff, the most critical portion of a flight. Undetected contaminants can cause engine failure by plugging the fuel lines or by replacing fuel with water.

It is the responsibility of the pilot-in-command of an aircraft to ensure that the aircraft has a sufficient quantity of the correct grade of uncontaminated fuel for each flight. But aviation mechanics must maintain the fuel systems in such a way that they can hold the full amount of fuel and deliver this fuel at the correct rate under all operating conditions. It is the responsibility of the person fueling an aircraft to use only the correct grade of fuel and to take all precautions to ensure that the fuel is free from water and other contaminants.

14 CFR Part 23—Airworthiness Standards: Normal Category Airplanes—provides requirements and guidance for the fuel systems of these aircraft. In this text, we will consider these requirements. Transport category airplanes have somewhat different requirements, and they are specified in 14 CFR Part 25.

The certification requirements in Part 23 have changed from being very prescriptive regulations to performance-based standards. This change came about as new technologies and advances in aircraft design outpaced the early design standards that the regulations were based on. An example of this change is the now obsolete Section 23.965, Fuel Tank Tests. This regulation stated that a fuel tank must be able to withstand a pressure of 3.5 psi without failure (a prescriptive requirement). The new amendment of the regulation, Section 23.2430, Fuel Systems, states that the fuel tank is to be designed to withstand the loads under likely operating conditions without failure and to retain fuel under all likely operating conditions and to minimize hazards to the occupants during any survivable emergency landing (performance basis).

14 CFR §23.2430 states the following:

(a) Each fuel system must—

    (1) Be designed and arranged to provide independence between multiple fuel storage and supply systems so that failure of any one component in one system will not result in loss of fuel storage or supply of another system;

    (2) Be designed and arranged to prevent ignition of the fuel within the system by direct lightning strikes or swept lightning strokes to areas where such occurrences are highly probable, or by corona or streamering at fuel vent outlets;

    (3) Provide the fuel necessary to ensure each powerplant and auxiliary power unit functions properly in all likely operating conditions;

(4) Provide the flight crew with a means to determine the total useable fuel available and provide uninterrupted supply of that fuel when the system is correctly operated, accounting for likely fuel fluctuations;

(5) Provide a means to safely remove or isolate the fuel stored in the system from the airplane;

(6) Be designed to retain fuel under all likely operating conditions and minimize hazards to the occupants during any survivable emergency landing. For level 4 airplanes, failure due to overload of the landing system must be taken into account; and

(7) Prevent hazardous contamination of the fuel supplied to each powerplant and auxiliary power unit.

(b) Each fuel storage system must—

(1) Withstand the loads under likely operating conditions without failure;

(2) Be isolated from personnel compartments and protected from hazards due to unintended temperature influences;

(3) Be designed to prevent significant loss of stored fuel from any vent system due to fuel transfer between fuel storage or supply systems, or under likely operating conditions;

(4) Provide fuel for at least one-half hour of operation at maximum continuous power or thrust; and

(5) Be capable of jettisoning fuel safely if required for landing.

(c) Each fuel storage refilling or recharging system must be designed to—

(1) Prevent improper refilling or recharging;

(2) Prevent contamination of the fuel stored during likely operating conditions; and

(3) Prevent the occurrence of any hazard to the airplane or to persons during refilling or recharging.

STUDY QUESTIONS: FUEL SYSTEM REQUIREMENTS

Answers are provided on page 169.

15. In the design of a fuel system, it _____ (is or is not) permissible for a fuel pump to draw fuel from more than one tank at a time.

16. In the design of a multiengine fuel system it _____ (is or is not) permissible for one tank outlet to feed both engines.

(continued)

17. If an engine supplied with a gravity fuel system requires 25 gallons of fuel per hour for takeoff, the fuel system must be capable of supplying _____ gallons per hour.

18. If an engine supplied with a pump-fed fuel system requires 25 gallons of fuel per hour for takeoff, the fuel system must be capable of supplying _____ gallons per hour.

19. A turbine engine fuel system must provide at least _____ percent of the fuel flow required by the engine under each intended operation condition and maneuver.

20. A conventional metal fuel tank must be able to withstand an internal pressure of _____ psi without leaking.

21. A nonmetallic fuel tank with walls supported by the aircraft structure (a bladder tank) must be able to withstand an internal pressure of _____ psi without leaking.

22. When the outlets of two fuel tanks are interconnected, the vent space above the fuel in the tanks must be _____ .

23. If the design landing weight of an airplane is less than its allowable takeoff weight, the airplane must have a _____ system installed.

Aircraft Fuel Systems

The weight of the fuel is a large percentage of an aircraft's total weight, and the balance of the aircraft in flight changes as the fuel is used. These conditions add to the complexity of the design of an aircraft fuel system. In small aircraft the fuel tank or tanks are located near the center of gravity so the balance changes very little as the fuel is used. In large aircraft, fuel tanks are installed in every available location and fuel valves allow the flight engineer to keep the aircraft balanced by scheduling the use of the fuel from the various tanks. In high-performance military aircraft, the fuel scheduling is automatic.

Gravity-Feed Fuel System for a Float Carburetor

The simplest fuel system is a gravity-feed system like those used on some of the small high-wing training airplanes.

The fuel is carried in two tanks, one in the root of each wing. The outlets of these tanks are interconnected and they flow into a simple ON/OFF fuel valve. Because the tank outlets are interconnected, the airspace above the fuel in the two tanks is also interconnected and the tanks vent to the atmosphere through an overboard vent in the top of the left tank.

The fuel flows from the shutoff valve through a strainer to the carburetor. A small, single-acting primer pump draws fuel from the strainer and sprays it into the intake manifold to furnish fuel for starting the engine.

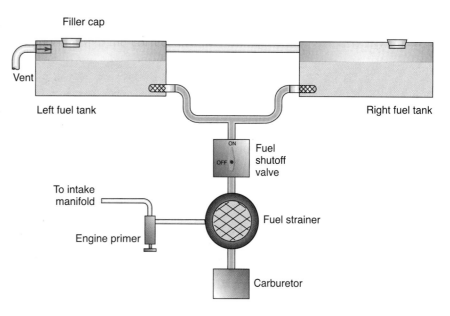

Figure 2-2. *Fuel system of a high-wing training airplane.*

Gravity-Feed System for a Fuel-Injected Engine

Figure 2-3 on the next page diagrams the fuel system of a high-wing airplane equipped with a fuel-injected engine.

The fuel flows by gravity from the main fuel tanks into small reservoir tanks and into the tank selector valve, which has three positions: OFF, LEFT ON, and RIGHT ON.

Fuel flows from the selector valve through a two-speed electric auxiliary pump that has a LOW and a HIGH position. After leaving the pump it passes through the main fuel strainer into the engine-driven fuel pump.

This engine us es a Teledyne-Continental fuel-injection system in which part of the fuel is returned by the mixture control to the pump through a check valve, and the selector valve to the reservoir of the tank that is being used.

A priming system uses a manually operated plunger-type pump that draws fuel from the strainer and sprays it into the entrance end of each of the two intake manifolds on the engine. More details of this pump are shown in Figure 2-3.

Low-Wing, Single-Engine Fuel System for a Float Carburetor

The fuel system in Figure 2-4 is found on some low-wing single-engine airplanes whose engines are equipped with float carburetors.

Fuel flows from the tanks to a fuel selector valve that has three positions, LEFT TANK ON, RIGHT TANK ON, and OFF. From the selector valve the fuel flows through a strainer and the pumps to the carburetor. The plunger-type electric pump and the diaphragm-type engine pump are connected in parallel. The electric pump moves the fuel for starting the engine, and as soon as it starts, the diaphragm pump supplies the fuel for normal operation. The electric pump is turned on for takeoff and landing to supply fuel in the event the engine pump should fail.

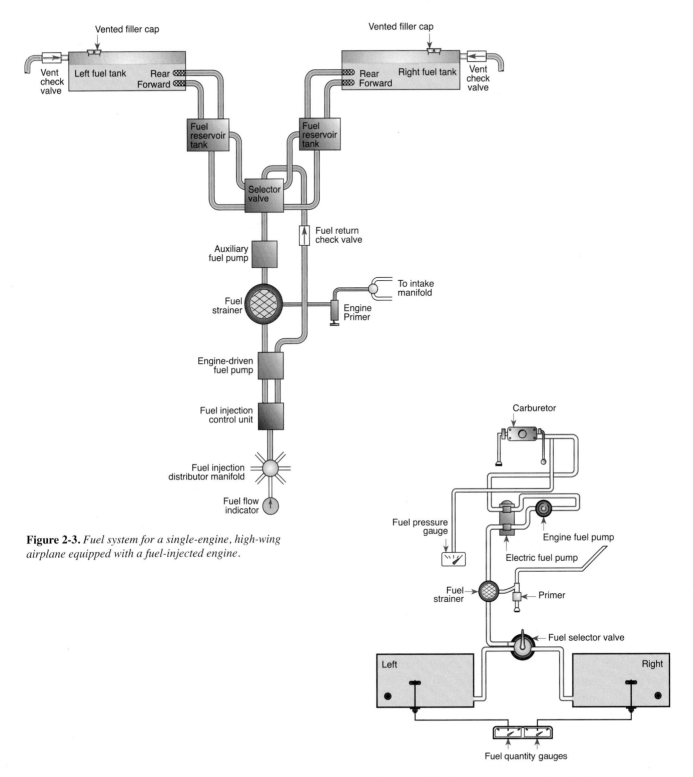

Figure 2-3. *Fuel system for a single-engine, high-wing airplane equipped with a fuel-injected engine.*

Figure 2-4. *Fuel system for a low-wing, single-engine airplane whose engine is equipped with a float carburetor.*

Low-Wing, Twin-Engine Fuel System for Fuel-Injected Engines

Figure 2-5 shows the fuel system for a low-wing, twin-engine airplane with fuel-injected engines. This airplane has two 51-gallon main fuel tanks, which are mounted on the wing tips, and two 36-gallon bladder-type auxiliary tanks, one in each wing. Two additional 26-gallon tanks can be installed in the nacelle lockers at the aft end of the engine nacelles. These locker tanks do not feed the engines directly, but are equipped with transfer pumps that allow the fuel to be pumped into the main tanks and from there to the engines.

This fuel system has a fuel selector valve for each engine. The valve for the left engine has the positions LEFT MAIN, RIGHT MAIN, LEFT AUXILIARY, and OFF. The valve for the right engine has the positions RIGHT MAIN, LEFT MAIN, RIGHT AUXILIARY, and OFF.

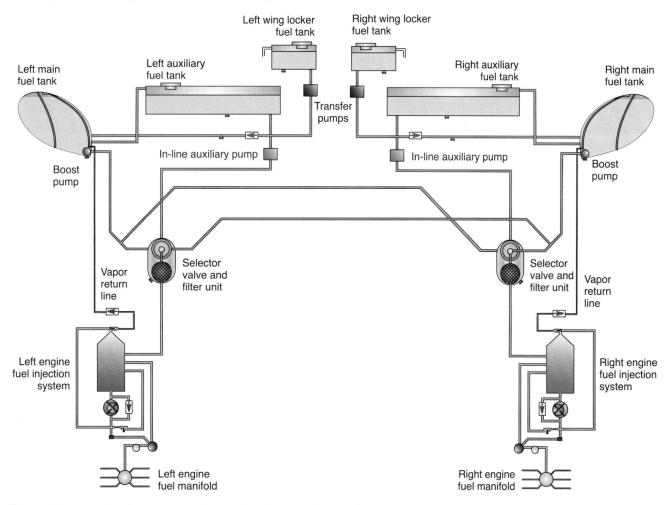

Figure 2-5. *Fuel system for a low-wing, twin-engine airplane with fuel-injected engines.*

Fuel flows from the selected tanks through the selector valves and the filters to the engine-driven pumps which are part of the Teledyne-Continental fuel-injection system. There is a small but steady stream of fuel through the vapor return lines from fuel-injector pumps to the main tanks. This return fuel picks up any vapors that have formed in the system and returns them to the tank, rather than allowing them to disturb the fuel metering.

The selector valves allow the pilot to operate either engine from either of the main fuel tanks and the left engine from the left auxiliary tank and the right engine from the right auxiliary tank. The fuel in the nacelle locker tanks can be pumped into the main tanks on their respective sides.

There is a submerged centrifugal-type auxiliary fuel pump in each of the main fuel tanks. These pumps are controlled by three electrical switches: for priming, for purging, and for backing up the engine-driven pumps for takeoff and landing. When the Prime switch is placed in the ON position, the auxiliary pump operates at high speed. When the Auxiliary Fuel Pump switch is placed in LOW position, the pump operates at low speed for purging the lines of vapor. When it is placed in the ON position, the pump operates at low speed, but in the event of the failure of the engine-driven pump, it automatically shifts to high speed. In the OFF position, the auxiliary pump does not operate.

Electric plunger-type pumps are installed in the lines between the wing locker tanks and the main tanks to transfer the fuel, and between the auxiliary tanks and the fuel selector valve to supply fuel to the fuel-injector pumps and prevent vapors forming in the lines between the auxiliary tanks and the injector pumps.

cross-feed valve. A valve in a fuel system that allows all engines of a multi-engine aircraft to draw fuel from any fuel tank.

Cross-feed systems are used to allow a multi-engine aircraft to maintain a balanced fuel condition.

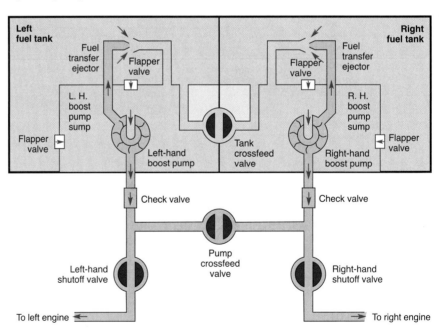

Figure 2-6. *Twin-engine cross-feed fuel system.*

Twin-Engine Cross-Feed Fuel System

The fuel system in Figure 2-6 has two fuel tanks, two shutoff valves, and two cross-feed valves. Either engine can draw fuel from either tank, or the tanks can be connected.

Each of these tanks has a boost-pump sump and a fuel transfer ejector to keep the boost-pump sumps full. Part of the boost-pump discharge flows through the ejector and creates a low pressure which pulls fuel from the tank into the sump. Flapper valves in the sump prevent fuel flowing from the sump back into the tank.

If either of the boost pumps should fail, the other pump can supply both engines through the pump cross-feed valve. The check valve prevents fuel from the tank with the functioning pump from flowing into the other tank under these conditions.

Four-Engine Manifold Cross-Feed Fuel System

Large aircraft have a number of fuel tanks that may be filled, drained, or used from a manifold that connects all tanks and all engines. Figure 2-7 shows such a system.

The characteristics of a manifold cross-feed fuel system are:

1. All tanks can be serviced through a single refueling receptacle. This pressure fueling reduces the chances of fuel contamination, as well as reducing the danger of static electricity igniting fuel vapors.

2. Any engine can be fed from any tank. This lets the pilot balance the fuel load to maintain good stability of the aircraft.

3. All engines can be fed from all tanks simultaneously.

4. A damaged tank can be isolated from the rest of the fuel system.

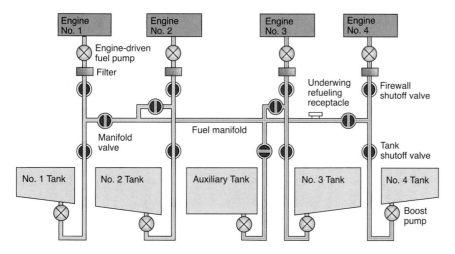

Figure 2-7. *A typical manifold cross-feed fuel system.*

ejector. A form of jet pump used to pick up a liquid and move it to another location. Ejectors are used to ensure that the compartment in which the boost pumps are mounted is kept full of fuel. Part of the fuel from the boost pump flowing through the ejector produces a low pressure that pulls fuel from the main tank and forces it into the boost-pump sump area.

boost pump. An electrically driven centrifugal pump mounted in the bottom of the fuel tanks in large aircraft. Boost pumps provide a positive flow of fuel under pressure to the engine for starting and serve as an emergency backup in the event an engine-driven pump should fail. They are also used to transfer fuel from one tank to another and to pump fuel overboard when it is being dumped.

Boost pumps keep pressure on the fuel in the line to the engine-driven pump, and in doing this, prevent vapor lock from forming in these lines.

Centrifugal boost pumps have a small agitator propeller on top of the pump impeller. This agitator releases the vapors in the fuel before the fuel leaves the tank.

manifold cross-feed fuel system. A type of fuel system commonly used in large transport category aircraft. All fuel tanks feed into a common manifold, and the dump chutes and the single-point fueling valves are connected to the manifold. Fuel lines to each engine are taken from the manifold.

Each tank has a boost pump and a tank shutoff valve, and each engine has a firewall shutoff valve. There is a manifold valve for each of the engines.

By opening the tank shutoff valve and the firewall shutoff valve, each engine is fed from its own fuel tank. And, by opening the manifold valve for any engine, the boost pump in the tank feeding that engine can pressurize the manifold. This allows pilot or flight engineer to balance the load in flight to maintain good stability.

This fuel system allows for single-point pressure fueling and defueling. This reduces the chances of fuel contamination, as well as reducing the danger of static electricity igniting fuel vapors.

Pressure fueling is done through an underwing fueling and defueling receptacle and a fuel control panel that contains all of the controls and gauges necessary for a person to fuel or defuel any or all of the tanks. When the aircraft is being refueled, the fueling hose is attached to the refueling receptacle on the manifold. All the manifold valves and tank valves are open and the firewall shutoff valves are closed. The valve on the fueling hose is opened and fuel flows into all the tanks. When a tank is full, or when it reaches the level preset on the fuel control panel, the valve for that tank shuts off. When all the tanks have the correct amount of fuel in them, the system automatically shuts off.

Helicopter Fuel System

Helicopters have unique requirements for their fuel systems. The spaces in which the fuel tanks can be located are far more limited than they are in an airplane because a helicopter has no wings in which the tanks can be installed. Another complication is that the center of gravity range is so limited that the fuel tanks as well as most of the payload must be located in close proximity to the rotor mast.

Figure 2-8 shows the airframe fuel system for a single-engine turbine-powered helicopter. The bladder-type fuel cell is mounted in the fuselage and is connected to the fuel filler port on the outside of the fuselage. Two centrifugal-type submerged boost pumps are mounted in the bottom of the tank, one forward and one aft. Fuel is picked up by the boost pumps and directed through integral check valves to a single fuel supply line. After the fuel leaves the tank, it passes through a solenoid-operated shutoff valve, through an airframe system filter, and through the engine filter to the engine fuel control unit.

bladder-type fuel cell. A plastic-impregnated fabric bag supported in a portion of an aircraft structure so that it forms a cell in which fuel is carried.

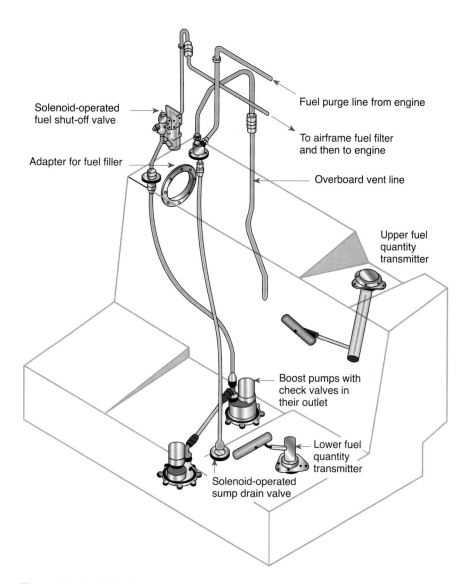

Solenoid-operated
fuel shut-off valve

Adapter for fuel filler

Fuel purge line from engine

To airframe fuel filter
and then to engine

Overboard vent line

Upper fuel
quantity
transmitter

Boost pumps with
check valves in
their outlet

Lower fuel
quantity
transmitter

Solenoid-operated
sump drain valve

Figure 2-8. *Simplified diagram of the fuel system of a turbine-engine-powered helicopter.*

Large Turbine-Engine Transport Fuel System

The fuel system of the Boeing 727 is typical of the systems used in this type of aircraft. The fuel is held in three tanks. Tanks 1 and 3 are located in the wings and have a nominal capacity of 12,000 pounds. Tank 2 has a nominal capacity of 24,000 pounds and consists of three sections. An integral section of tank 2 is located in each wing, and a bladder section is located in the wing center section. See Figure 2-9.

Tanks 1 and 3 have two centrifugal-type submerged boost pumps each that are driven by 3-phase AC motors. Tank 2 has four boost pumps of the same type. Each boost pump has a check valve in its outlet so fuel will not flow back into the tank through any pump if it is inoperative.

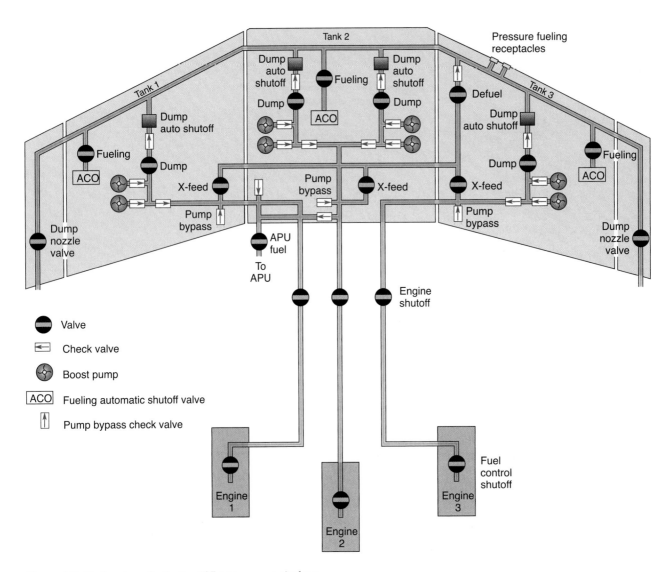

Figure 2-9. *Fuel system of a Boeing 727 jet transport airplane.*

The boost pumps in each tank feed their respective engines through electric motor-driven engine shutoff valves. Three cross-feed valves allow the boost pumps in any tank to supply fuel to any engine and to defuel any of the tanks or transfer fuel from one tank to another.

Vent lines in tanks 1 and 3 are connected to vent surge tanks outboard of their respective tanks. Vent lines in tank 2 are connected to both of the surge tanks. The vent-surge tank outlets are in a non-icing flush scoop on the lower surface of the wing tips. This scoop allows positive ram pressure to be in the tanks during all airplane attitudes.

The surge tanks are protected against the entry of flames in the vent duct. A flame-sensitive detector is mounted in each vent duct between the vent scoop and the surge tank. If a flame enters the duct, the detector will electrically discharge an inerting agent into the vent-surge tank which will prevent the flame from reaching the fuel tanks. The flight engineer has a test switch that tests the integrity of the system.

The electrically operated engine shutoff valves are operated by DC motors that are controlled by switches on the flight engineer's panel. When any fire pull handle is pulled, the engine fuel shutoff valve is closed and the switch on the flight engineer's panel is deactivated until the fire pull handle is pushed back in.

Fueling and Defueling

The Boeing 727 is equipped for pressure fueling and defueling, but provisions are also made for overwing fueling and suction defueling.

The single-point refueling panel (shown in Figure 2-10 on the next page), located in the leading edge of the right wing, contains two fueling hose couplings, fuel quantity indicators for the three tanks, and the control switches for the fueling valves.

Before fueling, test the fuel quantity indicators by turning the fueling test switch to ON. All three indicators should drive toward zero. When the switch is returned to its OFF position, the gauges will return to their original indication.

Connect the two fuel hoses and pressurize the fueling manifold. When the fueling valve switch is moved to the OPEN position, the valve opens and fuel flows from the fueling manifold into the tank. If the tank is to be completely filled, a float-operated shutoff valve, labeled ACO in Figure 2-9, will close the valve when the tank is full. If the tank is to be only partially filled, the fueling valve switch can be moved to the CLOSE position when the desired quantity is indicated on the fuel quantity gauge.

Tanks 1 and 3 have provisions for overwing fueling. Tank 2 does not have this provision, however it can be fueled from tanks 1 and 3 through their dump system. Open the dump valve in tank 1 or 3, and the fueling valve in tank 2. Turn on the boost pump in the tank furnishing the fuel. Fuel flows from this tank through the dump and pressure fueling manifold and then into tank 2 through its fueling valve.

Pressure defueling is done by connecting a fuel-servicing truck to the servicing manifold. Open all three of the cross-feed valves and turn on one or more boosts pump in each tank. Open the manually operated defuel valve and fuel will be pumped from the cross-feed manifold into the servicing manifold and into the servicing truck.

Suction defueling can be done by using the same connections and valve positions as for pressure defueling. Close the manifold vent shutoff valve at the fuel panel and use the suction provided by the servicing truck to get the fuel from the tanks. The fuel will flow from the tank through the pump-bypass check valves.

fire pull handle. The handle in an aircraft cockpit that is pulled at the first indication of an engine fire. Pulling this handle removes the generator from the electrical system, shuts off the fuel and hydraulic fluid to the engine, and closes the compressor bleed air valve. The fire extinguisher agent discharge switch is uncovered, but it is not automatically closed.

pressure fueling. The method of fueling used by almost all transport aircraft. The fuel is put into the aircraft through a single underwing fueling port. The fuel tanks are filled to the desired quantity and in the sequence selected by the person conducting the fueling operation.

Pressure fueling saves servicing time by using a single point to fuel the entire aircraft, and it reduces the chances for fuel contamination.

fuel jettison system. A system installed in most large aircraft that allows the flight crew to jettison, or dump, fuel to lower the gross weight of the aircraft to its allowable landing weight.

Boost pumps in the fuel tanks move the fuel from the tank into a fuel manifold. From the fuel manifold it flows away from the aircraft through dump chutes in each wing tip.

The fuel jettison system must be so designed and constructed that it is free from fire hazards.

Fuel Dumping

Fuel can be jettisoned in flight from all three tanks through either or both of the dump nozzles located in the wing tips. Fuel under boost pump pressure flows through the four electrically operated dump valves, through the automatic dump level control valves, into the fueling and dump manifold. The fuel leaves this manifold through the electrically operated dump nozzle valves and exits the aircraft through the dump nozzles.

The normal dumping rate is approximately 2,300 pounds per minute. The mechanically operated dump level control valves will shut the fuel off automatically when the level reaches 3,500 pounds in each tank. If these valves should not operate, the dumping can be terminated by closing the electrically operated dump valves.

Instruments and Controls

The switches and instruments for the fuel system are located at the single-point refueling panel in the leading edge of the right wing and at the flight engineer's panel.

Refueling Panel

The refueling panel has three fuel quantity gauges, one for each of the three tanks. These gauges indicate the usable fuel in each tank, measured in pounds. See Figure 2-10. Directly below each of these gauges is a guarded fueling shutoff valve switch and a valve-in-transit light. When the valve switch is moved, the light comes on until the valve reaches the position called for by the switch, and then goes out.

The fueling power switch controls power for the fueling operation with the external or APU power connected.

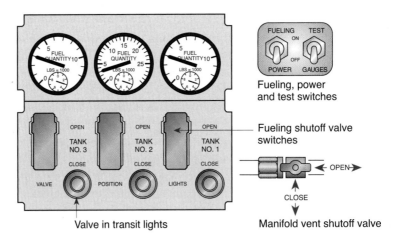

Figure 2-10. *Refueling panel controls and indicators.*

When the fueling test switch is moved to the ON position, all three indicators on the fueling panel are driven toward zero. The indicators on the flight engineer's panel are driven toward full. When the switch is turned to the OFF position, the indicators all return to their original position.

The manifold vent shutoff valve is a manual valve that is normally open, but is closed when the tanks are being defueled by suction.

Flight Engineer's Panel

The fuel system control switches and indicators on the flight engineer's panel are illustrated in Figures 2-11 and 2-12.

The digital total fuel quantity indicator indicates the total usable fuel aboard to the nearest 100 pounds. The three analog-type indicators give the usable amount of fuel in each of the three tanks. The large pointers indicate the thousands of pounds, and the small vernier pointers indicate the hundreds of pounds. These indicators are driven by a capacitance bridge system that compensates for variations in fuel temperature and density.

When the test switch for each indicator is depressed, the analog indicators move toward empty and the indication on the total quantity indicator increases. When the switch is released, the indications return to their normal values.

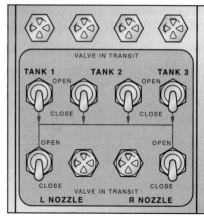

Figure 2-12. *Fuel dump control switches on the flight engineer's auxiliary panel.*

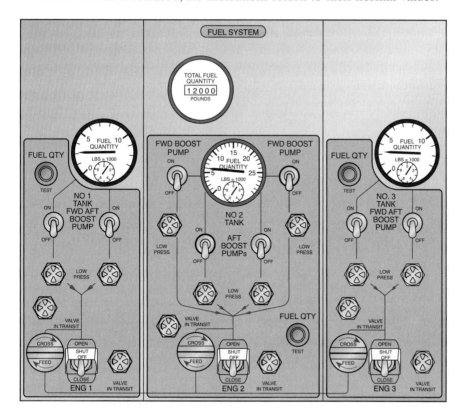

Figure 2-11. *Fuel system controls on the flight engineer's panel.*

The boost pump switches control the boost pumps. The low-pressure lights associated with each pump come on if the boost pump is not producing any pressure.

The engine fuel valve control switch controls the engine fuel valves as long as the fire pull handles are not pulled. When these handles are pulled, the valve control switch is disarmed and cannot operate until the fire pull handle is pushed back in. The valve-in-transit light comes on, indicating power to the valve motor, and it turns off when the valve reaches the position called for by the switch.

The cross-feed valve control switch is a rotary switch that has a bar on its knob that lines up with lines on the panel that show whether the valve is open or closed. When bar is aligned with the line, the engine fuel system is connected to the cross-feed manifold. See Figure 2-11.

The left and right dump nozzle valve switches and the dump valve switches are located on the flight engineer's auxiliary panel. Each switch has an accompanying valve-in-transit light that shows that there is power to the valve, and the light goes out when the valve reaches the position called for by the switch.

To dump fuel, open the appropriate nozzle valves and dump valves and turn on the boost pump or pumps. The fuel will dump until the dump level sensor in the tank shuts off the dump flow when the fuel in the tank reaches approximately 3,500 pounds.

STUDY QUESTIONS: AIRCRAFT FUEL SYSTEMS

Answers are provided on page 169.

24. Refer to Figure 2-2. Because fuel can feed from both tanks at the same time, the air space above the fuel in the tanks must be _____ .

25. The electric fuel pump and the engine fuel pump in Figure 2-4 are connected in _____ (series or parallel).

26. In the fuel system shown in Figure 2-5, vapors in the engine-driven fuel pump are returned to the _____ (main or auxiliary) fuel tanks.

27. In the cross-feed fuel system in Figure 2-6, the boost-pump sumps are kept filled by the fuel transfer _____ .

28. The manifold cross-feed system like that in Figure 2-7 allows any engine to be operated from any fuel tank. This allows the pilot to maintain a _____ fuel load to maintain good stability.

29. In the jet transport fuel system in Figure 2-9 the pressure for dumping fuel is provided by the _____ .

30. When pressure-fueling the jet transport fuel system in Figure 2-9, the fuel being directed into a tank is _____ (manually or automatically) shut off when the tank is full.

Fuel Tanks

Three types of fuel tanks are used in aircraft: built-up tanks, integral tanks, and bladder tanks.

Large fuel tanks have baffles to keep the fuel from surging back and forth, which could cause aircraft control difficulties. And some tanks have special baffles with flapper-type check valves around the tank outlet to prevent the fuel from flowing away from the outlet during certain uncoordinated flight maneuvers.

All fuel tanks have a low point, called a sump, with a drain valve or fitting which allows this sump to be drained from outside the aircraft. Any water or contaminants in the tank collect in the sump and are removed when the sump is drained.

All fuel tanks must be vented to the atmosphere, with the vents having sufficient capacity to allow the rapid relief of excessive pressure between the interior and the exterior of the tank. Some vent systems are designed to keep the pressure above the fuel in the tank the same as that at the fuel metering system air entrance.

If a gravity-fed fuel system can supply fuel from both tanks at the same time, the air space above the fuel in the tanks must be interconnected and vented overboard.

There is an additional hazard for bladder-type tanks. If the vent should become clogged, it is possible for the tank to collapse and pull away from its attachments. In addition, this action could easily cause blockage over the tank outlet before the tank is completely emptied.

Fuel tanks on small aircraft should be marked with the word "AVGAS" and the minimum grade or designation of fuel for the engine.

The fuel tanks on transport category aircraft must be marked with the word "JET FUEL," and the maximum permissible fueling and defueling pressures for pressure fueling systems.

Built-Up Fuel Tanks

Built-up tanks are made of sheet aluminum alloy or stainless steel and are riveted or welded. Some of the tanks in older aircraft are made of thin lead-coated steel called terneplate. These tanks use folded seams and are soldered to make them leak proof.

Some aircraft use fuel tanks ahead of the main spar in the wing that forms the leading edge of the wing. The components of these tanks are electrically seam-welded together, and to prevent their leaking, they are coated on the inside with a sealing compound.

Figure 2-13 shows a typical welded-aluminum fuel tank installed in the fuselage of an aircraft. The filler neck extends to the outside of the fuselage and is surrounded by a scupper, which collects any fuel that spills during fueling and carries it overboard through the drain line. The outlet line to the main fuel strainer is connected to a standpipe inside the tank, which puts the finger screen above the bottom of the tank and provides a sump to collect water and contaminants. The quick-drain valve at the bottom of the sump allows the sump to be drained during the walk-around inspection to check for the presence of water. The drain valve must also discharge clear of the airframe. A small perforated container of potassium dichromate crystals is mounted inside the tank in the sump area. The crystals change any water that collects in the sump into a weak chromate solution that inhibits corrosion.

Observe special caution when repairing a welded aluminum fuel tank, because the fuel vapors inside a tank can explode during the welding process if the tank is inadequately cleaned.

Before a fuel tank is welded, it should be thoroughly washed out with hot water and a detergent. Then live steam should be passed through the tank for at least 30 minutes. The steam vaporizes any fuel left in the tank and carries out the vapors.

After welding an aluminum fuel tank, remove all of the welding flux by scrubbing the weld area with a 5% solution of either sulfuric or nitric acid.

After the tank repairs have been completed, the tank should be pressure checked for leakage. Restrain the tank with restraints in the same location as those used in the aircraft, and apply regulated compressed air at a pressure of 3.5 psi. This does not sound like very much pressure, but consider a typical wing tank that is 24 inches wide and 36 inches long. This tank has an area of 864 square inches. When 3.5-psi air pressure is put into the tank, a force of 3,024 pounds acts on the top and bottom of the tank. If the tank is not adequately restrained, it will be damaged.

Integral Fuel Tanks

Almost all large aircraft and many small ones have a part of the structure sealed off and used as a fuel tank. This type of tank reduces weight and uses as much of the space as possible for carrying fuel.

scupper. A recess around the filler neck of an aircraft fuel tank. Any fuel spilled when the tank is being serviced collects in the scupper and drains to the ground through a drain line rather than flowing into the aircraft structure.

sump. A low point in an aircraft fuel tank in which water and other contaminants can collect and be held until they can be drained out.

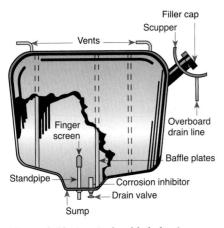

Figure 2-13. *A typical welded aluminum fuel tank.*

integral fuel tank. A fuel tank which is formed by sealing off part of the aircraft structure and using it as a fuel tank. An integral wing tank is called a "wet wing." Integral tanks are used because of their large weight saving.

The only way of repairing an integral fuel tank is by replacing damaged sealant and making riveted repairs, as is done with any other part of the aircraft structure.

Figure 2-14 shows an integral fuel tank used in a high-wing general-aviation airplane. All the seams are sealed with a rubber-like sealant that remains resilient so vibration will not crack it. Three inspection holes in the structure allow access to the inside of the tank for replacement of the fuel quantity probes or repairing any damaged sealant.

Integral fuel tanks must be thoroughly "inerted," or purged of any fuel vapors, before they can be repaired. This is done by allowing an inert gas such as carbon dioxide or argon to flow through the tank until all of the gasoline fumes have been purged. Both argon and carbon dioxide are heavier than air and will remain in the tank while the repairs are being made.

Integral tanks on large aircraft may be entered for inspection and repair. It is extremely important that before anyone enters these tanks, the tanks must be thoroughly purged by forcing a continuous flow of air through them for at least 2 hours. After purging the tank for the required time, test it to be sure that the vapor level is safe before allowing anyone to enter the tank. The person entering the tank must wear the proper protective clothing and an air supply respirator with full face mask. Another person, similarly equipped, must remain on the outside of the tank to monitor his or her progress and act as a safety agent for the person inside.

Many integral fuel tanks have a series of baffles with flapper-type check valves installed around the boost pumps to prevent fuel flowing away from the pump and the tank discharge line. This check valve allows fuel to flow to the boost pump, but it closes to prevent the fuel flowing away from it. Some tanks also have

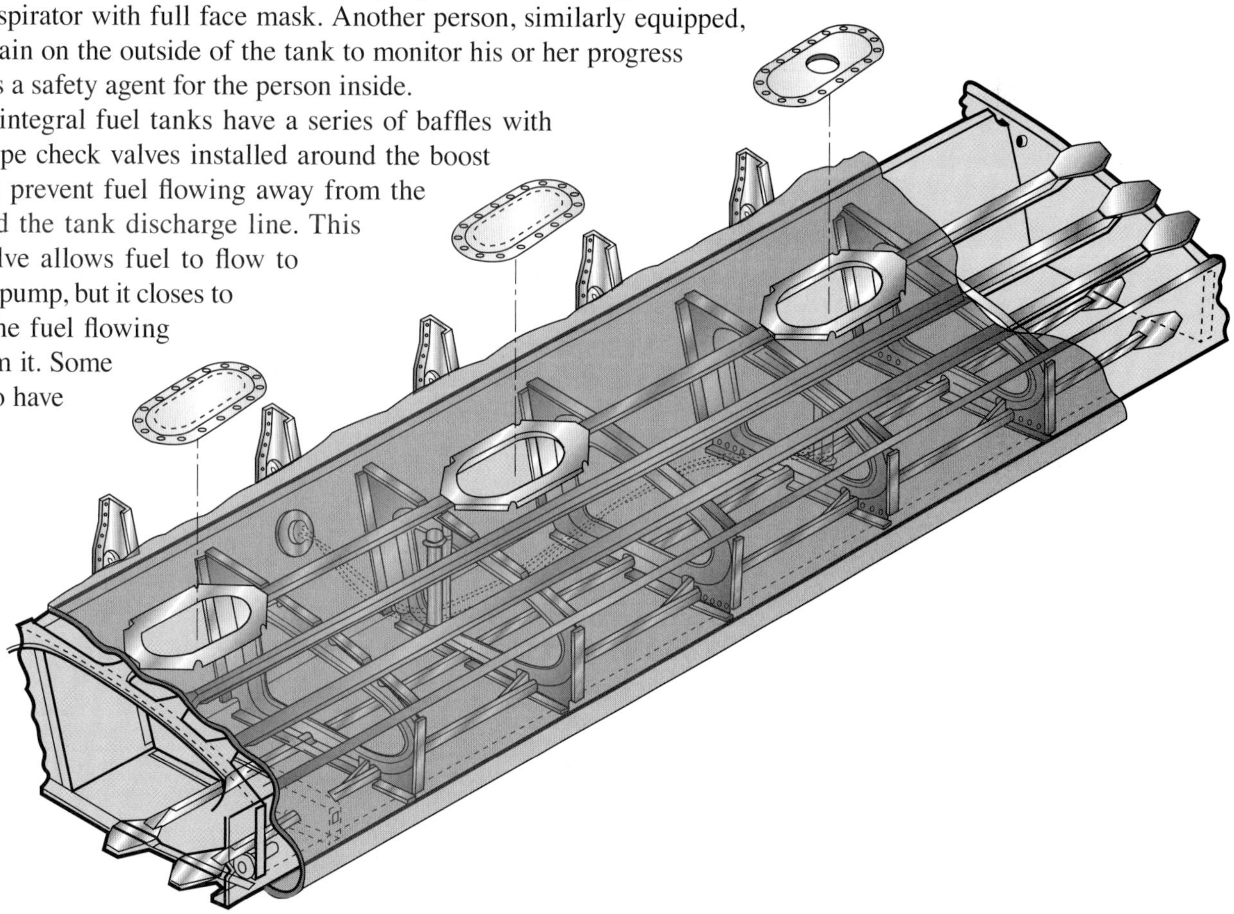

Figure 2-14. *An integral fuel tank is actually part of the structure that is sealed so it can carry the fuel without leaking.*

a pump-removal flapper-type check valve that allows a booster pump to be removed from the tank without having to first drain the tank.

Repair an integral fuel tank the same way you repair any other part of the structure with the exception that you must seal all seams with two-part sealant that is available in kit form from the aircraft manufacturer.

When new riveted joints are made in a fuel tank, the parts are fabricated, all rivet holes are drilled, and the metal parts cleaned with acetone or other approved fluid. A layer of sealant is applied to one of the mating surfaces and the parts are riveted together. After the riveting is completed, sealant is applied in a fillet as is shown in Figure 2-15.

Leaks are repaired by removing all of the old sealant from the area suspected of leaking. This is best done with a chisel-shaped tool made of hard fiber and the residue cleaned away with aluminum wool. Be sure that you do not use steel wool or sandpaper. These will break through any corrosion protective coatings and treatments, and steel wool will imbed dissimilar metal into the aluminum, setting up numerous galvanic corrosion points. Vacuum out all the chips, filings, and dirt, and thoroughly clean the entire area with acetone. Apply the sealant as shown in Figure 2-15, and allow it to cure as specified in the instructions that come with the sealer kit.

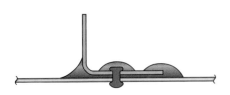

Figure 2-15. *Typical sealant application for a wing rib in an integral fuel tank.*

Bladder-Type Fuel Tanks

Some aircraft use rubberized fabric liners inside a part of the structure that has been especially prepared by covering all sharp edges of the supporting structure with chafing tape. Figure 2-16 shows a typical bladder-type installation in the inboard portion of the wing ahead of the main spar. These bladders are carefully folded and inserted into the wing through the available inspection holes. Inside the wing they are unfolded and attached to the structure with clamps, clips, or lacing. The interconnecting hoses are attached, and the clamps are torqued in place to complete the installation.

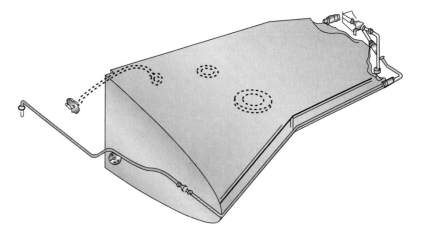

Figure 2-16. *Bladder-type fuel tank installed in the inboard portion of the wing ahead of the main spar.*

If bladder tanks are to remain empty for an extended period of time, wipe the inside of the tank with clean engine oil to prevent the rubber from drying out and cracking. See Figure 2-16.

A technician can repair bladder tanks by patching them, but it is usually more economical to send them to a repair station that is certificated for this specific repair. Technicians working in these shops are familiar with the bladders and can evaluate the condition of the tank and make all of the repairs that are needed to restore the cell to an airworthy condition.

Leaks in bladder cells are located by plugging all of the holes, inserting ammonia gas into the cell, and rounding the cell out with about ¾-psi air pressure. Place a white cloth saturated with a phenolphthalein solution over the cell. If there are any leaks, the ammonia gas will escape and react with the phenolphthalein and produce a bright red mark on the white cloth. Use extreme caution with these chemicals; they are very hazardous.

Maintenance and Inspection of Fuel Tanks

The maintenance and inspection of all fuel tanks have similarities, but there are also unique differences depending on the type of fuel tank. When inspecting fuel tanks, always be on the lookout for fuel stains or areas that appear damp or wet. Fittings that attach fuel lines, vents, or drains to a fuel tank are common areas for leaks and should be inspected carefully. Other common areas for leaks are gaskets on access panels and fuel quantity sending units.

Built-Up Fuel Tank Inspections

When inspecting built-up fuel tanks, pay special attention to mounting tabs or straps that secure the tank in place. These are areas of added stress and are prone to cracks and chaffing. Inspect welds and seams for cracks and the overall condition of the tank for corrosion. Some external areas around the tank may be difficult to see and may require opening additional inspection panels or using inspection mirrors or borescope equipment to see all areas around the tank. Using a flashlight, inspect the inside of the tank for condition and for debris or corrosion.

Integral Fuel Tank Inspections

Integral fuel tanks can be quite large and will often require the removal of access panels for inspection of the inside of the fuel tank. Inspect the inside of the tank for debris and corrosion. Check the security and condition of internally mounted lines, fuel quantity probes, vent valves, boost pumps and any other internally mounted equipment. Inspect the condition of internal sealant and gaskets. Repair damaged or missing sealant and replace gaskets as necessary.

Inspect the outside of the integral fuel tank for leaks and corrosion. Pay special attention to fittings and components that are attached to the outside of the fuel tank. Any areas that appear wet or stained should be carefully inspected.

Bladder-Type Fuel Tank Inspections

Inspect the inside of the tank with a flashlight and mirror, checking for security and attachment of the bladder to the fuel tank bay. The tank is held in place with snaps or cords that prevent the top and sides of the bladder from sagging into the tank area. If there are wrinkles in the bottom of the tank, or the bladder is collapsing into the tank area, some of the snaps may have come loose and need to be reconnected.

Inspect the condition of the bladder material. As the tanks age, the rubber compound of the tank will start to become brittle and crack and will eventually start to leak.

The external portions of the bladder tank are inspected for leaks and cracks. Fuel lines, vents, and fuel tank interconnections are often secured with clamps. Check the clamps for security and for any leaks. Do not overtighten these clamps as that can cause damage to the tanks.

Fuel Tank Filler Caps

For a component to which so little attention is paid, the fuel tank filler cap is vitally important. Fuel tanks are often located in the wings, and the filler opening is in a low pressure area during flight. If the cap does not seal properly, the low pressure will draw the fuel from the tank. Leaking filler caps will also allow water to enter the tank when the aircraft is parked outside in the rain.

Fuel tanks must be vented to the outside air. If air cannot enter the tank to take the place of the fuel as it is used, the resulting low pressure will cause fuel to cease flowing to the engine. If the tank is a bladder type, it will probably collapse and pull loose from its fastenings inside the structure. Some fuel tanks are vented through the filler cap, and others use vents that are independent of the cap. Be sure to install only the proper cap when replacing a filler cap. Many light aircraft in the past required a slight positive air pressure inside the fuel tank to ensure proper feed to the engine. These filler caps have a piece of tubing sticking up from the cap that must be pointed forward in flight.

One popular type of fuel filler cap, shown in Figure 2-17, seals the tank opening with an O-ring and vents the tank through a vent safety valve. This valve is closed when the air pressure in the tank and outside air are the same, but it opens when the pressure inside the tank is lower than the outside air pressure. It also acts as a safety valve and opens if the pressure in the tank should ever get as much as 5 psi above the pressure outside the tank.

An extremely serious problem develops if a reciprocating-engine-powered aircraft is inadvertently fueled with turbine engine fuel. Turbine engine fuel used in a reciprocating engine will detonate and destroy the engine. To prevent improper fueling, adapters may be installed in the fuel tank filler openings that prevent a jet fuel nozzle entering the tank.

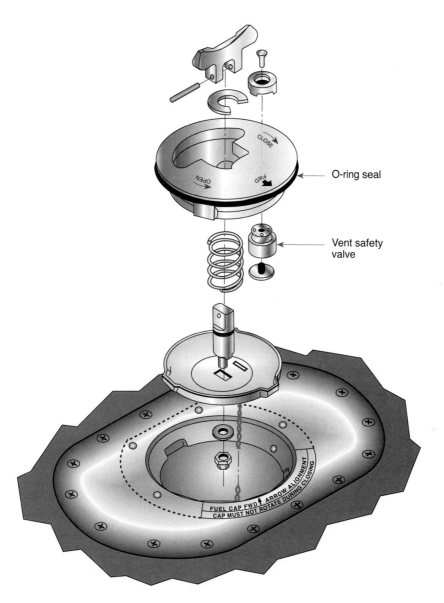

O-ring seal

Vent safety valve

Figure 2-17. *Fuel tank filler cap with a vent safety valve.*

Answers are provided on page 169.

31. Fuel is prevented from surging back and forth in a fuel tank by the installation of _____ inside the tank.

32. Water and other contaminants inside a fuel tank collect in the low point that is called the tank _____ .

33. The air pressure above the fuel in a fuel tank is kept the same as the pressure at the fuel metering system by fuel tank _____ .

34. The area around the fuel tank filler neck of a turbine engine aircraft that has a pressure fueling system must be marked with the maximum permissible fueling and defueling pressure and the words _____ .

35. Before making a welded repair to an aluminum fuel tank, wash it out with hot water and detergent and purge it with live steam for at least _____ minutes.

36. After a welded repair to an aluminum fuel tank is completed, the welded area should be washed with hot water and drained, then the area soaked with a 5% solution of _____ or _____ acid.

37. After a repair, a welded aluminum fuel tank must be leak tested with a pressure of _____ psi.

38. A part of the aircraft structure that is sealed off and used as a fuel tank is called a/an _____ fuel tank.

39. Integral fuel tanks on small general aviation airplanes can be purged of gasoline fumes by flowing _____ or _____ through the tank and allowing it to remain in the tank while repairs are being made.

40. Before a person can work inside an integral fuel tank, all of the vapors must be thoroughly purged from the tank by flowing air through the tank for at least _____ hours.

41. Bladder-type fuel cells are checked for leaks by filling the inside of the cell with _____ gas and covering the outside of the cell with a white cloth saturated with a _____ solution.

Fuel Pumps

Several types of fuel pumps are used in aircraft fuel systems. The simplest low-power, low-wing airplanes use a diaphragm pump on the engine and a plunger-type electrically operated auxiliary pump mounted in parallel with the engine pump. Larger reciprocating engines use sliding vane-type pumps driven by the engine and electrically driven centrifugal pumps inside the tanks for starting, backup, and fuel transfer. Turbine engine fuel pumps are normally gear, or eccentric sliding-vane type pumps.

Electrical Auxiliary Pumps

Fuel boost, or auxiliary, pumps are used to provide a positive flow of fuel from the tank to the engine. They are used for engine starting, as a backup for takeoff and landing, and, in many cases, to transfer fuel from one tank to another.

Plunger-Type Pumps

Many smaller general aviation aircraft use a plunger-type auxiliary fuel pump such as the one in Figure 2-18, installed in parallel with a diaphragm-type engine-driven pump.

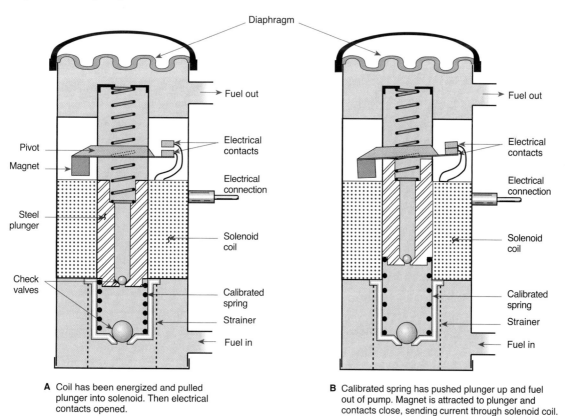

A Coil has been energized and pulled plunger into solenoid. Then electrical contacts opened.

B Calibrated spring has pushed plunger up and fuel out of pump. Magnet is attracted to plunger and contacts close, sending current through solenoid coil.

Figure 2-18. *An electrical plunger-type auxiliary fuel pump.*

These simple single-acting pumps have a steel plunger that is moved on its return stroke (downward as pictured) by an electromagnetic coil, and on its pumping stroke by a calibrated spring. In Figure 2-18A, the pump is shown at the beginning of its pumping stroke. When the switch is first turned on, the magnetic field pulls the steel plunger into the solenoid and opens the contacts. The calibrated spring then forces the plunger up, pushing fuel out of the top of the pump, simultaneously pulling more fuel into the bottom of the pump. When the plunger is out of the solenoid, as in Figure 2-18B, the magnet is attracted to it. As the magnet moves toward the plunger, the contact arm rotates on its pivot and the contacts close, sending current through the coil. This current produces a magnetic field that pulls the plunger back into the solenoid. As soon as the plunger is in the coil, the magnet is attracted to the steel case of the pump, and the contacts open, de-energizing the coil. The cylinder in which the plunger operates is nonferrous and the permanent magnet is not attracted to it.

When the pressure in the line to the carburetor is low, the pump cycles rapidly, but as the pressure in the discharge line rises, the fuel prevents the calibrated spring from forcing the plunger up as quickly, and the pump cycles slower. The calibrated spring determines the maximum pressure the pump can produce, and the spring inside the plunger dampens its stop at the end of the output stroke. The sealed air chamber above the output port diaphragm acts to dampen the output pressure pulses.

Centrifugal Boost Pump

Most of the larger aircraft that operate at high altitude use centrifugal boost pumps in the fuel tanks. These pumps supply fuel under positive pressure to the inlet of the engine-driven fuel pumps under conditions where the ambient pressure is too low to ensure a positive supply. Pressurizing the fuel lines prevents vapor lock at high altitude. Many of these boost pumps have a two-speed motor. Low speed is used to supply fuel to the engine for starting and as a backup for takeoff and landing. Operation of the pump at high altitude suppresses the formation of vapor in the system and prevents engine-driven pump cavitation. High speed is used to transfer fuel from one tank to another.

Figure 2-19 shows a centrifugal boost pump mounted on the outside of the tank, but a more common installation is seen in Figure 2-20, in which the electric motor is enclosed in an explosion-proof housing and submerged inside the tank.

A centrifugal boost pump is a variable-displacement pump, and it does not require a relief valve; its output pressure is determined by the impeller speed and the internal impeller clearances. The pressure produced by a single-speed centrifugal fuel pump is determined by the pump's design and its internal clearances and characteristics.

Outside mounted centrifugal boost pumps have a small agitator built onto the impeller that agitates the fuel before it enters the pump impeller. This causes the pump to release much of its vapors before it enters the fuel lines.

variable-displacement pump. A fluid pump whose output is determined by the demands placed on the system.

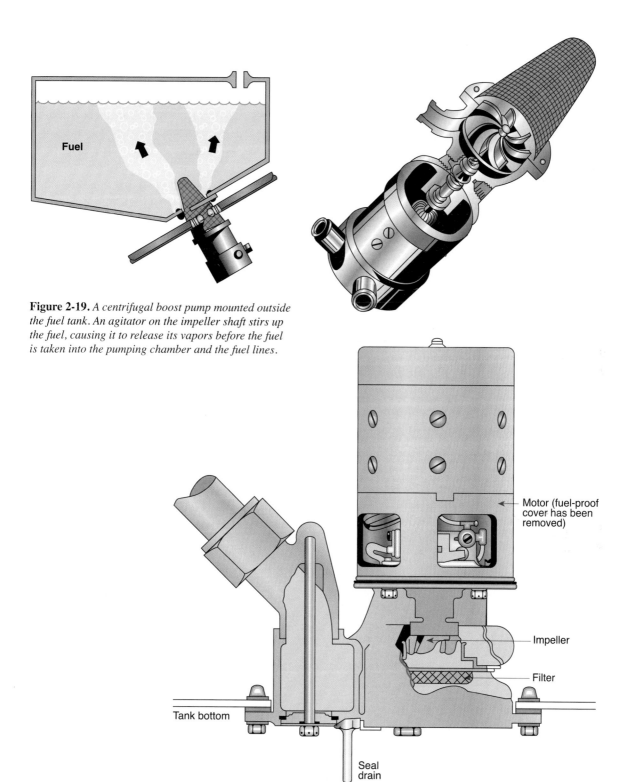

Figure 2-19. *A centrifugal boost pump mounted outside the fuel tank. An agitator on the impeller shaft stirs up the fuel, causing it to release its vapors before the fuel is taken into the pumping chamber and the fuel lines.*

Fuel

Motor (fuel-proof
cover has been
removed)

Impeller

Filter

Tank bottom

Seal
drain

Figure 2-20. *A submerged centrifugal boost pump. The motor is shown here with its fuel-proof case removed.*

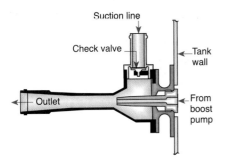

Figure 2-21. *An ejector pump uses a flow of fuel from the boost pump to produce a low pressure that draws fuel from the tank and sends it into the boost pump sump.*

Ejector Pump Systems

It is extremely important that submerged boost pumps always be completely covered with fuel to prevent pump cavitation and provide cooling for the pump motor. To prevent fuel flowing away from the pump in any flight attitude, some aircraft are equipped with boost pump sumps that are kept filled by an ejector pump system. See Figure 2-21. In Figure 2-22, the fuel tank has a surge box and a sump. The boost pump is installed in the sump, and some of its discharge is routed back into the tank through three ejector pumps.

An ejector pump is a type of jet pump that produces a low pressure when fuel from the boost pump flows through a venturi, as in Figure 2-21. Some of the fuel is taken from the discharge of the boost pump and directed through the ejector pump. This fuel flows through the venturi in the pump at high velocity, and the resulting low pressure draws fuel from the tank and from the surge box and discharges it into the boost pump sump.

The bulkhead between the surge box and the fuel tank has several flapper-type check valves that allow fuel to flow from the tank into the surge box, but prevent it from flowing in the opposite direction. These flapper valves ensure that fuel cannot flow away from the boost pump in any normal flight attitude.

Some aircraft also equip the boost pump sump with pump-removal flapper-type check valves that allow you to remove a booster pump from the tank without having to drain the tank first.

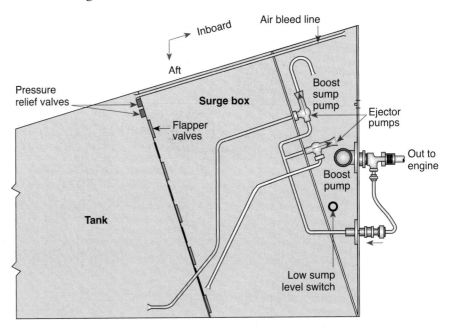

Figure 2-22. *This fuel tank has a surge box with flapper valves that allow the fuel to flow to the boost pump sump but prevent its flowing away from the pump. Ejector pumps draw fuel from the tank and the surge box into the boost pump sump.*

Engine-Driven Fuel Pumps

Three types of engine-driven fuel pumps are generally used on aircraft engines. The smallest engines use a diaphragm-type pump similar to that used on automobile engines, most of the large engines use vane-type pumps, and most turbine engines use gear-type pumps.

Diaphragm-Type Fuel Pump

Some of the smaller engines use diaphragm-type fuel pumps like the one in Figure 2-23. This type of pump is actuated by a plunger that is operated by an eccentric on one of the accessory gears or the camshaft. When the plunger presses against the rocker arm, the diaphragm is pulled down. This pulls fuel into the pump from the fuel tank. When the plunger drops away from the arm, a spring under the diaphragm pushes it up and forces the fuel out of the pump and into the carburetor. The pressure produced by the pump is determined entirely by the compressive strength of the diaphragm spring. This is a variable-displacement pump. When the demand of the engine is great, the pump moves a large volume of fuel, but when the demand is low, the fuel pump maximizes and hence minimizes the movement of the diaphragm, and very little fuel is moved.

The newest pumps use a sealing diaphragm under the top cap. The center casting ridge in this cap and the diaphragm form a pulsating chamber over the fuel intake port and a damping chamber over the outlet port.

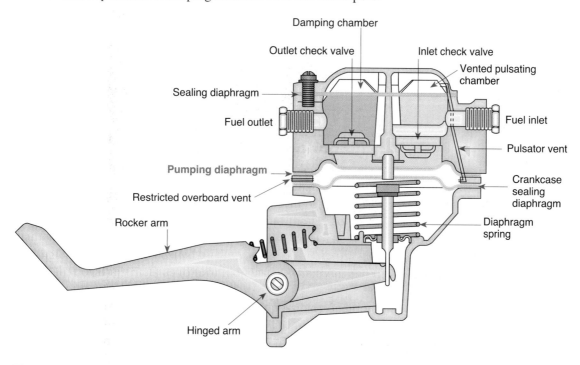

Figure 2-23. *A diaphragm-type engine-driven fuel pump is a variable-displacement pump that is normally installed in parallel with a plunger-type electric auxiliary pump.*

During the output stroke, the air trapped in the damping chamber compresses, absorbing some of the output energy. During the time of the intake stroke the compressed air in the damping chamber pushes on the outlet fuel till the outlet fuel and air pressure equalize. This action minimizes the pulsations in output pressure between output strokes.

The air vent from between the pumping and crankcase sealing diaphragm and the pulsating chamber oscillates the pulsator air pressure to increase the inlet stroke efficiency.

Diaphragm-type pumps are normally installed in parallel with a plunger-type auxiliary pump.

Vane-Type Fuel Pump

The most popular type of fuel pump for larger reciprocating engines is the vane-type pump shown in Figure 2-24. These pumps can be driven by the engine or by an electric motor.

As the pump rotor turns, steel vanes slide in and out of slots, changing the volume of the space between the rotor and the pump cylinder. On the inlet side of the pump this space increases its volume and pulls in fuel. On the discharge side its volume decreases and fuel is forced from the pump.

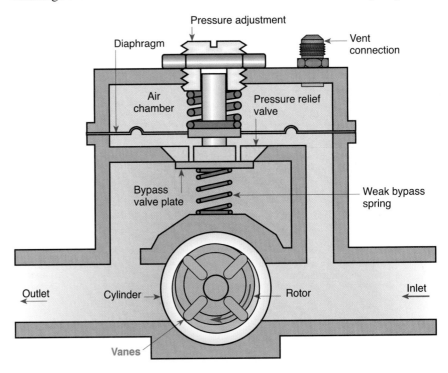

Figure 2-24. *A compensating vane-type fuel pump.*

A vane-type pump is a constant-displacement pump that moves a specific volume of fuel each time it rotates. Therefore it must have a relief valve to bypass back to the pump inlet all the fuel in excess of that required by the engine. When the outlet pressure rises above that for which the relief valve is set, the fuel lifts the relief valve from seat and the excess fuel returns to the inlet side of the vanes.

This pump is also called a compensated fuel pump. The compensating function maintains pump output pressure at a specific level above the air pressure at the inlet to the fuel metering device. This air pressure is directed into the pump through the vent connection. The diaphragm in the top of this pump is connected to the relief valve shaft and as the vent air pressure increases, the force on the diaphragm aids the relief valve spring and increases the pump output fuel pressure. A decrease in the inlet air pressure causes the pump outlet fuel pressure to decrease.

This compensation is useful in three ways. For a naturally aspirated engine the fuel pressure gauge will not fluctuate with altitude changes. The pump compensating chamber and the fuel pressure gauge vent chamber both sense ambient air pressure. Without the compensation, as the aircraft increases in altitude and ambient pressure decreases, the lower air pressure acting on the gauge mechanism will cause the gauge to indicate a higher fuel pressure. But with compensation, the lower pressure in the pump relief valve compensating chamber causes a decrease in fuel pressure that is equal to the ambient air pressure drop, and the fuel pressure gauge reading remains constant with altitude changes.

Secondly, if the pump compensating port is vented to the air at the entrance of a pressure carburetor, the carburetor's inlet fuel pressure from the pump will be held at a specific differential with its inlet air pressure. This condition is critical for consistent fuel metering by this type of carburetor.

The third compensated pump advantage is its ability to match the fuel metering device's inlet fuel pressure to its turbocharged inlet air pressure.

When used as an engine-driven pump, a vane-type pump is installed in series with the boost pump. For starting the engine, fuel flows from the boost pump into the pump inlet and forces the bypass valve plate on the bottom of the relief valve down. This allows fuel to flow to the engine with only a very slight pressure drop caused by the weak spring trying to hold the bypass valve closed.

constant-displacement pump. A fluid pump that moves a specific volume of fluid each time it rotates. Some form of pressure regulator or relief valve must be used with a constant-displacement pump when it is driven by an aircraft engine.

compensated fuel pump. A vane-type, engine-driven fuel pump that has a diaphragm connected to the pressure-regulating valve. The chamber above the diaphragm is vented to the carburetor upper deck where it senses the pressure of the air as it enters the engine.

The diaphragm allows the fuel pump to compensate for altitude changes and keeps the carburetor inlet fuel pressure a constant amount higher than the carburetor inlet air pressure.

Turbine-Engine Fuel Pump

The high fuel pressure required by turbine engines makes gear or piston pumps the most widely used types. The pump in Figure 2-25 is a constant-displacement, high-pressure pump with two gear-type pump elements. Each element is fitted with a shear section that will break if either element becomes jammed. The jammed element will stop, but the other element will continue to produce fuel pressure for the engine.

The gear-driven impeller at the inlet of the pump increases the fuel pressure from 15 to 45 psi before it enters the high-pressure gear sections of the pump. The two gear sections increase the pressure to about 850 psi and discharge it in a common outlet compartment in which the pump pressure relief valve is located. Pressure in excess of that for which the relief valve is set is bypassed to the gear section inlet.

shear section. A necked-down section of an engine-driven pump shaft that is designed to shear if the pump should seize. When the shear section breaks, the shaft can continue to turn without causing further damage to the pump or to the engine.

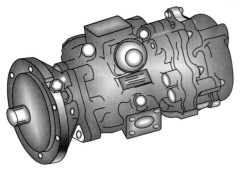

Figure 2-25. *Two-section, constant-displacement, gear-type fuel pump for a turbine engine.*

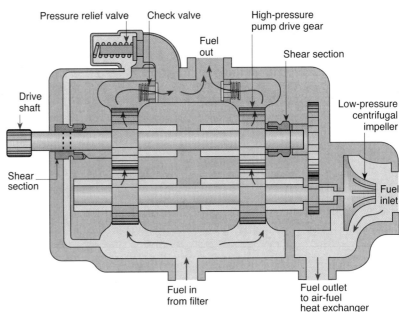

Pressure relief valve   Check valve   High-pressure pump drive gear

Fuel out

Shear section

Drive shaft

Low-pressure centrifugal impeller

Shear section

Fuel inlet

Fuel in from filter

Fuel outlet to air-fuel heat exchanger

44. The small agitator that spins with the impeller of a centrifugal boost pump is used to separate the _____ from the fuel before the fuel enters the lines to the carburetor.

45. Fuel is prevented from flowing away from the boost pump by flapper-type _____ in the fuel tank baffles.

46. Fuel is pulled into the boost pump sump from the fuel tank by a/an _____-type pump.

47. A diaphragm-type engine-driven pump is a _____ (constant or variable) -displacement pump.

48. The pressure produced by a diaphragm-type fuel pump is determined by the _____ .

49. A vane-type fuel pump is a _____ (constant or variable)-displacement pump.

50. Constant-displacement pumps _____ (do or do not) require a relief valve.

51. An engine-driven vane-type pump is installed in _____ (series or parallel) with the boost pump.

52. The air chamber on one side of the diaphragm in a compensated fuel pump senses the air pressure at the inlet to the _____ .

53. A gear-type fuel pump is a _____ (constant or variable)-displacement pump.

54. If the gears in a gear-type fuel pump should seize, the _____ on the drive shaft will prevent the engine being damaged.

Fuel Filters and Strainers

A review of aircraft accidents caused by powerplant failure shows a large portion of them are due to fuel contamination. Filters or strainers clogged with debris and water in the carburetor are chief offenders.

Types of Contaminants

Contaminants likely to be found in an aircraft fuel system include: water, solid particles, surfactants, and micro-organisms. The procedures to use to avoid fuel system contamination are covered later in this chapter.

Though always present in aviation fuel, water is now considered to be a major source of fuel contamination. Modern jet aircraft fly at altitudes where the temperature is low enough to cause water that is entrained, or dissolved, in the fuel to condense out and form free water. This free water can freeze, and the resulting ice will clog the fuel screens. This may be prevented by using an antifreeze additive in the fuel.

surfactant. A surface active agent, or partially soluble contaminant which is a by-product of fuel processing or of fuel additives. Surfactants adhere to other contaminants and cause them to drop out of the fuel and settle to the bottom of the fuel tank as sludge.

Sand blown into the storage tanks or in the aircraft fuel tanks during fueling operation or rust from unclean storage tanks are solid particles which clog strainers and restrict the flow of fuel.

Surfactants are partially soluble compounds which are by-products of the fuel processing or from fuel additives. Surfactants reduce the surface tension of the liquid contaminants and cause them to adhere to other contaminants and drop out of the fuel and form sludge.

Micro-organisms are one of the serious contaminants found in jet aircraft fuel tanks. Grown from airborne bacteria, these tiny organisms collect in the fuel and lie dormant until they come into contact with free water. The bacteria grow at a prodigious rate as they live in the water and feed on the hydrocarbon fuel and on some of the surfactant contaminants. The scum which they form holds water against the walls of the fuel tanks and causes corrosion. The antifreeze additive that is used with turbine engine fuel also acts as a biocidal agent and kills the micro-organisms, preventing them from forming the scum inside the tanks.

Required Fuel Strainers

All fuel systems are required to have a strainer in the outlet of each tank and at the inlet to the fuel metering system or the engine-driven pump. The strainer in the tank outlet is normally a coarse mesh finger screen that traps any large contaminants to prevent their obstructing the fuel line.

The main strainer, located before the inlet to the carburetor or fuel pump and in the lowest point in the system, may be similar to the gascolator in Figure 2-26. If the strainer is located in the lowest point in the system, it can trap any small amount of water that is present in the system. Most mainline strainers remove moisture from the fuel by allowing the fuel to flow into a large bowl. This causes the water to slow down and settle out of the fuel. Any heavier sediment also settles out in the same manner. The lighter sediment is trapped by the filtering screen as the fuel flows out of the strainer.

The filtering element of some of the larger fuel screens is made of a coarse screen formed into a cylinder with a cone in its center. This coarse screen is covered with a fine screen that does the actual filtering. Any water or contaminants in the fuel collect in the bottom of the strainer housing where they can be drained out on a daily or preflight inspection. See Figure 2-27.

Turbine engine fuel controls contain such close tolerance components that even the smallest contaminants can cause serious problems. For this reason, turbine engine fuel systems often use a microfilter that uses a replaceable cellulose filter element that is capable of removing foreign matter as small as 10 to 25 microns. A human hair has a diameter of approximately 100 microns. Such a filter is shown in Figure 2-28.

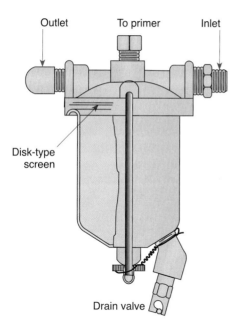

Figure 2-26. *A gascolator fuel filter is installed at the low point in the fuel system.*

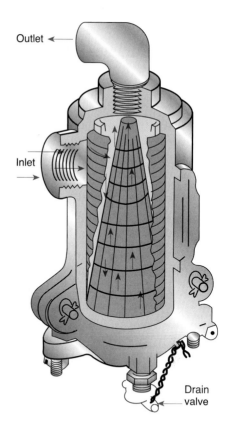

Figure 2-27. *A main fuel strainer.*

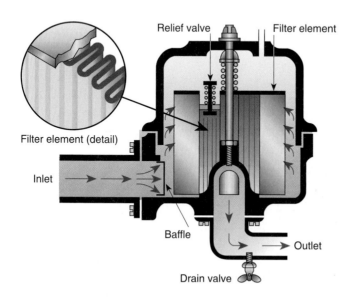

Figure 2-28. *Microfilter used in a turbine engine fuel system.*

Another type of filter that is widely used for turbine engine fuel systems is the wafer screen filter seen in Figure 2-29. The filtering element is a stack of wafer-type screen disks made of a 200-mesh bronze, brass, or stainless steel wire screen. This type of filter can remove very tiny particles from the fuel and at the same time can withstand the high pressures found in a turbine engine fuel system.

Some of the fuel filters used in jet transport aircraft have a pressure switch across the filtering element. If ice should form on the filter and block the flow of fuel, the pressure drop across the filter will increase enough to close the contacts and turn on a light on the flight engineer's panel, warning that ice is forming on the filter.

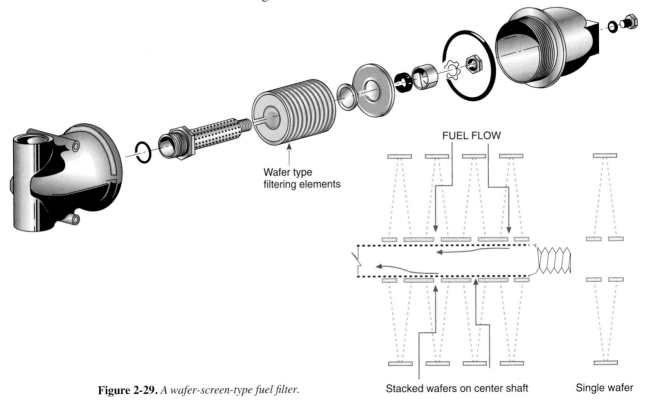

Wafer type filtering elements

FUEL FLOW

Stacked wafers on center shaft

Single wafer

Figure 2-29. *A wafer-screen-type fuel filter.*

57. Water can be prevented from freezing on the fuel screens by adding an _____ additive to the fuel.

58. Micro-organisms that form scum inside a fuel tank are killed by the _____ additive that is used in the fuel.

59. The main fuel strainers are located at the lowest point in the fuel system so it will trap and hold any _____ in the system.

60. The fuel filters on some jet transport aircraft have a pressure switch across the filtering element. This switch will turn on a warning light on the flight engineer's panel if _____ clogs the filter.

Fuel Valves

Aircraft fuel systems are complex and usually have several tanks, pumps, strainers and much plumbing. The valves that control the flow of fuel through these systems are vital components of the fuel system.

The valves must be capable of carrying all of the required fuel flow without an excessive pressure drop, and all valves must have some form of detent, a positive method of determining when they are in each marked position.

Plug-Type Valves

Some of the smaller aircraft use a simple plug-type selector valve in which a conical nylon or brass plug is rotated in a mating hole in the valve body. The plug is drilled in such a way that it can connect the outlet to any one of the inlets that is selected.

A spring-loaded pin anchored into the valve shaft slips into a detent when the cone is accurately aligned with the holes in the valve body. The pin slips into the detent notches in the washer when the two align. This detent allows the pilot to tell by feel when the valve is in its fully open or fully closed position. See Figure 2-30.

Poppet-Type Selector Valve

The poppet-type selector valve has many advantages over other types of hand-operated valves. It has a positive feel when any tank is in the full ON position and its design ensures that the line to a tank is either fully open or fully closed, with no possibility of an intermediate position.

Figure 2-31 shows a typical poppet-type selector valve. The handle rotates a cam which forces the poppet for the selected tank off its seat and fuel flows from that tank to the engine. Springs hold the poppets for all the other tanks tight against their seat. A spring-loaded indexing pin drops into a notch, or detent, in an indexing plate each time a poppet is fully off of its seat. It also drops into the notch when the valve in the OFF position and all of the poppets are seated.

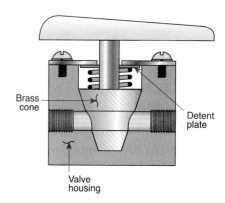

Figure 2-30. *Plug-type fuel selector or shutoff valve.*

detent. A spring-loaded pin or tab that enters a hole or groove when the device to which it is attached is in a certain position. Detents are used on a fuel valve to provide a positive means of identifying when the valve is in each of the selectable positions.

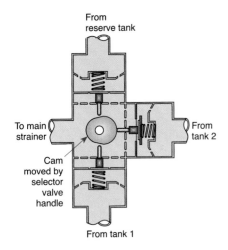

From reserve tank

To main strainer

From tank 2

Cam moved by selector valve handle

From tank 1

Figure 2-31. *A typical poppet-type fuel selector valve.*

Electric Motor-Operated Sliding Gate Valve

All large aircraft use electrically operated valves in their fuel systems. Common types of electrically operated valves are motor-driven gate valves and solenoid-operated poppet valves.

The valve in Figure 2-32 is a motor-driven gate valve. The geared output of a reversible electric motor drives a crank arm which moves the gate through a slot to cover the opening for the fuel line. Reversing the motor rotates the arm so it pulls the gate back and uncovers the fuel line opening. The gate is prevented from leaking by spring-loaded nylon seals, or O-rings that the gate slides between to cover the passage.

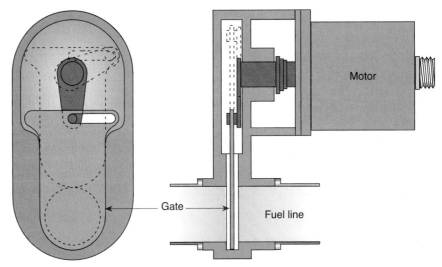

Motor

Gate

Fuel line

Figure 2-32. *Electric motor-operated sliding gate-type fuel valve.*

Solenoid-Operated Poppet-Type Fuel Shutoff Valve

The solenoid-operated poppet-type shutoff valve in Figure 2-33 uses a pulse of DC electricity in one circuit to open the valve and a pulse in another circuit to close it.

To open the valve, the opening solenoid is energized with a pulse of electricity. The magnetism produced by the pulse pulls the valve stem up until the spring behind the locking stem can force it into the notch in the valve stem. The locking stem holds the valve open.

To close the valve, the closing solenoid is energized with a pulse of electricity. The magnetism produced by this pulse pulls the locking stem back and allows the valve spring to close the valve.

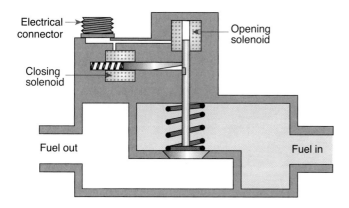

Figure 2-33. *Solenoid-operated shutoff valve.*

STUDY QUESTION: FUEL VALVES

Answer is provided on page 169.

61. A device on a fuel selector valve that allows the pilot to know when the valve is in each of the selectable positions is called a/an _____ .

Fuel Heaters

Because turbine-engine-powered aircraft fly at high altitudes where the temperature is very low, the fuel systems are susceptible to the formation of ice on the fuel filters.

A fuel temperature indicator on the flight engineer's panel warns when the fuel temperature is low enough for ice crystals to form in the fuel.

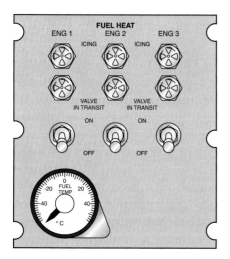

Figure 2-34. *Fuel heat control panel. The top lights indicate that ice is forming on the filters. The lower lights are on while the fuel heat valves are moving to the position called for by the fuel heat switch. The fuel heat switches open or close the valve that directs hot, high-pressure compressor bleed air into the heat exchanger. The fuel temperature gauge on the flight engineer's panel warns of the danger of ice clogging the fuel filters.*

Fuel filter icing lights warn that ice is forming on the fuel filter and restricting the flow of fuel. Fuel heat switches can open the fuel heat valves to direct hot, high-pressure compressor bleed air through the fuel heater to increase the temperature of the fuel.

Two types of fuel heaters can be used to prevent ice clogging the filters in turbine engine fuel systems: air-to-fuel and oil-to-fuel heat exchangers. Air-to-fuel systems use hot compressor bleed air for the source of heat, and oil-to-fuel systems use the heat from the engine lubricating oil.

Figure 2-35 shows a typical air-to-fuel heat exchanger. Cold fuel flows through the tubes in the heat exchanger, and the fuel temperature sensor controls the amount of warm air that flows around the tubes. Heat from the air enters the fuel and raises its temperature enough to prevent ice crystals forming on the fuel filter.

All the fuel that flows to the engine must pass through the heat exchanger, and it can raise the fuel temperature enough to thaw ice that has formed on the fuel screen.

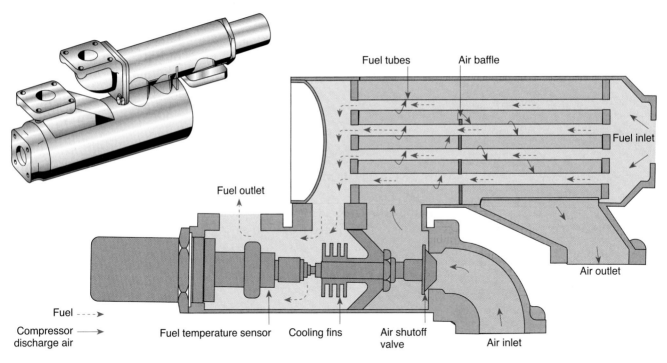

Figure 2-35. *An air-to-fuel heat exchanger for a jet aircraft.*

Fuel System Instruments

All aircraft, regardless of their size, must have some means of indicating the quantity of fuel in each tank. Other information that fuel system instrumentation must provide is fuel pressure, fuel flow, and fuel temperature.

Fuel Quantity Measuring Systems

Fuel quantity measuring systems range from extremely simple floats riding on the surface of the fuel to electronic systems that compensate for fuel temperature and indicate the number of pounds of fuel on board the aircraft.

Each fuel quantity indicator must be calibrated to read zero during level flight when the quantity of the fuel remaining in the tank is equal to the unusable fuel supply.

Direct-Reading Fuel Gauges

One simple type of direct-reading fuel quantity indicating system is a sight glass. A transparent tube connected between the top and the bottom of the fuel tank shows the level of the fuel in the tank. To make the level of the fuel easier to read, some of the tubes for shallow tanks are slanted, and the quantity is indicated against a calibrated scale behind the tube.

Some direct indicators use a simple varnish-coated cork float with a wire sticking through a hole in the fuel tank cap. The higher the wire protrudes from the tank, the more fuel there is. This type of system does not give an accurate indication of the amount of fuel in the tank, only a relative indication.

A combination of sight glass and cork has been used for fuel tanks in the wings of high-wing airplanes and in the upper wing of biplanes. A transparent tube, whose length is the same as the depth of the fuel tank, sticks out below the wing. A cork float rides on the top of the fuel in the tank and a wire protrudes from the bottom of the float. This wire rides inside the transparent tube and a knob, or indicator, on the end of the wire shows the level of the fuel in the tank.

Some fuel tanks have a float mounted on a wire arm that rides on the top of the fuel. See Figure 2-36. The wire arm moves a bevel gear which drives a pinion. Attached to the pinion is a pointer which rides over a dial to indicate the level of the fuel in the tank. All of this mechanism is sealed inside the fuel tank.

A similar type of indicator to that in Figure 2-36 mounts the pointer on the outside of the tank. A magnet on the pointer is magnetically coupled to a magnet inside the tank that is moved by the float arm mechanism. Movement of the float arm rotates the pointer, and there is no possibility of fuel leaking through this type of indicator.

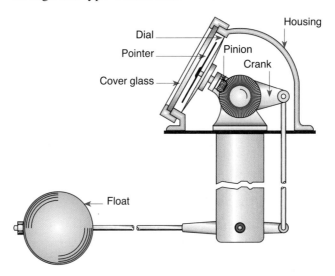

Figure 2-36. *A direct-reading fuel quantity gauge indicates the level of the fuel in the tank by converting the movement of the float arm into rotation of the pointer in front of the dial.*

Electrical Resistance-Type Fuel Quantity Indicating System

For many years the most widely used fuel quantity measuring system has been the electrical resistance-type system. These systems use a sender, or transmitter, that consists of a variable resistor mounted on the outside of the fuel tank and operated by an arm connected to a float that rides on the surface of the fuel in the tank. Movement of the arm is transmitted through a metal bellows-type seal to operate the wiper of the resistor.

There are two basic types of indicators used with this system. Both use current-measuring instruments calibrated in fuel quantity. When the tank is empty, the float is on the bottom and the resistive path to ground for the gauge circuit is maximum. This drives the indicator pointer to the EMPTY mark on the dial. When the tank is full, the float is near the top of the tank, the resistive path to ground is minimum, and the pointer is driven to the FULL mark.

Capacitance-Type Electronic Fuel Quantity Measuring System

The electronic (capacitance-type) fuel-quantity-indicating system has no moving parts inside the tank, and is more accurate than other types of systems used for measuring fuel quantity.

These systems use several capacitor-type probes extending across each tank from top to bottom. When the attitude of the aircraft changes, fuel rises in some probes and lowers in others, and the total capacitance of all probes remains constant. This makes the fuel-quantity indication independent of attitude changes.

The dielectric constant of the fuel changes with its temperature and thus its density. The system measures the weight, actually the mass, of the fuel rather than its volume. Cold fuel is denser than warm fuel, and there are more pounds in one gallon of cold fuel than there are in a gallon of warm fuel. Knowing the number of pounds of fuel available is more important than knowing the number of gallons, because the power produced by an aircraft engine is determined by the pounds of fuel burned, not the gallons.

capacitance-type fuel quantity measuring system. A popular type of electronic fuel quantity indicating system. The tank units are cylindrical capacitors, called probes, mounted across the tank from top to bottom, and the indicator is a servo-type instrument driven by a capacitance bridge and a signal amplifier. There are no moving parts of the system in the fuel tank.

The dielectric between the plates of the capacitance probes is made up of the fuel and the air above the fuel in the tank. The capacitance of the probe varies with the amount of fuel in the tank.

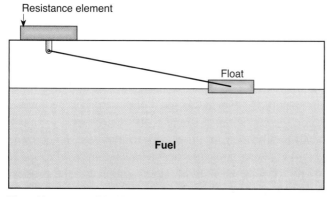

Float rides on top of fuel in tank and drives wiper across resistance element on the outside of tank through metal bellows-type seal.

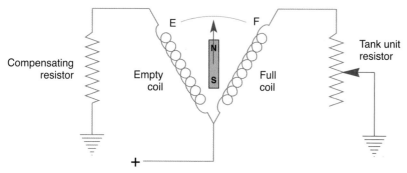

With this ratiometer indicator, when the tank is full, the tank unit resistance is minimum and current through the full coil inside the gauge is the maximum. A permanent magnet attached to the pointer pulls the pointer into alignment with the full coil.

Figure 2-37. *Electrical resistance-type fuel quantity indicator.*

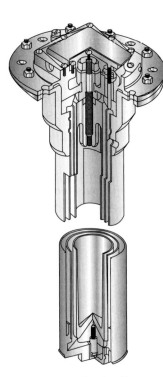

Flange-mounted tank unit

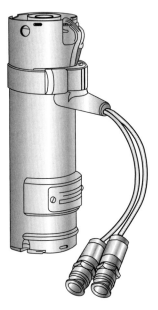

Internally-mounted tank unit

Figure 2-38. *Probes for a capacitance-type fuel quantity measuring system.*

By measuring the total capacitance of all of the capacitors in all of the fuel tanks, a totalizing system can indicate, on one instrument, the total number of pounds of fuel on board the aircraft.

The components in electronic (capacitance-type) fuel-quantity-indicating systems are:

- Capacitor probes mounted in the fuel tanks
- A bridge circuit to measure the capacitance of the probes
- An amplifier to increase the amplitude of the signal from the bridge circuit to a value high enough to drive the indicator
- An indicator mounted in the instrument panel to show the amount of fuel in the tanks

A capacitor is an electrical component made up of two conductors separated by a dielectric, or insulator. It stores an electrical charge, and the amount of charge it can store is determined by three things: the area of the plates, the separation between the plates, and the dielectric constant, or insulating characteristic, of the material between the plates.

Probes like those in Figure 2-38 extend across the fuel tanks from top to bottom. These probes are capacitors and are made of thin metal tubes that act as the plates. These plates have a fixed area, and they are separated by a fixed distance. The dielectric is the fuel or air inside the tank. Air has a dielectric constant, or K, of 1 and the fuel has a K of approximately 2, depending upon its temperature. When the tank is full, fuel is the dielectric and the probe has a given amount of capacity. As the fuel is used, the dielectric becomes less fuel and more air, and the capacitance of the probe decreases.

Several probes can be installed in a fuel tank to measure the quantity of fuel in odd-shaped tanks. These capacitors are connected in parallel and their total capacitance is the sum of the individual capacitances. The probes are connected into a bridge circuit and the indicator is servo-driven to make the bridge self-balancing.

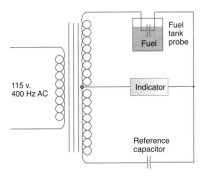

Simplified diagram of a capacitance bridge

Bridge circuit showing the way current in each half of bridge cancel out

Figure 2-39. *Capacitance bridge diagrams.*

Figure 2-39 is a simplified diagram of a basic capacitance bridge circuit. The bridge is excited with 400-hertz AC through the center-tapped secondary of a transformer. One half of the secondary winding is in series with the tank-unit capacitors and the other half is in series with a reference capacitor. The two halves of the center-tapped winding are 180° out of phase with each other, and if the capacitance of the tank units and the reference capacitor are exactly the same, their capacitive reactances will be the same, and the current through the top half of the bridge will exactly cancel the current through the bottom half. There will be no current flow through the indicator.

The self-balancing bridge in Figure 2-40 works in the same way as the one just considered. When the fuel level in the tank changes, the capacitance of the probes change and shift the phase of the current in the top half of the bridge. The bridge is now unbalanced and a signal is sent to the amplifier. The amplifier sends a resulting out-of-phase current through one set of windings in the two-phase motor inside the indicator. The other set of windings in the indicator motor is fed with a reference AC, and when the bridge is unbalanced, the motor will turn and drive the rebalancing potentiometer until the AC in the lower half of the bridge is in phase with that in the upper half. The bridge balances and the motor stops turning. The pointer of the fuel quantity indicator is attached to the motor shaft, and it indicates the number of pounds of fuel remaining in the aircraft.

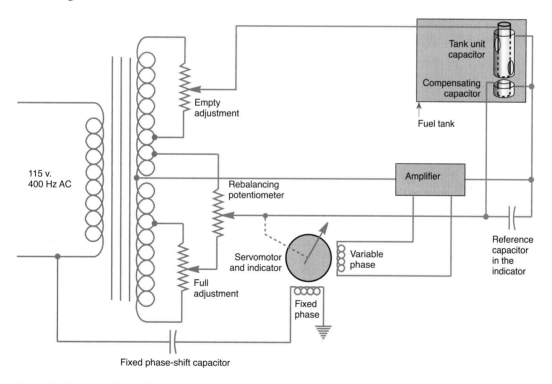

Figure 2-40. *A simplified self-balancing bridge circuit used in a capacitance-type fuel quantity indicating system.*

fuel totalizer. A fuel quantity indicator that gives the total amount of fuel remaining on board the aircraft on one instrument. The totalizer adds the quantities of fuel in all of the tanks.

drip stick. A fuel quantity indicator used to measure the fuel level in the tank when the aircraft is on the ground.

The drip stick is pulled down from the bottom of the tank until fuel drips from its open end. This indicates that the top of the gauge inside the tank is at the level of the fuel. Note the number of inches read on the outside of the gauge at the point it contacts the bottom of the tank, and use a drip-stick table to convert this measurement into gallons of fuel in the tank.

Aircraft instrument panel space is always limited, and one advantage of the capacitance-type fuel quantity indicating system is its ability to measure the fuel in several tanks and give the pilot an indication of the total number of pounds of fuel remaining on one indicator, called a totalizer.

A computerized fuel system indicates the amount of time remaining at the existing fuel flow rate, and is described in the section on fuel flow indication.

Drip Gauge and Sight Gauge

The fueling crew can use any of several types of external underwing fuel gaging devices to check the actual level of the fuel in the tank. These gauges give a purely physical indication of the fuel level in the tank and are used to verify the indications of the electronic measuring systems.

The drip stick is a hollow tube that mounts in the bottom of the fuel tank and sticks up to the top of the tank. To check the amount of fuel in the tank, the drip stick is unlocked and slowly pulled down until fuel begins to drip from its open end. The fuel quantity in the tank relates to the distance the drip

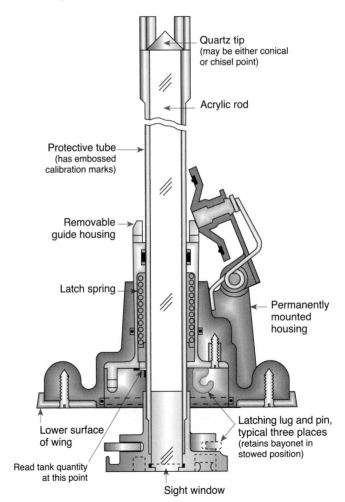

Figure 2-41. *Sight gauge for measuring the level of fuel in a tank from underneath the wing.*

Quartz tip
(may be either conical
or chisel point)

Acrylic rod

Protective tube
(has embossed
calibration marks)

Removable
guide housing

Latch spring

Permanently
mounted
housing

Lower surface
of wing

Latching lug and pin,
typical three places
(retains bayonet in
stowed position)

Read tank quantity
at this point

Sight window

stick is pulled from the tank before fuel begins to drip. Some drip sticks are graduated in inches or centimeters and a drip-stick table is used to convert the drip stick reading into pounds of fuel.

The sight gauge seen in Figure 2-41 works on the same basic principle as a drip stick, but no fuel actually drips from it. The gauge is a long acrylic plastic rod that sticks across the tank from bottom to top. To use the gauge, the technician unlocks it and pulls it down while watching the rod through the sight window. When the quartz tip is above the fuel, it reflects light back down the rod. As the rod is pulled and the tip enters the fuel, the amount of reflected light decreases. When the entire tip is in the fuel, no more light is reflected. The level of the fuel in the tank is at the point where the line of reflected light is visible, but is minimum in size. The amount of fuel is read on the calibrated scale opposite the reference mark on the bottom of the tank.

Fuel Flowmeters

Fuel quantity indication is an after-the-fact measurement. Much more useful information is obtained from the fuel flowmeters, which actually show the amount of fuel the engines are burning.

Flowmeters for Large Reciprocating Engines

Many large reciprocating engines use a vane-type flowmeter in the fuel line between the engine-driven pump and the carburetor. The measuring vane, shown in Figure 2-42, is moved by the flow of fuel, and is resisted by a calibrated hairspring. The more the vane is deflected by increased fuel flow, the greater the space between the apex of the vane and the chamber wall becomes. This is because the chamber is not circular, but is eccentric. This chamber design accommodates the increased volume of fuel that must pass through the unit as the fuel flow increases. Movement of the measuring vane is transmitted to the rotor of the Autosyn transmitter through a magnetic coupling, and the pointer on the Autosyn fuel-flow indicator in the cockpit follows the movement of the vane to indicate the fuel flow in gallons per hour. See Figure 2-43. This type of instrument is accurate and reliable, but shows only the volume of fuel

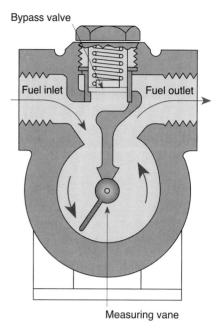

Figure 2-42. *Fuel chamber of a volume-type fuel flowmeter used with large reciprocating engines.*

Autosyn system. The registered trade name of a remote-indicating instrument system. An Autosyn system uses an electromagnet excited with 400-hertz AC for its rotor and a three-phase distributed-pole stator.

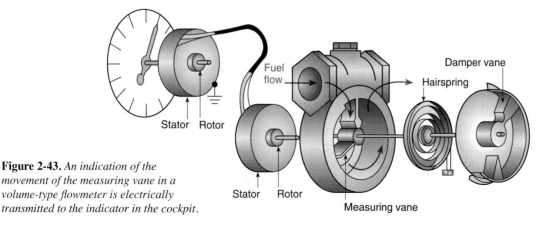

Figure 2-43. *An indication of the movement of the measuring vane in a volume-type flowmeter is electrically transmitted to the indicator in the cockpit.*

being used, not its mass. Some of the indicators used with this type of system have a scale on the inside of the gallons indication that gives the amount of fuel burned in pounds. This indication is only approximate, as it is based on the nominal weight of gasoline being six pounds per gallon. It does not take changes in fuel density into consideration.

Flowmeters for Fuel-Injected Horizontally Opposed Reciprocating Engines

The flowmeter used with fuel injection systems installed on horizontally opposed reciprocating engines does not measure mechanical movement. Rather, it measures the pressure drop across the injector nozzles as seen in Figure 2-44.

The principal fault of this arrangement is the fact that a plugged injector nozzle discharges less fuel than a clear nozzle, yet the pressure drop across it is greater than it is across a clear nozzle. Therefore the gauge will indicate a higher total flow rate when the flow is actually lower than when all nozzles are clear.

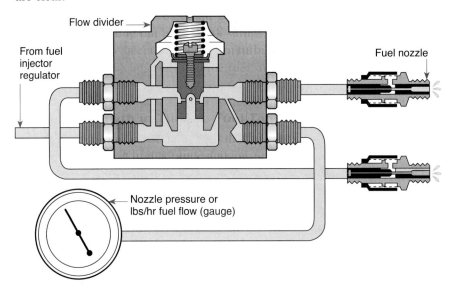

Figure 2-44. *The fuel flowmeter used with a fuel-injected horizontally opposed engine is a pressure gauge that measures the pressure drop across the injector nozzles.*

Computerized Fuel Flow System

Dedicated computers have found serious applications in all sizes of aircraft. One important computerized application is the Computerized Fuel Flow System, or CFS. This versatile instrument uses a small turbine rotor mounted in the fuel line between the fuel injection unit and the flow divider to which the fuel injection nozzles attach. All the fuel that flows to the cylinders must pass through the turbine, which spins at a speed proportional to the rate of fuel flow. As it spins, it interrupts a beam of light between a light-emitting diode and a phototransistor. The resulting pulses of light are converted into pulses of electricity and entered into the computer.

When the instrument is properly programmed with the amount of fuel on board at engine startup, it can inform the pilot of the number of pounds or gallons of fuel on board, the fuel flow in gallons or pounds per hour, the fuel time remaining at the present rate of flow, and the number of gallons of fuel used since the engine was initially started.

Flowmeters for Turbine Engines

Turbine engine fuel flow is measured in mass flow rather than volume flow, and the transmitting system is shown in Figure 2-45.

The impeller and the turbine are mounted in the main fuel line leading to the engine. The impeller, driven at a constant speed by a special three-phase motor, imparts a swirling motion to the fuel passing through it, and this swirling fuel deflects the turbine. The turbine is restrained by two calibrated restraining springs, and the amount it deflects is affected by both the volume and the density of the fuel.

The amount of turbine deflection is transmitted to an electrical indicator in the cockpit by a Magnesyn transmitter built into the flowmeter.

Magnesyn system. The registered trade name of a remote indicating instrument system. A Magnesyn system uses a permanent magnet as its rotor and a toroidal coil excited by 400-hertz AC as its stator.

A small magnet in the indicator follows the movement of a larger magnet in the transmitter.

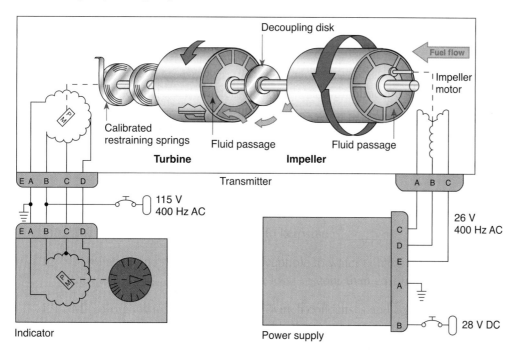

Figure 2-45. *Mass flowmeter used on a large turbine engine.*

Fuel Pressure Warning System

Most fuel pressure is measured with a differential-pressure gauge that measures the difference between the fuel pressure and the air pressure at the carburetor. These pressure gauges are sensitive enough for all normal operation, but an indicator with a more rapid response and positive indication is needed to warn the pilot of a dangerous drop in fuel pressure.

The fuel pressure warning system senses the pressure at the carburetor inlet and generates an electrical signal to give the first indication that a tank is empty and the selector valve should be switched to a full tank. As soon as the pump begins to draw air from the tank, the fuel pressure drops and the pressure warning system contacts close, sending an electrical signal which turns on a warning light or flashes a warning on an annunciator panel.

The pressure-sensitive mechanism is generally a bellows, and it can be adjusted to change the pressures at which it actuates. Maintenance and troubleshooting procedures for fuel pressure warning systems are found in the manufacturer's maintenance manuals.

Fuel Temperature Indicators

Fuel-temperature sensors are installed in the fuel tanks of some jet-powered aircraft to indicate to the flight engineer when the fuel is getting cold enough to begin forming ice crystals that could clog the fuel filters and shut off the flow of fuel to the engines.

When the fuel temperature gets near 0°C, hot compressor bleed air can be directed through the fuel heater to prevent the formation of ice.

STUDY QUESTIONS: FUEL SYSTEM INSTRUMENTS

Answers are provided on page 169.

65. Each fuel quantity indicator must be calibrated to read zero during level flight when the quantity of the fuel remaining in the tank is equal to the _____ fuel supply.

66. The tank unit used in an electronic fuel quantity indicating system is a/an _____ .

67. A capacitance-type fuel quantity indicating system measures fuel quantity in _____ (gallons or pounds).

68. The two things that make up the dielectric of the capacitor-type fuel probe are _____ and _____ .

69. A capacitance-type fuel quantity indicating system measures the weight of the fuel because the temperature of the fuel affects its _____ .

70. A volume of cold fuel contains _____ (more or less) heat energy than an equal amount of warm fuel.

71. Three things affect the capacitance of a capacitor; these are:

    a._____

    b._____

    c._____

72. A bridge circuit measures the capacitance of the fuel tank probes and a/an _____ increases the strength of the signal from this bridge to make it strong enough to drive the servo indicator.

73. The Autosyn-type fuel flowmeter transmits the movement of the metering vane from the engine to the cockpit _____ .

74. The flowmeter used on a fuel-injected horizontally opposed engine is actually a pressure gauge that measures the pressure drop across the _____ .

75. If a fuel injector nozzle becomes plugged and flows less fuel to the engine, the pressure-type fuel flowmeter will indicate a _____ (higher or lower) flow rate than when all nozzles are clear.

Fuel System Plumbing

The lines and fittings used in an aircraft fuel system carry highly flammable fuel through the aircraft. They must be of the highest quality materials and must be properly installed. This section discusses some of the requirements for fuel system plumbing.

Fuel Line Routing

The line must not chafe against control cables or airframe structure or come in contact with electrical wiring or conduit. Where physical separation of the fuel line from electrical wiring or conduit is impracticable, locate the fuel line below the wiring and clamp it securely to the airframe structure. In no case may the wiring be supported by the fuel line.

Fuel Line Alignment

Locate all bends accurately so that the tubing is aligned with all the support clamps and end fittings and is not drawn, pulled, or otherwise forced into place by them. Never install a straight length of tubing between two rigidly mounted fittings. Always incorporate at least one bend between such fittings to absorb strain caused by vibration and temperature changes.

Bonding

When fuel flows through a fuel line, it generates static electricity. If any portion of the system is electrically insulated from the aircraft structure, these charges can build up high enough to cause a spark.

All fuel system components must be electrically bonded and grounded to drain off all charges of static electricity before they can cause a spark.

Bond metallic fuel lines at each point where they are clamped to the structure. Integrally bonded and cushioned line-support clamps are preferred to other clamping and bonding methods.

Support of Fuel System Components

To prevent failure of the fuel lines, all fittings heavy enough to cause the line to sag should be supported by means other than the tubing.

Place support clamps or brackets for metallic lines as recommended in Figure 2-46.

Tubing O.D. (inch)	Approximate Distance Between Supports (inches)
1/8 to 3/16	9
1/4 to 5/16	12
3/8 to 1/2	16
5/8 to 3/4	22
1 to 1 1/4	30
1 1/2 to 2	40

Figure 2-46. *Support spacing for rigid fuel lines.*

STUDY QUESTIONS: FUEL SYSTEM PLUMBING

Answers are provided on page 169.

76. If a fuel line is routed through a compartment parallel with an electrical bundle, the fuel line should be _____ (above or below) the wire bundle.

77. It _____ (is or is not) permissible to clamp a wire bundle to a fuel line if a cushion clamp is used.

78. It _____ (is or is not) permissible to install a straight length of tubing between two rigidly mounted fittings.

79. The clamps used to support a fuel line should be _____ cushion clamps.

80. Fuel lines are bonded to the aircraft structure to prevent a buildup of _____.

81. A 1/2-inch O.D. fuel should be supported every _____ inches along the run of the line.

Fuel Jettisoning System

Transport category aircraft and general aviation aircraft are both allowed to have a higher takeoff weight than landing weight if they have a fuel jettisoning system. The jettisoning system allows the flight crew to dump enough fuel to lower the gross weight of the aircraft to its maximum allowable landing weight.

The fuel jettisoning system must be so designed that its operation is free from fire hazards and the fuel must discharge clear of any part of the aircraft. The system must be so designed that fuel or fumes will not enter any part of the airplane, and the jettisoning operation must not adversely affect the controllability of the airplane.

A fuel jettisoning system consists of lines, valves, dump chutes, and the chute operating mechanism, and the fuel is pumped overboard by boost pumps located inside the fuel tanks. The controls allow the flight personnel to close the dump valve to stop dumping during any part of the jettisoning operation.

Fuel tanks whose fuel can be jettisoned are equipped with a dump limit switch that will shut off the flow to the dump chute if the pressure drops below that needed to supply the engine with adequate fuel, or when the tank level reaches a preset dump shutoff level. This prevents more fuel from being jettisoned from any tank than is allowed by Federal Aviation Regulations.

Lateral stability of the aircraft is maintained while dumping fuel by having two separate and independent jettisoning systems, one for each side of the aircraft.

STUDY QUESTIONS: FUEL JETTISONING SYSTEM

Answers are provided on page 169.

82. If an aircraft is allowed to have a higher takeoff weight than its landing weight, it must have a _____ system.

83. Fuel is forced out of the jettisoning system by the _____ in the fuel tanks.

84. It _____ (is or is not) possible for the flight crew to terminate the fuel jettisoning operation at any time.

85. Lateral stability during fuel jettisoning is maintained by having _____ .

Fueling and Defueling

Aviation mechanics are often required to fuel aircraft and to maintain the fueling equipment, and so should be intimately familiar with fuel handling.

Each fuel bulk storage facility is protected from discharges of static electricity and from contamination as much as is practicable. It is the responsibility of the operator of these facilities to make absolutely certain that the proper grade of fuel is put into the fuel truck and that the truck is electrically grounded to the bulk facility when the fuel is being pumped. The fuel filters should be cleaned before pumping begins, and all of the water traps must be carefully checked for any indication of water.

It is extremely important to identify the fuel properly when fueling an aircraft. The use of fuel with a lower-than-allowed octane or performance rating can cause detonation, which can destroy an engine.

A number of reciprocating-engine-powered airplanes have crashed because they have been inadvertently fueled with turbine engine fuel. Turbine engine fuel will cause severe detonation when a reciprocating engine is operated at takeoff power.

When an aircraft is fueled from a tank truck, the driver must position the truck well ahead of the aircraft and headed parallel with the wings. The brakes must be set so there will be no possibility of the truck rolling into the aircraft. The truck sumps must be checked and a record made of the purity of the fuel.

The truck should be equipped with a fully charged fire extinguisher, ready for instant use if the need should arise. A static bonding wire should be attached between the truck and the aircraft and the truck should be grounded to the earth.

A ladder should be used if it is needed, and a soft mat should be placed over the top of the wing to keep the fuel hose from damaging the skin. The fuel nozzle must be free from any loose dirt which could fall into the tank, and when inserting the nozzle, special care must be taken not to damage the light metal of which the tank is made. The end of the nozzle must never be allowed to strike the bottom of the tank.

After the fueling operation is completed, replace the nozzle cover and secure the tank cap. Remove the wing mat and put all of the equipment back onto the truck and remove the hose and bonding wire and roll them back onto their storage reels.

The fueling and defueling procedures vary widely from aircraft to aircraft, and this makes it important to follow the instructions issued by the aircraft manufacturer. Normally, when defueling an aircraft that has fuel tanks in sweptback wings, you must defuel the outboard wing tanks first. This minimizes the twisting effect on the wing caused by the fuel being located behind the wing attachment points on the fuselage.

Pressure fueling, or single-point fueling, is used in large aircraft because of the tremendous amount of time saved by allowing the entire aircraft to be fueled from a single location. This not only saves time, but also makes for a much safer operation, as the pressure fueling reduces the chance of static electricity igniting fuel vapors.

When fueling an aircraft using the pressure fueling method, be sure the truck pump pressure is correct for the aircraft. The required pressures and the fueling procedures are normally shown on placards on the fuel control panel access door. No one should fuel an aircraft with a fuel pressure fueling system unless he or she has been thoroughly checked out on the procedure for the specific aircraft.

The fuel tank sumps and the main fuel strainer must be periodically drained to prevent contaminated fuel reaching the engine. Even if the aircraft is fueled from a truck or storage tank that is considered to be uncontaminated, the sumps and strainers should be checked because contamination may enter from other sources.

Fire Protection

All fueling operations must be done under conditions that allow for a minimum possibility of fire. All fueling and defueling operations should be done in the open, NEVER in a hangar.

All electrical equipment that is not absolutely necessary for the fueling operation should be turned off, and fueling should not be done in the proximity of radar operation. Radar systems radiate enough electrical energy that a spark could be caused to jump and ignite the fuel vapors.

Fires can be best brought under control with a carbon dioxide (CO_2) fire extinguisher. A dry-powder type extinguisher could be used as a last resort as it is an effective extinguishing agent, but it generates quite an expensive cleanup. Soda-acid or water-type extinguishers should not be used, because the fuel is lighter than water and will float away, spreading the fire. Both the dry-powder and the CO_2 should be swept back and forth across the base of the fire, allowing the agent to settle over the fuel source so it will cut off the supply of oxygen and extinguish the flame.

STUDY QUESTIONS: FUELING AND DEFUELING

Answers are provided on page 169.

86. When fueling an aircraft from a fuel truck, the truck should be positioned ahead of the aircraft and headed _____ (parallel to or perpendicular with) to the wings.

87. Before beginning the fueling operation, the aircraft and the fuel truck should be connected with a
_____ .

88. If a reciprocating engine is operated with turbine engine fuel, it will most likely be damaged by
_____ .

89. It _____ (is or is not) permissible to defuel an aircraft inside a hangar.

90. Pressure fueling is safer than overwing fueling because there is less danger of static electricity igniting the _____ .

91. The correct pressure to use for pressure fueling is normally noted on a placard in or adjacent to the
_____ .

92. Unless the service manual specifies otherwise, the outboard fuel tanks on an aircraft with swept-back wings should be defueled _____ (first or last).

Fuel System Contamination Control

Draining a sample of fuel from the main strainers has long been considered an acceptable method of assuring that the fuel system is clean. However, tests on several designs of aircraft have shown that this cursory sampling is not adequate to be sure that no contamination exists.

In one test reported to the FAA, three gallons of water were added to a half-full fuel tank. After time was allowed for this water to settle, it was necessary to drain 10 ounces of fuel before any water showed up at the strainer. In another airplane, one gallon of water was poured into a half-full fuel tank and more than a quart of fuel had to be drained out before water showed up at the strainer. The fuel tank sumps had to be drained before all of the water was eliminated from the system.

A commercial water test kit is available that consists of a small glass jar and a supply of capsules that contain a grayish-white powder. A 100-cc sample of fuel is taken from the tank or from the fuel truck and is put into the bottle. One of the test capsules is emptied into this sample of fuel, the lid is screwed onto the jar, and the sample is shaken for about 10 seconds. If the powder changes color from gray-white to pink or purple, the fuel has a water content of more than 30 parts per million, and it is not considered safe for use. This test is fail-safe because any error in performing it will show an unsafe indication.

Protection Against Contamination

Micronic filter. The registered trade name of a filter that uses a porous paper element.

All fuel tanks must have the discharge line from the tank protected by an 2- to 16-mesh finger screen. Downstream from this finger screen is the main strainer, usually of the fine-wire mesh type or of the paper Micronic type.

Each fuel tank is normally equipped with a quick-drain valve, where a sample of the fuel may be taken from each tank on the preflight inspection. When draining the main strainer, some fuel should flow with the tank selector set for each of the tanks individually. Drawing fuel when the selector valve is on the BOTH position will not necessarily drain all of the water that has collected in all of the fuel lines.

Importance of Proper Grade of Fuel

Aircraft engines are designed to operate with a specific grade of fuel, and they will operate neither efficiently nor safely if an improper grade is supplied to the engine.

The required minimum grade of fuel must be clearly marked on the filler cap of the aircraft fuel tanks, and the person fueling the aircraft must know the grade of fuel required and that the proper grade of fuel is being supplied.

If the tanks have been serviced with aviation gasoline of a lower grade than allowed or with turbine-engine fuel, the following procedure is recommended:

If the engine has not been operated:

1. Drain all improperly filled tanks.
2. Flush out all lines with the proper grade of fuel.
3. Refill the tanks with the proper grade of fuel.

If the engine has been operated:

1. Perform a compression check on all cylinders.
2. Inspect all cylinders with a borescope, paying special attention to the combustion chambers and to the domes of the pistons.
3. Drain the oil and inspect all oil screens.
4. Drain the entire fuel system, including all of the tanks and the carburetor.
5. Flush the entire system with the proper grade of fuel.
6. Fill the tanks with the proper grade of fuel.
7. Perform a complete engine run-up check.

Fuel System Troubleshooting

A schematic diagram of the fuel system is one of the most useful documents you can use when troubleshooting the system. The schematic diagram shows the components as they function in the system, but not necessarily as they are installed in the aircraft.

One of the most difficult problems to trace down in a fuel system is an internal leak. It is often possible to isolate a portion of a large-aircraft fuel system that has an internal leak by watching the fuel-pressure gauge and operating the selector valves. If the fuel pressure drops, or if the boost pumps must run continually to maintain the pressure, the selected portion of the system may have the internal leak.

You can check fuel valves in small aircraft for internal leakage by draining the strainer bowl, turning the valve off, and turning on the boost pump. If the valve is leaking internally, fuel will flow into the strainer bowl.

When inspecting any fuel system for leaks, turn on the boost pump, and visually inspect all valves located downstream of the pump for indication of leaks.

During the troubleshooting process, observe the fuel pressure warning system for indications of proper operation. The fuel pressure warning system may include warning lights and pressure gauges. If you are unsure if the system pressure is indicating correctly, an external pressure gauge may be connected into the system with a tee to verify system pressure.

Fuel System Maintenance and Inspection

Specific instructions for maintenance and inspection of fuel systems can be found in the aircraft maintenance manual. Every aircraft is different, and it is important to understand the system that you are working on.

Routine maintenance and inspection of fuel systems go hand-in-hand. As you perform maintenance on the fuel system, you are inspecting the components at the same time. When repairing or replacing any components in the fuel system, always refer to the aircraft maintenance manual for detailed instructions. In some cases, working on the fuel system may require defueling the aircraft. Follow the defueling instructions found in the aircraft maintenance manual.

When working on fuel systems, fuel spills may occur. Address fuel spills immediately to prevent further hazards from fires caused by sparks from electrical systems or other ignition sources. Small spills can be cleaned up with shop oil absorbent sweeping materials, while larger spills should be addressed by the local or airport fire department.

Fuel Lines and Plumbing

Inspect all lines for leaks, chafing, damage, and proper attachment. Verify that bonding straps are properly installed and are in good condition.

Fuel Filters and Screens

Fuel filters and screens are cleaned and inspected during routine maintenance inspections. Fuel screens or strainers are located at the outlet of fuel tanks and inlets to carburetors, fuel metering systems, and engine-driven fuel pumps. Fuel filters can be located in many different places, including engine bays, on the engine, or in the wing or fuselage. The filter elements should be cleaned and inspected for condition. Follow the maintenance manual instructions for the cleaning procedures for each type of filter.

Fuel Drains

Inspect all fuel drains for operation, checking for leaks, damaged gaskets and any obstructions. Fuel should be clear of any sediment or water. Any presence of rubber particles can often be a sign of hose deterioration.

Fuel Tanks and Vents

Inspect exterior openings of vents for obstructions. If the aircraft has a heated fuel vent, check for proper operation. Check fuel filler caps and anti-siphon valves for damage and attachment. Inspect the filler cap seals for flexibility, splits, cracks, or distortion. Inspect the general condition of the tanks as well as the exterior of the wing and fuselage for fuel leaks.

Required Placards

The specifications of required placards are found in the pilot's operating handbook/flight operations manual or in the aircraft maintenance manual.

Inspect fuel filler openings or access panels for required placards. Verify that selector valves are clearly marked for operation and limitations. Inspect quantity gauges for proper markings and associated placards.

Fuel Quantity Probes

Inspect for leaks at points of attachment. Open fuel tank access panels as necessary to inspect for condition, corrosion, and cleanliness. Check the fuel quantity gauges for operation. Calibration of fuel quantity systems is allowed on some aircraft. The calibration procedures, which may require specialized calibration equipment, will be found in the aircraft maintenance manual. When troubleshooting a fuel quantity system or replacing a fuel quantity probe, follow the aircraft manufacturer's instructions. After replacing a probe, check for leaks, proper operation, and proper calibration.

Fuel Temperature Probes

If the aircraft is equipped with fuel temperature probes, inspect for condition and security of attachment. Verify that the probes provide an accurate temperature. Consult the aircraft maintenance manual for additional inspections and for troubleshooting procedures.

Fuel Pumps

Inspect fuel pumps for leaks and security of attachment. Operate the pumps to check for proper operation.

Fuel Selector Valves, Firewall Shutoff Valves and Cross-feed Valves

Inspect all valves for leaks, condition, and security of attachment. Inspect all actuating mechanisms for condition and proper operation.

Check selector valves for ease of operation and proper system operation in each position. Verify the operation of firewall shutoff valves and cross-feed valves. Follow the instructions in the maintenance manual for the proper operation of the cross-feed system and for troubleshooting procedures.

Caution! If you need to replace a selector valve, make sure to connect all lines to the correct ports on the valve. Incorrect connections can result in fuel starvation to the engine.

Fuel Drain Collector Systems

Some turbine aircraft use fuel drain collector systems to capture fuel and oil from engine drain lines and fuel manifolds. Inspect the tank, pump, pump filter, and plumbing for leaks and security of attachment. Drain the tank as necessary.

STUDY QUESTIONS: FUEL SYSTEM MAINTENANCE AND INSPECTION

Answers are provided on page 169.

95. Fuel spills should be taken care of _____.

96. Fuel screens or strainers can be found

   a. _____

   b. _____

   c. _____

   d. _____

97. Fuel filters can be found

   a. _____

   b. _____

   c. _____

   d. _____

98. The presence of rubber particles found at a fuel drain may be a sign of _____.

99. The specifications for required fuel placards can be found in _____ or the aircraft _____.

100. Calibration procedures for fuel quantity systems will be found in _____.

101. Fuel selector valves should be checked for _____ and _____ operation in all positions.

102. After replacing a fuel valve, incorrect connections could cause _____.

103. Some turbine aircraft capture fuel and oil from drain lines in a _____.

Answers to Chapter 2 Study Questions

1. detonation
2. water
3. higher
4. low
5. low
6. 7
7. higher
8. octane, performance
9. tetraethyl lead
10. rubber
11. Jet A
12. more
13. corrosion
14. anti-icing
15. is not
16. is not
17. 37.5 gph
18. 31.25 gph
19. 100
20. 3.5
21. 2.0
22. interconnected
23. fuel jettisoning
24. interconnected
25. parallel
26. main
27. ejectors

28. balanced
29. boost pumps
30. automatically
31. baffles
32. sump
33. vents
34. JET FUEL
35. 30
36. nitric, sulfuric
37. 3.5
38. integral
39. argon, carbon dioxide
40. 2
41. ammonia, phenolphthalein
42. calibrated
43. variable
44. vapor
45. check valves
46. ejector
47. variable
48. diaphragm spring
49. constant
50. do
51. series
52. fuel metering device
53. constant
54. shear section

55. is not
56. freezes
57. antifreeze
58. antifreeze
59. water
60. ice
61. detent
62. a. compressor bleed air
    b. engine lubricating oil
63. compressor bleed air
64. can
65. unusable
66. capacitor
67. pounds
68. fuel, air
69. dielectric constant
70. more
71. a. area of the plates
    b. separation between the plates
    c. dielectric constant
72. amplifier
73. electrically
74. injector nozzles
75. higher
76. below
77. is not

78. is not
79. bonded
80. static electricity
81. 16
82. fuel jettisoning
83. boost pumps
84. is
85. two separate jettisoning systems
86. parallel to
87. static bonding wire
88. detonation
89. is not
90. fuel vapors

91. fueling control panel
92. first
93. schematic diagram
94. boost pumps
95. immediately
96. a. at fuel tank outlets
    b. at carburetor inlets
    c. in metering systems
    d. in engine-driven fuel pumps
97. a. in engine bays
    b. on the engine
    c. in the wing
    d. in the fuselage

98. hose deterioration
99. the pilot's operating handbook, maintenance manual
100. the aircraft maintenance manual
101. ease of operation, proper system
102. fuel starvation to the engine
103. drain collector system

CABIN ATMOSPHERE CONTROL SYSTEMS

3

Human Needs in Flight

Flight has become such a standard means of transportation, it's easy to forget the importance of the atmosphere control systems that make high- altitude flight possible. Unaided, people cannot survive at the high altitudes where most airliners fly. The air temperature is about −50°F (−45.6°C) and the atmospheric pressure is so low that the human body cannot get enough oxygen from the air to survive.

Without heating and pressurizing the air in an aircraft cabin, it would be impossible to fly at the high altitudes where turbine engines run most efficiently and where most bad weather can be avoided.

A complete cabin atmosphere control system regulates the pressure to force oxygen into our lungs, and temperature, humidity, and air movement to make the aircraft cabin comfortable.

Pressure

The human body requires oxygen. One way to provide this oxygen when flying at a high altitude is to increase the pressure of the air inside the aircraft cabin. When the air pressure inside the cabin is near to that on the earth's surface, enough oxygen will pass through the lungs and enter the blood stream to allow the brain and body to function normally.

Temperature

In the hot summertime, we feel comfortable when our bodies (which usually have a temperature of about 98°F) can pass off heat to the air around us. For this reason, the air in the aircraft cabin should be maintained in the comfort range of between 70°F (21°C) and 80°F (27°C).

In the wintertime, when the temperature of the outside air is much lower than that of our bodies, we lose heat from our bodies to the air so rapidly that we are uncomfortable. To allow our bodies to maintain their heat, heaters keep the temperature of the air inside the cabin within the comfort range.

Humidity

It is true that it is not only the heat, but also the humidity that makes summertime uncomfortable. Humidity is the amount of water vapor in the air, and it affects our comfort.

The human body has a natural air conditioning system that works best when the humidity is low. When our body is hot, water, or sweat, comes out of the pores of our skin, and air blowing over our bodies evaporates it. The heat that changes this water from a liquid into a vapor comes from our skin, and losing this heat makes us feel cooler.

But, when the humidity is high, the air already has a lot of water vapor in it and the sweat does not evaporate as readily. With less evaporation, less heat is removed, and we feel uncomfortable.

An effective cabin atmosphere control system maintains the humidity in the air at a level that allows our bodies to lose excessive heat, while at the same time containing enough moisture that our throats do not become dry.

Air Movement

We usually feel comfortable and alert when cool air blows over our face and head, as long as it blows at a rate fast enough to take away the unwanted heat but not hard enough to make us consciously aware of it.

Warm air feels comfortable when it blows over the lower part of our body, but it makes us drowsy and sluggish when it blows over our face and head.

A properly designed and operating cabin atmosphere control system moves air at the right temperature and moisture content over and around our bodies. This allows the flight crew to operate most efficiently and the passengers to be most comfortable.

The Atmosphere

The air that surrounds the earth is a physical mixture of gases made up of approximately 78% nitrogen, 21% oxygen, and traces of several other gases that include carbon dioxide and water vapor.

Oxygen is the most important gas in the air because no human or animal life can exist for more than a few minutes without it. Depriving our bodies of oxygen for even a few seconds can damage our brain. Nitrogen, which makes up the bulk of the air we breathe, is an inert gas. It provides volume to the air and dilutes the oxygen.

The earth's atmosphere extends upward for more than 20 miles, and since the gases that make up the atmosphere are compressible, the air near the surface is denser than the air higher up. As a result of this compression, about one half of the total atmosphere is below 18,000 feet.

While the pressure of the air changes with altitude, its composition remains relatively constant. There is the same percentage of oxygen in the air at sea level as there is at 30,000 feet, but because there is so little air at this altitude, the actual amount of oxygen is much less.

Standard Conditions

Standard conditions have been established for atmospheric pressure and temperature. Under these standards, the atmosphere is considered to press down on the surface of the earth with a pressure of 14.69 pounds per square inch. This much pressure will hold up a column of mercury 29.92 inches, or 760 millimeters, high. The pressure of the atmosphere decreases as the altitude increases, as is illustrated in Figure 3-1.

The standard temperature at sea level is 15°C, or 59°F. The temperature drops as the altitude increases until about 36,000 feet, which marks the beginning of the stratosphere, where the temperature stabilizes at −56.5°C (−69.7°F).

The density of air increases as its temperature decreases but it decreases as its pressure decreases. Decreased density lessens the aerodynamic drag of an aircraft, but the power the engines can develop also lessens as the density decreases. The temperature remains constant in the stratosphere, so the density change lessens as the altitude changes. For this reason, jet aircraft perform best at the beginning of the stratosphere, at an altitude of about 36,000 feet.

ICAO Standard Atmosphere						
Altitude Feet	Temperature		Pressure			Speed of Sound Knots
	°F	°C	In. Hg	Mm Hg	PSI	
0	59.00	15.0	29.92	760.0	14.69	661.7
1,000	55.43	13.0	28.86	733.0	14.18	659.5
2,000	51.87	11.0	27.82	706.7	13.66	657.2
3,000	48.30	9.1	26.82	681.2	13.17	654.9
4,000	44.74	7.1	25.84	656.3	12.69	652.6
5,000	41.17	5.1	24.90	632.5	12.23	650.3
6,000	37.60	3.1	23.98	609.1	11.77	647.9
7,000	34.04	1.1	23.09	586.5	11.34	645.6
8,000	30.47	-0.8	22.23	564.6	10.92	643.3
9,000	26.90	-2.8	21.39	543.3	10.51	640.9
10,000	23.34	-4.8	20.58	522.7	10.10	638.6
15,000	5.51	-14.7	16.89	429.0	8.30	626.7
20,000	-12.32	-24.6	13.75	349.5	6.76	614.6
25,000	-30.15	-34.5	11.12	284.5	5.46	602.2
30,000	-47.90	-44.4	8.885	226.1	4.37	589.5
35,000	-65.82	-54.2	7.041	178.8	3.64	576.6
*36,089	-69.70	-56.5	6.683	169.7	3.28	573.8
40,000	-69.70	-56.5	5.558	141.2	2.73	573.8
45,000	-69.70	-56.5	4.355	110.6	2.14	573.8
50,000	-69.70	-56.5	3.425	87.4	1.70	573.8
55,000	-69.70	-56.5	2.693	68.8	1.33	573.8
60,000	-69.70	-56.5	2.118	54.4	1.05	573.8
65,000	-69.70	-56.5	1.665	42.3	0.82	573.8
70,000	-69.70	-56.5	1.310	33.5	0.64	573.8
75,000	-69.70	-56.5	1.030	26.2	0.51	573.8
80,000	-69.70	-56.5	0.810	20.9	0.40	573.8
85,000	-64.80	-53.8	0.637	16.2	0.31	577.4
90,000	-56.57	-49.2	0.504	13.0	0.25	583.4
95,000	-48.34	-44.6	0.400	10.2	0.20	589.3
100,000	-40.11	-40.1	0.320	8.0	0.16	595.2
*Geopotential of the tropopause						

Figure 3-1. *Table of the ICAO Standard Atmosphere.*

The Characteristics of Oxygen

Oxygen is one of the most abundant chemical elements on the earth. It is found in the rocks and soil that make up the crust of the earth, and it accounts for most of the weight of the water that covers the majority of the earth. As a free gas, oxygen is one of the two major elements that make up the air that surrounds the earth.

Oxygen is colorless, odorless, and tasteless, and is extremely active chemically. This means that it unites with most of the other chemical elements to form compounds. Often it reacts with other elements so violently that it produces a large amount of heat and light.

Oxygen is produced commercially by lowering the temperature of air until it changes from a gas into a liquid. The oxygen is separated from the other gases by increasing the temperature enough for the various gases to boil off. Each of the constituent gases boils off at a different temperature.

Oxygen can also be produced in a very pure state by an electrolytic process in which electrical current is passed through water. The current causes the water to break down into its two chemical elements, hydrogen and oxygen.

Oxygen does not burn, but it supports combustion so well that you must take special care not to use oxygen where anyone is smoking or where there is any fire, hot metal, or open petroleum products.

Oxygen Partial Pressure

partial pressure. The percentage of the total pressure of a mixture of gases produced by each of the individual gases in the mixture.

Air is a physical mixture of gases rather than a chemical compound, and while the percentages of the gases remain constant, the amount of each gas in the air decreases as altitude increases.

Twenty-one percent of the gas in the air is oxygen, so the pressure caused by oxygen in the air is 21% of the total atmospheric pressure. Under standard sea level atmospheric conditions, oxygen exerts a pressure of 3.08 psi. This pressure forces oxygen into our lungs. At 10,000 feet, the total pressure is down to 10.10 psi, and the oxygen partial pressure is only 2.12 psi.

Generally speaking, there is not enough oxygen partial pressure in the air above 10,000 feet to allow the human body to function properly. If we fly at this altitude without supplemental oxygen for several hours, we will get a headache and will become fatigued.

At 15,000 feet, the oxygen partial pressure is down to 1.74 psi. Flight at this altitude for more than thirty minutes will cause us to become sleepy, and our judgment and coordination will be impaired.

At 35,000 feet, where the oxygen partial pressure is down to 0.76 psi, we can only function for about 15 to 30 seconds before losing consciousness.

There are two ways to increase the oxygen partial pressure while flying at high altitude: increase the pressure of the air in the cabin by pressurization, or provide supplemental oxygen for the occupants.

The Function of Oxygen

Gasoline is a compound of hydrogen and carbon. When it is mixed with air inside the cylinder of an aircraft engine, and its temperature is raised, it combines with the oxygen in the air. The hydrogen and carbon react with the oxygen and change into carbon dioxide (CO_2) and water (H_2O). When this change takes place, heat and light are released. The fuel is said to be burned, or oxidized.

The same kind of reaction, only not nearly so violent, takes place in our bodies when the oxygen we breathe furnishes our brain and muscles with the energy we need to operate.

When we inhale, our lungs fill with air, which is primarily a mixture of oxygen and nitrogen. A wonderfully complex system in our lungs separates the oxygen from the air and loads it onto the hemoglobin in our blood, which then carries it to our brain and to all our other organs that need oxygen. The oxygen reacts with hydrocarbons in our body to release the energy that we need.

In the human body, as in an aircraft engine, oxygen and carbon combine to form carbon dioxide. This CO_2 is picked up by the blood and carried back to the lungs where it is expelled into the air when we exhale.

We can go without food for days without suffering any permanent damage, but if our body is deprived of oxygen for even a short while, we develop a condition known as hypoxia. Its first symptoms are an increase in breathing rate, headaches, and a tingling sensation in the fingers. Judgment and vision are both impaired, and we become sleepy. Hypoxia degrades our night vision, and severe hypoxia causes unconsciousness and death.

14 CFR Part 91, *General Operating and Flight Rules*, gives the requirements for supplemental oxygen for unpressurized aircraft.

§91.211

(a) *General*. No person may operate a civil aircraft of U.S. registry—

(1) At cabin pressure altitudes above 12,500 feet (MSL) up to and including 14,000 feet (MSL) unless the required minimum flight crew is provided with and uses supplemental oxygen for that part of the flight at those altitudes that is of more than 30 minutes duration;

(2) At cabin pressure altitudes above 14,000 feet (MSL) unless the required minimum flight crew is provided with and uses supplemental oxygen during the entire flight time at those altitudes; and

(3) At cabin pressure altitudes above 15,000 feet (MSL) unless each occupant of the aircraft is provided with supplemental oxygen.

The Function of Carbon Dioxide

Our bodies produce carbon dioxide, most of which is expelled as we exhale, but we need a small amount of carbon dioxide to control the rate and depth of our breathing.

When we exercise or work hard, our blood contains an excess of carbon dioxide. This causes us to breathe deep and fast to get rid of this excess and take in the oxygen we need. Fear, stress, and pain also signal our lungs to breathe deeply, and under these conditions we get rid of much of the carbon dioxide we need. This condition, known as hyperventilation, causes symptoms similar to those of hypoxia, and can cause nausea and unconsciousness.

Altitude (Feet)	Effect
5,000	Deteriorated vision
10,000	Judgement and abilities impaired
14,000	Blurred thinking
16,000	Disorientation and belligerence
18,000	Possible unconciousness
Above 18,000	Unconciousness and possible death

Figure 3-2. *Effects of lack of oxygen on the human body.*

pressure altitude. The altitude in standard air at which the pressure is the same as the existing pressure.

MSL. Mean sea level. When the letters MSL are used with an altitude, it means that the altitude is measured from mean, or average, sea level.

The Threat of Carbon Monoxide

While our bodies need a small amount of carbon dioxide (CO_2), carbon monoxide (CO) serves no useful function, and we must guard against its presence. Only a small amount of CO can starve the brain by displacing the oxygen it needs.

CO is a colorless, odorless, tasteless, unstable gas that results from incomplete combustion of hydrocarbon fuels. It is found in the smoke and fumes from burning aviation fuels and lubricants, and in the smoke inhaled into our lungs from burning tobacco.

Hemoglobin is a part of our blood that carries oxygen from our lungs to our brain and all other organs that must have oxygen to function properly. But hemoglobin has a much higher affinity for CO than it has for oxygen. If CO is present in the air, the hemoglobin will fill up with it rather than with oxygen. When our brain is supplied with blood that does not have enough oxygen in it, we lose our ability to reason, and it becomes difficult to make correct decisions.

The effect of CO poisoning is cumulative; that is, breathing air that is even slightly contaminated with CO over a prolonged period of time is as bad as breathing a heavy concentration for a shorter period of time. Either will affect our ability to safely operate an aircraft.

The early stages of carbon monoxide poisoning are similar to any other form of oxygen starvation. First, we feel sluggish and too warm, and there is usually a tight feeling across the forehead. This is usually followed by a headache, ringing ears, and throbbing temples. If we don't heed the warning from these early symptoms, severe headaches, dizziness, unconsciousness, and even death will result.

Aircraft, especially those that use heat produced by the engine exhaust system, should be equipped with carbon monoxide detectors. These are simply small containers of colored chemical crystals that change their color in the presence of carbon monoxide. The color of the crystals warns occupants of an aircraft of the presence of carbon monoxide long before they could detect it by other means.

STUDY QUESTIONS: HUMAN NEEDS IN FLIGHT

Answers are provided on page 231.

1. A decrease in the temperature of the air causes the density to _____ (increase or decrease).

2. A decrease in the pressure of the air causes the density to _____ (increase or decrease).

3. The two gases that make up the majority of the atmosphere are _____ and _____.

4. Oxygen _____ (does or does not) burn.

5. Long exposure at an altitude of 10,000 feet without supplemental oxygen will result in _____ and fatigue.

6. A condition in which the human body is deprived of the oxygen it needs is called _____ .

7. The rate and depth of our breathing is controlled by _____ in our blood.

8. Carbon monoxide is dangerous because it takes the place of the _____ the brain needs to function.

The Physics of Cabin Atmosphere Control

To best understand the way a cabin atmosphere control system works, we should review some of the concepts of basic physics.

Heat

All matter is made up of extremely tiny particles called molecules. These molecules are too small to see, even with a high-powered microscope. And the molecules in all substances are held together by strong forces of attraction for each other.

All molecules contain heat energy, which causes them to move about in all directions. If a material contains only a small amount of heat energy, its molecules move about relatively slowly; but if heat is added, the molecules move faster. If it were possible to remove all the heat energy from a material, its molecules would stop moving altogether.

Heat energy can transfer from one object to another, and the transfer is always from an object with a high level of energy to one with a lower level of energy—from a hotter object to a cooler one.

When an object loses or gains heat energy, the molecules change their speed of movement enough that the object can actually change its physical state.

If a solid material such as a block of ice, a block of frozen water, sits in a pan, the molecules that make up the water are all moving about, but they don't have a great deal of energy. They all stay pretty much together so the ice holds its form and keeps its size and shape.

If the ice sits in a warm room, its molecules absorb some heat energy from the air, and their movement speeds up. As they speed up, they change their positions, and the block of ice changes form—it melts and turns into liquid water.

If the pan of water is put on a stove and heated, the molecules speed up even more. They move so fast that they leave the surface of the water and become steam, or water vapor.

Ice, water, and steam are all H_2O. They have the same chemical composition, but they are in different physical states, or conditions. The only difference is the amount of heat energy the H_2O has absorbed.

calorie. The amount of heat energy needed to raise the temperature of one gram of pure water 1°C.

British thermal unit (Btu). The amount of heat energy needed to raise the temperature of one pound of pure water 1°F.

sensible heat. Heat that is added to a liquid that causes a change in its temperature but not its physical state.

latent heat. Heat that is added to a material that causes a change in its state without changing its temperature.

specific heat. The number of Btu's of heat energy needed to change the temperature of one pound of a substance 1°F.

Units of Heat

There are two standard units of heat measurement, the calorie in the metric system and the British thermal unit, or Btu, in the U.S. Customary (U.S.) system. One calorie is the amount of heat energy needed to raise the temperature of one gram of pure water 1°C. One Btu is the amount of heat energy needed to raise the temperature of one pound of water 1°F.

Types of Heat

If a pan of water with a temperature of 80°F is placed on a stove and heated, the water will remain a liquid, but its temperature will increase. This is an example of sensible heat, heat added to a material that causes its temperature to change, but does not change its physical state.

Keep the pan of water on the stove, and its temperature will continue to rise, but only until the water begins to boil. As soon as it begins to boil, or change from a liquid into a vapor, its temperature stops rising.

It takes 970 Btu of heat energy to change one pound of water from a liquid into a vapor. This is called the latent heat of vaporization. When the water changes from a liquid into a vapor, this heat energy remains in it. When the water vapor cools enough to revert into a liquid, this same 970 Btu of heat energy is given up. The heat returned when the water vapor changes into a liquid is called the latent heat of condensation.

Specific heat is the number of Btu of heat energy needed to change the temperature of one pound of a substance 1°F. One Btu of heat energy will raise the temperature of one pound of water 1°F, so water has a specific heat of 1.0.

Refrigerant R-12 has a much lower specific heat. One Btu of heat energy will raise the temperature of 4.6 pounds of R-12 1°F. Its specific heat is 0.217.

Movement of Heat

Heat, like any other kind of energy, always moves from a high level of energy to a lower level. There are three ways this energy can move: by conduction, by convection, and by radiation.

If we touch a hot stove, we get burned. There is a big difference between the amount of heat energy in the stove and the heat energy in our skin. And, since our skin is in direct contact with the hot stove, this heat energy flows directly into our skin and burns it.

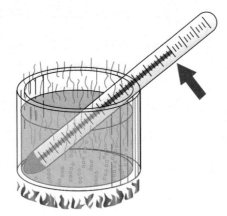

Figure 3-3. *Heat added to a liquid that causes it to change its temperature is called sensible heat.*

Figure 3-4. *Heat absorbed by a liquid as it changes to a gas without changing its temperature is called latent heat.*

The heat from the stove is transferred to our skin by conduction.

Convection is a method in which heat is transferred by vertical currents in a liquid or gas.

All of the water in a pan sitting on a hot stove will eventually become uniformly hot. But only the water on the bottom of the pan in direct contact with the hot metal is heated by conduction.

As this water gets hot, its molecules move faster, the water becomes less dense, and it rises. As it rises, it forces the colder water above it to go down to the bottom. This process continues until all of the water in the pan is heated.

The third way heat can be moved is by radiation. This is the method of heat transfer by electromagnetic waves.

Heat energy causes electromagnetic waves, much like radio waves, to radiate, or spread out, in all directions from an object. These waves can travel through space from one object to another without any contact between the objects, and can travel through a vacuum.

The tremendous amount of heat energy released by the sun reaches the earth by the process of radiation.

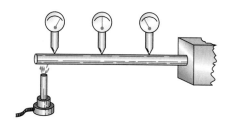

Figure 3-5. *Heat travels along this bar by conduction. The heat moves in the bar from a point of high heat energy to a point of lower heat energy.*

Temperature

Temperature is a measure of the amount of hotness or coldness of an object, and it is a measure of the effect of the heat energy an object has absorbed.

Temperature is measured on a scale that has two practical reference points. One of these is the temperature at which pure water changes from a liquid into a solid. At this point, the water has lost enough heat energy that the moving molecules slow down enough to turn the liquid into a solid. The other is the point at which water has gained enough heat energy to change from a liquid into a vapor. At this point, the molecules have sped up enough that they can no longer remain in liquid form, but they bounce out of the surface and become a gas.

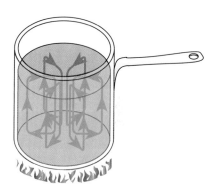

Figure 3-6. *Convection transfers heat through a fluid by vertical currents. Warm liquid is less dense than the colder liquid, and it rises. This forces the colder liquid down so it can be heated.*

Four different scales are used to measure temperature. Two of these scales, Fahrenheit and Celsius, are used in most of our everyday temperature measurements, and the other two, Kelvin and Rankine, are absolute temperature scales used primarily in scientific work.

The Fahrenheit temperature scale has 180 equal divisions between the point at which water freezes and the temperature at which it boils. The point at which water freezes is 32°F, and it boils 180 degrees higher, at 212°F. Absolute zero, or the temperature at which all molecules stop moving, is 460°F below zero or −460°F.

Celsius temperature has 100 equal divisions between the point at which water freezes and the point at which it boils. This is the reason Celsius temperature was formerly called Centigrade (100 graduations) temperature. Water freezes at 0°C and boils at 100°. Absolute zero is −273°C.

Absolute temperature is measured from the point at which all molecular movement stops, and the two absolute scales are used in scientific work.

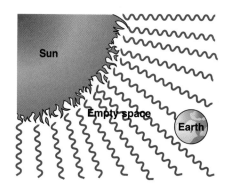

Figure 3-7. *Heat from the sun reaches the earth by radiation. Heat can transfer by radiation even through a vacuum.*

Kelvin temperature uses absolute zero as its zero value, and the divisions are the same as those used in Celsius temperature. Water freezes at 273°K and it boils at 373°K. To convert Celsius to Kelvin, add 273.

°K = °C + 273

For example, find the Kelvin temperature equivalent of 15°C.

°K = 15°C + 273° = 288°K

Rankine temperature also uses absolute zero as its zero value. Its divisions are the same as those used in Fahrenheit temperature. Water freezes at 492°R and boils at 672°R. To convert Fahrenheit to Rankine, add 460.

°R = °F + 460

For example, find the Rankine temperature equivalent of 59°F.

°R = 59°F + 460° = 519°R

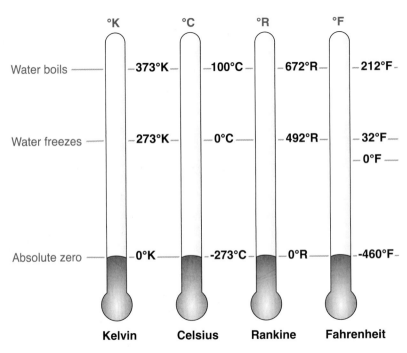

Figure 3-8. *The temperature scales.*

Pressure

Pressure is a measure of the amount of force that acts on a unit of area. It is always measured from a reference, and there are three commonly used references. Absolute pressure is measured from zero pressure, or a vacuum. In the U.S. measurement system it is expressed in terms of pounds per square inch, absolute (psia). Gauge pressure is measured from the existing atmospheric pressure, and is expressed in terms of pounds per square inch, gauge (psig). Differential pressure is the difference between two pressures and is noted as psid.

Units of Pressure

Most of the positive pressures (or pressure greater than that of the atmosphere), used in air conditioning system servicing are measured in pounds per square inch, gauge (psig). A typical high-side pressure gauge is calibrated from zero to about 500 psi.

Negative pressure (or pressure lower than that of the atmosphere), is typically measured in units of inches of mercury (in. Hg) and is called a vacuum. One inch of mercury is the amount of pressure that will hold up a column of mercury one inch high.

The pressure caused by the weight of the atmosphere pressing down on the surface of the earth is 14.69 pounds per square inch, and this much pressure will support a column of mercury 29.92 inches, or 760 millimeters high. This is called one atmosphere of pressure. For quick computations, a pressure of 1 psi is approximately the same as a pressure of 2 in. Hg.

A micron is one thousandth of a millimeter (0.001 mm). A vacuum measured in microns is often spoken of as a "deep vacuum." Its absolute pressure is so low that it will support a column of mercury only a few thousandths of a millimeter high.

micron ("micro meter"). A unit of linear measurement equal to one millionth of a meter, or one thousandth of a millimeter. A micron is also called a micrometer.

STUDY QUESTIONS: THE PHYSICS OF CABIN ATMOSPHERE CONTROL

Answers are provided on page 231.

9. The basic difference between ice, water, and steam is the amount of _____ each contains.

10. The basic unit of heat in the U.S. system is the _____ , and in the metric system it is the _____ .

11. Heat energy that causes a material to change its temperature is called _____ heat.

12. Heat energy that causes a material to change its physical state without changing its temperature is called _____ heat.

13. The two reference points used for measuring temperature are:

    a. _____

    b. _____

14. Absolute zero is the temperature at which there is no _____ motion.

15. The absolute temperature scale that uses the same graduations as the Celsius scale is the _____ scale.

(continued)

16. Pressure that is referenced from zero pressure is called _____ pressure.

17. Pressure that is referenced from the existing atmospheric pressure is called _____ pressure.

18. Pressure that is referenced from another pressure is called _____ pressure.

19. The number of Btu of heat energy needed to change the temperature of one pound of a substance one degree Fahrenheit is called the _____ of the substance.

20. Three methods of heat transfer are:

    a. _____

    b. _____

    c. _____

21. A vacuum is usually measured in units of _____ .

22. A "deep vacuum" is usually measured in units of _____ .

Aircraft Supplemental Oxygen Systems

There are two ways to provide high-flying aircraft with the oxygen needed to sustain life. The cabin can be pressurized to increase the total pressure of the air surrounding the occupants. This raises the partial pressure of the oxygen enough that it can enter the blood stream from the lungs. The other way is to furnish the occupants with supplemental oxygen. When the percentage of oxygen in the air is increased, its partial pressure becomes high enough to force it into the blood.

Types of Oxygen Supply

Oxygen can be carried in an aircraft in four ways: in its gaseous form, in a liquid form, as a solid chemical compound, and in some military aircraft the oxygen is extracted from the air by mechanical methods.

Gaseous Oxygen

Gaseous oxygen is stored in high-pressure steel cylinders that keep the oxygen under a pressure of between 1,800 and 2,400 pounds per square inch. At one time low-pressure oxygen systems were used in which the oxygen was carried in large cylinders under a pressure of 450 psi, but since these cylinders took up so much space in the aircraft, they are no longer used.

Gaseous oxygen has been carried in aircraft since World War I, when it was used by the Germans to allow their fleet of huge lighter-than-air Zeppelins to fly at a higher altitude than possible for British fighter aircraft.

High-flying aircraft between World Wars I and II carried gaseous oxygen in large, low-pressure tanks. In many installations the oxygen was fed to the pilot through a pipestem mouthpiece.

Most of the air battles of World War II were fought at high altitude. Air crews breathed gaseous oxygen from low-pressure cylinders. This oxygen was metered to the masks through continuous-flow or demand-type regulators.

Oxygen used for welding and cutting, for industrial chemical processes, and for hospital and ambulance use is not suited for use in aircraft oxygen systems because of its water content. Just a tiny drop of moisture can freeze in the regulator and shut off the flow of oxygen to the mask. Aircraft oxygen systems must be serviced exclusively with aviators' oxygen that meets military specifications MIL-O-21749 or MIL-O-27210. This oxygen is at least 99.5% pure and contains no more than 0.02 milligram of water per liter at 21.1°C (70°F).

aviators' oxygen. Oxygen that has had all of the water and water vapor removed from it.

Liquid Oxygen

Liquid oxygen (LOX) systems are used in most modern military aircraft because of their efficiency and small space requirements, but they find little application in civilian aircraft because of the special handling LOX requires.

LOX is a pale blue transparent liquid that boils under standard pressure at a temperature of about −180°F. To keep it in its liquid form, it is stored in a vented Dewar bottle, a special double-wall, spherical container made of steel. The inner surfaces of the container's double walls are reflective, which minimizes the transfer of heat by radiation, and all the air is pumped out of the space between the walls to minimize the transfer of heat by conduction.

The expansion rate of LOX is about 862:1. This means that one liter of LOX will produce about 862 liters of gaseous oxygen.

A converter in the oxygen system controls the gaseous oxygen that boils out of the liquid and delivers it to the oxygen regulator at the proper pressure.

Chemical Oxygen Generator

Chemical oxygen generators are used when oxygen is needed only occasionally as it is in smaller general aviation aircraft, or when it is used as an emergency backup in transport aircraft.

The active material, or candle, is made of sodium chlorate ($NaClO_3$) mixed with a binding material and molded into a specially shaped solid block. This candle is installed in a stainless steel case mounted in a heat shield. When oxygen is needed, a spring-loaded firing pin ignites a percussion cap which starts the sodium chlorate burning. As it burns, it releases a useful quantity of oxygen and heat. Insulation and a heat shield prevents the outside of the generator from becoming dangerously hot. Once the candle is ignited, it must burn until it is consumed because there is no way to shut it off.

chemical oxygen generator system. An oxygen system used for emergency or backup purposes. A candle, a solid block of a chemical that releases oxygen when it is burned, is installed in a special fireproof fixture. When oxygen is needed, the candle is ignited by a firing pin striking a percussion cap, and oxygen flows through flexible tubing to the masks.

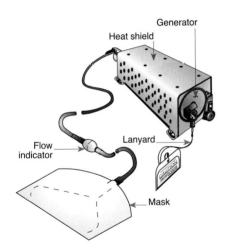

Figure 3-9. *A chemical oxygen generator with a simple rebreather-bag-type mask.*

Chemical oxygen generators are safe to store and handle, are lightweight, and in use they produce very little fire hazard. They have an extremely long shelf life but a time-limited service life.

With the exception of the routine inspection required for security of mounting and general condition, chemical oxygen generators require no attention or servicing until they have been used or their expiration date has been reached. When they are removed from an aircraft their firing pins must be covered with the appropriate caps, and any time they are to be transported, they must be properly packed and marked in such a way that identifies them as hazardous materials.

Chemical oxygen generator systems have the following characteristics:

- Once the candle is ignited, it releases oxygen at a predetermined rate which cannot be shut off or changed until the candle is exhausted.

- The storage capacity is about three times that of a gaseous oxygen system of the same weight.

- The system generators are inert below about 400°F even under severe impact.

- The distributing and regulating system is self-contained. It consists of a stainless steel cylinder attached to manifolded hose nipples, which contain orifices that ensure an equal flow to all masks.

Mechanically Separated Oxygen

The fire hazard of manufacturing and storing liquid oxygen aboard aircraft carriers and the difficulty of providing liquid oxygen at forward locations during battle conditions led the military services to study other ways of supplying oxygen for flight crews. One method that overcomes the dangers inherent with both high-pressure gaseous oxygen and liquid oxygen is mechanically separated breathing oxygen. This system is called OBOGS, or Onboard Oxygen Generating System.

The air we breathe is a physical mixture rather than a chemical compound, and its constituents, oxygen, nitrogen, and the traces of other gases, all have different physical characteristics. A patented material called a "molecular sieve" will pass oxygen, but effectively blocks nitrogen and the other gases. Compressor bleed air from the turbine engine is directed through containers of molecular sieve material, and only oxygen passes through it to the oxygen regulator. Part of the oxygen that passes through the sieve material is used to regularly back-flush the container and force all of the nitrogen and other gases out of the system.

Mechanically separated oxygen is used for many medical applications, and its use in aircraft is sure to increase.

Two Types of Oxygen Systems

Most small general aviation aircraft only require oxygen occasionally, and use a system that meters a continuous flow of oxygen whose amount is based on the altitude flown. Aircraft that regularly fly at altitudes above 18,000 feet typically have a diluter-demand system that meters oxygen based on the altitude flown, but directs it to the mask only when the user inhales. Aircraft that fly at very high altitudes, where the outside air pressure is too low to force oxygen into the lungs, use pressure-demand systems. These systems send oxygen to the mask under a slight positive pressure that forces it into the lungs.

Continuous-Flow Oxygen System

Continuous-flow systems, such as the one in Figure 3-10, are usually used in passenger oxygen systems and systems where oxygen is needed only occasionally. These systems are wasteful of oxygen, but because of their simplicity, they are the type installed in most small general aviation aircraft.

Unpressurized aircraft that fly at high altitudes may have a continuous-flow oxygen system for the passengers and a diluter-demand or pressure-demand system for the pilots.

The oxygen is carried in a steel, high-pressure bottle. The pressure is reduced from that in the bottle to between 300 and 400 psi by a pressure reducing valve, and the oxygen metered by a pressure regulator before it is delivered to the masks. A pressure relief valve is incorporated in the system to prevent damage in the event of a failure of the pressure reducing valve. If the pressure is relieved by the relief valve, a green "blowout" disk on the outside of the aircraft will blow out.

continuous-flow oxygen system. A type of oxygen system that allows a metered amount of oxygen to continuously flow into the mask. A rebreather-type mask is used with a continuous-flow system. The simplest form of continuous-flow oxygen systems regulates the flow by a calibrated orifice in the outlet to the mask, but most systems use either a manual or automatic regulator to vary the pressure across the orifice proportional to the altitude being flown.

pressure reducing valve. A valve used in an oxygen system to change high cylinder pressure to low system pressure.

pressure relief valve. A valve in an oxygen system that relieves the pressure if the pressure reducing valve should fail.

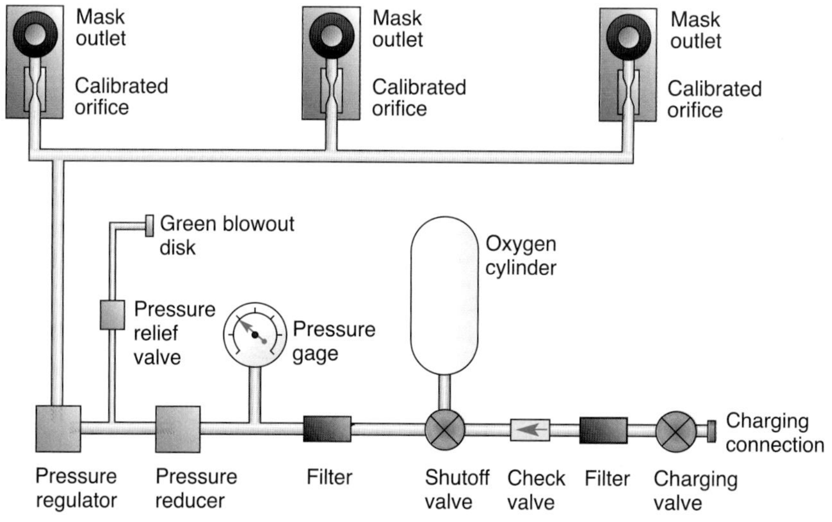

Figure 3-10. *A typical continuous-flow oxygen system.*

therapeutic mask adapter. A calibrated orifice in the mask adapter for a continuous-flow oxygen system that increases the flow of oxygen to a mask being used by a passenger who is known to have a heart or respiratory problem.

rebreather oxygen mask. A type of oxygen mask used with a continuous-flow system. Oxygen continuously flows into the bottom of the loose-fitting rebreather bag on the mask. The wearer of the mask exhales into the top of the bag. The first air exhaled contains some oxygen, and this air goes into the bag first. The last air to leave the lungs contains little oxygen, and it is forced out of the bag as the bag is filled with fresh oxygen. Each time the wearer of the mask inhales, the air first exhaled, along with fresh oxygen, is taken into the lungs.

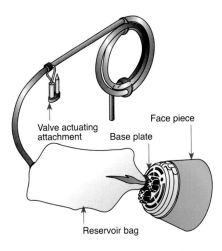

Figure 3-11. *Passenger oxygen mask.*

Continuous-Flow Regulators

There are automatic and manual continuous-flow oxygen regulators. The automatic regulator contains an aneroid that senses the altitude the aircraft is flying and meters the correct amount of oxygen accordingly. The manual regulator has a control that allows the pilot to adjust the flow based on the altitude of flight.

A calibrated orifice in the mask outlet determines the amount of oxygen the regulator delivers to the mask. The orifice for the pilot's mask usually meters more oxygen than those for the passenger masks, and some oxygen systems have provisions for a therapeutic mask outlet for passengers who have difficulty breathing or who have a known heart problem. The orifice in a therapeutic outlet allows approximately twice the normal flow.

Continuous-Flow Masks

Continuous-flow oxygen systems use rebreather-type oxygen masks. These masks may be as simple as a transparent plastic rebreather bag like the one in Figure 3-9. This mask is held loosely over the mouth and nose with an elastic band, and oxygen continuously flows into the bottom of the bag through a plastic hose that is plugged into the mask outlet.

When the user exhales, the air that was in the lungs for the shortest period of time is the first out, and it fills the bag. The last air expelled from the lungs has the least oxygen in it, and by the time it is exhaled, the bag is full and it spills out of the mask. When the user inhales, the first air to enter the bag, now enriched with pure oxygen, is rebreathed.

More sophisticated continuous-flow masks are used in pressurized aircraft. In the event of the loss of cabin pressure, an automatic turn-on valve sends oxygen into the passenger oxygen system. See Figure 3-13 on page 192. The oxygen pressure actuates the door actuator valve, which opens the door to the overhead mask compartment. A mask of the type in Figure 3-11 drops down. The passenger pulls on the mask tube, which opens the rotary, lanyard-operated valve and starts the flow of oxygen. The passenger then places the cup over his or her mouth and nose and breathes normally. Valves mounted in the base plate of the mask allow some cabin air to enter the mask and allow the air that has been exhaled from the lungs to leave it. At the beginning of the inhale, the pure oxygen from the bag is taken into the lungs. When the bag is empty, cabin air is taken in through one of the mask valves and mixes with oxygen flowing through the tube. The pure oxygen that is taken in first fills most of the lungs and is absorbed into the blood, and the diluted oxygen fills only that part of the respiratory system where no absorption takes place.

During the exhale, the air from the lungs leaves the mask through one of the valves while pure oxygen is flowing from the regulator into the reservoir bag to be ready for the next inhale.

Demand-Type Oxygen System

The cockpit crew of most commercial aircraft are supplied with oxygen through a diluter-demand system. This system meters oxygen only when the user inhales, and the amount of oxygen metered depends upon the altitude being flown. Figure 3-12 is a simplified diagram of a typical demand-type oxygen system.

Almost all pressurized turbine-powered aircraft have a demand-type oxygen system for the flight crew and a continuous-flow system as a backup for the passengers. Figure 3-13 shows this system. Two oxygen cylinders are installed in the aircraft, and selector valves allow either cylinder to supply the crew or the passengers.

Diluter-Demand-Type Regulator

Figure 3-14 shows a typical diluter-demand-type oxygen regulator, and Figure 3-15 shows the way this regulator operates.

For normal operation, the Supply lever is in the ON position, the Oxygen lever is in the NORMAL position, and the Emergency lever is OFF. Oxygen flows into the regulator through the supply valve, and when the user inhales, the pressure inside the regulator decreases and the demand valve opens, allowing oxygen to flow to the mask.

diluter-demand oxygen system. A popular type of oxygen system in which the oxygen is metered to the mask where it is diluted with cabin air by an airflow-metering aneroid assembly which regulates the amount of air allowed to dilute the oxygen on the basis of cabin altitude. The mixture of oxygen and air flows only when the wearer of the mask inhales. The percentage of oxygen in the air delivered to the mask is regulated, on the basis of altitude, by the regulator. A diluter-demand regulator has an emergency position which allows 100% oxygen to flow to the mask, bypassing the regulating mechanism.

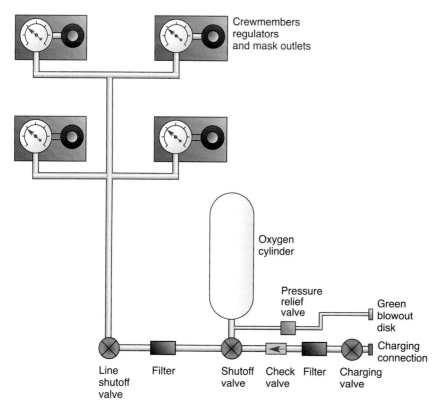

Figure 3-12. *A typical demand-type oxygen system.*

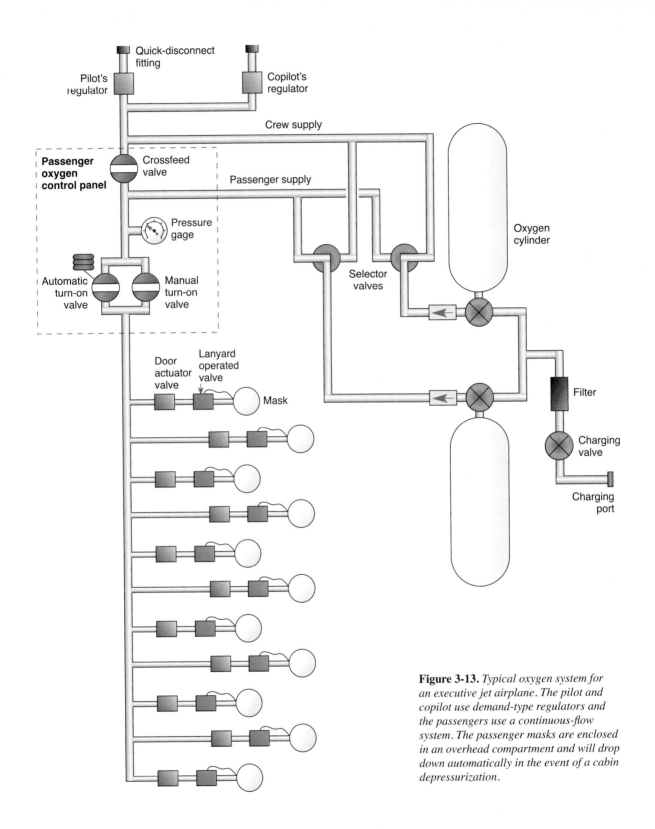

Figure 3-13. *Typical oxygen system for an executive jet airplane. The pilot and copilot use demand-type regulators and the passengers use a continuous-flow system. The passenger masks are enclosed in an overhead compartment and will drop down automatically in the event of a cabin depressurization.*

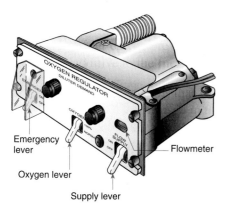

Figure 3-14. *A typical diluter-demand oxygen regulator.*

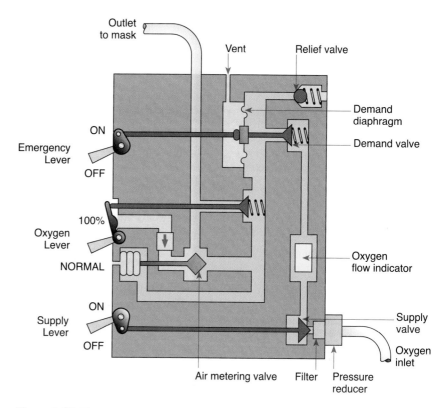

Figure 3-15. *The operational schematic of a diluter-demand oxygen regulator.*

The aneroid-operated air metering valve mixes cabin air with the oxygen. When the aircraft is flying at low altitudes, the user gets mostly cabin air and a small amount of oxygen. As the altitude increases, the aneroid progressively shuts off the cabin air and opens the oxygen line until, at approximately 34,000 feet, the cabin air is completely shut off and the mask receives 100% oxygen.

If there is smoke in the cockpit, or if the user feels a need for pure oxygen, the oxygen lever can be moved to the 100% position. The cabin air will be shut off from the regulator and only pure oxygen taken into the mask when the user inhales.

If the regulator malfunctions, the emergency lever can be placed in the ON position. This opens the demand valve and pure oxygen flows continually to the mask.

Pressure-Demand Oxygen Regulator

At altitudes above 40,000 feet the oxygen in the air has such a low partial pressure that even 100% oxygen must be forced into the lungs under a slight positive pressure from the regulator. Aircraft that operate at this altitude are equipped with pressure-demand regulators.

aneroid. An evacuated and sealed metallic bellows that is used as a pressure measuring element for absolute pressure.

pressure-demand oxygen system. A type of oxygen system used by aircraft that fly at very high altitude. This system functions as a diluter-demand system (*See* diluter-demand oxygen system) until, at about 40,000 feet, the output to the mask is pressurized enough to force the needed oxygen into the lungs, rather than depending on the low pressure produced when the wearer of the mask inhales to pull in the oxygen.

A pressure-demand regulator looks much like a diluter-demand regulator, but at altitudes above 40,000 feet, it supplies oxygen to the mask under a low positive pressure rather than depending upon the low pressure from the user's lungs to pull in the oxygen.

Gaseous Oxygen Cylinders

High-pressure oxygen cylinders, or bottles, carried in modern aircraft may be made of either heat-treated steel or Kevlar-wrapped aluminum alloy. They are painted green and have the words AVIATORS OXYGEN stenciled in letters one inch high.

These bottles must meet either ICC or DOT specification 3AA 1800 for the standard bottle or 3HT 1850 for the lightweight bottle. The specification number must be stamped on the bottle.

All oxygen bottles carried in aircraft must be hydrostatically tested within the required time interval. DOT 3AA 3000 cylinders must be tested to ⅔ of their working pressure every five years. DOT 3AA 1800 cylinders that meet the Department of Transportation (DOT) requirements spelled out in 49 CFR 173.34(e)(16) need be tested only every 10 years.

Lightweight cylinders, DOT 3HT 1850 must be hydrostatically tested every three years and must be retired from service after 24 years or 4,380 pressurizations, whichever occurs first. The date of the hydrostatic test must be stamped on the cylinder, near its neck.

Never let oxygen bottles become empty, nor let their pressure drop below about 50 psi. When the cylinder is empty, air containing water vapor may enter it and cause corrosion inside, where it is difficult to detect.

Up through World War II, oxygen was carried in low-pressure bottles. These steel bottles are much larger than the high-pressure bottles and are painted yellow. Oxygen inside them is under a pressure of approximately 450 psi.

Oxygen System Servicing

Servicing a gaseous oxygen system, though not complicated, requires strict attention to details and must be done in direct accordance with the instructions furnished by the aircraft manufacturer. Servicing consists of filling the system, purging it of all air, and checking the system for leaks.

Oxygen System Filling

Most oxygen systems are filled from an oxygen service cart similar to the one in Figure 3-16. This cart contains several oxygen bottles along with the necessary valves, gauges, service hoses, and an oxygen purifier. Some oxygen carts also carry bottles of compressed nitrogen. The valves of nitrogen bottles face in the opposite direction, to prevent the accidental connection of a nitrogen bottle into the oxygen system.

To fill an oxygen system, first purge the service line of all air by releasing some oxygen through it. Then connect it to the aircraft filler valve. Open the

hydrostatic test. A pressure test used to determine the serviceability of high-pressure oxygen cylinders. The cylinders are filled with water and pressurized to ⅔ of their working pressure. Standard-weight cylinders must be hydrostatically tested every five years, and lightweight cylinders (DOT 3HT) must be tested every three years.

lowest pressure bottle on the service cart and let it flow into the aircraft system until the system pressure reaches that in the bottle. Shut this bottle valve and then open the valve on the bottle with the next higher pressure.

The ambient temperature determines the final pressure required by the aircraft system. A pressure-temperature chart for each type of oxygen bottle should be on the service cart. Figure 3-17 is a typical pressure-temperature chart. If the ambient temperature is 90°F, the system should be charged until the pressure gauge reads 2,000 psi. When the temperature of the oxygen stabilizes, its pressure should be approximately 1,800 psi at 70°F.

Ambient Temperature °F	Filling Pressure For	
	1,800 psi At 70°F	1,850 psi At 70°F
0	1,600	1,650
10	1,650	1,700
20	1,675	1,725
30	1,725	1,775
40	1,775	1,825
50	1,825	1,875
60	1,875	1,925
70	1,925	1,975
80	1,950	2,000
90	2,000	2,050
100	2,050	2,100
110	2,100	2,150
120	2,150	2,200
130	2,200	2,250

Figure 3-17. *Pressure-temperature chart for filling an oxygen cylinder.*

ambient temperature. The temperature of the air surrounding a person or an object.

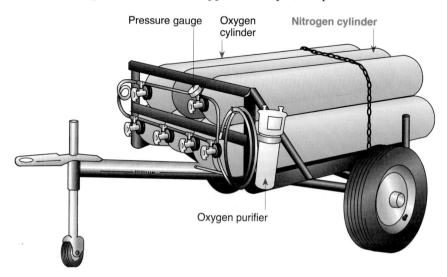

Pressure gauge   Oxygen cylinder   Nitrogen cylinder

Oxygen purifier

Figure 3-16. *A typical gaseous oxygen servicing trailer.*

Purging

If an oxygen system is opened and air has gotten into the lines, charge the system and purge it by letting oxygen flow through all the lines and masks for about ten minutes, until all the contaminating air has been removed.

purge. To remove all of the moisture and air from a cooling system by flushing the system with a dry gaseous refrigerant.

Leak Checking

If a loss of oxygen indicates a leak in the system, check the fittings by spreading a special nonpetroleum soap solution over all suspected areas and watching for bubbles. When you find a leak, release the pressure from the system before tightening any fittings.

Oxygen System Inspections

Chemical Oxygen Generator Systems

Inspect for security of mounting and general condition. Verify that the expiration date has not been exceeded and that the time remaining will be sufficient to reach the next scheduled inspection of the oxygen system.

Gaseous Oxygen Systems

Inspect the system on a regular basis in accordance with the aircraft maintenance instructions. Visually inspect all regulators, lines, and outlets for security of attachment and operation. Take a careful look at the masks, hoses, and fittings for condition. Plug the masks into the oxygen outlets to verify the flow of oxygen and clean the masks as required. Some masks used by the flight crew have microphones built into the masks. Check the microphones for operation. A quick-don mask is one that is stored or suspended close to the cockpit crew so that it can be accessed quickly. Check the storage quick release mechanism for operation and inspect the masks, hoses and regulators for condition and security.

Inspect the oxygen bottle, regulator, ON-OFF valve, and service lines and ports for security and condition. Actuate the ON-OFF valve from the cockpit and verify proper operation. Visually inspect servicing lines and ports for condition and security. Note and record the date of the last hydrostatic test that is stamped near the neck of the oxygen cylinder and re-test, as necessary. Verify the system is serviced to the proper pressure.

System Discharge Indication

The pressure relief valve in an installed gaseous oxygen system vents to a blowout plug on the side of the fuselage. If, for any reason, the pressure builds up in the system enough to open the pressure relief valve, the green disk over the outlet will blow out, showing that the oxygen system has discharged.

Special Precautions

Never use petroleum products on oxygen systems; there is a fire danger. The oxygen will react with oil or grease and produce enough heat to cause a fire. Never lubricate threaded fittings used in oxygen systems with any type of thread lubricant that contains petroleum. Teflon tape is generally approved to seal tapered pipe thread connections in an oxygen system, and a special water-base lubricant is used for other applications.

Fire Safety

Oxygen itself will not burn, but because it supports the combustion of other products, you should observe special safety precautions when working with oxygen. Some of these are:

1. Display "No Smoking" placards when an oxygen system is being serviced.

2. Provide adequate fire-fighting equipment in the immediate vicinity of the servicing.

3. Keep all tools and oxygen-servicing equipment free from oil or grease.

4. Avoid checking aircraft radio or electrical systems during the servicing operation.

Answers are provided on page 231.

23. When oxygen is needed for a backup in a pressurized aircraft the _____ system is used because of its simplicity, efficiency, and minimum maintenance required.

24. Aviators' oxygen is different from hospital oxygen because of its low _____ content.

25. The type of contaminant most generally found in gaseous oxygen systems is _____ .

26. In the onboard oxygen generating system (OBOGS), engine compressor bleed air flows through beds of a _____ material that mechanically filters the oxygen from the nitrogen and other constituents of the air.

27. The rate of release of the oxygen from a chemical oxygen generator system _____ (may or may not) be adjusted for the altitude flow.

28. The generators used in a chemical oxygen generator system are inert below _____°F even under a severe impact.

29. Supplemental oxygen is normally provided for passengers of a pressurized aircraft by the _____ (continuous-flow or demand)-type system.

30. In a continuous-flow oxygen system, the pressure of the oxygen in the high-pressure cylinder is reduced before it goes to the regulator by a/an _____ valve.

31. If the pressure reducer valve in a continuous-flow oxygen system should malfunction, a _____ valve will prevent damage to the system.

32. Two types of regulators that may be used in a continuous-flow oxygen system are _____ and _____ regulators.

33. The amount of oxygen a regulator will deliver to flow to a continuous-flow mask is determined by a _____ in the mask outlet.

34. The continuous-flow oxygen mask worn by a person with a known respiratory or heart problem should receive its oxygen from a _____ mask outlet.

35. A rebreather-bag-type oxygen mask is used with a _____ (continuous-flow or demand)-type oxygen system.

36. The cockpit crew of a pressurized aircraft normally have their supplemental oxygen supplied by a _____ (continuous-flow or demand)-type oxygen system.

(continued)

37. A diluter-demand oxygen regulator dilutes the oxygen it meters at the lower altitudes with _____ .

38. The demand valve on a diluter-demand oxygen regulator opens each time the wearer of the mask _____ .

39. High-pressure oxygen cylinders installed in an aircraft must meet the specifications of the _____ _____ or the _____ .

40. Oxygen cylinders are required to be _____ tested periodically and the date of the test stamped on it.

41. Standard high-pressure oxygen cylinders should be hydrostatically tested every _____ years.

42. Lightweight high-pressure oxygen cylinders should be hydrostatically tested every _____ years.

43. A lightweight high-pressure oxygen cylinder should be hydrostatically tested to a pressure of _____ psi.

44. A lightweight high-pressure oxygen cylinder should be retired from service after _____ years.

45. The pressure inside an oxygen bottle should never be allowed to drop below _____ psi.

46. High-pressure oxygen bottles are painted _____ .

47. Low-pressure oxygen bottles are painted _____ .

48. The amount of oxygen in a gaseous oxygen bottle is indicated by its _____ .

49. If a gaseous oxygen system is to be charged to 1,850 psi at 70°F when the ambient temperature is 60°F, the filling pressure should be _____ psi.

50. Any time an oxygen system has been opened, it should be purged for about _____ minutes to remove all of the air from the oxygen lines.

51. Thread lubricants used with oxygen system components must contain no _____ .

52. Leaks in an oxygen system are located by spreading a _____ soap solution over the suspected area and watching for bubbles.

53. A blowout plug on the side of the fuselage will be blown out if the oxygen system has been discharged through the _____ .

54. Thread lubricants approved for use in an oxygen system have a/an _____ base.

Aircraft Pressurization Systems

Although high altitude is a hostile environment in which the human body cannot subsist without a great deal of help, it is the ideal environment for high-speed flight. Turbine engines operate efficiently and the resistance caused by the low density air decreases drag. The humidity is low at high altitude, so weather conditions are excellent.

As early as the 1850s the American balloonist John Wise predicted that at high altitudes there was a fast moving "great river of air that could not only sweep him across the Atlantic ocean, but on around the world."

In the 1920s the U.S. Army Air Service experimented with pressurized flight. They built an oval steel tank in the cockpit of an airplane. There was a glass port through which the pilot could see, and the airplane controls were built into the tank. The tank was pressurized by a gear-driven supercharger, and the pilot was able to control an exhaust valve manually to maintain the pressure at the required level. An airplane flew with this system in 1921, but the experiment proved unsuccessful.

In 1934, Wiley Post, who had already proven his aeronautical expertise by flying twice around the world, once by himself, began to experiment with a pressure suit that would let him take advantage of high-altitude flight. Post's suit was made of rubberized fabric and topped with an aluminum helmet with a round porthole for him to see through. The suit was pressurized with air from the engine supercharger through two lines. One line ran direct, and the other wrapped around one of the exhaust stacks to pick up heat. The temperature inside the suit was controlled by metering the air from the two lines with needle valves. A liquid oxygen generator provided oxygen in the event of engine or supercharger failure.

Post's suit let him attain an altitude of 48,000 feet. He proved the existence of high-velocity winds at these altitudes, and his efforts spurred further study and development.

In 1936 Lockheed made a special version of their Model 10 Electra with a fully pressurized cabin. This airplane was powered by two turbosupercharged engines and was able to make flights to an altitude of 25,000 feet. The cabin altitude was maintained at 10,000 feet or less. The developments made by this airplane and the potential it created earned it the Collier trophy for the most valuable contribution to aircraft development in 1937.

In 1940, Transcontinental and Western Air put the Boeing 307B into service. This was the first airliner to have a fully pressurized cabin. Today all airliners and many general aviation aircraft are pressurized.

Principles of Pressurization

Aircraft are pressurized by sealing off a strengthened portion of the fuselage, called the pressure vessel, and pumping air into it. The cabin pressure is controlled by an outflow valve, usually located at the rear of the pressure vessel. The opening of this valve is controlled by the cabin pressure controller to regulate the amount of air allowed to leave the cabin.

Sources of Pressurization Air

Pressurization systems do not have to move a huge volume of air. Their function is to raise the pressure of the air inside closed containers. Small reciprocating-engine-powered aircraft receive their pressurization air from the compressor of the engine turbocharger. Large reciprocating-engine-powered aircraft have engine-driven air compressors to provide pressurization air, and turbine-powered aircraft use engine compressor bleed air.

Reciprocating-Engine-Powered Aircraft

Turbochargers are driven by engine exhaust gases flowing through a turbine. A centrifugal air compressor is connected to the turbine shaft. The compressor's output goes to the engine's cylinders to increase the manifold pressure and let the engine develop its power at altitude. Part of the compressed air is tapped off between the turbocharger and the engine and used to pressurize the cabin. This air passes through a sonic venturi, or flow limiter, and then through an intercooler into the cabin. See Figure 3-18.

Large reciprocating-engine-powered transports use either a positive-displacement Roots blower-type air compressor or a variable-displacement centrifugal compressor driven by the engine through an accessory drive or by an electric or hydraulic motor.

These large multi-engine airplanes have more than one cabin air compressor, and they are connected together through a delivery-air-duct check valve, or isolation valve, that prevents the loss of pressurization through a disengaged compressor.

Turbine-Engine-Powered Aircraft

Usually the air bled from a gas turbine engine compressor is free from contamination and can be used safely for cabin pressurization, but some aircraft use independent cabin compressors driven by compressor bleed air. See Figure 3-19 on page 202.

Some aircraft use a jet pump flow multiplier to increase the amount of air taken into the cabin. The jet pump is essentially a special venturi inside a line from the outside of the aircraft, like the one in Figure 3-20. A nozzle blows a stream of high-velocity compressor bleed air into the throat of the venturi, and this produces a low pressure that draws air in from the outside. This is mixed with the compressor bleed air and carried into the aircraft cabin.

---

pressure vessel. The strengthened portion of an aircraft structure that is sealed and pressurized in flight.

outflow valve. A valve in the cabin of a pressurized aircraft that controls the cabin pressure by opening to relieve all pressure above that for which the cabin pressure control is set. The outflow valve is controlled by the cabin pressure controller and it maintains the desired cabin pressure.

sonic venturi. A venturi in a line between a turbine engine or turbocharger and a pressurization system. When the air flowing through the venturi reaches the speed of sound, a shock wave forms across the throat of the venturi and limits the flow. A sonic venturi is also called a flow limiter.

Roots-type air compressor. A positive-displacement air pump that uses two intermeshing figure-8-shaped rotors to move the air.

jet pump. A special venturi in a line carrying air from certain areas in an aircraft that need an augmented flow of air through them. High-velocity compressor bleed air is blown into the throat of a venturi where it produces a low pressure that pulls air from the area to which it is connected. Jet pumps are often used in the lines that pull air through galleys and toilet areas.

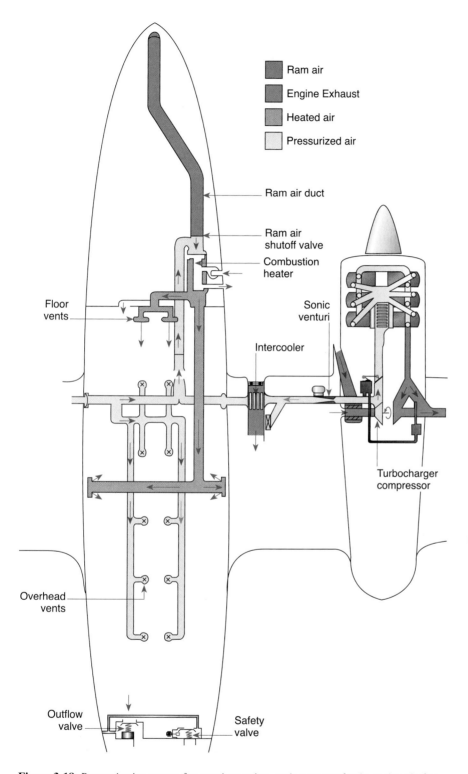

Figure 3-18. *Pressurization system for a reciprocating-engine-powered twin-engine airplane.*

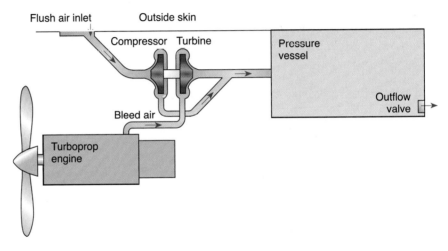

Figure 3-19. *Pressurization system of a turboprop airplane that uses compressor bleed air to drive a flow multiplier.*

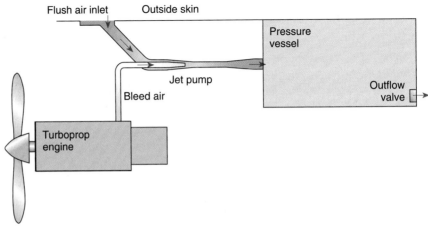

Figure 3-20. *A jet pump flow multiplier increases the air available for cabin pressurization.*

constant-differential mode. The mode of pressurization in which the cabin pressure is maintained a constant amount higher than the outside air pressure. The maximum differential pressure is determined by the structural strength of the aircraft cabin.

Modes of Pressurization

There are three modes of pressurization: the unpressurized mode, the isobaric mode, and the constant-differential mode. In the unpressurized mode, the cabin altitude is always the same as the flight altitude. In the isobaric mode, the cabin altitude remains constant as the flight altitude changes, and in the constant-differential mode, the cabin pressure is maintained a constant amount above that of the outside air pressure. This amount of differential pressure is determined by the structural strength of the pressure vessel.

The Unpressurized Mode

In the unpressurized mode, the outflow valve remains open and the cabin pressure is the same as the ambient air pressure.

The Isobaric Mode

In the isobaric mode, the cabin pressure is maintained at a specific cabin altitude as flight altitude changes. The cabin pressure controller begins to close the outflow valve at a chosen cabin altitude. The outflow valve opens and closes, or modulates, to maintain the selected cabin altitude as the flight altitude changes. The controller will maintain the selected cabin altitude up to the flight altitude that produces the maximum differential pressure for which the aircraft structure is rated.

The Constant-Differential Mode

Cabin pressurization puts the structure of an aircraft fuselage under a tensile stress as the pressure inside the pressure vessel tries to expand it. The cabin differential pressure, expressed in psid, is the ratio between the internal and external air pressure and is a measure of the stress on the fuselage. The greater the differential pressure, the greater the stress.

When the cabin differential pressure reaches the maximum for which the aircraft structure is designed, the cabin pressure controller automatically shifts to the constant-differential mode and allows the cabin altitude to increase, but maintains the maximum allowable pressure differential.

Pressurization Controls

The pressurization controller in Figure 3-21 provides the control signals for a typical pressurization system. The dial is graduated in cabin altitude up to approximately 10,000 feet. One knob sets the desired cabin altitude, another corrects the barometric scale, and the third knob sets the cabin rate of climb.

Pressurization Instruments

The main instruments used with a pressurization system are shown in Figure 3-22. These are a cabin rate-of-climb indicator and a combination cabin altitude and differential pressure gauge.

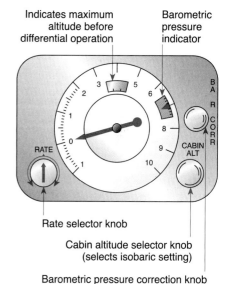

Indicates maximum altitude before differential operation

Barometric pressure indicator

Rate selector knob

Cabin altitude selector knob (selects isobaric setting)

Barometric pressure correction knob

Figure 3-21. *Typical cabin pressurization controller.*

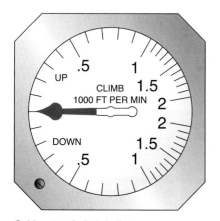

Cabin rate-of-climb indicator

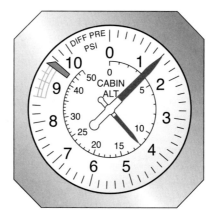

Combination cabin altimeter and differential pressure gage

Figure 3-22. *Typical instruments used with a cabin pressurization system.*

Cabin Air Pressure Regulator

The cabin pressure regulator maintains cabin altitude at a selected level in the isobaric range and limits cabin pressure to a preset differential value in the differential range by regulating the position of the cabin outflow valve. Normal operation of the regulator requires only the selection of the desired cabin altitude, the adjustment of the barometric scale, and the selection of the desired cabin rate of climb.

The regulator in Figure 3-23 is a typical differential-pressure-type regulator that is built into the normally closed, pneumatically operated outflow valve. It uses cabin altitude for its isobaric control and barometric pressure for the differential range of control. A cabin rate-of-climb controller controls the rate of pressure change inside the cabin.

There are two principal sections of this regulator: the head and reference chamber section, and the outflow valve and diaphragm section.

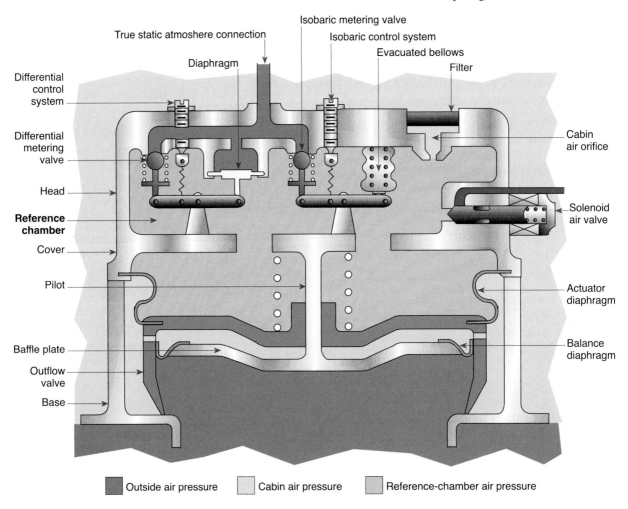

Figure 3-23. *A typical cabin pressure regulator.*

The balance diaphragm extends outward from the baffle plate to the outflow valve, creating a pneumatic chamber between the fixed baffle plate and the inner face of the outflow valve. Cabin air flowing into this chamber through holes in the side of the outflow valve exerts a force against the inner face of the valve that tries to open it. This force is opposed by the force of the spring around the valve pilot that tries to hold the outflow valve closed.

The actuator diaphragm extends outward from the outflow valve to the cover assembly, creating a pneumatic chamber between the cover and the outer face of the outflow valve. Air from the head and reference chamber section flows through holes in the cover, filling this chamber, exerting a force against the outer face of the outflow valve and helping the spring hold the valve closed.

The position of the outflow valve controls the amount of cabin air allowed to leave the pressure vessel, and this controls the cabin pressure. The position of the outflow valve is determined by the amount of reference-chamber air pressure (cabin air pressure) that presses on the outer face of the outflow valve.

Isobaric Control

The isobaric system of the cabin pressure regulator in Figure 3-23 incorporates an evacuated bellows, a rocker arm, a follower spring, and a ball-type isobaric metering valve. One end of the rocker arm is connected to the head by the evacuated bellows, and the other end of the arm holds the metering valve in a closed position against a passage in the head. A follower spring between the metering valve seat and a retainer on the valve causes the valve to move away from its seat as far as the rocker arm permits.

When the cabin pressure increases enough for the reference-chamber air pressure to compress the bellows, the rocker arm pivots about its fulcrum and allows the metering valve to move away from its seat an amount proportional to the compression of the bellows. When the metering valve opens, reference-chamber air flows from the regulator to the atmosphere through the true static atmosphere connection.

When the regulator is operating in the isobaric range, cabin pressure is held constant by reducing the flow of reference-chamber air through the metering valve. This prevents a further decrease in the reference pressure.

The isobaric control system responds to slight changes in reference-chamber pressure by modulating to maintain a substantially constant pressure in the chamber throughout the isobaric range of operation.

Anytime an increase in cabin pressure causes the isobaric metering valve to move toward the OPEN position, the reference pressure decreases and the outflow valve opens, decreasing the cabin pressure.

Differential Control

The differential control system incorporates a diaphragm, a rocker arm, a differential metering valve, and a follower spring. One end of the rocker arm is attached to the head by the diaphragm which forms a pressure-sensitive face between the reference chamber and a small chamber in the head. This small chamber is opened to atmosphere through a passage to the true static atmosphere connection.

Atmospheric pressure acts on one side of the diaphragm, and reference-chamber pressure acts on the other side. The opposite end of the rocker arm holds the metering valve in a closed position against a passage in the head. A follower spring between the metering valve seat and a retainer on the valve causes the valve to move away from its seat the amount the rocker arm allows.

When reference-chamber pressure becomes enough greater than the decreasing atmospheric pressure that it moves the diaphragm, the metering valve moves away from its seat an amount proportional to the movement of the diaphragm. When the metering valve opens, reference-chamber air flows to the atmosphere through the true static atmosphere connection and reduces the reference pressure. This causes the outflow valve to open and decrease the cabin pressure.

Cabin Rate of Climb

The cabin rate control determines the rate of pressure change inside the cabin by controlling the speed with which the outflow valve closes. If the cabin pressure is changing too rapidly (the cabin rate of climb is too great) the rate controller knob can be turned back to close the outflow valve faster.

Negative-Pressure Relief Valve

negative pressure relief valve. A valve that opens anytime the outside air pressure is greater than the cabin pressure. It prevents the cabin altitude ever becoming greater than the aircraft flight altitude.

A pressurized aircraft structure is designed to operate with the cabin pressure higher than the outside air pressure. If the cabin pressure were to become lower than the outside air pressure, the cabin structure could fail. Because of this design feature, all pressurized aircraft require some form of negative pressure relief valve that opens when the outside air pressure is greater than the cabin pressure.

The negative-pressure relief valve may be incorporated into the outflow valve, or it may be a separate unit.

Cabin Air Pressure Safety Valve

The cabin air pressure safety valve is a combination pressure relief, vacuum relief, and dump valve.

ambient pressure. The pressure of the air surrounding a person or an object.

The pressure relief valve prevents cabin pressure from exceeding a predetermined differential pressure above the ambient pressure.

The vacuum relief valve prevents ambient pressure from exceeding cabin pressure by allowing external air to enter the cabin when the ambient pressure is greater than the cabin pressure.

The dump valve is actuated by a switch in the cockpit. When the switch is in the ram, or auxiliary-ventilation, position, the solenoid air valve opens, dumping cabin air to the atmosphere. If the auxiliary ventilation position is selected while in cruising flight, the cabin pressurization will be dumped and the cabin pressure will decrease—the cabin altitude will rapidly increase until it is the same as the flight altitude.

The dump valve is also controlled by a squat switch on the landing gear so it will open when the aircraft is on the ground. This removes all positive pressure from the cabin and prevents the cabin from being pressurized when the aircraft is on the ground.

Augmented Airflow

Some aircraft use a jet pump (essentially a special venturi) in a line carrying air from certain areas that need increased airflow. Jet pumps are often used in the lines that pull air through galleys and toilet areas.

A nozzle blows a stream of high-velocity compressor bleed air into the throat of the venturi. This increases the velocity of the air flowing through the venturi and produces low pressure, which pulls air from the compartment to which it is connected.

Electronic Pressurization Controls

Most of the new generation aircraft use electronic controls to set the position of the outflow valves. These valves are opened or closed by AC or DC electric motors rather than by pneumatic pressure.

The signals to operate the outflow valves come from the pressure controller which can be set to operate in AUTO, STANDBY, or MANUAL mode. Normal operation is the automatic (AUTO) mode with other modes used for backup operation.

Pressurization System Checks

Pressurization systems on different aircraft may have similar components but the actual system operation could be quite different. Always follow the manufacturer's service instructions for operational checks, inspections, and troubleshooting. Specialized equipment and test boxes are required for some aircraft, while others may be pressurized by running the engines on the ground using special procedures. After maintenance is performed on the system, a flight test may be required to check all aspects of operation.

Pressurization System Maintenance

An often-neglected part of maintaining a pressurization system is the cleaning of seals and bellows. Follow the aircraft manual service instructions for determining the proper cleaning solution and carefully clean the seals on all doors, windows, emergency exits, outflow valves, and safety valves. In some cases, an additional conditioner may be recommended to extend the life and flexibility of the seals. A spray bottle with the specified cleaning solution can be used to spray into areas that are difficult to reach. This is often useful for cleaning the bellows of outflow and safety valves.

Visual Inspection

When inspecting an airplane with a pressurization system, remember that there are many places for air to escape. Visually inspect all door, window, and emergency exit seals for security and condition. The seals should not have any holes, and they need to be flexible to work well. An old seal may become brittle and start to fall apart. If this happens, the seal should be replaced.

Carefully inspect all windows, fuselage skins, and pressure bulkheads for cracks and signs of loose rivets and screws. Any of these issues could cause leaks or lead to future problems.

Inspect the outflow valve and safety valve for condition and security. Visually inspect the seals for holes or cracks. Inspect all lines and components that provide pressurized air to the cabin.

There may be many other systems that pass through the fuselage skins and pressure bulkheads. All of these "pass-throughs" are potential air leaks. Some of these potential leak areas are around control cables, torque tubes for flaps or landing gear, fuel lines, brake lines, oxygen lines, and electrical cables. Check all seals, bellows, and fittings for security and excessive gaps, considering that some gaps are necessary.

STUDY QUESTIONS: AIRCRAFT PRESSURIZATION SYSTEMS

Answers are provided on page 231.

55. Pressurization air for reciprocating-engine-powered general aviation aircraft is compressed by the _____ .

56. Two types of mechanical compressors used to supply pressurizing air for a reciprocating-engine-powered airplane are:

    a. _____

    b. _____

57. When two or more mechanical air compressors supply the cabin pressure for a pressurized aircraft, the loss of cabin pressure if one compressor should fail is prevented by a delivery air duct _____ valve.

58. In a turbine-engine-powered aircraft the air for pressurization comes from the _____ section of the engine.

59. The air used for pressurizing a turbine-engine-powered aircraft is called _____ air.

60. The cabin altitude is the same as the flight altitude when the aircraft is operating in the _____ mode.

61. The cabin altitude is maintained at a constant value as the flight altitude changes when the pressurization system is operating in the _____ mode.

62. The cabin pressure is maintained a given amount higher than the outside air pressure when the pressurization system is operating in the _____ mode.

63. The maximum differential pressure allowed in a pressurized aircraft is determined by the strength of the _____ .

64. The amount of air the cabin pressure regulator in Figure 3-23 allows to leave the cabin is determined by the _____ pressure.

65. When the cabin pressure regulator in Figure 3-23 is operating in the isobaric mode, cabin pressure is held constant by reducing the flow of reference-chamber air through the isobaric _____ valve.

66. Refer to Figure 3-23. Anytime an increase in cabin pressure causes the isobaric metering valve to move toward the OPEN position, the outflow valve _____ (opens or closes).

67. Refer to Figure 3-23. When the outside air pressure decreases enough that the difference between the cabin pressure and the outside pressure reaches the pressure-differential limit allowed by the airframe manufacturer, the differential metering valve _____ (opens or closes).

68. Refer to Figure 3-23. The isobaric metering valve is controlled by the _____ (bellows or diaphragm).

69. Refer to Figure 3-23. The differential metering valve is controlled by the _____ (bellows or diaphragm).

70. If the cabin rate of climb is too great, the rate control will cause the outflow valve to close _____ (faster or slower).

71. A negative-pressure relief valve is incorporated in a pressurization system to prevent cabin pressure ever becoming _____ (lower or higher) than the surrounding air pressure.

72. All positive pressure inside the cabin is relieved when the aircraft is on the ground by the _____ valve opening.

73. If "auxiliary ventilation" is selected on the pressurization control while cruising at altitude, cabin pressurization will be dumped, and the cabin altitude will _____ (increase or decrease).

74. Airflow is increased in some areas of an aircraft by using a _____ to augment the airflow.

Aircraft Heaters

Aircraft environmental control systems include heaters, cooling systems, pressurization systems, and supplemental oxygen.

The most widely used environmental control devices are heaters, which are installed in almost all aircraft, from the smallest trainers to the largest transport aircraft. In this section we discuss exhaust system heaters and combustion heaters. The section on air-cycle air conditioning systems discusses cabin heat taken from engine compressor bleed air.

Exhaust System Heaters

Most of the smaller aircraft use jackets, or shrouds, around part of the engine exhaust system to provide heat for the cabin. Air flows around the exhaust components, which function as a heat exchanger, before continuing to the cabin. The volume of heated air to the cabin is controlled by a cabin heat valve.

When the cabin heat valve is ON, the heated air is directed into the cabin. When it is OFF, this hot air is dumped overboard.

Aircraft that use this type of heater should have their exhaust system regularly inspected for cracks or other leaks. One acceptable way of checking exhaust systems is to remove the heater shroud, pressurize the system with the pressure discharge of a vacuum cleaner, and paint the outside of the system with a soap and water solution. Leaks will cause bubbles to appear.

Carbon monoxide detectors should be used in the cabin to detect any trace of carbon monoxide. These are simply small packets of crystals that are stuck to the instrument panel in plain sight of the occupants. These crystals are normally a bright color, but when they are exposed to carbon monoxide, they darken. They turn black when exposed to a level of CO that could cause illness.

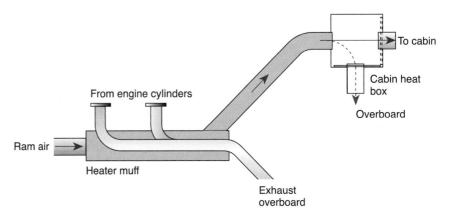

Figure 3-24. *A shroud around part of the exhaust system serves as a source of heat for some of the smaller aircraft cabins.*

Combustion Heaters

Some aircraft are heated with combustion heaters that use fuel from the aircraft fuel tanks. A typical combustion heater system schematic is shown in Figure 3-25.

combustion heater. A type of cabin heater used in some aircraft. Gasoline from the aircraft fuel tanks is burned in the heater.

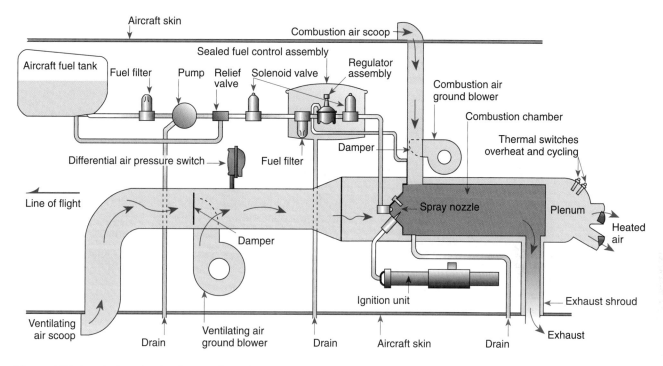

Figure 3-25. *A typical combustion heater schematic.*

Fuel flows from the tank through a filter and an electric fuel pump and relief valve, then through an overheat solenoid valve into the fuel control assembly. In this assembly there is another filter, a fuel-pressure regulator, and a thermostat-operated solenoid valve. From this assembly, the fuel flows to the spray nozzle inside the combustion chamber.

In flight, ventilating air flows into the air ducts from a scoop on the outside of the aircraft. On the ground, an electrically driven blower supplies ventilating air. This air flows through the heater housing to pick up heat and carry it where it is needed.

Combustion air is taken into the heater from the main air intake or from a separate outside air scoop, and the air pressure varies with the airspeed. A differential-pressure regulator or a combustion-air relief valve prevents too much air from entering the heater as the airspeed increases. An electrically driven blower ensures a consistent flow of air into the combustion chamber.

The heat produced by a combustion heater is controlled by a thermostat cycling switch that cycles the fuel on and off. When more heat is required, the fuel is turned on. When the correct temperature is reached, the fuel is turned off automatically. An overheat switch shuts the fuel off if the temperature at the discharge of the heater becomes too high.

Maintenance and Inspection

Routine inspection of combustion heaters is accomplished during 100-hour or annual inspections. Refer to the aircraft service instructions for maintenance and inspection details. Additional detailed inspection and troubleshooting procedures can be found in the service instructions from the combustion heater manufacturer. Note that Airworthiness Directives, service letters and service bulletins may be listed under the heater manufacturer and not necessarily under the aircraft manufacturer.

Routine servicing of combustion heaters will include inspection and cleaning of the heater fuel filters and spark plug. After the filters are reinstalled, the fuel system must be pressurized, and all connections carefully checked for traces of leaks. Visually inspect all components for condition and security. Check all controls for operation and verify full travel of air valves and dampers. Inspect air inlets, outlets, drains, and exhaust tubes for blockage or obstructions. Cracks in the combustion chamber may not be easily detected by a visual inspection, so the combustion chamber must be pressurized to check for cracks on a regular basis. This inspection is called a pressure decay test and is necessary to prevent exhaust gases and carbon monoxide from entering the cabin. After maintenance is complete, perform an operational check of the combustion heater.

STUDY QUESTIONS: AIRCRAFT HEATERS

Answers are provided on page 231.

75. Aircraft that are heated with exhaust system heaters should have _____ detectors installed on the instrument panel.

76. Two types of airflow through a combustion heater are _____ air and _____ air.

77. Too much combustion air is prevented from flowing through a combustion heater by either a combustion air _____ valve or a _____ regulator.

78. Regular maintenance of a combustion heater consists of cleaning or replacing the fuel _____ and checking all connections for _____ .

79. The temperature produced by a combustion heater is controlled by the thermostat which controls the _____ going to the heater.

Aircraft Cooling Systems

It has not been too many years since cooling aircraft was considered to be a needless expense both in weight and complexity. Airplanes flew in the low temperatures of high altitude and heating was the needed temperature control. Now, with people accustomed to more creature comfort, cooling systems are used to make the cabins more comfortable when the aircraft is on the ground.

Air-Cycle Cooling System

Transport aircraft use the compressor bleed air for pressurizing the cabins with temperature controlled air. Figure 3-26 shows the air conditioning system for a twin-engine jet transport airplane with the engines mounted on the aft fuselage. This airplane has two independent air conditioning systems that supply the cabin with heated and cooled air that is mixed to produce pressurizing air at the right temperature. Hot compressor bleed air is taken from the engines and from the auxiliary power unit. It passes through pressure

air-cycle cooling system. A system for cooling the air in the cabin of a turbojet-powered aircraft. Compressor bleed air passes through two heat exchangers where it gives up some of its heat; then it drives an expansion turbine where it loses still more of its heat energy as the turbine drives a compressor. When the air leaves the turbine it expands and its pressure and temperature are both low.

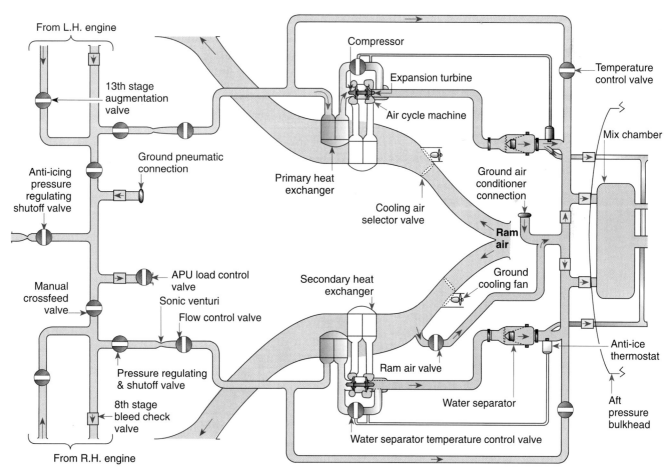

Figure 3-26. *Air conditioning system for a twin-engine jet transport airplane.*

regulating and shutoff valves, flow limiters, and flow control valves to the air-cycle machines where it is cooled. Some of the hot air is tapped off before it goes through the cooler, and is mixed with the cold air by a temperature control valve to get air of the correct temperature.

The cold air for cooling the airplane shown in Figure 3-26 is produced by removing heat energy from the hot compressor bleed air.

Hot compressor bleed air from the engines and the APU flows into the primary heat exchanger where it gives up some of its heat to ram air that flows through ducts.

After leaving the primary heat exchanger, it flows through the air-cycle machine where it is further compressed by the centrifugal compressor. The temperature rise caused by this compression allows more heat energy to be removed as the air flows through the secondary heat exchanger. After leaving this heat exchanger, the air gives up much of its energy as it spins the expansion turbine, which drives the air-cycle machine compressor. Still more energy is extracted in the last stage of cooling as the air expands upon leaving the turbine. When it leaves the expansion turbine, the air is cold.

As the air cools, moisture condenses out of it and is collected in the water separator. As the air leaves the air-cycle machine, it is so cold that the water will freeze in the water separator and shut off the flow of cooling air. To prevent this, the thermostat senses the temperature of the air leaving the water separator. If the temperature drops below 38°F, the water separator temperature control valve opens and lets warm air mix with the cold air to raise the temperature enough that the moisture will not freeze.

Temperature Control

The cabin air temperature is controlled by the temperature control valve taking the hot air that has bypassed the air-cycle machine and mixing it with the cold air as it leaves the water separator.

Maintenance, Inspection, and Troubleshooting

Air-cycle cooling system components may be found scattered throughout different sections of the airplane, and systems vary greatly from one aircraft type to the next. Instructions for maintenance, inspection, and troubleshooting will be found in the aircraft manufacturer's service instructions.

When inspecting and troubleshooting air-cycle systems, inspect the air ducts for leaks and verify that the multiple regulating and control valves are mounted securely and operate correctly. Inspect the expansion turbines for condition and make sure that they rotate freely.

Vapor-Cycle Cooling System

To better understand the way heat is moved in a vapor-cycle cooling system, consider the events that take place when heat from the sun is absorbed in the water of a lake.

When the sun shines on a lake during a hot summer day, some of the heat is absorbed by the water, which gets warmer. The warmed water on the surface evaporates, or changes from a liquid into a gas.

When the water evaporates, it takes some of the heat from the air immediately adjacent to the surface, and this air is cooled.

The water that evaporated from the surface of the lake is still water, only now it is in the form of invisible water vapor that is only slightly more than half as heavy as the air surrounding it. This water vapor still contains the energy from the sun that changed it from a liquid into a gas.

The lightweight water vapor rises in the air, and because the temperature of the air drops as altitude increases, the water vapor cools. Soon, its temperature becomes so low that it can no longer remain a vapor, and it changes back into a liquid, into tiny droplets that form clouds.

When the water vapor reverts into liquid water, the heat it absorbed from the sun is released, and this heat raises the temperature of the air surrounding the cloud.

Heat is moved in a vapor-cycle air cooling system in the same way it is moved from the surface of the lake to the air surrounding the clouds.

Under standard conditions, water is a liquid. If heat energy is added to a pan of water on a hot stove, and the temperature of the water goes up until it reaches 212°F, then the water boils. As long as the water is allowed to boil, its temperature will never rise above 212°F. But, if a tight-fitting lid is placed on the pan and more heat is added to the water, its temperature will go higher. The lid keeps pressure on the water, and it must get much hotter before it can boil.

A refrigerant such as R-134a (see description of R-134a on page 225) remains a liquid under standard pressure only at temperatures below −14.9°F. Above this temperature, it boils, or changes into a vapor.

R-134a in an open container will have a gauge pressure above it of 0 psig and its temperature will be −14.9°F. See Figure 3-27. If a lid with a closed

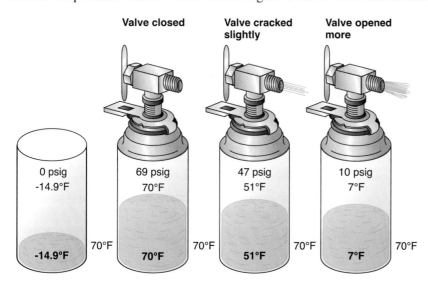

Figure 3-27. *There is a direct relationship between the temperature of R-134a and the pressure of the gas above it.*

valve is put on the container, the refrigerant reaches the temperature of the surrounding air, which in this case is 70°F. The pressure above the liquid reaches approximately 69 psig, where it stabilizes. If the valve is cracked slightly, some of the vapor escapes, the pressure drops and more liquid evaporates. When the pressure drops to approximately 47 psig, the temperature of the refrigerant drops to 51°F. If the valve is cracked still more, the pressure continues to drop and more refrigerant evaporates. When the pressure is down to 10 psig, the temperature of the refrigerant reaches 7°F.

To better understand the operation of a vapor-cycle cooling system, think of it as divided into two sides: the low side and the high side. The low side is the part of the system that picks up the heat, and the high side is the part of the system that gets rid of the heat.

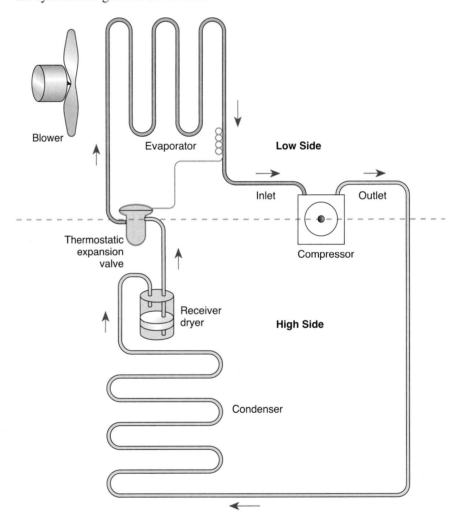

Figure 3-28. *A vapor-cycle cooling system is divided into a high side and a low side.*

The low side starts at the expansion valve, goes through the evaporator, and ends at the inlet of the compressor. The high side starts at the discharge of the compressor, goes through the condenser and the receiver-dryer, and ends at the expansion valve.

The pressure and the temperature are both low in the low side, and they are both high in the high side. See Figure 3-28.

The Compressor

The compressor is the heart of an air conditioning system. It moves the refrigerant through the system, and it divides the system into its high side and low side.

The compressor pulls the low-pressure refrigerant vapor from the evaporator and compresses it. And when the vapor is compressed, its pressure and temperature both go up.

The compressor carries a specified amount of special moisture-free refrigeration oil that lubricates and seals the compressor, and circulates through the system with the refrigerant.

Some compressors are driven from the aircraft engine by a V belt through an electromagnetic clutch. When the system calls for cooling, the clutch engages, and the pulley drives the compressor. When cooling is not needed, the clutch disengages and the pulley continues to turn, but the compressor is not driven. Other compressors are driven by an electric or hydraulic motor.

Typical air conditioning compressors use reed valves mounted in a valve plate between the top of the cylinders and the cylinder head.

compressor. The component in a vapor-cycle cooling system in which the low-pressure refrigerant vapors, after they leave the evaporator, are compressed to increase both their temperature and pressure before they pass into the condenser. Some compressors are driven by electric motors, others by hydraulic motors and, in the case of most light airplanes, are belt driven from the engine.

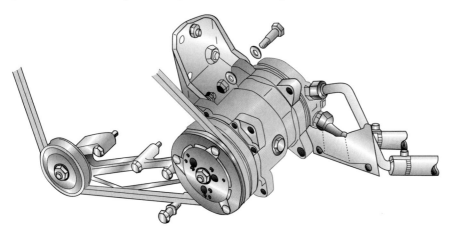

Figure 3-29. *A five-cylinder axial compressor that is belt-driven from the engine.*

The Compressor Drive System

When the compressor is driven by the engine with a V belt, an electromagnetic clutch inside a grooved pulley is used so the compressor can be engaged and disengaged as the demands of the system require. See Figure 3-30.

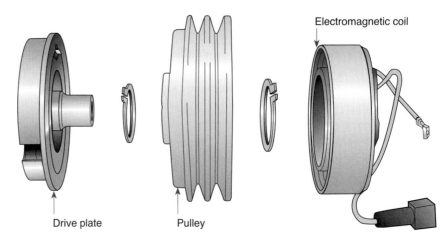

Figure 3-30. *Electromagnetic clutch for an engine-driven compressor.*

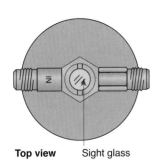

Top view   Sight glass

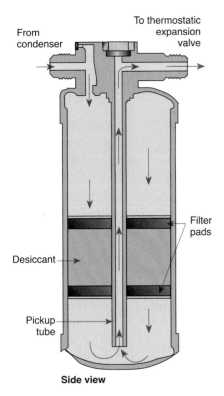

Side view

Figure 3-31. *Liquid refrigerant from the condenser is stored in the receiver-dryer.*

condenser. The component in a vapor-cycle cooling system in which the heat taken from the aircraft cabin is given up to the ambient air outside the aircraft.

The pulley is not rigidly connected to the compressor shaft, but it rides on a double-row ball bearing so it is free to turn without turning the compressor.

A clutch drive plate is keyed to the compressor shaft, and when the clutch is disengaged, there is a small amount of clearance between the plate and the pulley.

An electromagnetic coil is installed inside the pulley housing in such a way that when the air conditioning controls call for cooling, current flows through the coil, and a magnetic field is set up between the drive plate and the pulley. This magnetic field locks the pulley to the drive plate, and the pulley turns the compressor.

The compressor in some aircraft air conditioning systems is driven by a hydraulic motor whose pressure is supplied by an engine-driven pump.

A hydraulic manifold assembly contains a filter and a solenoid valve. When no cooling is required, the solenoid is de-energized and the valve allows fluid to bypass the motor and flow back to the reservoir. When the temperature control switch calls for cooling, the solenoid is energized and the valve shifts, closing off the return to the reservoir. The fluid flows through the pump so it can drive the compressor.

The Condenser

The refrigerant leaves the compressor as a hot, high-pressure gas, and flows to the condenser mounted where outside air can pass through its fins.

The condenser is made of high-pressure tubing wound back and forth, with thin sheet metal fins pressed over the tubes.

The hot refrigerant gas enters one side of the condenser and gives up some of its heat to the air flowing through the condenser fins.

When the system is working properly, about two thirds of the condenser is filled with refrigerant gas, and the rest contains liquid refrigerant.

The Receiver-Dryer

High-pressure, high-temperature liquid refrigerant leaves the condenser and flows into the receiver-dryer, which acts as a reservoir to hold the supply of refrigerant until it is needed by the evaporator. See Figure 3-31.

As the hot liquid refrigerant enters the receiver-dryer, it passes through a filter that removes any solid contaminants. Then it passes through a layer of a drying agent such as silica gel or activated alumina. This drying agent, called a desiccant, absorbs any moisture that may be circulating through the system in the refrigerant. Some receiver-dryers have two filters; the one below the desiccant prevents any particles of the desiccant getting into the system.

If moisture were allowed to remain in the system, it would mix with the refrigerant and form acids that could eat away the thin-wall tubing in the evaporator and cause leaks.

Another reason it is so important to remove all the moisture from the refrigerant is that it takes only a single drop of water to freeze in the expansion valve and block the flow of refrigerant into the evaporator. This stops the cooling action of the system.

Sometimes the refrigerant leaving the condenser has vapor in it, and the receiver-dryer acts as a separator. The liquid settles to the bottom and is picked up by the pickup tube that reaches almost to the bottom of the tank.

Some receiver-dryers include a sight glass that allows you to check the amount of refrigerant in the system. The sight glass is on the discharge side of the receiver-dryer, and if the system has enough refrigerant in it, only liquid flows to the expansion valve. But if the system is low on refrigerant, you will see bubbles in the sight glass.

Thermostatic Expansion Valves

The thermostatic expansion valve (TEV) is a metering device that measures the temperature of the discharge end of the evaporator to allow the correct amount of refrigerant to flow into the evaporator. All of the liquid refrigerant should be turned into a gas (it should evaporate) by the time it gets to the end of the evaporator coil.

Several types of thermostatic expansion valves are installed in aircraft air conditioning systems. This section discusses both internally and externally equalized TEVs.

Before discussing these valves, we must understand the term "superheat." Superheat is heat energy added to a refrigerant after it has changed from a liquid into a vapor. Refrigerant that has superheat in it is not hot, it is very cold.

Figure 3-32 shows a typical internally equalized thermostatic expansion valve. The outlet attaches to the inlet of the evaporator, and the inlet is connected to the tubing that comes from the receiver-dryer.

A diaphragm in the top of the valve rides on the top of two pushrods that press against the superheat spring.

receiver-dryer. The component in a vapor-cycle cooling system that serves as a reservoir for the liquid refrigerant. The receiver-dryer contains a desiccant that absorbs any moisture that may be in the system.

desiccant. A drying agent used in a refrigeration system to remove water from the refrigerant. A desiccant is made of silica-gel or some similar material.

sight glass. A small window in the high side of a vapor-cycle cooling system. Liquid refrigerant flows past the sight glass, and if the charge of refrigerant is low, bubbles will be seen. A fully charged system has no bubbles in the refrigerant.

thermostatic expansion valve (TEV). The component in a vapor-cycle cooling system that meters the refrigerant into the evaporator. The amount of refrigerant metered by the TEV is determined by the temperature and pressure of the refrigerant as it leaves the evaporator coils.

The TEV changes the refrigerant from a high-pressure liquid into a low-pressure liquid.

superheat. Heat energy that is added to a refrigerant after it changes from a liquid to a vapor.

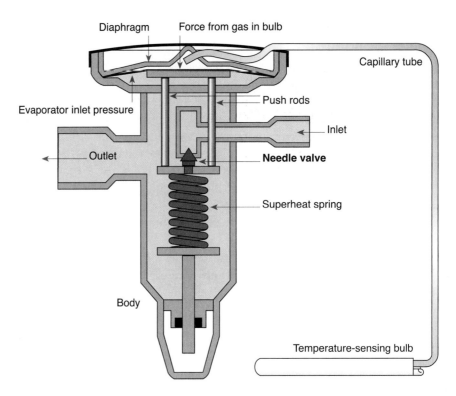

Figure 3-32. *Internally equalized thermostatic expansion valve.*

A capillary tube, which is a metal tube with a very small inside diameter, connects into the TEV just above the diaphragm. The end of this capillary tube is wound into a tight coil, and acts as the temperature pickup bulb. This bulb is clamped to the discharge line of the evaporator, and is wrapped with an insulating tape so it will not be affected by any temperature other than that of the evaporator discharge.

The capillary tube and the space above the diaphragm is partially filled with a highly volatile liquid. When the bulb is heated, the pressure of the vapor above the liquid increases. It produces a force that pushes the diaphragm down against the force caused by the superheat spring and the force caused by the evaporator inlet pressure acting on the bottom of the diaphragm. The temperature of the refrigerant in the discharge of the evaporator determines the amount of force that acts against the superheat spring.

A needle valve is located between the inlet and the outlet of the TEV. The position of the needle in the valve is determined by the balance between the force caused by the pressure of the gas above the diaphragm and the forces produced by the superheat spring and the pressure of the refrigerant in the evaporator.

When the system is started, the evaporator is warm, and the pressure inside the bulb is high, so the TEV allows the maximum amount of refrigerant to enter the evaporator.

volatile liquid. A liquid that easily changes into a vapor.

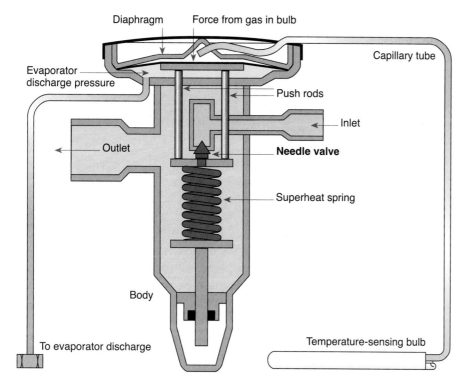

Figure 3-33. *Externally equalized thermostatic expansion valve.*

As the refrigerant evaporates, the temperature at the outlet of the evaporator drops and the pressure above the diaphragm decreases. This decreased pressure allows the superheat spring to close the needle valve and restrict the amount of refrigerant that flows into the evaporator. Just enough refrigerant is metered into the evaporator for it all to be turned into a gas by the time it reaches the end of the evaporator coils.

If the heat load inside the cabin of the aircraft increases, and all of the refrigerant is turned into a gas before it reaches the end of the evaporator coils, heat is added to the refrigerant vapor. This is superheat, and it increases the temperature of the refrigerant, but it does not increase its pressure. The increased temperature raises the pressure inside the bulb and on top of the diaphragm, and this forces the needle valve off its seat and allows more refrigerant to flow into the evaporator.

The amount of compression of the superheat spring is set at the factory, and it is important when installing a new TEV that the superheat setting be correct for the particular installation.

A TEV is equalized by having the pressure of the refrigerant inside the evaporator work on the bottom of the diaphragm. It works in such a way that it assists the superheat spring in opposing the force of the gas inside the temperature bulb. An internally equalized TEV has a passage inside the valve that allows the pressure at the inlet of the evaporator to press against the diaphragm.

evaporator. The component in a vapor-cycle cooling system in which heat from the aircraft cabin is absorbed into the refrigerant. As the heat is absorbed, the refrigerant evaporates, or changes from a liquid into a vapor. The function of the evaporator is to lower the cabin air temperature.

An externally equalized TEV is used with large evaporators that have a fair amount of pressure drop across the coils. This makes the outlet pressure significantly lower than the inlet pressure. An externally equalized TEV has a small tube connected to the discharge of the evaporator that carries this pressure to the space below the diaphragm.

The Evaporator

The evaporator is the part of the air conditioning system where the cold air is produced. It is made of a series of tubes over which thin sheet aluminum fins have been pressed. The area provided by the fins allows a maximum amount of heat to be picked up from the air inside the cabin and transferred into the refrigerant inside the evaporator tubing.

The evaporator is usually mounted inside a shroud in such a way that a blower can pull hot air from inside the cabin and force it through the evaporator fins. After the air leaves the evaporator, it blows over the occupants of the cabin. The blower is equipped with a speed control that allows the pilot to vary the amount of air blowing across the evaporator coils.

The thermostatic expansion valve is mounted at the inlet of the evaporator, and it breaks the refrigerant up into a fine mist and sprays it out into the coils. The refrigerant flowing through the coils picks up heat from the fins, is warmed, and turns into a gas. The air passing through the fins loses some of its heat and is cooled.

The temperature-sensing bulb of the TEV is clamped to the discharge line of the evaporator, and it is insulated with tape so it is not affected by any temperature except that caused by the refrigerant vapors inside the evaporator.

The temperature of the refrigerant vapor is controlled by regulating the amount of refrigerant allowed to enter the evaporator through the TEV. The vapor at the discharge of the evaporator is a few degrees warmer than the liquid refrigerant because of the superheat put into it. This superheat ensures that none of the refrigerant will be in its liquid state when it enters the inlet of the compressor because liquid refrigerant will damage the reed valves in the compressor.

reed valve. A thin, leaf-type valve mounted in the valve plate of an air conditioning compressor to control the flow of refrigerant gases into and out of the compressor cylinders.

In addition to absorbing heat from the air and cooling the air that is blown out into the cabin, the evaporator serves the very important function of dehumidifying the air. When warm, humid air is blown through the cold evaporator fins, the moisture condenses out of the air in the same way moisture condenses and forms as water on the outside of a glass holding a cold drink. This moisture drips down off the fins and collects in a pan, and is carried outside the aircraft through a drain tube. Pressurized aircraft have a float-operated drain valve in the drain line. When there is no water in the valve housing, the valve is closed. But when enough water collects in the housing, it raises the float, opens the valve and allows the water to be blown overboard. When there is no more water in the housing, the float drops down and the valve closes.

The fins on the evaporator must be kept open so that air can flow through them and add heat to the refrigerant. If the flow of air is blocked, the refrigerant cannot absorb enough heat, and the evaporator will get so cold that the moisture which condenses out of the air will freeze in the evaporator fins and block the air. The system will then stop producing cold air.

Service Valves

A vapor-cycle air conditioning system is a sealed system that operates under pressure. In order to measure the pressure in the system and to add refrigerant when the supply is low, provisions must be made for getting into the system while it is under pressure.

Schrader-type service valves are used on most aircraft air conditioning systems because of their light weight and reliability. A Schrader valve can be installed at any point in the system, and these valves keep the system closed until a service hose is screwed onto the valve. When the hose fitting is screwed down, a valve depressor inside the fitting presses down on the valve stem and opens the system.

Air Conditioning System Servicing Equipment

Because an air conditioning system is a sealed system, it requires specialized equipment to properly service it. The refrigerants currently used are considered to be a threat to the ozone and can no longer be vented to the atmosphere. In this section we will consider the manifold gauge set, the charging station, refrigerant recovery systems, and leak detectors.

The Manifold Gauge Set

The most useful single piece of service equipment for working with a vapor-cycle cooling system is a manifold gauge set, like the one in Figure 3-35 on the next page.

A manifold gauge set has two pressure gauges and two hand-operated valves, mounted on a manifold that has connections for three service hoses.

A red, high-pressure service hose attaches to a fitting connected directly to the high-side gauge. A blue, low-pressure hose attaches to a fitting connected to the compound low-side gauge. A yellow service hose connects to the center fitting.

The two valves shut off the center fitting from either of the two gauges, but they may be opened to connect the center hose to either the low side or the high side of the system.

The zero position of the compound low-side gauge is not at the end of the scale, but is placed in such a position that the pointer can move down scale to measure between zero and 30 inches of mercury vacuum, or up scale to measure from zero to 150 pounds per square inch pressure.

The high-pressure gauge is marked so it can measure from zero to 500 pounds per square inch.

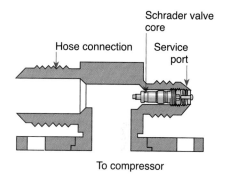

Detail of Schrader valve core

Figure 3-34. *Schrader-type valve air conditioning service valve.*

A manifold gauge set is used to measure the pressures that exist inside the air conditioning system, to evacuate the system of refrigerant, to pump down, or purge, the system of all water vapor, and to charge the system with refrigerant.

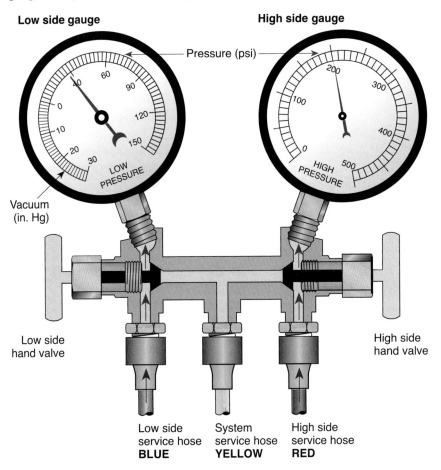

Figure 3-35. *The manifold gauge set is the most important single piece of equipment for servicing an air conditioning system.*

Charging Stand

A charging stand is a piece of equipment that contains everything needed to service an air conditioning system. All the equipment is mounted in a single unit that can easily be moved to the aircraft whose air conditioning system is being serviced.

A charging stand usually contains a cylinder of refrigerant and a heating system that allows the refrigerant to be heated to speed its entry into the system. This cylinder is fitted with valves that allow the refrigerant to be added to the system in either liquid or gaseous form.

A vacuum pump and a vacuum holding valve are included to allow a system to be pumped down and checked for leaks. All the hoses, adapters, and valves needed to connect the charging stand to the aircraft system are included.

charging stand. A handy and compact arrangement of air conditioning servicing equipment. A charging stand contains a vacuum pump, a manifold gauge set, and a method of measuring and dispensing the refrigerant.

Vacuum Pumps

When servicing an air conditioning system, you must remove every trace of moisture from the system. Water combines with the refrigerant to form hydrochloric acid, which can eat away the inside of the evaporator and condenser tubes and cause leakage. It also takes only a small droplet of water to freeze inside the thermostatic expansion valve and shut off the operation of the system.

Vacuum pumps may be of either the piston type or the rotary vane type and they are capable of producing a "deep vacuum," a very low absolute pressure. A good pump can produce a pressure as low as 29.99 inches of mercury (250 microns). At this extremely low pressure, water boils at a temperature of well below 0°F, and any water will turn into a vapor and be pulled out of the system.

Leak Detectors

An air conditioning system must be sealed so none of the refrigerant can leak out of it. Occasionally, though, a leak allows the refrigerant to escape. The leak must be found before the system is returned to service.

The only type of leak detector suited for servicing an aircraft air-conditioning system is an electronic oscillator-type leak detector. The oscillator produces a tone, and if even an extremely small trace of refrigerant is picked up by the pickup tube, the tone will change. An electronic leak detector is simple to use, extremely sensitive, and causes no danger when servicing the system.

Gaseous refrigerant is heavier than air, and the probe is passed below locations where leakage is suspected.

Refrigerant

The environmentally friendly R-134a (Tetrafluoroethane or HFC) is available in 13-ounce cans (commonly called one pound cans) that also contain some refrigerant oil for topping off systems. It is also available in larger disposable cylinders and in even larger refillable cylinders.

R-12 (Dichlorodifluoromethane or CFC) is no longer produced in the United States, but it is still available.

R-12 and R-134a are not interchangeable, and a system designed for R-12 must not be charged or topped off with R-134a.

Refrigeration Oil

The sealed air conditioning system is lubricated by a special high-grade refrigeration oil that circulates through the system with the refrigerant.

Fresh refrigeration oil is free of water, is a pale yellow color, almost clear, and has very little odor. Since refrigeration oil has a tendency to absorb moisture from the air, it must be kept in a tightly closed container until it is put into the system.

deep-vacuum pump. A vacuum pump capable of removing almost all of the air from a refrigeration system. A deep-vacuum pump can reduce the pressure inside the system to a few microns of pressure.

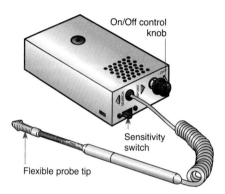

Figure 3-36. *An electronic oscillator-type leak detector detects extremely small refrigerant leaks and is safe for servicing aircraft air conditioning systems.*

Freon. The registered trade name for a refrigerant used in a vapor-cycle air conditioning system.

Air Conditioning System Checks

With the system turned on and the engine running at a fast idle, a normally-functioning air conditioning system will blow a stream of cold air out from the evaporator. All of the components in the high side of the system should feel hot or warm to the touch. All of the components in the low side of the system should feel cold or cool to the touch.

The actual temperature of the air as it leaves the evaporator depends on the air's humidity and the ambient air temperature, but it should be in the range of 35° to 45°F.

Visual Inspection

The entire air conditioning system should be checked visually for its condition. Begin with one part of the system and check it through the entire system.

Check the evaporator to be sure it is mounted securely and that there is a clear airflow path through its shroud.

The fins must be free of lint and dirt, and there must not be any fins bent over to obstruct the air flowing through them. The blower must operate at all speeds and not rub against its housing.

The sensor for the thermostatic expansion valve must be securely taped to the discharge of the evaporator, and covered so it will not be affected by any temperature other than that of the evaporator coil.

The thermostat switch must be secured in such a way that its sensor is in the fins of the evaporator so it can sense the temperature at the point the manufacturer specifies.

Check the compressor for security of mounting, for freedom of operation of the clutch, and for the proper belt tension. The load the compressor places on its mounting as it cycles on and off puts a big strain on the castings, so you should carefully inspect the area around which the compressor is mounted. Check the mounting bolts to be sure none of them have vibrated loose.

The condenser is much like the evaporator, except that it is made to withstand much higher temperatures and pressures. It must be inspected for security of mounting and for any bent or damaged fins. The housing that holds the condenser must be securely mounted in the aircraft structure, and it must be free from any obstruction to the airflow.

Many aircraft systems have a blower that forces air over the condenser when the aircraft is on the ground. Check this blower and its motor for proper operation, and be sure there is no indication that the blower is rubbing on its housing.

Check the receiver-dryer, which is usually located near the condenser, for proper and secure mounting. If it has a sight glass in it, check to see if there is an adequate supply of liquid refrigerant in the system. You shouldn't see any bubbles in the refrigerant.

Since the receiver-dryer is in the high side of the system, it is hot when the system is operating properly.

The entire air conditioning system is connected with hoses and tubing. Inspect every fitting and section of hose for any indication of oil leakage that would indicate a refrigerant leak.

All plumbing in the aircraft should be supported by the method the manufacturer specifies. If you install anything differently from the method used by the factory, the installation must be made according to approved data.

Operational Check

After a careful visual check confirms that the air conditioning system is properly mounted in the aircraft, you can give it an operational check. This check consists of connecting a manifold gauge set to the system and measuring the pressure of the refrigerant in the system.

Remove the protective cap from the service port in the high side of the system and, after checking to be sure the high-side valve on the manifold gauge set is closed, connect the high-side service hose to the valve. Open the high-side valve slightly and allow refrigerant to flow out of the center hose for about three to five seconds, then close the valve.

Remove the protective cap from the low-side service port and connect the low-side service hose. Open the low-side valve and allow refrigerant to flow out of the center hose for three to five seconds, then close the valve.

Allow the system to operate with the engine running at a relatively fast idle for about five minutes, with the blowers operating at high speed and the air conditioning controls calling for maximum cooling. After the system has run five minutes, check the evaporator air discharge temperature and the high-side pressure. The pressures are affected by the ambient temperature, but the pressures in Figure 3-37 are typical.

Ambient Temperature °F	High-Side Pressure psi	Low-Side Pressure psi
60°	105 – 110	4 – 8
70°	125 – 130	10 – 15
85°	170 – 180	15 – 30
100°	215 – 225	25 – 50
110°	255 – 260	30 – 60

Figure 3-37. *Pressures in a normally operating vapor-cycle air conditioning system.*

Installing a Partial Charge of Refrigerant

If the sight glass shows there is no refrigerant in the system, or if the pressure on the gauges of the manifold gauge set is below 50 psi, you must install a partial charge in the system before making any further operational checks.

Connect a can-tap valve to a one-pound can of refrigerant and puncture the can seal. Connect the valve to the center hose of the manifold gauge set and loosen the hose at the manifold. Open the can valve and allow refrigerant to flow through the hose for a few seconds to purge the hose of any air, then tighten the hose fitting.

Open the high-side manifold valve and allow refrigerant to flow into the system until the pressure is above 50 psi.

Leak Testing

A leakage of about ½ pound of refrigerant in a one-year period is not considered excessive, but a leak test must be performed if leakage is any greater than that.

With the system pressure above 50 pounds per square inch, hold the probe of an electronic leak detector below any point at which a leak is suspected. The detector changes the tone of the sound it produces when it detects a leak.

Air Conditioning System Servicing

Servicing an air conditioning system is different from other types of aircraft maintenance because the system is sealed and operates under pressure. Follow normal good operating practices in any type of maintenance work, and follow the instructions furnished by the aircraft manufacturer in detail. Some of the most commonly performed service procedures are as follows.

Discharging the System

When it is necessary to change any of the components in an air conditioning system or to replace contaminated refrigerant, drain the old refrigerant from the system. In the past this was done by connecting a manifold gauge set to the system and holding a shop towel over the end of the center hose, then slowly opening both the high- and low-side valves and allowing the refrigerant to escape into the atmosphere. R-12 is nontoxic, but it does displace oxygen from the area and it should not be discharged from a system in a closed area.

Concern for the environment changed the way R-12 was handled and recovery and recycling systems became a requirement. During servicing, refrigerant is emptied into a container in the recycling system and pumped through a series of filters to remove the refrigerant oil and to clean the refrigerant for reuse. Eventually, production of R-12 was phased out and has been replaced with R-134a. R134a is much better for the environment and is non-toxic, but the use of a recovery and recycling system is still a requirement. Unfortunately, R134a is not compatible with R12. In order to use R134a, R-12 systems must go through a process that coverts the system over to R-134a. It is important to check aircraft maintenance records to determine the type of refrigerant being used.

Replacing System Components

The procedure for replacing components in an air conditioning system is similar to that used for replacing components in any other aircraft system, except that the openings in the components must be kept capped until they are ready to be installed. Moisture is always present in the air, and the absolute minimum amount of moisture must be allowed to get into the system.

When installing hoses with hose clamps, lubricate the inside of the hose with clean refrigeration oil and work the fitting into the hose with a twisting motion.

Hoses that are screwed onto a component should be tightened by using two wrenches, one on the fitting in the component and one on the hose fitting. The use of two wrenches prevents straining the component.

Checking Compressor Oil

Compressors used in air conditioning systems are lubricated by oil sealed in the system. Any time the system is opened, it is a good idea to check the amount of oil in the compressor.

Because the compressors may be mounted in different ways on different aircraft, it is important that the instructions in the aircraft maintenance manual be followed to check the compressor oil. The oil in some compressors can be checked with the compressor installed on the engine; on other installations, the compressor must be removed and the oil checked with the compressor on the bench.

Flushing the System

If a system has been contaminated, it can be flushed by removing the receiver-dryer and flushing the system. This is done by connecting a can of refrigerant to the system and allowing the liquid refrigerant to flow through the system. Install a new receiver-dryer after the system has been flushed.

Evacuating the System

After the system has been repaired by replacing any faulty components and flushing the lines, all the air must be pumped out so any trapped moisture will be changed into water vapor and removed with a vacuum pump.

Connect a vacuum pump to the center service hose of the manifold gauge set, open both valves, and start the pump. Allow the pump to pull as much vacuum as it will, and hold the system at this low pressure for at least thirty minutes. After the system has been pumped down, close the valves on the manifold gauge set and check to see that there is no leak in the system. A leak would be indicated by a rise in the negative pressure shown on the low-side gauge.

Charging the System

After the system has been evacuated and is still under vacuum, close both valves on the manifold gauge set and disconnect the vacuum pump. Connect the hose to a container of refrigerant and purge the air from the hose.

Open the high-side valve and allow the amount of liquid refrigerant specified in the aircraft service instructions to flow into the system. The correct amount is usually specified in units of weight rather than volume.

If the full amount of refrigerant fails to flow into the system, close the high-side valve, turn the container of refrigerant upright, start the engine, and slowly open the low-side valve. Allow the compressor to pull enough refrigerant vapors into the system to give it a full charge. Filling the system

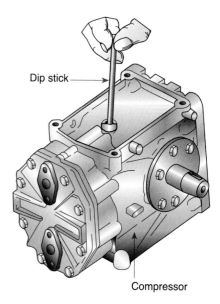

Dip stick

Compressor

Figure 3-38. *Checking the oil in a two cylinder in-line compressor.*

may be hastened by putting the cans of refrigerant in warm water, but be sure the temperature of the water is not higher than 125°F.

Never put liquid refrigerant into the low side of an operating system unless the low-side pressure is below 40 psi, and the ambient temperature is above 80°F. If the refrigerant has not all evaporated by the time it reaches the compressor it is likely to cause compressor damage.

When the system is fully charged and is operating properly with no bubbles visible in the sight glass, close both service valves and remove the manifold gauge set. Replace the protective caps over the service valves.

STUDY QUESTIONS: AIRCRAFT COOLING SYSTEMS

Answers are provided on page 231.

80. Heat for the cabin of a jet transport airplane is provided by _____ air.

81. In a jet transport airplane, hot compressor bleed air is mixed with cold air from the _____ machine to get air of the correct temperature for the cabin.

82. The first heat that is lost from the hot compressor bleed air in an air-cycle machine is removed by the _____ heat exchanger.

83. After the air leaves the primary heat exchanger it is heated as it is compressed by the _____ compressor.

84. After leaving the air-cycle machine centrifugal compressor the air gives up some of its heat as it passes through the _____ heat exchanger.

85. More heat is removed from the pressurizing air after it leaves the secondary heat exchanger as it spins the _____ which drives the centrifugal compressor.

86. The final stage of cooling is done when the air _____ upon leaving the turbine.

87. Moisture that condenses from the pressurizing air after it leaves the expansion turbine is removed by the _____ .

88. Water is prevented from freezing in the water separator by routing some _____ around the air-cycle machine to mix with cold air and raise its temperature.

89. In a vapor-cycle cooling system, heat from the cabin is absorbed into the refrigerant in the _____ .

90. Heat taken from the cabin is transferred into the outside air by the _____ .

91. The refrigerant enters the evaporator as a _____ (high or low)-pressure _____ (liquid or vapor).

92. The refrigerant leaves the evaporator as a _____ (high or low)-pressure _____ (liquid or vapor).

93. The refrigerant enters the condenser as a _____ (high or low)-pressure _____ (liquid or vapor).

94. The refrigerant leaves the condenser as a _____ (high or low)-pressure _____ (liquid or vapor).

95. The receiver-dryer holds the refrigerant in its _____ (liquid or vapor) state.

96. The two units that divide an air conditioning system into a high side and a low side are the _____ _____ and the _____ .

97. The component in an air conditioning system that increases both the temperature and the pressure of the gaseous refrigerant is the _____ .

98. Cycling of a compressor that is belt-driven from the aircraft engine is accomplished by using an electromagnetic _____ in the drive pulley.

99. The condenser is in the _____ (high or low) side of an air conditioning system.

100. The air conditioning system component that meters liquid refrigerant into the evaporator coils is the _____ .

101. The evaporator is in the _____ (high or low) side of an air conditioning system.

102. The air leaving the evaporator of a properly functioning air conditioning system should have a temperature of between _____°F and _____°F.

103. When using an electronic leak detector, the probe should be held _____ (above or below) a location of a suspected leak.

Answers to Chapter 3 Study Questions

1. increase
2. decrease
3. nitrogen, oxygen
4. does not
5. headaches
6. hypoxia
7. carbon dioxide
8. oxygen
9. heat energy
10. British thermal unit, calorie
11. sensible
12. latent
13. a. the freezing point of water
    b. the boiling point of water
14. molecular

15. Kelvin
16. absolute
17. gauge
18. differential
19. specific heat
20. a. conduction
    b. convection
    c. radiation
21. inches of mercury
22. microns
23. chemical oxygen candle
24. water
25. water
26. molecular sieve
27. may not
28. 400
29. continuous flow
30. pressure reducer
31. pressure relief
32. manual, automatic
33. calibrated orifice
34. therapeutic
35. continuous flow
36. demand
37. cabin air
38. inhales
39. Interstate Commerce Commission (ICC), Department of Transportation (DOT)
40. hydrostatically
41. 5
42. 3

43. 3,083
44. 24
45. 50
46. green
47. yellow
48. pressure
49. 1,925
50. 10
51. petroleum
52. nonpetroleum
53. pressure relief valve
54. water
55. turbocharger
56. a. Roots blower type
    b. Centrifugal type
57. check
58. compressor
59. compressor bleed
60. unpressurized
61. isobaric
62. constant differential
63. aircraft structure
64. reference chamber
65. metering
66. opens
67. opens
68. bellows
69. diaphragm
70. faster
71. lower
72. dump
73. increase

74. jet pump
75. carbon monoxide
76. combustion, ventilating
77. relief, differential-pressure
78. filter, leaks
79. fuel
80. compressor bleed
81. air cycle
82. primary
83. centrifugal
84. secondary
85. expansion turbine
86. expands
87. water separator
88. warm air
89. evaporator
90. condenser
91. low, liquid
92. low, vapor
93. high, vapor
94. high, liquid
95. liquid
96. thermostatic expansion valve, compressor
97. compressor
98. clutch
99. high
100. thermostatic expansion valve
101. low
102. 35, 45
103. below

AIRCRAFT INSTRUMENT SYSTEMS

4

An Overview of Aircraft Instruments

The progress attained in serious flight has been made possible by the development of accurate and dependable instruments. The first aircraft had no instruments at all, but as engines became more dependable, instruments were developed to tell the pilot the amount of fuel on board and the speed and temperature of the engine.

The first flight instruments were primitive altimeters and compasses. All flying had to be done when the horizon was visible because the pilot had no way to knowing when the aircraft was flying straight or turning. The development of a sensitive altimeter and gyro instruments allowed the first excursions into the realm of "blind flying." When radio became developed enough to be used as a navigation aid, true blind flight became possible. The first flight without any outside visual reference was made by Jimmy Doolittle in September of 1929.

Today, even small general aviation aircraft have sophisticated instruments that allow the pilot to know his or her exact location and to monitor the performance of the aircraft and its engine. With this knowledge, safe flight in almost all situations is a reality.

Most of the instruments used in the past and present give mechanical indications. Pointers rotate across calibrated dials in an analog fashion to indicate the values being measured. The mechanisms that convert the parameter being measured into rotation of a pointer are quite complex and delicate.

Today, with the rapid developments in solid-state electronics and microcomputer technology, much instrumentation uses solid-state pickups and light-emitting diodes or liquid crystal displays on the instrument panels.

This portion of the Aviation Mechanic Series discusses the basic operating principles of engine and flight instruments and many of the physical and electrical principles on which these instruments work.

Classifications of Aircraft Instruments

Aircraft instruments can be classified according to their function or their operating principles. Here, they are classified by their means of operation, and their function will be explained with each instrument.

Pressure Measuring Instruments

absolute pressure. Pressure referenced from zero pressure, or a vacuum.

Pressure is the amount of force acting on a given unit of area, and all pressure must be measured from some known reference. Absolute pressure is measured from zero pressure, or a vacuum. Gauge pressure is measured from the existing atmospheric pressure, and differential pressure is the difference between two pressures.

Absolute Pressure Instruments

The most accurate device for measuring absolute pressure is the mercury barometer, a glass tube about 34 inches long and one inch in diameter closed at one end and filled with mercury. Its open end is immersed in a bowl of mercury. See Figure 4-1. The mercury drops down in the tube and leaves an empty space, or a vacuum, above it. The weight of the air pressing down on the mercury in the bowl holds the mercury up in the tube at a height proportional to the pressure of the air. Standard atmosphere at sea level holds the mercury up in the tube until the top of the column is 29.92 inches, or 760 millimeters, above the top of the mercury in the bowl.

A mercury barometer is not a convenient instrument to carry in an aircraft, so the aneroid (no liquid) barometer has been developed. This instrument uses a sealed, evacuated, concentrically corrugated metal capsule as its pressure-sensitive mechanism.

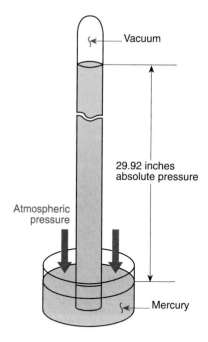

Figure 4-1. *A mercury barometer is the most accurate instrument to measure absolute pressure.*

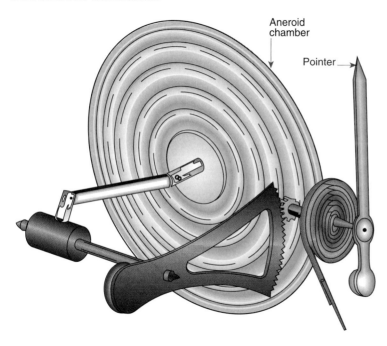

Figure 4-2. *An aneroid barometer mechanism.*

The concentric corrugations provide a degree of springiness that opposes the pressure of the air. See Figure 4-3. As the air pressure increases, the thickness of the capsule decreases, and as the pressure decreases, the capsule expands. A rocking shaft, sector gear, and pinion multiply the change in dimension of the capsule and drive a pointer across a calibrated dial.

aneroid. The sensitive component in an altimeter or barometer that measures the absolute pressure of the air. The aneroid is a sealed, flat capsule made of thin corrugated disks of metal soldered together and evacuated by pumping all of the air out of it. Evacuating the aneroid allows it to expand or collapse as the air pressure on the outside changes.

rocking shaft. A shaft used in the mechanism of a pressure-measuring instrument to change the direction of movement by 90° and to amplify the amount of movement.

sector gear. A part of a gear wheel that contains the hub and a portion of the rim with teeth.

pinion. A small gear that meshes with a larger gear, a sector of a gear, or a toothed rack.

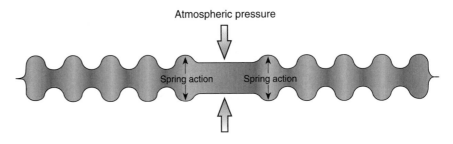

Atmospheric pressure

Spring action   Spring action

Figure 4-3. *The spring action of the corrugations opposes the pressure of the air to measure any changes in the air pressure.*

Absolute pressure is measured in an aircraft to determine altitude. The knob in the lower left-hand corner of the altimeter in Figure 4-4 adjusts the barometric scale in the window on the right side of the dial to set the pressure level from which the absolute pressure is referenced. The absolute pressure is expressed in feet of altitude from the referenced pressure level.

Figure 4-4. *An altimeter measures absolute pressure and displays it as feet of altitude above the pressure reference level that has been set into the barometric window.*

Gauge Pressure Instruments

Gauge pressure is measured from the existing barometric pressure and is actually the pressure that has been added to a fluid.

A Bourdon tube is typically used to measure gauge pressure. This tube is a flattened thin-wall bronze tube formed into a curve as in Figure 4-5. One end of the tube is sealed and attached through a linkage to a sector gear. The other end is connected to the instrument case through a fitting that allows the fluid to be measured to enter.

When the pressure of the fluid inside the tube increases, it tries to change the cross-sectional shape of the tube from flat to round. As the cross section changes, the curved tube tends to straighten out. This in turn moves the sector gear, which rotates the pinion gear on which the pointer is mounted.

Bourdon tube instruments measure relatively high pressures like those in engine lubricating systems and hydraulic systems. Lower pressures such as instrument air pressure, deicer air pressure, and suction are often measured with a bellows mechanism much like an aneroid capsule. Figure 4-6 shows this mechanism. The pressure to be measured is taken into the bellows. As the pressure increases, the bellows expands and its expansion rotates the rocking shaft and the sector gear. Movement of the sector gear rotates the pinion gear and the shaft on which the pointer is mounted.

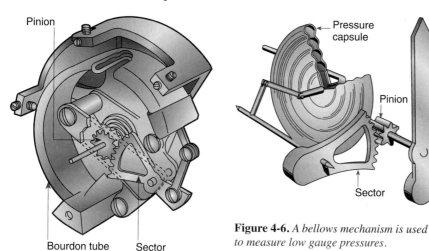

Figure 4-6. *A bellows mechanism is used to measure low gauge pressures.*

Figure 4-5. *A Bourdon tube mechanism is used to measure such gauge pressures as engine lubricating oil pressure and hydraulic fluid pressure.*

Differential Pressure Instruments

A differential pressure is simply the difference between two pressures. The indication on an airspeed indicator is caused by the difference between pitot, or ram, air pressure and static, or still, air pressure. Pitot pressure is taken into the inside of the diaphragm and static pressure is taken into the sealed instrument case. As the speed of the aircraft increases, the pitot pressure increases and the diaphragm expands, rotating the rocking shaft and driving the pointer across the dial.

A differential bellows like that in Figure 4-8 on the next page is a popular instrument mechanism that can be used to measure absolute, differential, or gauge pressure.

When a differential bellows is used to measure absolute pressure, as it is when used in a manifold pressure gauge, one of the bellows is evacuated and sealed and the other bellows senses the pressure inside the engine intake manifold.

differential pressure. The difference between two pressures. An airspeed indicator is a differential-pressure gauge. It measures the difference between static air pressure and pitot air pressure.

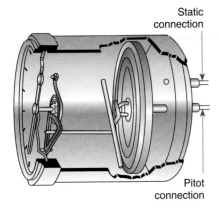

Figure 4-7. *An airspeed indicator is a differential pressure gauge which measures the difference between pitot, or ram air, pressure and static, or still air, pressure. The resulting differential pressure is displayed on the dial as knots, miles per hour, or kilometers per hour.*

airspeed indicator. A flight instrument that measures the pressure differential between the pitot, or ram, air pressure and the static pressure of the air surrounding the aircraft. This differential pressure is shown in units of miles per hour, knots, or kilometers per hour.

static air pressure. Pressure of the ambient air surrounding the aircraft. Static pressure does not take into consideration any air movement.

pitot pressure. Ram air pressure used to measure airspeed. The pitot tube faces directly into the air flowing around the aircraft. It stops the air and measures its pressure.

manifold pressure gauge. A pressure gauge that measures the absolute pressure inside the induction system of a reciprocating engine. When the engine is not operating, this instrument shows the existing atmospheric pressure.

When used to measure differential pressure, as it is when used as a fuel pressure gauge, onc bellows senses the air pressure at the carburetor inlet, and the other bellows senses the fuel pressure at the carburetor fuel inlet. A differential bellows can be used to measure gauge pressure by leaving one of the bellows open to the atmosphere and the other connected to the pressure to be measured.

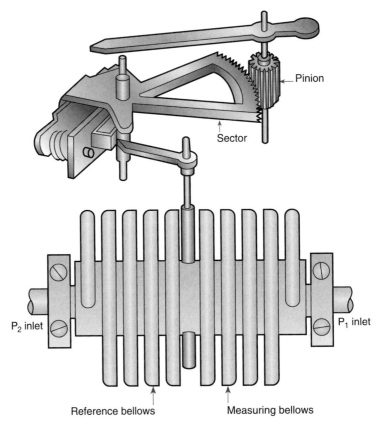

Figure 4-8. *Differential bellows mechanism that may be used to measure absolute, differential, or gauge pressure.*

STUDY QUESTIONS: PRESSURE MEASURING INSTRUMENTS

Answers are provided on page 304.

1. Pressure referenced from a vacuum is called _____ pressure.

2. An altimeter measures _____ (absolute, differential, or gauge) pressure.

3. Pressure referenced from the existing atmospheric pressure is called _____ pressure.

4. Engine oil pressure is an example of _____ (absolute, differential, or gauge) pressure.

5. A Bourdon tube instrument is used to measure _____ (absolute, differential, or gauge) pressure.

6. Pressure that is the difference between two pressures is called _____ pressure.

7. The pressure measured by an airspeed indicator is _____ (absolute, differential, or gauge) pressure.

Temperature Measuring Instruments

Pilots need to know the temperatures in aircraft that range all of the way from the low temperatures of the outside air at high altitude to the high temperatures of the engine exhausts. Three basic temperature measurement methods are discussed here: nonelectrical measurement, used for measuring outside air temperature and oil temperature in most small general aviation aircraft; resistance-change electrical instruments for measuring low temperatures; and thermocouple instruments for measuring high temperatures.

Nonelectrical Temperature Measurements

Most solids, liquids, and gases change dimensions proportional to their temperature changes. These dimensional changes may be used to move pointers across a dial to indicate changes in temperature.

Most small general aviation aircraft have an outside air temperature gauge protruding through the windshield. This simple thermometer is made of strips of two metals having different coefficients of expansion welded together, side by side, and twisted into a helix, or spiral. When this bimetallic strip is heated, one strip expands more than the other and the spiral tries to straighten out. A pointer is attached to the metal strip in such a way that, as the temperature changes, the pointer moves across a dial to indicate the temperature. During routine inspections, the outside air temperature gauge should be inspected to make sure that it is legible and accurate, and to verify that it is not loose or damaged.

helix. A screw-like, or spiral, curve.

Liquids also change their dimensions as their temperature changes. The most common example of this is the glass tube mercury thermometer often used in chemistry and physics laboratories and as home fever thermometers. These thermometers are simply thick-wall glass tubes that have a small reservoir on one end and a precision small-diameter bore through the entire length of the tube. The reservoir holds a supply of mercury that extends part-way up into the bore. When the temperature of the reservoir changes, the mercury expands or contracts, and its top end moves up or down against graduated marks that are engraved into the glass tube. Because of their delicacy, mercury thermometers find no practical use as aircraft instruments.

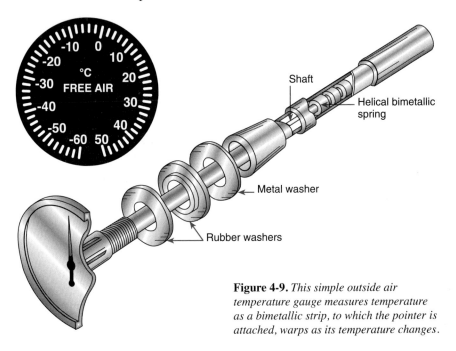

Figure 4-9. *This simple outside air temperature gauge measures temperature as a bimetallic strip, to which the pointer is attached, warps as its temperature changes.*

Temperature is also determined by measuring the pressure of the vapors above a highly volatile liquid. The vapor pressure varies directly as the temperature of the liquid.

A Bourdon tube is connected to a thin-wall, hollow metal bulb by a capillary tube. This is a length of copper tubing that has a very small inside diameter. The bulb is filled with a volatile liquid such as methyl chloride which has a high vapor pressure, and the entire bulb, capillary, and Bourdon tube are sealed as a unit. The bulb is placed where the temperature is to be measured and, as its temperature changes, the pressure of the vapors above the liquid changes. This pressure change is sensed by the Bourdon tube, which moves a pointer across a dial that is calibrated in degrees Fahrenheit or Celsius.

capillary tube. A soft copper tube with a small inside diameter. The capillary tube used with a vapor-pressure thermometer connects the temperature sensing bulb to the Bourdon tube. The capillary tube is protected from physical damage by enclosing it in a braided metal wire jacket.

Electrical Temperature Measurements

Two principles are used to measure temperature electrically, resistance change and voltage generation. The resistance of certain metals changes with their temperature, and this principle is used to measure relatively low temperatures such as oil temperature, outside air temperature, and carburetor air temperature. The voltage generation, or thermocouple principle, is used for measuring higher temperatures such as cylinder-head temperature and exhaust-gas temperature of both reciprocating and turbine engines.

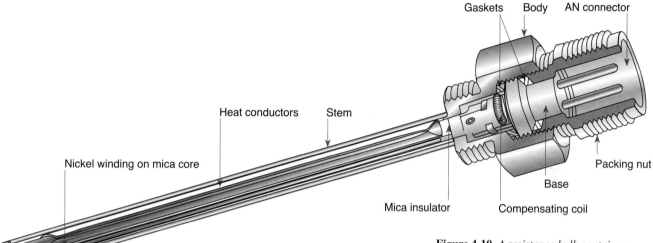

Figure 4-10. *A resistance bulb contains a length of nickel wire whose resistance changes linearly with changes in its temperature.*

Resistance-Change Instruments

A length of fine nickel wire wound around an insulator and enclosed in a thin-wall stainless steel tube serves as the pickup for resistance-change thermometers. See Figure 4-10. The resistance of the wire in this bulb changes from approximately 30 ohms at −70°F to 130 ohms at 300°F.

The resistance of the bulb is measured by either a Wheatstone bridge circuit like the one in Figure 4-11 or ratiometer circuits like those in Figures 4-12 and 4-13.

Wheatstone Bridge Circuit

Some resistance thermometers measure temperature changes by placing the bulb in one of the legs of a Wheatstone bridge, as in Figure 4-11.

The bridge is balanced and no current flows through the indicator when the ratio $R_1 : R_3$ is the same as the ratio of $R_2 : R_{Bulb}$. As the temperature sensed by the bulb decreases, the bulb resistance decreases and the bridge unbalances, sending current through the indicator that drives the needle toward the low side of the dial. An increase in temperature increases the bulb resistance and drives the indicator needle toward the high side of the dial.

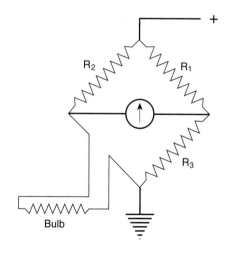

Figure 4-11. *A Wheatstone bridge circuit used to measure temperature.*

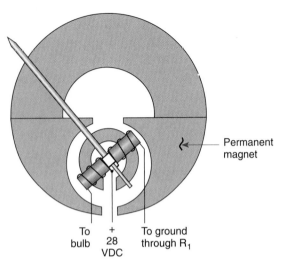

A Indicator has two coils mounted on its needle. These coils rotate over C-shaped core inside the strong magnetic field of the permanent magnet.

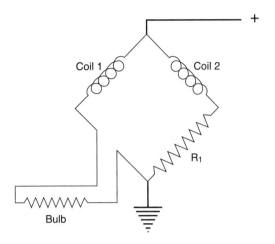

B Basic electrical circuit of the moving-coil ratiometer

Figure 4-12. *A moving-coil ratiometer.*

Ratiometer Circuits

There are two types of ratiometer circuits for measuring temperatures: moving-coil and moving-magnet ratiometers.

The moving-coil ratiometer in Figure 4-12 uses an instrument with two coils mounted on the indicator needle as seen in illustration A. The electrical circuit for this instrument is shown in illustration B. When the temperature is low and the bulb resistance is low, more current flows through coil 1 and the bulb than flows through coil 2 and resistor R_1. The resulting magnetic field pulls the needle toward the low side of the dial. When the temperature is high, the bulb resistance is high, and more current flows through coil 2 and R_1 than through coil 1 and the bulb, and the needle deflects toward the high side of the dial.

A moving-magnet ratiometer has its needle attached to a small permanent magnet that is influenced by the magnetic fields of two fixed coils arranged like those in Figure 4-13A.

Follow the circuit in Figure 4-13B to see the way this instrument measures temperature. When the temperature is low and the bulb resistance is low, more current flows through resistor A, the low-end coil, and the bulb, than flows through resistors A, E, and D. The magnetic field from the low-end coil pulls the needle on the permanent magnet toward the low side of the dial. When the temperature and the resistance of the bulb increase, current flows through resistors B, C, the high-end coil, and resistor D. The resulting magnetic field from the high-end coil moves the needle toward the high side of the dial.

Notice that this instrument can be used in either a 14-volt or a 28-volt aircraft depending upon the pin in the indicator to which the power is connected. A dropping resistor lowers the voltage if the instrument is used in a 28-volt aircraft.

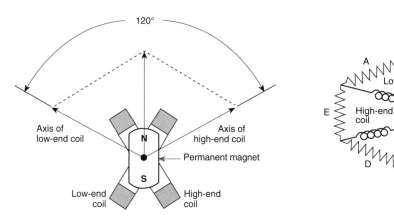

A Indicator has two fixed coils whose magnetic fields determine position of a small permanent magnet to which indicator needle is attached.

B Basic electrical circuit of a moving-magnet ratiometer

Figure 4-13. *A moving-magnet ratiometer.*

Thermocouple Instruments

Cylinder head temperature for reciprocating engines and exhaust gas temperature for both reciprocating and turbine engines are measured with thermocouple instruments. These instruments do not require any external power, since a thermocouple is an electrical generator.

A thermocouple used for measuring cylinder head temperature is a loop made of two different types of wire, as in Figure 4-14. One wire is made of constantan, a copper-nickel alloy, and the other wire is made of iron. One end of each wire is embedded in a copper spark-plug gasket or is joined inside a bayonet like that in Figure 4-15. This end of the loop is called the hot, or measuring, junction. The other ends of the wires are connected to the instrument movement to form the cold, or reference, junction. A voltage is produced between the two junctions that is proportional to the temperature

thermocouple. A loop consisting of two kinds of wire, joined at the hot, or measuring, junction and at the cold junction in the instrument. The voltage difference between the two junctions is proportional to the temperature difference between the junctions. In order for the current to be meaningful, the resistance of the thermocouple is critical, and the leads are designed for a specific installation. Their length should not be altered. Thermocouples used to measure cylinder head temperature are usually made of iron and constantan, and thermocouples that measure exhaust gas temperature for turbine engines are made of chromel and alumel.

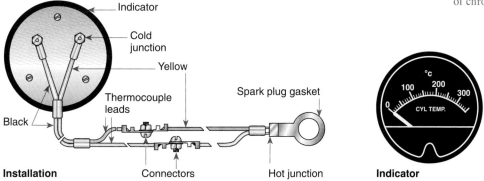

Figure 4-14. *A typical cylinder head temperature indicator installation using a spark plug gasket as the hot, or measuring, junction.*

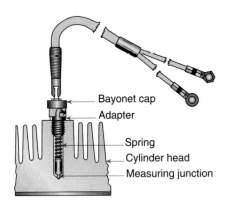

Figure 4-15. *A bayonet-type thermocouple for measuring cylinder head temperature.*

constantan. A copper-nickel alloy used as the negative lead of a thermocouple for measuring the cylinder head temperature of a reciprocating engine.

chromel. An alloy of nickel and chromium used as the positive element in a thermocouple for measuring exhaust gas temperature.

alumel. An alloy of nickel, aluminum, manganese, and silicon that is the negative element in a thermocouple used to measure exhaust gas temperature.

difference between the junctions. This voltage causes current to flow, and this current is measured on the indicator that is calibrated in degrees Celsius or degrees Fahrenheit.

Since the indicator is a current-measuring instrument, the resistance of the thermocouple leads must have a specific value. These leads usually have a resistance of either two or eight ohms, and their length must not be altered to suit the installation. If they are too long they may be coiled neatly so they will not cause any mechanical interference. If the resistance is too low, a special constantan-wire resistor may be installed in the negative lead.

For accurate temperature indication, the reference-junction temperature must be held constant. It is not practical to do this in an aircraft instrument, so the indicator needle is mounted on a bimetallic hairspring in such a way that it moves back as the cockpit temperature increases. This compensates for reference-junction temperature changes.

Higher temperatures, like those found in the exhaust gases of both reciprocating and turbine engines, are measured with thermocouples made of chromel and alumel wires. Chromel is an alloy of nickel and chromium and is used as the positive element in the thermocouple. Alumel is an alloy of nickel, aluminum, manganese, and silicon and is used as the negative element. Figure 4-16 shows a typical exhaust gas temperature system for a reciprocating engine. The thermocouple is mounted in the exhaust pipe, usually within about six inches of the cylinder.

The indicator is a current-measuring instrument similar to that used for measuring cylinder head temperature. See Figure 4-16.

The exhaust gas temperature (EGT) system for a turbine engine is similar to that for a reciprocating engine except that several thermocouples are used.

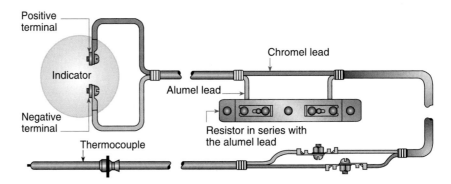

Figure 4-16. *A typical exhaust gas temperature indication system for installation on a reciprocating engine.*

These are arranged around the tail cone so they can sample the temperature in several locations. These indications are averaged to give one indication that is the average temperature of the gases leaving the turbine. Figure 4-17 shows a typical circuit for a turbine engine EGT system.

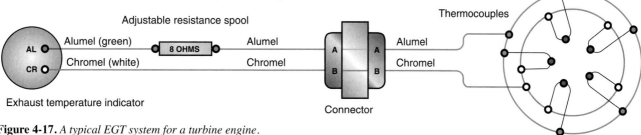

Figure 4-17. *A typical EGT system for a turbine engine.*

STUDY QUESTIONS: TEMPERATURE MEASURING INSTRUMENTS

Answers are provided on page 304.

8. A bimetallic-strip thermometer measures temperature because the two strips of metals have different coefficients of _____ .

9. A Bourdon tube thermometer measures temperature by measuring the pressure of the _____ of a volatile liquid.

10. The temperature-sensitive element in a resistance thermometer is a coil made of _____ wire.

11. As the temperature sensed by a resistance bulb increases, the resistance of the bulb _____ (increases or decreases).

12. Thermocouples used for measuring cylinder head temperature are usually made of _____ and _____ .

13. Most cylinder head temperature and exhaust gas temperature gauges are _____ (current or voltage) measuring instruments.

14. The thermocouple junction formed by the instrument movement of a cylinder head temperature gauge is the _____ (measuring or reference) junction.

15. Thermocouples used for measuring exhaust gas temperature are usually made of _____ and _____ .

16. The negative lead in an EGT thermocouple is made of _____ .

Mechanical Movement Measuring Instruments

Instruments that measure mechanical movement include all of the position-indicating lights as well as remote-indicating synchro systems. This section also discusses such devices as tachometers and accelerometers.

Position-Indicating Lights

There are a number of indications in an aircraft for which the only information needed is a simple yes or no. The flight crew needs to know if the landing gear is down and locked or if it is not down and locked, and if the cabin door is closed and locked or if it is not closed and locked. This information can be generated and displayed by simple switches and lights.

Precision switches, often called Microswitches after the trade name of the most popular manufacturer, detect a specific position of the item being measured. Figure 4-18 shows a typical precision switch. The operating plunger must be in a very specific position for the contacts to snap to their opposite condition. One switch can be placed on each of the three landing gears in such a way that their plunger will close the contacts only when each gear is fully down and correctly locked.

The down-and-locked position of the three landing gears may close switches that are in series. The indicator light will turn on only when all three switches are closed. In more modern installations, a signal may be sent from the three switches to a three-input AND gate circuit. When all three landing gears are down and locked, a signal at the output of the AND gate will cause a light to show that they are all down and locked.

Microswitch. The registered trade name for a precision switch that uses a short throw of the control plunger to actuate the contacts. Microswitches are used primarily as limit switches to control electrical units automatically.

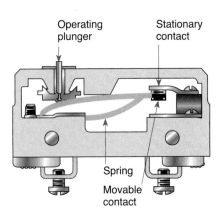

Figure 4-18. *A typical precision switch used to indicate that some device is in a specific position.*

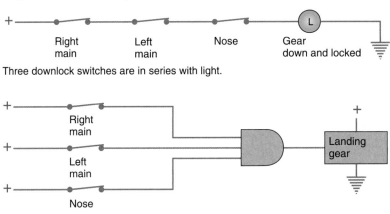

Three downlock switches are in series with light.

Electronic indicator is actuated by three switches connected to three inputs of an AND gate. Light on annunciator panel will illuminate only when all three gears are down and locked.

Figure 4-19. *A simplified diagram of a position indicating system that turns on a light only when all three landing gears are down and locked.*

Synchro Systems

A synchro system is a remote-indicating system in which the needle of an indicator moves in synchronization with the device whose movement is being monitored. There are three commonly used systems: the DC Selsyn system, the AC Magnesyn system, and the AC Autosyn system.

DC Selsyn System

A typical DC Selsyn system like that used to measure such movements as cowl flap position or stabilizer position is shown in Figure 4-20. A coil of resistance wire is wound around a circular form, and two wipers are driven by the device whose movement is being measured. One of the two wipers has a positive DC potential and the other is at ground potential. Current from these two wipers flows through the resistance element and then to the three coils inside the indicator. These coils are connected into a delta arrangement. As the wipers move over the resistance element, the current through the three coils changes and produces a moving magnetic field. A permanent magnet inside the coils locks with this field and rotates as the field changes. The pointer attached to the magnet moves across a calibrated dial to follow the movement being measured. The two wiper arms may be moved in relation to each other to adjust the position of the pointer on the dial when the device being measured is at either end of its travel.

synchro system. A remote instrument indicating system. A synchro transmitter is actuated by the device whose movement is to be measured, and it is connected electrically with wires to a synchro indicator whose pointer follows the movement of the shaft of the transmitter.

Selsyn system. A synchro system used in remote indicating instruments. The rotor in the indicator is a permanent magnet and the stator is a tapped toroidal coil. The transmitter is a circular potentiometer with DC power fed into its wiper. The transmitter is connected to the indicator in such a way that rotation of the transmitter shaft varies the current in the indicator toroidal coil. The magnet in the indicator follows the rotation of the transmitter shaft.

delta connection. A method of connecting three electrical coils into a ring or, as they are drawn on a schematic diagram as a triangle, a delta (Δ).

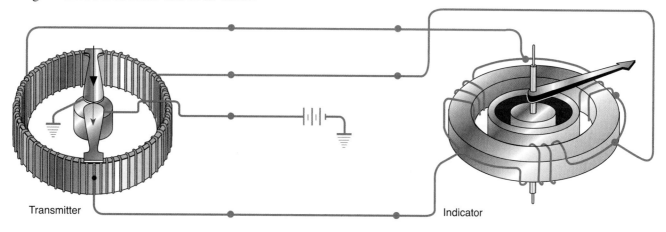

Figure 4-20. *A typical DC Selsyn system used to measure such mechanical movement as that of engine cowl flaps.*

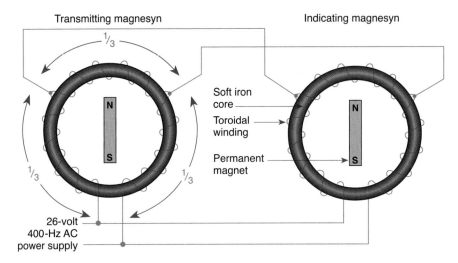

Figure 4-21. *A simplified circuit of a Magnesyn remote position indicating system.*

Magnesyn system. A synchro system used in remote indicating instruments. The rotors in a Magnesyn system are permanent magnets, and the stators are tapped toroidal coils, excited with 26-volt, 400-hertz AC. The rotor in the indicator will exactly follow the movement of the rotor in the transmitter.

toroidal coil. An electrical coil that is wound around a ring-shaped core of highly permeable material.

AC Magnesyn System

The Magnesyn (Magnetic Synchro) system is an AC remote-indicating system that uses permanent magnets for the moving elements and toroidal coils wound on highly permeable ring-type cores for the stationary elements.

The toroidal coils in the transmitter and indicator are tapped at two points and are connected as shown in Figure 4-21. The ends of the coils are excited with 26-volt, 400-Hz AC. A permanent magnet mounted on a shaft is free to rotate in the center of the coil. The magnet in the transmitter is driven by the device whose movement is to be measured, and the needle of the indicator is mounted on the shaft of the magnet in the indicator coil.

When no current is flowing in the coils, the flux from the permanent magnets flows through the ring-shaped cores surrounding them. But when current is flowing through the coils, the cores become magnetically saturated so they can no longer accept the flux from the permanent magnets. The coils are excited with 26-volt, 400-Hz AC so the cores become saturated and then demagnetized 800 times a second. This causes the flux from the permanent magnets to cut across the windings each time the flux from the AC in the windings drops through zero. The flux from the permanent magnets induces a voltage in the coils that causes a current to flow in the three segments of the coils. This current varies with the position of the magnets.

The magnet in the transmitter is considerably larger than that in the indicator, and the voltage it induces causes the small permanent magnet in the indicator to follow its movement.

One of the popular applications of the Magnesyn system is the Magnesyn remote-indicating compass. The compass transmitter is mounted in the wing or tail of the aircraft away from any interfering magnetic fields. This transmitter consists of a metal float, housing a rather large permanent magnet. The float rides inside a plastic housing that is filled with a damping liquid, and the toroidal coil is mounted on the outside of the housing. The magnet remains aligned with the earth's magnetic field, and as the airplane rotates around it, the current in the indicator coils changes, and the small permanent magnet in the indicator to which the pointer is attached retains its relationship with the magnet in the transmitter. The pointer attached to the magnet shaft rides over a calibrated dial to indicate the compass heading of the aircraft.

AC Autosyn System

The Autosyn (Automatic Synchro) system is used for many of the same purposes as the Magnesyn system, but it uses an electromagnet for its rotor. The Autosyn system, seen in Figure 4-22, uses delta-wound, distributed-pole, three-phase stators and single-phase rotors. The rotors are excited with 26-volt, 400-Hz AC. The AC in the rotor induces a voltage in the three-phase windings of the stator, and since the two stators are connected together in parallel, the voltages in the three stator windings of the indicator are exactly the same as those in the transmitter. The rotor in the transmitter is moved by the object whose movement is being measured, and as it moves, the magnetic field it induces in the three windings of the transmitter stator changes. The current in the indicator stator windings is the same as that in the transmitter stator, and the magnetic field it produces causes the rotor in the indicator to follow the rotor in the transmitter. See the cutaway view of an Autosyn indicator shown in Figure 4-23 on the next page.

Autosyn system. A synchro system used in remote indicating instruments. The rotors in an Autosyn system are two-pole electromagnets, and the stators are delta-connected, three-phase, distributed-pole windings in the stator housings. The rotors in the transmitters and indicators are connected in parallel and are excited with 26-volt, 400-hertz AC. The rotor in the indicator follows the movement of the rotor in the transmitter.

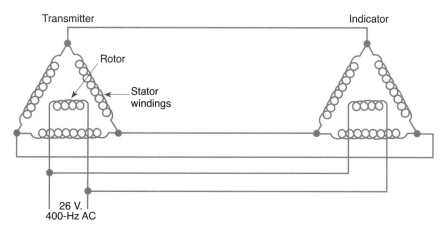

Figure 4-22. *A simplified circuit of an Autosyn remote position indicating system.*

Tachometers

One of the earliest aircraft instruments was a tachometer, used to let the pilot know the RPMs of the engine. Today, tachometers are required instruments in all powered aircraft, and their indications allow the pilots to monitor the performance of the engines. Tachometers for reciprocating engines indicate the engine speed in RPM times 100. Turbine-engine tachometers indicate the compressor speed in percent of the rated RPM.

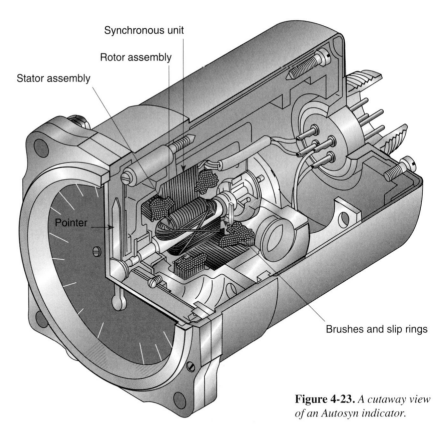

Figure 4-23. *A cutaway view of an Autosyn indicator.*

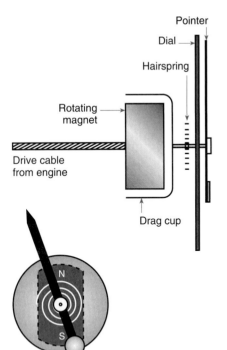

Figure 4-24. *A simplified diagram of a mechanically operated magnetic drag tachometer.*

The earliest tachometers were centrifugal instruments that used the same principle as the governors for steam engines. During World War II, a popular tachometer used a rather complicated clockwork mechanism that momentarily coupled a shaft from the engine directly to the indicating needle about once a second.

The mechanism in some modern mechanical tachometers resembles automobile speedometers, and the most popular electrical tachometer is based on a three-phase synchronous motor. New technology tachometers are digital electronic devices that count pulses from a tachometer generator or from the reciprocating-engine ignition system and display the engine speed in a digital format.

Mechanical Tachometer

The most widely used tachometer for smaller reciprocating engines is of the magnetic drag type. See Figure 4-24. A relatively small permanent magnet inside the instrument case is driven by a steel cable from the engine at one-half the crankshaft speed. Riding on the outside of this magnet, but not touching it, is an aluminum drag cup. A steel shaft attached to the outside center of this cup rides in bearings in the instrument so it is free to rotate. The instrument pointer is attached to this shaft and its rotation is restrained by a calibrated hairspring.

When the engine is operating, the magnet is spinning inside the instrument. As it spins, its lines of flux cut across the aluminum drag cup and induce an eddy current in it. This current produces a magnetic field which interacts with that of the rotating magnet and tries to drive the drag cup. But rotation of the cup is restrained by the calibrated hairspring so it rotates only a portion of a revolution. The pointer on the shaft moves in front of a dial that is marked in RPM times 100 to indicate the speed of the crankshaft.

This type of tachometer is mounted inside a steel case that prevents the magnetic flux produced by the rotating magnet from interfering with other instruments in the panel.

Most magnetic drag tachometers have an hourmeter built into them that is the counterpart to the odometer on an automobile speedometer. A series of drums with numbers on their outer surfaces are turned by a worm gear from the magnet drive shaft. The numbers on these drums indicate the number of hours the engine has run. The hours indication is derived from a shaft whose number of revolutions in a given time is a function of the speed of the engine. Because of this, the hours indication is accurate only at the cruise RPM of the engine. When replacing a magnetic drag tachometer, be sure to use one that is designed for the cruise RPM of the engine whose speed it is measuring. This RPM is stamped on the instrument case. The hours indication on this type of tachometer is normally considered sufficiently accurate for measuring inspection intervals and total engine operating time.

Magnetic drag tachometers are not known for their accuracy, and since engine RPM is extremely important, the tachometer indication should be checked with a stroboscopic tachometer any time there is reason to doubt the accuracy of the instrument.

Electric Tachometer

In the past, electric tachometers have used either an AC or DC permanent-magnet generator driven at one-half crankshaft speed. The voltage of these generators is proportional to their RPM, and this voltage was measured and displayed as RPM on the dial of a voltmeter. This system is limited because its accuracy depends on the strength of the permanent magnet in the generator, and this strength deteriorates with time.

A much more accurate system uses a three-phase permanent magnet generator on the engine that drives a small synchronous motor inside the indicator case. This motor in turn drives a magnet assembly and a drag disk such as the one in Figure 4-25 on the next page. The drag disk, with its calibrated hairspring and pointer, operates in exactly the same way as the drag cup in the mechanical tachometer. This instrument is inherently accurate, as the frequency of the generator is determined only by the RPM of the engine, and variations of the strength of the generator magnet have little or no effect on the accuracy.

RPM. Revolutions per minute

stroboscopic tachometer. A tachometer used to measure the speed of any rotating device without physical contact. A highly accurate variable-frequency oscillator triggers a high-intensity strobe light. When the lamp is flashing at the same frequency the device is rotating, the device appears to stand still.

hysteresis disk. A metal disk that is rigidly attached to the shaft, which drives the rotating magnet assembly. Lines of flux from the rotating magnetic field cut through the disk and induce eddy currents that develop a magnetic field in the disk. This field reacts with the rotating field to create a magnetic drag, which turns the disk.

The spring-loaded rotor produces starting and running torque at low speeds when the magnitude of the flux is low, but the hysteresis disk provides torque at high speed when the magnitude of the flux is great but the mass of the rotor prevents it from pulling into synchronization by itself. At the higher speeds the hysteresis disk moves the rotor to near synchronous speed.

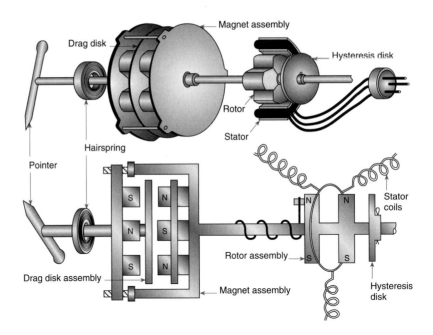

Figure 4-25. *Simplified diagram of a three-phase AC tachometer.*

Synchroscopes

Some tachometers designed for use on multi-engine aircraft have synchroscopes built into them. These instruments simply show a small disk in a cutout on the instrument dial. This disk is marked with light- and dark-colored segments so it is easy to see when it is turning. The disk is driven by two synchronous motor windings on its shaft, and these windings are excited by the output of the two engine tachometer generators. When the engines are turning at the same speed, the torque produced by the two windings cancel, and the disk remains still. But when one engine is turning faster than the other, one set of windings puts out more torque than the other and the disk rotates in the direction of the faster engine. The speed of rotation is one half of the difference in the speed of the two engines.

Accelerometers

In high-performance flight, it is often important to know the dynamic load acting on the aircraft. This load is a function of the force of acceleration and is indicated on an accelerometer in G units (gravity units).

The accelerometer mechanism shown in Figure 4-26 has a small lead weight that rides up and down on two polished steel shafts. When the aircraft is sitting still on the ground or is flying in smooth, straight, and level flight, the pointer-centering spring holds all three pointers pointing to 1G on the dial. This indicates that one force of gravity is acting on the aircraft. When the aircraft is pulled up sharply in flight, inertia acting on the weight pulls it down, and the main pointer and the +G pointers indicate a positive acceleration. When the aircraft returns to straight and level flight, the +G auxiliary pointer

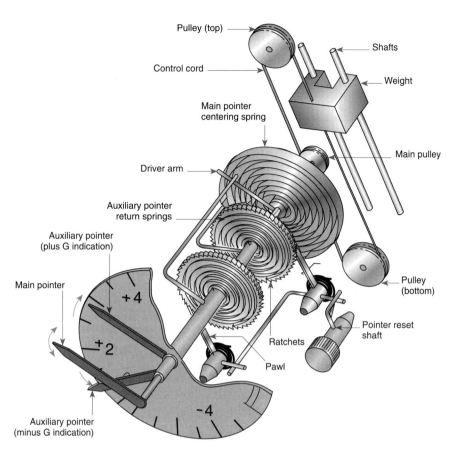

Figure 4-26. *An accelerometer gives the pilot an indication of the dynamic load acting on the aircraft.*

remains at the maximum positive acceleration and the main pointer returns to 1G. When the pilot forces the nose down suddenly, the weight moves up and the main and -G pointers move to indicate the negative acceleration. On return to straight and level flight, the -G pointer remains at the maximum negative acceleration and the main pointer returns to 1G. The two auxiliary pointers may be reset to 1G by pushing in the reset knob on the front of the instrument. This releases the pawls that hold the ratchets on the two auxiliary pointer shafts, and the auxiliary pointer-return springs return the pointers to 1G.

Angle of Attack Indicating Systems

The lift produced by an aircraft wing is a function of the air density and velocity, the size of the wing and shape of the airfoil, and the angle of attack. For many years the main instrument for indicating the approach to a stall has been the airspeed indicator. But this instrument does not tell the whole story. A stall can occur at any airspeed, but it can occur at only one angle of attack. For this reason, many airplanes have angle of attack indicators that allow them to safely fly at high angles of attack.

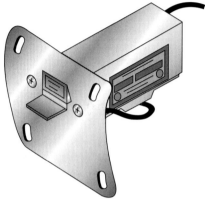

Stall-warning transmitter as it is installed in the leading edge of the wing

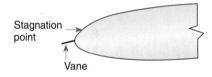

At low angles of attack, tab is below stagnation point and air holds it down, holding switch open.

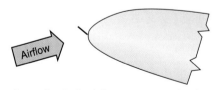

As angle of attack increases to point that a stall could occur, the stagnation point moves down, causing air to flow upward. This raises tab, closes switch and initiates a stall warning signal.

Figure 4-27. *A tab-type stall-warning indicator.*

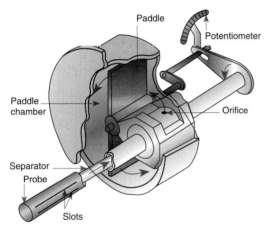

The airstream-direction detector senses the angle of attack the aircraft is flying by the pressure differential inside the paddle chamber.

The angle of attack indicator shows the actual angle of attack being flown.

Figure 4-28. *An angle of attack indicating system.*

angle of attack. The acute angle between the chord line of the wing and the relative wind.

angle-of-attack indicator. An instrument that measures the angle between the local airflow around the direction detector and the fuselage reference plane.

stagnation point. The point on the leading edge of a wing at which the airflow separates, with some flowing over the top of the wing and the rest below the wing.

Small general aviation airplanes such as those used for training have very simple indicators. One of the very simplest is an aural-type indicator. There is a hole at a very specific location in the leading edge of the wing near the root. Inside the wing, attached to this hole, is a reed that vibrates and makes a sound when air flows through it from inside the wing outward. When the angle of attack is low, air flows into this hole, and the reed does not vibrate. But when the angle of attack is high enough to warn of an impending stall, the air flows across the hole and creates a low pressure that draws air from inside the wing. As the air flows through the reed, it produces a sound loud enough to warn the pilot of an impending stall.

A more popular type of stall-warning device uses a small metal tab protruding from the leading edge of the wing at the stagnation point. This is the point at which the airflow separates into some flowing over the top of the wing and the rest below the wing. At low angles of attack, the air holds the tab down, but when the angle of attack increases, the stagnation point moves down, and as the wing approaches a stall, the air flows upward over the tab and raises it. This closes an electrical switch that turns on a stall warning light on the instrument panel or causes an electric stall warning horn to sound. Note that the stall-warning transmitter shown in Figure 4-27 (see previous page) has elongated mounting holes. This allows the transmitter to be adjusted up and down slightly if the stall warning is not activating at the correct airspeed. Always follow the instructions provided in the aircraft maintenance manual for making any adjustments.

For true precision flying, an angle of attack system as shown in Figure 4-28 may be installed. In this system the probe is installed so that it senses the direction of the airflow relative to a fuselage reference plane. As the angle of attack changes, relative amounts of air flowing into the two slots in the probe change. This causes the pressure inside the chambers formed by the upper and lower halves of the paddle to change. When the paddle moves, it moves the wiper of a potentiometer, which causes the pointer in the indicator to move over its dial to indicate the actual angle of attack.

Answers are provided on page 304.

17. A three-input digital logic AND gate can be used in a position indicating system to give the same information as three switches installed in _____ (series or parallel).

18. The moving element in the pickup for a DC Selsyn system is the wiper of a/an _____ .

19. The moving element in the indicator of a DC Selsyn system is a/an _____ .

20. The moving element in the transmitter for an AC Magnesyn system is a/an _____ .

21. The coil used in an AC Magnesyn system is a _____-wound coil.

22. The coil used in an AC Magnesyn system is tapped so it has _____ (how many) sections.

23. The moving element in the transmitter for an AC Autosyn system is a/an _____ .

24. The rotor of an AC Autosyn system has a _____ (single or three)-phase winding.

25. The stator of an AC Autosyn system has a _____ (single or three)-phase winding.

26. The Magnesyn and Autosyn remote indicating systems both are excited with _____-volt, _____-hertz AC.

27. The tachometer for a reciprocating engine gives the engine speed in RPM times _____ .

28. The magnetic drag tachometer measures engine RPM by the interaction of the magnetic field of the rotating permanent magnet and the field produced by _____ in the aluminum drag cup.

29. Most magnetic drag tachometers are mounted in cases made of _____ (steel or plastic).

30. Three-phase AC tachometers measure engine speed by the _____ (voltage or frequency) of the AC they produce.

31. An instrument that shows the pilot or flight engineer the difference in the speeds of the engines in a multi-engine aircraft is called a/an _____ .

32. The dynamic load acting on an aircraft in flight is indicated on an accelerometer in _____ units.

33. An accelerometer in an airplane that is not moving will indicate _____ (0G or 1G).

34. The airspeed of an airplane _____ (is or is not) always an indication of an impending stall.

(continued)

35. The most accurate stall warning systems measure the _____ .

36. Angle of attack indicating systems for high-performance aircraft sense the direction of the airflow over the aircraft relative to the fuselage _____ .

Direction-Indicating Instruments

All certificated aircraft are required to have some type of magnetic direction indicator. The magnetic compass is one of the simplest of all instruments and is one of the oldest. The origin of the magnetic compass dates back to the early sea peoples who discovered that a piece of lodestone, when suspended in the air or floated on a chip of wood, would always point toward the North Star. The simple concept of the magnetic compass has not changed since these early days, and the physical appearance of the aircraft compass has changed very little over the decades. Modern navigation systems have relegated the magnetic compass to a backup status, but its familiar face is present even in jet transport aircraft with their panels full of exotic electronic displays.

The earth is a huge permanent magnet, with magnetic north and south poles located near, but not at, the geographic poles. The magnets in a magnetic compass align with the earth's field and serve as a directional reference for the pilot.

The magnets are attached to the bottom of a metal float suspended on a pivot riding in a cup-shaped jewel in a bowl of compass fluid. Mounted around the float is a ring-shaped dial, called a card, marked with the directions. The four cardinal compass points are marked with the letters N, E, S, and W, and there are marks every five degrees. The alternate marks, which represent 10-degree increments, are longer than the 5-degree marks. Every 30-degree mark has the value of the heading marked above it with the last zero omitted.

A glass lens is mounted in the front of the instrument, and a straight vertical marker, called a lubber line, allows the pilot to relate the heading of the aircraft to the specific degree mark on the card.

The compass is filled with compass fluid, a highly refined petroleum product similar to kerosine. This fluid damps the oscillations of the compass card. Since the bowl is completely full of fluid, a diaphragm or bellows assembly like the one in Figure 4-29 must compensate for changes in volume of the fluid as its temperature changes.

Compass Errors

The magnetic compass requires no electrical power, and needs no other components to function. But it has three basic errors to be aware of: variation, deviation, and dip errors.

lodestone. A magnetized piece of natural iron oxide.

cardinal compass points. The four principal directions on a compass: North, East, South, and West.

lubber line. A reference on a magnetic compass and directional gyro that represents the nose of the aircraft. The heading of the aircraft is shown on the compass card opposite the lubber line.

compass fluid. A highly refined, water-clear petroleum product similar to kerosine. Compass fluid is used to damp the oscillations of magnetic compasses.

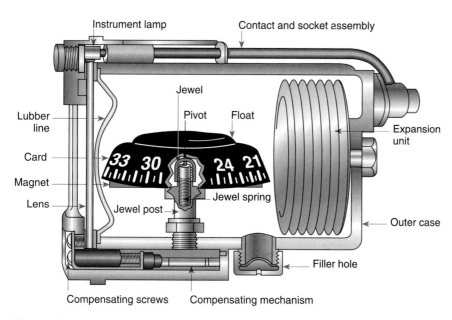

Figure 4-29. *A cutaway view of a direct-reading magnetic compass.*

Variation

The magnetic compass error caused by the fact that the earth's magnetic and geographic poles are not at the same location is called variation error. In land navigation, this is called declination error.

The compass magnets always align with the earth's magnetic field, and the lines of force of this field leave the earth at its magnetic north pole and return at its magnetic south pole. All aeronautical charts are drawn with reference to the earth's geographic north and south poles. Since the magnetic and geographic poles are not at the same physical location, the compass indication cannot be used directly with an aeronautical chart.

Aeronautical charts have isogonic lines drawn across them, and anywhere along a given isogonic line, there is a specific angular difference between the magnetic north pole and the geographic pole. For example, along the 15° east isogonic line that passes roughly through Denver, Colorado, the compass points to a location that is 15° east of the geographic north pole. When a pilot flying in the area of Denver wants to fly due east (090°), he or she must subtract this 15° and fly a magnetic course of 075°.

There is one line along which magnetic and geographic poles are in alignment. This is called the agonic line and it runs roughly through Chicago, Illinois. See Figure 4-30. East of the agonic line, the compass points to a location that is west of true north and the variation must be added to the true direction to find the magnetic course. The variation error is the same regardless of the heading the aircraft is flown, but it varies with the location on the earth's surface, and it continually changes. These changes, while small, are great enough that the position of the isogonic lines are redrawn on aeronautical charts each time the charts are revised.

isogonic line. A line drawn on an aeronautical chart along which the angular difference between the magnetic and geographic north poles is the same.

agonic line. A line drawn on an aeronautical chart along which there is no angular difference between the magnetic and geographic north poles.

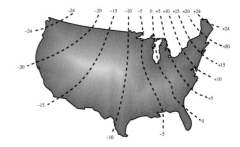

Figure 4-30. *Isogonic lines of equal compass variation.*

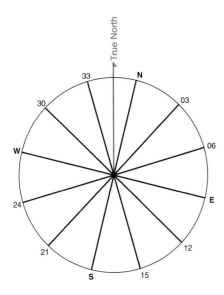

Figure 4-31. *Compass roses are laid out on many airports to be used to swing magnetic compasses.*

compass rose. A location on an airport where an aircraft can be taken to have its compasses "swung." Lines are painted on the rose to mark the magnetic directions in 30° increments.

compass swinging. A maintenance procedure that corrects a magnetic compass for deviation error. The aircraft is aligned on a compass rose, and the compensating magnets in the compass case are adjusted to get the compass to align with the direction marked on the rose. After the deviation error is minimized on all headings, a compass correction card is completed and mounted on the instrument panel next to the compass.

deviation error. An error in a magnetic compass caused by localized magnetic fields in the aircraft. Deviation error, which is different on each heading, is compensated by the technician "swinging" the compass. A compass must be compensated so the deviation error on any heading is no greater than 10 degrees.

Deviation

The floating magnets in a compass are affected not only by the earth's magnetic field, but by all other magnetic fields near them. They align with the composite field produced by the earth's field and the magnetic influence of steel structural members, current-carrying wires, and steel instrument cases. The effect of this composite field varies with the heading of the aircraft, and a correction must be made by the pilot for each different heading flown. Deviation error is minimized by two small permanent magnets inside the compensating mechanism in the compass.

Many airports have a compass rose on which an airplane is placed to swing the compass to minimize the deviation error. The compass rose is usually painted on a taxi strip well away from any magnetic interference caused by electrical power lines or buried pipes. The north-south line is aligned exactly magnetic north and south, and intersecting lines are laid out every 30°. See Figure 4-31.

A compass is "swung," to compensate it for deviation error, by following these steps:

1. Taxi the airplane onto the compass rose and align it along the north-south line, pointing north. Leave the engine running at a speed that allows the alternator to produce current.

2. Using a nonmagnetic screwdriver, turn the N-S compensating screw seen in Figure 4-32 until the compass reads N (360°).

3. Move the airplane until it aligns with the east-west line, pointed east. Adjust the E-W compensating screw until the compass reads E (090°).

4. Move the airplane until it aligns with the north-south line, pointed south. Adjust the N-S screw to remove one half of the N-S error. Record the compass indication with the radio off and again with it on.

5. Move the airplane until it aligns with the east-west line, pointed west. Adjust the E-W screw to remove one half of the E-W error. Record the compass indication with the radio off and again with it on.

6. Move the airplane until it aligns with the 300° line and record the compass indication with the radio both off and on.

7. Continue to move the airplane until it aligns with each line in the compass rose and record the compass indications with the radio both off and on.

8. Make a compass correction card similar to the one in Figure 4-33.

There should be no compass error greater than 10° on any heading. If there is an error greater than this, the cause must be found and corrected. Some part of the structure may have to be demagnetized, some equipment may have to be moved, or some electrical wires may have to be rerouted.

FOR	000	030	060	090	120	150
STEER						
RDO. ON	001	032	062	095	123	155
RDO. OFF	002	031	064	094	125	157

FOR	180	210	240	270	300	330
STEER						
RDO. ON	176	210	243	271	296	325
RDO. OFF	174	210	240	273	298	327

Figure 4-32. *The deviation compensating screws on a magnetic compass.*

Figure 4-33. *A compass correction card.*

The compass is lighted with a tiny DC light bulb. The wiring used to carry the current to and from this bulb should be twisted and grounded at a location well away from the compass. Twisting the wires effectively cancels the magnetic fields caused by the current.

Dip Errors

The earth's magnetic field leaves the surface vertically at the North Pole and re-enters vertically at the South Pole. Near the equator, the field parallels the surface of the earth. The compass magnets align with the magnetic field, and near the poles, the magnetic field pulls one end of the magnet down. To compensate for this tilt, the compass float is weighted so it will float relatively level in all but the extremely high latitudes. This tilt and its correction cause two errors: acceleration error and northerly turning error.

When an aircraft accelerates while flying on an east or west heading, the inertia of the dip-compensating weight causes the compass card to swing toward the north. When it decelerates on either of these headings, the inertia causes the card to swing toward the south.

When an aircraft is flying on a northerly heading and is banked for a turn, the downward pull of the vertical component of the magnetic field causes the card to start to move in the direction opposite to the direction of the turn. When banking for a turn from a southerly heading, the card starts to turn in the correct direction, but it turns faster than the airplane is turning.

Vertical-Card Magnetic Compass

The traditional magnetic compass in Figure 4-32 has a built-in error potential in reading the heading indication. Notice that when the aircraft is flying on a northerly heading, the indications for easterly directions are on the west side

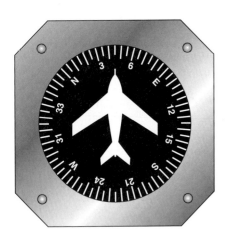

Figure 4-34. *A vertical-card magnetic compass minimizes the error of turning in the wrong direction to reach a desired heading.*

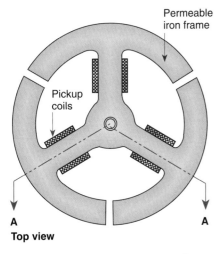

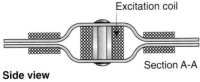

Figure 4-35. *The flux valve has a highly permeable segmented-ring frame suspended as a pendulum. An excitation coil mounted in the center of the frame carries 400-Hz AC which magnetically saturates the frame 800 times each second.*

of the compass. The reason is that the pilot is looking at the back side of the compass card, and the airplane turns around the card. This error potential is minimized by the vertical card compass in Figure 4-34.

The dial of the instrument is driven by gears from the magnet, which is mounted on a shaft rather than floating in a bowl of liquid. Oscillations of the magnet are damped by eddy currents induced into a damping cup. The nose of the symbolic airplane serves as the lubber line, and it is easy for the pilot to immediately visualize the direction to turn to reach a given heading.

Inspection of Magnetic Compass Systems

Inspect the magnetic compass for security and obvious defects. Visually inspect the fluid level and turn the instrument lights on to check the operation of the light bulb. Verify that the compass correction card is mounted close to the compass and is legible. Compass correction cards are often in a location where they are in direct sunlight and are prone to fading.

Flux Gate Compass System

The magnetic compass has so many limitations that much study has been made to determine direction relative to the earth's magnetic field by methods other than simply observing a card or dial attached to a floating magnet.

The successful New York-to-Paris flight by Charles Lindbergh in 1927 was made possible, in part, by an earth inductor compass that overcame the oscillation and dip errors and minimized the deviation error. A wind-driven generator was mounted behind the cabin where magnetic interference from the engine was minimum. This generator contained coils in which the earth's magnetic field induced a voltage whose phase was altered by the heading of the aircraft. A controller allowed Lindbergh to set in the compass heading he wished to fly.

An electrical indicator on the instrument panel showed him when his actual heading was either to the right or left of the desired heading. By keeping the needle centered, he was able to fly a constant heading. Modern flux-gate compasses work on this same basic principle, but the hardware has been vastly improved.

A flux valve like the one in Figure 4-35 is mounted in a location in the aircraft where magnetic interference is minimum, often near a wing tip or in the vertical fin. The sensitive portion of the flux valve consists of a highly permeable segmented-ring frame, suspended as a pendulum and sealed in a housing filled with a damping fluid, as in Figure 4-36. A coil is mounted in the center of the frame and is excited with 400-Hz AC. Pickup coils are wound around each of the three legs, and they are connected into a Y-circuit as shown in Figure 4-38 on page 264.

When the aircraft is flying, the earth's magnetic field is picked up by the permeable frame. During each peak of the excitation AC, the frame is magnetically saturated and rejects the earth's field. But 800 times a second, as

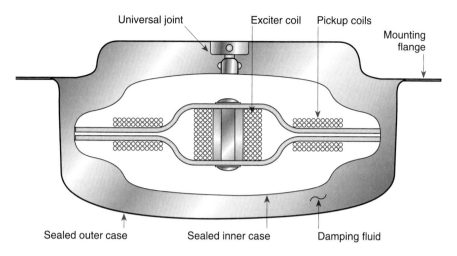

Figure 4-36. *The flux valve is sealed inside a case which is suspended as a pendulum in a housing filled with a damping fluid.*

eddy current damping. Decreasing the amplitude of oscillations by the interaction of magnetic fields.

In the case of a vertical-card magnetic compass, flux from the oscillating permanent magnet produces eddy currents in a damping disk or cup. The magnetic flux produced by the eddy currents opposes the flux from the permanent magnet and decreases the oscillations.

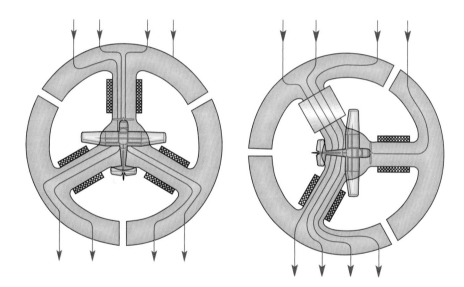

Figure 4-37. *When the frame is not saturated, it accepts flux from the earth's magnetic field. This flux cuts across the windings of the three pickup coils. The heading of the aircraft determines the voltage relationships existing in the coils.*

the AC drops back through zero, the earth's field cuts across the windings of the three pickup coils and induces a voltage in them. The relationship of the voltage in each of the three coils is determined by the heading of the aircraft.

The output of the three pickup coils in the flux valve is fed into the flux-valve synchro in Figure 4-38. The three-phase voltage in the stator causes its rotor to follow the rotation of the aircraft relative to the earth's magnetic field. The voltage output of this rotor is fed into a compass-slaving amplifier whose output excites one phase of a two-phase slaving torque motor. This motor applies a force to the slaved attitude gyro, causing it to precess and rotate its gimbals until the rotor of the flux-valve synchro is in a position determined by the relationship of the earth's magnetic field and the pickup coils. Also connected to the gyro gimbals and the flux-valve synchro rotor is the rotor of the heading synchro. As the gyro turns to indicate the rotation of the aircraft relative to the earth's magnetic field, the rotor of the heading synchro turns. This causes the rotor in the movable-dial synchro to rotate the dial of the remote gyro heading indicator.

As we will see in the study of some of the electronic navigation systems, the flux gate compass system is an extremely important component in many modern flight instruments.

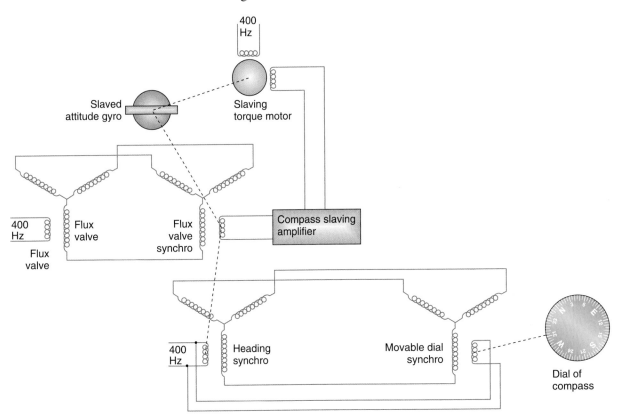

Figure 4-38. *A basic schematic diagram of a flux gate compass system.*

Answers are provided on page 304.

37. The reference mark in a magnetic compass that allows the pilot to determine the exact compass heading is called the _____ .

38. The marks on a magnetic compass card are spaced every _____ degrees.

39. The magnetic and geographic poles of the earth _____ (are or are not) at the same location.

40. Variation error of a compass _____ (does or does not) change with the heading of the aircraft.

41. The compass error caused by local magnetic fields is called _____ (deviation or variation).

42. Deviation error of a compass _____ (does or does not) change with the heading of the aircraft.

43. A technician swings a compass to minimize and plot the _____ (variation or deviation) error.

44. The maximum deviation error allowed for a magnetic compass is _____ degrees.

45. The magnetic fields caused by the current used to power the built-in compass light are minimized by _____ the wires carrying the current.

46. Two compass errors caused by the vertical component of the earth's magnetic field are:

    a. _____

    b. _____

47. The nose of the symbolic airplane on a vertical-card magnetic compass serves as the _____ .

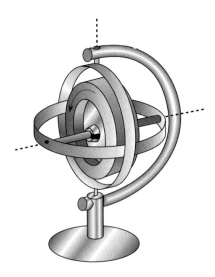

Figure 4-39. *A spinning gyroscope mounted in a double gimbal will remain in the same attitude, relative to the earth, even if its stand is moved, tilted, or twisted.*

gyro (gyroscope). The sensing device in an autopilot system. A gyroscope is a rapidly spinning wheel with its weight concentrated around its rim. Gyroscopes have two basic characteristics that make them useful in aircraft instruments: rigidity in space and precession. *See* rigidity in space and precession.

rigidity in space. The characteristic of a gyroscope that prevents its axis of rotation tilting as the earth rotates. This characteristic is used for attitude gyro instruments.

gimbal. A support that allows a gyroscope to remain in an upright condition when its base is tilted.

attitude indicator. A gyroscopic flight instrument that gives the pilot an indication of the attitude of the aircraft relative to its pitch and roll axes. The attitude indicator in an autopilot is in the sensing system that detects deviation from a level-flight attitude.

Gyroscopic Instruments

A gyroscope is a small wheel with its weight concentrated in its rim. When it spins at a high speed, it exhibits two interesting characteristics: rigidity in space and precession. Directional gyros and gyro horizons are attitude gyros, and they make use of the characteristic of rigidity in space. Rate gyros such as turn and slip indicators and turn coordinators use the characteristic of precession.

Attitude Gyros

If a gyroscope is mounted in a double gimbal like the one in Figure 4-39 and spun at a high speed, it will remain in the attitude in which it was spun even though the stand in which it is mounted is moved, tilted, or twisted. This is the characteristic of rigidity in space and is used in attitude gyro instruments.

Attitude Indicator

The gyro in the attitude indicator seen in Figure 4-40 is mounted in a double gimbal with its spin axis vertical. The older attitude indicator, normally called a gyro horizon, or artificial horizon, has a simple horizon bar that retains its relationship with the gyro as the aircraft pitches and rolls. The amount the aircraft rotates about its pitch and roll axes is indicated by the relationship of the horizon bar with the miniature airplane in the center of the instrument face. This miniature airplane is fixed in its relationship with the aircraft.

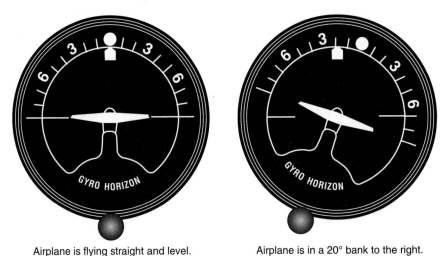

Airplane is flying straight and level.   Airplane is in a 20° bank to the right.

Figure 4-40. *The horizon bar of the gyro horizon remains level with the natural horizon, and the miniature airplane attached to the instrument case depicts the attitude of the aircraft relative to the horizon.*

Modern attitude indicators have replaced the simple horizon bar with a two-color dial like the one in Figure 4-41. The top of this dial is blue to represent the sky and the bottom is brown for the earth. Straight horizontal lines, marked in degrees, align with the miniature airplane to indicate the amount of pitch, and angled lines all pointing into the center indicate the degree of bank.

Heading Indicator

A heading indicator is an attitude gyro instrument with the spin axis of the gyro in a horizontal plane. It senses rotation about the vertical axis of the aircraft. The early heading indicators were called directional gyros, or simply DGs. These instruments had a drum-type card much like that of a floating-magnet compass surrounding the gyro. Modern heading indicators use vertical cards shown in Figure 4-42.

A gyro heading indicator is not a direction-seeking instrument, and it must be set to agree with the magnetic compass. The gyro remains rigid in space and the aircraft turns around it. The symbolic airplane on the glass is fixed, and as the heading of airplane changes, the card rotates and the indication under the extended nose of the airplane is the actual heading. Markers around the instrument dial at 45° and 90° increments make it easy for a pilot to turn 45°, 90°, or 180° without having to do any mental arithmetic.

Rate Gyros

Rate gyros are mounted in single gimbals, and they operate on the characteristic of precession. A force acting on a spinning gyroscope is felt, not at the point of application, but at a point 90° from the point of application in the direction of rotation.

In Figure 4-43, an upward force is applied to one end of the gyro shaft. This is the same as a force applied to the top of the wheel. Rather than tilting the shaft upward, the force is felt at the right side of the wheel, which is 90° from the point of application in the direction the wheel is rotating. Precession causes the upward force on the shaft to rotate the shaft in a counterclockwise direction

Figure 4-41. *A modern attitude indicator has the horizon bar replaced with a two-color dial to indicate sky and ground..*

Figure 4-42. *A vertical-card gyro heading indicator.*

heading indicator. A gyroscopic flight instrument that gives the pilot an indication of the heading of the aircraft.

precession. The characteristic of a gyroscope that causes a force to be felt, not at the point of application, but at a point 90° in the direction of rotation from that point.

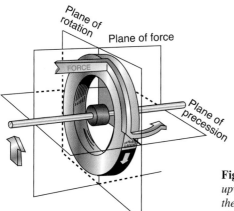

Figure 4-43. *Precession of a gyroscope. An upward force on one end of the shaft causes the gyro to rotate in a counterclockwise direction as viewed from above.*

turn and slip indicator. A rate gyroscopic flight instrument that gives the pilot an indication of the rate of rotation of the aircraft about its vertical axis.

A ball in a curved glass tube shows the pilot the relationship between the centrifugal force and the force of gravity. This indicates whether or not the angle of bank is proper for the rate of turn. The turn and slip indicator shows the trim condition of the aircraft and serves as an emergency source of bank information in case the attitude gyro fails. Turn and slip indicators were formerly called needle and ball and turn and bank indicators.

(when viewed from above) in a horizontal plane. Figure 4-43 summarizes this action. The plane of rotation, plane of force, and plane of precession are all at 90° to each other. An upward force in the plane of the force will cause a counterclockwise rotation in the plane of precession.

Turn and Slip Indicator

The turn and slip indicator in Figure 4-44 is the oldest gyroscopic instrument used in aircraft. It was originally called a needle and ball, then a turn and bank indicator, and in the last couple of decades, it has been more accurately called a turn and slip indicator.

The turn mechanism in this instrument is a gyro wheel mounted in a single gimbal with its spin axis horizontal and the axis of the gimbal aligned with the longitudinal axis of the aircraft. When the aircraft yaws, or rotates about its vertical axis, a force is applied to the front and back of the gimbal, which, because of precession, causes the gimbal to lean over. This leaning is restrained by a calibration spring, and the amount the gimbal leans over is determined by the rate at which the aircraft is yawing. See Figure 4-45.

The rotation of the gimbal drives a paddle-shaped pointer across the instrument dial. There are no graduation numbers on the dial, just an index mark at the top. The calibration spring is adjusted so that the needle moves over with its left edge aligned with the right edge of the index mark when the aircraft is yawing at the rate of 3° per second. This is called a standard-rate turn and will result in a 360° turn in two minutes.

Since fast airplanes must turn at a rate of yaw less than 3° per second, turn and slip indicators for these airplanes are calibrated so that when the left edge of the needle is aligned with the right edge of the index mark, the airplane is yawing 1½ degrees per second. The dials of four-minute turn indicators have, in addition to the index mark, two doghouse-shaped marks located one needle-width away from each side of the index mark. When the needle is aligned with one of the doghouses, the airplane is making a 3° per second turn.

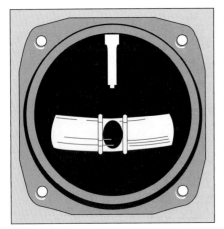

Two-minute turn indicator

4 MIN TURN

Four-minute turn indicator

Figure 4-44. *Turn and slip indicators.*

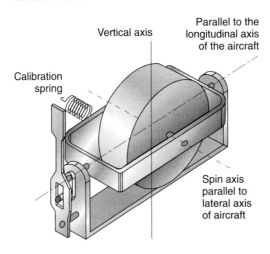

Vertical axis

Parallel to the longitudinal axis of the aircraft

Calibration spring

Spin axis parallel to lateral axis of aircraft

Figure 4-45. *The rate gyro in a turn and slip indicator precesses an amount that is proportional to the rate of rotation about its vertical axis.*

The ball in a turn and slip indicator shows the pilot when the turn is coordinated; that is, when the angle of bank is correct for the rate of turn. In a coordinated turn the force of gravity and the centrifugal force are balanced and the ball remains in the center of the curved glass tube, between the two wires. If the rate of turn is too great for the angle of bank, the centrifugal force is greater than the force of gravity and the ball rolls toward the outside of the turn. If the angle of bank is too great for the rate of turn, the effect of gravity is greater than the centrifugal force and the ball rolls toward the inside of the turn.

Figure 4-46. *A turn coordinator.*

Turn Coordinator

A turn and slip indicator measures rotation only about the vertical axis of the aircraft. But a turn is started by banking the aircraft, or rotating it about its roll axis. When the aircraft is banked, the lift produced by the wings has a horizontal component that pulls the aircraft around in curved flight. An instrument that could sense roll as well as yaw would allow the pilot to keep the aircraft straight and level better than a turn and slip indicator. To this end, the turn coordinator in Figure 4-46 was developed.

A turn coordinator is much like a turn and slip indicator except that the gimbal axis is tilted upward about 30°. This allows it to sense both roll and yaw. The needle has been replaced by a small symbolic airplane, and marks by the wing tips indicate a standard rate turn.

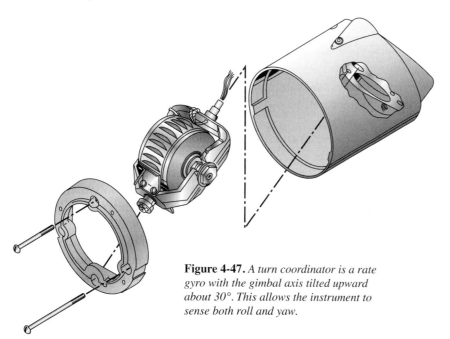

Figure 4-47. *A turn coordinator is a rate gyro with the gimbal axis tilted upward about 30°. This allows the instrument to sense both roll and yaw.*

Answers are provided on page 304.

48. Attitude gyros operate on the gyroscopic principle of _____ (rigidity in space or precession).

49. Attitude gyros are mounted in _____ (single or double) gimbals.

50. An attitude indicator senses rotation about the _____ and _____ axes of an aircraft.

51. The spin axis of the gyro in an attitude indicator is _____ (horizontal or vertical).

52. The heading indicator senses rotation about the _____ axis of the aircraft.

53. The spin axis of the gyro in a heading indicator is _____ (horizontal or vertical).

54. A gyro heading indicator _____ (is or is not) a direction-seeking instrument.

55. Rate gyros operate on the gyroscopic principle of _____ (rigidity in space or recession).

56. A rate gyro is mounted in a _____ (single or double) gimbal.

57. A turn and slip indicator senses rotation about the _____ axis of the aircraft.

58. The spin axis of the gyro in a turn and slip indicator is _____ (horizontal or vertical).

59. A one-needle-width turn with a two-minute turn indicator means that the aircraft is yawing _____ degrees per second.

60. When the needle of a four-minute turn indicator is aligned with one of the doghouses, the aircraft is yawing _____ degrees per second.

61. A turn coordinator senses rotation of an aircraft about its _____ and _____ axes.

Aircraft Instrument Systems

Knowing the basic operating principles of the various types of instruments will help understand the way these instruments relate to the entire aircraft. This section discusses the various systems in which specific instruments are installed.

Pitot-Static Systems

One of the most important instrument systems is the pitot-static system. This system serves as the source of the pressures needed for the altimeter, airspeed indicator, and vertical speed indicator.

A tube with an inside diameter of approximately ¼ inch is installed on the outside of an aircraft in such a way that it points directly into the relative airflow over the aircraft. This tube, called a pitot tube, picks up ram air pressure and directs it into the center hole in an airspeed indicator.

Small holes on either side of the fuselage or vertical fin or small holes in the pitot-static head sense the pressure of the still, or static, air. This pressure is taken into the case of the altimeter, airspeed indicator, and vertical speed indicator.

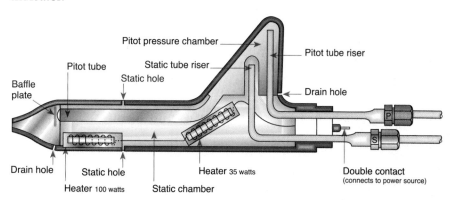

Figure 4-48. *An electrically heated pitot-static head.*

Figure 4-48 shows a typical pitot-static head. Ram, or impact, air is taken into the front of the head and directed up into the pitot pressure chamber. It is taken out of this chamber through the pitot-tube riser to prevent water from getting into the instrument lines. Any water that gets into the pitot head from flying through rain is drained overboard through drain holes in the bottom of the front of the head and in the back of the pressure chamber. Static air pressure is taken in through holes or slots in the bottom and sides of the head. An electrical heater in the head prevents ice from forming on the head and blocking either the static holes or pitot air inlet.

Pitot-static systems for light airplanes are similar to the one in Figure 4-49. The pitot tube for these aircraft is connected directly to the center opening of the airspeed indicator. The two flush static ports, one on either side of the fuselage, are connected together and supply pressure to the airspeed

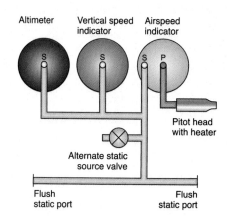

Figure 4-49. *A typical pitot-static system for a small general aviation airplane.*

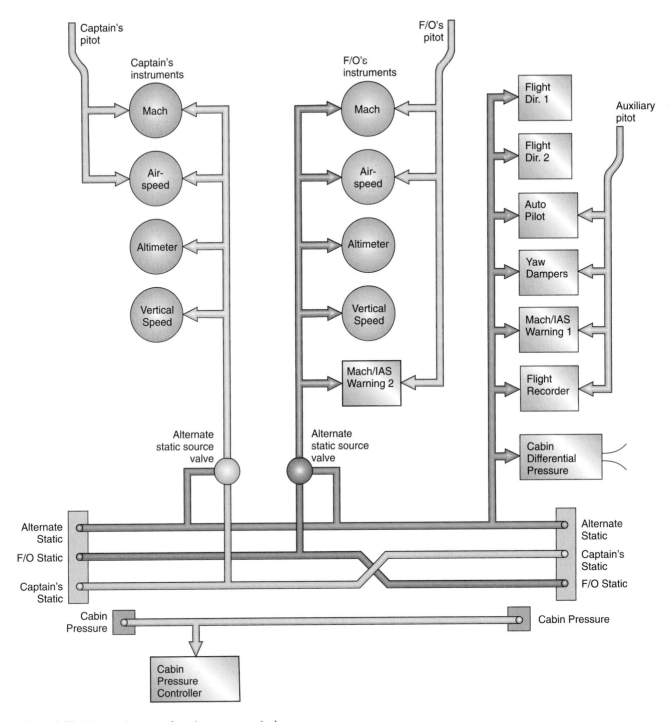

Figure 4-50. *Pitot-static system for a jet transport airplane.*

indicator, altimeter, and vertical-speed indicator. An alternate static air valve is connected into this line to supply static air to the instruments if the outside static ports should ever cover over with ice. The alternate air is taken directly from the cockpit of unpressurized aircraft, but pressurized aircraft pick it up from outside of the pressure vessel. When inspecting a pitot-static system, always actuate the alternate static source to verify that it is working correctly. It is common to see a slight jump in the vertical speed indicator when opening or closing the alternate static source. You may also see a small amount of water come out of the drain when actuating the alternate static source valve. Alternate static sources are usually designed to be at the low spot in the static system. This allows any accumulated water from condensation to be easily drained when actuating the alternate static source.

Large jet transport aircraft have a more complex pitot-static system. Figure 4-50 shows such a system. The pitot tube on the left side of the aircraft supplies the captain's Machmeter and airspeed indicator. Static pressure for all of the captain's instruments is obtained from the captain's static source, but the alternate static source valve allows this to be taken from the alternate static sources.

The right-hand pitot tube supplies pitot air pressure to the first officer's Machmeter, airspeed indicator, and No. 2 Mach/Indicated Airspeed warning system. All the first officer's static instruments connect to the F/O static source, and can also be connected to the alternate static source.

The auxiliary pitot tube picks up ram air for the auto pilot, yaw dampers, No. 1 Mach/IAS warning system, and flight recorder. The alternate static source supplies air to these instruments plus the two flight directors and the reference for cabin differential pressure.

Airspeed Indicators

An airspeed indicator is a differential pressure indicator that takes ram, or pitot, air pressure into a diaphragm assembly and static air pressure into the instrument case. See Figure 4-51. As the aircraft flies faster, the diaphragm expands, and this expansion is transmitted through the rocking shaft and sector gear to the pinion which is mounted on the same shaft as the pointer.

The indication on the airspeed indicator is called indicated airspeed (IAS), and two corrections must be applied before this is of value in precision flying.

The air passing over the aircraft structure does not flow smoothly over all parts, and its flow pattern changes with the airspeed. The pressure of the air picked up by the static ports changes with the airspeed, and this change in pressure causes an error in the airspeed indication called position error. When indicated airspeed is corrected for position error, the result is calibrated airspeed (CAS). Equivalent airspeed (EAS) and true airspeed (TAS) are obtained by correcting CAS for compressibility and nonstandard temperature and pressure. This correction is done by the pilot with a flight computer.

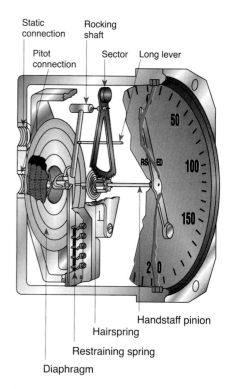

Figure 4-51. *Cutaway view of an airspeed indicator.*

indicated airspeed (IAS). The airspeed as shown on an airspeed indicator with no corrections applied.

calibrated airspeed (CAS). Indicated airspeed corrected for position error. See position error.

position error. The error in pitot-static instruments that is caused by the static ports not sensing true static air pressure. Position error changes with airspeed and is usually greatest at low airspeeds.

equivalent airspeed (EAS). Calibrated airspeed corrected for errors caused by the compressibility of the air inside the pitot tube.

compressibility. The change in air density due to compression. At relatively low airspeeds, this change is small and no correction is needed. However, at high airspeeds, generally above 200 knots IAS, or at altitudes above 10,000 feet, compressibility effects become more significant and require that corrections be made.

true airspeed (TAS). Equivalent airspeed corrected for nonstandard pressure and temperature.

knot. A speed measurement that is equal to one nautical mile per hour. One knot is equal to 1.15 statute mile per hour.

True Airspeed Indicator

A true airspeed indicator contains a temperature-compensated aneroid bellows that modifies the movement of the levers as the pressure and temperature change. The pointer indicates the true airspeed being flown.

An airspeed indicator installed in many of the small general aviation aircraft is called a True Speed indicator. See Figure 4-52. This instrument has two cutouts in the dial, with a movable subdial which has altitude graduations visible in one cutout and true airspeed visible in the other. A knob on the front of the instrument allows the pilot to rotate the subdial to align the existing outside air temperature with the pressure altitude being flown. When these two parameters are aligned, the instrument pointer will show on the subdial the true airspeed being flown.

Maximum-Allowable Airspeed Indicator

An airplane is limited to a maximum true airspeed by structural considerations and also by the onset of compressibility at high speeds. As the air becomes less dense at high altitude, the indicated airspeed for a given true airspeed decreases. Relatively low-performance airplanes have a fixed red line on the instrument dial which is the never-exceed mark (V_{NE}), but airplanes that fly at high altitudes often use a maximum-allowable airspeed indicator. This instrument has two pointers: one, the ordinary airspeed indicator pointer and the other, a red or red and black-striped or checkered pointer that is actuated by an aneroid altimeter mechanism. This pointer shows the maximum indicated

Figure 4-52. A True Speed indicator is an airspeed indicator with a manually rotated subdial that allows the pilot to correct the indicated airspeed for nonstandard pressure and temperature. The true airspeed indication is read at the end of the pointer on the white subdial.

airspeed allowed for the altitude being flown, and it moves down the dial as the altitude increases. The small numbers on the dial indicate the limiting Mach numbers for the altitude being flown.

The indicator in Figure 4-53 is a combination pointer and drum indicator. The white pointer shows at a glance that the airspeed is something over 400 knots, and the number in the center of the drum is 31. The indicated airspeed shown here is 431 knots.

Machmeter

The airspeed limit placed on many airplanes is caused not by structural strength, but by the onset of compressibility and the formation of shock waves as the airplane approaches the speed of sound. For this reason many airplanes are Mach limited. For the pilot to know just how near the aircraft is to the speed of sound, a Machmeter such as the one whose dial is seen in Figure 4-54 may be installed.

A Machmeter uses an airspeed indicator mechanism whose pointer movement is modified by an altimeter aneroid. The dial is calibrated in Mach numbers, and the pointer shows the pilot, at a glance, the relationship between the speed of the aircraft and the speed of sound. The Machmeter in Figure 4-54 shows that the airplane is flying at Mach .83, which is 83% of the speed of sound.

Mach number. The ratio of the speed of an airplane to the speed of sound under the same atmospheric conditions. An airplane flying at Mach 1 is flying at the speed of sound.

Figure 4-53. *The dial of a maximum-allowable airspeed indicator.*

Figure 4-54. *This Machmeter shows that the airplane is flying at 83% of the speed of sound.*

Altimeters

A pneumatic, or pressure, altimeter is actually an aneroid barometer whose dial is calibrated in feet of altitude above some specified reference level.

Some of the very early altimeters had a range of approximately 10,000 feet and had a knob that allowed the pilot to rotate the dial. Before takeoff, the dial was rotated to indicate zero feet if the flight was to be local, or, more accurately, to the surveyed elevation of the airport. This simple altimeter did not take into consideration the changes in barometric pressure along the route of flight that have a great effect on the altimeter indication.

The altimeter that has been used for all serious flying since the 1930s is the three-pointer sensitive altimeter, a recent version of which is seen in Figure 4-55.

The long pointer of the three-pointer altimeter in Figure 4-55 makes one round of the dial for every 1,000 feet. The dial is calibrated so that each number indicates 100 feet and each mark indicates 20 feet. The short pointer makes one round of the dial for every 10,000 feet, and each number represents 1,000 feet. The third pointer is actually a partial disk with a triangle that rides around the outer edge of the dial so that each number represents 10,000 feet. A cutout in the lower part of this disk shows a barber-pole striped subdial. Below 10,000 feet, the entire striped area is visible, but above this altitude the solid part of the disk begins to cover the stripes, and by 15,000 feet all the stripes are covered.

The altimeter in Figure 4-55 shows a pressure altitude of 10,180 feet. The small window in the right side of the dial shows the barometric scale. This scale is adjusted by the altitude set knob. When this knob is turned, both the barometric scale and the pointers move. Before takeoff and when flying below approximately 18,000 feet, the pilot sets the barometric scale to the altimeter setting given by the control tower or by an air traffic controller for an area within 100 miles of the aircraft. The altimeter setting is the local barometric pressure corrected to mean sea level. When the barometric scale is adjusted to the correct altimeter setting, the altimeter shows indicated altitude, which is the altitude above mean, or average, sea level. By keeping the barometric scale adjusted to the current altimeter setting, the pilot can tell the height of the aircraft above objects whose elevations are marked on the aeronautical charts.

When the aircraft is flying above 18,000 feet, the barometric scale must be adjusted to 29.92 inches of mercury, or 1013 millibars. This causes the altimeter to measure the height above standard sea-level pressure. This is called pressure altitude, and even though its actual distance from mean sea level varies from location to location, all aircraft flying above 18,000 feet are flying at pressure altitudes, and vertical separation is accurately maintained.

Figure 4-55. *A three-pointer sensitive altimeter.*

altimeter setting. The barometric pressure at a given location corrected to mean (average) sea level.

pressure altitude. The altitude read on an altimeter when the barometric scale is set to the standard sea level pressure of 29.92 inches of mercury.

Some of the modern altimeters are drum-pointer-type indicators like that in Figure 4-56. The barometric scale of this instrument shows both inches of mercury and millibars, and it has a single pointer that makes one round for 1,000 feet. A drum counter shows the altitude directly. The altimeter in Figure 4-56 shows an indicated altitude of −165 feet.

Encoding Altimeter

Air traffic control radar displays returns from the aircraft that ATC controls. These returns show not only location of the aircraft, but also the pressure altitude the aircraft is flying. An encoding altimeter supplies the pressure altitude, in increments of 100 feet, to the transponder that replies to the ground radar interrogation. Some encoding altimeters are the indicating instrument used by the pilot, and others are blind instruments that have no visible display of the altitude. They only furnish this information to the transponder.

14 CFR §91.217 requires that the indication from the encoding altimeter not differ more than 125 feet from the indication of the altimeter used by the pilot to maintain flight altitude.

Figure 4-56. *A drum-pointer-type altimeter.*

Altimeter Replacement

When replacing an altimeter, make sure that the replacement altimeter is of the same type and has the same maximum altitude rating as the original altimeter. The aircraft Illustrated Parts Catalog may list more than one altimeter that is approved for replacement, so care must be taken to order the correct one.

Vertical-Speed Indicators

A vertical-speed indicator (VSI), often called a rate-of-climb indicator, is an unusual type of differential pressure gauge. It actually measures only changing pressure. Static pressure is brought into the instrument case from the static air system. This air flows into a diaphragm capsule similar to the one used in an airspeed indicator and into the instrument case through a calibrated restrictor.

When the aircraft is flying at a constant altitude, the air pressure is not changing and the pressures inside the capsule and inside the instrument case are the same. The indicating needle is horizontal and represents no vertical speed. When the aircraft goes up, the air becomes less dense and the pressure inside the capsule changes immediately, but the calibrated restrictor causes the pressure inside the case to change more slowly. As long as the aircraft is going up, the pressure is changing, and the needle deflects to indicate the number of hundred feet per minute the altitude is changing. When the altitude is no longer changing, the pressure inside the case becomes the same as that inside the capsule, and the needle returns to zero. When the aircraft descends, the pressure becomes greater and the indicator shows a downward vertical speed.

Figure 4-57. *A vertical-speed indicator.*

Instantaneous Vertical-Speed Indicator

A vertical-speed indicator cannot show a climb or descent until it is actually established. For this reason, there is a noticeable lag in its indication, and the VSI is not able to detect the changes in pitch attitude that precede the actual change in altitude. To make the VSI more useful for instrument flying, the instantaneous vertical-speed indicator, or IVSI, has been developed. This instrument uses two accelerometer-actuated air pumps, or dashpots, installed across the capsule. When the aircraft is flying level, the IVSI indicates zero, but when the pilot drops the nose to begin a descent, the accelerometer causes a slight pressure increase inside the capsule, and the indicator needle immediately deflects downward. As soon as the actual descent begins, the changing pressure keeps the needle deflected. When the pilot raises the nose to begin a climb, the accelerometer causes a slight pressure drop inside the capsule and the needle immediately deflects upward.

STUDY QUESTIONS: PITOT-STATIC SYSTEMS

Answers are provided on page 304.

62. The instruments that connect to the static air system are the _____ , _____ , and _____ .

63. The instrument that connects to the pitot system is the _____ .

64. Ice is prevented from forming on a pitot-static head by a/an _____ .

65. If the static ports on the side of an aircraft ice over in flight, the pilot can restore service to the static instruments by opening the _____ valve.

66. The airspeed as read directly from the airspeed indicator is called _____ airspeed.

67. Indicated airspeed corrected for position error is called _____ airspeed.

68. Calibrated airspeed corrected for nonstandard pressure and temperature is called _____ airspeed.

69. The indication of a true airspeed indicator is modified by a/an _____ bellows that compensates for pressure and temperature changes.

70. As altitude increases, the maximum allowable indicated airspeed _____ (increases or decreases).

71. When an airplane is flying at 75% of the speed of sound, it is flying at Mach _____ .

72. When the barometric scale of an altimeter is adjusted to the local altimeter setting, the altitude shown is the height above _____ . This is called _____ altitude.

73. When the barometric scale of an altimeter is set to 29.92 inches of mercury, the altimeter is showing _____ altitude.

74. When aircraft fly at an altitude of 18,000 feet or above, the barometric scale of the altimeter should be adjusted to _____ inches of mercury or _____ millibars.

75. An encoding altimeter furnishes altitude information to the _____ which transmits this information to the air traffic controller on the ground.

76. An encoding altimeter must agree with the altimeter used by the pilot to maintain flight altitude within _____ feet.

77. A vertical-speed indicator measures the rate of _____ of the static pressure surrounding the aircraft.

78. One limitation of a vertical-speed indicator is that its indication _____ (lags or leads) the actual pressure changes.

79. An instantaneous vertical speed indicator uses _____-actuated air pumps to start the indication when the aircraft pitches up or down.

Gyro Instrument Power Systems

Gyro instruments are essential for safe flight when the natural horizon is not visible. Almost all current production aircraft are equipped with at least an attitude gyro and a gyroscopic heading indicator. These instruments are backed up by a turn and slip indicator or turn coordinator and an airspeed indicator.

For safety, the attitude gyros may be electrically driven and the rate gyro driven by air, or the attitude instruments may be air driven and the rate gyro electrically driven. By using this type of power arrangement, failure of either the instrument air source of the electrical power will not deprive the pilot of all of the gyro instruments. Some gyroscopic instruments are dual powered. The gyro wheel contains the windings of an electric motor, and buckets are cut into its periphery so it can also be spun by a jet of air.

Gyro Pneumatic Systems

The gyro wheels in pneumatic flight instruments are made of brass and have notches, or buckets, cut in their periphery. Air blows through a special nozzle into the buckets and spins the gyro at a high speed. See Figure 4-58.

There are two ways of producing the airflow over the gyro wheels: suction and pressure. The air can be evacuated from the instrument case, and air

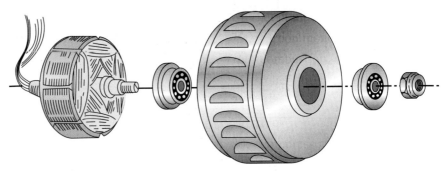

Figure 4-58. *This dual-powered gyro has buckets cut into its periphery so it can be driven by air. It also has a fixed winding inside the gyro that allows it to be driven as an electric motor.*

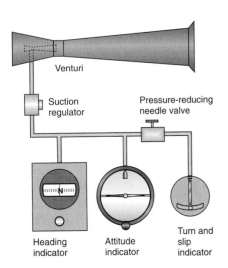

Figure 4-59. *A gyro instrument system using a venturi tube for the source of suction.*

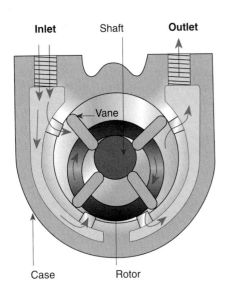

Figure 4-60. *A vane-type air pump can be used either to evacuate the instrument case or to provide a flow of pressurized air to drive the instrument gyros.*

drawn in through a filter flows through the nozzles to drive the gyro. Or, air moved by a vane-type air pump can be directed through the nozzles to spin the gyros.

Suction Systems

Some gyro instrument-equipped aircraft do not have an air pump, and the gyros on these aircraft must be driven by low pressure produced by a venturi tube mounted on the outside of the fuselage. Air flowing through the venturi produces a low pressure inside the instrument case. Air flows into the instrument cases through built-in filters to spin the gyros. See Figure 4-59. The gyro horizon and directional gyros used in these systems each require four inches of mercury suction to drive the gyro at its proper speed, and the turn and slip indicator requires two inches of mercury.

A venturi tube capable of providing enough airflow through the three instruments is mounted on the outside of the fuselage. The line connecting the venturi tube to the instruments contains a suction regulator. This regulator is adjusted in flight to provide four inches of mercury suction at the cases of the heading indicator and the attitude indicator. A needle valve between the attitude instruments and the turn and slip indicator is then adjusted to provide two inches of mercury suction at the case of the turn and slip indicator.

Venturi systems are not dependable for flight into instrument meteorological conditions because the venturi tube will likely ice up and become inoperative.

Modern aircraft equipped with pneumatic gyros use vane-type air pumps similar to the one in Figure 4-60. Two types of air pumps are wet pumps and dry pumps.

Wet Vacuum Pump System

Wet vacuum pumps were the only type of pump available for many years. These pumps have steel vanes riding in a steel housing. They are lubricated by engine oil taken in through the base of the pump. This oil seals, cools, and lubricates the pump and is then removed from the pump with the discharge air. Before this air is dumped overboard or used for inflating deicer boots, the oil is removed by routing the air through an air-oil separator. The oily air is blown through a series of baffles where the oil collects and is drained back into the engine crankcase, and the air is either directed overboard or to the deicer distributor.

wet-type vacuum pump. An engine-driven air pump that uses steel vanes. These pumps are lubricated by engine oil drawn in through holes in the pump base. The oil passes through the pump and is exhausted with the air. Wet pumps must have oil separators in their discharge line to trap the oil and return it to the engine crankcase.

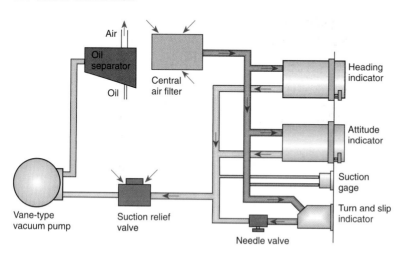

Figure 4-61. *A wet-pump vacuum system used to drive gyro instruments.*

The air to drive the gyros is taken in through a central air filter, and then flows directly to the nozzles in the heading indicator, attitude indicator, and turn and slip indicator. The cases of the heading and attitude indicators are connected to the suction side of the system, and the case of the turn and slip indicator is also connected to the suction side, but there is a needle valve in the line. Air flows from the instruments through the suction-relief valve to the pump and then is discharged. The suction-relief valve is a spring-loaded flat disk valve that opens at a preset amount of suction to allow air to enter the system. If the spring is set with too much compression, the suction will have to be greater to allow the disk to offseat and allow air to enter the system. The suction relief valve is adjusted to four inches of mercury as read on the instrument panel suction gauge, and the needle valve in the turn and slip line is adjusted so there will be a suction of two inches of mercury in the turn and slip case.

Dry Air Pump Systems

Dry air pumps have almost completely replaced wet pumps for instrument air systems. These pumps are lighter in weight and require no lubrication or oil separators in their discharge lines. They can drive instruments with either the suction they produce or by their positive air pressure.

Dry air pumps are vane-type pumps with the rotors and vanes made of a special carbon compound that wears in microscopic amounts to provide the needed lubrication.

Figure 4-62 shows a typical twin-engine dual vacuum pump system for gyro instruments. Each pump is connected to a manifold check valve through a vacuum regulator that allows just enough outside air to enter the system to maintain the desired suction.

In case either pump should fail, the manifold check valve will prevent the inoperative side of the system interfering with the working side. The manifold is connected to the outlet ports of the attitude indicator and the heading indicator and to the suction gauge. The inlet ports of both indicators are connected to an inlet air filter. The line that goes to the filter also goes to the suction gauge so that it reads the pressure drop across the gyros. The

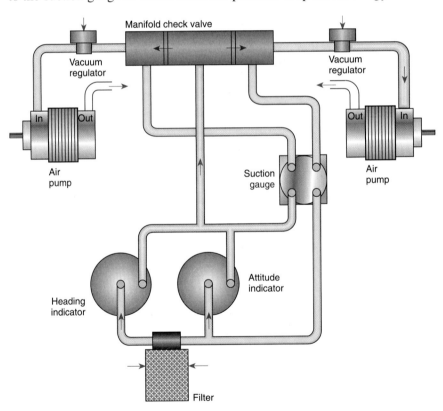

Figure 4-62. *A twin-engine vacuum system for gyros.*

suction gauge has two red buttons visible when the pumps are not operating, but as soon as either pump is producing a vacuum, its button pulls into the instrument and is not visible. The lines to these pump-failure buttons are taken off of the manifold before the check valves.

Pressure System

Many modern airplanes fly at altitudes so high, there is not enough ambient air pressure to drive the gyro instruments. For these aircraft, the output of the air pumps can be used to drive the gyros. A typical twin-engine pressure-instrument system is seen in Figure 4-63.

The inlets of the pumps are fitted with an inlet filter and the outlet air flows through a pressure regulator that vents all the air above the pressure for which it is adjusted. The air then flows through an in-line filter and into the manifold check valve to the inlet of the gyro instruments. After passing through the gyros, the air is vented into the cabin. Pump-failure buttons on the pressure gauge pop out to show when either pump is not producing the required pressure.

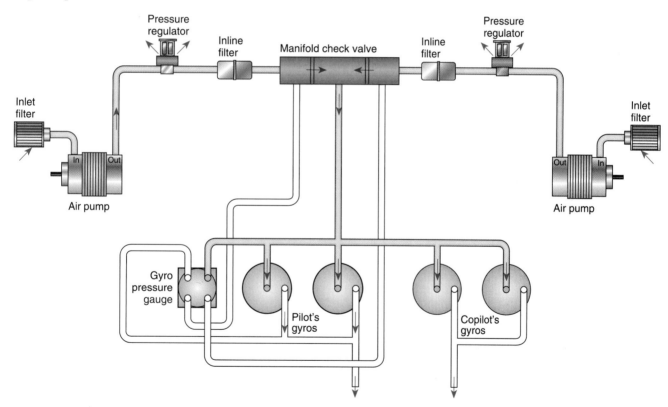

Figure 4-63. *A twin-engine pressure system for gyros.*

Troubleshooting and Maintenance

In order to troubleshoot air-driven gyro systems, you must first understand whether the system is a pressure system or a vacuum system. Start by inspecting the filters to see that they are in good condition and are properly installed. Regulator filters should be replaced every 100 hours of operation or at each annual inspection. Central vacuum filters or pressure system inlet filters should normally be replaced every 500 hours, or at each annual inspection.

Most vacuum and pressure systems will include a gauge or button indicator that will show when a pump has failed. Vacuum pumps are generally replaced every six years and the output will decrease as they wear out. If the pump is new but the pressure is low, check carefully for leaks and for pinched or kinked tubes in the plumbing before adjusting the regulator.

When adjusting the regulator, you must first bend the locking tabs flat to allow the adjustment to be made. After adjustment, bend the tabs back up to lock the adjustment arm in place. See Figure 4-64.

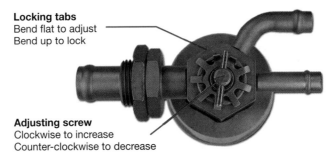

Locking tabs
Bend flat to adjust
Bend up to lock

Adjusting screw
Clockwise to increase
Counter-clockwise to decrease

Figure 4-64. *Regular adjustment with locking tabs.*

STUDY QUESTIONS: GYRO INSTRUMENT POWER SYSTEMS

Answers are provided on page 304.

80. An aircraft that has pneumatic attitude gyros normally has rate gyros that are driven by _____ .

81. A "wet" vacuum pump is lubricated with _____ .

82. A "dry" vacuum pump does not need any lubrication because the vanes and rotor are made of _____ .

83. The discharge from a vacuum pump is often used to furnish compressed air for the _____ system.

84. Aircraft that operate at high altitudes have their pneumatic gyro instruments driven by a _____ (vacuum or pressure) system.

Automatic Flight Control Systems

Automatic flight has been investigated since the early days of aviation, and in 1914, Lawrence Sperry demonstrated successful automatic flight in a Curtiss C-2 flying boat. In 1933 Wiley Post had an experimental Sperry automatic pilot installed in his Lockheed *Vega*, the *Winnie Mae*. He had flown around the world in this airplane in 1931 with Harold Gatty as his navigator, but with the automatic pilot, he completed a similar flight alone.

Automatic flight is important, not only because it frees the human pilot from continuously flying the aircraft, but it flies the aircraft with a greater degree of precision and can navigate by coupling onto the various electronic navigation aids. Many modern high-performance fighter aircraft are designed to be conditionally stable and cannot be flown manually, but must be flown with automatic flight control systems.

Early automatic pilots used two attitude gyro instruments, a directional gyro and an artificial horizon. Pneumatic pickoffs from these gyros controlled three balanced oil valves that supplied hydraulic fluid to one side or the other of linear servo cylinders in the aileron, rudder, and elevator control systems.

Modern automatic flight control systems use attitude gyros, rate gyros, altimeter aneroids, and signals from various electronic navigation aids to program the desired flight profile that the aircraft can follow with extreme precision. These pickoffs and servos are now considered to be input and output devices for the flight computers.

The simplest autopilot is a single-axis wing-leveler using a single canted rate gyro that senses roll or yaw and sends a signal to pneumatic servos in the aileron system that keeps the wings level. Three-axis autopilots are the most common type. Pitch errors are corrected by the elevator channel, roll errors are corrected by the aileron channel, and a heading is maintained by the rudder channel.

A yaw damper is installed in many swept wing airplanes to counteract Dutch roll, which is an undesirable low-amplitude oscillation about both the yaw and roll axes. These oscillations are sensed by a rate gyro and signals are sent to the rudder servo that provides the correct rudder movement to cancel these oscillations.

Further integration of automatic flight control systems includes auto-throttle systems which, when coupled with the autopilot system, can set the desired engine power and parameters for all phases of flight, up to and including auto landings. These complex systems were once only seen on large commercial aircraft, but new advances in technology are bringing these capabilities to general aviation, including single-engine aircraft.

An automatic flight control system consists of four subsystems: command, error-sensing, correction, and follow-up.

The pilot programs the desired flight parameters into the command subsystem. The error-sensing subsystem detects when the aircraft is not in the condition called for by the command. A signal is sent to the correction subsystem, which moves a control to achieve the appropriate changes. The

automatic flight control system (AFCS). The full system of automatic flight control that includes the autopilot, flight director, horizontal situation indicator, air data sensors, and other avionics inputs.

automatic pilot. An automatic flight control device that controls an aircraft about one or more of its three axes. The primary purpose of an autopilot is to relieve the pilot of the control of the aircraft during long periods of flight.

canted rate gyro. A rate gyro whose gimbal axis is tilted so it can sense rotation of the aircraft about its roll axis as well as its yaw axis.

yaw damper. An automatic flight control system that counteracts the rolling and yawing produced by Dutch roll. *See* Dutch roll.

Dutch roll. An undesirable, low-amplitude oscillation about both the yaw and roll axes that affects many swept wing airplanes. Dutch roll is minimized by the use of a yaw damper.

follow-up subsystem senses the changes in the parameter and removes the error signal as soon as the correction is completed.

Command Subsystem

flight controller. The component in an autopilot system that allows the pilot to maneuver the aircraft manually when the autopilot is engaged.

The command subsystem is the portion of the automatic flight control system that allows the pilot to program the aircraft to do what is needed. A sketch of a typical controller is seen in Figure 4-65.

To engage the autopilot, the pilot depresses the AP button. An indicator light shows that it is engaged. Depressing the HDG button ties the system to the horizontal situation indicator and the aircraft will fly the heading that is selected on it.

Depressing the NAV button commands the aircraft to fly along the VOR radial or RNAV course selected on the appropriate navigation source.

Depressing the APPR button causes the system to capture the chosen ILS localizer and follow it to the runway. If a back-course approach is to be made, the pilot can depress the REV button to see back-course information. When the GS button is depressed, the light will indicate that it is armed, and when the aircraft intercepts the glide slope, it will lock on it and will descend along its electronic path.

Depressing the ALT button commands the aircraft to fly to a selected barometric altitude and hold it.

The YAW button engages the rudder trim, which automatically trims the rudder for changes in airspeed.

Rotating the TURN knob commands the aircraft to initiate a banked turn to the left or right.

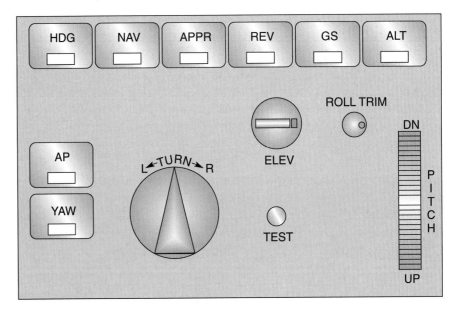

Figure 4-65. *The controller for a typical automatic flight control system.*

The PITCH control can be moved to the UP or DN position to command a change in pitch attitude. When it is released, it returns to its spring-loaded center position.

The ELEV indicator shows whether or not the elevator is in its neutral position, and indicates any needed pitch-trim changes.

The ROLL TRIM allows the pilot to trim the aircraft about its roll axis when no other command is active.

Most of the commands mentioned above can be checked on the ground during inspection of the autopilot system. The aircraft maintenance manual will provide guidance on the exact procedures.

Error-Sensing Subsystem

Gyros normally do error-sensing. The gyro in an attitude indicator senses any deviation from level flight, either in pitch or roll. The gyro in a heading indicator senses any deviation from the heading selected by the pilot. The amount of error signal is related to the amount the aircraft has deviated from its chosen attitude or heading.

Rate gyros are used in some simpler automatic flight control systems to sense deviation from the selected flight condition. These instruments normally use a canted-rate gyro such as that used in a turn coordinator to sense rotation about both the roll and yaw axes. When the aircraft rolls or yaws, the gyro rolls over, or precesses, an amount proportional to the rate of deviation. A signal is sent to the appropriate servos to return the aircraft to a condition of level flight.

Because of the ease with which modern electronic systems can interface with automatic flight control systems, the output from the VOR and ILS as well as other navigation systems can be used to produce error signals. The pilot can tune to the appropriate localizer frequency on the VHF nav receiver and command the aircraft to follow an ILS approach. Any time the aircraft deviates from the glide slope or the localizer, an error signal is established that returns the aircraft to the desired flight path.

Altimeters can be included in the error-sensing subsystem. If the pilot has commanded the aircraft to fly to a given altitude, an error signal is established when the aircraft is not at that altitude, and the controls are adjusted to cause it to attain that altitude and level off. The altitude-hold command causes an error signal any time the aircraft departs from the specified altitude.

Correction Subsystem

The error-sensing subsystem acts as the brains of the system to detect when a correction is needed. Its signal is sent to the controller and then to the servos, which act as the muscles of the system.

Some automatic flight control systems have hydraulic servos that are balanced actuators in the control cable system as seen in Figure 4-66A. When fluid is directed to one side of the piston, the piston moves and pulls on the

servo. The component in an autopilot system that actually applies the force to move the flight control surfaces.

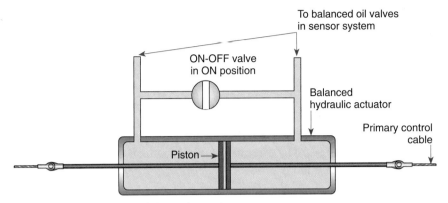

A Hydraulic servo using a balanced actuator

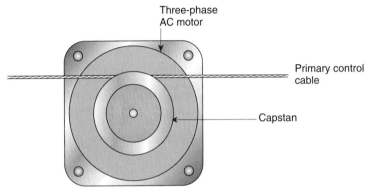

B Capstan driven by a three phase AC motor in the primary control system

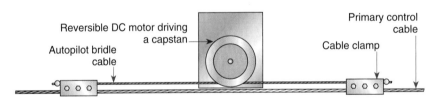

C The capstan, driven by a reversible DC motor, pulls on the bridle cable which is clamped to the primary control cable.

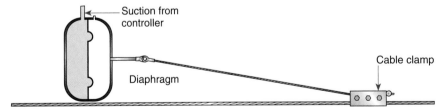

D Pneumatic servo for a wing-leveler autopilot. Two such servos are used to pull the aileron cables in the correct direction.

Figure 4-66. *Automatic flight control servos.*

cable to move the appropriate control. To turn this type of autopilot off, the valve between the two sides of the servo cylinder is opened and the piston is free to move back and forth as the controls are moved.

Some systems use electric motors with drum-type capstans mounted on their shafts as servos. In some installations the primary control cable is wrapped around the capstan, Figure 4-66B. In other installations a smaller bridle cable is wrapped around the capstan and secured to the primary control cable with clamps as shown in Figure 4-66C.

Some smaller wing-lever autopilots use a canted-rate gyro for the sensor and two pneumatic servos like the one in Figure 4-66D. The small cable attached to the diaphragm in this servo is clamped to the primary aileron cable. When the rate gyro senses a roll or yaw, it shifts an air valve and directs suction to the servo that pulls on the correct aileron cable to return the aircraft to level flight. As long as the wings remain level, the airplane cannot turn.

Electric servos have the unusual requirement that they must start, stop, and reverse their direction rapidly when the controller directs, and they must have sufficient torque to move the controls. Some of the larger aircraft use three-phase AC motors to drive the capstan, and the smaller aircraft use DC motors. See Figure 4-66.

balanced actuator. A linear hydraulic actuator that has the same area on each side of the piston.

Follow-Up Subsystem

The follow-up system stops the control movement when the surface has deflected the proper amount for the signal sent by the error sensor. There are two basic types of follow-up systems, rate and displacement.

The rate follow-up used on some of the smaller autopilot systems takes its signals from a canted-rate gyro that senses both roll and yaw. When the aircraft rolls or yaws, a signal is generated by the rate gyro that relates to both the direction and rate of deviation. The signal is amplified and sent to the servos, which move the aileron, and in some installations the rudder, to bring the aircraft back to straight and level flight.

A displacement follow-up system uses position pickups on each of the primary flight controls. When a signal from the error-sensing system causes a control to deflect, the position pickup follows the movement of the surface and nulls out the signal from the error sensor when the surface attains the correct deflection.

For example, if the left wing drops, the gyro senses an error and sends a signal to the aileron servo that moves the left aileron down. When the aileron moves an amount proportional to the amount the wing has dropped, the follow-up system generates a signal equal in amplitude, but opposite in polarity, to the error signal and cancels it.

The left wing is still down and the aileron is deflected, and since the signals have canceled, the autopilot does not call for any more aileron deflection. As the aerodynamic forces bring the wing back to its level-flight attitude, an error signal opposite to the one that started the action is produced. This signal is

follow-up signal. A signal in an autopilot system that nulls out the input signal to the servo when the correct amount of control surface deflection has been reached.

gradually canceled, and by the time the wing is level, the aileron is in the streamlined position and there is no overshooting or oscillation.

Inspection of Autopilot Servos

There are many different types of autopilot servos, so it is important for you to consult the aircraft maintenance instructions for detailed inspection requirements. The following are general inspections that are common to most systems.

Inspect all servos for security of mounting and condition. If the servo uses a capstan, inspect the cable that wraps arounds the capstan for wear spots and broken cables. Inspect the ends of the bridle cable for security of attachment to the primary control cable.

Autopilot servos use a clutch mechanism that allows the pilot to override the autopilot system. While the autopilot is turned on and operating, make sure that the autopilot servos can be overridden by operating the flight controls. Some aircraft provide instructions in the maintenance manual for setting the servo clutch "break-out" tensions. If instructions are not provided in the maintenance manual, the clutch settings are set or adjusted by the autopilot manufacturer or by an FAA-authorized repair station.

Stability Augmentation and Flight Envelope Protection

The use of the previously described correction and follow-up subsystems, within the capabilities of the automatic flight control system, allows for stability augmentation and flight envelope protection systems. Some aircraft, such as advanced fighter aircraft, are inherently unstable and require stability augmentation systems to enable the pilot to control the aircraft. Command signals from the pilot are sent via the flight control computers to the flight control actuators, which then correctly position the flight controls.

The flight envelope protection systems on some aircraft constantly monitor the aircraft and are designed to prevent the pilots from exceeding certain parameters. In some cases, the system will prevent the aircraft from being stalled and will automatically drop the nose of the aircraft if it gets too slow. This same system may prevent the airplane from exceeding a set bank angle or exceeding maximum aerodynamic loads.

Flight Director Indicator and Horizontal Situation Indicator

One advance in flight instrumentation is the flight director, shown in Figure 4-67. This instrument functions like an attitude indicator with the addition of the "bow-tie-shaped" steering bars. The triangular delta symbol represents the airplane, and the steering bars are controlled by the autopilot command and error-sensing systems. Rather than sending the signals to the appropriate servos to actually control the aircraft, the signals are sent to the steering bars that tell the pilot what to do. The flight director in Figure 4-67 is telling the pilot to pitch the nose up and turn to the right. The flight director shows

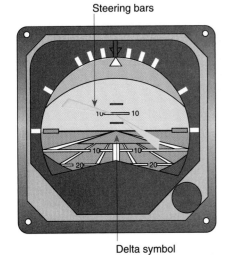

Steering bars

Delta symbol

Figure 4-67. *The bow-tie steering bars in this flight director show the pilot that the aircraft should be pitched up and turned to the right. The object is to fly the delta symbol so that it rests in the V of the steering bars.*

the pilot the changes to make in pitch and roll in the same way the horizontal situation indicator (HSI) shows the pilot the proper changes to make in directional flight.

The HSI in Figure 4-68 shows the pilot the relationship of the aircraft to the VOR radial or ADF bearing, the magnetic direction, the desired course and heading, and also the relationship of the aircraft to the glide slope.

The pilot wants to approach the VOR station by flying inbound on the 120° radial. This gives a course of 300° to the station. This is set into the HSI with the course select knob. The airplane is flying a compass heading of 330° as shown opposite the lubber line, and is slightly to the left of the desired course as is shown by the lateral deviation bar which is to the right of the airplane symbol. If the pilot continues on this heading, the 330° radial will be intercepted, but the pilot has turned the heading select knob until the selected heading marker, or "bug," is over 315°. This commands the autopilot to change the heading of the airplane 15° to the left. In this case the pilot believes that the 15° difference between the heading and the course will correct for wind drift and allow the airplane to track inbound on the 120° radial.

HSI. Horizontal Situation Indicator.

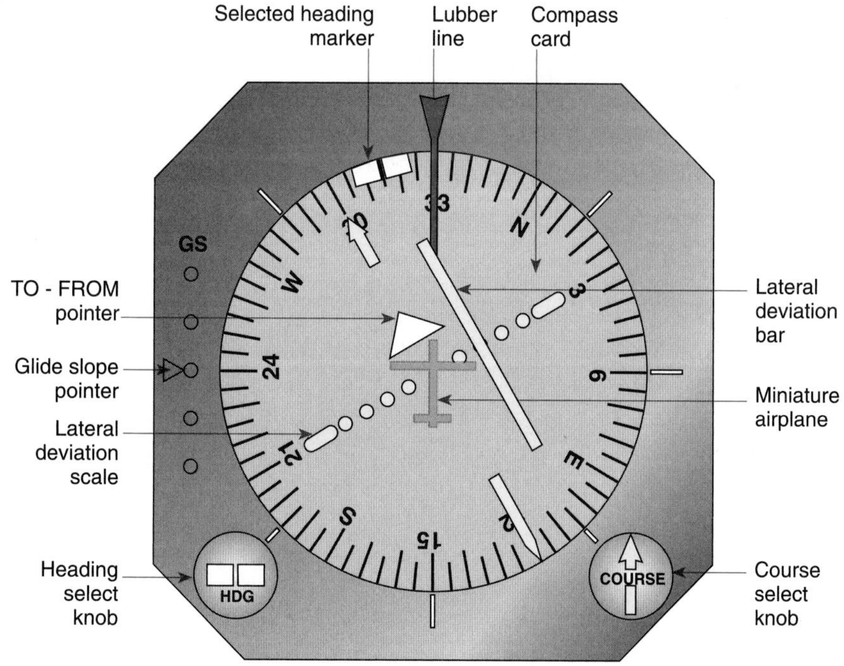

Figure 4-68. *This horizontal situation indicator (HSI) shows the pilot to be inbound to the station on the 120° radial. The selected course is 300°, the heading is 330°, and the pilot has selected a change in heading to 315°.*

Glass Cockpits

The mechanical and electrical instruments with which we are familiar are often derogatorily called "steam gauges" because new technology is making them obsolete. This new technology, the "glass cockpit" replaces many of these single function instruments with multifunction displays (MFD), which display the most critical information on one or more flat-panel electronic displays.

This type of instrumentation is more accurate than the older instrumentation and since it is computer-based, it is programmable so it can be kept compatible with new technology as it develops.

Until recently, these instruments were available only for military and jet transport aircraft, and these systems are discussed in Chapter 5. But now they are available for general aviation aircraft.

Photo ©Cessna Aircraft Co.

Figure 4-69. *The glass panel multifunction displays replace many separate instruments and reduce the workload for the pilot.*

Answers are provided on page 304.

85. The four subsystems of an automatic flight control system are:

    a. _____

    b. _____

    c. _____

    d. _____

86. The pilot is able to maneuver the aircraft when the autopilot is engaged by turning knobs or pressing buttons on the _____ .

87. Most autopilot systems sense deviation from straight and level flight with _____ .

88. The type gyro used by a wing-lever type of autopilot is a/an _____ (attitude or rate) gyro.

89. The component in an automatic flight control system that actually applies force to move the control surface is the _____ .

90. Autopilot servos are driven by signals supplied by the _____ .

91. The subsystem in an autopilot that stops the control movement when its deflection is correct for the amount of error is called the _____ system.

92. The two types of follow-up systems are the _____ and the _____ systems.

Visual Warning Systems

Annunciator Panel

The annunciator panel (Figure 4-70) is a group of warning and status lights located in plain sight of the pilot. These lights are identified by the condition or name of the system they represent and are color coded to show the status of the condition they announce. The color red is reserved for warnings that require immediate action. Yellow (often called amber) is for cautions or non-normal conditions. If action is not taken on a caution, it could lead to a more serious condition. Green is used to show that the system is turned on and operating normally or to show a normal condition (such as landing gear down and locked). White is normally used to indicate that a system has been turned on (e.g., landing light or pitot heat turned on).

Figure 4-70. *Annunciator panel.*

Master Caution

A master caution light and warning horn is often used along with an annunciator panel to bring additional awareness to the flight crew. The master caution is centrally located or positioned to be readily visible. See Figure 4-71. The light will flash and the horn will sound when one of the warnings on the annunciator panel is activated. The caution warning can be canceled by the crew, but the warning light of the system that caused the warning will remain illuminated until the issue is resolved. Canceling the master caution resets the system to be available to warn of new or repeat faults.

Figure 4-71. *Master caution light.*

Master Caution Troubleshooting

Troubleshooting an intermittent master warning or caution begins with identifying the aircraft system or subsystem that is causing the warning. Even if the initial master warning or caution is very brief, there will be a corresponding system that is causing the indication. Once the underlying system is identified, further troubleshooting can then occur, focusing on the system causing the warning.

Aural Warning Systems

Transport aircraft operating under 14 CFR Part 25 have stringent requirements for aural warning systems. Figure 4-72 shows some examples of aural warnings used on transport aircraft.

Warning System	Stage of Operation	Signal	Cause of Signal
Landing gear	Landing	Continuous horn	Landing gear is not down and locked and power lever(s) reduced to idle.
Mach warning	In flight	Clacker	EAS or Mach number limits exceeded
Flight controls	Takeoff	Intermittent horn	Thrust levers are advanced and any of these conditions exist: 1. Speed brakes not down 2. Flaps not in takeoff range 3. APU exhaust door is open 4. Stabilizer not in takeoff setting
Pressurization	In flight	Intermittent horn	If cabin pressure becomes equal to atmospheric pressure at the specific altitude
Fire warning	Any stage	Continuous bell	Any overheat condition or fire in any engine or nacelle, or main wheel or nose wheel well, APU engine or any compartment having fire warning system installed. Also when fire warning system is being tested.
Communications	Any stage	High chime	Any time captain's call button is pressed at external power panel forward, or rearward cabin attendant's panel
Communications	Any stage	Two-tone or high-low chime or single low chime	When a signal has been received by an HF or VHF communications system and decoded by the Selcal decoder

Figure 4-72. *Aural warning signals used in transport category aircraft.*

Answers are provided on page 304.

93. The takeoff warning system alerts the flight crew when a flight control is not properly set prior to takeoff. This system is activated by a switch on the _____ .

94. The aural signal for a fire in an engine compartment is a/an _____ .

95. The aural signal for a flight control being in an unsafe condition for takeoff is a/an

   _____ .

96. The aural signal for the landing gear being in an unsafe condition for landing is a/an

   _____ .

Instrument Installation and Maintenance

Aircraft instrument maintenance is different from any other maintenance. According to 14 CFR §65.81(a), a certificated mechanic may perform or supervise the maintenance, preventive maintenance, or alteration of an aircraft or appliance, or a part thereof, for which he or she is rated (but excluding major repairs to, and major alterations of propellers, and *any repair to, or alteration of, instruments.*)

Aviation mechanics are authorized to perform the required 100-hour inspections on instruments and instrument systems and to conduct the static system checks. They can remove and replace instruments and instrument components and replace the range markings on instruments if these marks are on the outside of the glass and do not require opening the instrument case.

Any actual repair or calibration to an instrument must be made by the instrument manufacturer or by an FAA-certificated repair station approved for the particular repair to the specified instrument.

Instrument Range Marking

Some instruments have colored range marks that let the pilot see at a glance whether a particular system or component is operating in a safe and desirable range of operation or in an unsafe range. The colored marks direct attention to approaching operating difficulties. Figure 4-73 shows the colors used and the meaning of each.

Color and type of mark	Meaning
Green arc	Normal operating range
Yellow arc	Caution range
White arc	Special operations range
Red arc	Prohibited range
Red radial line	Do not exceed indication
Blue radial line	Special operating condition

Figure 4-73. *Meanings of instrument range mark colors.*

Instrument	Range Marking	Instrument	Range Marking
Airspeed indicator		**Oil temperature gauge**	
White arc	Flap operating range	Green arc	Normal operating range
Bottom	Flaps-down stall speed	Yellow arc	Precautionary range
Top	Maximum airspeed for flaps-down flight	Red radial line	Maximum and/or minimum permissible oil temperature
Green arc	Normal operating range		
Bottom	Flaps-up stall speed	**Tachometer (Reciprocating engine)**	
Top	Maximum airspeed for rough air	Green arc	Normal operating range
Blue radial line	Best single-engine rate of climb airspeed	Yellow arc	Precautionary range
		Red arc	Restricted operating range
Yellow arc	Structural warning area	Red radial line	Maximum permissible rotational speed
Bottom	Maximum airspeed for rough air		
Top	Never-exceed airspeed	**Tachometer (Turbine engine)**	
Red radial line	Never-exceed airspeed	Green arc	Normal operating range
		Yellow arc	Precautionary range
Carburetor air temperature		Red radial line	Maximum permissible rotational speed
Green arc	Normal operating range		
Yellow arc	Range where carburetor ice is most likely to form	**Tachometer (Helicopter)**	
		Engine tachometer	
Red radial line	Maximum allowable inlet air temperature	Green arc	Normal operating range
		Yellow arc	Precautionary range
		Red radial line	Maximum permissible rotational speed
Cylinder head temperature		Rotor tachometer	
Green arc	Normal operating range	Green arc	Normal operating range
Yellow arc	Operation approved for limited time	Red radial line	Maximum and minimum rotor speed for power-off operational conditions
Red radial line	Never-exceed temperature		
		Torque indicator	
Manifold pressure gauge		Green arc	Normal operating range
Green arc	Normal operating range	Yellow arc	Precautionary range
Yellow arc	Precautionary range	Red radial line	Maximum permissible torque pressure
Red radial line	Maximum permissible manifold absolute pressure		
		Exhaust gas temperature indicator (Turbine engine)	
Fuel pressure gauge		Green arc	Normal operating range
Green arc	Normal operating range	Yellow arc	Precautionary range
Yellow arc	Precautionary range	Red radial line	Maximum permissible gas temperature
Red radial line	Maximum and/or minimum permissible fuel pressure		
Oil pressure gauge			
Green arc	Normal operating range		
Yellow arc	Precautionary range		
Red radial line	Maximum and/or minimum permissible oil pressure		

Figure 4-74. *Range markings for specific instruments.*

bezel. The rim that holds the glass cover in the case of an aircraft instrument.

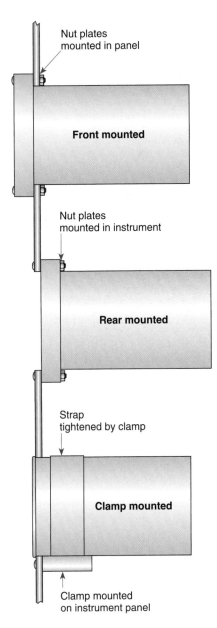

Nut plates
mounted in panel

Front mounted

Nut plates
mounted in instrument

Rear mounted

Strap
tightened by clamp

Clamp mounted

Clamp mounted
on instrument panel

Figure 4-75. *Instrument mounting methods.*

It is the responsibility of the aviation mechanic installing an instrument in an aircraft and a mechanic conducting an inspection to ensure the instruments are properly marked for the aircraft in which they are being installed. Type Certificate Data Sheets for the aircraft and the engine specify the range marks that are required.

Some instruments have the range marking on the glass rather than on the dial, and instruments marked in this way must have a slip mark to show if the glass has slipped and the marks are no longer properly aligned. The slip mark is a white line painted across the instrument bezel and onto the glass at the bottom of the instrument. If the glass should slip and get the markings out of alignment with the numbers on the dial, the slip mark will be broken and the pilot warned that the range markings are not correct.

Instrument Removal and Installation

A mechanic is allowed to install instruments in an instrument panel, and it is his or her responsibility on an inspection to be sure that the instruments are secure in their mounting and that all the hoses and wires attached to the instruments are in good condition and do not interfere with any of the controls.

Many of the electrical instruments are mounted in iron or steel cases to prevent interference from outside magnetic fields. Lines of magnetic flux cannot flow across iron or steel, and these cases entrap the lines of flux, rather than allowing them to affect nearby instruments. Even with this precaution, electrical instruments should not be mounted near the magnetic compass, and the wires carrying current into the compass light should be twisted to prevent the lines of flux from this small current from causing a compass error.

Most instruments are installed in the panel with four brass machine screws that screw either into brass nuts mounted in holes in the instrument case or into nut plates installed in the panel. Because panel space is so limited, many modern instrument cases are flangeless and are held in clamps attached to the back of the panel. The instrument is connected to its electrical harness or hose and slipped through the hole in the panel until it is flush and properly aligned, then the clamp-tightening screw in the panel is turned to tighten the clamp around the instrument case.

Care should be taken when installing and removing instruments as they can be damaged if jarred. When removing instruments, support the instrument behind the panel to prevent it from dropping down on top of other instruments. If the instrument is held in place with a clamp-type bracket, loosen the clamp-tightening screw only enough to slide the instrument out the front of the panel. If the screw is removed all the way, the clamp will fall down behind the panel and will need to be reinstalled.

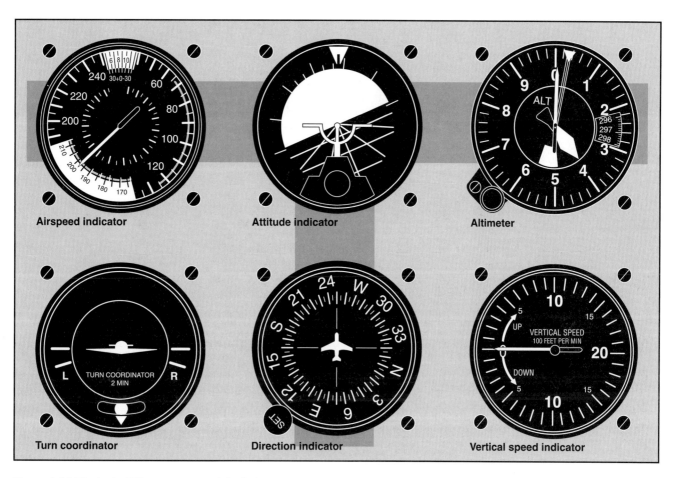

Figure 4-76. *The basic "T" arrangement of the flight instruments.*

For many years the arrangement of the instruments in the panel was haphazard, at best. The directional gyro and gyro horizon were much larger than the other instruments and were often placed in inappropriate locations. Now that instrument flight has become so important, there is a standard arrangement for basic flight instruments. This is known as the basic "T" arrangement.

Aircraft instrument panels are shock-mounted to absorb low-frequency, high-amplitude shocks. The type, size, and number of shock mounts required for an instrument panel are determined by the weight of the complete panel unit with all of the instruments installed. For heavy panels, two shock mounts like those in Figure 4-77A are mounted between brackets attached to the structure and to the panel. Lighter weight panels are supported from the structure with the type of shock mounts shown in Figure 4-77B. Any time a panel is supported by shock mounts, a bonding strap must be installed across the mounts to carry any return current from the instruments into the aircraft structure. When inspecting instrument installation, check the bonding straps to be sure that they are in good condition and securely fastened.

shock mounts. Resilient mounting pads used to protect electronic equipment by absorbing low-frequency, high-amplitude vibrations.

bonding. The process of electrically connecting all isolated components to the aircraft structure. Bonding provides a path for return current from the components, and it provides a low-impedance path to ground to minimize radio interference from static electrical charges. Shock-mounted instrument panels have bonding braids connected across the shock mounts, so that return current from the instruments can flow into the main structure and thus return to the alternator or battery.

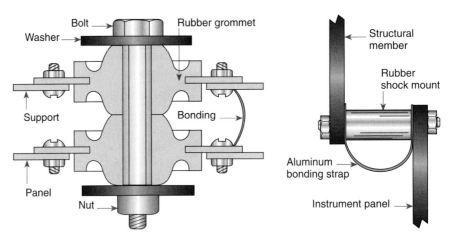

A Double shock mounts used for heavy panels   B Shock mount for relatively lightweight panels

Figure 4-77. *Instrument panel shock mounts.*

Instrument Maintenance

An aircraft instrument in need of any repair or alteration must be returned to the instrument manufacturer or to a certificated repair station approved for the particular instrument. A mechanic can install instruments and inspect them, but is not authorized to do any type of repair or alteration.

Such operations as replacing range markings on the outside of the instrument glass, tightening loose mounting screws, tightening leaking B nuts in the plumbing, and retouching chipped case paint are not considered to be instrument repairs or alterations and may be done by an appropriately rated mechanic.

Instruments that have a leaking case or a cracked glass or instruments that are fogged or whose pointers will not zero must be replaced.

Static System Leak Checks

Altimeters, vertical speed indicators, and airspeed indicators all connect to the static air system. As the airplane goes up in altitude, the static air pressure lowers, and the altimeter indicates a higher altitude. The air pressure inside the airspeed indicator case lowers, and the pitot pressure can more easily expand the diaphragm capsule.

If the static pressure line should become disconnected inside a pressurized cabin in flight, the static pressure in the instrument cases will increase. This will cause the altimeter to read a lower altitude and the airspeed indicator to indicate a lower airspeed.

A certificated aviation mechanic with an Airframe rating can check the static air system for leakage as is required by 14 CFR §91.411 and described in 14 CFR Part 43, Appendix E. All openings into the static system are closed, and a negative pressure, or suction, of 1.07 inches of mercury is applied to the static system, to cause an equivalent altitude increase of 1,000 feet to be indicated on the altimeter. The line to the tester is then shut off and the altimeter is watched. It must not leak down more than 100 feet in one minute.

If a leak is indicated, isolate portions of the system and check each portion systematically. Begin at the connection nearest the instruments and check it. If this is good, reseal the connection and check the next portion, working your way out to the static ports until the leak is found.

A static system leak checker may be made from components that can be purchased from a surgical supply house. You will need an air bulb such as is used for measuring blood pressure and two or three feet of thick-walled surgical hose. Slip the hose over the suction end of the bulb as seen in Figure 4-78 and clamp it in place with a hose clamp.

To check the system, close the pressure bleed-off valve and then squeeze the air bulb to expel as much air as possible. Hold the suction hose firmly against the static pressure opening and slowly release the bulb while watching the altimeter and vertical speed indicator. Do not release the bulb rapidly enough for the needle on the VSI to peg. When the altimeter indicates an increase in altitude of 1,000 feet, pinch the hose to trap the suction in the system, and hold it for one minute. The altimeter indication should not decrease by more than 100 feet.

Most aircraft have more than one static port, and when performing this test, the port not used must be taped over to prevent it interfering with the test. One handy method of doing this is to use black plastic electrical tape to make a large X over the static port. This tape is easy to remove without damaging the finish, and the large black X is so easy to see that you are not likely to forget and leave the static port covered.

The pressure end of the checker can be used for checking the integrity of the pitot system.

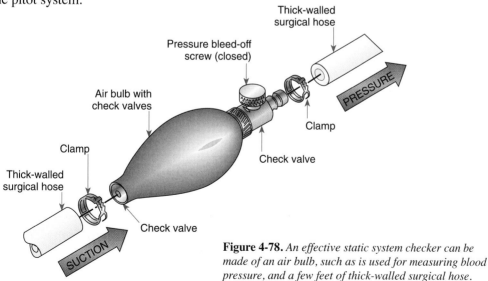

Figure 4-78. *An effective static system checker can be made of an air bulb, such as is used for measuring blood pressure, and a few feet of thick-walled surgical hose.*

Pitot-Static System Test

While a certified aviation mechanic with an Airframe rating can check the static system for leaks, a certified repair station, or the aircraft manufacturer, must perform the IFR pitot-static inspection that is required every 24 months for flight under IFR. This test includes a performance and error test of the altimeter (typically to 20,000-foot altitude), a leak check of the pitot-static system, and a test of altitude reporting equipment (encoder). In addition, there is a 24-month requirement for inspecting the output of the transponder. This inspection checks the outputs of the transponder for frequency accuracy and proper power output and is required for all aircraft that fly in controlled airspace, regardless of whether the aircraft is flown under IFR.

Instrument Handling

Aircraft instruments are delicate and sensitive devices that require special care in handling. Many of the cases of airspeed indicators, vertical speed indicators, and manifold pressure gauges are made of thermosetting plastic and can be cracked if the fittings are overtightened. Be sure to observe the caution marked on these instruments, and do not blow into the openings.

Cylinder head temperature and exhaust gas temperature gauges are thermocouple-type instruments whose moving coils are damped through the thermocouple. When the thermocouple is not connected, the instrument is not damped and the pointer can swing violently enough to knock it out of balance, which will result in inaccurate indications. Any time a thermocouple instrument is not connected to its thermocouple, a loop of uninsulated wire should be wrapped around the terminals to short-circuit them and allow damping current to flow. Be sure that this wire is removed before the thermocouple is connected.

Gyro instruments are especially easy to damage by rough handling. If the instrument is fitted with a caging device, cage it when it is not in the panel. Never handle a gyro instrument when the rotor is spinning, and when preparing it for shipment to a repair facility, use only the packing boxes specified by the manufacturer or the repair shop. Some gyro instruments require special handling, and when packing this type of instrument be sure to follow all instructions in detail.

cage. To lock the gimbals of a gyroscopic instrument so it will not be damaged by abrupt flight maneuvers or rough handling.

Instrument System Caution

Use extreme caution when washing aircraft to not spray water into pitot tubes or static ports. Water and pressure can both cause damage to the aircraft instruments.

This same caution applies to using compressed air. You should never use compressed air during maintenance or troubleshooting of a pitot-static instrument system due to the risk of damaging the instruments.

Answers are provided on page 304.

97. An aviation mechanic with an Airframe rating _____ (is or is not) permitted to make a minor repair to an airspeed indicator.

98. An aviation mechanic with a Powerplant rating _____ (is or is not) permitted to calibrate an oil temperature gauge.

99. An aviation mechanic with an Airframe rating _____ (is or is not) permitted to perform an instrument system static check on an aircraft.

100. Instruments can be repaired only by the manufacturer or by a/an _____ approved by the FAA for the particular instrument.

101. The proper range marks for an instrument may be found in the _____ _____ for the aircraft or engine.

102. The white arc on an airspeed indicator is the _____ range.

103. The yellow arc on an airspeed indicator is the _____ area.

104. An airspeed indicator is marked to show the best rate of climb speed with one engine inoperative with a _____ radial line.

105. A red arc on a tachometer indicates a _____ range.

106. A green arc on an instrument indicates the _____ range.

107. A white slip mark between the instrument bezel and the glass is required when the instrument range marks are on the _____ .

108. The maximum or minimum safe operating limits are indicated on an instrument dial with a _____ .

109. An Aviation Mechanic certificate with an Airframe rating _____ (is or is not) authorization to replace a cracked glass in an aircraft instrument.

110. The person responsible for making sure an instrument is properly marked when it is installed in an aircraft is the instrument _____ .

111. There are two ways instruments can be held in the instrument panel. These are:

    a. _____

    b. _____

(continued)

112. Aircraft instrument panels are usually shock mounted to absorb _____ (low or high)-frequency, _____ (low or high)-amplitude shocks.

113. A certificated aviation mechanic with Airframe and Powerplant ratings _____ (may or may not) perform minor repairs to engine instruments.

114. The result of the instrument static pressure line becoming disconnected inside a pressurized cabin during high altitude cruising flight will be that the altimeter will read _____ (high or low) and the airspeed indicator will read _____ (high or low).

115. The maximum altitude loss permitted during an unpressurized aircraft instrument static pressure system integrity check is _____ feet in _____ minute(s).

116. The minimum requirements for testing and inspection of instrument static pressure systems required by 14 CFR §91.411 are contained in 14 CFR Part _____ Appendix _____ .

117. When performing the static system leakage check required by 14 CFR §91.411, the mechanic uses a _____ (positive or negative) pressure.

118. If a static pressure system check reveals excessive leakage, the leak(s) may be located by isolating portions of the line and testing each portion systematically, starting at the _____ (instrument or static port) end of the system.

Answers to Chapter 4 Study Questions

1. absolute
2. absolute
3. gauge
4. gauge
5. gauge
6. differential
7. differential
8. expansion
9. vapor
10. nickel
11. increases
12. iron, constantan
13. current

14. reference
15. chromel, alumel
16. alumel
17. series
18. variable resistor
19. permanent magnet
20. permanent magnet
21. toroidal
22. three
23. electromagnet
24. single
25. three
26. 26,400

27. 100
28. eddy currents
29. steel
30. frequency
31. synchroscope
32. G
33. 1G
34. is not
35. angle of attack
36. reference plane
37. lubber line
38. 5
39. are not

40. does not
41. deviation
42. does
43. deviation
44. 10
45. twisting
46. a. acceleration error
    b. northerly-turning error
47. lubber line
48. rigidity in space
49. double
50. roll, pitch
51. vertical
52. vertical
53. horizontal
54. is not
55. precession
56. single
57. vertical
58. horizontal
59. 3
60. 3
61. roll, yaw
62. airspeed indicator, altimeter, vertical speed indicator
63. airspeed indicator
64. electric heater
65. alternate static air
66. indicated

67. calibrated
68. true
69. aneroid
70. decreases
71. .75
72. mean sea level, indicated
73. pressure
74. 29.92, 1013
75. transponder
76. 125
77. change
78. lags
79. accelerometer
80. electricity
81. engine oil
82. carbon
83. deicer
84. pressure
85. a. command
    b. error-sensing
    c. correction
    d. follow-up
86. controller
87. gyros
88. rate
89. servo
90. controller
91. follow-up

92. rate, displacement
93. thrust lever
94. continuous bell
95. intermittent horn
96. continuous horn
97. is not
98. is not
99. is
100. 100. repair station
101. Type Certificate Data Sheets
102. flap operating
103. structural warning
104. blue
105. restricted operating
106. normal operating
107. glass
108. red radial line
109. is not
110. installer
111. a. screws
     b. clamps
112. low, high
113. may not
114. low, low
115. 100, 1
116. 43, E
117. negative
118. instrument

COMMUNICATION AND NAVIGATION SYSTEMS

5

Communication Systems

For many years the only electronics involved in aviation were used for communication and navigation, and all electronic equipment was classified simply as "radio." Today's aircraft employ vast quantities of electronic equipment, much of it unrelated to either communication or navigation. This equipment is now classified as avionics. This section considers the portion of avionics that deals with communication and navigation, and the section on electronic instrument systems discusses some of the other aspects of avionics.

Components in the communication and electronic navigation systems are considered aircraft instruments, and as such, can only be repaired by the manufacturer or by an FAA-certificated repair station. To perform certain tuning operations on radio transmitters, mechanics must hold the appropriate license issued by the Federal Communications Commission (FCC). Each radio transmitter installed in an aircraft used for international flights must have an FCC-issued radio station license, and this license must be displayed in the aircraft. Each person operating a radio transmitter was formerly required to hold at least a valid restricted radio telephone permit. This requirement has been lifted and is no longer required when operating an aircraft radio station that operates only on VHF frequencies and does not make foreign flights.

Basic Radio Theory

Radio is a method of transmitting intelligence from one location to another by means of electromagnetic radiation.

A block diagram of an extremely basic radio transmitter is shown in Figure 5-1. This transmitter contains a crystal-controlled oscillator that produces alternating current with a very accurate frequency in the radio frequency (RF) range. This is above approximately 10 kilohertz (10,000 cycles per second). The intelligence to be transmitted is changed into an audio frequency (AF) electrical signal by the microphone, and this AF modulates, or changes, the

avionics. The branch of technology that deals with the design, production, installation, use, and servicing of electronic equipment mounted in aircraft.

antenna. A special device used with electronic communication and navigation systems to radiate and receive electromagnetic energy.

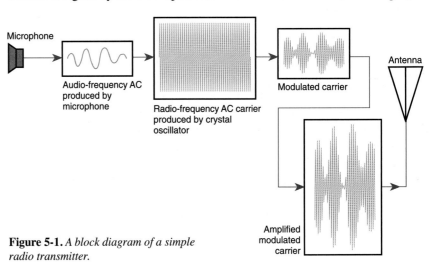

Figure 5-1. *A block diagram of a simple radio transmitter.*

carrier so that its voltage varies in exactly the same way as the voltage from the microphone. Notice that both sides of the modulated carrier are the same as the AF signal. The voltage of the modulated carrier is amplified so that it has enough power to radiate into space when it goes to the antenna.

The signal radiates out into space from the transmitter antenna, and is picked up by the receiving antenna, as is shown in Figure 5-2. As this signal travels through space it becomes weakened, or attenuated, and contaminated with electromagnetic noise. The signal-to-noise ratio is an indication of the efficiency of the receiver to eliminate as much noise as possible without decreasing the desired signal.

The signal picked up by the antenna is a very weak imitation of the amplified modulated RF signal that was sent to the transmitter antenna. The weak modulated RF signal is amplified, and then demodulated. This removes the RF carrier but leaves both halves of the AF signal. Since the resultant voltage of the AF signal is zero, one half must be removed. This is done in the detector,

signal-to-noise ratio. The ratio of the power of the received signal to the power of the noise that is interfering with the signal.

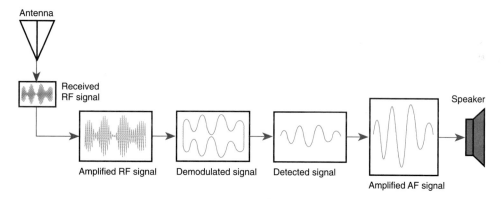

Figure 5-2. *A block diagram of a simple radio receiver.*

or rectifier. The resulting voltage has the same waveform as that produced by the microphone attached to the transmitter. This signal has too low a voltage to be useful, so it is amplified and then used to drive a speaker. The audio output of the speaker is the same as the input to the microphone.

The transmitter uses a crystal oscillator to produce an accurately controlled carrier frequency, and only this one frequency radiates from the transmitter antenna. The receiver antenna picks up not only the signal from the desired transmitter, but signals from every other transmitter in the area as well as electromagnetic radiation from all sorts of electrical devices. In order for a receiver to be useful, it must filter out every frequency except the one that is wanted. To do this, it employs a special superheterodyne circuit. See Figure 5-3.

The antenna picks up all the radio signals in the area, and they are taken into a tunable preamplifier. This preamplifier uses an electronic filter circuit that passes only the frequency to which the receiver is tuned and sends all of

superheterodyne circuit. A sensitive radio receiver circuit in which a local oscillator produces a frequency that is a specific difference from the received signal frequency. The desired signal and the output from the oscillator are mixed, and they produce a single, constant intermediate frequency. This IF is amplified, demodulated, and detected to produce the audio frequency that is used to drive the speaker.

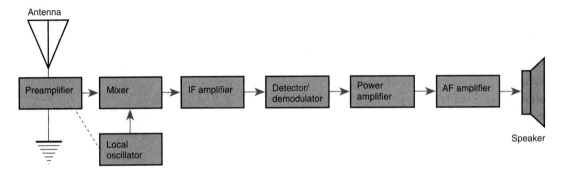

Figure 5-3. *A simplified block diagram of a superheterodyne receiver.*

the other frequencies to ground. To better understand filters, review the section on filters in the *General* textbook of this Aviation Mechanic Series. In this explanation, we will consider the receiver to be a broadcast receiver tuned to 1,200 kilohertz. The preamplifier amplifies any signal with a frequency of 1,200 kHz and passes all other frequencies to ground.

A tunable local oscillator is included in this circuit. The frequency of this oscillator is varied so it is always a specific frequency higher than the frequency to which the preamplifier is tuned. For most broadcast band receivers, the frequency of the local oscillator is always 455 kilohertz higher than the frequency tuned on the preamplifier. In this case, the local oscillator produces a signal with a frequency of 1,655 kilohertz (1,200 + 455).

The signals from the preamplifier and the local oscillator are sent to the mixer. When signals with two frequencies are mixed, they produce two other signals, one with a frequency that is the sum of the original two frequencies and the other with a frequency that is the difference between the two. The four signals will have frequencies of 1,200 kHz, 1,655 kHz, 2,855 kHz (1,200 + 1,655), and 455 kHz (1,655 − 1,200). The four signals from the mixer are sent

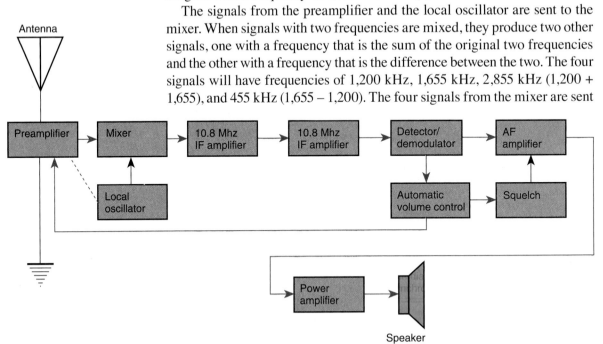

Figure 5-4. *A simplified block diagram of a VHF superheterodyne communication receiver.*

into the intermediate frequency (IF) amplifier. This is a very narrow-band amplifier that is tuned to 455 kHz. It amplifies the 455 kHz signal and attenuates, or diminishes, all other frequencies.

The amplified 455 kHz signal is sent to the detector/demodulator, which removes the 455 kHz IF carrier and leaves the AF envelope that has both halves of the audio signal. The detector rectifies the AF signal and removes one half of the envelope. The resulting signal is an exact copy of the AF that modulated the carrier that is being received. The AF signal is amplified by a power amplifier stage and drives the speaker. The output of the speaker is the same as the input to the microphone at the transmitter.

Communication receivers such as those used in aircraft are more sensitive than the normal household broadcast receiver, and they have more stages. Figure 5-4 shows a block diagram of a very high frequency (VHF) communication receiver.

sensitivity. A measure of the signal strength needed to produce a distortion-free output.

The signal is picked up on the antenna and amplified by the tuned preamplifier. The local oscillator produces a frequency that is 10.8-megahertz different from the frequency to which the preamplifier is tuned. These two frequencies are fed into the mixer where they produce a 10.8-MHz intermediate frequency. This IF is amplified by two stages of IF amplification and sent into the detector/demodulator, where it emerges as an audio frequency signal that duplicates the AF produced by the microphone at the transmitter.

selectivity. The ability of a radio receiver to separate desired signals from unwanted signals.

To hold the output constant as the input signal voltage changes, some of the output from the detector goes to an automatic volume control (AVC). This is fed back into the preamplifier in such a way that it increases the pre-amp amplification when the signal is weak and attenuates it when the signal is too strong.

Some of the detector output is sent into a squelch circuit that controls the audio frequency amplifier. When no signal is being received, the AF amplifier output is attenuated, or decreased, so the background noise that makes a hissing sound in the speaker is not loud enough to be annoying. But as soon as a signal is received, the attenuation is removed, allowing the audio output to be loud enough to be comfortably heard.

noise (electrical). An unwanted electrical signal within a piece of electronic equipment.

The output of the AF amplifier goes to a power amplifier where it is further amplified so it can drive the speaker.

Modulation

As you have seen in the simplified explanation of a transmitter and receiver, the carrier wave that is generated in the transmitter is just that, a device that carries the information from the transmitter to the receiver. The carrier has a frequency high enough to produce electromagnetic waves that radiate from the antenna, and this frequency is accurately controlled so that a sensitive receiver can select the carrier from a specific transmitter and reject the carriers from all other transmitters.

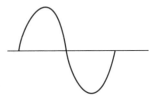
Waveform of the audio frequency used to modulate the carrier

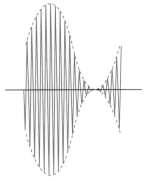
Amplitude of the modulated carrier varies with amplitude of modulating AF

Figure 5-5. *Amplitude modulation.*

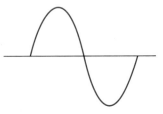
Waveform of audio frequency used to modulate the carrier

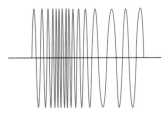
Frequency of modulated carrier varies with amplitude of modulating AF

Figure 5-6. *Frequency modulation.*

The carrier itself serves no function other than to carry the signal from the transmitter to the receiver, and the carrier is routed to ground after the intelligence is removed from it. It is the intelligence, or information, produced by the microphone or other type of input device that is important. The process of placing intelligence on a carrier is called modulation, and there are several ways to do it. Three ways most often used in aviation communication equipment are amplitude modulation (AM), frequency modulation (FM), and single-sideband (SSB).

Amplitude Modulation (AM)

Amplitude modulation, or AM, is a method of modulation in which the voltage of the carrier is changed by the audio signal. Figure 5-5 shows a sine-wave audio signal that has been used to modulate a carrier. The voltage of the resulting carrier varies with the voltage of the modulating audio frequency.

Frequency Modulation (FM)

Man-made interference, such as that caused by electric motors and ignition systems, and natural interference, like that caused by lightning in the atmosphere, amplitude-modulate all radio signals in their vicinity. Frequency modulation is used to obtain interference-free communication.

The voltage variations of the audio frequency signal produced by a microphone are used to change the frequency of the carrier. As shown in Figure 5-6, as the voltage of the AF rises in a positive direction, the frequency of the carrier increases, and as it goes negative, the frequency of the carrier decreases.

The amplitude of an FM carrier is held constant by limiter circuits, and any interference, which amplitude-modulates the carrier, is clipped off so it does not appear in the output.

When an FM signal is received, the deviations in frequency are changed into amplitude variations in an audio-frequency voltage that is amplified and used to drive the speaker.

Single-Sideband (SSB)

Both AM and FM are limited in that they require a wide band of frequencies for their transmission. For example, if a 25-MHz carrier is modulated with an audio-frequency signal that contains frequencies up to 5,000 hertz, the transmitted signal occupies a band of frequencies from 24.995 to 25.005 megahertz. This band includes the carrier, the lower sideband, which is the carrier frequency minus the modulating frequency; and the upper sideband, which is the carrier frequency plus the modulating frequency.

Figure 5-7 shows the advantages of SSB over AM. The upper illustration shows the bandwidth required for an AM signal, and the lower illustration shows the bandwidth required for an SSB signal. The carrier and the upper sideband have been removed.

All the information needed is carried in either one of the sidebands, and it is inefficient use of energy to transmit the carrier and both the upper and lower sidebands. Removing the carrier and one of the sidebands and using all of the available energy for transmitting the other sideband give the transmitter a much greater range.

Radio in the United States typically uses the lower sideband, but the upper sideband is used overseas. When an SSB transmission is picked up by an AM receiver, it is heard as a muffled noise because it has no carrier to mix with to produce an audible tone. But inside the SSB receiver, a carrier of the proper frequency is inserted and the original sound is reproduced.

At present, SSB is the primary type of transmission for communication in the high frequency (HF) band. Its advantages are:

- By eliminating one sideband and the carrier, all transmission energy is used in the remaining sideband.

- An SSB signal occupies a smaller portion of the frequency spectrum.

Radio Waves

When a high-frequency AC signal is placed on a special conductor called an antenna, two fields exist: electric fields, called E fields; and magnetic fields, called H fields. In Figure 5-8 on the next page, view A shows an electrical generator connected between the two halves of the antenna. View B shows the development of the magnetic field whose strength is determined by the amount of current flowing. Since this is AC, which periodically reverses, the current is not uniform throughout the antenna, but is minimum at the end of each section, where it reverses, and maximum in the center. The current flows in the direction shown by the arrow I for one alternation and then reverses during the next. C shows the development of the electric field. The polarity is shown for one alternation, and the intensity of the E field is determined by the amount of voltage. D shows the two fields that exist in the antenna at the same time.

When the AC changes fast enough, the fields do not entirely collapse before the next buildup occurs, and some of the energy is radiated out into space as an electromagnetic, or radio, wave. This wave has two components, the electric wave and the magnetic wave. The waves are at right angles to each other, and both are at right angles to the direction of propagation, or the direction the wave is traveling. See Figure 5-9.

When a radio wave leaves the transmitter antenna, it travels out in space at the speed of light, 186,000 miles per second, or 300,000,000 meters per second. When this wave strikes the antenna of a radio receiver, it generates a voltage that is a much weaker replication of the voltage in the transmitter antenna.

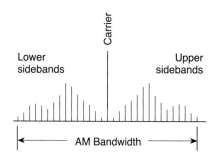

An AM transmitter must transmit carrier and both upper and lower sidebands. This requires much power and twice the bandwidth needed for the information.

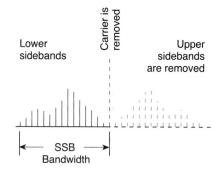

An SSB transmitter removes carrier and transmits only one sideband, in this case, the lower sideband.

Figure 5-7. *Advantage of SSB over AM.*

A Transmitter is actually an AC generator placed between two halves of the antenna.

Antenna

Generator

B Alternating current flowing in antenna produces magnetic field whose strength varies along length of antenna. Direction of field reverses with each alternation.

I →

H Field

+ −

C Voltage that exists between the ends of antenna produces an electric field. Polarity of this field reverses with each alternation of the AC.

E Field

+
+ +
+
+
+
+ +

−
−
−
−

D Magnetic (H) and electric (E) fields exist in antenna at same time.

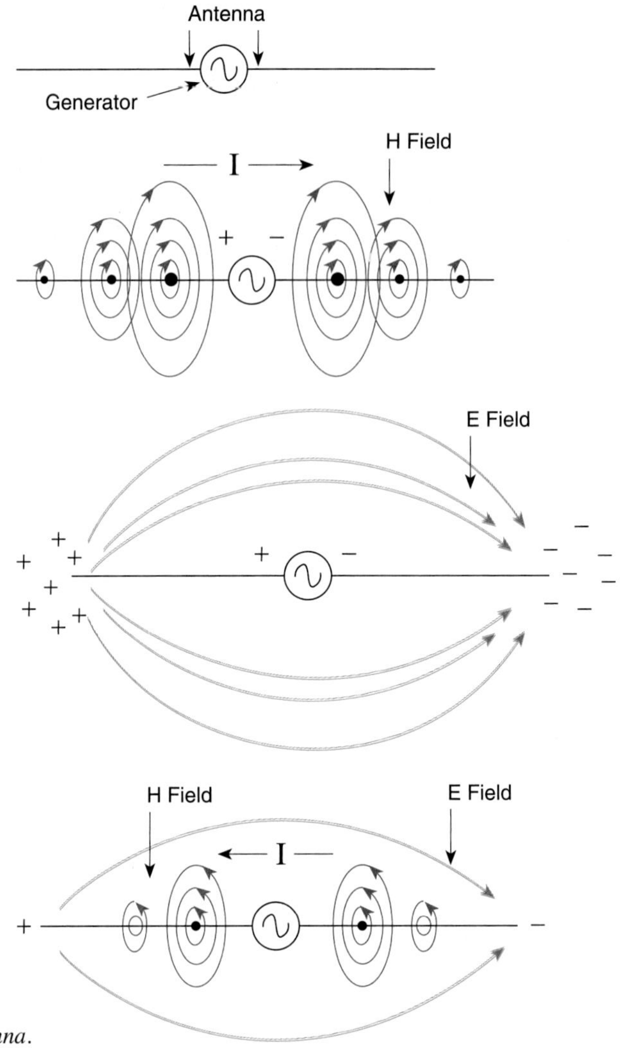

H Field

E Field

← I —

+

−

Figure 5-8. *Fields surrounding a radio antenna.*

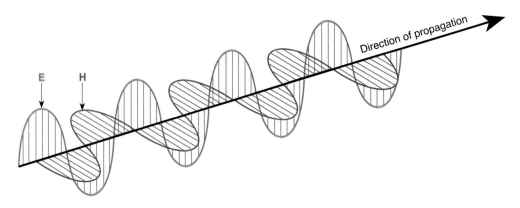

E   H

Direction of propagation

Figure 5-9. *A radio wave has two components, an electric wave (E) and a magnetic wave (H). These waves are at right angles to each other and both are at right angles to the direction the wave is traveling.*

Polarization

To induce the maximum amount of voltage into the receiving antenna, the antenna must be installed in such a way that it is perpendicular to the magnetic, H, field, and parallel to the electric, E, field in the radio waves. When the transmitting antenna is vertical, the E field is vertical, and the radiation is said to be vertically polarized. The maximum reception is picked up with a vertical antenna. When the transmitting antenna is horizontal, the radiation is horizontally polarized, and is best received on a horizontal antenna.

Wavelength

A radio wave is essentially a sine wave that radiates from the transmitting antenna. There is a definite relationship between the length of the wave and its frequency, and this relationship is extremely important. The higher the frequency, the shorter the distance between the ends of the wave. This relationship is seen in the formula in Figure 5-10.

λ = v ÷ f
λ = wavelength in meters
v = velocity of light (300,000,000 meters per second for radio waves) ÷ 1,000,000
f = frequency in megahertz

Example: Find the length of a VHF wave whose frequency is 108 megahertz.

λ = v ÷ f
  = 300 ÷ 108
  = 2.8 meters

Figure 5-10. *Relationship between frequency and wavelength.*

Frequency Allocation

Radio did not become a successful means of communication until a method was devised to separate one frequency of electromagnetic energy from all the others. This is commonly done by the use of electronic filters, and it has reached an extremely high level of perfection.

It is now practical to produce many frequencies in a transmitter by using only a single high-precision crystal in a circuit called a synthesizer. The oscillators inside the receivers are also crystal-controlled and it is common practice to have adjacent communication channels separated by 25 kilohertz. In order to operate in certain European airspace, the aircraft must have the capability of selecting frequency spacing of 8.33 kHz. Typically, there is a switch in the cockpit to make the 25/8.33 selection.

Band and Function	Frequency
Very low frequency (VLF)	**3 – 30 kHz**
Low frequency (LF)	**30 – 300 kHz**
Loran C	100 kHz
ADF	200 – 1,700 kHz
Medium frequency (MF)	**300 kHz – 3 MHz**
Commercial broadcast	535 kHz – 1.6 MHz
High frequency (HF)	**3 – 30 MHz**
HF communications	2 – 25 MHz
Very high frequency (VHF)	**30 – 300 MHz**
Marker beacons	75 MHz
ILS localizer	108.1 – 111.95 MHz
VOR	108.0 – 117.95 MHz
VHF communications	118.0 – 135.975 MHz
Ultrahigh frequency (UHF)	**300 MHz – 3 GHz**
ILS glideslope	320 – 340 MHz
DME	960 MHz – 1.215 GHz
Secondary surveillance radar	1.03 GHz and 1.09 GHz
Superhigh frequency (SHF)	**3 – 30 GHz**
Radar altimeter	2.2 – 2.4 GHz
Weather radar (C band)	5.5 GHz
Doppler radar (X band)	8.8 GHz
Weather radar (X band)	9.4 GHz
Doppler radar (K band)	13.3 GHz
Extremely high frequency (EHF)	**30 – 300 GHz**

Figure 5-11. *Frequency allocation for aviation navigation and communication.*

Since it is possible to separate frequencies accurately, the usable range of frequencies has been divided and bands assigned for various communication and navigation purposes. The frequencies used for aviation communication and navigation are shown in Figure 5-11.

Communication radios use highly sensitive and selective transmitters and receivers for two-way communication between aircraft and ground stations or between aircraft in flight.

Aircraft flying over the oceans typically use HF communication because it can travel great distances. HF equipment operates in the frequency range of 2 to 25 megahertz and is normally single-sideband.

Very high frequency (VHF) radio transmissions operate in the 118.000 to 135.975 megahertz range. This frequency range is used for air traffic control (ATC) communication and for communication between civil aircraft operated domestically. VHF communication use single-channel simplex operation in which a single frequency is used for both transmitting and receiving (single-channel), but only one person can talk at a time (simplex). This differs from duplex communication where both people can talk at the same time, as on a telephone.

VHF. Very High Frequency.

Radio Wave Propagation

When a radio wave is transmitted from the antenna it moves out along three paths, depending primarily upon its frequency. These paths are surface waves, sky waves, and space waves, as in Figure 5-12.

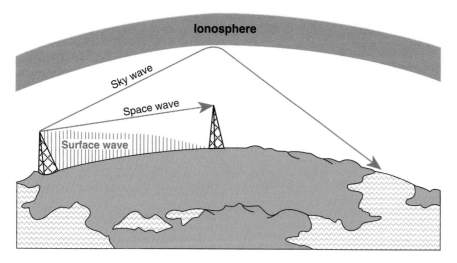

Figure 5-12. *Electromagnetic energy radiated from a transmitter antenna travels in surface waves, sky waves, or space waves, depending primarily on its frequency.*

The lower frequencies such as VLF, LF, and MF normally follow the curvature of the earth in surface waves. These waves travel great distances and are used for very long-distance communication and navigation. Commercial broadcast signals follow this path in the daytime.

HF communication and commercial broadcast at night are carried primarily by sky waves. This energy tries to radiate into space, but it bounces off the ionosphere and returns to the earth at a distance from the transmitter. This "skip distance," as it is called, varies and is responsible for the fading of many signals heard from a long distance.

Frequencies in the VHF and higher bands follow a straight line from the transmitting antenna to the receiving antenna and are said to travel by space waves.

skip distance. The distance from a radio transmitting antenna to the point on the surface of the earth the reflected sky wave first touches after it has bounced off of the ionosphere.

Antenna

An antenna is a special conductor connected to a radio transmitter to radiate the electromagnetic energy produced by the transmitter into space. An antenna is also connected to the receiver to intercept this electromagnetic energy and carry it into the receiver circuits, where it is changed into signals that can be heard and used. The characteristics that make an antenna good for transmitting also make it good for receiving.

dipole antenna. A straight-wire, half-wavelength, center-fed radio antenna. The length of each of the two arms is approximately one fourth of the wavelength of the center frequency for which the antenna is designed.

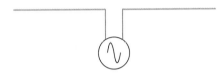

A A dipole antenna has its strongest field perpendicular to its length.

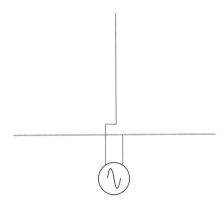

B A vertical whip antenna is omnidirectional. Its field strength is equal in all directions.

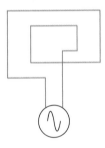

C A loop antenna is highly directional. Its maximum strength is in line with its plane and decreases sharply perpendicular to its plane.

Figure 5-14. *Directional characteristics of typical antennas.*

coaxial cable. A special type of electrical cable that consists of a central conductor held rigidly in the center of a braided outer conductor.

Coaxial cable, or coax, as it is normally called, is used for attaching radio receivers and transmitters to their antenna.

Three characteristics of an antenna are critical: its length, polarization, and directivity. For an antenna to be most efficient, its length must be one-half the wavelength of the signal being transmitted or received, as shown in Figure 5-13. This length allows the antenna current to be maximum.

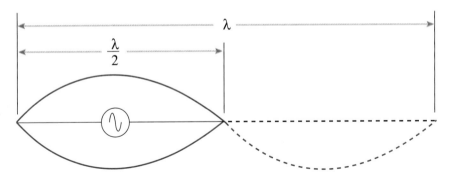

Figure 5-13. *For maximum efficiency, an antenna should have a length of one-half the wavelength it is carrying.*

When the transmitting antenna is vertical, its electric field is vertical and the magnetic field is horizontal. It is picked up best by a vertical antenna. Most LF, MF, and HF communication use horizontally polarized antennas, and higher frequency systems use vertically polarized antennas.

Figure 5-14 shows three types of antennas and their directional characteristics. The dipole antenna in **A** transmits its signal strongest in a direction perpendicular to its length. The vertical whip antenna in **B** has a uniform field strength in all directions and is called an omnidirectional antenna. The loop antenna in **C** is highly directional. Its strength is sharply reduced in the direction perpendicular to its plane.

Transmission Lines

In order for a transmitter to get the maximum amount of energy into its antenna, and for the receiving antenna to get the maximum amount of energy into its receiver, the antennas must be connected to the equipment with a special type of conductor called a coaxial cable. This cable has a central conductor surrounded by a special insulating material. This is, in turn, surrounded by a braided metal shield. All of this is encased in a protective plastic coating. A coaxial cable, commonly called coax, has a specified characteristic impedance that must be matched to the antenna and the transmitter or receiver. Normally this impedance is 50 ohms.

Coax is relatively rugged, but care must be exercised to not allow it to become overheated, and it must not be bent around a radius smaller than 10 times the cable diameter. Anything that distorts the spacing between the central conductor and the outer conductors can change the characteristics of the coax and decrease the efficiency of the installation.

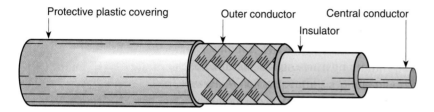

Protective plastic covering   Outer conductor   Central conductor

Insulator

Figure 5-15. *Coaxial cable is used to connect transmitters and receivers to their antenna.*

Communication Radio Antenna

In the past, long-wire trailing antennas were used for HF communication. But advances in communication technology have developed tuned antennas that are actually part of the aircraft structure. Other aircraft use a copper-clad steel wire enclosed in a polyethylene covering run from outside the fuselage above the cockpit to the top of the vertical fin.

VHF communication uses the frequencies between 118 and 136 megahertz, which are just above the VOR frequencies, and the antenna used is normally a quarter-wavelength, vertically polarized whip. The metal in the aircraft structure provides the other quarter-wavelength to make the antenna electrically a half-wavelength long. Many whip antennas are bent so they can also pick up horizontally polarized signals.

Broad-band blade antennas provide more efficient transmission and reception than simple whips.

Aircraft Communication Addressing and Reporting System (ACARS)

ACARS is a communication link between an airliner in flight and the airline's main ground facilities. Data is collected in the aircraft by the digital flight data acquisition unit, which interfaces with the communication systems, navigation systems, engines, flight controls, automatic flight control system, landing gear, cabin doors, and the flight management computer. Status messages are compiled and coded to compress them. The compressed message is then transmitted via the VHF data link, HF data link, or SATCOM to a datalink service provider (DSP) on the ground. The signal is then sent by ground line to the airline's operations center or air navigation service provider (ANSP). Here it is routed to the appropriate departments.

Replies from the airline ground facilities regarding weather and dispatch updates or other pertinent data are sent via ground line to the Chicago facility and then transmitted from the appropriate remote station. Information received in the aircraft is decoded and printed so the appropriate flight crewmember can have a hard copy of the information.

Information transferred between the aircraft and the ground facility by ACARS greatly increases safety and efficiency of operation.

ACARS (Aircraft Communication Addressing and Reporting System). A two-way communication link between an airliner in flight and the airline's main ground facilities. Data is collected in the aircraft by digital sensors and is transmitted to the ground facilities. Replies from the ground may be printed out so the appropriate flight crewmember can have a hard copy of the response.

Honeywell Aerospace has developed a system similar to ACARS, but for business jet aircraft: the AFIS® (Airborne Flight Information System). It is a powerful, two-way datalink communication system that provides worldwide access to datalink communications by way of both VHF and satellite communication networks. AFIS is controlled through the aircraft's flight management system (FMS) and it provides convenient menu-driven access to services directly on the aircraft's cockpit display unit (CDU).

One of the AFIS system's greatest strengths is its flexibility. It allows pilots to meet their individual communications needs from almost anywhere in the world. With AFIS, pilots always have the best information available at their fingertips. Some AFIS important features are:

- Access to essential digital ATC services, communications, winds aloft, and weather.

- AFIS flight plan uplink into the FMS saves time and enhances safety by reducing waypoint entry errors.

- Automatic or manual switching between VHF and satellite modes.

- Automatic position reporting and aircraft-event triggers enhance flight following.

Selective Calling (SELCAL)

The flight crew members of a modern airliner have such a heavy work load that they are not able to spare the concentration needed to monitor the frequencies used by the airline company in order to select from all of the traffic only the messages directed at their specific aircraft. The radio communication facilities operated by the FAA cannot be used for any purpose other than the control of air traffic, and therefore no company business can be conducted on these frequencies.

An airline ground facility can communicate with any of its aircraft in flight through a DSP. DSP assigns a four-tone code to each aircraft, and when it needs to communicate with a particular aircraft, this code is used. When the receiver in the aircraft identifies its code, the SELCAL decodes it and operates a chime or a light to alert the crew to the fact that a message is being directed to them. The crew can then use the appropriate receiver to hear the message.

Audio Integrating System (AIS)

Modern airliners have a complex interphone system that allows flight crewmembers to communicate with each other and ground crewmembers to communicate with the flight crew or with other members of the ground crew. The pilots and flight attendants can make announcements to the passengers, and the conversations in the cockpit are recorded for investigative use in the event of an air crash. Each of the subsystems of the AIS of a large jet transport aircraft are considered below.

Flight Interphone

All communications from the flight deck, both internal and external, are directed through audio selection panels at each one of the crew stations. By using switches on these panels, the crewmembers can receive and transmit on any of the VHF or HF transceivers, can listen to any of the navigation receivers, and can talk over the interphone or the public address system.

Cabin Interphone

The cabin interphone control panel allows communication between the flight attendants and the captain and allows either the flight attendants or the captain to make announcements over the public address (PA) system. The pilot has full priority over all others in making PA announcements.

Service Interphone

Phone jacks are located throughout the aircraft that allow service personnel to communicate with each other. A switch on the flight engineer's panel connects the service and flight interphone systems.

Passenger Address

Good communication between the flight crew and the passengers is extremely important in airline flying. There are four levels of priority assigned to the passenger address system. Announcements by the pilot have first priority, then announcements by the flight attendants. Prerecorded announcements follow as third level, and finally boarding music. A chime is produced when the pilot turns on the "fasten seat belt" or "no smoking" signs.

Note: Required passenger information lights such as "Fasten Seat Belt" and "No Smoking" are typically called ordinance lights.

Prerecorded emergency announcements may be initiated by the pilot or by a flight attendant, and these messages are initiated automatically in the event of a cabin depressurization.

Passenger Entertainment

Passenger entertainment systems, commonly referred to as in-flight entertainment (IFE) systems, have evolved dramatically since their introduction. Early tape deck systems provided a limited number of audio-only channels for music and a movie channel for listening to the movie that was shown on drop-down screens that extended from overhead panels located in select locations around the cabin.

Modern IFE systems use fiber-optic cables to provide a wide selection of movies and channels to screens located in the seat back in front of each passenger. Even this approach is evolving, since most passengers now have access to cellphones, tablets, and laptops. Airlines are finding it more cost effective to provide Bluetooth and Wi-Fi access to IFE systems, thereby reducing the weight and cost of seat-back entertainment systems.

Ground Crew Call

The ground crew has a flight-deck call button in the nosewheel well that, when depressed, sounds a low chime on the flight deck and illuminates a ground-crew call light. When the ground-crew call button on the flight deck is depressed, a horn in the nosewheel well sounds. When the chime or the horn sounds, the appropriate crewmembers can use the interphone system to communicate with the one who initiated the call.

Cockpit Voice Recorder

The cockpit voice recorder, or CVR, is an important device for determining the cause of an aircraft accident. An endless tape allows for 30 minutes of recording, and then it is automatically erased and recorded over. There are four inputs to the recording heads: the microphones of the captain, the first officer, the flight engineer, and a microphone that picks up received audio and cockpit conversations. These microphones are always "hot" and do not require any type of keying.

The pickups are all in the cockpit, but the actual tape recorder is in a fire-resistant box usually located near the tail of the aircraft, and is painted bright orange so that it is easily identified among the wreckage.

Emergency Locator Transmitter (ELT)

An Emergency Locator Transmitter (ELT) is a small, self-contained, battery powered transmitter that was developed to assist in locating downed aircraft. There are two types of ELTs, Technical Standard Order (TSO) C-91a analog units that operate on 121.5 MHz and 243.0 MHz, and the newer TSO C-126 digital ELTs that operate on 406.025 MHz. The digital ELT can be encoded with the owner's contact information, pertinent aircraft data and with the aircraft's position data. This can help search and rescue (SAR) forces locate the aircraft more quickly after a crash than is possible with the older analog ELTs. Digital ELTs also transmit a stronger signal than the older analog ELTs, and the 406.025 MHz ELTs also incorporate a low-power 121.5 MHz homing transmitter to aid searchers in finding the aircraft in the terminal phase of the search.

Both the Federal Communications Commission (FCC) and the FAA require that the 406.025 MHz ELTs be registered with the National Oceanic and Atmospheric Administration (NOAA). The NOAA maintains the owner registration database for U.S.-registered 406.025 MHz ELTs, and operates the United States' portion of the Cospas–Sarsat satellite distress alerting system, which is designed to detect activated ELTs.

If a properly registered 406.025 MHz ELT is activated, the Cospas–Sarsat satellite system can decode the owner information and provide that data to the appropriate (SAR) center. The center then telephones or contacts the owner to verify the status of the aircraft. If the aircraft is safely secured in a hangar, a costly ground or airborne search is avoided, and if the ELT has been inadvertently actuated it can be deactivated.

area mics. The "hot" microphones in the aircraft cockpit, which are not required to be keyed.

key (verb). To initiate an action by depressing a key or a button.

ELT (emergency locator transmitter). A self-contained radio transmitter that automatically begins transmitting on the emergency frequencies any time it is triggered by a severe impact parallel to the longitudinal axis of the aircraft.

Cospas–Sarsat. An international search and rescue system that uses satellites to detect and locate emergency beacons carried by ships, aircraft, or individuals. The system consists of a network of satellites, ground stations, mission control centers, and rescue coordination centers.

If an "armed" ELT is subject to crash-generated forces, it is designed to automatically activate and continuously emit its respective signals, analog or digital, for at least 48 hours.

The Cospas–Sarsat system has announced the termination of satellite monitoring and reception of the 121.5 MHz and 243.0 MHz frequencies in 2009, but they will continue to monitor the 406.025 MHz frequency. After the termination date, those aircraft with only 121.5 MHz or 243.0 MHz ELTs will have to depend upon either a nearby Air Traffic Control facility receiving the alert signal or an overflying aircraft monitoring 121.5 MHz or 243.0 MHz detecting the alert.

ELTs are installed as far aft in the fuselage as it is practical to place them, and they are connected to a flexible whip antenna. The installation must be such that orients the inertia switch so that it is sensitive to a force of approximately 5G along the longitudinal axis of the aircraft.

When an ELT is properly installed, it requires little maintenance other than ensuring that it remains securely mounted and connected to its antenna. There must be no evidence of corrosion, and the battery must be replaced according to a specific schedule. Nonrechargeable batteries must be replaced or chargeable batteries recharged when the transmitter has been used for more than one cumulative hour, or when it has reached 50% of its usable life, or if it is rechargeable 50% of its useful life of charge. The date required for its replacement must be legibly marked on the outside of the transmitter case and recorded in the aircraft maintenance records. During routine inspections of the aircraft, such as 100-hour or annual inspections, the aviation mechanic will be looking for this date while inspecting the ELT.

An ELT can be tested by removing it from the aircraft and taking it into a shielded or screened room to prevent the radiation of signals that could trigger a false alert.

An operational check of analog, 121.5/243 MHz, ELTs may be made during the first 5 minutes after any hour. If operational tests must be made outside of this period, they should be coordinated with the nearest FAA control tower or FSS. Tests should be no longer than three audible sweeps, and if the antenna is removable, a dummy load should be substituted during test procedures.

Digital 406.025 MHz ELTs should only be tested in accordance with the unit's manufacturer instructions.

Additional information on testing ELTs can be found in the most current revision of FAA Advisory Circular AC 91-44, titled *Operational and Maintenance Practices for Emergency Locator Transmitters and Receivers*.

The pilot should check at the end of each flight to be sure that the ELT has not been triggered. Depending upon the type of ELT installed, this is done by tuning the VHF receiver to 121.5 MHz or the UHF receiver to 406.025 MHz and listen for the tone. If no tone is heard, the ELT is not operating.

Answers are provided on page 381.

1.   Each radio transmitter installed in an aircraft used for international flights must have an FCC-issued _____ license.

2.   To perform certain tuning operations on radio transmitters, mechanics must hold the appropriate license issued by the _____ .

3.   The radio-frequency carrier used in a radio transmitter is produced by a/an _____-controlled oscillator.

4.   A superheterodyne circuit is used in a radio _____ (receiver or transmitter).

5.   Most communication between civilian aircraft and ground facilities is in the _____ (HF, VHF, or UHF) frequency band.

6.   Most radio communication by aircraft operating over the oceans is done in the _____ (HF, VHF, or UHF) frequency band.

7.   SSB is the primary type of transmission for communication in the _____ (HF or VHF) band.

8.   One difference between AM and SSB radio communication is that SSB communication requires a _____ (wider or narrower) band of frequencies for its transmission.

9.   The two fields that exist in a radio antenna are the:

   a. _____

   b. _____

10. Radio waves travel through space at a speed of _____ miles per second, or _____ meters per second.

11. Radio waves emitted from a vertical whip antenna are best picked up by a _____ (vertical or horizontal) antenna.

12. A radio wave with a frequency of 136 MHz has a wavelength of _____ meters.

13. VHF radio communication travel primarily by the _____ (ground, sky, or space) waves.

14. Three critical characteristics of a radio antenna are:

   a._____

   b._____

   c._____

15. For an antenna to be most effective, its length should be _____ (¼ or ½) of a wavelength.

16. A loop antenna _____ (is or is not) directional.

17. An antenna is connected to a transmitter with a _____ cable.

18. The system that allows an airline ground facility to monitor conditions existing in an aircraft in flight is called the _____ .

19. When an airline ground facility wishes to contact one of its aircraft in flight the _____ system is used.

20. A prerecorded emergency announcement in flight may be automatically initiated over a large aircraft's passenger address system in the event of a _____ .

21. Emergency locator transmitters operate on one or more frequencies. These are 121.5 MHz, 243 MHz, and _____ MHz.

22. Most ELTs are powered by _____ (the aircraft electrical system or a self-contained battery).

23. An ELT is activated by an inertial switch that senses impact forces that are parallel to the _____ (lateral or longitudinal) axis to the aircraft.

24. An ELT is normally installed in the aircraft as far _____ (aft or forward) as possible.

25. When activated, the battery installed in an ELT must be capable of furnishing power for signal transmission for at least _____ hours.

26. An ELT battery must be replaced when it has been installed for _____ percent of its rated usable life.

27. The replacement date for an ELT battery must be legibly marked on the outside of the _____ .

28. Operation of an analog ELT may be verified by tuning the VHF receiver to _____ MHz and activating the transmitter momentarily.

29. If you are going to operationally check an analog ELT, the test should be performed within _____ minutes after any hour.

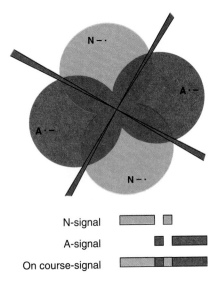

N-signal

A-signal

On course-signal

Figure 5-16. *The low-frequency, four-course radio range was the earliest successful radio navigation system. When the pilot heard the overlapping signals as a solid tone, the airplane was flying along one of the four course legs.*

Electronic Navigation Systems

Air travel became practical when radio navigation made it possible for pilots to navigate without having to depend upon visual recognition of landmarks.

Much early radio navigation made use of the fact that a loop antenna was highly directional. Some airplanes had a wire loop wound inside the fuselage, behind the cabin. If the pilot tuned in a commercial broadcast station and turned the airplane until the volume was minimum, the airplane would fly to the station. There were a number of problems with this simple system; not the least was the problem of 180° ambiguity. The same minimum volume would be obtained when the aircraft was flying directly away from the station as when it was flying directly toward it. To be assured of flying to the station, the pilot had to listen carefully to the change in volume. If the signal got louder, the aircraft was, indeed, flying toward the station.

The first really practical radio navigation system was the low-frequency, four-course radio range. Radio transmitters were located on the airports and along the designated Federal airways. The antenna system for these ranges transmitted overlapping figure-eight-shaped signals. See Figure 5-16. One set of antennas transmitted the International Morse code letter N (— •), and the other set transmitted the letter A (• —). These characters were so spaced that, in the area where they were received with equal strength, the pilot heard a continuous tone. An identification signal was transmitted every 30 seconds.

When flying into an airport equipped with this system, the pilot would tune the receiver to the radio range frequency and identify the station. The signal heard would be an A or an N along with the identifier. An orientation pattern was flown until the pilot heard the continuous tone and then turned toward the station. If the turn was made in the correct direction, the signal became louder, but if it was made in the wrong direction, the signal faded. By flying a heading that kept the solid tone with increasing volume, the pilot approached the antennas. When directly over the antenna, the signal built up quite strong and then faded rapidly. This was called the cone of silence and identified the aircraft position as directly over the antenna.

The low-frequency, four-course range had serious limitations. It operated in the low-frequency range that was highly susceptible to interference from atmospheric static. During bad weather, when the system was needed most, it was least reliable. Variations in the strength of the two signals often caused the legs to swing in such a way that they could lead the pilot over dangerous terrain. Finally, successful use of this system required a high degree of skill on the part of the pilot.

Automatic Direction Finder (ADF)

Another early use of electronics as navigation aids was the radio direction finder (RDF). A large loop of wire was installed inside the airplane, usually across the fuselage behind the cabin. When the radio was tuned to a low- or medium-frequency (LF or MF) station, the volume would change with the heading of the airplane. The volume was lowest when the plane was headed directly toward or away from the station, and the loudest when the wings were pointed toward the station. The only way to determine whether the station was ahead or behind the station was to carefully note whether the volume increased or decreased as you flew along. If the volume increased, you were headed toward the station.

Some improvements were made in RDF, but during World War II the popular rotating-loop automatic direction finder (ADF) was perfected and it continues in use today. When the ADF receiver is tuned to an LF/MF nondirectional radio beacon (NDB), or to an AM commercial broadcast station, the needle on the ADF indicator points to the station's transmitting antenna regardless of the heading or position of the aircraft. The indicator gives the relative bearing between the aircraft and the station. When the needle points to 0°, the nose of the aircraft is pointing directly to the station. With the needle pointing at 180°, the station is directly behind the aircraft. If the needle points at 090°, the station is off the right wingtip. When flying directly toward a station, the needle will point to 0°, and when the station is crossed, the needle will swing to 180°.

An ADF receiver operates in the LF and MF frequency bands and has inputs for two different antennas, a loop and a long-wire-type sense antenna. The output of the loop antenna varies with the direction between the plane of the loop and the station being received. The output of the sense antenna is omnidirectional, meaning that its signal strength is the same in all directions. The field of the two antennas, when mixed in the ADF receiver, is heart-shaped with a very definite and sharp null. See Figure 5-17.

When the frequency of a radio beacon is selected on the ADF receiver, the signals from the two antennas mix and a voltage is generated in the receiver that causes the loop-drive motor to rotate the loop. The loop will rotate until the combined field is the weakest, the null. The needle always indicates the direction of the station from the nose of the aircraft in a clockwise direction.

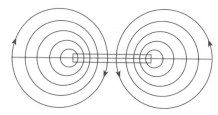

The loop antenna is highly directional with the maximum strength received when the antenna is pointing either directly toward or away from the transmitting antenna.

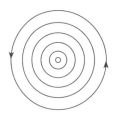

The sense antenna is omnidirectional. It receives with equal strength from all directions.

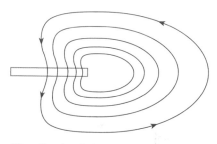

When the signals from the loop and the sense antennas are combined, the field from the sense antenna cancels the field from one side of the loop and adds to that of the other side. The resulting field is heart-shaped with a definite and sharp null.

Figure 5-17. *Reception patterns for ADF antennas.*

nondirectional beacon (NDB). A LF/MF radio beacon transmitting nondirectional signals. When a NDB is installed in conjunction with an instrument landing system (ILS) marker, it is called a compass locator.

relative bearing. The number of degrees measured clockwise between the heading of the aircraft and the direction from which the bearing is taken.

Figure 5-18 is a highly simplified block diagram of a rotating-loop ADF system. The output of the loop antenna is amplified and mixed with the output of the sense antenna. This combined signal is amplified by a tuned amplifier that filters out all but the desired signal. The signal is mixed with the output of a local oscillator to produce an intermediate frequency (IF). The IF is amplified, demodulated, and detected and sent to an audio power amplifier and then to the speaker. A voltage is taken from the output of the detector, filtered and amplified, and used to drive the loop-drive motor. This voltage has the correct polarity to drive the loop in the proper direction to reach its null position. The needle of the ADF indicator is driven by the same signal, and it shows the position of the station relative to the nose of the aircraft in a clockwise direction.

The beat frequency oscillator (BFO) connected to the IF amplifier is used when the ADF receiver is tuned to an unmodulated transmitter. The transmissions from radio beacons in some foreign countries are not modulated, and in order to hear the station, a signal is generated in a BFO that is near that of the IF amplifier. When the BFO signal mixes with the IF, an audio signal is produced whose frequency is the difference between the two signals. In the United States, almost all radio beacons are modulated, so the BFO is not switched in.

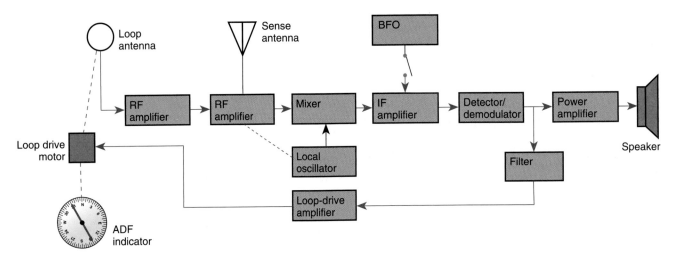

Figure 5-18. *A simplified block diagram of a rotating-loop ADF.*

The principle of the ADF has changed very little over the years, but the hardware has changed dramatically to keep up with the state of the art. Modern high-speed aircraft do not use an actual long-wire sense antenna, but part of the structure is made to function in the same way as the long wire. The rotating loop antenna has been replaced with a nonrotating fixed loop as seen in Figure 5-19.

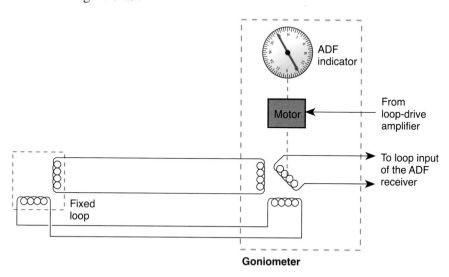

Goniometer

Figure 5-19. *A simplified block diagram of an ADF fixed loop and the goniometer that produces the loop input for the ADF receiver. The motor that drives the goniometer rotor also drives the needle of the indicator.*

The nonrotating loop is actually two fixed-loop antennas connected to two fixed stator windings in a resolver, or goniometer. The fields of the two stator windings induce a voltage in the rotor, and this voltage is sent into the loop input of the RF amplifier in the ADF receiver. The signal is processed in the receiver in the way shown in Figure 5-18. The output of the loop-drive amplifier drives a small motor inside the ADF indicator that drives the rotor of the goniometer until it aligns with the null produced by the of the two fixed coils and the output of the sense antenna. The motor also rotates the needle of the ADF indicator so that it indicates the direction of the station received relative to the nose of the aircraft.

One of the latest types of ADF indicators has a movable card that shows the aircraft magnetic heading at the top of the instrument. This allows the head of the needle to indicate the magnetic bearing to the station and the tail of the needle to indicate the magnetic bearing from the station. See Figures 5-22 and 5-23 (on page 335) that illustrate a movable-card radio magnetic indicator (RMI) and its use as an ADF indicator.

While the use of ADF navigation has been an integral part of the aerospace system for many years, the use of ADF was generally replaced with VOR systems and, with the advent of GPS systems, is becoming virtually obsolete.

goniometer. Electronic circuitry in an ADF system that uses the output of a fixed loop antenna to sense the angle between a fixed reference, usually the nose of the aircraft, and the direction from which the radio signal is being received.

magnetic bearing. The direction to or from a radio transmitting station measured relative to magnetic north.

Very High Frequency Omnidirectional Range Navigation System (VOR)

VOR. Very high frequency Omni Range navigation.

Immediately after the end of World War II, the Civil Aeronautics Administration, forerunner of the present FAA, realized that the tremendous growth of aviation as a serious means of transportation would demand better radio navigation facilities than the low-frequency, four-course system then in use. Aircraft approaching or departing from a busy airport should be able to use more than four courses. Also, the system should not operate in the low frequency band, which is susceptible to all types of atmospheric interference. Finally, the inherent accuracy of the system should be in the ground equipment. The accuracy of the equipment in an aircraft would relate to the type of flying being done and the amount of money the user was willing to spend for precision. This allowed relatively inexpensive equipment to be installed in light aircraft that operated under visual flight rules (VFR) and yet allowed airliners and military aircraft to navigate with a high degree of precision.

VOR operates in the 108- to 118-MHz band with 50-kHz channel spacing, making 360 channels available. VOR transmitters located along the airways have about 200 watts of output power and are usable for approximately 200 nautical miles. Terminal VORs (TVOR) are located on the airports, and they operate with about 50 watts of output power and have a usable range of approximately 25 nautical miles.

terminal VOR. A low-powered VOR that is normally located on an airport.

VOR is a phase-comparison type of navigation system that provides direction to a station, and when it is combined with distance measuring equipment (DME), it provides a specific fix. Since VOR is such a popular navigation system, it has been developed to a very high degree of sophistication, especially in the presentation of information to the pilot. This text discusses the basic principles as they apply to the early type of display, and the way the new systems relate.

The VOR ground station transmits two signals modulated with 30-hertz on the same frequency. One signal is an omnidirectional reference signal and the other is a rotating signal. The ground station is set up in such a way that the two signals are in phase as the rotating signal sweeps past magnetic north. They get farther apart until it sweeps past 180° magnetic, and then are back in phase at 360°.

The equipment in the aircraft consists of the horizontally polarized antenna, the VHF VOR receiver, the omni bearing selector (OBS), the course deviation indicator (CDI), and the TO/FROM indicator.

CDI. Course Deviation Indicator.

The antenna is a horizontally polarized V-dipole that is installed above the aircraft cabin or on the vertical fin. The more modern antenna is a "towel rack" that mounts on the vertical fin and acts as a highly efficient horizontal dipole.

The receiver may be the VHF communication receiver with the additional circuitry needed to process the VOR signals and also the circuitry to process the instrument landing system (ILS) localizer signals. The localizer signals are in the same frequency range as the terminal VOR signals, and the localizer uses the same instrument as is the VOR, but its operation is entirely different. The localizer is described with the ILS on page 337.

Follow the block diagram in Figure 5-20 to see the way the VOR functions. The VOR signal from the receiver contains an AM 30-Hz variable signal (this is the one that rotates), and a 10-kHz subcarrier that is frequency modulated with a 30-Hz reference signal.

A 10-kHz filter passes the FM reference signal and it is demodulated to remove the subcarrier and is passed into the omni bearing selector as a 30-Hz signal. The OBS is a variable phase shifter that can shift the phase of the reference signal. When it is shifted, the OBS indicator shows the number of degrees it has been shifted.

A 30-Hz filter passes the variable signal, and it is put into the phase detector with the output from the OBS. The phases of the two signals are compared and they drive the needle of the course-deviation indicator.

Another phase detector is parallel to the one that drives the course-deviation, or L-R, indicator, but this one is in series with a 90° phase shifter. Its signals are always 90° out of phase with the signals that drive the L-R indicator. The output of this phase detector drives the TO-FROM indicator.

localizer. The portion of an instrument landing system that directs the pilot along the center line of the instrument runway.

left-right indicator. The course-deviation indicator used with a VOR navigation system.

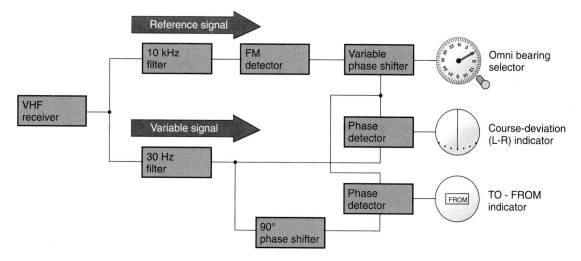

Figure 5-20. *A simplified block diagram of the VOR circuitry in a VOR receiver.*

Figure 5-21 shows the way the VOR operates. The pilots in airplanes A and B can select the frequency of the VOR station on the receiver and identify it by the three-letter code identifier or the voice identifier. He or she then turns the OBS knob until the needle of the L-R indicator centers. It will center at two different settings of the OBS. In this case, it centered when the OBS read 030° and the TO-FROM indicator indicated FROM. This means that if the airplane were turned to a heading of 030°, it would be flying *from* the station. It will also center on 210° and the TO-FROM indicator will indicate TO. If the airplane is turned to a heading of 210°, it will go *to* the station.

The pilots in airplanes C and D will also have the L-R indicator centered when the OBS reads 030° and 210°. When it reads 030°, the TO-FROM indicator will indicate TO, and when it reads 210°, the TO-FROM will indicate FROM. If either of these two airplanes was turned to a heading of 030°, it would go to the station. When the aircraft is off the radial, the needle will deflect toward the radial by an amount proportional to the amount it is off course. The needle will deflect full scale when the aircraft is approximately 15° off course.

Notice one important fact about VOR. It has nothing to do with the heading of the aircraft; it is only sensitive to the location of the aircraft directionally in relation to the station. This is different from ADF, which computes the direction of the station relative to the direction the nose of the aircraft is pointed.

radial. A directional line radiating outward from a radio facility, usually a VOR.

When an aircraft is flying outbound on the 030° radial, it is flying away from the station on a line that has a magnetic direction of 030° from the station.

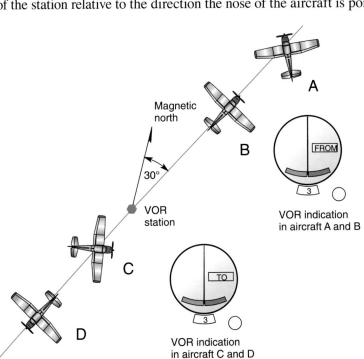

Figure 5-21. *The indication of a VOR has nothing to do with the heading of the aircraft. It is entirely dependent upon the location of the aircraft relative to the station.*

Radio Magnetic Indicator (RMI)

In an effort to minimize the number of instruments on a modern instrument panel and to combine information from various indicators to make their interpretation easier, the radio magnetic indicator, or RMI, has been developed and is now widely used. This instrument combines the remote indicating compass with the indicators for the ADF and VOR.

A flux-gate compass drives the dial of the instrument, and the head of the VOR needle points to the TO bearing to the station. Figure 5-22 shows the dial of an RMI, and Figure 5-23 shows the location and heading of the aircraft relative to the two radio stations.

The single arrow that indicates for the VOR is pointing to 150°. This is the TO bearing to the station, and if the aircraft were turned to a heading of 150° it would go to the station. This places the aircraft on the 330° radial (180° + 150° = 330°). VOR radials are always numbered by the magnetic direction FROM the station.

The flux-gate compass has rotated the dial of the indicator to show that the aircraft is flying with a magnetic heading of 315°. The dial has turned until 315° is under the marker at the top of the instrument, which is the lubber line. This means that there is probably a wind from the west and the aircraft is crabbing 15° to the left to prevent the wind blowing it off the 330° radial.

The double arrow that indicates for the ADF shows that the station being received on the ADF is to the left of the aircraft between the wing and the nose. The station has a magnetic bearing from the aircraft of 255°. Remember that an ADF arrow always points to the station relative to the nose of the airplane, which is the top of the indicator. See Figures 5-22 and 5-23.

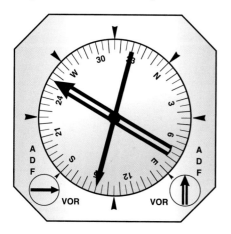

Figure 5-22. *An RMI shows the magnetic heading of the aircraft, the VOR radial on which it is flying, and the magnetic direction from the aircraft to a station being received on the ADF.*

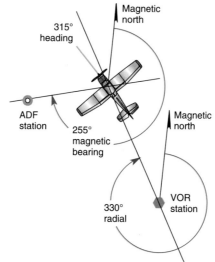

Figure 5-23. *This is the position of the aircraft shown by the instrument in Figure 5-22. It is heading 315° magnetic and is flying outbound on the 330° radial from the VOR. The ADF station has a magnetic bearing from the aircraft of 255°.*

Instrument Landing System (ILS)

VOR, ADF, and RNAV allow navigation between airports, but it is the ILS, or instrument landing system, that allows pilots to get safely on the ground once they've reached their destination.

The ILS system has been used for years, and is extremely efficient. The system consists of these electronic components: compass locators for the outer marker and the middle marker, localizer, marker beacons, and glide slope. This system is illustrated in Figure 5-24.

localizer. The portion of an instrument landing system that directs the pilot along the center line of the instrument runway.

glide slope. The portion of an instrument landing system that provides the vertical path along which an aircraft descends on an instrument landing.

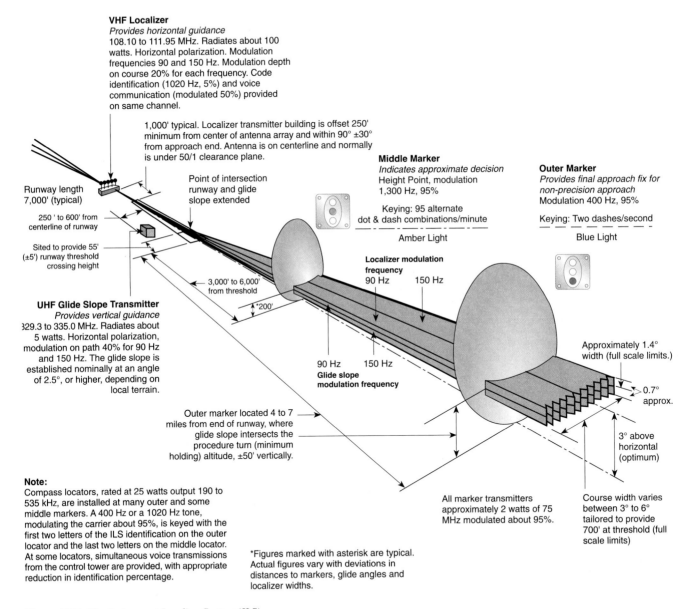

VHF Localizer
Provides horizontal guidance
108.10 to 111.95 MHz. Radiates about 100 watts. Horizontal polarization. Modulation frequencies 90 and 150 Hz. Modulation depth on course 20% for each frequency. Code identification (1020 Hz, 5%) and voice communication (modulated 50%) provided on same channel.

1,000' typical. Localizer transmitter building is offset 250' minimum from center of antenna array and within 90° ±30° from approach end. Antenna is on centerline and normally is under 50/1 clearance plane.

Runway length 7,000' (typical)

250 ' to 600' from centerline of runway

Sited to provide 55' (±5') runway threshold crossing height

Point of intersection runway and glide slope extended

Middle Marker
Indicates approximate decision
Height Point, modulation 1,300 Hz, 95%

Keying: 95 alternate dot & dash combinations/minute

Amber Light

Outer Marker
Provides final approach fix for non-precision approach
Modulation 400 Hz, 95%

Keying: Two dashes/second

Blue Light

Localizer modulation frequency
90 Hz   150 Hz

3,000' to 6,000' from threshold

*200'

UHF Glide Slope Transmitter
Provides vertical guidance
329.3 to 335.0 MHz. Radiates about 5 watts. Horizontal polarization, modulation on path 40% for 90 Hz and 150 Hz. The glide slope is established nominally at an angle of 2.5°, or higher, depending on local terrain.

90 Hz   150 Hz
Glide slope modulation frequency

Outer marker located 4 to 7 miles from end of runway, where glide slope intersects the procedure turn (minimum holding) altitude, ±50' vertically.

Approximately 1.4° width (full scale limits.)

0.7° approx.

3° above horizontal (optimum)

Note:
Compass locators, rated at 25 watts output 190 to 535 kHz, are installed at many outer and some middle markers. A 400 Hz or a 1020 Hz tone, modulating the carrier about 95%, is keyed with the first two letters of the ILS identification on the outer locator and the last two letters on the middle locator. At some locators, simultaneous voice transmissions from the control tower are provided, with appropriate reduction in identification percentage.

All marker transmitters approximately 2 watts of 75 MHz modulated about 95%.

Course width varies between 3° to 6° tailored to provide 700' at threshold (full scale limits)

*Figures marked with asterisk are typical. Actual figures vary with deviations in distances to markers, glide angles and localizer widths.

Figure 5-24. *The Instrument Landing System (ILS).*

Compass Locators

Compass locators are low-frequency nondirectional beacons that operate between 190 and 535 kHz. They transmit a continuous carrier and keyed identifier and have a range of approximately 15 miles. When the ADF is tuned to the published frequency of the compass locator at the outer marker, the aircraft can fly directly to the marker that begins the instrument approach. Compass locators are typically installed at the outer marker and the middle marker.

Localizer

A localizer is a VHF facility that provides course guidance down the extended center line of the instrument runway from approximately 18 miles out to the point of touchdown. The localizer uses the same receiver, antenna, and indicator as the VOR, but operates on an entirely different principle.

The localizer antenna arrays are located at the far end of the instrument runway, and they transmit a horizontally polarized signal on frequencies between 108.10 and 111.95 MHz. The carrier is transmitted with two sets of antenna. The signal from one set is modulated with a 90-Hz tone and the signal from the other is modulated with a 150-Hz tone. Refer to Figure 5-24. The antennas that radiate the 90-Hz tone have a pattern that is about $1\frac{1}{2}°$ to 3° wide and it extends from the center line of the instrument runway toward the left side, as viewed from the approach end. The pattern of the 150-Hz modulated signal is on the right side of the runway center line.

When the VHF Nav receiver is tuned to a localizer frequency, the VOR circuitry is switched out and the localizer circuitry activated. The signal from the antenna is taken into the receiver and passed through two filters. One filter passes the 90-Hz tone and the other passes the 150-Hz tone. This audio signal is rectified and changed to a DC voltage that drives the pointer of the same Left-Right indicator that is used with the VOR. When the aircraft is to the right of the runway center line, it is in the 150-Hz modulation area, and the needle deflects to the left, showing that the runway is to the left. The needle deflects full scale when the aircraft is approximately 2.5° off of the center line. This translates to about 1,500 feet at five miles out, but becomes less as the runway is approached. If the aircraft moves to the left of the runway center line, it is in the 90-Hz area and the needle is driven to the right, indicating that the runway is to the right of the aircraft. While the localizer indicator is the same instrument used with VOR, when it is displaying the localizer, it is approximately four times as sensitive as it is when it is displaying VOR.

The localizer signals extend from both ends of the instrument runway. When the aircraft is approaching the runway from the end that has the glide slope, it is said to be making a front-course approach and the pilot turns toward the needle when the aircraft is off course. When approaching from the opposite end of the runway, the aircraft is making a back-course approach. When the aircraft drifts off course the pilot must turn it away from the needle to get back on course. This, you will notice, differs from the way VOR is flown.

back course. The reciprocal of the localizer course for an ILS (Instrument Landing System).

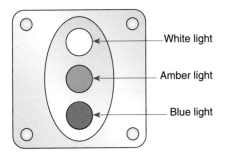

Figure 5-25. *A three-light display for the marker beacons located along an ILS approach.*

The blue light illuminates in a series of dashes to indicate passage over the outer marker (OM).

The amber light illuminates in a series of alternate dots and dashes to indicate passage over the middle marker (MM).

The white light illuminates in a series of dots to indicate passage over the inner marker (IM).

UHF. Ultrahigh Frequency

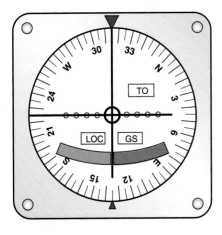

Figure 5-26. *An ILS indicator.*

Marker Beacons

The outer marker beacon transmitter is located between four and seven miles from the end of the runway. This is a low-power 75-MHz transmitter that radiates its signal straight up. The outer marker is modulated with a 400-Hz audio tone in a series of dashes.

When the aircraft is directly above the outer marker, this signal is received and the modulation is filtered. The 400-Hz modulation turns on a blue light in the three-light display on the instrument panel and the pilot hears the series of 400-Hz dashes.

When the aircraft is about 3,500 feet from the threshold of the runway, it passes over the middle marker. This is the same type of transmitter and antenna, but it is modulated with a 1,300-Hz tone in a series of alternating dots and dashes. When this modulation is filtered, it turns on the amber light and the pilot hears the dots and dashes.

Some instrument landing systems have an inner marker that uses the same type of transmitter and antenna. This is located at the point at which the aircraft should be at its decision height. It is modulated with a 3,000-Hz tone in a series of dots, and its filtered audio signal turns on the white light.

Glide Slope

The glide slope transmitter and antenna are located about 750 to 1,250 feet from the approach end of the runway and offset about 250 to 600 feet from the runway center line. It transmits a highly directional signal that is approximately 1.4° wide and is angled upward from the transmitter at an angle of approximately 3°.

The signal from the glide slope is transmitted on one of 40 UHF channels between 329.30 MHz and 335.00 MHz, and the antenna is a small UHF dipole that is sometimes built into the front of the VOR/localizer antenna.

Each glide slope channel is paired with a specific localizer frequency and is automatically selected when the pilot tunes the VHF nav receiver to the localizer frequency. Two signals using the same carrier are transmitted from the antenna system in such a way that they overlap to form the glide slope. The upper signal is modulated with a 90-Hz tone and the lower signal is modulated with a 150-Hz tone.

When the signal is received, the audio modulations are filtered and converted into DC voltages that drive the horizontal cross pointer seen in Figure 5-26. If the aircraft is above the glide slope, it is in the 90-Hz modulation and the pointer is driven downward to show the pilot to fly down. If the aircraft is below the glide slope, it is in the 150-Hz modulation and the pointer is driven up to instruct the pilot to fly up.

Radar Beacon Transponder

Radar is one of the most important devices for the control of aircraft along our airways and in busy terminal areas. The primary radar at an air traffic control center sends out highly directional pulses of UHF or SHF energy. This energy travels in a straight line, and if it does not hit anything, it continues out into space and does not return, but if it hits an aircraft, part of the energy is reflected back to the ground antenna. This is a large dish antenna that is able to collect the faint echo of the energy reflected from the aircraft. This returned energy is processed by the receiver and displayed on a radar scope as a bright dot with azimuth and distance on the radar screen which is a Planned Position Indicator (PPI) See Figure 5-31 on page 349.

With the large number of aircraft in the air at any one time, air traffic controllers need to identify the dot on the scope made by a specific aircraft. Secondary Surveillance Radar (SSR) is used for this purpose. The ground equipment of the SSR is an interrogating unit with an antenna that is mounted on the highly directional rotating dish antenna of the primary radar. Several coded pulse trains are transmitted from the SSR antenna to the aircraft. Civil aircraft utilize two of these pulse trains, the first set of pulses is Mode A, or the location pulses, and the second set is Mode C, the altitude reporting pulses.

The airborne portion of this system is the transponder that contains a receiver and a transmitter that can respond to a received signal with any of 4,096 discrete codes. See Figure 5-27.

The ground controller assigns the pilot of an aircraft a specific code to select on the transponder. When the transponder is operating, it receives the pulse of energy from the ground station transmitted at 1030 MHz, delays for a specific number of microseconds, then replies on 1090 MHz with the assigned code. Instead of being just dots on a crowded scope, the controller can filter out and eliminate all of the aircraft other than those responding with the assigned code. The returns for these aircraft appear as a double slash on the controller's radar scope. If the controller wants to know which one of the returns is from the particular aircraft, the pilot may be asked to indent. To do this, the pilot pushes the IDENT button on the instrument. The return signal modifies the two-slash image so the controller can easily identify the image for the specific aircraft.

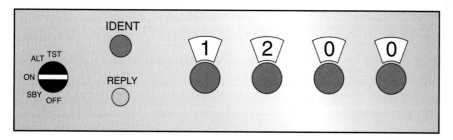

Figure 5-27. *The control head of an ATC transponder.*

When Mode C, or ALT, is selected on the control, the transponder receives a signal from the encoding altimeter and responds with a code that places an alphanumeric display beside the double slashes showing the pressure altitude at which the aircraft is flying.

The controls for a typical transponder are seen in Figure 5-27 (see previous page). The four selector knobs allow the pilot to select the code the controller requests. The selector switch on the left has an OFF, STANDBY, ON, ALT, and TEST position. There is also an IDENT button and a REPLY light. When the switch is in the OFF position, the transponder is turned off. When it is in the STANDBY position, the equipment is warmed up, but it is not replying to any interrogations. In the ON position, it replies with the selected code when it is interrogated. When the ALT position is selected it replies with the altitude code as furnished by the encoding altimeter. When the IDENT button is pressed, the return is modified so the controller can instantly identify the aircraft. The reply light blinks each time the transponder replies to a ground interrogation.

Because of the increased use of SSR, mode-S has been developed as a solution to the frequency congestion on 1090 MHz. Mode-S (mode select) does this by assigning individual aircraft a permanent mode-S address from the internationally assigned registration number. This allows a specific aircraft to be interrogated in such a way that no other aircraft will reply. Mode-S is designed to be compatible with the current radio beacon system, and it can interrogate current transponders and mode-S transponders can reply to the current interrogations.

Transponder Checks

Because an accurate reply is so important, the FAA requires that all transponders be checked every 24 calendar months and found to comply with the requirements that are specified in 14 CFR Part 43, Appendix F.

Traffic Alert/Collision Avoidance System (TCAS)

The crowded skies and busy workloads of the flight crews make traffic avoidance extremely important. When operating under Visual Flight Rules, it is the responsibility of the pilot-in-command of an aircraft to see and avoid any traffic, and when operating under Instrument Flight Rules, it is the responsibility of the air traffic controller to space the aircraft so there is no danger of in-flight collisions. But, with the large number of aircraft in the air around busy airports, visual contact is sometimes not possible and as a result there have been several fatal accidents.

TCAS is a computerized avionics system that reduces the danger of midair collisions between aircraft. It does this by monitoring the airspace around the aircraft independent of air traffic control. The FAA requires TCAS on all commercial turbine powered transport aircraft with more than 30 passenger seats or a maximum takeoff weight greater than 33,000 pounds,

pressure altitude. The altitude in standard air at which the pressure is the same as the existing altitude. The pressure altitude furnished to the transponder is independent of the indication on the pilot's altimeter.

alphanumeric symbols. Symbols made up of all of the letters in our alphabet, numerals, punctuation marks, and certain other special symbols.

and TCAS is available for installation in all mode-C (altitude-reporting) transponder-equipped aircraft. In a glass cockpit aircraft, the TCAS information is shown on the navigation display; on aircraft equipped with mechanical instruments, the TCAS display is incorporated in the instantaneous vertical speed indicator.

TCAS operates by the communication between aircraft with correctly operating transponders. Several times each second the transponder transmits an interrogation on 1030 MHz and all the other properly equipped aircraft within a specified range respond on 1090 MHz. These continuous interrogation-response cycles are fed into a computer, which builds a three-dimensional map of all the aircraft within range showing their bearing, altitude and velocity. The computer extrapolates this current position data and by anticipating future positions it determines whether or not a potential collision threat exists. TCAS then instructs the pilots of conflicting aircraft, by visual display and synthesized voice, of the proper maneuvers to avoid collision.

There are two TCAS systems in general use, TCAS I and TCAS II. TCAS I is primarily intended for general aviation aircraft and it monitors the airspace within a range of approximately 40 miles of the aircraft. It provides information on the approximate bearing and altitude of the conflicting aircraft and generates a collision warning traffic advisory (TA) that warns the pilot of another aircraft in near proximity with the voice announcement "*traffic, traffic*", but it does not provide any suggested maneuvers to avoid collision. When the threat no longer exists, the system states "*clear of conflict.*"

TCAS II is used in most commercial aircraft. It has all the features of TCAS I, but it also provides a resolution advisory (RA) which suggests to the pilot the corrective action to take. An RA may announce "*descend, descend*" to one of the conflicting aircraft, and "*climb, climb*" to the other aircraft to provide maximum separation.

The display for a TCAS uses such symbols as:

- Open diamond represents a surveillance target.

- Solid diamond represents a proximity target (an aircraft within a vertical distance of ±1,200 feet, and lateral distance of 6 nautical miles).

- Yellow circle is a TA that indicates that a threat aircraft is within 20 to 48 seconds of the closest point of contact.

- Red square is an RA that indicates that a threat aircraft is within 35 seconds of the closest point of contact.

- Altitude symbols show the relative vertical separation between the aircraft. A plus (+) indicates the conflicting aircraft is above your aircraft, and a minus (–) indicates that it is below.

- Trend vectors are arrows next to the aircraft symbol that shows whether the conflicting aircraft is climbing or descending.

Distance Measuring Equipment (DME)

VOR gives the pilot the direction from the station, but it tells nothing about the distance from the station. In order to get a definite location fix, two VOR receivers would have to be used. DME, or distance measuring equipment, has been developed and is installed in most modern aircraft to give the pilot an actual readout of the distance of the aircraft from the station.

DME is a UHF pulse system that is actually part of the military TACAN (Tactical Air Navigation) system that gives military pilots both direction and distance from the station. VOR and TACAN stations are installed at the same location and are called VORTAC stations. Civilian pilots receive their direction information from the VOR and their distance from the DME.

DME operates on a frequency in the band between 987 and 1,213 MHz and is tuned with the VOR. The antenna is a short UHF blade mounted on the belly of the aircraft.

In operation, the DME transmits approximately 150 pairs of randomly-spaced pulses each second. The ground station receives these pulses as well as the pulses from every other aircraft flying in the area and retransmits them all. The DME receives all of these retransmitted pulses and locks onto the pulse pairs it recognizes as having the same spacing as those it transmitted.

When the DME recognizes the pulse pairs it transmitted, it measures the difference between the time they were transmitted and the time the retransmitted pulses were received. This time difference in microseconds is converted into nautical miles and displayed on the DME indicator. This distance is called slant-line distance because it is the distance through the air to the station, and not the distance over the ground. When the aircraft is directly over the station at an altitude of 6,000 feet it will indicate that it is about one nautical mile from the station. It is one mile above the station.

Modern DME has circuits in it that measure the change in distance for a given time and give direct readout of the ground speed, and time en route to the station.

Area Navigation (RNAV)

The main limitation of VOR as a navigation system is that it can only direct the pilot to or from VOR stations, and often flights must be made to some location that does not have a VOR. This limitation has been overcome with Area Navigation, or RNAV, as it is generally called.

If a pilot wants to fly directly to an airport that does not have a VOR on the field, but is located near a VORTAC station, a way point can be set on the field that appears to the RNAV receiver to be a VOR station. The way point is established by entering the radial and the distance from the VORTAC into the RNAV. In Figure 5-28, the destination airport is 36 miles from the VORTAC station on its 140° radial. The RNAV knows the radial on which the aircraft is located and its distance from the VORTAC. By knowing the length and direction of two sides of a triangle, the RNAV computer can easily

DME. Distance Measuring Equipment.

TACAN (Tactical Air Navigation). A radio navigation facility used by military aircraft for both direction and distance information. Civilian aircraft receive distance information from a TACAN on their DME.

VORTAC. An electronic navigation system that contains both a VOR and a TACAN facility.

determine the direction of a straight line from the aircraft to the destination airport and the distance to the airport.

The RNAV uses a course deviation indicator similar to that used with VOR to show any deviation from a straight line between the aircraft present position and the way point. As the aircraft flies toward the way point, the computer keeps track of the decreasing distance and displays on its indicator the distance to go, the ground speed, and the estimated time en route. Some sets can display the estimated time of arrival.

There is one important difference between the CDI of a VOR and that of an RNAV. Deviation from the desired course on a VOR is an angular deviation. The actual distance the aircraft is off course depends upon its distance from the station. Deviation on an RNAV indicator is a linear deviation. If the indicator shows the aircraft to be 2 nautical miles off course, this distance will not change as the aircraft approaches the way point.

Global Positioning System (GPS)

The global positioning system (GPS) is fast taking over as the navigation system of choice for both the military and civilian aircraft in America and worldwide. GPS is a satellite-based system that uses a network of 24 satellites placed into orbit by the U.S. Department of Defense (DOD). It was originally intended for use only by the military, but since the 1980s its full capability has been available for civilian use. GPS works in any weather conditions, anywhere in the world, 24 hours a day and there are no user fees for GPS.

The accuracy is in the system, not in the equipment used, which varies from the simple hand-held receivers to the elaborate equipment used by the military and the airlines. GPS involves three segments: the space segment, the control segment, and the user segment.

The Space Segment

The space segment consists of 24 satellites, 21 are active and 3 are operational spares that can immediately replace any that fail. These satellites are held in six orbital planes approximately 12,000 miles above the earth's surface, and are located in their orbit in such a way that at least four of them can always be received by a GPS receiver, they travel at about 7,000 miles per hour and circle the earth twice a day.

GPS satellites are powered by solar energy and have small rocket boosters to keep them in the correct orbit. Each satellite transmits a series of digital signals with a power of 50 watts or less on several frequencies. These signals allow the receiver to identify the specific satellite, give its exact location in its orbit, and tell the exact time the signal was transmitted. Civilian GPS receivers use signals transmitted on the L1 frequency of 1575.42 MHz.

GPS signals contain four different kinds of information; an identifier which allows you to know which satellites are being received, ephemeris data which gives the exact location of each satellite, the condition of the satellite, and the exact time.

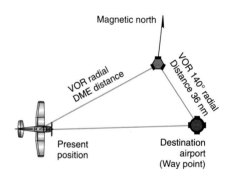

Figure 5-28. *RNAV is able to direct an aircraft to a way point that is defined in terms of a radial from a VORTAC station and the distance in nautical miles between the station and the way point. The computer in the RNAV solves the trig problem of finding the length and direction of the unknown side of a triangle when the length and direction of the other two sides are known.*

Figure 5-29. *This hand-held GPS receiver has a moving map display and a terrain clearance feature. Lowrance Airmap 600C.*

database. A body of information that is available on any particular subject.

The Control Segment

There are five control stations located around the world. Four of these are unmanned monitoring stations and the fifth is the master control station. The monitoring stations receive continuous data from the satellites and forward it to the master station. The master station tracks each satellite and knows its exact location, altitude, and velocity, and it sends to the satellites any corrections that they need.

The User Segment

The user segment is the receiver and its display. The corrected signals from the satellites allows the receiver to know the exact time the signal was transmitted and the exact time it was received. These signals travel at the speed of light—186,000 miles per second, and by knowing the speed and the time traveled, the receiver can determine the exact distance between the satellite and the aircraft.

By measuring this distance between several of the satellites, the receiver can determine the user's position and display it in units of longitude and latitude, or actually show the location on a moving map.

When a GPS receiver is locked onto the signals from three satellites it can calculate a two-dimensional position (latitude and longitude) and can track movement. By locking onto four or more satellites, the receiver can also determine the user's altitude. By knowing the exact location of the aircraft, the GPS can compute such other information as speed, bearing, track, distance traveled, distance to destination and much more.

The most popular type of display for GPS is the moving map, in either a small handheld unit (see Figure 5-29) or integrated into the multifunction display such as the one in Figure 5-30. An updatable database card containing such data as VOR information, communications frequencies, airport data, and Flight Service Station references is used to program the display.

To use GPS for navigation, enter the identifier or latitude/longitude location of your destination. The display shows such information as the bearing and distance to the location, the ground speed and the estimated time enroute and much more.

Figure 5-30. *This panel-mounted GPS display is included in this multifunction display. Garmin GNS-480.*

Wide Area Augmentation System (WAAS)

GPS alone does not meet the FAA's navigation requirements for accuracy and integrity, and for this reason WAAS was developed. WAAS is required to provide a position accuracy of 7.6 meters or better both laterally and vertically, at least 95% of the time. But actual performance measurements have shown it typically provides better than 1.0 meters laterally and 1.5 meters vertically throughout most of the contiguous United States. WAAS was developed by the FAA for use in precision flight approaches and the airports were not required to install and maintain precision approach equipment.

WAAS, like the normal GPS is composed of three main segments; the Ground segment, the Space segment, and the User segment.

The Ground Segment

The ground segment is composed of about 25 precisely surveyed reference stations which monitor and collect information on the GPS signals, and then send their data to the two master stations. The master stations use the data from the reference stations to generate the needed corrections. These corrections are then sent to ground uplink stations which transmit them to the satellites in the space segment for broadcast to the user segment.

The Space Segment

The space segment consists of multiple geosynchronous communication satellites which broadcast the messages generated by the master stations for reception by the user segment. These satellites also broadcast the same type of range information as normal GPS satellites, effectively increasing the number of satellites available for a GPS position fix.

geosynchronous satellite. A satellite whose orbital track over the earth repeats itself regularly.

The User Segment

The user segment is the GPS and WAAS receiver, which uses the information broadcast from each GPS satellite to determine its location and the current time, and receives the WAAS corrections from the Space segment. These corrections improve its accuracy.

WAAS resolves most GPS limitation with its ease of use, and high degree of accuracy, and it does not require expensive on-airport facilities, and it works just as well between airports, allowing aircraft to fly directly from one airport to another, rather than having to follow routes dictated by ground facilities.

Inertial Navigation System (INS)

The INS is an extremely accurate navigation system that does not depend upon outside navigation signals to direct the pilot to any chosen destination. The INS has three accelerometers and three attitude gyros mounted at right angles to each other on a gyro-stabilized inertial platform that remains parallel to the earth's surface regardless of the earth's rotation or the airplane's position or attitude.

The exact location of the aircraft in terms of latitude and longitude is entered into the INS computer before the aircraft is pushed back from the gate, and as the aircraft moves, the computer integrates the signals from the accelerometers with time to track the movement of the aircraft longitudinally, laterally, and vertically.

The latitude and longitude of the aircraft are continually updated in the computer, and the direction, distance, and time to any way point entered into the computer are displayed for the pilot to see. This information is also fed into the automatic flight control system to direct the aircraft to fly to the way point.

Microwave Landing System (MLS)

MLS was considered by the FAA to be a replacement for the Instrument Landing System (ILS) because it allowed multiple approach paths instead of the single approach path allowed by ILS. In the United States, this has been replaced by WAAS, but it is still used to some extent in Europe.

Radar and Radio Altimeters

Pneumatic altimeters measure the absolute pressure of the air in which the aircraft is flying. By adjusting a reference pressure level in the barometric window, the altimeter will show the height, in feet, above this reference level. This instrument does not show the height of the aircraft above the terrain over which it is flying, and it is not adequate for the extreme precision needed for some of the very-low-visibility instrument approaches approved for modern, well-equipped aircraft.

Radar altimeters were developed during World War II when certain types of bombing and torpedo release demanded an extremely accurate knowledge of the height of the aircraft above the surface of the water. These altimeters transmitted a pulse of energy vertically downward, which hit the surface and bounced back and was received. The lapsed time between transmission and reception was measured and displayed on an instrument in terms of feet of altitude.

Modern aircraft use radio altimeters which, instead of transmitting pulses of energy, transmit a 50-MHz frequency-modulated continuous-wave signal on a carrier frequency of 4,300 MHz. The modulation causes the frequency of this wave to vary from 4,250 to 4,350 MHz, and this variation occurs 100 times each second.

This signal is transmitted downward by a directional antenna, and it strikes the ground and bounces back to the aircraft where it is received on another antenna. The frequency of the signal changes a specific number of Hertz each second, and the transmitted energy travels a specific number of feet each second. The equipment measures the difference in frequency between the signal transmitted and that received, and the difference relates to the distance the wave has traveled from the aircraft to the ground and back to the aircraft.

The distance, in feet, between the aircraft and the surface is displayed on an instrument. The pilot is able to set the decision height into the instrument. When the aircraft descends to this height above the ground, a light warns that the decision must be made to continue the approach to landing, or if the approach lights are not visible, to execute a missed approach.

Terrain Awareness Warning System (TAWS)

The Ground Proximity Warning System (GPWS), developed in the 1970s, prevented many accidents caused by controlled flight into terrain; however, the wide acceptance of GPS and WAAS has given us a far better system—the Enhanced Ground Proximity Warning System (EGPWS). This system is so satisfactory that the FAA requires its installation in certain aircraft; since the name "EGPWS" is a proprietary name, the FAA has selected the name Terrain Awareness Warning System (TAWS).

The GPWS senses the nearness of the ground by monitoring the radar altimeter to determine the actual height above the ground, and the air data computer, instrument landing system, and landing gear and flap position to determine if the aircraft is properly configured for its distance from the ground. If it is too near the ground for its location or configuration, the system warns the pilot. But the TAWS computer receives position information from a GPS receiver, and compares that position with the internal terrain or obstacle database. It also receives aircraft configuration and air-data information to create a four-dimensional position of latitude, longitude, altitude and time. It compares this position with the onboard database of terrain, obstacles and runways to determine if any conflicts exist. If a possible conflict is detected between the predicted flight path of the aircraft and terrain, visual and audible warnings are given to the pilot.

There are three general categories of TAWS that are designed provide a warning with enough time for the flight crew to take appropriate action.

Terrain Depiction Systems

These systems contain databases of terrain elevations taken from government charts that show the terrain in color that depict elevations above sea just as on sectional charts. These systems can only give pilot the general awareness of the terrain and no audible or visual warnings are given.

Class-B Terrain Avoidance Warning Systems

Class-B TAWS equipment is required for turbine-powered airplanes operated under Part 91 with six or more passenger seats and for turbine-powered airplanes operated under Part 135 with six to nine passenger seats. This equipment includes these basic functions:

- Forward-looking terrain avoidance that looks ahead and below the aircraft flight path to provide a suitable alert if a potential threat exists.

- Premature descent alert uses the predicted flight path information determined from an approach navigation source and its own airport database to determine if the aircraft is below the normal approach path for the nearest runway. If a conflict is detected, a warning is given to the pilot.

- Attention alerts provides appropriate visual and audio alerts for both cautions and warnings.

- Indications of imminent contact with the ground provides indications of possible terrain conflicts for the following conditions:
  - Excessive rates of descent.
  - Negative climb rate or altitude loss after takeoff.
  - Voice callout "five hundred" when the aircraft descends to 500 feet above the terrain or nearest runway elevation.

Class-A Terrain Avoidance Warning Systems

Class-A TAWS equipment is required for turbine-powered airplanes operated under Part 121, airline and Part 135 charter, of 10 or more passenger seats. In addition to all of the requirements of Class-B, this equipment includes:

- Terrain awareness display on a multi-function display.

- Indications of imminent contact with the ground and additional indications of possible terrain conflict such as:
  - Excessive closure rate to terrain.
  - Flight into terrain when not in landing configuration.
  - Excessive downward deviation from an ILS glideslope.

Radar

One of the most important developments to come out of World War II was that of radar (RAdio Detection And Ranging). This system, brought to a high level of operation by the British, allowed ships and aircraft to be detected and tracked when they could not be seen because of distance or clouds.

Radar transmits a pulse of high-energy electromagnetic waves at a super-high frequency from a highly directional antenna. This pulse travels from the antenna until it strikes an object, then part of the energy is reflected and it returns to the antenna and is directed into the receiver. The returned pulse is displayed as a light dot on a cathode-ray tube at a specific distance and direction from a reference on the tube.

A basic primary radar system can be explained by using the block diagram in Figure 5-31.

The synchronizer is the timing device that produces the signals that synchronize the functions of the transmitter, receiver, and indicator. The modulator produces pulses of high-voltage DC that are built up and stored until a timing, or trigger, pulse from the synchronizer releases them into

cathode-ray tube. A display tube used for oscilloscopes and computer video displays.

An electron gun emits a stream of electrons that is attracted to a positively charged inner surface of the face of the tube. Acceleration and focusing grids speed the movement of the electrons and shape the beam into a pinpoint size. Electrostatic or electromagnetic forces caused by deflection plates or coils move the beam over the face of the tube.

The inside surface of the face of the tube is treated with a phosphor material that emits light when the beam of electrons strikes it.

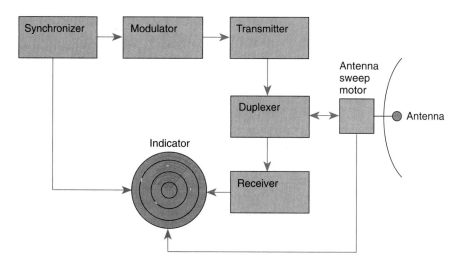

Figure 5-31. *A simplified block diagram of a primary radar system.*

the transmitter. In the transmitter, the high-voltage pulses are changed into pulses of SHF energy of extremely short duration. These pulses are directed into the duplexer, which acts as an automatic selector switch, connecting the transmitter to the antenna, and then disconnecting it and connecting the antenna to the receiver. The pulse of SHF energy is radiated from a short dipole antenna and is focused by a parabolic reflector into a beam. The beam of SHF electromagnetic energy travels in a straight line until it hits some object, and then some of it bounces back and is picked up by the reflector and focused on the antenna and is carried into the duplexer. The duplexer, again acting as a switch, directs the returned energy into the receiver. The receiver manipulates this energy so it is usable by the indicator.

The returned energy is displayed on a cathode-ray tube (CRT) indicator, such as the one in Figure 5-32, as a bright spot of light. The location of the spot is determined in azimuth by the position of the antenna when the return was received, and in its distance from the center of the scope by the time between the transmission of the energy and the reception of the returned energy. In this way, the location of the spot shows the direction and distance between the antenna and the object causing the return.

As the antenna rotates, the sweep on the indicator follows it and leaves a light dot for each return. The phosphors on the inside of the CRT have a characteristic called persistence that causes them to continue to glow for a short time after the sweep has past. This persistence allows the returns to remain on the indicator long enough to form a meaningful pattern.

Radar has made precision control of air traffic possible. All of the airways are covered by radar surveillance, and the terminal radar control is able to track all of the aircraft in the vicinity of the airports. Precision-radar-controlled approaches assist pilots in safe landings in all types of weather conditions.

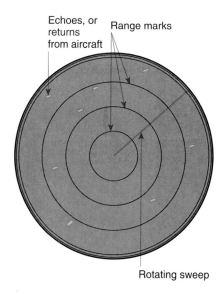

Figure 5-32. *A circular, or P-scan, PPI radar indicator.*

Band	Application	Frequency
	Radar altimeter	2.2 – 2.4 GHz
C	Weather radar	5.4 GHz
X	Doppler radar	8.8 GHz
X	Weather radar	9.4 GHz

Figure 5-33. *Radar bands and their frequency ranges.*

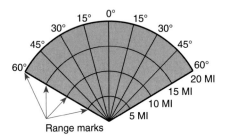

Figure 5-34. *The fan-shaped PPI scope commonly used with weather radar. Different distance scales can be selected.*

PPI (Plan Position Indicator). A type of radar scope that shows both the direction and distance of the target from the radar antenna. Some radar antenna rotate and their PPI scopes are circular. Other antenna oscillate and their PPI scopes are fan shaped.

Weather Radar

Weather radar, the most widely used airborne radar, is available for general aviation aircraft as well as airliners.

Weather radar operates in the same way as the primary radar previously described. Its purpose is to detect turbulence and display it in such a way that the pilot can alter the flight direction to avoid it.

Turbulence is often associated with clouds that contain rain, and when rain is present, the radar beam will reflect from the droplets and furnish a return. The electromagnetic energy has a frequency that gives the best return from the water droplets. Most current weather radar operates in the X or the C band. X-band radar has a frequency of 9.4 GHz and a wavelength of approximately 3.2 cm. C-band radar has a frequency of 5.4 GHz and a wavelength of approximately 5.5 cm. See Figure 5-33.

The typical modern weather radar uses a flat-plate planar-array antenna rather than a dipole and parabolic reflector. The beam sweeps approximately 60° to either side of the nose of the aircraft and the returns are displayed on a fan-shaped plan position indicator (PPI) scope similar to that in Figure 5-34.

Most modern weather radars have color displays. The intensity of the returned energy determines the color of the display on the screen. Minimum precipitation shows up as a green return, medium precipitation shows up as yellow, and heavy precipitation shows up as a red area.

Automatic Dependent Surveillance–Broadcast (ADS-B)

ADS-B, or Automatic Dependent Surveillance–Broadcast, is a key part of the FAA's Next Generation Air Transportation System (NextGen) for improving air transportation safety and efficiency. The traditional use of radar for tracking aircraft position has its drawbacks due to time delays and physical obstructions, such as mountains. ADS-B equipped aircraft use accurate GPS data along with transponder information to transmit information about aircraft speed, altitude, and location to ground-based ADS-B stations, as well as directly to other aircraft. Air traffic control is able to see the location of aircraft based on the transmissions to the ground-based stations.

The transmission portion of ADS-B is called ADS-B Out and the aircraft receiving portion is called ADS-B In. The ADS-B In technology uses a display where the information of other aircraft is displayed and will often include collision avoidance software. The FAA mandated that all aircraft flying in controlled airspace in the United States be equipped with ADS-B Out technology by January 1, 2020. ADS-B In is not required but does provide a significant safety enhancement. The minimum required equipment to meet the ADS-B Out mandate is a WAAS-enabled GPS system, a 1090 MHz Mode S transponder, and an ADS-B approved processor.

Lightning Detector System

It has long been known that an ADF radio would home in on a thunderstorm as well as on a conventional radio transmitter. This principle is made use of in the Stormscope® lightning detector system.

Weather radar requires precipitation to produce its return, but the Stormscope does not. Turbulence is caused by the upward and downward movement of air currents, and as these currents move against each other, static electrical charges build up. The voltage increases until it has an opportunity to discharge to an area that has an opposite charge. It often builds up to such a high value that the discharge is the visible lightning with which we are all familiar. Discharges at a lower voltage are not visible, but are intense enough to be detected by the Stormscope.

The Stormscope works essentially in the same way as an ADF. It has a fixed loop and sense antenna built into a single unit, a computer and processor, and a small-diameter visual display. When the unit is turned on, it picks up the static electricity discharges from within the storm and shows each discharge on the display as a small green dot. The azimuth location of the dot is determined in the same way ADF determines the direction to a station. The distance is determined by the computer, which among other things measures the intensity of the discharge and places the dot a specific distance from the center of the display. The Stormscope detects only electrical discharges and is not affected by rain.

The L-3 Stormscope® WX-950 in Figure 5-35 offers real-time weather avoidance capability. It features two modes of operation for precise thunderstorm mapping.

In the Cell Mode, the Stormscope displays storm cells with better cell definition and range, allowing for easier interpretation for navigating around the areas to avoid, allowing both traffic and lightning to share the same

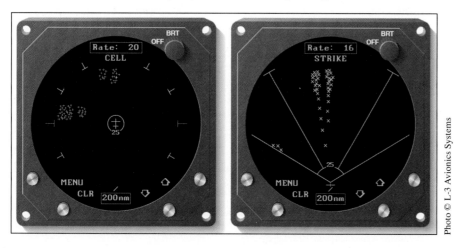

Photo © L-3 Avionics Systems

Figure 5-35. *Stormscope in the 360° view in Cell Mode and in the 120° view in Strike Mode.*

display. In Strike Mode, the Stormscope detects and maps individual strikes, allowing you to monitor sporadic electrical activity that may indicate the beginnings of a storm.

Maintenance and Operation of High Power/High Frequency Systems

Extra caution must be taken when working around systems that produce high power or very high frequencies (such as weather radar or SATCOM systems). Never operate these systems when anyone is close to the antennas, as the output of these systems can cause physical harm to humans. Standing in front of an operating weather radar antenna is much like being in front of a microwave oven that is operating with the door open. If you are inside the airplane and are going to operate one of these systems, always announce your actions to others in the area so that they know to stay clear.

Always follow the aircraft manufacturer's instructions when operating and troubleshooting these systems.

STUDY QUESTIONS: ELECTRONIC NAVIGATION SYSTEMS

Answers are provided on page 381.

30. The old four-course radio range operated in the _____ (low or high)-frequency range.

31. The Automatic Direction Finder (ADF) operates in the _____ and _____ bands.

32. An ADF system requires two antenna. These are a/an _____ and a/an _____ antenna.

33. The loop antenna used with an ADF system _____ (is or is not) a directional antenna.

34. The indication on an ADF indicator _____ (does or does not) change as the heading of the aircraft changes.

35. VOR navigation equipment operates in the _____ (VHF or UHF) band.

36. The antenna used with a VOR system is _____ (horizontally or vertically) polarized.

37. The antenna and receiver used for VOR are also used for the _____ (glide slope or localizer) portion of the instrument landing system.

38. The indication on a VOR Course Deviation Indicator _____ (does or does not) change as the aircraft heading changes.

39. When a Radio Magnetic Indicator is driven by a VOR, the needle points to the _____ (TO or FROM) bearing.

40. The dial of an RMI indicates the _____ (true or magnetic) heading of the aircraft.

41. Compass locators used with an ILS operate in the _____ (LF, VHF, or UHF) band.

42. The signals from the compass locators are received by the _____ (ADF or VOR) receiver.

43. The portion of an ILS that provides guidance down the center line of the instrument runway is the _____ .

44. The localizer used with an ILS operates in the _____ (LF, VHF, or UHF) band.

45. When the Left-Right indicator is used with a localizer signal, it is _____ (more or less) sensitive than it is when it is used with a VOR signal.

46. The glide slope used with an ILS operates in the _____ (LF, VHF, or UHF) band.

47. The carrier transmitted by a marker beacon used with an ILS has a frequency of _____ MHz.

48. A pilot _____ (does or does not) manually tune the glide slope receiver.

49. A transponder can reply to the ground interrogator on any of _____ (how many) codes the pilot can select.

50. When Mode C is selected on the transponder, the altitude data is taken from the _____ .

51. When a radar controller needs to identify a particular aircraft on his radar scope, he asks the pilot to push the _____ button on the transponder.

52. The TCAS operates on signals from other airplanes in the vicinity whose transponders are operating in Mode _____ .

53. The TCAS computer builds a three-dimensional map of all the aircraft within range showing their _____, _____, and _____ .

54. If a Class II TCAS detects two aircraft on a potential collision course, it will warn one aircraft to _____ and the other one to _____ .

55. Distance Measuring Equipment (DME) is a _____ (pulse or phase comparison) system.

56. DME operates in the _____ (VHF or UHF) band.

(continued)

57. The distance shown on a DME indicator _____ (is or is not) the actual distance over the ground from the location of the aircraft to the station.

58. RNAV is able to direct a pilot to a way point that has been defined and entered into the equipment as the radial and distance from a/an _____ .

59. The deviation indicator for an RNAV receiver shows the _____ (angular or linear) deviation from the desired course.

60. A fully functioning GPS uses _____ (how many) satellites.

61. To get a three dimensional fix (latitude, longitude, and altitude) a GPS receiver must be locked onto _____ or more satellites.

62. The most popular type of display for GPS is the _____ .

63. The two main advantages of WAAS over GPS is its _____ and _____ .

64. The inertial navigation system (INS) _____ (is or is not) dependent upon ground-based electronic signals.

65. A radar altimeter shows the pilot the actual height of the aircraft above _____ (the ground or sea level).

66. The TAWS has essentially replaced the _____ .

67. The TAWS receives its location data from the _____ .

68. The TAWS warns the flight crew of a dangerous situation with both visual and _____ warnings.

69. Weather radar returns show energy that is reflected from _____ .

70. An area of the heaviest precipitation shows up on a color weather radar as _____ (green, yellow, or red).

71. The Stormscope system detects electrostatic discharges within a storm and it _____ (does or does not) require water for its signal.

Electronic Instrument Systems

One reason aviation is such a fascinating branch of science is the speed with which it changes. And in no aspect have changes occurred as rapidly as they have in the field of instrumentation and control. Miniaturization of electronic components has made possible the development of circuits that could never have been built with vacuum tubes or even with discrete components such as transistors and coils.

It was integrated circuits that made electronic computers practical, and it was the replacement of analog computers with digital computers that made possible the electronic instrument systems that are used in modern aircraft.

Microcomputers

Computers operate with numbers, and an electrical computer must assign a definite value of voltage to each digit. Using the decimal number system requires the computer to be able to manipulate ten different values, or conditions, and this requires precision measurement and complicates the process of computing. But there are other number systems than the decimal system. The binary number system will do everything the decimal system will do, and it uses only two conditions: 0 and 1 or, electrically, voltage and no voltage.

Computers have become such an important part of our life that we use them every day whether we recognize it or not. Almost all schools and many homes have personal computers, or PCs, and most businesses have access to larger computers. In this text, we are not concerned with these devices, but rather we want to examine the principle on which the many dedicated computers that are part of an aircraft instrument or control system operate.

dedicated computer. A small digital computer, often built into an instrument or control device, that contains a built-in program that causes it to perform a specific function.

Figure 5-36 is a very simple diagram of a digital computer. This computer has three components: a central processing unit, or CPU, a memory, and input/output devices.

The CPU is the heart of the computer and it contains a clock, a control unit, and an arithmetic/logic unit (ALU). The memory contains all of the instructions and data stored in the form of binary numbers, called words. The input devices receive signals from temperature, position, or pressure sensors, and commands from the pilot. The output devices can be anything from a video display to electric motors or other types of actuators.

The memory section contains two types of memory, ROM and RAM. ROM, or Read-Only Memory, is permanent memory built into the computer and cannot be changed. ROM contains the instructions that allow the computer to start up and perform a number of diagnostic tests to assure that everything is working as it should. It also contains all the steps the computer should take to process signals from the input devices and give the desired results in the output.

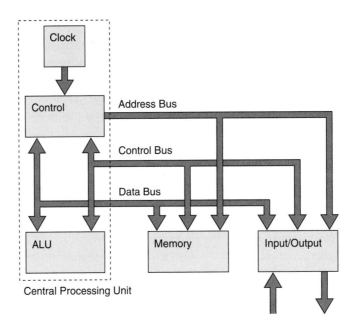

Figure 5-36. *An extremely simplified block diagram of a dedicated digital computer.*

The RAM, or Random-Access Memory, is a read-write memory in which data can be held in storage until it is needed and then called out and manipulated by the ALU and put back into storage. RAM is called volatile memory, because anything that is in it when the power is turned off is lost.

Let's consider a hypothetical dedicated computer designed to maintain cylinder head temperature within an optimum range and warns the pilot if it gets out of this range. The aircraft has a digital cylinder head temperature indicator with a two-line remarks display such as the one in Figure 5-37. Up to a temperature of 100°C, the light bars on the indicator are green. Between 100°C and 230°C, they are blue, and above 230°C, they are red. Above 260°C, the bars flash.

These are the requirements for this computer:

1. The cowl flaps are to be open when aircraft is on the ground.

2. The cowl flaps should close when the aircraft becomes airborne.

3. The cowl flaps should be automatically regulated to maintain the CHT between 100°C and 248°C.

4. When the temperature is between 100°C and 230°C, the display reads AUTO-LEAN OK.

5. When the temperature reaches 230°C, the readout in the bottom of the instrument displays AUTO-RICH ONLY.

6. If the temperature reaches 248°C, the display reads TIME LIMITED. A timer begins, and when it counts five minutes, the display flashes the words TIME LIMIT EXCEEDED.

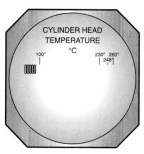

CHT is 90°C. Bars are green, and no remarks are displayed.

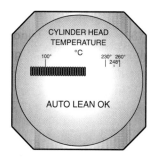

CHT is 185°C. Bars are blue, and notation shows that engine can be operated with carburetor mixture set to AUTO LEAN.

CHT is 235°C. Bars are red, and notation shows AUTO RICH must be used.

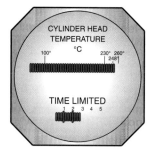

CHT is 250°C. Bars are red, and engine is in time limited range. It has been operating in this range for almost 3 minutes out of the allowable 5 minutes.

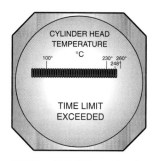

CHT is still 250°C and has been above 248°C limit for more than the allowable 5 minutes. TIME LIMIT EXCEEDED warning is flashing.

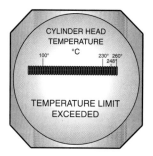

CHT is 260°C and light bars and TEMPERATURE LIMIT EXCEEDED warning is flashing.

Figure 5-37. *This type of digital cylinder head temperature indicator can be driven by a computer. Each bar in the display represents 5°C.*

7. If the temperature reaches 260°C, the light bars flash and the display flashes the words TEMPERATURE LIMIT EXCEEDED.

The computer takes these basic steps, and while it takes a while for us to read them, the computer steps through them continuously. Each step takes only a few thousandths of a second.

1. When the master switch is turned on, the first signal from the clock tells the control to clear all of the storage areas in the computer and perform all of the necessary diagnostic tests.

2. The next signal from the clock tells the control to fetch the first instruction. The program in ROM tells the control to determine from the landing gear squat switch (an input device) if weight is on the landing gear.

3. If the squat switch says that weight is on the landing gear, an instruction is sent to the controller signaling the cowl flap motor to open the cowl flaps.

4. The clock continually tells the control to fetch instructions from the memory. These steps amount to a loop of instructions that tell the

controller to sense the input from the CHT thermocouple and light up the correct light bars on the indicator display.

5. The loop of instructions also continually monitors the landing gear squat switch, and when it signals that the weight is off of the landing gear, an instruction is sent that causes the cowl flap motor (an output device) to close the cowl flaps.

6. The loop continues to search all of the input devices until the temperature sensor indicates that the CHT has reached 100°C. At this time the display at the bottom of the indicator shows the words AUTO-LEAN OK.

7. The loop continues to search all of the input devices until the temperature sensor indicates that the CHT has reached 230°C. At this time the display at the bottom of the indicator changes to show the words AUTO-RICH ONLY.

8. The loop continues to search all of the input devices until the temperature sensor shows that the CHT has reached 248°C. A signal is sent to the cowl flap motor to open the cowl flaps enough to keep the temperature below 248°C. Any time the loop detects that the CHT is above 248°C, the display shows the words TIME-LIMITED. The control directs a display on the CHT indicator to light up a bar graph that shows the length of time the engine is allowed to operate in this temperature range. Each 15 seconds a red bar lights up.

9. If the loop sampling the temperature finds that it remains above 248°C for the full five minutes that are allowed, the display changes to TIME LIMIT EXCEEDED, and the display flashes.

10. If the temperature sampled by the loop ever reaches 260°C, the light bars and the display TEMPERATURE LIMIT EXCEEDED flash.

Digital Indicating and Control Systems

Digital electronics has opened an extremely wide door for new developments.

Liquid crystal displays (LCDs) are used as multifunction displays (MFDs) in the modern glass cockpits. A single MFD replaces a number of mechanical analog-type indicators and has the added advantage that only those indicators that show abnormal conditions are displayed. In addition to displaying instrument indications, LCDs may be used to display check lists and operational history of the portions of the system that are showing trouble, suggest corrective action, and display any performance reduction caused by the malfunction.

Digital systems lend themselves to self-examination of their operating condition and the diagnosis of faults that are detected. This is done by the portion of the system known as BITE, or Built-In Test Equipment. BITE checks the system, and when a malfunction is detected it traces it to the nearest line replaceable unit, or LRU, and informs the flight crew of the action that should be taken. LRUs may be replaced by the mechanic on the flight line.

MFD. Multi-Function Display

glass cockpit. An aircraft instrument system that uses a few cathode-ray-tube displays to replace a large number of mechanically actuated instruments.

BITE. Built-In Test Equipment

In this section of the text we will discuss three digital instrument systems that are presently in use: Electronic Flight Instrument System (EFIS), Engine Indicating and Crew Alerting System (EICAS), and Electronic Centralized Aircraft Monitor (ECAM) system.

Electronic Flight Instrument Systems (EFIS)

EFIS consists of a pilot's display system and a copilot's display system. Each system has two color CRT display units: an electronic attitude director indicator (EADI), and an electronic horizontal situation indicator (EHSI). These indicators are driven by symbol generators and are controlled by display controllers. See Figure 5-38.

The symbol generators receive data from such sensors as those listed in Figure 5-39 and process it. This data is then sent to the appropriate indicator. The center symbol generator can be switched by the display controllers so it will furnish data to either set of indicators in the event that their symbol generator should fail.

LRU. Line Replaceable Unit

EFIS. Electronic Flight Instrument System

EICAS. Engine Indicating and Crew Alerting System

ECAM. Electronic Centralized Aircraft Monitor

EHSI. Electronic Horizontal Situation Indicator

EADI. Electronic Attitude Director Indicator

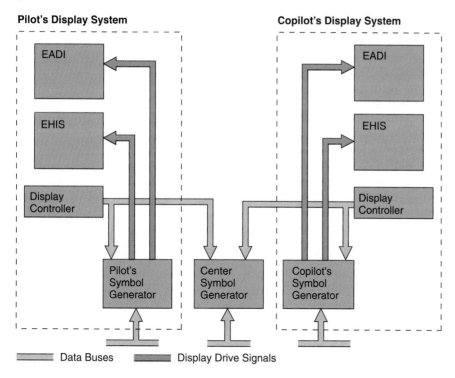

Pilot's Display System

Copilot's Display System

- Data Buses
- Display Drive Signals

Figure 5-38. *Simplified block diagram of an Electronic Flight Instrument System.*

data bus. A wire or group of wires that are used to move data within a computer system.

VOR
DME
ILS
Radio altimeter
Weather radar
Inertial reference system
Flight control computer
Flight management computer
Display controller

Figure 5-39. *Typical sources of data that are fed into the symbol generators for an EFIS.*

The EADI shows such information as the pitch and roll attitude of the aircraft, the flight director commands, deviation from the localizer and glide slope, selected airspeed, ground speed, radio altitude, and decision height.

The display controller allows the pilot to select the appropriate mode of operation for the current flight situation.

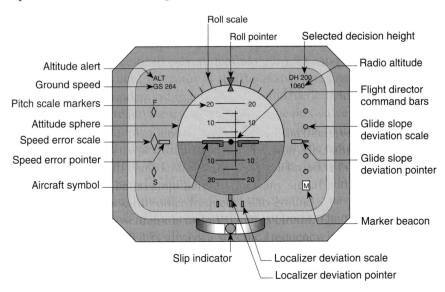

Figure 5-40. *An electronic attitude director indicator, an EADI.*

The EHSI has four selectable modes: MAP, PLAN, ILS, and VOR.

In the MAP mode the EHSI takes its signals from the flight management computer and shows its display against a movable map display. This display shows heading and track information, distance to go, ground speed, and estimated time of arrival. It shows the location of various airports, navaids, and way points. And it also shows the wind speed and direction.

In the PLAN mode, the EHIS shows a static map with the active route of the flight plan drawn out on it.

In the VOR mode, the display shows the compass rose with heading and course information. In the ILS mode, the heading and localizer and glide slope information are shown. Information furnished by the weather radar is shown on the EHSI when it is in the expanded scale format of both the VOR and ILS modes.

When any function such as navigation (NAV), compass (HDG), localizer (LOC) or glide slope (GS) shown on the EHSI is not operative, or if the signals being received or used are too weak to give a proper indication, a warning flag will show up that warns the pilot not to depend upon that function.

way point. A phantom location created in certain electronic navigation systems by measuring direction and distance from a VORTAC station or by latitude and longitude coordinates from loran or GPS.

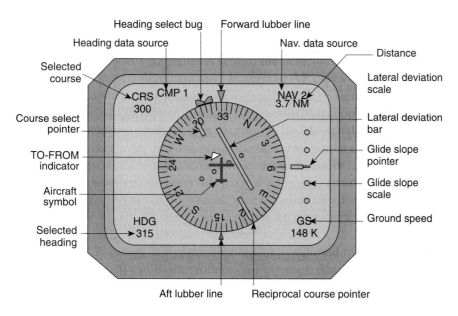

Figure 5-41. *An electronic horizontal situation indicator, an EHSI, in the VOR mode.*

Engine Indicating and Crew Alerting System (EICAS)

The EICAS, or engine indicating and crew alerting system, takes the place of a myriad of individual instruments and furnishes the needed information to the flight crew. A typical EICAS senses the parameters shown in Figure 5-42, and in addition it interfaces with such systems as the maintenance control display panel (MCDP) of the flight control computer (FCC), the thrust management system (TMS), the electronic engine control (EEC), the flight management computer (FMC), the radio altimeter, and the air data computer (ADC).

The EICAS consists of two color CRT displays, mounted one above the other. See Figure 5-43 on the next page. The right-hand side of the upper display shows the engine primary displays such as EPR, EGT, and N_1 speed. These parameters are shown in the form of an analog display with the actual value in digits. The left-hand side of the display shows warnings and cautions.

The lower display shows engine secondary parameters such as N_2 and N_3 speeds, fuel flow, oil quantity, oil pressure, and oil temperature, and engine vibration. The status of systems other than engine systems may be displayed as well as maintenance data.

Caution and warning lights as well as aural signals back up the displays on the EICAS.

Electronic Centralized Aircraft Monitor System (ECAM)

The ECAM system monitors the functions and condition of the entire aircraft and displays the information on two color CRT displays that are mounted side by side in the cockpit. The left-hand display shows the status of a system, and

Engine sensors

> Compressor speeds
> N_1, N_2, and N_3
> Engine pressure ratio
> Exhaust gas temperature
> Fuel flow
> Oil pressure
> Oil quantity
> Oil temperature
> Vibration

System sensors

> Hydraulic quantity
> Hydraulic pressure
> Control surface positions
> Electrical system voltage
> Electrical system current
> Electrical system frequency
> Generator drive temperature
> Environmental control system
> temperatures
> APU exhaust gas temperature
> APU speed
> Brake temperature

Figure 5-42. *Parameters sensed by the EICAS.*

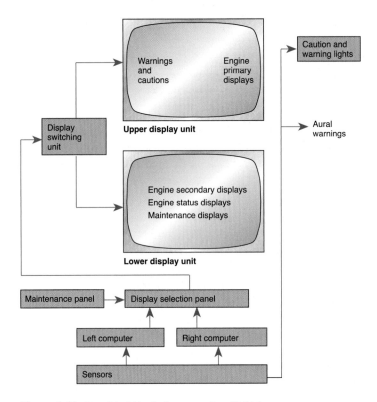

Figure 5-43. *Simplified block diagram of an EICAS.*

the right-hand display shows diagrams and additional information about the system on the left-hand display.

Three automatic display modes can be selected: flight-phase, advisory, and failure-related modes. A manually selected mode displays diagrams and information about the various systems in the aircraft.

The automatic flight-phase mode is normally displayed and it shows the conditions for the current phase of flight. These phases are: preflight, takeoff, climb, cruise, descent, approach, and after-landing. The failure-related mode has priority over the other modes. When some parameter exceeds its operating limit, a diagram of the system appears in the right-hand display and the recommended corrective action is shown on the left-hand display.

When some unit fails, the failure-related mode actuates, and the left-hand display shows the flight crew any changes that must be made in the operation of the aircraft as a result of the failure.

Air Data Computer

Small aircraft sample static air pressure to drive the altimeter and vertical speed indicator. In addition, pitot, or ram, air pressure is sampled to work with the static pressure to give an indication of airspeed.

Large aircraft also sample static and pitot pressures, but, rather than simply driving the mechanical instruments, these pressures are taken into an air data computer. In this computer they expand bellows in a conventional manner, but these bellows operate electrical pickoffs that convert the pressures into digital signals that are used by the various instruments and other computers.

Altitude information is used by the autopilot in its altitude-acquire and altitude-hold modes. It is used by the transponder to furnish pressure altitude information to the ATC ground radar. It is used to determine rate of altitude change and is furnished to the Mach module to convert indicated airspeed into Mach number. It is also used by the cabin-pressure computer and the flight recorder.

Airspeed information is used by the flight director and the autopilot and is used with the altitude information to produce Mach number. A total air temperature pickup converts air temperature into an electrical signal which is used to convert indicated airspeed into true airspeed.

In order to allow more aircraft to fly at the most efficient altitude, the FAA has issued a Reduced Vertical Separation Minimums (RVSM) between Flight Levels 290 and 410 (29,000 and 41,000 feet pressure-altitude). This reduces the required vertical separation from 2,000 feet to 1,000 feet for aircraft that meet the requirements for RVSM. The aircraft must be able to hold an assigned altitude within ±65 feet, and to do this, the static air pressure of the existing air must be accurately measured. To do this, there is a Static System Error Corrector for the air data computer.

Any distortion of the aircraft structure in the area of the static ports can give an erroneous static pressure indication. These areas are so sensitive that paint flakes, or even scratches in the paint can cause an unacceptable error. For this reason some aircraft are required to have all paint in the area of the static air pickup points removed. It is advisable to always check the current Aircraft Maintenance Manual or instructions for continued airworthiness (ICA) before performing any work in these areas.

Flight Management Computer System (FMCS)

The FMCS is a single-point system that allows a flight crew to initiate and implement a flight plan and to monitor its operation. The FMCS is the point at which the flight crew inputs the information to initialize the inertial reference units (IRUs).

The FMCS consists of two Flight Management Computers (FMCs) and two control display units (CDUs). An extensive data base that contains all of the navigational and operational information needed for the flight can be stored in the two FMCs. The CDUs have an alphanumeric key pad that allows the flight crew to display and update data and to call up any of the information stored in its data base. The output of the key pad is displayed on a portion of

FMC. Flight Management Computer

the display called the scratch pad. This information can be transferred to the appropriate data field by pressing one of the line select keys along either side of the display. Figure 5-44 shows an example of an FMCS.

Some of the major functions performed by the FMCS are:

- Receives and transmits digital data to and from the various systems on board the aircraft.

- Checks to determine that all of the received data is valid.

- Formats and updates data and sends it to the CDU for display on the scratch pad.

- Provides alerting and advisory messages to the CDU for display on the scratch pad.

- Performs a self-test during the power-up operation, and on request. Any failures are recorded on nonvolatile memory for use at a later date.

- Computes the aircraft's current position, velocity and altitude.

- Selects and automatically tunes the VORs and DMEs.

- Determines the aircraft position by measuring the distance from two automatically tuned DME stations.

- Computes velocity by using the IRU inputs, and altitude by using IRU and ADC inputs.

- Monitors aircraft and engine parameters and computes and displays the vertical path of the flight profile.

- Compares the actual lateral position of the aircraft with its desired position and generates steering commands, which are then input to the appropriate flight control computer (FCC).

- Compares the actual vertical profile data with the desired altitude and altitude rate and generates pitch and thrust commands, which are input to the appropriate FCC and thrust management computer (TMC).

- Provides navigational data to the EFIS symbol generators.

Figure 5-44. *FMS-4200 Flight Management System.*

Head-Up Displays

Head-up displays (HUDs) were initially developed for military aircraft but are becoming more common in commercial and business aircraft and are even finding their way into general aviation and experimental aircraft. A head-up display provides information to the pilot on a transparent screen so that the pilot does not need to lower his or her eyes to the instrument panel to see the same information. The most common information displayed is flight and navigation information, but new systems may include traffic alerts, flight plan information, autopilot modes, warning annunciations, and even synthetic vision depictions of terrain and obstacles.

Figure 5-45. *View through the HUD of a Boeing 787-200 during an approach to landing.*

STUDY QUESTIONS: ELECTRONIC INSTRUMENT SYSTEMS

Answers are provided on page 381.

72. The three basic components in a digital computer are:

    a. _____

    b. _____

    c. _____

73. Two types of memory in a digital computer are:

    a. _____

    b. _____

74. RAM _____ (does or does not) allow data to be written into the memory as well as read from it.

75. RAM is normally _____ (volatile or nonvolatile).

76. The self-diagnostic portion of a digital system installed in an aircraft is called _____ .

77. A component that can be changed by the mechanic on the flight line is called a/an_____ .

(continued)

78. The unit in an EFIS that receives and processes the input signals from the aircraft and engine sensors and sends it to the appropriate display is the _____ .

79. The unit in an EFIS that allows the pilot to select the appropriate system configuration for the current flight situation is the _____ .

80. The two displays that are part of an EFIS are:

    a. _____

    b. _____

81. When a warning flag appears on an EHSI or HSI for a function such as NAV, HDG, or GS, the function is _____ .

82. Three engine primary parameters that are displayed on the upper display of an EICAS are:

    a. _____

    b. _____

    c. _____

83. The mode that takes priority over all of the other display modes in an ECAM is the _____ mode.

84. The air data computer uses total air temperature to convert indicated airspeed into _____ .

85. The air data computer uses altitude information to convert indicated airspeed into _____ .

86. Scratches, paint flakes, or any surface distortion near the _____ can cause an erroneous static pressure indication.

87. A single-point system that allows a flight crew to initiate and implement a flight plan and monitor its operation is the _____ .

Electronic Systems Installation and Maintenance

The electrical and electronic systems are some of the most important systems in a modern aircraft. These aircraft have many complex electronic devices that must be properly installed and maintained. They must have the proper type and amount of electrical power, they must have adequate cooling, and their sensitive pickups must be protected from interference by electromagnetic radiation from other devices.

Most of the components in these electronic systems must be repaired only by FAA-certificated repair stations that are approved for the specific work, and the aviation mechanic must be able to restore a malfunctioning system to its normal operation by replacing only the faulty components.

The profitability of modern airline operation depends upon every flight departing on schedule, and any maintenance-caused delay must be kept to an absolute minimum. Because of this, the manufacturers have designed into the aircraft built-in test equipment, or BITE. When a system malfunctions, BITE checks it out and informs the flight crew of the system status and the action that must be taken to restore normal operation. BITE normally traces the problem down to a line replaceable unit, or LRU, that can be replaced at the next stop.

Troubleshooting aircraft electrical and electronic systems is usually accomplished with the power on for checking proper operation. Multimeters can be a valuable tool to trace power through a circuit, but be careful to not short across terminals with the multimeter leads.

General aviation maintenance is not as structured as airline maintenance and the aviation mechanic must often design the installation of electrical and electronic systems. This section discusses the installation and maintenance of electrical and electronic systems in general aviation aircraft.

Approval for the Installation of Electronic Equipment

The addition of any equipment to an aircraft constitutes an alteration, and must be made according to approved data. If the equipment to be installed is included in the equipment list that is furnished with the aircraft, its installation is considered to be a minor alteration. The installation may be done and the aircraft approved for return to service by an aviation mechanic holding an Airframe rating.

Much of the newer equipment is not included in the equipment list, but its approval for installation has been obtained by the manufacturer of the equipment in the form of a Supplemental Type Certificate (STC). Instructions for its installation are included with the STC. The installation can be done by an aviation mechanic holding an Airframe rating, and when the installation is completed, the work must be inspected for conformity with the approved data by an aviation mechanic holding an Inspection Authorization. Installation of any electronic equipment that is done according to an STC constitutes a major alteration, and its completion must be recorded and submitted to the FAA on an FAA Form 337.

When equipment is installed without the use of an STC, approval must be obtained from the local FAA District Office before the work is begun. Approval for some installations is quite complex and may require engineering approval.

Required Placards for Communication and Navigation Equipment

When you are inspecting the communication and navigation equipment on an aircraft, remember to check for required placards. Placards can become faded or damaged over time and should be replaced if they are difficult to read. The location and content of placards can be found in the manufacturer's service instructions and the aircraft flight manual (AFM) or pilot's operating handbook (POH).

Electrical Considerations

All electrical and electronic components must have an uninterrupted supply of electricity that has the correct voltage, and if AC, the correct frequency and phase. The system must be so designed that an adequate supply of current can reach the equipment, and all of the wiring terminations must be of an approved type that prevents accidental disconnection and minimizes the chance of improper connection.

Load Limits

Generators or alternators are the primary sources of electrical energy in an aircraft. Their combined output must be great enough that the total connected electrical load does not exceed their current rating, and the system must keep the battery fully charged.

Most multi-engine aircraft have normal electrical loads that exceed the capacity of either alternator alone. If one engine or alternator should fail, the flight crew must be able to reduce enough of the electrical load to bring the required current down until it is within the rating of the remaining alternator. This must be done without turning off any system or component that is essential to the safety of flight.

Aircraft that have complex electrical and electronic systems normally have loadmeters installed between the alternator and the system bus. These indicators are calibrated in the percentage of the alternator rated output, and by monitoring their indication, the flight crew can keep the electrical load safely below the alternator maximum output.

Circuit Protection

All electrical systems must have fuses or circuit breakers installed as close to the main power buses as practical to protect the wiring from overheating.

Electronic equipment must also be protected from voltage spikes. These spikes are lethal to solid-state electronic components, and during the starting and shutdown procedure all of the sensitive electronic components are especially vulnerable. To protect them, almost all aircraft electrical systems have some provision for isolating the avionics bus from the main electrical system. Figure 5-46 shows two such systems. A switch-type circuit breaker

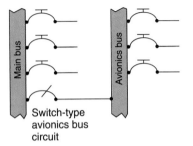

Switch-type circuit breaker is used to isolate avionics bus from main bus when engine is being shut down or started.

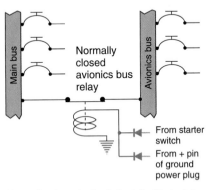

Normally closed relay is installed to isolate avionics bus from main bus when engine is being started or when ground power unit is plugged in.

Figure 5-46. *Avionics bus protection.*

can be installed that should be opened before the engine is shut down and closed only after the engine is started. This system works, but the avionics bus can be isolated automatically by installing a normally closed relay between the two buses. Without power on the relay coil, the relay is closed and the avionics bus has power. But when the engine starter switch is closed, or when the ground power unit is plugged in, current flows in the relay coil and the contacts are opened, preventing voltage spikes damaging anything attached to the avionics bus.

Wiring

The wiring practices used for avionics installations must be the same as those used for other electrical systems in an aircraft, except that special attention must be paid to the effect of electromagnetic fields radiating from wires carrying AC. Much avionic equipment is extremely sensitive to electromagnetic radiation, and the wires carrying signals are protected from this interference by shielding them.

A shielded wire is encased in a metal braid that intercepts any radiated energy and conducts it to ground rather than allowing it to cause interference. Since intercepted current flows in the shielding, the fields from this current are minimized by grounding the shielding at only one point, rather than at both of its ends.

Bundling and Routing

Wires that carry alternating current are normally not bundled with wires that carry the signals into sensitive avionic equipment. Be very careful when installing an electronic component to follow the instructions from the manufacturer in detail. Some wires are required to be twisted, and others must be shielded. In some cases, such as data cables, the twisted pairs of wires will be shielded, and then the bundle of twisted pairs will be shielded as well.

Wires that have high energy going through them, such as strobe lights, radio transmission cables, and spark plug ignition leads, are shielded to prevent interference with other electrical systems. These wires should be routed separately from other electrical systems to minimize electrical interference.

Wire bundles, also known as wire harnesses, should be tied with special plastic straps or waxed cord. The bundles should be attached to the structure with cushion clamps. The edges of any hole in a structural member through which the wire passes must be protected with a rubber grommet. Most wire bundles are installed so they parallel the structural members, but certain critical wires, such as transmission lines, are run as directly as possible to minimize their length.

1. Cut outer insulation back about 1/4 inch from end of cable and remove insulation from braid.

2. Separate braid and fan it out, being careful not to break any strands.

3. Remove about 1/8 inch of insulation from around center conductor, being very careful not to nick conductor when insulation is cut.

4. Slip nut, washer, gasket, and clamp over wire.

5. Fold strands of outer conductor back over tapered clamp and trim them flush with end of taper.

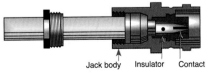

6. Tin exposed inner conductor with good grade of 60-40 resin-core solder. Slip center contact over end until it butts flush against the dielectric. Very carefully solder it to conductor. Heat contact with soldering iron and flow solder through hole in contact body. Do not burn insulation and use only enough solder to form good connection. Slip insulator and connector over end of cable and secure it with nut.

Figure 5-47. *Proper installation of a connector on a coaxial cable.*

Transmission Lines

For the maximum amount of energy to be transferred between a piece of avionic equipment and its antenna, the impedance of the antenna and that of the equipment must be matched. For this reason, antennas are normally connected to the equipment with coaxial cable that has a very specific characteristic impedance.

Coaxial cable, or coax, as it is normally called, has an inner conductor, a heavy insulation, an outer conductor braid, and a plastic insulation around the entire cable. Figure 5-47 shows the proper way to install a connector on a piece of coax.

The coax, furnished with certain pieces of avionics equipment, has been cut to the required length and its length should not be changed. If the cable is too long, it should be carefully coiled up and attached to the aircraft structure with cushion clamps. Normally coax may be run directly between the equipment and the antenna, and it should not be bundled with other wires.

It is a good practice when installing a coaxial cable to secure it firmly along its entire length with cushion clamps every two feet or so. The spacing between the inner and outer conductors is critical and the cable must not be crushed. Because of this, coax should not be bent with a radius smaller than 10 times the cable diameter.

When coax cable passes through bulkheads, ribs, or close to other parts of aircraft structure, the cable should be supported so that it cannot sag and chafe against the surrounding structure. It is also good practice to use abrasion protection, such as rubber grommets or caterpillar grommets, on any structure that the coax passes through.

Protection from Electrostatic Discharge Damage

Most of the new sensitive electronic equipment in aircraft is highly susceptible to electrostatic discharge (ESD) damage. The normal rubbing of our clothing on our bodies builds up a high voltage that can transfer into the equipment when we handle it. This high voltage can cause enough current to flow to destroy some of the sensitive integrated circuit components. To prevent damaging any of this equipment, be sure that your body is completely discharged by touching a nearby section of grounded metal. Many newer commercial aircraft that have equipment bays for mounting electronic equipment will have an ESD grounding strap that is permanently mounted in the equipment bay. Attach this strap to your wrist before removing or installing any of the electronic boxes. If electrical equipment allows for servicing, such as the replacement of an internal card, always work on an ESD bench that is electrically grounded and includes a wrist grounding strap. Always attach the wrist grounding strap before beginning any work on the equipment and ensure that the other end of the strap is securely grounded to the work bench.

Weight and Balance

The installation of any avionics equipment affects the empty weight of the aircraft, its CG, and its useful load. The weight-and-balance record must be updated to show the change in the empty weight and empty-weight CG of the aircraft. The addition of equipment decreases the useful load, and if the installation is ahead of the forward limit or behind the aft limit, it is possible for it to move the aircraft EWCG outside of its allowable limits.

Cooling

Electronic equipment and electronic instruments often produce heat that must be carried away to prevent the equipment from being damaged. Installations in large aircraft produce so much heat that special ducts from the air conditioning system are routed to blow cool air over or through the installation racks. Smaller aircraft often have dedicated avionics cooling fans or air intakes on the outside of the fuselage, with a scoop opening forward to pick up ram air for cooling. These systems normally require some form of baffle to prevent water from getting into the equipment when the aircraft is flown in rain.

Inspection of Panel-Mounted Radios and Equipment

The installation of panel-mounted radios and electronic equipment should be inspected during routine inspections of the cockpit area. Verify that radios are fully seated into their electrical connection sockets, as any loose connections can cause intermittent operation. The method of securing radios in an instrument panel varies widely from one manufacturer to the next. Radios may be held in place with quarter-turn fasteners, by hidden clips that are pushed out of the way with special pins, or by recessed screws that are only accessible through small holes in the faceplate of the radio. Always check with the maintenance manual before trying to remove a radio. In addition to mounting security, operate the panel lights to verify the dimming operation of the radio internal lighting.

Shock Mounting

Electronic equipment is easily damaged by vibration. To prevent this, much of the equipment is mounted in special shock-mounted racks like the one in Figure 5-48. The equipment is slid into the rack and the locking screws are tightened to hold it tightly in place. When the equipment is slid into the rack, pins in the electrical connector fit into sockets in the rack, and electrical connection is made with the aircraft system.

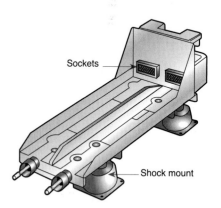

Figure 5-48. *A typical shock-mounted electronic equipment rack. When the equipment is slid into the rack, electrical contact is made between the plugs on the equipment and the sockets installed in the rack.*

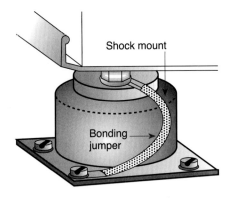

Figure 5-49. *All shock-mounted equipment must have provisions for carrying the return current back to the aircraft structure. Bonding jumpers should be as short as practical and must not produce any appreciable voltage drop.*

When electronics are installed in a stationary instrument panel, the installation must be strong enough to withstand a 2.0-G load forward, 1.5 G sideways, 6.6 G downward, and 3.0 G upward.

Shock mounts such as the typical mount seen in Figure 5-49 are designed to isolate the equipment from high-frequency, low-amplitude vibration. They allow considerable freedom of movement of the equipment, and before the installation is complete, be sure to check for the full deflection of the mount to be sure that the equipment cannot move enough to contact adjacent equipment or the aircraft structure itself. Be sure that the permanently installed wiring is not strained when the equipment deflects.

The shock mounts are not only vibration isolators, they are also electrical insulators, and provisions must be made for carrying all of the return current from the equipment back into the aircraft structure. Braided tinned copper bonding jumpers seen in Figure 5-49 must be installed to carry this current. The braid must be large enough to carry the current, and the voltage drop across the jumper must be negligible. The resistance between the equipment rack and the aircraft structure must not be more than three milliohm (0.003 ohm).

During inspection of the shock mounts, verify that the rubber portion is not torn, is still flexible, and has not become age hardened. Check the attachment hardware for proper installation and security. Inspect the equipment rack for security and condition and any quick release mechanisms for proper installation and safety.

Some electronic equipment may be mounted under the seats. When this type of installation is made, you must prove that there will be at least one inch of clearance when the seat is deflected to its maximum. This deflection is measured when the seat is loaded with 6.6 times the amount the seat is designed to carry. Most seats are designed to carry 170 pounds, and so it must be loaded with 1,122 pounds to check the clearance.

Bonding and Static Protection

Bonding

The different parts of a metallic structure airplane are electrically connected through a process called bonding. Bonding all components of the aircraft together provides a low resistance electrical path between all sections of the aircraft structure. This low resistance path is often used as the common electrical ground plane and negative return path to the battery.

Bonding the aircraft structure together also provides increased lightning protection and decreases the likelihood of damage to control surface hinges, hinge bearings, and electrical wires as well as reduces radio interference caused by static discharge between different parts of the structure.

Bonding and lightning protection of composite aircraft requires that a conductive layer (commonly copper or aluminum mesh) be added just below the exterior surface of the aircraft. This conductive layer is constructed within the layers of the composite materials and includes provisions for attachment of jumpers at control surface hinge locations.

Static Protection

The movement of air over an aircraft surface can cause a buildup of static electricity. When the voltage builds up high enough, electrons will jump to some component that has a lower voltage. This electron movement is in the form of a spark which causes enough electromagnetic radiation to interfere with the sensitive radio receivers. Two steps can be taken to minimize static interference, bond all of the movable structural components together, and install static dischargers on all of the control surfaces.

Bonding jumpers are normally made of tinned copper wire braid and are fastened between the movable components and the main structure. When a static charge builds up, it finds a low-resistance path to flow to the main structure. With all of the structure at the same electrical potential, there is no static discharge.

Be sure to remove all of the paint and anodized film before installing the jumpers, and install them as shown in Figure 5-50. There should be no more than four terminals installed at any one point. The jumpers should be as short as practicable and the resistance across the jumper should be no more than three milliohm (0.003 ohm).

Static electrical charges tend to build up as air flows over the control surfaces, and to prevent this buildup, many control surfaces have static dischargers installed on their trailing edges (Figure 5-51). These dischargers carry the static charges into the atmosphere before their voltage builds up high enough

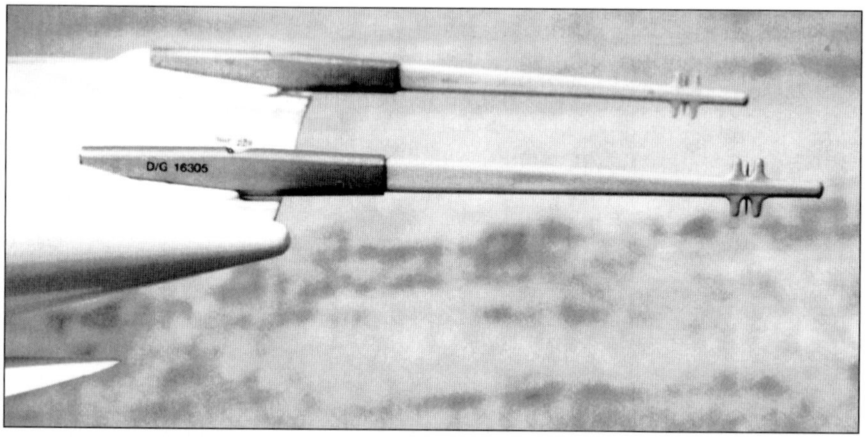

static dischargers. Devices connected to the trailing edges of control surfaces to discharge static electricity harmlessly into the air. They discharge the static charges before they can build up high enough to cause radio receiver interference.

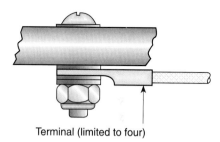

Terminal (limited to four)

Figure 5-50. *Method of attaching a bonding jumper to a flat surface.*

Kuflic Photography

Figure 5-51. *Nullfield static dischargers are installed on the trailing edges of control surfaces to carry static electrical charges into the atmosphere, before they build up a high enough voltage to interfere with the electronic equipment.*

to cause the high current to flow that causes radio interference. By the proper design and location of these dischargers, the static charges will be dissipated while their current level is low.

Static dischargers, also known as static wicks or static discharge wicks, come in different shapes and sizes based on the discharge requirements and the speed of the aircraft. Low speed static wicks tend to be much more flexible than those required for high speed. See Figure 5-52.

For static discharge wicks to be effective, they must be properly grounded to the mounting surface of the aircraft. When inspecting static discharge wicks, make sure that they are mounted securely and that there is very little resistance between the mounting base and the airframe. Check that the ends are not frayed excessively, and replace as necessary.

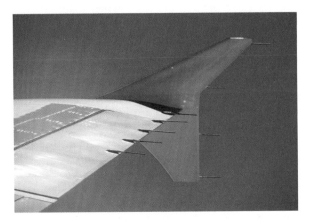

Figure 5-52. *Several static wicks on the wingtip and winglet of an Airbus A319.*

Antenna Installation

Regardless of the excellence of the equipment, no radio installation is better than its antenna. Each piece of equipment must have a specific antenna, and this antenna must be mounted in a specific location for the most efficient operation. Most antennas are used for both reception and transmitting. They are connected to the equipment through a duplexer, which is an electrically operated switch that switches the antenna to the transmitter when the press-to-talk switch on the microphone is closed.

Types of Antenna

The length, polarization, and location of an antenna is of extreme importance in getting the most efficient transmission and reception from the installed equipment. The types of antennas used with several pieces of avionic equipment are examined here.

VHF Communication

VHF transmitters and receivers use a vertically polarized antenna that may be mounted either above or below the aircraft fuselage. Some of the simpler installations use wire whip antennas like the one in Figure 5-53, while the more efficient installations use a broad-band blade antenna like the one in Figure 5-54. Some wire antennas are bent aft at about a 45° angle, which allows them to receive horizontally as well as vertically polarized signals.

A VHF communication antenna is a quarter-wavelength antenna that uses the metal of the aircraft as the other quarter wavelength to give the antenna the required half wavelength. When installing this type of antenna on a fabric-covered aircraft, you must provide a ground plane. This is done by using strips of aluminum foil or a piece of aluminum screen wire that extends out for approximately one-quarter wavelength from the center of the antenna on the inside of the fabric.

The VHF system can be checked for operation by tuning the radio to a frequency where local operations are occurring. If there is a weather reporting station (ATIS) at your local airport, you can check reception by tuning to this station. To check the transmission of the VHF system, a common practice is to call another aircraft or ground control for a radio check.

HF Communication

Aircraft that fly over the water for long distances rely on high-frequency communications. The lower frequencies used by this equipment require long antenna. The horizontally polarized radiation used by HF communications allows long wires to be used. These are often installed between a point above the cockpit and the tip of the vertical fin. The wire is often a copper-plated steel wire, but the more efficient systems use an antenna wire encased in a plastic sheath to minimize precipitation static.

Some modern high-speed aircraft have the HF communications antennas built into some part of the structure, such as the leading edge of the vertical fin.

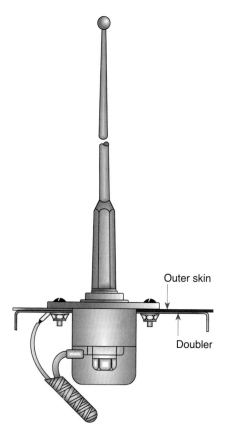

Figure 5-53. *Installation of a wire-type VHF communication antenna. This type of antenna is often bent back at an angle of 45° to allow it to receive both vertically and horizontally polarized signals.*

Figure 5-54. *Broad-band VHF communications blade-type antenna.*

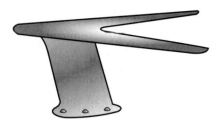

Figure 5-55. *A typical "ram's horn" VOR/ LOC antenna. Some antennas of this type have a small horizontally polarized UHF dipole glide slope antenna mounted in the front of the housing.*

VOR/LOC

The VOR and the localizer function of the ILS share the same antenna. Figure 5-55 shows a "ram's-horn" VHF V-dipole antenna. The favored location for this type of antenna is on top of the aircraft above the cabin with the apex pointing forward.

Some more modern high-efficiency VOR antennas are of the type shown in Figure 5-56. The two antennas are designed to mount on the upper section of the vertical stabilizer of a single-finned airplane or on either side of a helicopter tail boom. The two antennas are connected together through a phasing coupler to provide a single 50-ohm input in the VOR, localizer, and glide slope bands.

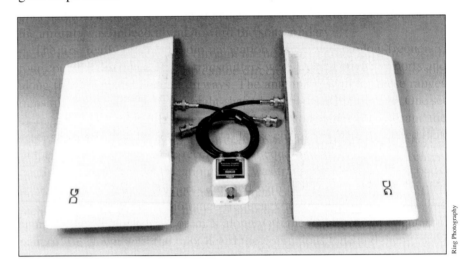

Figure 5-56. *VOR/LOC/GS antenna system that mounts on the sides of the upper portion of the vertical fin of a single-fin airplane or on the sides of the tail boom of a helicopter.*

Glide Slope

The glide slope portion of the ILS operates in the UHF range. Its antenna is a UHF dipole mounted near the front of the aircraft, sometimes on the same mast as the VOR/LOC antenna. Some general aviation aircraft mount the glide slope antenna inside the cabin in roughly the same location as the rear view mirror in an automobile.

Marker Beacons

Marker beacons transmit horizontally polarized signals vertically upward on a frequency of 75 MHz. They are received in the aircraft by an antenna like the one in Figure 5-57, mounted on the bottom of the fuselage.

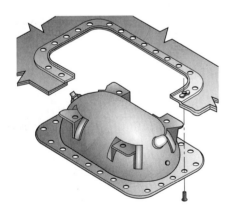

Figure 5-57. *A flush-mounted marker beacon receiver antenna.*

ADF

The automatic direction finder requires two antenna, a loop and a sense antenna. The loop has traditionally been a rotating device enclosed in a rather large housing. Now, almost all ADF installations use fixed loops mounted in thin streamlined housings below the fuselage. Since the metal in the aircraft affects the reception of the signal by the loop antenna, the loop must be mounted on the fuselage center line. Some faster aircraft have the loop antennas mounted flush with the aircraft skin.

Because the LF and MF bands are relatively close together, the same antenna used as the ADF sense antenna for picking up LF NDBs can also pick up standard commercial broadcast stations.

Figure 5-58. *ADF fixed-loop antenna.*

DME

Distance measuring equipment uses a short, vertically polarized UHF whip or blade antenna. It is mounted on the center line of the bottom of the fuselage as far from any other antenna as is practical. This location is chosen to prevent an interruption in DME operation by the antenna being blanked by the wing when the aircraft is banked. See Figure 5-59.

ATC Transponder

The air traffic control transponder uses the same type of antenna as the DME. It is also mounted on the bottom center line of the fuselage. It and the DME antenna must be as far apart as practical. Both installations require that the coax between the equipment and the antenna be as short as possible.

Figure 5-59. *A typical UHF blade antenna such as is used with the DME and ATC transponder.*

Radio Altimeter

Radio altimeters transmit vertically downward and receive their reflected signal from the surface beneath them. This system requires two antennas mounted on the bottom of the fuselage. In most installations these antennas are flush with the skin.

ELT

The emergency locator transmitter antenna typically uses a thin wire whip antenna mounted as far aft in the fuselage as possible, but ahead of the empennage. It is usually mounted on top of the fuselage, where it is least likely to be damaged.

$D = 0.000327\,AV^2$

D = Drag, or air load, on the antenna, in pounds

0.000327 = a constant

A = Frontal area of the antenna in square feet

V = Never exceed airspeed of the aircraft in miles per hour

Figure 5-60. *Formula for finding the air load on an antenna.*

Antenna Structural Attachment

When you attach an antenna to an aircraft structure, consider not only the radiation pattern and interference from other antennas or electromagnetic fields, but the structural aspects as well. The installation must be made in such a way that all of the air loads are transmitted into the aircraft structure rather than concentrating in the skin.

You can find detailed guidelines for installing antennas in FAA Advisory Circular 43.13-2B, *Acceptable Methods, Techniques, and Practices—Aircraft Alterations,* Chapter 3, which also includes recommended locations for various types of antennas. For example, a GPS antenna should always be mounted on the top of the fuselage in order to have a line-of-sight view of GPS satellites.

Most antennas in small general aviation aircraft are attached to the fuselage skin. This skin is normally too thin to support the antenna by itself, so a doubler must be installed inside the fuselage to absorb some of the loads from the antenna and carry them into the skin so that there are no stress concentrations. A gasket or sealant is used between an antenna mast and the fuselage skin to prevent the entry of moisture into the fuselage.

The person designing an antenna installation must prove to the FAA that the installation is strong enough to carry all the air loads.

The formula used in Advisory Circular 43.13-2B for determining the air loads is shown in Figure 5-60.

We can use the formula in Figure 5-60 to find the air load imposed on an antenna with a frontal area of 0.137 square feet installed on an aircraft with a V_{NE} of 275 mph. In this installation the antenna would have to withstand an air load of 3.39 pounds.

$$D = 0.000327\,AV^2$$

$$= 0.000327 \cdot 0.137 \cdot 275^2$$

$$= 0.000327 \cdot 0.137 \cdot 75,625$$

$$= 3.39 \text{ pounds}$$

Flutter and vibration must also be considered in the installation of an antenna. When any rigid antenna is mounted on a vertical stabilizer, the flutter and vibration characteristics must be carefully evaluated, as the weight and air loads on the antenna can change the resonant frequency of the vertical surface. If the particular antenna has not been previously approved for installation on the vertical fin, be sure to have the installation approved by the FAA before beginning the actual work.

When an automatic direction finder is installed on a particular type of aircraft for the first time, check the loop antenna for quadrantal error.

Quadrantal error is caused when the metal in the aircraft structure distorts the electromagnetic field of the received signal. It causes azimuth inaccuracies, which are greatest between the four cardinal points with respect to the center line of the aircraft.

Antenna Inspection

When performing an inspection on an aircraft, pay specific attention to the antennas. Antennas may become damaged by erosion from rain or other foreign objects. Antennas on the bottom of an aircraft are often damaged by rocks and debris during takeoffs and landings. Carefully inspect the aircraft structure that the antennas are mounted on for cracks and corrosion.

STUDY QUESTIONS: ELECTRONIC SYSTEMS INSTALLATION AND MAINTENANCE

Answers are provided on page 381.

88. The installation of a piece of electronic equipment that is included in the aircraft equipment list is considered to be a _____ (minor or major) alteration.

89. When a piece of electronic equipment is installed on an aircraft according to the data included with a Supplemental Type Certificate, the work must be recorded on an FAA Form _____ .

90. The primary source of electrical energy in an aircraft is the _____ (battery or alternator).

91. Fuses and circuit breakers are required in an aircraft electrical system to protect the _____ (equipment or wiring).

92. Electromagnetic radiation is prevented from interfering with signals carried to sensitive avionic equipment by using _____ wires.

93. Coaxial cable _____ (should or should not) be included in a bundle with other wires.

94. Coaxial cable should be secured along its entire length at intervals of approximately every _____ feet.

95. Coaxial cable should not be bent with a bend radius of less than _____ times the diameter of the cable.

96. Before working on any electronic component containing integrated circuit devices, wear a wrist strap that connects your body to electrical _____ .

97. When electronic equipment has been installed or removed from an aircraft, appropriate changes must be made in the _____ records.

98. Heat from the electronic equipment installed in a large aircraft is removed by cold air produced in the _____ system.

(continued)

99. Bonding jumpers for connecting a shock-mounted equipment rack to the aircraft structure are normally made of braided _____ .

100. If electronic equipment is installed beneath a seat, the seat must not deflect to closer than _____ inch(es) from the equipment when the seat is loaded with 6.6 times the load it is designed to hold.

101. Static dischargers help eliminate radio interference by dissipating static electricity into the atmosphere at a _____ (high or low) current level.

102. The VHF V-dipole antenna mounted on top of the cabin or on the vertical fin is used by the _____ and the _____ .

103. The antenna for the marker beacon is mounted on the _____ (top or bottom) of the fuselage.

104. When a hole is cut in the aircraft skin for an antenna, the strength that has been lost is replaced by riveting a/an _____ in place inside the skin.

105. Commercial broadcast stations are usually received by the ADF _____ (loop or sense) antenna.

106. Before installing a rigid antenna on a vertical fin, the installation must be carefully evaluated for _____ and _____ characteristics.

107. When an automatic direction finder is installed on a particular type of aircraft for the first time, it is important that the loop antenna be checked for _____ error.

108. The preferred location for a VOR antenna on a single-engine aircraft is on top of the cabin, with the apex of the V pointing _____ (aft or forward).

109. The DME antenna is normally mounted on the center line of the aircraft fuselage on the _____ (bottom or top).

Answers to Chapter 5 Study Questions

1. Radio Station License
2. Federal Communications Commission
3. crystal
4. receiver
5. VHF
6. HF
7. HF
8. narrower
9. a. magnetic
   b. electric
10. 186,000, 300,000,000
11. vertical
12. 2.2
13. space
14. a. length
    b. polarization
    c. directivity
15. ½
16. is
17. coaxial
18. Aircraft Communication Addressing and Reporting System (ACARS)
19. Selective Calling (SELCAL)
20. cabin depressurization
21. 406.025
22. self contained battery
23. longitudinal
24. aft
25. 48
26. 50
27. transmitter case
28. 121.5
29. 5
30. low
31. low, medium
32. loop, sense
33. is
34. does
35. VHF
36. horizontally
37. localizer
38. does not
39. TO
40. magnetic
41. LF
42. ADF
43. localizer
44. VHF
45. more
46. UHF
47. 75
48. does not
49. 4,096
50. encoding altimeter
51. IDENT
52. C
53. a. bearing
    b. altitude
    c. velocity
54. climb, descend
55. pulse
56. UHF
57. is not
58. VORTAC
59. linear
60. 24
61. 4
62. moving map
63. a. accuracy
    b. integrity
64. is not
65. the ground
66. Ground Proximity Warning System (GPWS)
67. GPS receiver
68. audible
69. water
70. red
71. does not
72. a. central processing unit
    b. memory
    c. input/output devices
73. a. ROM (Read Only Memory)
    b. RAM (Random Access Memory)
74. does
75. volatile
76. BITE
77. LRU
78. symbol generator
79. display controller
80. a. Electronic Attitude Director Indicator (EADI)
    b. Electronic Horizontal Situation Indicator (EHSI)
81. inoperative
82. a. EGT
    b. EPR
    c. N_1 speed

83. failure-related

84. true airspeed

85. Mach number

86. static air pickup points

87. Flight Management
    Computer System

88. minor

89. 337

90. alternator

91. wiring

92. shielded

93. should not

94. 2

95. 10

96. ground

97. weight and balance

98. air conditioning

99. tinned copper

100. 1

101. low

102. VOR, localizer

103. bottom

104. doubler

105. sense

106. flutter, vibration

107. quadrantal

108. forward

109. bottom

ICE CONTROL AND RAIN
REMOVAL SYSTEMS

6

Ice Control Systems

Ice affects both engines and airframes and accounts for a large number of aircraft accidents. Reciprocating-engine-powered aircraft are susceptible to carburetor ice, which shuts off the airflow to the engine. Structural ice forms on the airfoil surfaces and adds weight, as well as disturbing the smooth flow of air needed to produce lift.

There are two types of ice control systems: anti-icing systems, which prevent the formation of ice, and deicing systems, which remove ice after it has formed. Both of these systems are discussed here.

A complete ice control system consists of:

- Surface deicers
- Windshield ice control
- Powerplant ice control
- Brake deicers
- Heated pitot heads

Dangers of In-Flight Icing

Some aircraft are certificated for flight into known icing conditions, but wise pilots know that in reality, the ice control systems on these aircraft only give them time to fly out of the icing conditions, not enough to remain in them deliberately. No aircraft can withstand unrestricted exposure to icing.

In addition to the dangers caused by added weight and the disruption to the aerodynamics of the airplane, ice can also build up on the windshield, preventing the pilots from being able to see out. This becomes dangerous if the ice is still on the windshield when the pilots are trying to land the airplane.

Three types of structural ice affect aircraft in flight: rime ice, glaze ice, and frost. Rime ice is a rough, opaque ice that forms when small droplets of water freeze immediately upon striking the aircraft. It builds up slowly, causes a great deal of drag, and deforms the airfoil, increasing the stall speed of the aircraft. Rime ice is relatively easy to break loose with deicer boots.

Glaze ice is the most dangerous ice. It forms on aircraft flying through supercooled water or freezing rain. Glaze ice adds a great amount of weight and is difficult for the boots to break loose.

Three factors must be present for rime or glaze ice to form on an aircraft in flight. There must be visible moisture in the air, which can be in the form of rain, drizzle, or clouds. The surface of the aircraft must be below the freezing temperature of water, and the drops of water must be of the appropriate size for the formation of ice.

rime ice. A rough ice that forms on aircraft flying through visible moisture, such as a cloud, when the temperature is below freezing. Rime ice disturbs the smooth airflow as well as adding weight.

glaze ice. Ice that forms when large drops of water strike a surface whose temperature is below freezing. Glaze ice is clear and heavy.

frost. Ice crystal deposits formed by sublimation when the temperature and dew point are below freezing.

supercooled water. Water in its liquid form at a temperature well below its natural freezing temperature. When supercooled water is disturbed, it immediately freezes.

sublimation. A process in which a solid material changes directly into a vapor without passing through the liquid stage.

ethylene glycol. A form of alcohol used as a coolant for liquid-cooled engines and as an anti-icing agent.

isopropyl alcohol. A colorless liquid used in the manufacture of acetone and its derivatives and as a solvent and anti-icing agent.

Frost forms on an aircraft when the surface temperature is below freezing and water sublimates from the air, or changes directly from water vapor into ice crystals without passing through the liquid state. Frost does not add appreciable weight, but the tiny ice crystals create a rough surface that increases the thickness of the boundary layer and adds so much drag that flight may be impossible. All traces of frost must be removed before flight. Do this by sweeping it off with a long-handled push broom or by spraying the aircraft with a mixture of ethylene glycol and isopropyl alcohol.

Types of Ice Control Systems

Three types of ice control systems are considered here: ice detection systems, anti-ice systems, and deice systems.

Ice Detection Systems

Ice control systems should be turned on when needed, but not used when there is no danger of ice formation. Ice is easy to see in some conditions, but some locations on the aircraft are not visible and require other methods besides visual detection.

Ice on the windshield and on the wings in the daytime is easy to see before it builds up to a dangerous level. Aircraft manufacturers recognize the importance of visual ice detection and provide ice lights on the outside of the aircraft cabin that shine out along the wings' leading edges so that ice build-up can be detected at night.

Some jet transport aircraft have electronic ice detectors mounted in critical locations that are not visible to the flight crew. These detectors are small probes that vibrate at a specific frequency monitored by a small built-in dedicated computer. When ice forms on the probe its vibrating frequency decreases, and when it drops to a predetermined value the computer turns on an ice-warning light. This alerts the flight crew so they can turn on the appropriate ice control system. At the same time, current is sent through heaters surrounding the probe to melt the ice so the probe can again vibrate freely. As long as the probe continues to detect ice, the ice-warning light remains on, but when it no longer ices up, the ice warning light goes out.

Anti-Icing Systems

anti-icer system. A system that prevents the formation of ice on an aircraft structure.

Critical areas on an aircraft where ice should not be allowed to form include carburetors, pitot tubes, windshields, turbine engine air inlets, and any components that are located ahead of the these inlets. On some aircraft, such as the Boeing 727, this includes the upper VOR antenna. Anti-icing systems prevent ice from forming on these components. There are three types of anti-icing systems: electrical, thermal, and chemical.

Deicing Systems

Components of an aircraft that do not lend themselves to anti-icing are protected by deicing systems. Ice is allowed to form, and then its bond with the surface is broken and the ice is removed by the air flowing over the surface or by centrifugal force. Most airfoils and propellers are protected by deicing systems.

Pitot-Static System Ice Protection

Pitot heads installed on aircraft that are likely to encounter icing have an electrical heater built into them to prevent ice clogging their air inlet. This heater produces enough heat to damage the head if there is no cooling air flowing over it, so it should not be turned on while the aircraft is on the ground except for brief preflight checking.

You can ensure that the heater is operating properly in flight by watching the ammeter when the pitot heat is turned on. The heater draws enough current that the ammeter will show its operation.

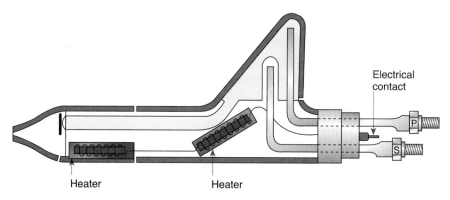

Figure 6-1. *The heater in a pitot-static head effectively prevents ice from blocking the source of pitot and static air pressures.*

Some flush static ports have heaters built into them, but on most aircraft there are two separate ports located at widely separated locations. It is unlikely that both ports will ice over at the same time. In the unlikely event that both should become plugged, the system is equipped with an alternate static air source valve that allows the pilot to select alternate air. This picks up static air from a location inside the aircraft where ice will not form.

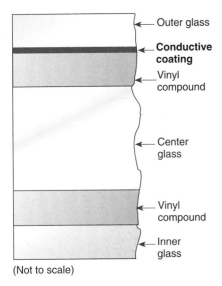

Figure 6-2. *The heated windshield of a jet transport aircraft is made of several layers of glass and vinyl with a conductive film deposited on the inner surface of the outer glass.*

thermistor. A special form of electrical resistor whose resistance varies with its temperature.

tempered glass. Glass that has been heat-treated to increase its strength. Tempered glass is used in birdproof heated windshields for high-speed aircraft.

Windshield Ice Protection

Aircraft that routinely fly into icing conditions have some method of preventing ice from forming on the windshield and obstructing the pilot's visibility. Three types of ice control are: double-panel windshields with warm air blown through the space between the panels, anti-icing fluid sprayed on the outside of the windshield, and electrically heated windshields. Most modern aircraft use electrically heated windshields.

Windshields for jet transport aircraft are extremely strong, as they must not only withstand all of the air loads but must be strong enough to withstand, without penetration, a direct strike by a four-pound bird at the designed cruising speed of the aircraft. In addition to preventing the formation of ice on these windshields, the heat keeps the thermoplastic vinyl layers from becoming brittle, and this prevents the windshield from shattering if it should be struck by a bird in flight.

Figure 6-2 shows the makeup of a jet transport windshield. It is made of three layers of tempered glass with inner layers of a thermoplastic vinyl compound. An electrically conductive film is deposited on the inside surface of the outer glass.

Windshields like the one in Figure 6-2 use 400-Hz AC. Voltage is increased by autotransformers to force enough current through the high resistance of the conductive film to produce the required heat. Thermistor-type temperature sensors laminated into the windshield measure its temperature and send this data to the AC controller, which sends just enough current through the conductive film to keep the windshield at the correct temperature.

Surface scratches or tiny chips in the tempered glass often cause stresses inside the panel that break the electrically conductive film. This allows arcing across the breaks which can cause local hot spots. If arcing occurs near one of the heat sensors, it can distort the heat control system.

Some business jet and turboprop airplanes have windshields made of two layers of tempered glass with a layer of a vinyl compound between them. A fine-wire heating element is embedded in this vinyl material.

The heating element is supplied with DC through a two-position switch and a temperature controller. Thermistor-type sensors embedded in the vinyl layer sense the windshield temperature. When the windshield anti-ice switch is in the NORMAL position, the sensors cause the controller to send current into the heating element until the windshield temperature rises to approximately 110°F. When this temperature is reached, current stops until the windshield cools to 90°F. The controller cycles current through the heating element to maintain the temperature within the set limits.

When severe icing is encountered, the switch can be moved to the HIGH position. This sends additional current through a small section of the heating element to raise the temperature of a critical area of the windshield.

This type of windshield ice control is strictly anti-icing, as it does not produce enough heat to melt off a heavy accumulation of ice that could form before the heat is turned on. Enough heat is generated, however, that this system should not be turned on while the aircraft is on the ground except for a momentary check of its operation. An adequate flow of air is required over the windshield to prevent damage.

Some of the smaller general aviation aircraft have heated anti-icing panels on the outside of the windshield. A panel of this type is shown in Figure 6-3. This panel is made of two sheets of plate glass separated by a layer of vinyl compound. A fine resistance wire embedded in the vinyl is heated with DC, supplied through a connector enclosed in a streamlined housing near the panel. The panel is removable and is installed only on flights when icing conditions are likely. Prior to entering possible icing conditions, the system is turned on, and once it is in operation, temperature sensors cycle the power to maintain a temperature of approximately 100°F.

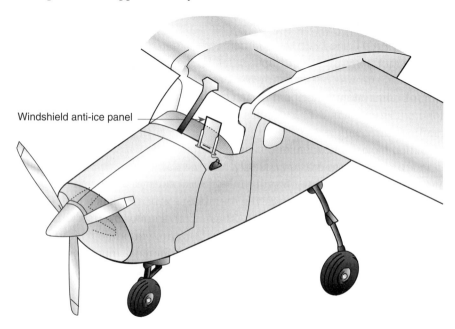

Windshield anti-ice panel

Figure 6-3. *A removable heated panel may be installed on some of the smaller general aviation aircraft to provide an ice-free area in the windshield directly in front of the pilot.*

Airfoil Ice Protection

Ice formation on the wings of early aircraft was one of the hindrances to scheduled airline flights. Ford Trimotors and Curtiss Condors, with their exposed wires and struts, had so many places to collect ice that there would not have been much profit in deicing the airfoil surfaces. But when the stream-lined, slick-skin, cantilever airplanes such as the Boeing 247, the Douglas DC-2, and the Northrop *Alpha*, started flying in airline service, engineers and operators realized that if they could remove ice from the wings of these

A When system is not operating, suction holds all three tubes deflated and tight against leading edge.

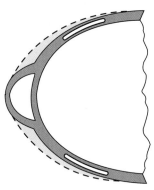

B When system is first turned on, center tube inflates and cracks the ice. Center tube remains inflated for specific number of seconds, then deflates.

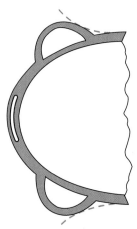

C Outer two tubes inflate and raise cracked ice from surface so wind can blow it away.

Figure 6-4. *The operating cycle of a typical three-spanwise-tube deicer boot.*

airplanes, all-weather flight schedules could be realistic. In about 1932, the B.F. Goodrich Company developed the inflatable boot deicer that is still in use today.

Turbine-powered aircraft have a ready supply of hot compressed air from their engine compressors, and these aircraft often used thermal deicers and anti-icers for their wings.

Pneumatic Deicer System

Pneumatic deicer systems have boots made of soft pliable rubber or rubberized fabric attached to the leading edges of the wings and empennage. These boots contain inflatable tubes. There are several boot designs, some having as few as three and others as many as 10 spanwise tubes. Other boots have chordwise tubes.

The surface ply of the boots is made electrically conductive so it will dissipate the static electrical charges that build up as air flows over them. If this charge did not flow off the boot, the voltage could build up high enough to discharge through the boot to the skin, and in doing so burn a hole in the boot.

The typical three-spanwise-tube boot in Figure 6-4 shows the operation of this system. When the system is not in operation, suction from the engine-driven vacuum pump holds the tubes deflated and tight against the leading edge (A).

When icing is encountered in flight, the pilot allows ice to form over the boots, then turns the system on. Air from the discharge side of the vacuum pump inflates the center tube in the boot (B) to crack the ice. The timer holds the center tube inflated for a specific number of seconds, then deflates it and inflates the two outer tubes. These tubes lift the cracked ice so air can get under it and blow it from the surface (C).

When the pneumatic deicer system was first developed, there were no good adhesives to bond the boots to the wing, and the B.F. Goodrich Company devised the Rivnut to provide a threaded hole in the thin metal of the leading edges of the wings and empennage. Some of the older installations still use machine screws and Rivnuts to secure the boots. These installations are easily identified by a metal fairing strip that covers the edges of the boots.

All modern installations use an adhesive to bond the boots to the surface. When a surface-bonded boot is installed, all the paint must be removed from the area to which the boot is to be bonded. The metal must be perfectly clean, and the bonding material must be applied in strict accordance with the instructions furnished by the maker of the boots.

Single-Engine Airplane Deicing System

Small aircraft equipped for flight into known icing conditions have a wing and empennage deicing system similar to the one in Figure 6-5. The engine-driven air pump (vacuum pump) used for the gyro instruments supplies the necessary 18- to 20-psi positive pressure to operate the boots and the suction used to hold them tight against the leading edges when the system is not operating. If the air pump uses engine oil as a lubricant ("wet"-type), an oil separator must be installed in its discharge side to remove the lubricating oil. This oil collects on a series of baffles and drains back into the engine crankcase. Dry-type air pumps have carbon vanes and require no lubrication, and so do not require an oil separator.

When the deicing system is not operating, the shuttle valve is held over so that suction from the air pump holds the boots deflated and tight against the leading edges of the surfaces.

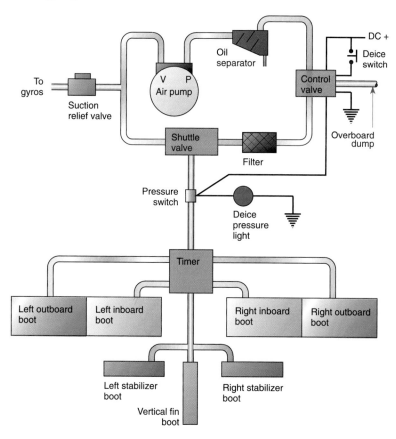

Figure 6-5. *Wing and empennage deicing system for a single-engine airplane that is approved for flight into known icing conditions.*

When ice has formed on the wings, the pilot depresses the momentary-on deice switch. This opens the control valve, allowing air pressure to reach the shuttle valve and move the shuttle over so air pressure can reach the timer. The timer begins a sequence of operation that inflates the empennage boots for about six seconds, then the inboard wing boots for six seconds, and finally the outboard wing boots for six seconds. When there is sufficient pressure at the boots for proper inflation, the deice pressure light on the instrument panel illuminates. When the cycle is completed, the control valve opens the passage to the overboard dump, and the shuttle moves over so the suction can again hold the boots tightly against the skin.

Multi-Engine Airplane Deicing System

The pneumatic deicing system used on large aircraft works in the same way as the system just described, except there are larger boots and more components. Figure 6-6 diagrams a typical deicing system for a twin-engine airplane. This system has wet-type air pumps on both engines. The discharge air from these pumps flows through oil separators and check valves into the deicer control valve. When the system is turned OFF, the air discharges overboard, and when it is turned ON, the air flows to the distributor valve/timer. An electric motor drives the distributor valve in a timed sequence to the center tube of the outboard boots, then to the outer tubes of the outboard boots. The boots on the empennage then inflate and deflate, then the center tubes, and finally the outer tubes on the inboard wing boots inflate and deflate.

The boots actuate symmetrically to keep the airflow disturbances even on both sides of the aircraft. This minimizes any flight or control problems caused by these disturbances.

When the system is turned OFF, the distributor valve connects the suction side of the air pumps to the boots to hold them tightly against the leading edges. A suction-relief valve installed between the check valves and the distributor valve regulates the amount of suction that is applied to the boots.

Proper actuation of the deicer system may be determined by watching the pressure and suction gauges. The pressure gauge fluctuates as the timer sequences the different boots, but the suction gauge remains steady since the vacuum side of the pump is not used during normal operation of the system.

Turbine-engine aircraft have a ready source of warm compressor bleed air for anti-icing, and they normally use thermal ice control. Some of the smaller turbine engines do not have an adequate quantity of bleed air for thermal ice control, but do have enough for inflating pneumatic deicing boots. Systems that use compressor bleed air for this purpose have a pressure regulator that lowers the pressure to the correct value and a venturi downstream of the regulator that produces suction when the boots are not inflated. This suction holds the tubes deflated and tight against the leading edges.

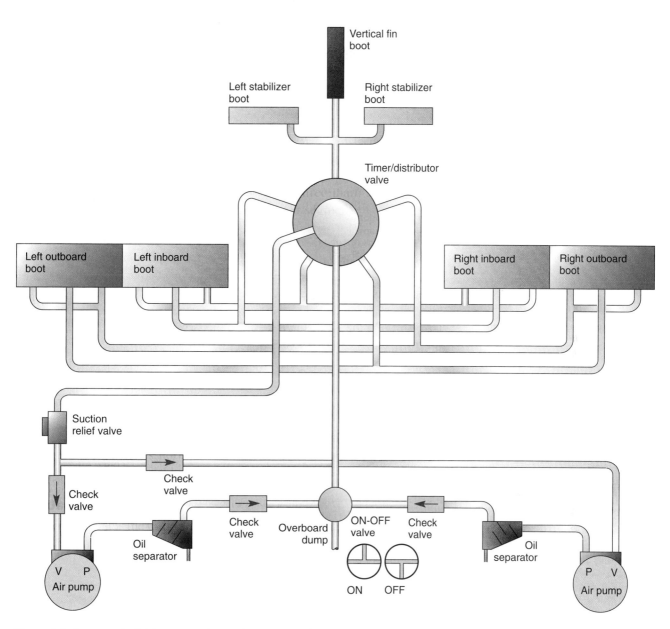

Figure 6-6. *A pneumatic deicing system for a twin-engine airplane.*

Thermal Ice Control Systems

Large turbine-engine-powered aircraft use hot compressor bleed air to prevent the formation of ice on the airfoils. This anti-icing system is operated in flight when icing conditions are first encountered or when they are expected to occur. It keeps the leading-edge devices warm with a continuous flow of heated air.

Some thermal ice control systems may be used as deicers as well as anti-icers. These systems allow much hotter air to flow through the leading edges, but for shorter periods of time and in a cyclic sequence. When these are used as deicers, ice is allowed to accumulate, then the leading edge is heated, and the ice breaks off.

The Boeing 727 uses hot air to protect the wings, engines, and upper VHF antenna from ice. Hot compressor bleed air flows from the two outboard engines through wing anti-ice control valves to a common manifold and then to the wing anti-ice ducts. The two inboard leading-edge flap sections and all eight leading edge slats are protected. After passing through the leading-edge flaps, the air is vented into the wing leading edge cavity, and air from the slats is vented into the inner slat cavity and then overboard through the slat-track openings and drain holes.

Overheat warning switches in the wing anti-ice ducting warn of overheating when the system is operating either on the ground or in the air. Temperature sensors are installed in the bleed air supply ducts downstream of the anti-ice valves, and this temperature is shown on the flight engineer's panel.

Some hot air is tapped off from the wing anti-ice ducting and used to provide anti-ice protection to the upper VHF radio antenna. This antenna is mounted on top of the fuselage in such a location that if ice were to form on it and break off, it would be ingested into the center engine.

Some large reciprocating-engine-powered airplanes use thermal ice control systems with the heat supplied by either combustion heaters or augmenter tubes installed around the exhaust system.

Combustion heaters burn aviation gasoline from the main fuel tanks, and the amount of heat they produce is controlled by thermoswitches. These switches turn the fuel off when the temperature reaches the upper limit and turn it back on when the lower control temperature is reached.

Brake Deice System

Some aircraft operate in climates where they regularly encounter freezing rain that can cause the brakes to seize. When the brake deice system is actuated, compressor bleed air is directed through the brake assemblies to melt any ice that may have formed.

Brake deice systems can be used at any time the aircraft is on the ground, but should not be used when the outside air temperature is well above freezing. In flight, a timer prevents them from being used for more than approximately 10 minutes. This prevents overheating in the wheel well.

augmenter tube. A long, stainless steel tube around the discharge of the exhaust pipes of a reciprocating engine. Exhaust gases flow through the augmenter tube and produce a low pressure that pulls additional cooling air through the engine. Heat may be taken from the augmenter tubes and directed through the leading edges of the wings for thermal anti-icing.

Powerplant Ice Protection

Powerplant ice affects both reciprocating and turbine engines. Most reciprocating engines are prone to carburetor or induction system icing, and turbine engines are mostly bothered by ingestion of ice that has broken off of some portion of the aircraft ahead of the intake.

Reciprocating Engines

Carburetor ice is the most prevalent type of powerplant ice and it can affect the safety of flight when there is no visible moisture in the air and no danger of other types of ice forming. A float-type carburetor acts as a very effective mechanical refrigerator. Liquid fuel is sprayed into the induction air in the form of tiny droplets that evaporate, or change from a liquid into a vapor. Heat is required to make this change, and it comes from the air flowing through the carburetor. When heat energy is removed from the air, the air's temperature drops enough to cause moisture to condense out and freeze in the throat of the carburetor. This ice chokes off the air flowing into the cylinders and causes the engine to lose power. Severe carburetor icing can cause engine failure. There is about a 70°F drop in temperature when the fuel evaporates, and carburetor ice can form when the outside air temperature is as high as 100°F if the humidity is high.

Carburetor ice is typically prevented by heating the air before it is taken into the carburetor. Aircraft certificated under Federal Aviation Regulation Part 23, which have a sea-level engine with a venturi carburetor, must be able to increase the temperature of the induction air by 90°F. Aircraft with altitude engines must be able to provide a temperature rise of 120°F. This heating is normally done by routing the air around the outside of some part of the exhaust system before taking it into the carburetor. The heated air bypasses the inlet air filter, and carburetor heat should not be used for ground operation.

Fuel-injected engines are not bothered by carburetor ice, but ice can form on the intake air filter and choke off the air flowing into the engine. These aircraft typically have an alternate air valve that allows air from inside the engine cowling to be taken into the fuel injection unit if the screen should ice over.

Some larger engines spray isopropyl alcohol into the throat of the carburetor. This coats the venturi and throttle valves so ice will not stick to the carburetor.

Most carburetor ice forms at the point the liquid fuel droplets evaporate, and this is in the carburetor body where the airflow would be disturbed by a temperature probe. Flight tests have shown a definite relationship between the temperature of the air entering the carburetor and the temperature of the air at the point of fuel evaporation. A temperature probe can be installed at the carburetor air inlet, and as long as the air temperature it senses remains above a specific value, there is little chance of carburetor ice forming. The pilot can control the temperature of this air by using the carburetor heat control.

sea-level engine. A reciprocating engine whose rated takeoff power can be produced only at sea level.

altitude engine. A reciprocating engine whose rated sea level takeoff power can be produced to an established higher altitude.

Turbine Engines

Turbine engines are susceptible to damage from chunks of ice that get into the compressor, so anti-icing systems are used to prevent the formation of ice ahead of the compressor inlet. Many aircraft have air passages in the compressor inlet case, inlet guide vanes, nose dome, and nose cowling. Hot compressor bleed air flows through these passages to prevent the formation of ice.

Ice can form when the engine is operated at high speed on the ground when the temperature is as high as 45°F if the air is moist. The high velocity of the inlet air creates a pressure drop that lowers the temperature of the air enough for ice to form.

In flight the anti-icing system is turned on before entering areas of visible moisture (rain or clouds) when the inlet temperature is between about 40°F and 5°F. Below 5°F, there is so little moisture in the air that ice is not likely to form.

Sometimes turbine-powered aircraft sit on the ground and water collects in the compressor and freezes. If this should happen, direct a flow of warm air through the engine until all of the ice is melted and the rotating parts turn freely.

Propellers

Ice on a propeller changes its airfoil shape and creates an unbalanced condition. Both of these conditions produce vibration and can damage the engine as well as the airframe. The earliest propeller ice control, and a system that is still in use, is chemical anti-icing. A mixture of isopropyl alcohol and ethylene glycol is carried in a tank in the aircraft and when icing conditions are anticipated, some of it is pumped into a slinger ring around the hub of the propeller and then out along the leading edges of the blades. Some propellers have molded rubber feed shoes bonded to the blade roots to help concentrate the flow of fluid along the portions of the blade that are most susceptible to ice formation. Keeping the blade surfaces perfectly smooth and waxed assists in preventing ice from sticking when it forms.

Propellers are deiced with an electrothermal system that has rubber boots bonded to the leading edge of the blades. These boots have electrical heating elements embedded in them that are supplied with current from a propeller deicing timer.

Figure 6-8 (see page 398) is the electrical schematic diagram of a typical electrothermal deicing system used on a twin turboprop airplane. Current flows from the bus through the 20-amp Auto Prop Deice circuit breaker/ switch into the deicer timer unit. When the manual-override relays are not energized, this current flows through brushes riding on slip rings mounted on the propeller spinner bulkhead into the heating elements bonded to the propeller blades. The slip rings are connected to the heater elements through flexible conductors that allow the blades to change their pitch angle. See Figure 6-8.

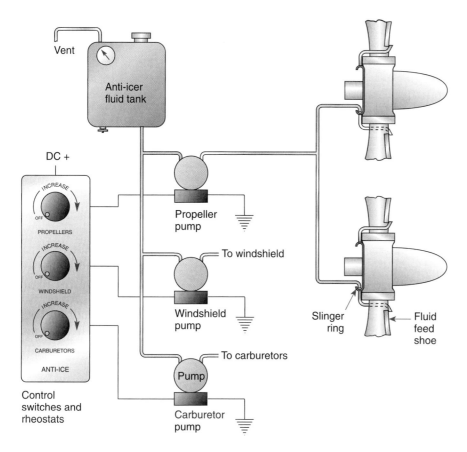

Figure 6-7. *A typical chemical anti-icing system for a propeller.*

The timer sends current through the right propeller for about 90 seconds, then switches over and sends current through the left propeller for 90 seconds.

Some propeller deicing systems have two separate heating elements on each blade. Current flows through the right propeller outboard element for somewhere around 30 seconds, then through the right propeller inboard element for the same length of time. After the right propeller is deiced, the timer shifts over and sends current through the left propeller outboard elements and then through the left propeller inboard elements.

Current cycles of the two propellers are controlled by the timer as long as the propeller Auto Prop Deice switch is ON. When the Manual Prop Deicer switch is held in its momentary ON position, the two manual-override relays are energized and current flows directly from the bus to the blades without going through the timer.

The pilot can easily tell whether the deicing system is operating correctly in the AUTOMATIC mode by watching the propeller ammeter. It will show a flow of current each time one of the heater elements draws current.

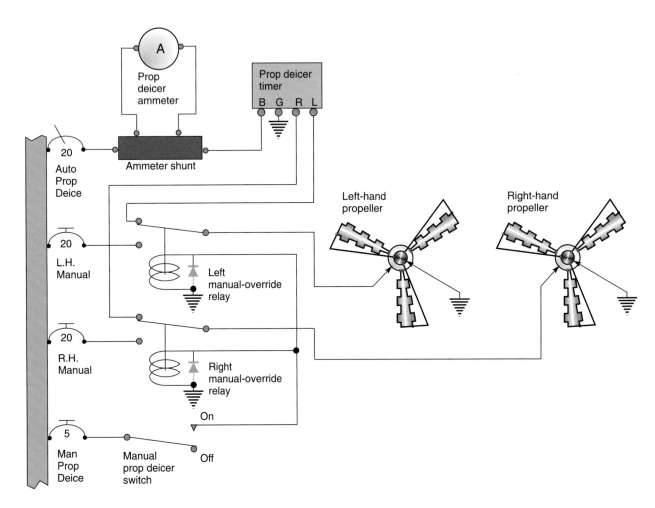

Figure 6-8. *Electrothermal propeller deicing system.*

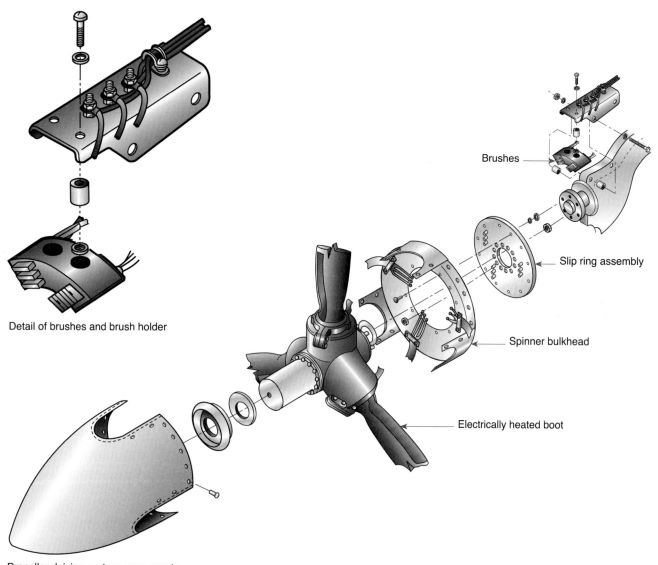

Detail of brushes and brush holder

Brushes

Slip ring assembly

Spinner bulkhead

Electrically heated boot

Propeller deicing system components

Figure 6-9. *Electrothermally deiced propeller.*

Water Drain System Ice Protection

The water lines, drain masts, toilet drain lines, and waste water drains that are located in areas where they are exposed to freezing temperatures in flight are protected by electrically heated hoses or by ribbon or blanket heaters. All of these heaters have thermostats built into them that prevent them from overheating.

Ground Deicing and Anti-Icing

Aircraft operating in the winter months are often faced with the problem of taking off into conditions of snow and ice. Federal Aviation Regulations prohibit takeoff when snow, ice, or frost is adhering to the wings, and it is the responsibility of the aviation mechanic to operate the equipment that deices and anti-ices the aircraft.

Test data shows that ice, snow, or frost formations with a thickness and surface roughness similar to medium or coarse sandpaper on the leading edge and upper surface of a wing can reduce wing lift by as much as 30 percent and increase drag by as much as 40 percent. For this reason, all snow, ice, and frost must be removed.

Small aircraft that have been sitting in the open and are covered with snow may be prepared for flight by sweeping the snow off with a brush or broom, making very sure that there is no frost left on the surface. Frost, while adding very little weight, roughens the surface enough to destroy lift. An engine heater that blows warm air through a large hose may be used for deicing, but take care to prevent melted ice from running down inside the aircraft structure and refreezing.

FPD. Freezing-point depressant.

There are two methods of ground ice control for large aircraft: deicing and anti-icing, and there are two types of freezing-point depressant (FPD) fluids in use: Type I and Type II. Deicing and anti-icing may be accomplished by two procedures: the one-step procedure and two-step procedure.

Deicing is the removal of ice that has already formed on the surface, and anti-icing is the protection of the surface from the subsequent formation of ice. Just before takeoff large aircraft are both deiced and anti-iced.

The FPD fluids used for icing protection are made up of propylene/diethylene and ethylene glycols with certain additives. These fluids are mixed with water to give them the proper characteristics.

Type I FPD fluids contain a minimum of 80% glycols and are considered "unthickened" because of their relative low viscosity. Type I fluid is used primarily for deicing, because it provides very limited anti-icing protection.

Type II FPD fluids contain a minimum of 50% glycols and are considered "thickened" because of added agents that enable the fluid to be deposited in a thicker film and to remain on the aircraft surfaces until time of takeoff. These fluids are used for deicing and anti-icing and provide greater protection than Type I fluids against ice, frost, or snow formation on the ground.

Deicing and anti-icing may be done with the one-step or the two-step procedure. In the one-step procedure, the FPD fluid is mixed with water that is heated to a nozzle temperature of 140°F (60°C) and sprayed on the surface. The heated fluid is very effective for deicing, but the residual FPD fluid film has very limited anti-icing protection. Anti-icing protection is enhanced by using cold fluids. In some instances, the final coat of fluid is applied in a fine mist, using a high trajectory to allow the fluid to cool before it touches the aircraft skin.

For the two-step procedure, the first step is deicing, and heated fluid is used. The second step is anti-icing and cold fluid is used, so it will remain on the surface for a longer period of time.

STUDY QUESTIONS: ICE CONTROL SYSTEMS

Answers are provided on page 411.

1. Two types of ice control are:

    a. _____

    b. _____

2. The ice control system that prevents the formation of ice is the _____ system.

3. The ice control system that removes ice after it has formed is the _____ system.

4. Frost on an aircraft wing _____ (does or does not) constitute a hazard to flight.

5. A pitot head is anti-iced with a/an _____ (electric or hot air) heater.

6. An operational check of a pitot-static tube heater may be made by watching the _____ when the heater is turned on.

7. Frost may be removed from an aircraft by spraying it with a deicing fluid that normally contains _____ and _____ .

8. Electrically heated windshields that use a conductive film as the heating element are energized with _____ (AC or DC).

9. The temperature of an electrically heated windshield is sensed by _____-type sensors laminated between the glass panels.

10. A breakdown of the electrically conductive film inside an electrically heated windshield can cause _____ .

(continued)

11. Three methods of preventing ice from forming on a windshield and obstructing pilot visibility are:

    a. _____

    b. _____

    c. _____

12. The fluid that is used for anti-icing propeller blades is a mixture of _____ and _____ .

13. Current for the heating elements in an electrothermal deicing system for a propeller is carried from the airframe into the propeller through _____ and _____ .

14. Reciprocating-engine-powered aircraft get the air for inflating the deicer boots from a/an _____ .

15. Deicing systems are turned on _____ (before or after) icing is encountered.

16. Deicer boots are attached to modern aircraft leading edges with a/an _____ .

17. Before installing a surface-bonded deicer boot to the leading edge of an aircraft wing, the paint must be _____ (cleaned or removed).

18. The oil that is used to lubricate a "wet" vacuum pump is removed from the discharge air by a/an _____ .

19. Deicer boots are actuated symmetrically to minimize control problems caused by disturbance of the _____ .

20. The inflation sequence of a pneumatic deicer boot system is controlled by a _____ / timer.

21. The amount of suction used to hold the deicing boots deflated when the system is not operating is controlled by a/an _____ valve.

22. During normal operation of a pneumatic deicer system, the air pressure gauge will _____ (fluctuate or remain steady).

23. During normal operation of a pneumatic deicer system, the suction gauge will _____ (fluctuate or remain steady).

24. The component in a multi-engine pneumatic deicing system that directs suction into the boots when the system is not operating is the _____ .

25. Two sources of heat for thermal ice control on reciprocating-engine-powered aircraft are:

 a. _____

 b. _____

26. The temperature of the air produced by a combustion heater is controlled by cycling the _____ (fuel or ignition) on and off.

27. Carburetor ice _____ (can or cannot) form when the outside air temperature is above 70°F.

28. Visible moisture _____ (is or is not) required for the formation of carburetor ice.

29. The heat for eliminating carburetor ice normally comes from the _____ .

30. Fuel-injected engines have an alternate source of induction system air to use in the event the _____ ices over.

31. When carburetor heat is used, the intake air _____ (is or is not) filtered.

32. A carburetor heater system for a sea-level engine should be able to increase the temperature of the air by _____°F.

33. Ice is prevented from sticking to the throttle valve and venturi in a carburetor by spraying _____ into the carburetor inlet.

34. If the compressor of a turbine engine is immobile because of ice, the ice should be melted with _____ .

35. Type I FPD fluids are used primarily for _____ (anti-icing or deicing).

36. Heated FPD fluids are most effective for _____ (anti-icing or deicing).

37. For most effective anti-icing, the FPD fluid is applied _____ (hot or cold).

Figure 6-10. *Rain control panel located in the overhead control area of a jet transport cockpit.*

Rain Removal Systems

Rain removal systems are used in most larger aircraft to keep the windshield free of water so the pilot can see for the approach and to maneuver the aircraft safely on the ground.

Small general aviation aircraft have acrylic windshields that are easy to scratch, so windshield wipers are not used. Rain is prevented from obstructing visibility on these aircraft by keeping the windshield waxed with a good grade of paste wax. Water does not spread out on the waxed surface, but balls up and is blown away by the propeller blast.

Large aircraft have tempered glass windshields and a rain removal system that may be mechanical, chemical, or pneumatic.

Mechanical systems use windshield wipers similar to those used on automobiles except that they are able to withstand the high air loads caused by the speed of the aircraft. The wipers for the pilot and the copilot are driven independently, so if one drive malfunctions, there will still be clear visibility on the other side. The wipers may be driven by electric motors or hydraulic or pneumatic actuators, and all systems have speed controls and a position on the control switch that drives the blades to a stowed, or park, position.

Windshield wipers should never be operated on a dry windshield because they will scratch the expensive glass. When you must operate them for maintenance purposes, flush the windshield with water and operate the wipers while the glass is wet.

Chemical rain repellent is a syrupy liquid carried in pressurized cans in the rain repellent system. When flying in heavy rain with the windshield wipers operating, the pilot depresses the rain repellent buttons. This opens solenoid valves for a specific length of time and allows the correct amount of liquid to spray out along the lower portion of the windshield. The windshield wipers then spread the repellent evenly over the glass, and when rain strikes the treated surface it balls up rather than spreading out. The water is carried away by the high velocity of the air flowing over the windshield.

Chemical rain repellent should not be discharged onto a dry windshield because it will smear and be difficult to remove. It can restrict visibility if it is sprayed on the windshield when there is not enough rain to allow it to be spread out smoothly.

Another method of controlling rain on aircraft windshields is the use of a blast of high-velocity hot turbine engine compressor bleed air. This air is blown across the windshield from ducts similar to that in Figure 6-11. The air forms a barrier that prevents the rain from hitting the windshield glass.

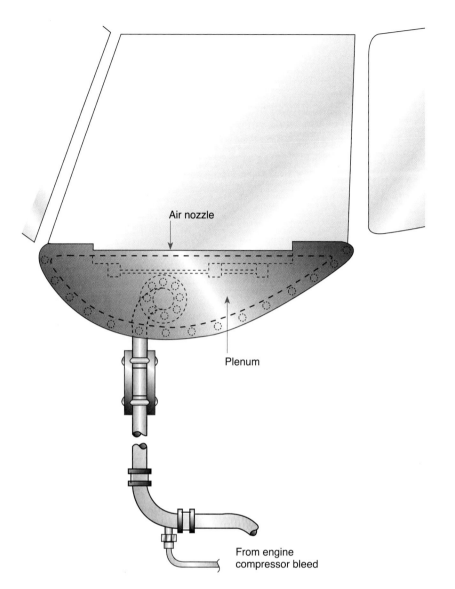

Air nozzle

Plenum

plenum. An enclosed chamber in which air can be held at a pressure higher than that of the surrounding air.

From engine compressor bleed

Figure 6-11. *Pneumatic rain removal system.*

Answers are provided on page 411.

38. Acrylic plastic windshields on small general aviation aircraft are treated to ease the removal of rain by coating them with a smooth coat of _____ .

39. Three types of rain removal systems for large aircraft are:

    a. _____

    b. _____

    c. _____

40. Chemical rain repellent _____ (should or should not) be applied to a dry windshield.

41. The air for a pneumatic rain removal system comes from the _____ .

Inspection and Maintenance of Ice Control and Rain Removal Systems

It is important to understand the airplane that you are working on and how each of these systems work before you inspect or perform maintenance on the systems. This information can be found in the manufacturer's instructions for continued airworthiness.

Chemical deice and anti-ice fluids may be used on some aircraft for any, or all, ice protection systems. Care should be taken when working around these chemicals, and you should follow all safety precautions that pertain to the fluid being used. Follow the manufacturer's instructions for handling, cleaning spills, and proper storage.

Pitot-Static Systems

Pitot-static ice protection is accomplished by electrical heaters built into the pitot tubes and static ports. All modern pitot tubes have heaters, but many static ports, especially on smaller aircraft, do not have heaters.

Inspection

Inspect pitot tubes and static ports for security and visually check all openings to make sure that they are clear and not blocked.

Testing and Troubleshooting

Most pitot-static heaters can be checked on the ground by turning on the pitot-static heater and briefly touching the pitot tubes and static ports. Caution should be taken as the pitot tubes can heat up very quickly and become very hot. Remove ground pitot covers before turning the pitot heat on. Some pitot-static heat systems are disabled on the ground as, without cooling air flowing over them, they can overheat and damage the components. These systems will usually have a test button that can be actuated on the ground for a few seconds to test the components.

If the heater is not working, turn the system on and check for proper voltage at the component and check for a good electrical ground. If the voltage is correct and the ground is good, the problem is most likely in the heating element. This can be verified by disconnecting the electrical connection and checking the resistance of the heating element. If there is no resistance, the element is broken and should be replaced.

Windshield Ice Protection

Common windshield ice protection systems are heated windshields or chemical fluids that are sprayed onto the windscreen. Caution should be used when cleaning all aircraft windshields and especially heated windshields. Heated windshields are very expensive and can be ruined by using the wrong cleaner. Use only the recommended cleaning methods, which is often lots of water and mild soap. Use only a clean, soft cloth or sponge or use your bare hand. Dry windshields should never be rubbed with a dry cloth, as this can cause scratches and builds up static that can attract dust.

Inspection

Inspect electrically heated windshields and windshield panels for security and condition of all electrical connections. Check for delamination between the layers of the windshield. A small amount of delamination may be acceptable, and the limits will be detailed in the aircraft maintenance instructions. Inspect the mounting screws for security. Some aircraft manufacturers specify retorquing the windshield mounting screws at set inspection intervals. Follow the maintenance instructions to operationally check the windshield heat (checking for heat and proper current draw). Some aircraft limit the amount of time that windshield heat can be operated on the ground.

For inspection of fluid windshield ice protection systems, check condition and security of all lines and spray nozzles. Check mounting, condition and operation of the fluid pump. Some systems require checking for proper fluid flow by measuring a set number of ounces of fluid within a specified number of seconds. Check fluid level and service as required.

Pneumatic Deicer Systems

Maintenance

Deicer boots are made of rubber and should be cleaned with a mild soap and water solution. Any grease or oil must be removed with a rag damp with naphtha or Varsol and then the entire area washed with soap and water. Small holes in the boots may be patched with cold patches similar to those used for bicycle tubes (but not the same material). Use only patching material provided by the boot manufacturer and follow its repair procedures in detail.

The boots may be periodically resurfaced with a black, conductive neoprene cement to seal any tiny pinholes and ensure that the boots remain electrically conductive.

Inspection and Operational Checks

Inspect all boots, pneumatic lines, and system components for condition and security. Check rubber hoses for age hardening and cracking.

The operation and testing of pneumatic boots on the ground requires a source of pressurized air to inflate the boots. This can be done by running the aircraft engines and using the aircraft source of air or by using a ground test set that regulates the air to the proper pressure. When the system is operating normally, different sections of the pneumatic boots will operate at different times as controlled by the control valve and timer. Verify that the boots are cycling in the correct sequence and for the proper length of time. Inspect for leaks and proper inflation of each boot.

Propeller Ice Protection Systems

The most common form of propeller ice protection is the use of electrically heated boots that are bonded to the propeller blades. Electrical power is supplied through a system timer that cycles between propellers, propeller blades, or inner and outer sections of the individual boots. Power is transferred from the timer to the rotating propeller through a set of carbon blocks that are mounted on the engine. The carbon blocks ride on slip rings that are mounted on the back of the propeller. The sections of the slip ring are then connected with wires to the heating elements of the boots.

Inspection and Operational Checks

Inspect the propeller boots for security and visible breaks in the heating element. Check the wires that run from the boots to the slip ring for security and chafing. Inspect the carbon brushes for wear and replace as necessary. Check the brush block for security and for proper alignment of the brushes to the slip ring. Inspect the wires from the brush block to the timer for security and chafing.

Check the operation of the boots and timers by turning the system on. Do not run the system on the ground any longer than necessary to verify that each of the boots and boot sections are working correctly.

> **Caution!** Deice boots on composite propellers should not be operated on the ground without the engines running. The cooling air flowing over the propellers is necessary to prevent the composite blades from overheating and delaminating. The proper operation of the deice boots is verified by checking for the correct amperage on the propeller ammeter while the engine is running.

Thermal Ice Control Systems

Thermal ice control systems on large aircraft provide heated air to the leading edges of the wings, stabilizers, and engine nacelles. The inspection and maintenance of these systems focuses primarily on the control valves, ducting, and manifolds that distribute the hot air.

Inspection and Maintenance

Visually inspect ducts and manifolds for security, condition, and distortion, paying special attention to all seals and bellows for obvious leaks. When replacing ducts, or when leaks are suspected, the system can be pressurized in accordance with the aircraft maintenance instructions. The amount of leakage is not allowed to exceed a specified amount. Leaks can often be detected by listening for the escaping air. Smaller leaks can be found by spraying a mixture of soapy water over the suspected area and watching for bubbles.

Windshield Wiper Systems

Never operate windshield wipers on a dry windshield. This causes scratches that can eventually require replacement of a very expensive windshield.

Inspection and Maintenance

Inspect wiper motors and arms for condition and security. Check adjustment of the tension springs that provide the proper pressure of the blade to the windscreen. Verify speed control operation and that the park position stows the blade in the correct location. Inspect the wiper blade for condition and replace as necessary. Follow the aircraft manufacturer's instructions for replacing the wiper blade.

Windshield Pneumatic Rain Removal System

Inspection and Maintenance

Pneumatic rain removal systems are simple systems with few moving parts. Bleed air from the engine is controlled by a valve that supplies air to the windshield plenum and air nozzle.

Inspect bleed air lines for condition, security, and leaks. Inspect the control valve for security and the air plenum and nozzle for cracks and proper attachment.

STUDY QUESTIONS: INSPECTION AND MAINTENANCE OF ICE CONTROL AND RAIN REMOVAL SYSTEMS

Answers are provided on page 411.

42. Care should be taken when working with deicer _____ and _____, and to follow all _____ safety instructions.

43. If a pitot heater is not working and an ohmmeter shows that there is no resistance in the heating element, the _____ is broken.

44. Windshield ice protection systems prevent ice by the use of:

    a. _____

    b. _____

45. Using the wrong cleaner on a windshield can _____ the windshield.

46. The limits for windshield delamination can be found in _____.

47. Rubber deicer boots should be cleaned with _____ and _____.

48. Grease and oil on deicer boots can be removed with _____ or _____.

49. Electrical power for propeller deicer boots is transferred from the engine to propeller through _____ and _____.

50. Composite propeller deice boots _____ (can/should not) be operated on the ground without the engines running.

51. For ice control on large aircraft, _____ is provided to the leading edges of the wings and stabilizers.

52. Operating windshield wipers on a dry windshield may cause _____.

53. Pneumatic windshield rain removal systems use _____ from the engines.

Answers to Chapter 6 Study Questions

1. a. anti-ice system
    b. deice system
2. anti-ice
3. deice
4. does
5. electric
6. ammeter
7. ethylene glycol, isopropyl alcohol
8. AC
9. thermistor
10. arcing
11. a. warm air blown between laminated glass panels
    b. chemical anti-icing fluid sprayed on the outside
    c. electrically heated windshields
12. isopropyl alcohol, ethylene glycol
13. brushes, slip rings
14. engine-driven air pump
15. after
16. adhesive

17. removed
18. oil separator
19. airflow
20. distributor valve
21. suction relief
22. fluctuate
23. remain steady
24. distributor valve
25. a. combustion heaters
    b. augmenter tubes around the exhaust
26. fuel
27. can
28. is not
29. exhaust system
30. air filter
31. is not
32. 90
33. isopropyl alcohol
34. warm air
35. deicing
36. deicing
37. cold

38. wax
39. a. mechanical
    b. chemical
    c. pneumatic
40. should not
41. turbine engine compressor
42. fluids, chemicals, manufacturer's
43. heating element
44. a. heated windshields
    b. chemical fluids
45. ruin
46. the aircraft maintenance manual
47. mild soap, water
48. naphtha, Varsol
49. carbon brushes, slip rings
50. should not
51. heated air
52. scratches
53. bleed air

FIRE PROTECTION SYSTEMS

7

Fire Protection

Aircraft carry large volumes of highly flammable fuel in a lightweight, vibration-prone structure. This structure also carries engines that continually produce extremely hot exhaust gases. Add a complex electrical system with motors and relays that produce sparks, and radio and radar transmitters that emit electromagnetic radiation, and you have an ideal environment for fires.

Yet the fire detection and protection systems available in modern aircraft are so effective, there are relatively few fires in the air.

Requirements for Fire

Fire is the result of a chemical reaction between some type of fuel and oxygen. When this reaction occurs, energy is released in the form of heat and light.

For a fire to start, there must be fuel, oxygen, and a high enough temperature to start the reaction. Fires may be extinguished by removing the fuel or oxygen or by reducing the temperature to a level below that needed for the reaction.

The National Fire Protection Association has categorized fires and identified the types of extinguishing agents best used on each type. The four categories are Classes A, B, C, and D.

Class A fires are fueled by solid combustible materials such as wood, paper, and cloth. These fires typically occur in aircraft cabins and cockpits, so any extinguishing agent used for Class-A fires must be safe for the occupants.

Class B fires are fueled by combustible liquids such as gasoline, turbine-engine fuel, lubricating oil, and hydraulic fluid. Class-B fires typically occur in engine compartments.

Class C fires involve energized electrical equipment. These fires can occur in almost any part of an aircraft and they demand special care because of the danger of electrical shock.

Class D fires are those in which some metal such as magnesium burns. These fires typically occur in the brakes and wheels, and burn with a ferocious intensity. Never use water on a burning metal, it only intensifies the fire.

Fire Detection Systems

A complete fire detection system consists of fire detectors, overheat detectors, rate-of-temperature-rise detectors, smoke detectors, and carbon monoxide detectors. We will discuss each of these.

Requirements for a fire detection system:

1. The system must not give false warnings under any flight or ground operating condition.

2. The system must give a rapid indication of a fire and accurately identify its location.

3. The system must accurately indicate when a fire has been extinguished.

4. The system must sound a warning if a fire re-ignites.

5. The system must continue to indicate the presence of a fire as long as the fire exists.

6. The integrity of the system must be able to be tested from the cockpit.

7. Detectors must not be damaged by exposure to oil, water, vibration, extremes of temperature, and the handling encountered in normal maintenance.

8. Detectors must be lightweight and adaptable to any mounting position.

9. Detector circuitry must operate directly from the aircraft electrical system.

10. The detector circuitry must require a minimum of electrical current when it is not indicating a fire.

11. Each detection system should actuate an audible alarm and a cockpit light that shows the location of the fire.

12. There must be a separate detection system for each engine.

Fire Detectors and Overheat Detection Systems

A fire detector system warns the flight crew of the presence of a fire that raises the temperature of a particular location to a predetermined high value. An overheat detector initiates a warning when there is a lesser increase in temperature over a larger area. Most of these detection systems turn on a red light and sound a fire-warning bell.

Thermoswitch-Type Fire Detection System

The single-terminal bimetallic thermoswitch-type spot detector circuit uses a number of spot detectors such as the one in Figure 7-1 installed in a circuit like the one in Figure 7-2. When a fire occurs in the area protected by one of the detectors, the detector is heated, and strips on which the contacts are mounted distort and close the contacts, completing the circuit between the loop and ground.

The circuit in Figure 7-2 will signal the presence of a fire even if the loop of wire connecting the detectors is broken. During normal operation the detectors get their power from both ends of the loop, and if the loop is broken at any one point, all of the detectors still have power. If any one detector senses a fire, its contacts will close and provide a ground for the fire-warning light.

Closing the fire-warning test switch energizes the test relay, removes power from one end of the loop and grounds it, turning on the fire-warning light and sounding the bell. If there is an open in the wire between the detectors, there will be no ground for the warning light, and it will not illuminate.

Another type of thermoswitch spot detector installed in some aircraft have two terminals. Instead of completing the circuit to ground when a fire is detected, the detector completes the circuit between the two conductors connected to their terminals. These two-terminal thermoswitches are connected between two loops, and the system can tolerate either an open circuit or a short to ground in either of the loops without affecting the operation of the system.

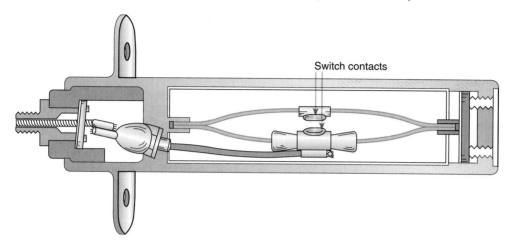

Figure 7-1. *A single-terminal bimetallic thermoswitch fire detector.*

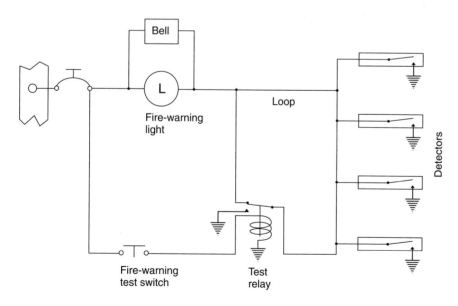

Figure 7-2. *Circuit for a single-terminal thermoswitch fire detector system.*

Follow the circuit in Figure 7-3 to see the way the two-terminal thermo-switch system works. When there is no fire, Loop 2 is connected to the positive voltage, and Loop 1 is connected to ground, both through the normally-closed contacts of the relay.

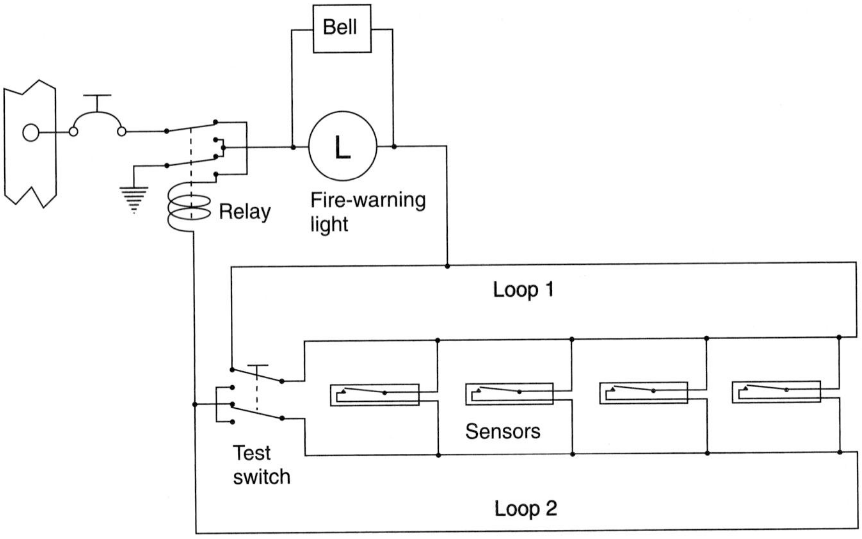

Figure 7-3. *Circuit for a two-terminal thermoswitch fire detector system.*

If there is a short to ground in Loop 1, nothing happens because Loop 1 is already at ground potential. If there is a short to ground in Loop 2, the fault current energizes the relay and places Loop 2 at ground potential. The relay makes Loop 1 positive, or "hot."

Both ends of the two loops are connected to the test switch, and a single open in either of the loops has no effect on the operation of the system.

When the test switch is depressed, the circuit between the two loops is completed. Current flows through the relay coil, all of Loops 1 and 2, and back to ground through the fire-warning light and bell. Pressing the test switch checks the integrity of the entire system.

Rate-of-Temperature-Rise Detection System

A thermoswitch-type detection system initiates a fire warning when any of the individual detectors reaches a predetermined temperature. But because a fire can have a good start before this temperature is reached, the thermo-couple-type fire-warning system is used. This system initiates a fire warning when the temperature at any specific location in the monitored compartment rises a great deal faster than the temperature of the entire compartment.

two-terminal spot-type fire detection system. A fire detection system that uses individual thermoswitches installed around the inside of the area to be protected.

These thermoswitches are wired in parallel between two separate circuits. A short or an open circuit can exist in either circuit without causing a fire warning.

thermocouple fire detection system. A fire detection system that works on the principle of the rate-of-temperature-rise. Thermocouples are installed around the area to be protected, and one thermocouple is surrounded by insulation that prevents its temperature from changing rapidly.

In the event of a fire, the temperature of all the thermocouples except the protected one will rise immediately and a fire warning will be initiated. In the case of a general overheat condition, the temperature of all the thermocouples will rise uniformly and there will be no fire warning.

Thermocouple-type fire-warning systems are often installed in engine compartments where normal operating temperatures are quite high, but the rise to this temperature is gradual.

A thermocouple is made of two different types of wire welded together, and the point at which the wires are joined is called a junction. When several thermocouples are connected in series in a circuit, a voltage will exist within the circuit that is proportional to the difference in the temperatures of the various junctions.

The sensors used with a thermocouple system are similar to the one in Figure 7-4. These sensors have a piece of each of the two thermocouple wires, typically iron and constantan, welded together and mounted in the housing that protects them from physical damage, yet allows free circulation of air around the wires. They form the measuring junctions of the thermocouple, and all of them are connected in series with the coil of a sensitive relay and a test thermocouple. See Figure 7-5.

The sensors are mounted at strategic locations around the monitored compartment. One sensor is mounted inside a thermal insulating shield that protects it from direct air circulation, yet allows it to reach the temperature of the air within the compartment. This sensor is called the reference junction.

When there is no fire, all of the junctions are the same temperature and no current flows in the thermocouple circuit. When the engine is started and the temperature of the engine compartment rises, the temperatures of all of the thermocouples rise together and there is still no current flow. But if there is a fire, the temperature of one or more of the thermocouples will rise immediately while the temperature of the insulated reference thermocouple

thermocouple. An electrical device consisting of a loop made of two different types of wire. A voltage is generated in a thermocouple that is proportional to the difference in the temperatures of the two points where the dissimilar wires join. This voltage difference causes current to flow.

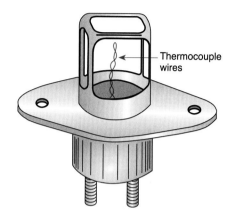

Figure 7-4. *A thermocouple fire sensor.*

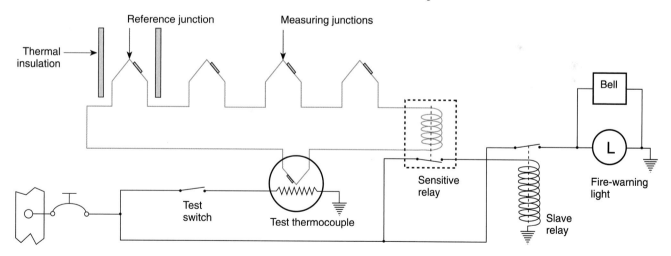

Figure 7-5. *A rate-of-temperature-rise fire-detection circuit.*

continuous-loop fire-detection system. A fire-detection system that uses a continuous loop of two conductors separated with a thermistor-type insulation.

Under normal temperature conditions, the thermistor material is an insulator, but if it is exposed to a fire, the thermistor changes into a conductor and completes the circuit between the two conductors, initiating a fire warning.

rises much more slowly. As long as there is a difference in temperatures between any of the junctions, there is a difference in voltage between them. Not much current, but enough to energize the sealed sensitive relay, flows in the thermocouple circuit. The contacts of the sensitive relay close and carry enough current to the coil of the slave relay to close its contacts and allow current to flow to the fire-warning light and bell.

A thermocouple fire detection system is tested by closing the test switch and holding it closed for a specified number of seconds. Current flows through the heater inside the test thermocouple housing and heats the test junction. Since this junction is in series with all the other junctions, there is a voltage difference, and thus enough current flows to energize the sensitive relay and initiate a fire warning.

Continuous-Loop Detector Systems

Engine compartments, APU installations, and wheel wells are difficult locations to monitor for fire, and continuous-loop-type detectors are often used in these areas rather than individual detectors such as thermoswitches or thermocouples. There are two types of continuous-loop fire and overheat detection systems: thermistor and pneumatic.

Thermistor-Type Continuous-Loop Systems

There are two configurations of thermistor-type continuous loop elements: single-conductor and two-conductor elements.

The single-conductor element has a center conductor supported in a thin-wall inconel tube by ceramic beads. See Figure 7-6. An electrical connection

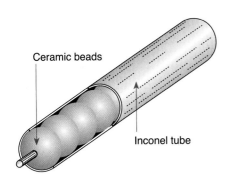

Figure 7-6. *A single-conductor continuous-loop fire detector element.*

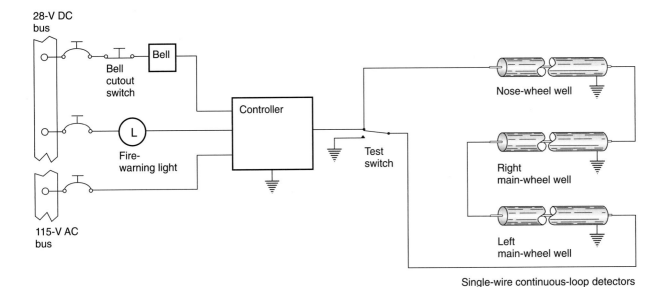

Figure 7-7. *Single-conductor continuous-loop fire detection circuit.*

is made to the conductor, and the outside tube is grounded to the airframe. The space between the beads is filled with a eutectic (low melting-point) salt whose resistance drops drastically when it melts. When any portion of the tube gets hot enough to melt the salt, the resistance between the center conductor and the outside tube drops, and signal current flows to initiate a fire warning. When the fire is extinguished, the molten salt solidifies and its resistance increases enough that the fire-warning current no longer flows.

The two-conductor loop is also mounted in an inconel tube, and it has two parallel wires embedded in a thermistor material whose resistance decreases as its temperature increases. One of the wires is grounded to the outer tube, and the other terminates in a connector and is connected to a control unit that continuously measures the total resistance of the sensing loop. By monitoring the resistance, this unit will detect a general overheat condition as well as a single hot spot. See Figure 7-8.

eutectic material. An alloy or solution that has the lowest possible melting point.

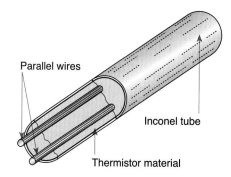

Figure 7-8. *Two-conductor continuous-loop fire detector element.*

thermistor material. A material with a negative temperature coefficient that causes its resistance to decrease as its temperature increases.

Pneumatic-Type Continuous-Loop System

The pneumatic fire detection system also uses a continuous loop for the detection element, but this loop is made of a sealed stainless steel tube that contains an element which absorbs gas when it is cold, but releases this gas when it is heated.

One type of pneumatic fire detection system is the Lindberg system. The stainless steel tube which makes up the loop contains the gas-absorbing element and the gas, and is connected to a pressure switch as is seen in Figure 7-9. When the loop, which is installed around the monitored area, is heated in a local area by a fire or by a general overheat condition, the gas is released and its pressure closes the pressure switch. Closing this switch completes the circuit for one of the windings of a transformer and allows the 115-volt, 400-Hz power from the aircraft electrical system to illuminate the fire-warning light and sound the fire-warning bell.

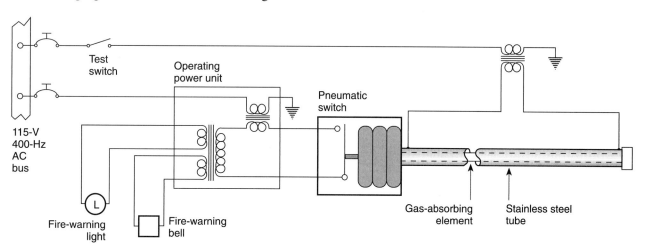

Figure 7-9. *The operating principle of a Lindberg pneumatic fire detector.*

This system is tested by closing the test switch. This allows low-voltage AC to flow through the tubing in the loop. This current heats the loop and causes the release of enough gas to close the pressure switch and initiate a fire warning.

The Systron-Donner pneumatic fire detection system also uses a continuous loop for the detection element, but this loop contains two gases and a titanium center wire with the capacity to absorb an amount of hydrogen gas that is proportional to its temperature. See Figure 7-10.

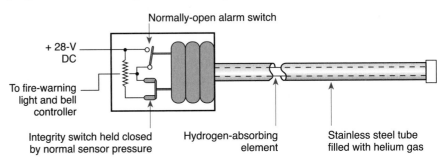

Figure 7-10. *Operating principle of a Systron-Donner pneumatic fire and overheat detector.*

The tube is filled with helium gas under pressure, and at normal temperature, the helium produces a pressure that is proportional to the average temperature of the entire tube. When the average temperature of the tube reaches the value for which the warning system is set, the pressure of the helium gas becomes great enough to close a set of normally open contacts in the detector housing and initiate a fire-warning signal.

Any time an actual fire increases the temperature of a localized area of the tube, the center wire will release enough hydrogen gas to increase the pressure inside the housing to close the contacts and initiate a fire warning.

When the fire is extinguished, the temperature drops and the center wire absorbs enough hydrogen gas to lower the pressure in the housing so the contacts can snap open and restore the system to a condition to detect the fire if it should re-ignite.

There are two switches in the housing; one is normally open, and it closes to signal the presence of a fire when the pressure of either the hydrogen or helium gas increases enough to close it. The other is called the integrity switch and it is held closed by the normal pressure of the helium gas in the tube. If a break should occur in the tube and the helium pressure is lost, the integrity switch will open, and when the test switch is closed, no current can flow to initiate the fire-warning system. The failure of the warning light to illuminate shows that the system is faulty.

Smoke and Flame Detectors

Certain areas in an aircraft can produce a great deal of smoke before any flames actually appear, and it is important in these areas to detect the first indication of smoke. Baggage and cargo compartments are typically protected by smoke detectors, of which there are four types: CO detectors, photoelectric detectors, ionization-type detectors, and visual detectors. CO detectors measure the level of carbon monoxide in the air. Photoelectric detectors indicate the presence of smoke in air drawn from a compartment by measuring the refraction of a beam of light shined through the sample of air. Ionization-type detectors measure the current that flows through ionized air, and visual detectors detect the presence of smoke by actually viewing samples of air that are drawn through the smoke detector chamber.

Flame detectors are usually light detectors that are sensitive to infrared radiation. These detectors are mounted in an electrical circuit that amplifies their voltage enough to initiate a fire-warning signal.

Carbon Monoxide Detectors

Carbon monoxide is a colorless, odorless gas that is a byproduct of incomplete combustion of almost all hydrocarbon fuels and is present in all smoke. It is lethal even in small concentrations, and its presence must be detected early.

CO detectors are not usually used in cargo and baggage compartments as are other smoke detectors, but are used in the cabin and cockpit areas. The most widely used CO detectors are small cards with a transparent pocket containing silica gel crystals that are treated with a chemical that changes color when it is exposed to CO. Normally the crystals are yellow or tan, but when they are exposed to CO, they change color to green or black. The more drastic the change, the higher the content of CO in the air. These small detectors have an adhesive backing that allows them to be attached to the instrument panel, in easy view of the flight crew to warn of the presence of CO. They must be periodically replaced with fresh indicators.

As an aviation mechanic, inspect the CO detectors on a regular basis. If the color has changed significantly, it could be an indication of a dangerous condition caused by an exhaust leak coming through the cabin heat system or from a combustion heater failure.

smoke detector. A device that warns the flight crew of the presence of smoke in cargo and/or baggage compartments. Some smoke detectors are of the visual type, others are photoelectric or ionization devices.

infrared radiation. Electromagnetic radiation whose wavelengths are longer than those of visible light.

carbon monoxide detector. A packet of chemical crystals mounted in the aircraft cockpit or cabin where they are easily visible. The crystals change their color from yellow to green when they are exposed to carbon monoxide.

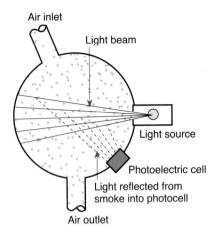

Figure 7-11. *A photoelectric smoke detector allows a current to flow that is proportional to the amount of light refracted by the smoke particles in the detector chamber.*

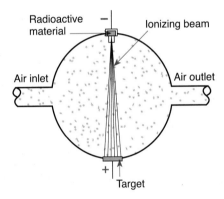

Figure 7-12. *Smoke in the detector chamber of an ionization-type smoke detector lowers the degree of ionization and decreases the current flowing to the external circuit.*

Photoelectric Smoke Detectors

Air from the monitored compartment is drawn through the detector chamber and a light beam is shone on it. A photoelectric cell installed in the chamber senses the light that is refracted by smoke particles. The photocell is installed in a bridge circuit that measures any changes in the amount of current it conducts. When there is no smoke in the air flowing through the chamber, no light is refracted, and the photocell conducts a reference amount of current. When there is smoke in the air, some of the light is refracted and sensed by the photocell, and its conductivity changes, changing the amount of current. These changes in current are amplified and used to initiate a smoke-warning signal. See Figure 7-11.

Ionization-Type Smoke Detectors

Ionization-type smoke detectors work on the basic principle of those detectors found in many homes. A tiny amount of radioactive material is mounted on one side of the detector chamber. This material bombards the oxygen and nitrogen molecules in the air flowing through the chamber and ionizes it to the extent that a reference amount of current can flow across the chamber through the ionized gas to an external circuit. Smoke flowing through the chamber changes the level of ionization and decreases the current. When the current is reduced to a specific amount, the external circuit initiates a smoke-warning signal. See Figure 7-12.

Visual Smoke Detectors

Some jet transport aircraft have visual-type smoke detectors similar to the one in Figure 7-13 installed on the flight engineer's panel. The inside of the chamber is painted nonreflective black, and glass observation windows let the flight engineer see inside the chamber. A light shines across the chamber in such a way that it will illuminate any smoke that is present. Air, pulled from the compartments that are being monitored, flows through the detection chamber. When there is no smoke in this air, no light is visible in the window, but when there is smoke, the light strikes it, and can be seen in the window.

Since no light is visible when there is no smoke, a green indicator light on the front of the detector illuminates to show the flight engineer when the light is on.

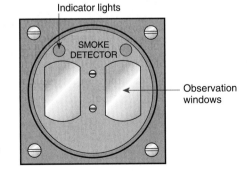

Figure 7-13. *Visual-type smoke indicator allows the flight engineer to actually observe the air sampled from a compartment for traces of smoke.*

Answers are provided on page 441.

1. Three requirements for a fire are:

    a. _____

    b _____

    c. _____

2. A fire that involves solid combustibles such as paper and upholstery is a Class _____ fire.

3. A fire that involves burning metals is a Class _____ fire.

4. A fire that involves energized electrical equipment is a Class _____ fire.

5. A fire that involves liquid fuels such as gasoline and oil is a Class _____ fire.

6. In thermoswitch fire-detection systems using several thermoswitches and a single indicator light, the switches are wired in _____ (series or parallel) with each other, and the entire combination of switches is in _____ (series or parallel) with the light.

7. The fire detection system that can operate properly when there is either an open or a short circuit in either of its two loops is the _____ (single-terminal or two-terminal) thermoswitch system.

8. The fire detection system that initiates a fire warning when there is an excessive rate of temperature rise in the monitored compartment is the _____ (thermocouple or thermoswitch) system.

9. Current flows in a fire-warning thermocouple circuit because of the voltage produced by the difference in the _____ of any of the junctions.

10. The two-conductor continuous-loop fire detector _____ (does or does not) detect a general overheat condition as well as a local hot spot.

11. A pneumatic fire detection system _____ (does or does not) warn of a general overheat condition as well as a fire.

12. Carbon monoxide is usually detected by chemical crystals that change their _____ (color or electrical resistance) when they are exposed to CO.

13. Flame detectors are light detectors that are sensitive to _____ (visual light or infrared radiation).

(continued)

14. Photoelectric smoke detectors are usually used to monitor _____ (engine or cargo) compartments.

15. Some of the air in an ionization-type smoke detector is ionized by a tiny piece of _____ material.

16. The light that actuates a visual smoke indicator _____ (is or is not) visible to the flight crew.

Fire-Extinguishing Systems

Fire protection systems divide themselves logically into two categories: fire detection and fire extinguishing. The fire-extinguishing systems furthermore divide into hand-held and installed systems. Here we will consider the various types of fire-extinguishing agents, then the hand-held extinguishers, and finally, the installed systems.

Fire-Extinguishing Agents

Since fire is the chemical reaction between a fuel with oxygen, it can be controlled by interfering with this reaction. This can involve removing the fuel, smothering the fuel with a substance that excludes the oxygen, or lowering the temperature of the fuel. The most effective method for extinguishing aircraft fires involves using a chemical compound that combines with the oxygen to prevent it from combining with the fuel.

Water

Class A fires can be extinguished with an agent, such as water, that lowers the temperature of the fuel. Small hand-held fire extinguishers contain water that is adequately protected with an antifreeze agent. When the handle of these extinguishers is twisted, the seal in a carbon dioxide (CO_2) cartridge is broken, and the CO_2 pressurizes the water and discharges it in the form of a spray. When the water evaporates and changes from a liquid to a vapor, it absorbs heat from the air above the fire and lowers its temperature enough to cool the burning Class-A fuel enough to cause the fire to go out.

Never use water on Class B, C, or D fires. Most flammable liquids float on water, and the use of water on Class B fires will only spread the fire. Water conducts electricity, and its use on a Class C fire constitutes a definite danger of electrocution. Water sprayed on the burning metal in a Class D fire will actually intensify the fire rather than extinguish it.

Inert Cold Gas Agents

Carbon dioxide (CO_2) and liquid nitrogen (N_2) are both effective fire-extinguishing agents. They both have very low toxicity.

Carbon Dioxide (CO_2)

CO_2 is heavier than air, and when it is sprayed on a fire it remains on the surface and excludes oxygen from the combustion process, and the fire goes out. CO_2 has been a favored extinguishing agent for many years. It is relatively inexpensive, nontoxic, safe to handle, and has a long life in storage.

CO_2 extinguishers are found in almost all maintenance shops, on most flight lines, and in most ground vehicles. Most of the older aircraft had hand-held CO_2 extinguishers mounted in fixtures in the cabins and cockpits and fixed CO_2 extinguishing systems in the engine nacelles. These airborne extinguishers have been replaced in modern aircraft by more efficient types.

Hand-held CO_2 extinguishers can be used to extinguish fires in energized electrical equipment, but they should not be used unless the nozzles are made of a nonconductive material. Fortunately most nozzles are made of pressed nonconductive fiber.

CO_2 is usually a gas, and it is stored in steel bottles under pressure. When it is released, it expands and cools enough to change into a finely divided snow of dry ice.

dry ice. Solidified carbon dioxide. Dry ice sublimates, or changes from a solid directly into a gas, at a temperature of −110°F (−78.5°C).

Dry Chemical Agents

Dry chemical fire extinguishers spray out a very fine powder of sodium bicarbonate (baking soda) $NaHCO_3$, potassium bicarbonate $KHCO_3$, or ammonium phosphate (($NH_4)_3PO_4$) that completely covers the burning fuel and prevents oxygen from reaching the flames.

Dry chemical fire extinguishers can be used on Class A, B, and C, fires. They are effective, but require an extensive clean-up after the fire is extinguished. They are the extinguisher of choice for Class D fires involving burning magnesium metal, such as fires in aircraft brakes.

Liquid Nitrogen (N_2)

N_2 is more effective than CO_2, but because it is a cryogenic liquid, it must be kept in a Dewar bottle. Some military aircraft use N_2 for inerting fuel tanks and have it available for use in fire-extinguishing systems, primarily for use in extinguishing powerplant fires.

cryogenic liquid. A liquid which boils at temperatures of less than about 110°K (−163°C) at normal atmospheric pressures.

Dewar bottle. A vessel designed to hold liquefied gases. It has double walls with the space between being evacuated to prevent the transfer of heat. The surfaces in the vacuum area are made heat-reflective.

Halogenated Hydrocarbons

This classification of fire-extinguishing agents includes the most widely used agents today, as well as some of the agents used in the past that are no longer considered suitable.

These agents are hydrocarbon compounds in which one or more of the hydrogen atoms have been replaced with an atom of one of the halogen elements such as fluorine, chlorine, or bromine.

In the process of combustion, the molecules of the fuel combine with those of oxygen in an orderly fashion, but if one of the halogen compounds is mixed with the oxygen this combination is interrupted and may be stopped entirely; the fire will go out.

One of the earliest halogenated hydrocarbons to find widespread use as a fire-extinguishing agent for use in aircraft was carbon tetrachloride, generally known as carbon tet or by its trade name, Pyrene. When a stream of liquid Pyrene is sprayed on a fire from a hand-pump-type extinguisher, it evaporates and extinguishes the flame. There are serious drawbacks to carbon tet; it is unstable in the temperatures of the flame and it converts into a toxic gas known as phosgene. It also has a harmful cumulative toxic effect on the human body, and so is no longer used as a fire-extinguishing agent nor as a dry-cleaning fluid.

The two most widely used halogenated hydrocarbons are bromotrifluoromethane ($CBrF_3$), widely known as Halon 1301, and bromochlorodifluoromethane ($CBrClF_2$), known as Halon 1211. Both of these compounds, often called by the trade name Freon, have a very low toxicity. Halon 1301 is the least toxic of all commonly used agents. Both are very effective as fire-extinguishing agents. They are noncorrosive, evaporate rapidly, leave no residue, and require no cleanup or neutralization. Halon 1301 does not require any pressurizing agent, but Halon 1211 may be pressurized with nitrogen or with 1301.

Hand-Held Fire Extinguishers

Federal Aviation Regulations Part 135 *Commuter and On-Demand Operations* requires that passenger-carrying aircraft operated under this part have at least one hand-held fire extinguisher located on the flight deck and at least one in the passenger compartment. For years, the most popular extinguishers have been CO_2 type, but modern developments have made Halon 1301 and Halon 1211 the extinguishers of choice. These extinguishing agents are the least toxic of all and they are effective on almost all types of fires likely to be encountered in an aircraft cabin. These extinguishers are available in small, medium, and large sizes. The small extinguishers are adequate for fires of up to one square foot in area, medium extinguishers are adequate for fires up to two square feet in area, and the large sizes are adequate for fires up to five square feet.

Halon 1301. A halogenated hydrocarbon fire-extinguishing agent that is one of the best for extinguishing cabin and powerplant fires. It is highly effective and is the least toxic of the extinguishing agents available. The technical name for Halon 1301 is bromotrifluoromethane.

Halon 1211. A halogenated hydrocarbon fire-extinguishing agent used in many HRD fire-extinguishing systems for powerplant protection. The technical name for Halon 1211 is bromochlorodifluoromethane.

Freon. The registered trade name for many of the halogenated hydrocarbons used as fire extinguishants and refrigerants.

Extinguishers using Halon 1211 use compressed nitrogen for a propellant, but Halon 1301 has enough pressure that it does not require a separate propelling agent. All Halon extinguishers have built-in pressure gauges to indicate the pressure of the extinguishant.

Hand-held CO_2 extinguishers are still used in many aircraft. The two-pound size is usually installed in aircraft cabins. The state of charge of a CO_2 extinguisher is determined by weighing it. The weight of the empty container and nozzle is stamped on the valve.

Dry chemical fire extinguishers use compressed nitrogen to expel a dry powder such as sodium bicarbonate or potassium bicarbonate. Dry chemical is an effective extinguishing agent, but should never be used in an aircraft cockpit in-flight, as the loose powder in the air obstructs visibility.

Installed Fire-Extinguishing Systems

Aircraft use two types of installed fire-extinguishing systems: the CO_2 systems installed in the engine compartments of older aircraft, and the high-rate-discharge (HRD) systems used on most modern jet transport aircraft.

Carbon Dioxide Extinguishing Systems

Installed CO_2 systems were the primary systems for most twin-engine and four-engine transport aircraft up through the World War II era.

CO_2 is carried in steel bottles and is often pressurized with compressed nitrogen to aid in expelling the CO_2 under very low temperature conditions. The bottles have a remotely operated valve and are connected to a selector handle that allows the pilot to select the engine into which the CO_2 will be discharged. When the engine is selected, the T-shaped handle is pulled. The bottle is emptied into the power section of the engine through a perforated aluminum tube that surrounds the engine. Some of the larger systems had two bottles that allowed the pilot to release the second bottle into the fire if it was not extinguished by the first one.

CO_2 systems have two indicator disks, one red and one yellow, located on the outside of the fuselage near the bottles. If the bottles are discharged by the pilot actuating the T-handle, the yellow disk will blow out. If the area around the bottles becomes overheated enough to raise the pressure of the gas to a dangerous level, the red disk will blow out and the system will automatically discharge. On the normal walk-around inspection, the flight crewmember can tell, from these disks, the condition of the CO_2 system.

High-Rate-Discharge (HRD) Extinguishing Systems

Most modern turbine-engine-powered aircraft have their powerplant areas protected by two or more spherical or cylindrical HRD bottles of Halon 1211 or 1301. A charge of compressed nitrogen is usually placed in the container to ensure that the agent is dispersed in the shortest time possible. The containers are sealed with a frangible disk that is broken when a cutter is fired into it by

HRD. High-rate-discharge

frangible. Breakable, or easily broken.

a powder charge, or squib, which is ignited when the pilot closes the agent discharge switch. The entire contents of the bottle are discharged within about 0.08 second after the agent discharge switch is closed.

Figure 7-14 shows a cross-sectional view of a typical spherical HRD bottle. The cartridge is electrically ignited, which drives the cutter into the disk and releases the agent. The strainer prevents any of the broken disk from getting into the distribution system.

The safety plug is connected to a red indicator disk on the outside of the engine compartment. If the temperature of the compartment in which the bottle is mounted rises enough to increase the pressure of the gas to a dangerous level, the safety plug melts and releases the gas. As the gas vents to the atmosphere, it blows out the red indicator disk, showing that the bottle has been discharged because of an overheat condition. If the bottle is discharged by normal operation of the system, a yellow indicator disk blows out. The gauge shows the pressure of the agent and the gas in the container.

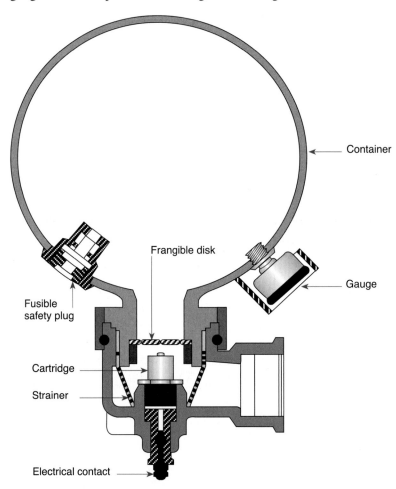

Figure 7-14. *A typical HRD container for protecting an engine compartment.*

Answers are provided on page 441.

17. A water fire extinguisher _____ (should or should not) be used on a burning metal.

18. CO_2 fire extinguishers should not be used on an electrical fire unless the discharge horn is made of a _____ (metal or nonmetallic material).

19. A dry chemical fire-extinguishing agent extinguishes a fire by preventing _____ from reaching the flame.

20. A dry chemical fire extinguisher _____ (is or is not) suitable for extinguishing inflight cockpit fires.

21. The proper fire-extinguishing agent to use to extinguish a fire in an aircraft brake is _____ .

22. A fire-extinguishing agent that is also used to inert fuel tanks is _____ .

23. Carbon tetrachloride is _____ (toxic or nontoxic).

24. The least toxic of all popular fire-extinguishing agents other than water is _____ .

25. The state of charge of a hand-held fire extinguisher may be determined by weighing it. This is true of a _____ (CO_2 or Halon) extinguisher.

26. The state of charge of a hand-held fire extinguisher may be determined by a pressure gauge built into the valve head. This is true of a _____ (CO_2 or Halon) extinguisher.

27. If an installed CO_2 fire-extinguishing system is discharged in the normal manner, the _____ (yellow or red) disk on the outside of the fuselage is blown out.

28. The agent in an HRD container is discharged when the sealing disk is ruptured by a cutter driven by a _____ .

29. The Freon, or Halon, fire-extinguishing agent in an HRD bottle is propelled from the bottle by a charge of compressed _____ .

30. If an HRD fire extinguisher bottle is discharged because of an overheat condition, the _____ (yellow or red) disk on the outside of the fuselage is blown out.

31. Halon 1301 _____ (is or is not) corrosive to aluminum.

Complete Fire Protection System

A complete fire protection system incorporates both the detection and the extinguishing systems. In this section, we will consider the complete fire protection system installed in a typical twin-engine jet transport aircraft.

There are fire/overheat detectors for both engines, fire detectors for the APU and the wheel wells, overheat detectors for the wing/body caused by pneumatic duct leaks, and smoke detectors in the lavatories.

Engine Fire Detection and Extinguishing

Each engine has two gas-pressure type overheat/fire detector loops identified as loop A and loop B, each loop has four detectors, located on the fan case and the engine core section.

If there is a break in one of the loops, the gas will escape and the fault switch in the detector element will open and the amber fault light on the engine fire extinguishing-overheat/fire protection panel will illuminate (Figure 7-15). A general overheat condition in the engine compartment will increase the pressure of the gas in the detector loop enough to close the overheat switch in the detector element and illuminate the amber overheat light on the panel.

If the temperature in the engine compartment increases enough to indicate the presence of a fire, the gas pressure in the detector loop will become great enough to close the fire switch in the fire detector. See Figure 7-16.

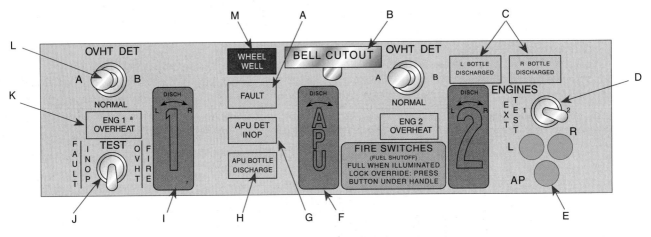

A. Engine detector **FAULT** light (amber)
B. Fire warning **BELL CUTOUT** switch
C. **ENGINE BOTTLE DISCHARGED** lights (amber)
D. **EXTINGUISHER TEST** switch
E. **EXTINGUISHER TEST** lights (green)
F. **APU FIRE WARNING** switch (red)
G. **APU DETECTOR INOP** light (amber)

H. **APU BOTTLE DISCHARGED** light (amber)
I. **ENGINE FIRE WARNING** switch (red) (2)
J. **FAULT/INOP** and **OVHT/FIRE** test switch
K. **ENGINE OVERHEAT** light (amber) (2)
L. **ENGINE OVERHEAT DETECTOR** switch (2)
M. **WHEEL WELL FIRE WARNING LIGHT** (red)

Figure 7-15. *Engine fire extinguishing-overheat fire protection panel.*

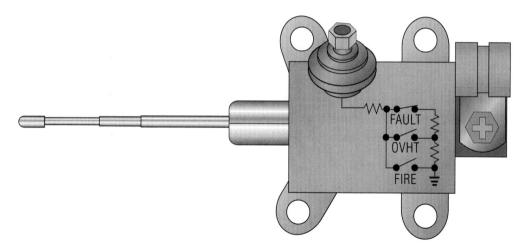

Figure 7-16. *Engine fire detector element.*

This condition activates the aural warning unit to give the bell sound, it illuminates the red light in the engine fire warning switch and the switch handle for that engine unlocks. When this switch handle is pulled, these things happen:

1. Engine fuel shut-off valve is closed

2. Thrust-reverser control power goes off

3. Spar fuel valve closes

4. Power to engine-driven pump low-pressure-warning system goes off

5. Bleed-air valve closes

6. Hydraulic shut-off valve closes

When the fire warning switch handle is turned clockwise, 28-volts DC is sent to the squib in the right fire extinguishing bottle and the powder charge in that squib is ignited. The disk is broken and the Halon extinguishing agent is emptied into the protected area. Turning the switch counterclockwise sends voltage to the left bottle and it releases its Halon gas. When either bottle is emptied, the appropriate bottle-discharged light on the overheat/fire protection panel comes on.

The plumbing that carries the fire extinguishing agent from the bottles to the engines are marked with brown color-coding tape that has a series of diamonds to aid technicians who are color-blind or for use in dim light.

APU Fire Detection and Extinguishing

The APU is protected by its own fire-detection and extinguishing system. When a fire is detected in the APU compartment or near the tailpipe, the aural warning unit produces a bell sound and the red light in the APU fire

APU. Auxiliary power unit.

warning switch illuminates, the switch unlocks, and the APU automatically shuts down. Turning the switch either clockwise or counterclockwise sends voltage to the squib in the APU fire extinguisher bottle. The powder charge is ignited and the Halon gas is released into the APU compartment. When the bottle is discharged, the APU bottle-discharged light on the overheat/fire protection panel illuminates. A fire-warning light in the APU ground control panel in the main wheel well flashes, and the intermittent fire-warning horn sounds. The APU fire extinguisher bottle can also be discharged from the ground control panel. See Figure 7-17.

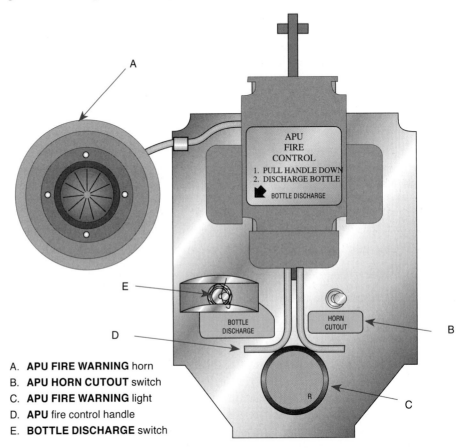

A. **APU FIRE WARNING** horn
B. **APU HORN CUTOUT** switch
C. **APU FIRE WARNING** light
D. **APU** fire control handle
E. **BOTTLE DISCHARGE** switch

Figure 7-17. *APU fire extinguishing ground control panel.*

Lower Cargo Compartment Smoke Detectors and Fire Suppression

The two lower cargo compartments, forward and aft, are protected by smoke detectors and a bottle of nitrogen-pressurized Halon 1301 fire extinguishing agent.

The Cargo Fire Control panel in the cockpit (Figure 7-18) allows the flight crew to monitor the electronic smoke detectors in the two compartments. If smoke is detected, the aural warning unit sounds the alarm and the forward or aft extinguishing circuit may be armed by pressing the appropriate ARM button. Then when the DISCHARGE button is pressed, the squib in the bottle ignites the powder charge that discharges enough Halon into the compartment to protect it for about 60 minutes. When the bottle is discharged, the amber DISCH light comes on.

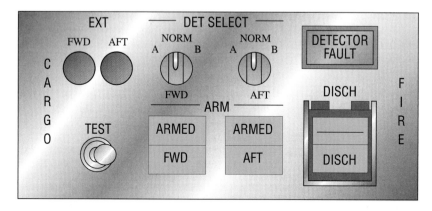

Figure 7-18. *Cargo smoke detection and fire suppression panel.*

Wheel Well Overheat Monitoring

The wheel well is monitored for an overheat condition by a thermistor-type loop detector. If an overheat condition exists, a signal is sent to the compartment overheat detection control module in the electronic equipment compartment. Here a code is generated by the BITE (built-in test equipment) that advises maintenance of the overheat condition. At the same time it illuminates the red WHEEL WELL fire warning light on the overheat/fire protection panel in the cockpit.

Wing and Body Overheat Monitoring

The cargo compartment and air conditioning equipment compartments are monitored with thermistor type detectors for an indication of an overheat condition. If the temperature in these areas rises above about 255°F a signal is sent to the BITE, which generates a code that advises of the condition.

The wing leading edges and engine strut cavities are monitored in the same way to advise that a temperature of greater than about 310°F has been reached.

Lavatory Smoke Detection and Fire Extinguisher

The ever-present danger of some thoughtless passenger disobeying the no-smoking-in-the-lavatory rule and endangering the flight has required the lavatories to be equipped with electronic smoke detectors and fire extinguishers. In case of a fire, the extinguisher sprays the area below the wash basin and in the trash bin area with an inert gas that extinguishes the fire.

When smoke is detected, the red SMOKE DETECT light on the lavatory smoke detector control panel (Figure 7-19) illuminates and the appropriate smoke location indicator comes on notifying the flight crew of the problem.

If a fire exists, eutectic plugs in the extinguisher bottle melt and the inert gas is automatically released. There is a temperature indicator strip near the trash bin that indicates the highest temperature reached at this location.

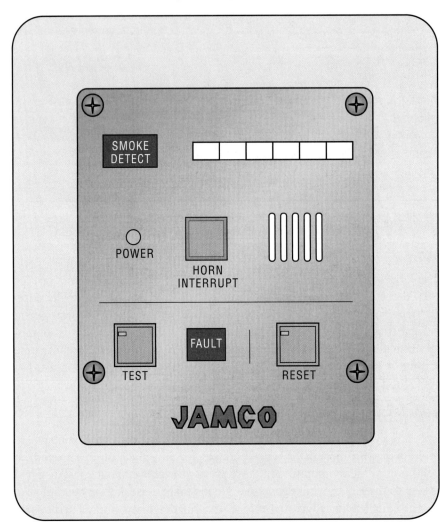

Figure 7-19. *Lavatory smoke detector control panel.*

Maintenance and Servicing of Fire-Detector Systems

The detector elements used in fire and overheat protection systems are precision devices that require special care and attention for their installation and servicing. About the only maintenance required by a fire detection system is replacing damaged sensors and ensuring that all of the wiring is properly supported and in good condition. Detailed system descriptions for specific aircraft, along with inspection, maintenance, and servicing instructions, will be found in the aircraft maintenance manual.

Operational checks for detection of smoke, toxic fumes, overheat, fire, and fire-protection systems are normally accomplished through built-in test functions. Pressing the test button checks the continuity of the system and activates the alarm signal and indicator lights. Aircraft maintenance instructions will detail the operation, maintenance, and inspection for each of these systems. Some systems, such as cargo bay smoke detectors, are in multiple locations throughout the aircraft and should be inspected to make sure that the inlets are not blocked and allow air to freely pass to them.

The sensors used in the continuous-loop-type systems are particularly subject to damage from careless handling during routine engine maintenance. They should be carefully checked for dented, kinked, or crushed sections, as any damage of this type can cause a false fire warning. When replacing continuous-loop sensor elements, be sure to follow the instructions in the aircraft service manual in detail. Support the elements as shown in the service manual and be sure to maintain the required clearance between the elements and the aircraft structure.

The locations for all of the components in a fire detection system have been chosen with special care by the engineers of the aircraft manufacturer, and all the components must be maintained in the exact location specified. Detectors actuate at different temperatures, and it is especially important to use only detectors with the correct part number when replacing one.

Some of the specific items to inspect are:

1. Check for abrasion of the loop caused by the elements rubbing on the cowling, accessories, or structural members.

2. Be sure that there are no pieces of safety wire or metal particles that could short-circuit a spot detector.

3. Be sure that no rubber grommets in the mounting clamps have an indication of damage from oil or overheating, and be sure that all grommets are properly installed. The slit in the grommet should face the outside of the nearest bend to prevent the element from chafing on the clamp. See Figure 7-20.

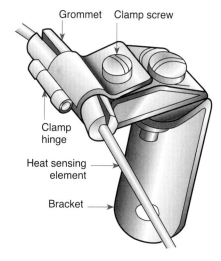

Figure 7-20. *Typical fire-detector loop clamp showing the correct way of installing the grommet.*

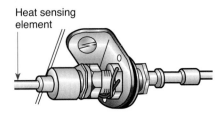

Figure 7-21. *Correct attachment of a fire-detector loop to the aircraft structure.*

4. Check for loose nuts or broken safety wire at the ends of the sensing elements. Follow the manufacturer's instructions regarding the torque to use and the types of washers, if any, that are to be used. See Figure 7-21.

5. replacing a thermocouple sensor, be sure that the wires are connected to the proper terminal of the sensor. The fact that the two elements of the thermocouple are made of different metals makes this important.

Troubleshooting Fire-Detection Systems

In order to effectively troubleshoot a fire-detection system, you must first understand the system that you are working on. After understanding the system, the next step is to use the troubleshooting procedures provided by the manufacturer.

The following procedures are general guidelines that can be used in most systems and go hand-in-hand with the inspection items listed earlier in this section.

1. Intermittent alarms can be a challenge to find and are often found by applying pressure to different components in the system to see if you can re-create the problem. Check for loose connections and loose clamps that might allow wires or sensing elements to short out.

2. Inspect for kinks in the detection loop. If there is a kink, carefully unbend the kink and see if the problem goes away. Even if the problem does go away, there is a chance that there was internal damage to the loop and the problem will return. If the problems returns, replace the section of the loop with the suspected damage.

3. False alarms can be isolated to the major sections of the system. Disconnect the sensing loop from the control box. If the alarm still sounds, the problem is in the control box. If the alarm goes away, the problem is in the sense loop. If the sense loop has multiple sections, disconnect the sections from each other and then reconnect them one at a time until the alarm sounds. This will isolate the problem to one section of the loop.

4. If the test switch on the control box does not cause the alarm to sound, there are several possibilities to check out. First, check that the control unit is receiving power and that the sense loop is connected. If so, disconnect the loop and check the resistance of the loop detector element. If it is a single conductor loop, there should be no continuity between the center conductor and the outer tube. If it is a two-conductor loop, there should be no continuity between the two wires. If no fault is found after these steps, the control unit itself may be faulty or the test switch may have malfunctioned.

Maintenance and Servicing of Fire-Extinguishing Systems

Bottles of fire-extinguishing agent must be kept fully charged. Most of these bottles have gauges mounted directly on them. The pressure of the agent varies with its temperature, and for this pressure to be meaningful, a correction must be made. Figure 7-22 is a typical chart showing the allowable limits for the indicated pressure. If the pressure falls outside of the allowable range, the container must be removed and replaced with one that is properly charged.

To find the allowable pressure range for an agent temperature of 33°F, see Figure 7-22.

For this problem, we must interpolate:

Between 30° and 40°F (an increase of 10 degrees) the minimum pressure changes from 209 to 230 psi, an increase of 21 psi. That works out to be a 2.1 psi per degree of temperature rise. With the same temperature rise, the maximum pressure changes from 295 to 317 psi, or 22 psi. This is 2.2 psi per degree of temperature rise.

For 33 degrees, the minimum pressure would be 215.3 psi (209 + 6.3), and the maximum pressure would be 301.6 psi (295 + 6.6).

When inspecting a fire-extinguishing system, check all components for security of attachment and proper servicing. Check agent bottles for correct pressure and for the presence of the red and yellow discharge indicator disks. Check the date of the last hydrostatic pressure test of the agent bottles. Aircraft-mounted fire-extinguishing bottles must be hydrostatically tested every five years.

The discharge cartridges for an HRD container are life-limited components, and the replacement date is calculated from the date stamped on the cartridge. To inspect the cartridge for expiration, it is necessary to remove the cartridge from the discharge valve. To access the cartridge, remove the electrical leads and discharge line to gain access to the discharge valve. The service life of the cartridge is specified by the manufacturer in years and is measured from the date of manufacture.

Fire extinguisher discharge cartridges are not normally interchangeable between valves. The distance the contact point protrudes from the cartridge may vary from one cartridge to another, and care must be taken if a cartridge is removed from the discharge valve that the correct cartridge is reinstalled in the valve. If the wrong cartridge is used, there is a possibility that there will not be electrical continuity.

It is extremely important when checking the electrical connections to the container to use the recommendations of the manufacturer. Make sure that the current used to test the wiring is less than that required to detonate the squib.

When working on fire-extinguishing systems, and in the areas where an accidental discharge would dispense the fire-extinguishing agent, it is recommended that the mechanic wear adequate personal protective equipment (PPE). At a minimum, this includes a respirator mask and a face shield.

Container Pressure Versus Temperature

Temperature °F	Container Pressure (PSIG)	
	Minimum	Maximum
-40	60	145
-30	83	465
-20	105	188
-10	125	210
0	145	230
10	167	252
20	188	275
30	209	295
40	230	317
50	255	342
60	284	370
70	319	405
80	356	443
90	395	483
100	438	523

Figure 7-22. *Fire extinguisher pressure/ temperature chart.*

Answers are provided on page 441.

32. Six things that are done when the fire-warning switch handle in the cockpit is pulled are:

    a. _____

    b. _____

    c. _____

    d. _____

    e. _____

    f. _____

33. The fire-extinguishing agent _____ (is or is not) discharged when the fire-warning switch handle is pulled.

34. The tubing that carries fire-extinguishing agents is color coded with a stripe of _____ (what color) tape and a series of _____ (what symbol).

35. Maintenance of a fire detection system consists of _____ (repair or replacement) of damaged components.

36. Based on the chart in Figure 7-22, the allowable range of agent pressure at a temperature of 85°F is _____ to _____ psig.

37. If the pressure gauge on an HRD bottle shows that the container pressure is too low for the existing temperature, the mechanic must _____ (replace or refill) the container.

38. Fire extinguisher discharge cartridges _____ (are or are not) normally interchangeable between valves.

Answers to Chapter 7 Study Questions

1. a. fuel
    b. oxygen
    c. high enough temperature
2. A
3. D
4. C
5. B
6. parallel; series
7. two-terminal
8. thermocouple
9. temperature
10. does
11. does
12. color
13. infrared radiation
14. cargo
15. radioactive

16. is not
17. should not
18. nonmetallic material
19. oxygen
20. is not
21. dry chemical
22. nitrogen
23. toxic
24. Halon 1301
25. CO2
26. Halon
27. yellow
28. powder charge
29. nitrogen
30. red
31. is not

32. a. Engine fuel shut-off valve is closed
    b. Thrust-reverser control power goes off
    c. Spar fuel valve closes
    d. Power to engine-driven pump low-pressure-warning system goes off
    e. Bleed-air valve closes
    f. Hydraulic shut-off valve closes
33. is not
34. brown, diamonds
35. replacement
36. 376, 463
37. replace
38. are not

AIRCRAFT INSPECTION

8

Inspections

Inspection is one of the most important functions of an aviation mechanic. As aircraft grow in complexity, it becomes more important to detect any possible trouble before it gets serious. To assist the mechanic in this important function, aircraft manufacturers furnish a detailed inspection check list in the service manual for each aircraft. In addition, the Federal Aviation Administration has listed in Appendix D of 14 CFR Part 43 *Maintenance, Preventive Maintenance, Rebuilding, and Alteration,* the scope and detail of items to be included in annual and 100-hour inspections. Appendix E of this same regulation gives the requirements for altimeter system tests and inspections, and Appendix F gives the requirements for ATC transponder tests and inspections.

The *General* textbook of this Aviation Mechanic Series covers the requirements for the various inspections, primarily from the legal standpoint. It discusses the authorization needed to conduct the inspections, how often they must be conducted, and what records must be kept. In this section of the *Airframe* text, we want to look at inspections from the practical standpoint and refer you to the *General* text for the legal implications.

Required Inspections

We will consider the inspections in order of their complexity, from the preflight inspection to some of the special inspections, and finally to inspections that involve the entire aircraft.

Preflight Inspection

preflight inspection. A required inspection to determine the condition of the aircraft for the flight to be conducted. It is conducted by the pilot-in-command.

The preflight inspection is not a maintenance inspection, but many pilots do not know how to give an aircraft a good preflight. You may be able to help a pilot learn just what to look for. The inspection described here is typical for light airplanes, and should always be modified to agree with the information furnished in the pilot's operating handbook for the particular aircraft.

Preflight Inspection Sequence

1. Begin the inspection inside the cabin. Check to be sure the ignition switch or magneto switches are OFF, and the flight controls are unlocked. Turn the master switch ON and check the indication of the fuel quantity indicator. Turn the master switch OFF, and be sure that the avionics master switch is OFF so the sensitive electronic equipment will not be damaged during the engine start procedure.

   Check to be sure that the proper paperwork is in the aircraft and that the aircraft has been inspected within the required time interval for the type of inspection under which it is operating. There should be a current registration certificate, a certificate of airworthiness, and a radio-station license. If the aircraft is not operating for hire, it should

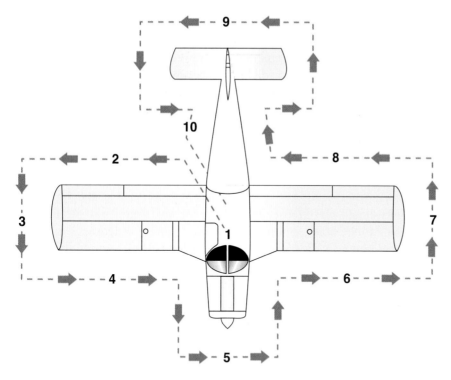

Figure 8-1. *Recommended preflight walk-around inspection of a small training airplane.*

have had an annual inspection within the past 12 months. If it is operating for hire, it should also have had a 100-hour inspection within the past 100 hours of operation or evidence of being operated under a progressive inspection system.

2. Walk along the trailing edge of the right wing and check the flap and aileron. The flap should be in its fully up position and there should be no looseness that could indicate worn attachment fittings. You should be able to move the aileron through its full travel without any binding or any unusual noise. The aileron should not be loose on its hinges, which would indicate worn hinges or hinge bolts. If the bolt that connects the control cable to the aileron horn is visible, it should be checked for proper safety. Check the cable to be sure that its fitting pivots freely on the horn.

3. Walk around the wing tip and check it for any indication of "hangar rash." The wing tip light should be secure and show no indication of damage.

4. Walk along the leading edge and check top and bottom for any indication of dents or damage. There should be no dirt or anything that could disrupt the smooth airflow over the top of the wing. Remove the chain, cable, or rope used to tie the aircraft down.

   Drain a sample of fuel from the fuel tank quick-drain. This fuel should be clean and free from any trace of water, and its color should

control horn. The arm on a control surface to which the control cable or push-pull rod attaches to move the surface.

hangar rash. Scrapes, bends, and dents in an aircraft structure caused by careless handling.

indicate that it is of the grade specified for the aircraft. Grade 100 fuel is green, 100-low lead is blue, and grade 80 is red. Dispose of this fuel sample using whatever method is allowed by the airport.

Remove the fuel cap and look at the amount of fuel in the tank. Fuel gauges are not known for their accuracy, and this is the one chance the pilot has to be absolutely positive of the amount of fuel in the tanks. Be sure to replace the fuel cap properly.

Check the condition of the landing gear. Most fixed-gear airplanes have wheel pants installed, so you will not be able to inspect the tire thoroughly, but check it to see that its inflation appears to be proper. The shock strut should have several inches of piston visible, and the torsion links should not be loose, indicating excessive wear. The hydraulic line going to the brake should show no sign of wear or leakage, and there should be no indication of leaking hydraulic fluid around the brake. The wheel pant should be secure, with no cracks or looseness. There should be no mud that could interfere with the wheel.

5. Walk around the nose of the aircraft. Check the windshield for cleanliness and for any indication of cracks, scratches, or other damage.

Check the engine oil quantity, and be sure the dipstick is properly secured. Check as much of the engine as is visible for any indication of oil or fuel leakage, or anything that may be loose. Check the air inlets for any kind of obstruction. If the aircraft has been tied down outside for any length of time, check especially for any indication of bird nests that have been built inside the cowling.

Drain a sample of fuel from the main strainer and check it for indication of water.

If it is winter, check the end of the crankcase breather to be sure it is not clogged with ice.

Check the propeller and spinner. There should be no nicks or pits along the leading edge of the blades, and there should be no looseness in the spinner. Propeller spinner bulkheads are noted for cracking and they should be checked for any indication of cracks or missing screws.

Check the nosewheel. There should be no looseness or cracks in the wheel pant, and the torsion links and the shimmy damper should show no indication of excessive looseness or wear. The shock strut should show the proper amount of extension, and when the nose is depressed, the strut should return to its original extension.

6., 7. and 8. Walk around the left wing, noting the same things as on the right wing. On many airplanes, the stall warning pickup is in the leading edge of the left wing. Check this for freedom and proper operation.

9. Walk around the empennage. Check the movable surfaces for freedom of movement and for any indication of looseness or wear. Remove the tail tie-down.

    Pay particular attention to the trim tab or stabilizer adjustment mechanism. Trim tab hinges are subject to a good deal of wear, and worn tab hinges can allow the tab to flutter.

    Check the ELT antenna for security of mounting.

10. Check the baggage compartment to ensure that there is nothing in it that should not be there, and that everything in the compartment is properly secured. Check to see that the door closes and locks securely so it will not cause any airflow distortion.

    When you return to the cockpit, check all of the controls for freedom of movement, and be sure that when the wheel is rotated to the left, the left aileron moves up and the right aileron moves down. When the wheel is pulled back, the trailing edge of the movable surface should move up. The flaps should move smoothly through their entire range of travel. The trim tab should operate smoothly and the indicator should show its position. It should be positioned correctly for takeoff. When the master switch is turned on, the electric gyros should begin to spin up without any excessive noise. When the radio is turned on, tune it to 121.5 MHz temporarily to be sure the ELT has not been inadvertently triggered into operation.

    The seat belts and shoulder harness should be in good condition, and the cabin door should close tightly and the door lock should operate freely.

Special Inspections

You must give special inspections to any aircraft that has experienced a rough or overweight landing or flown into severe turbulence. Inspect the powerplant according to the manufacturer's recommendations after a propeller strike or a sudden stoppage. These inspections are described in the *Powerplant* textbook of the Aviation Mechanic Series.

If an aircraft has experienced a rough or overweight landing, jack it up and inspect the entire landing gear for damage. Remove the tires and check the wheels by eddy current inspection, especially in the bead seat area. Check the inside of the tires for any indication of broken cords.

If the aircraft has flown through severe turbulence, check the entire structure for any indication of deformation or cracks. Check the skins for any waviness and the rows of rivets for any indication of rivets that have tipped. You'll need to do further in-depth inspection if you find any of these problems.

Altimeters and Static Systems

14 CFR §91.411 specifies that no person may operate an airplane or helicopter in controlled airspace under Instrument Flight Rules unless, within the preceding 24 calendar months, each static pressure system, each altimeter instrument, and each automatic pressure altitude reporting system has been tested and inspected and found to comply with the provisions of 14 CFR Part 43, Appendix E.

Static System Check

The check of the static system is described in 14 CFR §25.1325. It may be conducted by a certificated mechanic holding an Airframe rating (14 CFR §91.411(b)(3)).

For unpressurized aircraft, the static air system is evacuated to a pressure of one inch of mercury or until the altimeter indicates an increase of 1,000 feet. The pressure is trapped and held for one minute, and the altimeter should not change its indication by more than 100 feet.

For pressurized aircraft, the system is evacuated to a pressure that is equal to the maximum certificated cabin differential pressure. This is held for one minute, and the altimeter should not change its indication by more than 2% of the equivalent altitude of the maximum cabin differential pressure, or 100 feet, whichever is greater.

An air bulb like the one in Figure 8-2 can generate an adequate source of suction to check the static system. You can obtain the bulb, which is the type used for measuring blood pressure, and the thick-walled surgical tubing from a surgical supply company.

To perform the static system check on an unpressurized aircraft, follow these steps:

1. Seal off one of the static ports with pressure-sensitive tape. Black electrical tape is good for this purpose because it is highly visible, and you are not likely to forget and leave it in place when the check is completed. Do not use transparent tape, because it is too easy to forget to remove it.

2. Check the alternate static source valve to be sure that it is in the closed, or normal, position.

3. Squeeze the air bulb (see Figure 8-2) to expel as much air as possible and hold the suction hose firmly against the static port opening.

4. Slowly release the bulb to apply suction to the system until the altimeter shows an increase of 1,000 feet. (On a pressurized aircraft, this increase must be the altitude equivalent of the maximum cabin differential pressure for which the aircraft is certificated.)

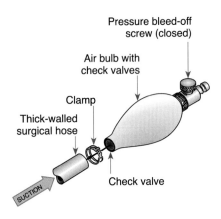

Figure 8-2. *Equipment for checking an instrument static system for leaks.*

5. Pinch the hose tightly to trap the suction in the system and hold it for one minute. The altimeter should not change its indication more than 100 feet. (The altimeter indication in a pressurized aircraft is allowed to change 2% of the altitude increase used for the test).

6. If the altimeter does not change its indication more than the allowable amount, carefully tilt the hose away from the static port, allowing air to enter the system slowly.

7. Remove the tape from the unused static port.

The altimeter or automatic pressure altitude reporting equipment must be checked by the manufacturer of the airplane or helicopter or by a certificated repair station properly equipped and approved for this procedure.

The tests specified in 14 CFR Part 43, Appendix E are:

- Scale error to the maximum normally expected operating altitude of the aircraft

- Hysteresis

- After effect

- Friction

- Case leak

- Barometric scale error

ATC Transponder

An aircraft's ATC transponder must be inspected once every 24 calendar months according to the requirements in 14 CFR Part 43, Appendix F. These inspections must be conducted by a certificated repair station having the proper equipment and approved for this specific function.

The tests specified in 14 CFR Part 43, Appendix F are:

- Radio reply frequency

- Suppression

- Receiver sensitivity

- Radio-frequency peak output power

- Mode S diversity transmission channel isolation

- Mode S address

- Mode S formats

- Mode S all-call interrogations

- ATCRBS-only all-call interrogations

- Squitter

Major Inspections

The FAA requires all certificated aircraft to have a major inspection on a periodic basis. These inspections are all similar in content but differ in how often they are performed and in who is authorized to perform them.

The FAA requires in 14 CFR § 43.15 that each annual and 100-hour inspection be conducted by following a checklist. This checklist may be compiled by the mechanic performing the inspection or may be one furnished by the manufacturer of the aircraft. Progressive inspections require a description of the work to be done, and this description must be followed in detail. All of these inspections must include at least all of the items listed in Appendix D of 14 CFR Part 43, which are reproduced in Figure 8-3.

You can substitute a progressive inspection for the annual and 100-hour inspection under certain conditions.

Large airplanes, turbojet multi-engine airplanes, turbopropeller-powered multi-engine airplanes, and turbine-powered rotorcraft must be inspected on an inspection program similar to that used by air carriers.

These programs are adapted to the aircraft and to the specific conditions under which they operate, and they may be taken from:

1. The continuous airworthiness inspection program currently in use by an air carrier operating under 14 CFR Part 121, 127, or 135.

2. An aircraft inspection program approved for a carrier operating under 14 CFR Part 135.

3. A current inspection program recommended by the aircraft manufacturer.

4. Any other inspection program established by the registered owner or operator and approved by the Administrator.

Annual Inspection

All aircraft operating under 14 CFR Part 91, except large and turbine-powered multi-engine airplanes and those operating under a progressive inspection, must have an annual inspection and be approved for return to service once every 12 calendar months. The requirements for these inspections are covered in 14 CFR §91.409.

An annual inspection is identical to a 100-hour inspection except that it must be conducted by an aviation mechanic who holds an Inspection Authorization (IA). The aviation mechanic conducting a 100-hour inspection does not need to hold an Inspection Authorization.

If an annual inspection has expired, the aircraft can be flown to a point where the inspection can be conducted only if the FAA issues a special flight permit for the flight.

---

air carrier. An organization or person involved in the business of transporting people or cargo by air for compensation or hire.

Continuous Airworthiness Inspection Program. An inspection program that is part of a continuous airworthiness maintenance program approved for certain large airplanes (to which 14 CFR Part 125 is not applicable), turbojet multi-engine airplanes, turbopropeller-powered multi-engine airplanes, and turbine-powered rotorcraft.

Inspection Authorization (IA). An authorization that may be issued to an experienced aviation mechanic who holds both an Airframe and Powerplant rating. It allows the holder to conduct annual inspections and to approve an aircraft or aircraft engine for return to service after a major repair or major alteration.

APPENDIX D—Scope and Detail of Items (as Applicable to the Particular Aircraft) to be Included in Annual and 100-Hour Inspections

(a) Each person performing an annual or 100-hour inspection shall, before that inspection, remove or open all necessary inspection plates, access doors, fairing, and cowling. He shall thoroughly clean the aircraft and aircraft engine.

(b) Each person performing an annual or 100-hour inspection shall inspect (where applicable) the following components of the fuselage and hull group:

(1) *Fabric and skin*—for deterioration, distortion, other evidence of failure, and defective or insecure attachment of fittings.

(2) *Systems and components*—for improper installation, apparent defects, and unsatisfactory operation.

(3) *Envelope, gas bags, ballast tanks, and related parts*—for poor condition.

(c) Each person performing an annual or 100-hour inspection shall inspect (where applicable) the following components of the cabin and cockpit group:

(1) *Generally*—for uncleanliness and loose equipment that might foul the controls.

(2) *Seats and safety belts*—for poor condition and apparent defect.

(3) *Windows and windshields*—for deterioration and breakage.

(4) *Instruments*—for poor condition, mounting, marking, and (where practicable) improper operation.

(5) *Flight and engine controls*—for improper installation and improper operation.

(6) *Batteries*—for improper installation and improper charge.

(7) *All systems*—for improper installation, poor general condition, apparent and obvious defects, and insecurity of attachment.

(d) Each person performing an annual or 100-hour inspection shall inspect (where applicable) components of the engine and nacelle group as follows:

(1) *Engine section*—for visual evidence of excessive oil, fuel, or hydraulic leaks, and sources of such leaks.

(2) *Studs and nuts*—for improper torquing and obvious defects.

(3) *Internal engine*—for cylinder compression and for metal particles or foreign matter on screens and sump drain plugs. If there is weak cylinder compression, for improper internal condition and improper internal tolerances.

(4) *Engine mount*—for cracks, looseness of mounting, and looseness of engine to mount.

(5) *Flexible vibration dampeners*—for poor condition and deterioration.

(6) *Engine controls*—for defects, improper travel, and improper safetying.

(7) *Lines, hoses, and clamps*—for leaks, improper condition and looseness.

(8) *Exhaust stacks*—for cracks, defects, and improper attachment.

(9) *Accessories*—for apparent defects in security of mounting.

(10) *All systems*—for improper installation, poor general condition, defects, and insecure attachment.

(11) *Cowling*—for cracks, and defects.

(e) Each person performing an annual or 100-hour inspection shall inspect (where applicable) the following components of the landing gear group:

(1) *All units*—for poor condition and insecurity of attachment.

(2) *Shock absorbing devices*—for improper oleo fluid level.

(3) *Linkages, trusses, and members*—for undue or excessive wear fatigue, and distortion.

(4) *Retracting and locking mechanism*—for improper operation.

(5) *Hydraulic lines*—for leakage.

(6) *Electrical system*—for chafing and improper operation of switches.

(7) *Wheels*—for cracks, defects, and condition of bearings.

(8) *Tires*—for wear and cuts.

(9) *Brakes*—for improper adjustment.

(10) *Floats and skis*—for insecure attachment and obvious or apparent defects.

(f) Each person performing an annual or 100-hour inspection shall inspect (where applicable) all components of the wing and center section assembly for poor general condition, fabric or skin deterioration, distortion, evidence of failure, and insecurity of attachment.

(g) Each person performing an annual or 100-hour inspection shall inspect (where applicable) all components and systems that make up the complete empennage assembly for poor general condition, fabric or skin deterioration, distortion, evidence of failure, insecure attachment, improper component installation, and improper component operation.

(h) Each person performing an annual or 100-hour inspection shall inspect (where applicable) the following components of the propeller group:

(1) *Propeller assembly*—for cracks, nicks, binds, and oil leakage.

(2) *Bolts*—for improper torquing and lack of safetying.

(3) *Anti-icing devices*—for improper operations and obvious defects.

(4) *Control mechanisms*—for improper operation, insecure mounting, and restricted travel.

(i) Each person performing an annual or 100-hour inspection shall inspect (where applicable) the following components of the radio group:

(1) *Radio and electronic equipment*—for improper installation and insecure mounting.

(2) *Wiring and conduits*—for improper routing, insecure mounting, and obvious defects.

(3) *Bonding and shielding*—for improper installation and poor condition.

(4) *Antenna including trailing antenna*—for poor condition, insecure mounting, and improper operation.

(j) Each person performing an annual or 100-hour inspection shall inspect (where applicable) each installed miscellaneous item that is not otherwise covered by this listing for improper installation and improper operation.

Figure 8-3. *Items that must be checked on each annual, 100-hour, or progressive inspection. This is Appendix D of 14 CFR Part 43.*

One-Hundred-Hour Inspection

All aircraft operated for hire and all aircraft used for flight instruction for hire are required by 14 CFR §91.409(b) to have a complete inspection once every 100 hours of flight. This inspection, which includes both the airframe and the powerplant, is identical to the annual inspection except that it may be performed by an aviation mechanic who holds both Airframe and Powerplant ratings, but it does not require an Inspection Authorization (IA).

An annual inspection can take the place of a required 100-hour inspection, and each 100-hour inspection can be used as an annual inspection if it is conducted by a mechanic holding an Inspection Authorization.

The 100-hour limitation can be exceeded by not more than 10 hours while en route to a place where the inspection can be performed. But if the time is extended, the extension must be subtracted from the time to the next inspection. If an inspection is due at 1,200 hours, but at this time the airplane is away from its home base, it has until 1,210 hours, if needed, to reach the place where the inspection can be performed. The excess time used must be included in the time for the next 100-hour inspection. If the inspection was performed at 1,208 hours, the next 100-hour inspection would still be due at 1,300 hours.

Progressive Inspection

progressive inspection. An inspection that may be used in place of an annual or 100-hour inspection. It has the same scope as an annual inspection, but it may be performed in increments so the aircraft will not have to be out of service for a lengthy period of time.

downtime. Any time during which an aircraft is out of commission and unable to be operated.

Progressive inspections may be used instead of annual and 100-hour inspections to keep the downtime to a minimum while performing the inspection. The inspection is conducted in small increments under an approved schedule that will ensure that the complete inspection equivalent to an annual inspection is completed within a period of 12 calendar months.

To put an aircraft on a progressive inspection program, the owner or operator must submit a written request to the local FAA Flight Standards District Office (FSDO). This request must include:

1. The name of the certificated mechanic holding an Inspection Authorization who will supervise or conduct the progressive inspection;

2. A detailed inspection procedures manual including:

   a. An explanation of the progressive inspection, including the continuity of inspection responsibility, the making of reports and the keeping of records, and technical reference materials,

   b. An inspection schedule, specifying the interval in hours or days when routine and detailed inspections will be performed and including instructions for exceeding an inspection interval by not more than 10 hours while en route, and for changing an inspection interval because of service experience, and

   c. Sample routine and detailed inspection forms and instructions for their use;

3. Description of the housing and equipment for disassembly and proper inspection of the aircraft; and

4. Statement that the appropriate current technical information for the aircraft is available.

The frequency and detail of the progressive inspection must ensure that the aircraft, at all times, will be airworthy and will conform to all applicable FAA Aircraft Specifications, Type Certificate Data Sheets, Airworthiness Directives, and other approved data.

If the progressive inspection is discontinued, the owner or operator must immediately notify the local FAA FSDO in writing of the discontinuance. After discontinuance, the first annual inspection is due within 12 calendar months after the last complete inspection under the progressive program. If 100-hour inspections are required, they are required based upon the date the annual inspection was completed.

Large Aircraft Inspections

Large airplanes, turbojet multi-engine airplanes, turbopropeller-powered multi-engine airplanes, and turbine-powered rotorcraft operated under 14 CFR Part 91 must be inspected on an inspection program specified in 14 CFR §91.409 (e) and (f). This inspection program is not the same as the progressive inspection described in 14 CFR §43.15(d).

These programs are adapted to the aircraft and to the specific conditions under which they operate, and they may be taken from:

1. The continuous airworthiness inspection program currently in use by an air carrier operating under 14 CFR Part 121, 127, or 135;

2. An aircraft inspection program approved for a carrier operating under 14 CFR Part 135;

3. A current inspection program recommended by the aircraft manufacturer; or

4. Any other inspection program established by the registered owner or operator and approved by the Administrator.

The Conduct of an Annual or 100-Hour Inspection

All annual, 100-hour, and progressive inspections begin with an examination of the aircraft records, a survey of the appropriate maintenance information, the actual inspection of the aircraft, and the completion of the required records. Here, we will examine each of these steps.

Type Certificate Data Sheets (TCDS). The official specifications of an aircraft, engine, or propeller issued by the Federal Aviation Administration.

TCDS lists pertinent specifications for the device, and it is the responsibility of the mechanic and/or inspector to ensure, on each inspection, that the device meets these specifications.

Airworthiness Directive (AD note). A notice sent out by the FAA to the registered owner of an aircraft notifying him or her of an unsafe condition that has been found on his aircraft. Compliance with AD notes is compulsory.

Examination of the Aircraft Records

All the aircraft records must be examined, and these include:

- Type of inspection program and time since last inspection;

- Total time on the airframe;

- Current status of life-limited parts;

- Time since last overhaul of parts required to be overhauled on a specific time basis;

- List of current major alterations to the airframe, engine, propeller, rotor, or any appliance;

- Status of any applicable Airworthiness Directives. This must show the date and method of compliance, and if it is a recurring AD, the date the next compliance is required; and

- Determine if additional inspections or service items are due during the inspection. Certain airframe inspections may be at longer time frame intervals (such at 600 hours or 1,000 hours) or based on engine cycles. Other inspection items are based on calendar inspections, such as every 5 years.

These records may be in the form of a logbook or some other method that has been approved by the FAA. Keeping these records on computers is a modern practice.

Survey of Maintenance Information

The Type Certificate Data Sheets for the aircraft, engine, and propeller must be available to allow the mechanic to be sure the aircraft adheres to its specifications for certification.

All the Airworthiness Directives that apply to the aircraft, engine, propeller, and all appliances must be researched. It is extremely important that no applicable AD be missed, and with the large number of ADs currently issued, it is wise to subscribe to a service that compiles all the ADs and service bulletins and makes them available in the form of loose-leaf record books, microfiche, or computer data.

Check Airworthiness Alerts and manufacturer's service bulletins and letters to find out whether or not the aircraft needs special attention in any area.

Some equipment may have been installed according to a Supplemental Type Certificate (STC). The installation must conform to the data furnished with the STC.

life-limited parts. Life-limited parts are those that require replacement after a set number of flight hours or cycles. Refer to manufacturer's instructions on the proper recording of cycles, which may refer to takeoffs and landings or engine starts, or a combination of both.

Airworthiness Alert. A notice sent by the FAA to certain interested maintenance personnel, identifying problems with aircraft gathered from Malfunction and Defect Reports. These problems are being studied at the time the Airworthiness Alert is issued but have not been fully evaluated at the time the material went to press.

Supplemental Type Certificate (STC). An approval issued by the FAA for a modification to a type certificated airframe, engine, or component.

More than one type certificate can be issued for the same basic alteration to a type certificated product (aircraft, engine, or propeller), but each holder must prove to the FAA that the alteration meets all of the requirements of the original type certificate.

Inspection of the Aircraft

Before starting the actual inspection, run up the engine to check the operation of all its systems and to get warm fresh oil covering the cylinder walls for the compression test. Check every airframe control for proper operation and operate all systems to detect any problems that may need correction.

Follow the written checklist specified for the aircraft. This list must include at least all of the items listed in 14 CFR Part 43, Appendix D. This is the information in Figure 8-3. (See page 451.) The requirements for a powerplant inspection are covered in the *Powerplant* textbook of the Aviation Mechanic Series.

Always follow the manufacturer's instructions as written and do not add or take away from the scope of the inspections that are provided. Adding to the specified instructions can lead to over-inspecting beyond what was intended and conversely, taking away from the scope will cause intended inspection items to be missed entirely.

The primary method of detecting problems is through careful visual inspection. Visual inspection may be enhanced with a bright light and magnifying lens. Suspected discrepancies such as cracks can be explored further by taking a clear digital picture and then zooming in on the picture to enlarge details.

The more important airframe items to be checked on a typical high-performance single-engine airplane during an annual, 100-hour, or progressive inspection are listed here with notes showing some of the things to look for.

Fuel System

1. **Fuel strainers.** Drain all fuel strainers, clean the bowls and filters, and replace them. Pressure-check the system for leaks. Safety the filters.

2. **Fuel sump drains.** Drain a quantity of fuel from all of the tank and system sump drains. Check the drained fuel for indications of water or other contaminants. Check the drain for leakage.

3. **Fuel selector valve and placards.** Check for freedom of movement of the selector valve control. Determine that there is a definite feel for the valve in each position. There should be no indication of fuel leakage around the selector valve or the lines attached to it. All the required placards should be installed and legible.

4. **Auxiliary fuel pump.** This pump should operate properly with no indication of leaks. The electric wires going to the pump should be properly supported and in good condition.

5. **Engine-driven fuel pump.** This pump should be securely mounted on the engine with no indication of oil leaks around the base or fuel leaks around the lines attached to it.

6. **Fuel quantity indicators and sensing units.** These should be checked for any indication of fuel leakage, and the wires should be securely attached and supported. The indicator should agree with the amount of fuel known to be in the tank.

7. **Fuel lines.** Check all lines for security of mounting and for any indication of chafing. Check for fuel dye stains around all fittings.

8. **Engine primer.** The primer typically uses a small-diameter copper line that is susceptible to breakage after it has been hardened from vibration. Check it at the primer pump and at the engine. Tug on the line to see if it will pull out of the fitting. Check the entire system for indication of fuel leaks.

Landing Gear

1. **Brake wheel units.** Check the brake linings for excessive wear. Check the calipers for freedom and for any indication of corrosion or rust. Check the hydraulic line for indication of leaks. Check the disk for indications of rust or pitting and for any indication of warpage.

2. **Tires.** Check for any indication of weather-checking of the sidewall, cuts across any of the tread lands, and any indication of uneven wear. Check the tread depth. Check the inflation pressure when the loaded weight of the aircraft is on the wheels.

3. **Main gear wheels.** Check for any indication of damage to the flanges and for any indication of cracks. Check the balance weights for security of mounting.

4. **Wheel bearings.** Remove the bearings, clean them, and check all of the rollers and races for indication of flaking or brinelling. Repack the bearings with the proper grease, and torque the axle nut according to the aircraft manufacturer's instructions, and safety it.

5. **Shock absorbers.** Check the oleo strut for proper extension and for any indication of rust or corrosion. Check the torsion links for looseness or wear and for any indication of damage. Check for proper safety of all bolts securing the torsion links. Lubricate the torsion links as specified by the aircraft manufacturer.

6. **Nose gear.** Check the nose-gear shock strut, torsion links, and shimmy damper for any indication of excessive wear or looseness. Check the tire for uneven wear and for any evidence of damage. Clean, inspect, and pack the nose-gear wheel bearings and torque the axle nut and safety it. Check the entire nose-gear steering mechanism for looseness and for freedom of all of the bearings in the steering links.

7. **Landing gear retraction.** Place retractable landing gear aircraft on jacks to perform a gear retraction test. Be sure to follow all of the manufacturer's instructions for jacking the aircraft, and use the proper power supply for performing the retraction test.

Systematically check all of the wiring and switches in the indicating system for security of mounting and the integrity of all connections. Check all of the hydraulic lines for any indication of leakage or wear. Check the uplocks, downlocks, and all of the door operating linkage for proper rigging and alignment. Lubricate any components specified by the aircraft manufacturer.

Perform the number of retraction and extension cycles specified by the manufacturer, and check to be sure that there is the required clearance between all parts of the landing gear and the structure when the gear is retracted. Check to be sure that the doors are all flush with the structure when the gear is up. Check to be sure that the hydraulic reservoir is full of the proper type of hydraulic fluid.

Airframe

1. **Structure.** Inspect all external portions of the aircraft for any indication of damage or corrosion. Remove all fairings and inspection covers. Examine the edges of all skins for any indication of deformed rivets or puffed paint that would indicate corrosion under the paint. Sight along the surface of the skins for any indication of wrinkles.

Inspect the internal aircraft structure for cracks, deformation, and corrosion. Reference the section on Cleaning and Corrosion Control in the *General* textbook of the Aviation Mechanic Series for a good understanding of the different types of corrosion, what they look like, and how to prevent corrosion. Pay special attention to areas of high stress, such as wing-to-fuselage attachments, wing spars, carry-through spars, horizontal and vertical stabilizer attachments, flight control installations, landing gear installations, and engine mount attachments.

Aircraft structure that warrants a more detailed inspection of defects can be inspected using penetrant inspection, ultrasonic inspection, or radiographic inspection. Reference the Detecting Corrosion section in the previously mentioned chapter of the *General* textbook for descriptions of these special inspections.

2. **Windshield and windows.** Check all transparent plastic for scratches, cracks, or crazing and for any evidence of damage. All windows that can be opened should function smoothly and close and lock completely.

3. **Doors.** Check all door hinges and locks. The locks should secure the door properly and function with no binding. Check all of the door seals for proper functioning.

4. **Bilge areas.** Remove all of the inspection covers below the floor rug, and carefully examine the bilge area for entrapped dirt or water and for any indication of corrosion. Make sure that all drain holes are open. Check all of the control cables in this area and perform any lubrication specified by the manufacturer.

5. **Seats and seat rails.** Carefully examine the seat rails for any indication of worn holes and for cracks or damages to the rails. Examine the seat locking pins to be sure that they are working properly and are not worn. The pin should easily and smoothly extend for the correct distance into the holes in the rail.

6. **Seat belts and harness.** Examine the seat belts and shoulder harness for any indication of fraying or wearing. The attachment points should be secure, and the belts and harnesses should be of the approved type for the aircraft and must include the proper TSO markings.

7. **Control columns, chains, and cables.** Examine the controls for full and unobstructed travel. Examine the chains and sprockets to be sure that the sprockets are secure on the control yoke and the chains ride freely over the sprockets. Examine all of the control cables, especially as they pass over pulleys, to be sure that the cable is not frayed and the pulleys turn freely. Check all of the turnbuckles for the proper safety.

8. **Rudder pedals and brake cylinders.** Check the rudder pedals for any indication of wear or looseness. Check the brake master cylinders for indication of leakage and for the condition of the hoses. Fill the brake reservoirs with the proper fluid.

9. **Avionics equipment.** Check to be sure that all avionics equipment listed in the current equipment list is actually installed and that no equipment is installed that is not included in the equipment list. Check all of the avionics for operation.

10. **Instruments.** Check all instruments for loose or broken glass and for any indication of damage. All required range marking should be in place. Be sure that a current compensation card is installed for the compass and for any other instruments that require such a card. Check behind the panel to see that no hoses or wires are chafing or are obstructing the free movement of the controls.

    When the master switch is turned on, the electrical gyro instruments should begin to spin up. They should operate with no excessive noise, and when the power is turned off, they should have the coast-down time specified in the service manual.

11. **Air filters.** Clean or replace all of the air filters in the gyro instruments.

12. **Instrument panel.** Check the shock mounts to be sure that they are adequately supporting the instrument panel and do not allow it to contact the structure. Check the bonding straps that electrically connect the instrument panel to the aircraft structure. Be sure that all of the required placards are on the panel.

13. **Heating and defrosting systems.** Check all of the ducting and controls for the heating and defrosting system. The controls should work freely and all of the hoses should be of the proper type and correctly installed.

14. **Lights, switches, and circuit breakers.** Check all interior and exterior lights to be sure they operate as they should. All switches should operate properly and should be properly labeled. All circuit breakers should be labeled, and the wires attached to them should be secure. If the aircraft uses fuses, the correct fuses should be installed and the proper spare fuses should be available.

15. **Pitot-static system.** If the aircraft is operated under Instrument Flight Rules, the altimeter and static system must be checked every 24 months as described in the section under special inspections. If these special checks do not have to be made, at least check the static system for leaks. Check the pitot system to be sure that it does not have any leaks. Check the pitot heater. Turn it on for a few seconds and then turn it off. The pitot head should be warm.

16. **Stall warning system.** Check the stall warning system for operation. If an electrical system is used, check the stall-warning vane for freedom and be sure that the stall-warning horn or light operates when the vane is lifted. If the mechanical-reed type of system is used, be sure that it sounds when a suction is placed over its entry hole.

17. **Antennas and cables.** All antennas should be securely mounted on the aircraft, and the coaxial cables firmly attached. There should be no corrosion or indication of water leaking into the structure around the antenna, and there should be no cracks in the structure that could be caused by the antenna vibrating. The coaxial cable should be secured to the structure and it should not interfere with any of the controls or control cables.

18. **Battery, battery box, and cables.** Check the battery box and the area surrounding it for any indication of corrosion. The inside of the box should be adequately protected with a tar-based paint or with polyurethane enamel. The battery should be secure in the box with no looseness. There should be no corrosion on the battery cables and the cables should be tight. Lead-acid batteries should be checked for proper water level. Check all of the hardware on nickel-cadmium batteries for condition and for any indication of burning.

19. **Emergency Locator Transmitter.** Check the ELT for security of mounting and connection to its antenna. The ELT should be of the approved type and the battery replacement or recharge date should be legibly marked on the outside of the case. The battery must have been replaced or recharged within the allowable time. Turn on the VHF radio receiver and tune it to 121.5 to be sure that the ELT is not transmitting.

20. **Oxygen system.** Check the oxygen bottles to be sure that they are the correct type and that they have been hydrostatically tested within the required time interval. The bottles should be filled. The masks and hoses should be in good condition and be properly stowed.

21. **Deicer system.** The deicer boots should be checked for condition and security of attachment. The distributor valve and all plumbing should be checked, and during engine run-up, the system should be checked for proper operation.

Control System

1. **Cables and control surfaces.** Systematically check all of the control cables, turnbuckles, pulleys, brackets, cable guards, and fairleads. Begin at the cockpit control and go all the way to the horn on the control surface. There should be no rust or corrosion on the cables, and all pulleys should turn freely. Be sure that the control surfaces move in the correct direction when the cockpit control is moved. Be sure that no part of the control system rubs against the structure during full travel of the controls.

2. **Control surface travel.** Check the control surface travel to be sure that it is the same as that specified in the Type Certificate Data Sheets for the aircraft. The stop on the control surface should be reached before the stop in the cockpit, and there should be a slight amount of springback in the control system.

3. **Flaps.** The wing flaps should operate freely throughout all of their range, and electric flaps with automatic stops should stop at the correct number of degrees. The flap tracks should show no excessive wear or looseness.

4. **Trim adjustment devices.** The trim tabs or adjustable stabilizer jackscrews should be inspected for security and for any indication of binding or unusual wear. There should be no looseness in any tab actuating mechanism as this can lead to flutter. The indicator in the cockpit should agree with the position of the tabs.

Record of the Inspection

After the inspection is complete, it must be recorded in the aircraft maintenance records as specified in 14 CFR §43.11. The record must be concluded
with a statement like the one in Figure 8-4 if the aircraft passed, and the one
in Figure 8-5 if it failed.

An annual inspection is valid for 12 calendar months, and a calendar
month ends at midnight of the last day of the month in which the inspection
is completed. If an annual is completed on June 4 of this year, it will expire
at midnight of June 30 next year.

Date _____

I certify that this aircraft has been inspected in accordance with a/an (insert type)
inspection and was determined to be in an airworthy condition.

Signed _____
Certificate type and number _____

Figure 8-4. *Typical statement approving an aircraft for return to service after it has passed
an annual or 100-hour inspection.*

Failed Inspection

If the aircraft does not pass the inspection, a list of all the discrepancies
and items that kept it from meeting its airworthiness requirements should
be included in the maintenance entry, and a signed and dated list of these
items must be furnished to the owner or lessee (14 CFR §43.11(b)). These
discrepancies do not have to be corrected by the mechanic performing the
inspection, but can be corrected by any mechanic who holds the appropriate
certification. When they are corrected and signed off in the maintenance
record, the aircraft is legal for flight.

If any of the discrepancies require a major repair, an aviation mechanic
may make the repair and initiate an FAA Form 337, but the repair must be
checked for compliance with approved data. The aircraft must be approved
for return to service and the Form 337 signed by an aviation mechanic holding
an Inspection Authorization.

FAA Form 337. The FAA form that must
be filled in and submitted to the FAA
when a major repair or major alteration
has been completed.

Date _____

I certify that this aircraft has been inspected in accordance with a/an (insert type)
inspection and a list of discrepancies and unairworthy items dated (date) has been
provided for the aircraft owner or operator.

Signed _____
Certificate type and number _____

Figure 8-5. *Typical statement disapproving an aircraft for return to service after it has
failed an annual or 100-hour inspection.*

STUDY QUESTIONS: AIRCRAFT INSPECTIONS

Answers are provided on page 464.

1. A preflight inspection _____ (is or is not) considered to be a maintenance inspection.

2. The method of nondestructive inspection best suited for checking wheels after an overweight landing is the _____ method.

3. An aviation mechanic holding an Airframe rating can conduct the _____ (static system or altimeter) tests required by 14 CFR §91.411.

4. The maximum leakage that is allowed for a static air system that has been evacuated until the altimeter indicates a change of 1,000 feet is _____ feet in one minute.

5. Altimeters used in IFR flight must be checked for accuracy every _____ calendar months.

6. The tests required for an altimeter are described in 14 CFR Part _____ Appendix E.

7. An ATC transponder must be checked every _____ calendar months.

8. An aviation mechanic certificate with an Airframe rating _____ (is or is not) the authorization needed to perform the required tests on an ATC transponder.

9. An annual inspection _____ (is or is not) more comprehensive than a 100-hour inspection.

10. An aircraft that is due for an annual inspection may be flown to a place where the inspection can be performed if the FAA grants a/an _____ permit for the flight.

11. A 100-hour inspection of an aircraft _____ (does or does not) include an inspection of the powerplant.

12. A person conducting a 100-hour inspection on an aircraft must hold both an Airframe and Powerplant rating. An Inspection Authorization _____ (is or is not) required.

13. A person conducting an annual inspection on an aircraft must hold both an Airframe and Powerplant rating. An Inspection Authorization _____ (is or is not) required.

14. An aircraft operating under the 100-hour inspection system of 14 CFR Part 91 can be operated for a maximum of _____ hours beyond the 100-hour inspection period, if necessary, in order to reach a place where the inspection can be performed.

15. The operating conditions that make a 100-hour inspection mandatory are found in 14 CFR Part _____ .

16. An annual inspection _____ (can or cannot) be substituted for a 100-hour inspection.

17. A 100-hour inspection can be treated as an annual inspection if the inspector holds a/an _____ _____ .

18. An entire progressive inspection must be completed within _____ calendar months.

19. The record of compliance with all applicable Airworthiness Directives must include the date and _____ of their compliance.

20. The permanent records of an aircraft must include these things:

    a. _____

    b. _____

    c. _____

    d. _____

    e. _____

    f. _____

21. The recommended statement for approving or disapproving an aircraft for return to service after a 100-hour or annual inspection is found in 14 CFR _____ .

22. An annual inspection that is completed on March 15 of this year will expire on midnight of March _____ next year.

23. If an aircraft fails an annual or 100-hour inspection, a signed and dated list of all the discrepancies and unairworthy items that keep it from meeting its airworthiness requirements must be furnished to the _____ or _____ .

24. If an aircraft fails an annual inspection because of a discrepancy that requires a major repair, the repair can be made by an appropriately rated mechanic. The person returning the aircraft for return to service _____ (is or is not) required to hold an Inspection Authorization (IA).

25. If an aircraft has failed an annual inspection because of several items that require minor repairs, the repairs can be made and the aircraft approved for return to service by an appropriately rated aviation mechanic. The aviation mechanic approving the aircraft for return to service _____ (is or is not) required to hold an Inspection Authorization.

26. Large airplanes and turbine-powered multi-engine aircraft operated under 14 CFR Part 91 must be inspected in accordance with an inspection program authorized under Subpart E of 14 CFR §91.409 (e) and (f). This inspection _____ (is or is not) the same as the progressive inspection covered in 14 CFR §43.15(d).

Answers to Chapter 8 Study Questions

1. is not
2. eddy current
3. static system
4. 100
5. 24
6. 43
7. 24
8. is not
9. is not
10. special flight
11. does
12. is not
13. is
14. 10
15. 91
16. can
17. Inspection Authorization
18. 12
19. method

20. a. Type of inspection program
     b. Total time on airframe
     c. Current status of life-limited parts
     d. Time since last overhaul of parts required to be overhauled on a specific time basis
     e. List of current major alterations
     f. Status of applicable Airworthiness Directives

21. 43
22. 31
23. owner, lessee
24. is
25. is not
26. is not

POTABLE WATER AND WASTE SYSTEMS

9

Auxiliary Systems

In larger aircraft, there are multiple systems designed for passenger safety and comfort. For passenger and crew comfort, potable water and lavatory waste systems allow aircraft to travel long distances while meeting passenger needs.

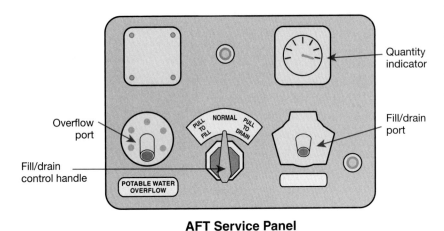

AFT Service Panel

Figure 9-1. *Airbus A320 potable water service panel.*

Potable Water

Potable water systems are designed to supply fresh water for galleys and lavatories. Potable water, which is suitable for drinking, is stored in one or more tanks that normally range in size from 30 to 50 gallons. The system is comprised of servicing ports for filling and draining, holding tanks, monitoring and pressurization systems, water heaters, and distribution lines.

To service specific aircraft, consult the manufacturer's service manual. The following instructions are generic but will be similar for most aircraft.

The potable water system is serviced on the ground through the service panel that is accessed from outside the airplane. See Figures 9-1 and 9-2. To fill the tank, remove the cap from the Fill/Drain port and connect the ground service hose to the port. Turn the Fill/Drain control handle to the "Pull to Fill" position and pull the handle out to the mechanical stop. Turn the pump on the service vehicle to on. Water will begin to flow into the tank and the

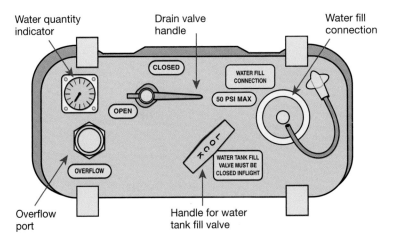

Figure 9-2. *Water service panel on Boeing 757-300.*

quantity indicator will reflect the amount of water in the tank. When the tank is full, the Tank Full indicator light will come on and the Fill/Drain handle will automatically return to the normal position. If the tank is overfilled, water will flow from the overflow port on the panel. Verify that the quantity indicator shows full. Turn the pump on the service vehicle off, disconnect the fill hose, reinstall the cap onto the Fill/Drain port, and close the service panel.

Just as the aircraft is pressurized, potable water systems need to be pressurized with air to provide water flow through all phases of flight. The source for pressurizing the water tank comes either from a dedicated air compressor or from the aircraft pneumatic system, or a combination of both. The tank pressurization system includes pressure regulators and pressure relief valves to maintain the system at the proper pressure.

Refer to Figure 9-3 for a potable water system on a Boeing 737. Note that in this diagram, the drain water from the lavatory sinks and galleys, commonly referred to as gray water, does not go to a holding tank and is drained directly overboard the aircraft. These sinks are seldom used on the ground and if they are, the amount of water that drains out is very small. Inflight, the water exits

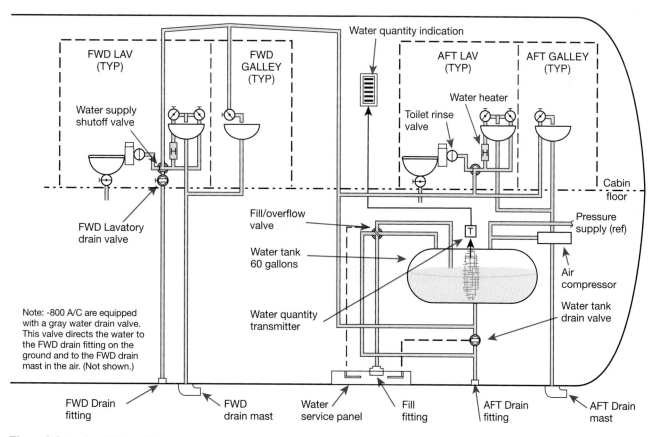

Figure 9-3. *Boeing 737 potable water system.*

through heated drain masts that prevent the water from running back along the fuselage. See Figures 9-4 and Figure 9-5. Due to high aircraft speeds and altitudes, water drained overboard dissipates and vaporizes before reaching the ground.

Not all aircraft dump the gray water overboard. Gray water in some aircraft drains into the lavatory waste system tank.

Figure 9-4. *Forward and aft cabin gray water drain masts.*

Figure 9-5. *Closeup view of drain mast.*

Lavatory Waste Systems

Like most aircraft systems, lavatory waste systems have evolved over the years. The two most common systems still in use are the closed waste system, also known as a recirculating system, and the more efficient vacuum waste system, which has generally replaced closed waste systems.

Closed Waste System

Closed waste systems use a single toilet waste system for each lavatory or may combine two or more closely located lavatories to a single tank (Figure 9-6). The waste collection tanks are pre-charged with a blue chemical liquid known as SkyKem for the flushing agent. SkyKem aids in removing odors and disinfecting the toilet bowl. When the toiled is flushed, a timer starts and activates a pump that pumps filtered SkyKem fluid from the holding tank into the toilet bowl, washing debris into the tank. After approximately 10 seconds, the timer turns the pump off.

Aircraft that use closed waste systems will have multiple lavatory service panels to service each of the tanks.

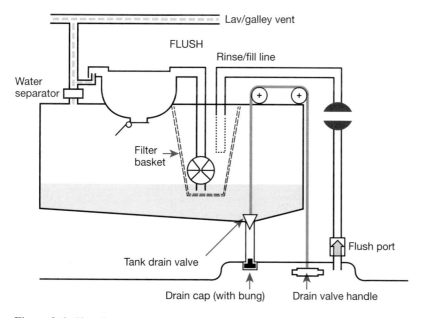

Figure 9-6. *Closed waste system.*

Vacuum Waste Systems

Vacuum waste systems are used in new aircraft due to multiple advantages over recirculating systems. These advantages include:

- Weight savings due to the use of a single holding tank and less pre-charge liquid weight.

- Lavatories do not need dedicated space for holding tanks and can be made smaller.

- A single exterior service panel for most aircraft.

- It is easier to move lavatories around for different cabin configurations.

- When the toilet is flushed, cabin air is drawn into the waste system and purged overboard, reducing odors.

See Figure 9-7 for a typical vacuum waste system. The vacuum waste system starts with a specially designed toilet bowl with steep sides and very slippery surface. The outlet of each toilet is controlled by a normally closed

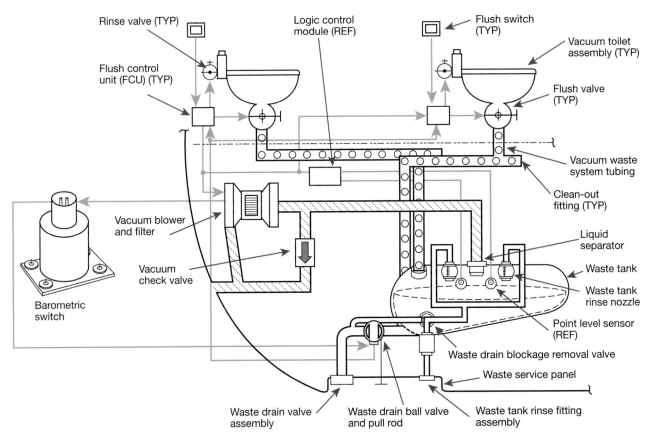

Figure 9-7. *Typical vacuum waste system.*

flush valve, which is connected via lines to a single waste holding tank. The waste holding tank is maintained at a negative pressure. The negative pressure is provided by a vacuum generator at lower altitudes. Above 16,000 feet, the differential pressure between the cabin and ambient air provides adequate negative pressure.

When the flush button is pressed in the lavatory, a signal is sent to the flush control unit. The flush control unit directs the flush valve to open and, in some cases, to open a rinse valve that sends a small amount of potable rinse water into the toilet bowl. When the flush valve opens, the vacuum in the holding tank draws the waste from the toilet bowl to the holding tank. When the flush cycle is complete, the control unit shuts off the rinse water and closes the flush valve.

The waste holding tank is pre-charged with a small amount of water. When servicing the tank, water enters through spray nozzles that rinse the inside of the tank to remove residues while the tank drain is open. After rinsing, and the drain valve is closed, and the water level is set to the specified pre-charge level. Liquid level sensors in the tank send a signal to a central data center where the tank level is monitored by the flight crew.

The vacuum connection at the top of the waste tank includes a water separator to ensure that only air is passed on to the vacuum system. The air traveling into the vacuum system is purged overboard, aiding in the removal of odors.

Lavatory Waste System Servicing

The following instructions are generic in nature, but most waste systems will have similar service procedures. For specific aircraft, follow the instructions provided in the manufacturer's service manual. Always use recommended personal protective equipment (PPE) when servicing lavatory systems. At a minimum, use eye protection, rubber gloves and a protective apron or protective outerwear.

1. First, you will need to locate the service access panel and open the panel. See Figure 9-8. If the system is a vacuum waste system, opening the service panel will disable the vacuum system to prevent the toilet system from operating while it is being serviced.

2. At the main waste drain connection in the service panel, there is both a drain cap and a drain valve for added security. Open the drain cap and connect the large drain hose from the service cart. Actuate the lever that opens the secondary valve. With the hose connected and the secondary valve open, locate the tank drain handle and pull the handle down. This opens the valve at the outlet of the waste tank allowing the contents to drain into the service cart.

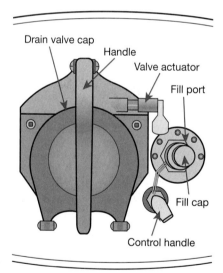

Figure 9-8. *Typical waste system service panel.*

3. Remove the cap on the water fill port and connect the freshwater line. On the service cart, turn on the water pump. Water will enter the tank through spray nozzles that rinse the inside of the tank. After rinsing, close the main tank drain valve and allow the tank to fill to the proper pre-charge level. Turn off the water, disconnect the fill line, and reinstall the cap on the fill port.

4. Close the service panel drain valve and disconnect the large drain hose.

5. Close the drain valve cap and close the service panel door.

Water and Waste Tank Ice Protection

The plumbing for potable water and lavatory waste systems is located in areas of the aircraft that may encounter freezing temperatures. In order to prevent water in the lines from freezing and disabling the systems, electric heating elements and blankets are used to heat the lines. Thermostats located in or near the lines turn on the heating elements when temperatures drop below a set level.

Maintenance and Inspection of Potable Water and Waste Systems

The maintenance and inspection of potable water and lavatory waste systems is similar to other aircraft systems but has additional areas and concerns to consider.

1. Perform an operational check on all components. Verify adequate water pressure and draining at each lavatory sink and galley. If hot water heaters are installed, check each heater for proper operation by turning on the hot water faucet. Flush each lavatory, observing operation and correct cycling and timing of the components.

2. Inspect all components, connections, and lines for security of attachment and leaks. Pay special attention to areas below lines, tanks, and lavatories for areas that are damp. Chemicals and waste materials are very corrosive and can cause extensive corrosion in the aircraft structure. The areas below lavatories have historically been areas of corrosion. Some of these areas are difficult to inspect and corrosion can spread before being detected. Remove heat and insulation blankets as necessary to inspect lines and aircraft structure.

3. Inspect all control panels and indicators for proper operation.

Answers are provided on page 474.

1. Water that is suitable for drinking is called _____ water.

2. Servicing of the potable water system is accessed by an _____.

3. Different methods for pressurizing potable water tanks are by:

    a. _____

    b. _____

    c. _____

4. Water drained from sinks and galleys is handled differently in different aircraft. Two methods of dealing with this water is by draining

    a. _____.

    b. _____.

5. Lavatory waste systems still in use are the:

    a. _____

    b. _____

6. The most common type of lavatory waste system in use today is the _____ waste system.

7. The advantages of a vacuum waste system over recirculating systems are:

    a. _____

    b. _____

    c. _____

    d. _____

    e. _____

8. In respect to cabin pressure, the vacuum waste system holding tank is held at a _____ (negative or positive) pressure.

9. When servicing a vacuum waste system, opening the service panel will disable the _____.

(continued)

10. Water lines and plumbing in potable water and waste systems is protected from freezing by:

a. _____

b. _____

11. When inspecting lavatory waste systems, the areas below lavatories are common areas for _____.

Answers to Chapter 9 Study Questions

1. potable
2. external service panel
3. a. dedicated air compressors
   b. the aircraft pneumatic system
   c. combination of the two methods above
4. a. it directly overboard
   b. the water into the lavatory holding tank
5. a. closed waste system (or recirculating system)
   b. vacuum waste system
6. vacuum

7. a. weight savings
   b. lavatories can be made smaller
   c. use of a single external servicing panel
   d. flexible cabin configurations
   e. reduced odors
8. negative
9. vacuum system
10. a. electric heating elements
    b. insulation blankets
11. corrosion

Glossary

absolute pressure. Pressure measured from zero pressure, or a vacuum.

absolute zero. The point at which all molecular motion ceases. Absolute zero is −460°F and −273°C.

AC 43.13-1B. The advisory circular used by mechanics that contains examples of accepted methods, techniques, and practices for aircraft inspection and repair.

AC 43.13-2B. The advisory circular used by mechanics and repair stations that contains acceptable methods, techniques, and practices for the inspection and alteration of aircraft.

ACARS (Aircraft Communication Addressing and Reporting System). A two-way communication link between an airliner in flight and the airline's main ground facilities. Data is collected in the aircraft by digital sensors and is transmitted to the ground facilities. Replies from the ground may be printed out so the appropriate flight crew-member can have a hard copy of the response.

actuator. A fluid power device that changes fluid pressure into mechanical motion.

ADC. Air data computer.

ADF. Automatic direction finder.

ADI. Attitude director indicator.

aerodynamic drag. The total resistance to the movement of an object through the air. Aerodynamic drag is composed of both induced drag and parasite drag. See induced drag and parasite drag in Volume 1 Glossary.

aerodynamic lift. The force produced by air moving over a specially shaped surface called an airfoil. Aerodynamic lift acts in a direction perpendicular to the direction the air is moving.

agonic line. A line drawn on an aeronautical chart along which there is no angular difference between the magnetic and geographic north poles.

air carrier. An organization or person involved in the business of transporting people or cargo by air for compensation or hire.

air-cycle cooling system. A system for cooling the air in the cabin of a turbojet-powered aircraft. Compressor bleed air passes through two heat exchangers where it gives up some of its heat; then it drives an expansion turbine where it loses still more of its heat energy as the turbine drives a compressor. When the air leaves the turbine it expands and its pressure and temperature are both low.

airspeed indicator. A flight instrument that measures the pressure differential between the pitot, or ram, air pressure and the static pressure of the air surrounding the aircraft. This differential pressure is shown in units of miles per hour, knots, or kilometers per hour.

Airworthiness Alert. A notice sent by the FAA to certain interested maintenance personnel, identifying problems with aircraft that have been gathered from Malfunction and Defect Reports. These problems are being studied at the time the Airworthiness Alert is issued but have not been fully evaluated by the time the material went to press.

Airworthiness Directive (AD note). A notice sent out by the FAA to the registered owner of an aircraft notifying him or her of an unsafe condition that has been found on the aircraft. Compliance with AD notes is mandatory.

alphanumeric symbols. Symbols made up of all of the letters in our alphabet, numerals, punctuation marks, and certain other special symbols.

alternator. An electrical generator that produces alternating current. The popular DC alternator used on light aircraft produces three-phase AC in its stator windings. This AC is changed into DC by a six-diode, solid-state rectifier before it leaves the alternator.

altimeter setting. The barometric pressure at a given location corrected to mean (average) sea level.

altitude engine. A reciprocating engine whose rated sea-level takeoff power can be produced to an established higher altitude.

alumel. An alloy of nickel, aluminum, manganese, and silicon that is the negative element in a thermocouple used to measure exhaust gas temperature.

ambient pressure. The pressure of the air surrounding a person or an object.

ambient temperature. The temperature of the air surrounding a person or an object.

American Wire Gauge. The system of measurement of wire size used in aircraft electrical systems.

amplifier. An electronic circuit in which a small change in voltage or current controls a much larger change in voltage or current.

analog electronics. Electronics in which values change in a linear fashion. Output values vary in direct relationship to changes of input values.

analog-type indicator. An electrical meter that indicates values by the amount a pointer moves across a graduated, numerical scale.

aneroid. The sensitive component in an altimeter or barometer that measures the absolute pressure of the air. The aneroid is a sealed, flat capsule made of thin corrugated disks of metal soldered together and evacuated by pumping all of the air out of it. Evacuating the aneroid allows it to expand or collapse as the air pressure on the outside changes.

angle-of-attack indicator. An instrument that measures the angle between the local airflow around the direction detector and the fuselage reference plane.

annunciator panel. A panel of warning lights in plain sight of the pilot. These lights are identified by the name of the system they represent and are usually covered with colored lenses to show the meaning of the condition they announce.

antenna. A special device used with electronic communication and navigation systems to radiate and receive electromagnetic energy.

anti-icing additive. A chemical added to the turbine-engine fuel used in some aircraft. This additive mixes with water that condenses from the fuel and lowers its freezing temperature so it will not freeze and block the fuel filters. It also acts as a biocidal agent and prevents the formation of microbial contamination in the tanks.

APU (auxiliary power unit). A small turbine or reciprocating engine that drives a generator, hydraulic pump, and air pump. The APU is installed in the aircraft and is used to supply electrical power, compressed air, and hydraulic pressure when the main engines are not running.

arcing. Sparking between a commutator and brush or between switch contacts that is caused by induced current when a circuit is broken.

attenuate. To weaken, or lessen the intensity of, an activity.

attitude indicator. A gyroscopic flight instrument that gives the pilot an indication of the attitude of the aircraft relative to its pitch and roll axes.

The attitude indicator in an autopilot is in the sensing system that detects deviation from a level-flight attitude.

augmenter tube. A long, stainless steel tube around the discharge of the exhaust pipes of a reciprocating engine. Exhaust gases flow through the augmenter tube and produce a low pressure that pulls additional cooling air through the engine compartment. Heat may be taken from the augmenter tubes and directed through the leading edges of the wings for thermal anti-icing.

autoignition system. A system on a turbine engine that automatically energizes the igniters to provide a relight if the engine should flame out.

automatic flight control system (AFCS). The full system of automatic flight control that includes the autopilot, flight director, horizontal situation indicator, air data sensors, and other avionics inputs.

automatic pilot (autopilot). An automatic flight control device that controls an aircraft about one or more of its three axes. The primary purpose of an autopilot is to relieve the pilot of the control of the aircraft during long periods of flight.

Autosyn system. A synchro system used in remote indicating instruments. The rotors in an Autosyn system are two-pole electromagnets, and the stators are delta-connected, three-phase, distributed-pole windings in the stator housings.

The rotors in the transmitters and indicators are connected in parallel and are excited with 26-volt, 400-Hz AC. The rotor in the indicator follows the movement of the rotor in the transmitter.

aviators oxygen. Oxygen that has had almost all of the water and water vapor removed from it.

avionics. The branch of technology that deals with the design, production, installation, use, and servicing of electronic equipment mounted in aircraft.

azimuth. A horizontal angular distance, measured clockwise from a fixed reference direction to an object.

back course. The reciprocal of the localizer course for an ILS (Instrument Landing System). When flying a back-course approach, the aircraft approaches the instrument runway from the end on which the localizer antennas are installed.

barometric scale. A small window in the dial of a sensitive altimeter in which the pilot sets the barometric pressure level from which the altitude shown on the altimeter is measured. This window is sometimes called the "Kollsman" window.

base. The electrode of a bipolar transistor between the emitter and the collector. Varying a small flow of electrons moving into or out of the base controls a much larger flow of electrons between the emitter and the collector.

bezel. The rim that holds the glass cover in the case of an aircraft instrument.

bilge area. A low portion in an aircraft structure in which water and contaminants collect. The area under the cabin floorboards is normally called the bilge.

bipolar transistor. A solid-state component in which the flow of current between its emitter and collector is controlled by a much smaller flow of current into or out of its base. Bipolar transistors may be of either the NPN or PNP type.

BITE. Built-in test equipment.

black box. A term used for any portion of an electrical or electronic system that can be removed as a unit. A black box does not have to be a physical box.

bladder-type fuel cell. A plastic-impregnated fabric bag supported in a portion of an aircraft structure so that it forms a cell in which fuel is carried.

bonding. The process of electrically connecting all isolated components to the aircraft structure. Bonding provides a path for return current from electrical components, and a low-impedance path to ground to minimize static electrical charges. Shock-mounted components have bonding braids connected across the shock mounts.

boost pump. An electrically driven centrifugal pump mounted in the bottom of the fuel tanks in large aircraft. Boost pumps provide a positive flow of fuel under pressure to the engine for starting and serve as an emergency backup in the event an engine-driven pump should fail. They are also used to transfer fuel from one tank to another and to pump fuel overboard when it is being dumped.

Boost pumps prevent vapor locks by holding pressure on the fuel in the line to the engine-driven pump. Centrifugal boost pumps have a small agitator propeller on top of the impeller to force vapors from the fuel before it leaves the tank.

Bourdon tube. A pressure-indicating mechanism used in most oil pressure and hydraulic pressure gauges. It consists of a sealed, curved tube with an elliptical cross section. Pressure inside the tube tries to straighten it, and as it straightens, it moves a pointer across a calibrated dial.

Bourdon-tube pressure gauges are used to measure temperature by measuring the vapor pressure in a sealed container of a volatile liquid, such as methyl chloride, whose vapor pressure varies directly with its temperature.

British thermal unit (Btu). The amount of heat energy needed to raise the temperature of one pound of pure water 1°F.

bus. A point within an electrical system from which the individual circuits get their power.

cage (*verb*). To lock the gimbals of a gyroscopic instrument so it will not be damaged by abrupt flight maneuvers or rough handling.

calendar month. A measurement of time used by the FAA for inspection and certification purposes. One calendar month from a given day extends from that day until midnight of the last day of that month.

calibrated airspeed (CAS). Indicated airspeed corrected for position error. See position error.

calorie. The amount of heat energy needed to raise the temperature of one gram of pure water 1°C.

canted rate gyro. A rate gyro whose gimbal axis is tilted so it can sense rotation of the aircraft about its roll axis as well as its yaw axis.

capacitance-type fuel quantity measuring system. A popular type of electronic fuel quantity indicating system that has no moving parts in the fuel tank. The tank units are cylindrical capacitors, called probes, mounted across the tank, from top to bottom.

The dielectric between the plates of the probes is either fuel or the air above the fuel, and the capacitance of the probe varies with the amount of fuel in the tank. The indicator is a servo-type instrument driven by the amplified output of a capacitance bridge.

capillary tube. A soft copper tube with a small inside diameter. The capillary tube used with a vapor-pressure thermometer connects the temperature sensing bulb to the Bourdon tube. The capillary tube is protected from physical damage by enclosing it in a braided metal wire jacket.

carbon monoxide detector. A packet of chemical crystals mounted in the aircraft cockpit or cabin where they are easily visible. The crystals change their color from yellow to green when they are exposed to carbon monoxide.

carbon-pile voltage regulator. A type of voltage regulator used with high-output DC generators.

Field current is controlled by varying the resistance of a stack of thin carbon disks. This resistance is varied by controlling the amount the stack is compressed by a spring whose force is opposed by the pull of an electromagnet. The electromagnet's strength is proportional to the generator's output voltage.

cathode-ray tube. A display tube used for oscilloscopes and computer video displays.

An electron gun emits a stream of electrons that is attracted to a positively charged inner surface of the face of the tube. Acceleration and focusing grids speed the movement of the electrons and shape the beam into a pinpoint size. Electrostatic or electromagnetic forces caused by deflection plates or coils move the beam over the face of the tube. The inside surface of the face of the tube is treated with a phosphor material that emits light when the beam of electrons strikes it.

CDI. Course deviation indicator.

CDU. Control display unit.

centering cam. A cam in the nose-gear shock strut that causes the piston to center when the strut fully extends. When the aircraft takes off and the strut extends, the wheel is straightened in its fore-and-aft position so it can be retracted into the wheel well.

charging stand (air conditioning service equipment). A handy and compact arrangement of air conditioning servicing equipment. A charging stand contains a vacuum pump, a manifold gauge set, and a method of measuring and dispensing the refrigerant.

chemical oxygen candle system. An oxygen system used for emergency or backup use.

Solid blocks of material that release oxygen when they are burned are carried in special fireproof fixtures. When oxygen is needed, the candles are ignited with an integral igniter, and oxygen flows into the tubing leading to the masks.

chromel. An alloy of nickel and chromium used as the positive element in a thermocouple for measuring exhaust gas temperature.

circuit breaker. An electrical component that automatically opens a circuit any time excessive current flows through it.

A circuit breaker may be reset to restore the circuit after the fault causing the excessive current has been corrected.

clamp-on ammeter. An electrical instrument used to measure current without opening the circuit through which it is flowing. The jaws of the ammeter are opened, slipped over the current-carrying wire, and then clamped shut. Current flowing through the wire produces a magnetic field which induces a voltage in the ammeter that is proportional to the amount of current.

coaxial cable. A special type of electrical cable that consists of a central conductor held rigidly in the center of a braided outer conductor. Coaxial cable, commonly called coax, is used for attaching radio receivers and transmitters to their antenna.

collective pitch control. The helicopter control that changes the pitch of all of the rotor blades at the same time. Movement of the collective pitch control increases or decreases the lift produced by the entire rotor disk.

combustion heater. A type of cabin heater used in some aircraft. Gasoline from the aircraft fuel tanks is burned in the heater.

compass fluid. A highly refined, water-clear petroleum product similar to kerosine. Compass fluid is used to damp the oscillations of magnetic compasses.

compass rose. A location on an airport where an aircraft can be taken to have its compasses "swung." Lines are painted on the rose to mark the magnetic directions in 30° increments.

compass swinging. A maintenance procedure that minimizes deviation error in a magnetic compass. The aircraft is aligned on a compass rose, and the compensating magnets in the compass case are adjusted so the compass card indicates the direction marked on the rose. After the deviation error is minimized on all headings, a compass correction card is completed and mounted on the instrument panel next to the compass.

compensated fuel pump. A vane-type, engine-driven fuel pump that has a diaphragm connected to the pressure-regulating valve. The chamber above the diaphragm is vented to the carburetor upper deck where it senses the pressure of the air as it enters the engine.

The diaphragm allows the fuel pump to compensate for altitude changes and keeps the carburetor inlet fuel pressure a constant amount higher than the carburetor inlet air pressure.

compound gauge (air conditioning servicing equipment). A pressure gauge used to measure the pressure in the low side of an air conditioning system. A compound gauge is calibrated from zero to 30 inches of mercury vacuum, and from zero to about 150-psi positive gauge pressure.

compressor (air conditioning system component). The component in a vapor-cycle cooling system in which the low-pressure refrigerant vapors, after they leave the evaporator, are compressed to increase both their temperature and pressure before they pass into the condenser.

Some compressors are driven by electric motors, others by hydraulic motors and, in the case of most light airplanes, are belt driven from the engine.

condenser (air conditioning system component). The component in a vapor-cycle cooling system in which the heat taken from the aircraft cabin is given up to the ambient air outside the aircraft.

conductor (electrical). A material that allows electrons to move freely from one atom to another within the material.

constant differential mode (cabin pressurization). The mode of pressurization in which the cabin pressure is maintained a constant amount higher than the outside air pressure. The maximum differential pressure is determined by the structural strength of the aircraft cabin.

constant-speed drive (CSD). A special drive system used to connect an alternating current generator to an aircraft engine. The drive holds the generator speed (and thus its frequency) constant as the engine speed varies.

constantan. A copper-nickel alloy used as the negative lead of a thermocouple for measuring the cylinder head temperature of a reciprocating engine.

contactor (electrical component). A remotely actuated, heavy-duty electrical switch. Contactors are used in an aircraft electrical system to connect the battery to the main bus.

continuity tester. A troubleshooting tool that consists of a battery, a light bulb, and test leads. The test leads are connected to each end of the conductor under test, and if the bulb lights up, there is continuity. If it does not light up, the conductor is open.

Continuous Airworthiness Inspection Program. An inspection program that is part of a continuous airworthiness maintenance program approved for certain large airplanes (to which 14 CFR Part 125 is not applicable), turbojet multi-engine airplanes, turbopropeller-powered multi-engine airplanes, and turbine-powered rotorcraft.

continuous-duty solenoid. A solenoid-type switch designed to be kept energized by current flowing through its coil for an indefinite period of time. The battery contactor in an aircraft electrical system is a continuous-duty solenoid. Current flows through its coil all the time the battery is connected to the electrical system.

continuous-flow oxygen system. A type of oxygen system that allows a metered amount of oxygen to continuously flow into the mask. A rebreather-type mask is used with a continuous-flow system.

The simplest form of continuous-flow oxygen systems regulates the flow by a calibrated orifice in the outlet to the mask, but most systems use either a manual or automatic regulator to vary the pressure across the orifice proportional to the altitude being flown.

continuous-loop fire-detection system. A fire-detection system that uses a continuous loop of two conductors separated with a thermistor-type insulation. Under normal temperature conditions, the thermistor material is an insulator; but if it is exposed to a fire, the thermistor changes into a conductor and completes the circuit between the two conductors, initiating a fire warning.

control horn. The arm on a control surface to which the control cable or push-pull rod attaches to move the surface.

conventional current. An assumed flow of electricity that is said to flow from the positive terminal of a power source, through the external circuit to its negative terminal. The arrowheads in semiconductor symbols point in the direction of conventional current flow.

conversion coating. A chemical solution used to form an airtight oxide or phosphate film on the surface of aluminum or magnesium parts. The conversion coating prevents air reaching the metal and keeps it from corroding.

crabbing. Pointing the nose of an aircraft into the wind to compensate for wind drift.

cross-feed valve (fuel system component). A valve in a fuel system that allows any of the engines of a multi-engine aircraft to draw fuel from any fuel tank.

Cross-feed systems are used to allow a multi-engine aircraft to maintain a balanced fuel condition.

CRT. Cathode-ray tube.

cryogenic liquid. A liquid which boils at temperatures of less than about 110°K (−163°C) at normal atmospheric pressures.

current. A general term used for electrical flow. *See* conventional current.

current limiter. An electrical component used to limit the amount of current a generator can produce. Some current limiters are a type of slow-blow fuse in the generator output. Other current limiters reduce the generator output voltage if the generator tries to put out more than its rated current.

cyclic pitch control. The helicopter control that allows the pilot to change the pitch of the rotor blades individually, at a specific point in their rotation. The cyclic pitch control allows the pilot to tilt the plane of rotation of the rotor disk to change the direction of lift produced by the rotor.

database. A body of information that is available on any particular subject.

data bus. A wire or group of wires that are used to move data within a computer system.

dedicated computer. A small digital computer, often built into an instrument or control device, that contains a built-in program that causes it to perform a specific function.

deep-vacuum pump. A vacuum pump capable of removing almost all of the air from a refrigeration system. A deep-vacuum pump can reduce the pressure inside the system to a few microns of pressure.

delivery air duct check valve. An isolation valve at the discharge side of the air turbine that prevents the loss of pressurization through a disengaged cabin air compressor.

delta connection (electrical connection). A method of connecting three electrical coils into a ring or, as they are drawn on a schematic diagram as a triangle, a delta (D).

derated (electrical specification). Reduction in the rated voltage or current of an electrical component. Derating is done to extend the life or reliability of the device.

detent. A spring-loaded pin or tab that enters a hole or groove when the device to which it is attached is in a certain position. Detents are used on a fuel valve to provide a positive means of identifying the fully on and fully off position of the valve.

detonation. An explosion, or uncontrolled burning of the fuel-air mixture inside the cylinder of a reciprocating engine. Detonation occurs when the pressure and temperature inside the cylinder become higher than the critical pressure and temperature of the fuel. Detonation is often confused with preignition. *See* preignition in Volume 1 Glossary.

deviation error. An error in a magnetic compass caused by localized magnetic fields in the aircraft.

　　Deviation error, which is different on each heading, is compensated by the technician "swinging" the compass.

　　A compass must be compensated so the deviation error on any heading is no greater than 10 degrees.

Dewar bottle. A vessel designed to hold liquefied gases. It has double walls with the space between being evacuated to prevent the transfer of heat. The surfaces in the vacuum area are made heat-reflective.

differential pressure. The difference between two pressures. An airspeed indicator is a differential-pressure gauge. It measures the difference between static air pressure and pitot air pressure.

differential-voltage reverse-current cutout. A type of reverse-current cutout switch used with heavy-duty electrical systems. This switch connects the generator to the electrical bus when the generator voltage is a specific amount higher than the battery voltage.

digital multimeter. An electrical test instrument that can be used to measure voltage, current, and resistance. The indication is in the form of a liquid crystal display in discrete numbers.

diluter-demand oxygen system. A popular type of oxygen system in which the oxygen is metered to the mask, where it is diluted with cabin air by an airflow-metering aneroid assembly which regulates the amount of air allowed to dilute the oxygen on the basis of cabin altitude.

　　The mixture of oxygen and air flows only when the wearer of the mask inhales. The percentage of oxygen in the air delivered to the mask is regulated, on the basis of altitude, by the regulator.

　　A diluter-demand regulator has an emergency position which allows 100% oxygen to flow to the mask, bypassing the regulating mechanism.

dipole antenna. A half-wavelength, center-fed radio antenna. The length of each of the two arms is approximately one fourth of the wavelength of the center frequency for which the antenna is designed.

DME. Distance measuring equipment.

downtime. Any time during which an aircraft is out of commission and unable to be operated.

downwash. Air forced down by aerodynamic action below and behind the wing of an airplane or the rotor of a helicopter. Aerodynamic lift is produced when the air is deflected downward. The upward force on the aircraft is the same as the downward force on the air.

drip stick. A fuel quantity indicator used to measure the fuel level in the tank when the aircraft is on the ground. The drip stick is pulled down from the bottom of the tank until fuel drips from its open end. This indicates that the top of the gauge inside the tank is at the level of the fuel. Note the number of inches read on the outside of the gauge at the point it contacts the bottom of the tank, and use a drip-stick table to convert this measurement into gallons of fuel in the tank.

dry air pump. An engine-driven air pump which uses carbon vanes. Dry pumps do not use any lubrication, and the vanes are extremely susceptible to damage from solid airborne particles. These pumps must be operated with filters in their inlet so they will take in only filtered air.

dry ice. Solidified carbon dioxide. Dry ice sublimates, or changes from a solid directly into a gas, at a temperature of −110°F (−78.5°C).

dummy load (electrical load). A noninductive, high-power, 50-ohm resistor that can be connected to a transmission line in place of the antenna. The transmitter can be operated into the dummy load without transmitting any signal.

dynamic stability. The stability that causes an aircraft to return to a condition of straight and level flight after it has been disturbed from this condition.

When an aircraft is disturbed from straight and level flight, its static stability starts it back in the correct direction; but it overshoots, and the corrective forces are applied in the opposite direction. The aircraft oscillates back and forth on both sides of the correct condition, with each oscillation smaller than the one before it. Dynamic stability is the decreasing of these restorative oscillations.

EADI. Electronic attitude director indicator.

ECAM. Electronic centralized aircraft monitor.

eccentric bushing. A special bushing used between the rear spar of certain cantilever airplane wings and the wing attachment fitting on the fuselage. The portion of the bushing that fits through the hole in the spar is slightly offset from that which passes through the holes in the fitting. By rotating the bushing, the rear spar may be moved up or down to adjust the root incidence of the wing.

eddy current damping (electrical instrument damping). Decreasing the amplitude of oscillations by the interaction of magnetic fields.

In the case of a vertical-card magnetic compass, flux from the oscillating permanent magnet produces eddy currents in a damping disk or cup. The magnetic flux produced by the eddy currents opposes the flux from the permanent magnet and decreases the oscillations.

EFIS. Electronic Flight Instrument System.

EHSI. Electronic horizontal situation indicator.

EICAS. Engine Indicating and Crew Alerting System.

ejector. A form of jet pump used to pick up a liquid and move it to another location. Ejectors are used to ensure that the compartment in which the boost pumps are mounted is kept full of fuel. Part of the fuel from the boost pump flowing through the ejector produces a low pressure that pulls fuel from the main tank and forces it into the boost-pump sump area.

electromotive force (EMF). The force that causes electrons to move from one atom to another within an electrical circuit. Electromotive force is an electrical pressure, and it is measured in volts.

electron current. The actual flow of electrons in a circuit. Electrons flow from the negative terminal of a power source through the external circuit to its positive terminal. The arrowheads in semiconductor symbols point in the direction opposite to the flow of electron current.

ELT (emergency locator transmitter). A self-contained radio transmitter that automatically begins transmitting on the emergency frequencies any time it is triggered by a severe impact parallel to the longitudinal axis of the aircraft.

EMI. Electromagnetic interference.

equalizing resistor. A large resistor in the ground circuit of a heavy-duty aircraft generator through which all of the generator output current flows.

The voltage drop across this resistor is used to produce the current in the paralleling circuit that forces the generators to share the electrical load equally.

ethylene dibromide. A chemical compound added to aviation gasoline to convert some of the deposits left by the tetraethyl lead into lead bromides. These bromides are volatile and will pass out of the engine with the exhaust gases.

ethylene glycol. A form of alcohol used as a coolant for liquid-cooled engines and as an anti-icing agent.

eutectic material. An alloy or solution that has the lowest possible melting point.

evacuation (air conditioning servicing procedure). A procedure in servicing vapor-cycle cooling systems. A vacuum pump removes all the air from the system. Evacuation removes all traces of water vapor that could condense out, freeze, and block the system.

evaporator (air conditioning component). The component in a vapor-cycle cooling system in which heat from the aircraft cabin is absorbed into the refrigerant. As the heat is absorbed, the refrigerant evaporates, or changes from a liquid into a vapor. The function of the evaporator is to lower the cabin air temperature.

FAA Form 337. The FAA form that must be filled in and submitted to the FAA when a major repair or major alteration has been completed.

fairing. A part of a structure whose primary purpose is to produce a smooth surface or a smooth junction where two surfaces join.

FCC. Federal Communications Commission.

FCC. Flight Control Computer.

fire pull handle. The handle in an aircraft cockpit that is pulled at the first indication of an engine fire. Pulling this handle removes the generator from the electrical system, shuts off the fuel and hydraulic fluid to the engine, and closes the compressor bleed air valve. The fire extinguisher agent discharge switch is uncovered, but it is not automatically closed.

fire zone. A portion of an aircraft designated by the manufacturer to require fire-detection and/or fire-extinguishing equipment and a high degree of inherent fire resistance.

fixed fire-extinguishing system. A fire-extinguishing system installed in an aircraft.

flameout. A condition in the operation of a gas turbine engine in which the fire in the engine unintentionally goes out.

flash point. The temperature to which a material must be raised for it to ignite, but not continue to burn, when a flame is passed above it.

flight controller. The component in an autopilot system that allows the pilot to maneuver the aircraft manually when the autopilot is engaged.

flying wing. A type of heavier-than-air aircraft that has no fuselage or separate tail surfaces. The engines and useful load are carried inside the wing, and movable control surfaces on the trailing edge provide both pitch and roll control.

FMC. Flight Management Computer.

follow-up signal. A signal in an autopilot system that nulls out the input signal to the servo when the correct amount of control surface deflection has been reached.

forward bias. A condition of operation of a semiconductor device such as a diode or transistor in which a positive voltage is connected to the P-type material and a negative voltage to the N-type material.

FPD. Freezing point depressant.

fractional distillation. A method of separating the various components from a physical mixture of liquids.

The material to be separated is put into a container and its temperature is increased. The components having the lowest boiling points boil off first and are condensed. Then as the temperature is further raised, other components are removed. Kerosine, gasoline and other petroleum products are obtained by fractional distillation of crude oil.

frangible. Breakable, or easily broken.

Freon. The registered trade name for a refrigerant used in a vapor-cycle air conditioning system.

frost. Ice crystal deposits formed by sublimation when the temperature and dew point are below freezing.

fuel-flow transmitter. A device in the fuel line between the engine-driven fuel pump and the carburetor that measures the rate of flow of the fuel. It converts this flow rate into an electrical signal and sends it to an indicator in the instrument panel.

fuel jettison system. A system installed in most large aircraft that allows the flight crew to jettison, or dump, fuel to lower the gross weight of the aircraft to its allowable landing weight.

Boost pumps in the fuel tanks move the fuel from the tank into a fuel manifold. From the fuel manifold it flows away from the aircraft through dump chutes in each wing tip.

The fuel jettison system must be so designed and constructed that it is free from fire hazards.

fuel totalizer. A fuel quantity indicator that gives the total amount of fuel remaining on board the aircraft on one instrument. The totalizer adds the quantities of fuel in all of the tanks.

gauge pressure. Pressure referenced from the existing atmospheric pressure.

General Aviation Airworthiness Alerts. Documents published by the FAA that provide an economical interchange of service experience and cooperation in the improvement of aeronautical product durability, reliability, and safety. Alerts include items that have been reported to be significant, but which have not been fully evaluated at the time the material went to press.

generator. A mechanical device that transforms mechanical energy into electrical energy by rotating a coil inside a magnetic field. As the conductors in the coil cut across the lines of magnetic flux, a voltage is generated that causes current to flow.

generator series field. A set of heavy field windings in a generator connected in series with the armature. The magnetic field produced by the series windings is used to change the characteristics of the generator.

generator shunt field. A set of field windings in a generator connected in parallel with the armature. Varying the amount of current flowing in the shunt field windings controls the voltage output of the generator.

GHz (gigahertz). 1,000,000,000 cycles per second.

gimbal. A support that allows a gyroscope to remain in an upright condition when its base is tilted.

glass cockpit. An aircraft instrument system that uses a few cathode-ray-tube displays to replace a large number of mechanically actuated instruments.

glaze ice. Ice that forms when large drops of water strike a surface whose temperature is below freezing. Glaze ice is clear and heavy.

glide slope. The portion of an ILS (Instrument Landing System) that provides the vertical path along which an aircraft descends on an instrument landing.

goniometer. Electronic circuitry in an ADF system that uses the output of a fixed loop antenna to sense the angle between a fixed reference, usually the nose of the aircraft, and the direction from which the radio signal is being received.

ground. The voltage reference point in an aircraft electrical system. Ground has zero electrical potential. Voltage values, both positive and negative, are measured from ground. In the United Kingdom, ground is spoken of as "earth."

ground-power unit (GPU). A service component used to supply electrical power to an aircraft when it is being operated on the ground.

gyro (gyroscope). The sensing device in an autopilot system. A gyroscope is a rapidly spinning wheel with its weight concentrated around its rim. Gyroscopes have two basic characteristics that make them useful in aircraft instruments: rigidity in space and precession. *See* rigidity in space and precession.

Halon 1211. A halogenated hydrocarbon fire-extinguishing agent used in many HRD fire-extinguishing systems for powerplant protection. The technical name for Halon 1211 is bromochlorodifluoromethane.

Halon 1301. A halogenated hydrocarbon fire-extinguishing agent that is one of the best for extinguishing cabin and powerplant fires. It is highly effective and is the least toxic of the extinguishing agents available. The technical name for Halon 1301 is bromotrifluoromethane.

hangar rash. Scrapes, bends, and dents in an aircraft structure caused by careless handling.

heading indicator. A gyroscopic flight instrument that gives the pilot an indication of the heading of the aircraft.

heat exchanger. A device used to exchange heat from one medium to another. Radiators, condensers, and evaporators are all examples of heat exchangers. Heat always moves from the object or medium having the greatest level of heat energy to a medium or object having a lower level.

helix. A screw-like, or spiral, curve.

hertz. One cycle per second.

holding relay. An electrical relay that is closed by sending a pulse of current through the coil. It remains closed until the current flowing through its contacts is interrupted.

homebuilt aircraft. Aircraft that are built by individuals as a hobby rather than by factories as commercial products. Homebuilt, or amateur-built, aircraft are not required to meet the stringent requirements imposed on the manufacture of FAA-certificated aircraft.

HRD. High-rate-discharge.

HSI. Horizontal situation indicator.

hydrocarbon. An organic compound that contains only carbon and hydrogen. The vast majority of our fossil fuels such as gasoline and turbine-engine fuel are hydrocarbons.

hydrostatic test. A pressure test used to determine the serviceability of high-pressure oxygen cylinders. The cylinders are filled with water and pressurized to $\frac{5}{3}$ of their working pressure.

Standard-weight cylinders (DOT 3AA) must be hydrostatically tested every five years, and lightweight cylinders (DOT 3HT) must be tested every three years.

hypoxia. A physiological condition in which a person is deprived of the needed oxygen. The effects of hypoxia normally disappear as soon as the person is able to breathe air containing sufficient oxygen.

IFR. Instrument flight rules.

indicated airspeed (IAS). The airspeed as shown on an airspeed indicator with no corrections applied.

induced current. Electrical current produced in a conductor when it is moved through or crossed by a magnetic field.

infrared radiation. Electromagnetic radiation whose wavelengths are longer than those of visible light.

INS. Inertial Navigation System.

Inspection Authorization (IA). An authorization that may be issued to an experienced aviation mechanic who holds both an Airframe and Powerplant rating. It allows the holder to conduct annual inspections and to approve an aircraft or aircraft engine for return to service after a major repair or major alteration.

integral fuel tank. A fuel tank which is formed by sealing off part of the aircraft structure and using it as a fuel tank. An integral wing tank is called a "wet wing." Integral tanks are used because of their large weight saving.

The only way of repairing an integral fuel tank is by replacing damaged sealant and making riveted repairs, as is done with any other part of the aircraft structure.

intermittent-duty solenoid. A solenoid-type switch whose coil is designed for current to flow through it for only a short period of time. The coil will overheat if current flows through it too long.

IRS. Inertial Reference System.

IRU. Inertial Reference Unit.

iso-octane. A hydrocarbon, C_8H_{18}, which has a very high critical pressure and temperature. Iso-octane is used as the high reference for measuring the antidetonation characteristics of a fuel.

isobaric mode. The mode of pressurization in which the cabin pressure is maintained at a constant value regardless of the outside air pressure.

isogonic line. A line drawn on an aeronautical chart along which the angular difference between the magnetic and geographic north poles is the same.

isopropyl alcohol. A colorless liquid used in the manufacture of acetone and its derivatives and as a solvent and anti-icing agent.

jet pump. A special venturi in a line carrying air from certain areas in an aircraft that need an augmented flow of air through them. High-velocity compressor bleed air is blown into the throat of a venturi where it produces a low pressure that pulls air from the area to which it is connected.

Jet pumps are often used in the lines that pull air through galleys and toilet areas.

key (verb). To initiate an action by depressing a key or a button.

kHz (kilohertz). 1,000 cycles per second.

Kollsman window. The barometric scale window of a sensitive altimeter. *See* barometric scale.

labyrinth seal. A type of seal in a Roots blower cabin supercharger that is made in the form of knife edges riding in step-shaped grooves. Air pressure is dropped in each section of the seal, and any oil in the air is trapped in the grooves.

landing gear warning system. A system of lights used to indicate the condition of the landing gear. A red light illuminates when any of the gears are in an unsafe condition, a green light shows when all of the gears are down and locked, and no light is lit when the gears are all up and locked.

An aural warning system is installed that sounds a horn if any of the landing gears are not down and locked when the throttles are retarded for landing.

latent heat. Heat that is added to a material that causes a change in its state without changing its temperature.

left-right indicator. The course-deviation indicator used with a VOR navigation system.

life-limited parts. Life-limited parts are those that require replacement after a set number of flight hours or cycles.

linear change. A change in which the output is directly proportional to the input.

loadmeter. A current meter used in some aircraft electrical systems to show the amount of current the generator or alternator is producing. Loadmeters are calibrated in percent of the generator rated output.

localizer. The portion of an ILS (Instrument Landing System) that directs the pilot along the center line of the instrument runway.

lodestone. A magnetized piece of natural iron oxide.

logic flow chart. A type of graphic chart that can be made up for a specific process or procedure to help follow the process through all of its logical steps.

LORAN A. LOng Range Aid to Navigation. A hyperbolic navigation system that operates with frequencies of 1,950 kHz, 1,850 kHz, and 1,900 kHz. LORAN has been decommissioned and is no longer used for aircraft navigation.

LRU. Line replaceable unit.

lubber line. A reference on a magnetic compass and directional gyro that represents the nose of the aircraft. The heading of the aircraft is shown on the compass card opposite the lubber line.

Magnesyn system. The registered trade name of a synchro system used for remote indicating instruments. The rotors in a Magnesyn system are permanent magnets, and the stators are tapped toroidal coils, excited with 26-volt, 400-hertz AC. The rotor in the indicator accurately follows the movement of the rotor in the transmitter.

magnetic bearing. The direction to or from a radio transmitting station measured relative to magnetic north.

manifold cross-feed fuel system. A type of fuel system commonly used in large transport category aircraft. All fuel tanks feed into a common manifold, and the dump chutes and the single-point fueling valves are connected to the manifold. Fuel lines to each engine are taken from the manifold.

manifold pressure gauge. A pressure gauge that measures the absolute pressure inside the induction system of a reciprocating engine. When the engine is not operating, this instrument shows the existing atmospheric pressure.

master switch. A switch in an aircraft electrical system that can disconnect the battery from the bus and open the generator or alternator field circuit.

MFD. Multi-function display.

MHz (megahertz). 1,000,000 cycles per second.

microbial contaminants. The scum that forms inside the fuel tanks of turbine-engine-powered aircraft that is caused by micro-organisms.

These micro-organisms live in water that condenses from the fuel, and they feed on the fuel. The scum they form clogs fuel filters, lines, and fuel controls and holds water in contact with the aluminum alloy structure. This causes corrosion.

micro-organism. An organism, normally bacteria or fungus, of microscopic size.

Microswitch. The registered trade name for a precision switch that uses a short throw of the control plunger to actuate the contacts. Microswitches are used primarily as limit switches to control electrical units automatically.

millivoltmeter. An electrical instrument that measures voltage in units of millivolts (thousandths of a volt).

MSL. Mean sea level. When the letters MSL are used with an altitude, it means that the altitude is measured from mean, or average, sea level.

MTBF. Mean Time Between Failures.

multimeter. An electrical test instrument that consists of a single current-measuring meter and all of the needed components to allow the meter to be used to measure voltage, resistance, and current. Multimeters are available with either analog- or digital-type displays.

NDB. Nondirectional beacons.

negative pressure relief valve (pressurization component). A valve that opens anytime the outside air pressure is greater than the cabin pressure. It prevents the cabin altitude ever becoming greater than the aircraft flight altitude.

noise (electrical). An unwanted electrical signal within a piece of electronic equipment.

nonvolatile memory. Memory in a computer that is not lost when power to the computer is lost.

normal heptane. A hydrocarbon, C_7H_{16}, with a very low critical pressure and temperature. Normal heptane is used as the low reference in measuring the antidetonation characteristics of a fuel.

NPN transistor. A bipolar transistor made of a thin base of P-type silicon or germanium sandwiched between a collector and an emitter, both of which are made of N-type material.

null position. The position of an ADF loop antenna when the signal being received is canceled in the two sides of the loop and the signal strength is the weakest.

octane rating. A rating of the antidetonation characteristics of a reciprocating engine fuel. It is based on the performance of the fuel in a special test engine. When a fuel is given a dual rating such as 80/87, the first number is its antidetonating rating with a lean fuel-air mixture, and the higher number is its rating with a rich mixture.

open wiring. An electrical wiring installation in which the wires are tied together in bundles and clamped to the aircraft structure rather than being enclosed in conduit.

oscilloscope. An electrical instrument that displays the waveform of the electrical signal it is measuring.

outflow valve (pressurization component). A valve in the cabin of a pressurized aircraft that controls the cabin pressure by opening to relieve all pressure above that for which the cabin pressure control is set.

overvoltage protector. A component in an aircraft electrical system that opens the alternator field circuit any time the alternator output voltage is too high.

parabolic reflector. A reflector whose surface is made in the form of a parabola.

parallel circuit. A method of connecting electrical components so that each component is in a path between the terminals of the source of electrical energy.

paralleling circuit. A circuit in a multi-engine aircraft electrical system that causes the generators or alternators to share the electrical load equally.

paralleling relay. A relay in a multi-engine aircraft electrical system that controls a flow of control current which is used to keep the generators or alternators sharing the electrical load equally.

The relay opens automatically to shut off the flow of paralleling current any time the output of either alternator or generator drops to zero.

partial pressure. The percentage of the total pressure of a mixture of gases produced by each of the individual gases in the mixture.

performance number. The antidetonation rating of a fuel that has a higher critical pressure and temperature than iso-octane (a rating of 100). Iso-octane that has been treated with varying amounts of tetraethyl lead is used as the reference fuel.

petrolatum-zinc dust compound. A special abrasive compound used inside an aluminum wire terminal being swaged onto a piece of aluminum electrical wire. When the terminal is compressed, the zinc dust abrades the oxides from the wire, and the petrolatum prevents oxygen reaching the wire so no more oxides can form.

petroleum fractions. The various components of a hydrocarbon fuel that are separated by boiling them off at different temperatures in the process of fractional distillation.

phased array antenna. A complex antenna which consists of a number of elements. A beam of energy is formed by the superimposition of the signals radiating from the elements. The direction of the beam can be changed by varying the relative phase of the signals applied to each of the elements.

phenolic plastic. A plastic material made of a thermosetting phenol-formaldehyde resin, reinforced with cloth or paper. Phenolic plastic materials are used for electrical insulators and for chemical-resistant table tops.

pinion. A small gear that meshes with a larger gear, a sector of a gear, or a toothed rack.

plenum. An enclosed chamber in which air can be held at a pressure higher than that of the surrounding air.

PNP transistor. A bipolar transistor made of a thin base of N-type silicon or germanium sandwiched between a collector and an emitter, both of which are made of P-type material.

position error. The error in pitot-static instruments caused by the static ports not sensing true static air pressure. Position error changes with airspeed and is usually greatest at low airspeeds.

potentiometer. A variable resistor having connections to both ends of the resistance element and to the wiper that moves across the resistance.

PPI (plan position indicator). A type of radar scope that shows both the direction and distance of the target from the radar antenna. Some radar antenna rotate and their PPI scopes are circular. Other antenna oscillate and their PPI scopes are fan shaped.

precession. The characteristic of a gyroscope that causes a force to be felt, not at the point of application, but at a point 90° in the direction of rotation from that point.

preflight inspection. A required inspection to determine the condition of the aircraft for the flight to be conducted. It is conducted by the pilot-in-command.

press-to-test light fixture. An indicator light fixture whose lens can be pressed in to complete a circuit that tests the filament of the light bulb.

pressure altitude. The altitude in standard air at which the pressure is the same as that of the existing air. Pressure altitude is read on an altimeter when the barometric scale is set to the standard sea level pressure of 29.92 inches of mercury.

pressure-demand oxygen system. A type of oxygen system used by aircraft that fly at very high altitude. This system functions as a diluter-demand system until, at about 40,000 feet, the output to the mask is pressurized enough to force the needed oxygen into the lungs, rather than depending on the low pressure produced when the wearer of the mask inhales to pull in the oxygen. (*See* diluter-demand oxygen system.)

pressure fueling. The method of fueling used by almost all transport aircraft. The fuel is put into the aircraft through a single underwing fueling port. The fuel tanks are filled to the desired quantity and in the sequence selected by the person conducting the fueling operation.

Pressure fueling saves servicing time by using a single point to fuel the entire aircraft, and it reduces the chances for fuel contamination.

pressure reducing valve (oxygen system component). A valve used in an oxygen system to change high cylinder pressure to low system pressure.

pressure relief valve (oxygen system component). A valve in an oxygen system that relieves the pressure if the pressure reducing valve should fail.

progressive inspection. An inspection that may be used in place of an annual or 100-hour inspection. It has the same scope as an annual inspection, but it may be performed in increments so the aircraft will not have to be out of service for a lengthy period of time.

purge (air conditioning system operation). To remove all of the moisture and air from a cooling system by flushing the system with a dry gaseous refrigerant.

PVC. Polyvinylchloride. A thermoplastic resin used to make transparent tubing for insulating electrical wires.

quick-disconnect fitting. A hydraulic line fitting that seals the line when the fitting is disconnected. Quick-disconnect fittings are used on the lines connected to the engine-driven hydraulic pump. They allow the pump to be disconnected and an auxiliary hydraulic power system connected to perform checks requiring hydraulic power while the aircraft is in the hangar.

radial. A directional line radiating outward from a radio facility, usually a VOR.

When an aircraft is flying outbound on the 330° radial, it is flying away from the station on a line that has a magnetic direction of 330° from the station.

range markings. Colored marks on an instrument dial that identify certain ranges of operation as specified in the aircraft maintenance or flight manual and listed in the appropriate aircraft Type Certificate Data Sheets or Aircraft Specifications. Color coding directs attention to approaching operating difficulties.

Airspeed indicators and most pressure and temperature indicators are marked to show the various ranges of operation.

These ranges and colors are the most generally used:

Red radial line, do not exceed.

Green arc, normal operating range.

Yellow arc, caution range.

Blue radial line, used on airspeed indicators to show best single-engine rate of climb speed.

White arc, used on airspeed indicators to show flap operating range.

RDF. Radio direction finding.

rebreather oxygen mask. A type of oxygen mask used with a continuous-flow oxygen system. Oxygen continuously flows into the bottom of the loose-fitting rebreather bag on the mask. The wearer of the mask exhales into the top of the bag. The first air exhaled contains some oxygen, and this air goes into the bag first. The last air to leave the lungs contains little oxygen, and it is forced out of the bag as the bag is filled with fresh oxygen. Each time the wearer of the mask inhales, the air first exhaled, along with fresh oxygen, is taken into the lungs.

receiver-dryer. The component in a vapor-cycle cooling system that serves as a reservoir for the liquid refrigerant. The receiver-dryer contains a desiccant that absorbs any moisture that may be in the system.

reed valve. A thin, leaf-type valve mounted in the valve plate of an air conditioning compressor to control the flow of refrigerant gases into and out of the compressor cylinders.

relay. An electrical component which uses a small amount of current flowing through a coil to produce a magnetic pull to close a set of contacts through which a large amount of current can flow. The core in a relay coil is fixed.

retard breaker points. A set of breaker points in certain aircraft magnetos that are used to provide a late (retarded) spark for starting the engine.

reverse bias. A voltage placed across the PN junction in a semiconductor device with the positive voltage connected to the N-type material and the negative voltage to the P-type material.

rigid conduit. Aluminum alloy tubing used to house electrical wires in areas where they are subject to mechanical damage.

rigidity in space. The characteristic of a gyroscope that prevents its axis of rotation tilting as the earth rotates. This characteristic is used for attitude gyro instruments.

rime ice. A rough ice that forms on aircraft flying through visible moisture, such as a cloud, when the temperature is below freezing. Rime ice disturbs the smooth airflow as well as adding weight.

RMI. Radio magnetic indicator.

rocking shaft. A shaft used in the mechanism of a pressure-measuring instrument to change the direction of movement by 90° and to amplify the amount of movement.

Roots-type air compressor. A positive-displacement air pump that uses two intermeshing figure-8-shaped rotors to move the air.

RPM. Revolutions per minute.

schematic diagram. A diagram of an electrical system in which the system components are represented by symbols rather than drawings or pictures of the actual devices.

Schrader valve. A type of service valve used in an air conditioning system. This is a spring-loaded valve much like the valve used to put air into a tire.

scupper. A recess around the filler neck of an aircraft fuel tank. Any fuel spilled when the tank is being serviced collects in the scupper and drains to the ground through a drain line rather than flowing into the aircraft structure.

sea-level engine. A reciprocating engine whose rated takeoff power can be produced only at sea level.

sector gear. A part of a gear wheel containing the hub and a portion of the rim with teeth.

selcal system. Selective calling system. Each aircraft operated by an airline is assigned a particular four-tone audio combination for identification purposes. A ground station keys the signal whenever contact with that particular aircraft is desired. The signal is decoded by the airborne selcal decoder and the crew alerted by the selcal warning system.

Selsyn system. A DC synchro system used in remote indicating instruments. The rotor in the indicator is a permanent magnet and the stator is a tapped toroidal coil. The transmitter is a circular potentiometer with DC power fed into its wiper which is moved by the object being monitored. The transmitter is connected to the indicator in such a way that rotation of the transmitter shaft varies the current in the sections of the indicator toroidal coil. The magnet in the indicator on which the pointer is mounted locks with the magnetic field produced by the coils and follows the rotation of the transmitter shaft.

semiconductor diode. A two-element electrical component that allows current to pass through it in one direction, but blocks its passage in the opposite direction. A diode acts in an electrical system in the same way a check valve acts in a hydraulic system.

sensible heat. Heat that is added to a liquid causing a change in its temperature but not its physical state.

sensitivity. A measure of the signal strength needed to produce a distortion-free output in a radio receiver.

series circuit. A method of connecting electrical components in such a way that all the current flows through each of the components. There is only one path for current to flow.

series-parallel circuit. An electrical circuit in which some of the components are connected in parallel and others are connected in series.

servo amplifier. An electronic amplifier in an autopilot system that increases the signal from the autopilot enough that it can operate the servos that move the control surfaces.

SHF. Superhigh frequency.

shielded wire. Electrical wire enclosed in a braided metal jacket. Electromagnetic energy radiated from the wire is trapped by the braid and is carried to ground.

shock mounts. Resilient mounting pads used to protect electronic equipment by absorbing low-frequency, high-amplitude vibrations.

shunt winding. Field coils in an electric motor or generator that are connected in parallel with the armature.

sight glass (air conditioning system component). A small window in the high side of a vapor-cycle cooling system. Liquid refrigerant flows past the sight glass, and if the charge of refrigerant is low, bubbles will be seen. A fully charged system has no bubbles in the refrigerant.

silicon controlled rectifier (SCR). A semiconductor electron control device. An SCR blocks current flow in both directions until a pulse of positive voltage is applied to its gate. It then conducts in its forward direction, while continuing to block current in its reverse direction.

skip distance. The distance from a radio transmitting antenna to the point on the surface of the earth the reflected sky wave first touches after it has bounced off of the ionosphere.

slow-blow fuse. An electrical fuse that allows a large amount of current to flow for a short length of time but melts to open the circuit if more than its rated current flows for a longer period.

smoke detector. A device that warns the flight crew of the presence of smoke in cargo and/or baggage compartments. Some smoke detectors are of the visual type, others are photoelectric or ionization devices.

solenoid. An electrical component using a small amount of current flowing through a coil to produce a magnetic force that pulls an iron core into the center of the coil. The core may be attached to a set of heavy-duty electrical contacts, or it may be used to move a valve or other mechanical device.

sonic venturi. A venturi in a line between a turbine engine or turbocharger and a pressurization system. When the air flowing through the venturi reaches the speed of sound, a shock wave forms across the throat of the venturi and limits the flow. A sonic venturi is also called a flow limiter.

specific heat. The number of Btu's of heat energy needed to change the temperature of one pound of a substance 1°F.

split bus. A type of electrical bus that allows all of the voltage-sensitive avionic equipment to be isolated from the rest of the aircraft electrical system when the engine is being started or when the ground-power unit is connected.

split-rocker switch. An electrical switch whose operating rocker is split so one half of the switch can be opened without affecting the other half.

Split-rocker switches are used as aircraft master switches. The battery can be turned on without turning on the alternator, but the alternator cannot be turned on without also turning on the battery. The alternator can be turned off without turning off the battery, but the battery cannot be turned off without also turning off the alternator.

squib. An explosive device in the discharge valve of a high-rate-discharge container of fire-extinguishing agent. The squib drives a cutter into the seal in the container to discharge the agent.

stagnation point. The point on the leading edge of a wing at which the airflow separates, with some flowing over the top of the wing and the rest below the wing.

starter-generator. A single-component starter and generator used on many of the smaller gas-turbine engines. It is used as a starter, and when the engine is running, its circuitry is shifted so that it acts as a generator.

static dischargers. Devices connected to the trailing edges of control surfaces to discharge static electricity harmlessly into the air. They discharge the static charges before they can build up high enough to cause radio receiver interference.

stroboscopic tachometer. A tachometer used to measure the speed of any rotating device without physical contact. A highly accurate variable-frequency oscillator triggers a high-intensity strobe light. When the lamp is flashing at the same frequency the device is rotating, the device appears to stand still.

sublimation. A process in which a solid material changes directly into a vapor without passing through the liquid stage.

sump. A low point in an aircraft fuel tank in which water and other contaminants can collect and be held until they can be drained out.

supercooled water. Water in its liquid form at a temperature well below its natural freezing temperature. When supercooled water is disturbed, it immediately freezes.

superheat. Heat energy that is added to a refrigerant after it changes from a liquid to a vapor.

superheterodyne circuit. A sensitive radio receiver circuit in which a local oscillator produces a frequency that is a specific difference from the received signal frequency. The desired signal and the output from the oscillator are mixed, and they produce a single, constant intermediate frequency. This IF is amplified, demodulated, and detected to produce the audio frequency that is used to drive the speaker.

Supplemental Type Certificate (STC). An approval issued by the FAA for a modification to a type certificated airframe, engine, or component.

More than one STC can be issued for the same basic alteration, but each holder must prove to the FAA that the alteration meets all the requirements of the original type certificate.

surfactant. A surface active agent, or partially soluble contaminant, which is a by-product of fuel processing or of fuel additives. Surfactants adhere to other contaminants and cause them to drop out of the fuel and settle to the bottom of the fuel tank as sludge.

surveyor's transit. An instrument consisting of a telescope mounted on a flat, graduated, circular plate on a tripod. The plate can be adjusted so it is level, and its graduations oriented to magnetic north. When an object is viewed through the telescope, its azimuth and elevation may be determined.

synchro system. A remote instrument indicating system. A synchro transmitter is actuated by the device whose movement is to be measured, and it is connected electrically with wires to a synchro indicator whose pointer follows the movement of the shaft of the transmitter.

TACAN (Tactical Air Navigation). A radio navigation facility used by military aircraft for both direction and distance information. Civilian aircraft receive distance information from a TACAN on their DME.

takeoff warning system. An aural warning system that provides audio warning signals when the thrust levers are advanced for takeoff if the stabilizer, flaps, or speed brakes are in an unsafe condition for takeoff.

TCAS. Traffic Alert Collision Avoidance System.

tempered glass. Glass that has been heat-treated to increase its strength. Tempered glass is used in birdproof, heated windshields for high-speed aircraft.

terminal strips. A group of threaded studs mounted in a strip of insulating plastic. Electrical wires with crimped-on terminals are placed over the studs and secured with nuts.

terminal VOR. A low-powered VOR that is normally located on an airport.

tetraethyl lead (TEL). A heavy, oily, poisonous liquid, $Pb(C_2H_5)_4$, that is mixed into aviation gasoline to increase its critical pressure and temperature.

therapeutic mask adapter. A calibrated orifice in the mask adapter for a continuous-flow oxygen system that increases the flow of oxygen to a mask being used by a passenger who is known to have a heart or respiratory problem.

thermistor. A special form of electrical resistor whose resistance varies with its temperature.

thermistor material. A material with a negative temperature coefficient that causes its resistance to decrease as its temperature increases.

thermocouple. A loop consisting of two kinds of wire, joined at the hot, or measuring, junction and at the cold junction in the instrument. The voltage difference between the two junctions is proportional to the temperature difference between the junctions.

In order for the current to be meaningful, the resistance of the thermocouple is critical, and the leads are designed for a specific installation. Their length should not be altered. Thermocouples used to measure cylinder head temperature are usually made of iron and constantan, and thermocouples that measure exhaust gas temperature for turbine engines are made of chromel and alumel.

thermocouple fire detection system. A fire detection system that works on the principle of the rate-of-temperature rise. Thermocouples are installed around the area to be protected, and one thermocouple is surrounded by thermal insulation that prevents its temperature changing rapidly.

In the event of a fire, the temperature of all the thermocouples except the protected one will rise immediately and a fire warning will be initiated. In the case of a general overheat condition, the temperature of all the thermocouples will rise uniformly and there will be no fire warning.

thermostatic expansion valve (TEV). The component in a vapor-cycle cooling system that meters the refrigerant into the evaporator.

The amount of refrigerant metered by the TEV is determined by the temperature and pressure of the refrigerant as it leaves the evaporator coils.

The TEV changes the refrigerant from a high-pressure liquid into a low-pressure liquid.

TMC. Thrust management computer.

toroidal coil. An electrical coil wound around a ring-shaped core of highly permeable material.

total air temperature. The temperature a column of moving air will have if it is stopped.

TR unit. A transformer-rectifier unit. A TR unit reduces the voltage of alternating current and changes it into direct current.

transducer. A device that changes energy from one form to another. Commonly used transducers change mechanical movement or pressures into electrical signals.

transformer rectifier. A component in a large aircraft electrical system used to reduce the AC voltage and change it into DC for charging the battery and for operating DC equipment in the aircraft.

tricresyl phosphate (TCP). A chemical compound, $(CH_3C_6H_4O)_3PO$, used in aviation gasoline to assist in scavenging the lead deposits left from the tetraethyl lead.

trimmed flight. A flight condition in which the aerodynamic forces acting on the control surfaces are balanced and the aircraft is able to fly straight and level with no control input.

trip-free circuit breaker. A circuit breaker that opens a circuit any time an excessive amount of current flows regardless of the position of the circuit breaker's operating handle.

troubleshooting. A procedure used in aircraft maintenance in which the operation of a malfunctioning system is analyzed to find the reason for the malfunction and to find a method for returning the system to its condition of normal operation.

turn and slip indicator. A rate gyroscopic flight instrument that gives the pilot an indication of the rate of rotation of the aircraft about its vertical axis.

A ball in a curved glass tube shows the pilot the relationship between the centrifugal force and the force of gravity. This indicates whether or not the angle of bank is proper for the rate of turn.

The turn and slip indicator shows the trim condition of the aircraft and serves as an emergency source of bank information in case the attitude gyro fails. Turn and slip indicators were formerly called needle and ball and turn and bank indicators.

two-terminal spot-type fire detection system. A fire detection system that uses individual thermoswitches installed around the inside of the area to be protected. These thermoswitches are wired in parallel between two separate circuits. A short or an open circuit can exist in either circuit without causing a fire warning.

Type Certificate Data Sheets (TCDS). The official specifications of an aircraft, engine, or propeller issued by the Federal Aviation Administration.

The TCDS lists pertinent specifications for the device, and it is the responsibility of the mechanic and/or inspector to ensure, on each inspection, that the device meets these specifications.

UHF. Ultrahigh frequency.

vapor lock. A condition in which vapors form in the fuel lines and block the flow of fuel to the carburetor.

vapor pressure. The pressure of the vapor above a liquid needed to prevent the liquid evaporating. Vapor pressure is always specified at a specific temperature.

VFR. Visual flight rules.

VHF. Very high frequency.

vibrator-type voltage regulator. A type of voltage regulator used with a generator or alternator that intermittently places a resistance in the field circuit to control the voltage. A set of vibrating contacts puts the resistor in the circuit and takes it out several times a second.

volatile liquid. A liquid that easily changes into a vapor.

voltmeter multiplier. A precision resistor in series with a voltmeter mechanism used to extend the range of the basic meter or to allow a single meter to measure several ranges of voltage.

VOR. Very high frequency Omni Range navigation.

VORTAC. An electronic navigation system that contains both a VOR and a TACAN facility.

way point. A phantom location created in certain electronic navigation systems by measuring direction and distance from a VORTAC station or by latitude and longitude coordinates from Loran or GPS.

wet-type vacuum pump. An engine-driven air pump that uses steel vanes. These pumps are lubricated by engine oil drawn in through holes in the pump base. The oil passes through the pump and is exhausted with the air. Wet-type pumps must have oil separators in their discharge line to trap the oil and return it to the engine crankcase.

wire bundle. A compact group of electrical wires held together with special wrapping devices or with waxed string. These bundles are secured to the aircraft structure with special clamps.

zener diode. A special type of solid-state diode designed to have a specific breakdown voltage and to operate with current flowing through it in its reverse direction.

zero-center ammeter. An ammeter in a light aircraft electrical system located between the battery and the main bus. This ammeter shows the current flowing into or out of the battery.

Index

long-wire, 321
loop, 320
marker beacon, 376
polarization, 317
radio altimeter, 377
vertical whip, 320
VHF communication, 375
VOR/LOC, 376
anti-icing
additive, 108
ground, 400
system, 386
antiskid brake system, 48
antiskid control box, 49
APU. *See* auxiliary power unit
area navigation, 342
aromatic additives, 107
ATC transponder inspection, 449
atmospheric conditions, standard, 176–232
attitude indicator, 266
audio integrating system (AIS), 322
audio wave propagation, 316
augmenter tube, 394
aural warning systems, 295
autoignition system, 51
Automatic Dependent Surveillance–Broadcast
    (ADS-B), 350
automatic direction finder (ADF), 329
automatic flight control system (AFCS), 285–292
automatic pilot, 285
autopilot
correction subsystem, 287
error-sensing subsystem, 287
follow-up subsystem, 289
servos, 288
Autosyn system, 155, 251
auxiliary fuel pump, 116
auxiliary power unit (APU), 61
fire detection and extinguishing, 433
aviation gasoline, 105
aviators' oxygen, 187
avionics, 57, 57–58, 310
avionics cooling, 371
avionics protection, 57

B

barometer, mercury, 237
barometric pressure, 238
barometric scale, 238
barrier-type terminal strip, 70
battery circuits, 18
battery contactor, 11, 18, 20
bipolar transistor, 11
BITE (Built-In Test Equipment), 358, 367
bladder-type fuel tank, 110, 130
bonding, electrical, 299, 372
boost pump, 117, 124
Bourdon tube, 238, 239, 242
brake deicers, 385
BTU (British thermal unit), 182

C

cabin
air pressure regulator, 204
air pressure safety valve, 206
interphone, 323
negative-pressure relief valve, 206
rate of climb, 206
temperature comfort range, 175
calibrated airspeed (CAS), 273
canted rate gyro, 285
capacitance bridge, 152
capillary tube, 242
carbon dioxide, 179, 427
carbon dioxide fire extinguisher, 163
carbon monoxide, 180
carbon monoxide detector, 423
carburetor, float-type, 112, 113
CAS. *See* calibrated airspeed
cathode-ray tube, 348
Celsius temperature, 183
centrifugal-type auxiliary fuel pump, 116
chemical oxygen generator, 187, 188, 195
chromel, 246
circuit
complex, 16
landing and taxi light, 43
navigation light, 43
parallel, 15
series, 15
series-parallel, 15

E

EAS. *See* equivalent airspeed
ECAM. *See* electronic centralized aircraft monitor (ECAM)
eddy current damping, 263
EFIS. *See* electronic flight instrument systems
EHIS. *See* electronic horizontal situation indicator
EHSI. *See* electronic horizontal situation indicator
EICAS. *See* engine indicating and crew alerting system
ejector pump, 116
electrical
    bonding, 299
    fuses, 76
    load limits, 368
    switches, 7, 76
    terminal strips, 70
    wire
        bundling, 74, 75
        identification, 72, 73
        size chart, 65
        splices, 72
        terminals, 70–71
electrical symbols, Appendix A, 95–98
electrical system
    inspection and maintenance, 79
    requirements, 4
    terms, 5
    troubleshooting, 82–89
electrical wire size chart, 65
electron current, 6
electron flow, 6
electronic attitude director indicator, 359–360
electronic centralized aircraft monitor (ECAM), 359, 361
electronic flight instrument systems (EFIS), 359
electronic horizontal situation indicator (EHSI), 359–361
electronic pressurization control, 207
electrostatic discharge damage, 370
ELT. *See* emergency locator transmitter
emergency locator transmitter (ELT), 324, 460
engine, altitude, 395
engine-driven fuel pump, 116
engine indicating and crew alerting system
    (EICAS), 359, 361
equivalent airspeed (EAS), 273
essential bus, 61

ethylene dibromide, 107
ethylene glycol, 386, 396
evaporator, 221
exhaust gas temperature measuring system, 246
exhaust system heater, 210

F

FAA Flight Standards District Office, 452
Fahrenheit temperature, 183
FCC (Federal Communications Commission), 310
fire detection systems, 415–425
    maintenance and servicing, 437
    rate-of-temperature-rise, 418
    troubleshooting, 438
fire detector, 416
    continuous-loop, 420
        pneumatic-type, 421
        thermistor-type, 420
    Lindberg pneumatic, 421
    spot-type, 417
    Systron-Donner pneumatic, 422
    thermocouple-type, 418, 419
    thermoswitch-type, 416
fire extinguisher
    carbon dioxide, 429
    high-rate discharge, 429
fire-extinguishing agents, 426
fire-extinguishing systems, maintenance and
    servicing of, 439
fire protection during fueling, 163
fire protection system
    jet transport airplane, 432–436
    maintenance, 437
    servicing, 439
fire pull handle, 121
fires, types of, 415
flapper valve, 117
flash point, 107
flight
    controller, 286
    director, 290
    interphone, 323
flight envelope protection, 290
flight management computer system (FMCS), 363
flow multiplier, 200, 202
flux gate compass, 262, 264

light fixture, press-to-test, 45
line replaceable unit (LRU), 358, 367
liquid nitrogen, 427
liquid oxygen, 187
loadmeter, 38
localizer, 333, 336–337
logic flow chart, 89
   troubleshooting, 89–91
low-frequency, four-course radio range, 328
LRU. *See* line replaceable unit
lubber line, 258

M
Machmeter, 273, 275
Mach number, 275
Magnesyn system, 157
magnetic compass, 258–262
   vertical-card, 261
maintenance information, 454
manifold gauge set, 223, 230
manifold pressure gauge, 240
manifold vent shutoff valve, 123
marker beacon, 338
mass fuel flowmeter, 157
master caution, 294
master switch, 18
maximum-allowable airspeed indicator, 274
MFD. *See* multi-function display
microbial contaminants, 108
microcomputers, 355
micrometer, 185
Micronic filter, 164
micron of pressure, 185
micro-organism, 142
Microswitch, 27, 248
microwave landing system (MLS), 346
millivoltmeter, 38
MLS. *See* microwave landing system
moving-magnet ratiometer, 244
multi-engine airplane deicing system, 392
multifunction display (MFD), 292, 358
multimeter, 92
   digital, 92, 93

N
National Fire Protection Association, 415
navigation light circuit, 43
normal heptane, 107
northerly turning error, 261

O
octane rating, 106
ohmmeter, 84
oil-to-fuel heat exchanger, 148
omni bearing selector, 332
one-hundred-hour inspection, 450, 452
open wiring, 75
oscilloscope, 94
outflow valve, 200
overheat detection systems, 416
overvoltage protector, 24–29
oxygen
   aviators', 187
   characteristics, 177
   functions, 178
   gaseous, 186, 196
   gaseous cylinders, 194–195
   liquid, 187
   mechanically separated, 188
   rebreather mask, 190
   therapeutic mask, 190
oxygen partial pressure, 178
oxygen regulator, 191–194
   diluter-demand, 191
   pressure-demand, 193
oxygen servicing trailer, 195
oxygen system
   continuous-flow, 189–190
   diluter-demand, 191
   discharge indication, 196
   filling, 194
   inspection and maintenance, 195–196
   leak testing, 195
   purging, 195
   safety, 196

P
parallel circuit, 15
paralleling circuit, 28, 32, 35